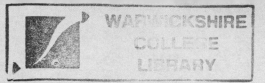
Services Marketing

About the authors

Prof. Dr. Manfred Bruhn is head of the Department of Marketing at the Center for Business and Economics (WWZ) at the University of Basel (Switzerland) and honorary professor at the Technical University Munich (TUM). He has been teaching in marketing and management at all levels, as well as in further education, for more than 25 years. He is author of more than 30 German and international textbooks and management books, amongst them, *Relationship Marketing* (Pearson Education). Manfred Bruhn authors aproximately 20 articles a year for publications such as the *European Journal of Marketing*, the *Journal of Relationship Marketing* and *Total Quality Management*, as well as many German marketing and business journals. He is also editor of several anthologies, a marketing encyclopedia, as well as the *Swiss Journal of Business Research and Practice*. As a counsellor for top management at some major global corporations and a member of several companies' supervisory boards, he is closely connected to business practice.

Dr. Dominik Georgi is head of the Services Management group at the Department of Marketing, University of Basel (Switzerland). He teaches marketing and management courses at all levels and researches in the fields of services marketing, service quality, relationship marketing and value management. He has authored books on topics such as the cost-benefit analysis of quality management as well as the dynamics of customer relationships. He has also published many articles in international marketing and management journals, anthologies, encyclopedias and business magazines. Dominik Georgi is also a reviewer for several international journals. He frequently consults with service corporations on topics such as value management and customer relationship management, as well as service quality and customer satisfaction measurement and management.

Manfred Bruhn
and Dominik Georgi

Services Marketing
Managing the Service Value Chain

FT Prentice Hall
FINANCIAL TIMES

An imprint of **Pearson Education**
Harlow, England · London · New York · Boston · San Francisco · Toronto · Sydney · Singapore · Hong Kong
Tokyo · Seoul · Taipei · New Delhi · Cape Town · Madrid · Mexico City · Amsterdam · Munich · Paris · Milan

Pearson Education Limited
Edinburgh Gate
Harlow
Essex CM20 2JE
England

and Associated Companies throughout the world

Visit us on the World Wide Web at:
www.pearsoned.co.uk

First published 2006

ISBN-13: 978-0-27368-157-1
ISBN-10: 0-27368-157-5

British Library Cataloguing-in-Publication Data
A catalogue record for this book is available from the British Library

Library of Congress Cataloging-in-Publication Data
Bruhn, Manfred.
    Services marketing : managing the service value chain / Manfred Bruhn and Dominik Georgi.
        p. cm.
    Includes bibliographical references and index.
    ISBN 0-273-68157-5
    1. Service industries--Marketing--Management. 2. Customer
services--Marketing--Management. 3. Business logistics--Management. I. Georgi, Dominik. II. Title.

    HD9980.5.B78 2005
    658.8--dc22

                                                                        2005053044

10 9 8 7 6 5 4 3 2 1
10 09 08 07 06

Typeset in 10pt Palatino by Pantek Arts Ltd, Maidstone, Kent
Printed by Ashford Colour Press Ltd., Gosport

The publisher's policy is to use paper manufactured from sustainable forests.

Contents

List of figures   xi

List of tables   xv

Preface   xvi

Guided tour   xx

Publisher's acknowledgements   xxii

Part 1 Basic concept: The Service Value Chain

Chapter 1 Managing the service process by the Service Value Chain   5

It's all about value   7
   Services marketing in action 1.1: Strong competition in many service industries   7
Services are processes   13
The Service Value Chain   16
   Services marketing in action 1.2: Grocery market share through customer retention   19
   Services marketing in action 1.3: Service Value Chain in the tourism industry   20
Summary   22
Case study: Creating value at Ritz-Carlton   27

**Chapter 2 Value creation by services marketing: Service Value Chain and
Service Profit Chain   31**

Integrating the Service Value Chain and the Service Profit Chain   33
Customer value   36
   Services marketing in action 2.1: Customer segmentation based on customer
      profitability in a Scandinavian bank   41
Value-driving customer behaviours   44
   Services marketing in action 2.2: Customer migration analysis   46
How customers evaluate services   48
   Services marketing in action 2.3: Different sides of the same coin   50
Value contribution of the Service Value Chain   57
Summary   58
Case study: The Service Profit Chain at a UK grocery store   61
Case study: The Service Profit Chain at Canadian Imperial Bank of
Commerce (CIBC)   64

Part 2   Primary value processes: Managing interactions and relationships

Chapter 3   The customer interaction process: Managing customer integration, the service encounter and service recovery   71

Value creation by service interactions   73
Customer integration   74
Producing a service in the service encounter   76
   Services marketing in action 3.1: Critical incidents of a cruise operator   81
Service recovery   91
   Services marketing in action 3.2: Service recovery at Club Med Cancun   97
   Services marketing in action 3.3: Successful and unsuccessful recovery
     strategies in retailing   100
Summary   102
Case study: Fujitsu Consulting: Mobile operators creating value by service
   interactions   106

Chapter 4   The customer relationship process: Managing customer acquisition, retention and recovery   109

Value contribution of customer relationships   110
Understanding customer relationships   113
   Services marketing in action 4.1: Customer relationship lifecycle   115
Understanding and managing relational behaviours   118
   Services marketing in action 4.2: Tesco Clubcard   123
   Services marketing in action 4.3: Who has the best loyalty programme?   124
   Services marketing in action 4.4: Switching processes of bank customers   129
   Services marketing in action 4.5: Reducing customer defection in the credit
     card industry   133
   Services marketing in action 4.6: Experiences with managing relationships
     across industries   135
Relationship quality: Customer perceptions of their relationships to service
   providers   136
Summary   139
Case study: Tesco's Clubcard   142

Part 3   Secondary value processes: Creating service value

Chapter 5   Defining the benefit part of service value: The service product   147

Value contribution of the service product   148
   Services marketing in action 5.1: Core service drives customer switching   149
   Services marketing in action 5.2: Tetra Pak: Designing the service programme
     according to the customer's value chain   150

Elements of the service product   151
    Services marketing in action 5.3: Pizza Hut celebrates successful delivery to space   153
    Services marketing in action 5.4: The impact of after sales service on customer
      perceptions   160
    Services marketing in action 5.5: Importance of core and relational service aspects
      differ according to gender   161
    Services marketing in action 5.6: Leading Hotels extends its line   165
Decisions regarding the service product   167
    Services marketing in action 5.7: Service innovation at FTSE:
      The FTSE4Good Index for socially responsible investment   170
    Services marketing in action 5.8: Online in air   171
    Services marketing in action 5.9: Service innovation in hospital foodservice   172
    Services marketing in action 5.10: easyJet: Focus on price via externalisation   181
    Services marketing in action 5.11: Product elimination by financial service
      providers   182
    Services marketing in action 5.12: Time-lapse of the Iridium story   184
Summary   185
Case study: Recreational Equipment (REI): The greatest shop in the world   188

Chapter 6   Defining the cost part of service value: Service pricing   191

Value contribution of pricing   192
 Determining service price   194
    Services marketing in action 6.1: UK banks' pricing practices for current account
      and payments services   197
    Services marketing in action 6.2: Pricing for a new recreational centre   201
    Services marketing in action 6.3: Multi-step synthetic pricing for a hotel   206
Strategic options of price discrimination   208
    Services marketing in action 6.4: Examples of membership-related price
      discrimination   211
    Services marketing in action 6.5: Price bundling at Royal Bank of Scotland   214
    Services marketing in action 6.6: Last-minute birthday package   216
    Services marketing in action 6.7: Price discrimination at Werder Bremen   219
Summary   220
Case study: Restructuring the pricing strategy of an Australian football club   224

Chapter 7   Delivering service value: Managing service delivery   226

Value contribution of service delivery   227
Place of service delivery   228
    Services marketing in action 7.1: Food de luxe at home in Barcelona   229
    Services marketing in action 7.2: Mobile learning gains foothold   232
    Services marketing in action 7.3: Groundbreaking new service delivers museum-
      quality high resolution art and photography into the home on flat panel
      TVs and PCs   233
    Services marketing in action 7.4: Customer 'run' on Mediamarkt due to
      marketing tricks   236
    Services marketing in action 7.5: Evaluation of service locations by a pizza
      restaurant chain   239

Timing of service delivery 241
   Services marketing in action 7.6: Effectiveness of a 24-hour freeway patrol
     service 244
   Services marketing in action 7.7: Delivering furniture: A race with the customer 245
Channels of service distribution and delivery 246
   Services marketing in action 7.8: Channel preferences of bank customers 257
   Services marketing in action 7.9: Value effects of multi-channelling 258
   Services marketing in action 7.10: External channel conflicts in the life
     insurance industry 259
Summary 260
Case study: Multi-channelling at Mövenpick Wein Corporation 263

Chapter 8   Communicating service value: Service communications and branding   267

Value contribution of branding and communications 268
   Services marketing in action 8.1: McDonald's recovery 269
Interactional, relational and brand communications 270
   Services marketing in action 8.2: Wasted communications opportunities by
     UK banks 274
Service branding and communications 275
   Services marketing in action 8.3: Interbrand's brand value ranking 277
   Services marketing in action 8.4: Brand image messages of US universities 280
   Services marketing in action 8.5: Means–end chain of students at the University
     of New Hampshire 281
Instruments of service communications 283
   Services marketing in action 8.6: Permission marketing by Amex 289
   Services marketing in action 8.7: Car race at Times Square 290
Integrated communications 293
   Services marketing in action 8.8: Integrated advertisements by service firms 294
Summary 296
Case study: Virgin Mobile: Growth through branding and communications in a
   saturated market 299

Part 4   Secondary value processes: Managing service resources for value

Chapter 9   Managing employees, tangibles and technology for value   304

Managing the behaviour of service employees 306
   Services marketing in action 9.1: Restructuring at Barclays 307
   Services marketing in action 9.2: The McDonald's training programme 314
   Services marketing in action 9.3: Compensation drives attraction and retention
     of restaurant managers 316
   Services marketing in action 9.4: Attracting and selecting new employees
     at McDonald's 317
Managing the tangibles of a service 319
   Services marketing in action 9.5: Cleanliness as a tangible quality dimension
     in hotels 323

Managing service technology   324
    Services marketing in action 9.6: Customer motivation and productivity through
       technology in Conduit call centres   326
    Services marketing in action 9.7: Driving value through technology   329
    Services marketing in action 9.8: Questions for the implementation of
       service technologies   333
Summary   334
Case study: Service orientation through employee commitment at Novotel London   337
Case study: British Airways: Improving value through self-service kiosks   340

Chapter 10   Service capacity management   343

Value contribution of capacity management   345
    Services marketing in action 10.1: Managing service capacity by service
       communications   346
Gaps between service demand and capacity   347
Determinants of service capacity management   349
    Services marketing in action 10.2: Shopping habits affected by football event   350
Options for managing service capacity   351
    Services marketing in action 10.3: Demand level analysis for the foodservice
       industry   354
    Services marketing in action 10.4: Ticketing procedure for Football World
       Championship 2006   360
    Services marketing in action 10.5: Price-related capacity management at
       Germanwings   362
    Services marketing in action 10.6: Yield management at American Airlines   367
Summary   368
Case study: Capacity adjustments at McDonald's   371

Part 5   The external and internal environment of value-oriented services marketing

**Chapter 11   Services marketing and the markets: Market strategies, international
services marketing, service networks and service outsourcing   379**

Market segment strategies   381
Market development through international services marketing   383
    Services marketing in action 11.1: Cost and revenue synergies of international
       affairs at Air France-KLM   383
    Services marketing in action 11.2: The rise and fall of coffee shops in Switzerland 385
    Services marketing in action 11.3: International insurers going to China   386
    Services marketing in action 11.4: Tesco's international success   389
    Services marketing in action 11.5: The Big Mac Index   391
Strategies regarding other providers   392
Service outsourcing strategy   392
    Services marketing in action 11.6: Citibank's technology outsourcing   393
Service network strategy   396

Services marketing in action 11.7: Advertising agency network of the year   397
Services marketing in action 11.8: The alliances battle   399
Summary   404
Case study: IKEA's globalisation strategy   407
Case study: Networking at Nexcom   408

Chapter 12   Services marketing and the service firm: Implementing and controlling   411
services marketing

Value contribution of services marketing implementation and control   412
Implementing services marketing: Adapting a service firm's structure,
    systems and culture   413
    Services marketing in action 12.1: Marketing decisions in the airline industry   416
    Services marketing in action 12.2: Service profit responsibility at Reuters   417
    Services marketing in action 12.3: Problems with implementing customer
        value orientations   423
    Services marketing in action 12.4: Bonus culture in investment banks   426
Controlling services marketing: Assessing services marketing's value drivers   427
    Services marketing in action 12.5: Value drivers of department stores   431
    Services marketing in action 12.6: Application of the relationship blueprint   434
Summary   437
Case study: Value drivers in the airline industry   440

Glossary   442

Bibliography   449

Index   467

Supporting resources

Visit **www.pearsoned.co.uk/bruhn** to find valuable online resources

For instructors
- An Instructor's Manual, including sample answers for selected material in the book
- Customisable PowerPoint slides, including key figures and tables from the main text

For more information please contact your local Pearson Education sales representative or visit **www.pearsoned.co.uk/bruhn**

List of figures

Figure 1.1:	Learning objectives of Chapter 1	6
Figure 1.2:	Developmental stages of services marketing	10
Figure 1.3:	Services are processes	13
Figure 1.4:	Primary value processes	17
Figure 1.5:	Relationship of bonding and market share for UK grocery stores	19
Figure 1.6:	Typical Service Value Chain in the tourism industry	20
Figure 1.7:	Framework of value-oriented services marketing and outline of the book	23
Figure 1.8:	Learning summary for Chapter 1	25
Figure 2.1:	Service Value Chain and Service Profit Chain	32
Figure 2.2:	Learning objectives of Chapter 2	32
Figure 2.3:	Original Service Profit Chain	34
Figure 2.4:	Original and generalised Service Profit Chain	34
Figure 2.5:	Integration of Service Value Chain and Service Profit Chain	35
Figure 2.6:	Generic customer value components	37
Figure 2.7:	Calculation scheme for the customer contribution margin	40
Figure 2.8:	ABC-analysis based on customer sales	41
Figure 2.9:	Customer segments for a particular Scandinavian bank based on customer profitability and transaction volume	42
Figure 2.10:	CLV differences across industries	44
Figure 2.11:	Customer segmentation regarding customer behaviours	47
Figure 2.12:	GAP model of service quality	51
Figure 2.13:	Hierarchical structure of service quality dimensions	53
Figure 2.14:	SERVQUAL item battery	55
Figure 2.15:	Overview of expectation types	56
Figure 2.16:	Learning summary for Chapter 2	59
Figure 2.17:	Operationalisation of profit chain variables	62
Figure 2.18:	Relationships within the Service Profit Chain	63
Figure 2.19:	Service Profit Chain of Canadian Imperial Bank of Commerce (CIBC)	65
Figure 3.1:	Learning objectives of Chapter 3	73
Figure 3.2:	Examples of services with different challenges for initiating a service interaction	75
Figure 3.3:	Service encounter elements in service production	77
Figure 3.4:	Types of service encounters	78

Figure 3.5:   Examples of positive and negative critical incidents   79
Figure 3.6:   Measures for managing the customer roles   88
Figure 3.7:   Blueprint for a corner shoeshine   89
Figure 3.8:   Blueprint of a flight with an airline   92
Figure 3.9:   Effects of service failures   93
Figure 3.10:   Effects of service recovery   95
Figure 3.11:   Service recovery measures   100
Figure 3.12:   Evaluation of service recovery strategies   101
Figure 3.13:   Learning summary for Chapter 3   104
Figure 4.1:   Learning objectives of Chapter 4   110
Figure 4.2:   Value effects of a customer relationship   112
Figure 4.3:   Relationships and episodes of interactions   113
Figure 4.4:   Customer relationship lifecycle   115
Figure 4.5:   Empirical findings on profit generated per customer in
                different sectors   116
Figure 4.6:   Examples of service guarantees   119
Figure 4.7:   Customer retention activities   122
Figure 4.8:   Types of defection processes   131
Figure 4.9:   Critical path of a customer relationship   132
Figure 4.10:   Index of the ability to win back lost customers by
                UK companies   135
Figure 4.11:   Relationship value chain   137
Figure 4.12:   Measures to manage trust and familiarity   138
Figure 4.13:   Learning summary for Chapter 4   139
Figure 5.1:   The service product pyramid   147
Figure 5.2:   Learning objectives of Chapter 5   148
Figure 5.3:   Value chain of a food manufacturer   150
Figure 5.4:   Types of supplementary services   153
Figure 5.5:   E-services versus classical services   162
Figure 5.6:   Structure of a service programme   163
Figure 5.7:   The Sixt service programme   164
Figure 5.8:   Types of service innovations   168
Figure 5.9:   Service innovation process   174
Figure 5.10:   Forms of service prototyping   176
Figure 5.11:   Externalisation and internalisation   180
Figure 5.12:   Financial service elimination strategies   182
Figure 5.13:   Learning summary for Chapter 5   186
Figure 6.1:   Learning objectives of Chapter 6   192
Figure 6.2:   Forms of charges for current account and payments services   198
Figure 6.3:   Sample profile   201
Figure 6.4:   Multi-step synthetic service pricing   205
Figure 6.5:   Multi-step synthetic service pricing for a hotel   207
Figure 6.6:   Criteria for service price discrimination   209
Figure 6.7:   Points of time of banks introducing service bundling   213

Figure 6.8:   Learning summary for Chapter 6   221
Figure 7.1:   Learning objectives of Chapter 7   227
Figure 7.2:   Criteria for decisions regarding service locations   237
Figure 7.3:   Location evaluation form by DoubleDave's pizza restaurant
                chain   240
Figure 7.4:   Dimensions of service timing   241
Figure 7.5:   One-to-one service delivery   246
Figure 7.6:   Types of service delivery multiplication   247
Figure 7.7:   Multiplication of personal service delivery without
                geographical extension   248
Figure 7.8:   Multiplication with geographical extension   249
Figure 7.9:   Electronic service delivery   251
Figure 7.10:   Learning summary for Chapter 7   261
Figure 8.1:   Learning objectives of Chapter 8   268
Figure 8.2:   Value contribution of service communications   269
Figure 8.3:   Value-oriented types of service communication   271
Figure 8.4:   Potential advertising opportunity wasted by banks each year
                compared to other industries   274
Figure 8.5:   Brand-related profit chain   277
Figure 8.6:   Consequences of consumers' behaviour according to the
                means–end approach   279
Figure 8.7:   Exemplar individual ladders   281
Figure 8.8:   Means–end ladder of the University of New Hampshire   282
Figure 8.9:   Types of service communication instruments   284
Figure 8.10:   Dimensions of personal communication quality   285
Figure 8.11:   Modes of nonverbal communication   286
Figure 8.12:   Options for customising internet communications   288
Figure 8.13:   Options of service communications for making services
                tangible   292
Figure 8.14:   Learning summary for Chapter 8   296
Figure 9.1:   Types of service resources   304
Figure 9.2:   Learning objectives of Chapter 9   305
Figure 9.3:   Internal and external Service Profit Chain   306
Figure 9.4:   Instruments of managing service employee behaviour   310
Figure 9.5:   Incentives for motivating service employees   318
Figure 9.6:   Value effects of service tangibles   319
Figure 9.7:   Types of service tangibles   321
Figure 9.8:   Value effects of service technologies   327
Figure 9.9:   Types of service technologies   330
Figure 9.10:   Issues of service technology implementation   332
Figure 9.11:   Learning summary for Chapter 9   335
Figure 10.1:   Learning objectives of Chapter 10   344
Figure 10.2:   Value effects of service capacity management   345
Figure 10.3:   Determinants of service capacity management decisions   349

Figure 10.4: Options for managing service capacity   351
Figure 10.5: Strategies for long-term capacity determination   355
Figure 10.6: Options for short-term capacity adjustments   357
Figure 10.7: Options for demand adjustments   359
Figure 10.8: Types of waiting lines and their advantages and disadvantages   364
Figure 10.9: Learning summary for Chapter 10   369
Figure 11.1: Decisions regarding consumer and provider markets   380
Figure 11.2: Learning objectives of Chapter 11   381
Figure 11.3: Market segment strategies of a service provider   382
Figure 11.4: Types of international penetration strategy   388
Figure 11.5: Big Mac Index   391
Figure 11.6: Value creation by service networks   398
Figure 11.7: Alliances between airlines   400
Figure 11.8: Capacity shares in the intercontinental airline market   400
Figure 11.9: Partners of British Airways in the supply chain   402
Figure 11.10: Dimensions of the quality of cooperation between firms   403
Figure 11.11: Learning summary for Chapter 11   405
Figure 12.1: Learning objectives of Chapter 12   412
Figure 12.2: Model of a process organisation   419
Figure 12.3: Example of a relationship process organisation   420
Figure 12.4: Structure of customer information systems   421
Figure 12.5: Examples of customer-oriented remuneration systems   423
Figure 12.6: Types of company culture   425
Figure 12.7: Instruments for managing company culture   426
Figure 12.8: Categories of value drivers   429
Figure 12.9: Structure of value drivers according to the Service Profit Chain   430
Figure 12.10: Drivers of value-oriented services marketing   430
Figure 12.11: Exemplary relationship blueprint and questions for identifying
              value drivers   434
Figure 12.12: Learning summary for Chapter 12   437

List of tables

Table 1.1:   Students' expenditure on services in the UK 2002/2003   5
Table 2.1:   Sample CLV calculation   43
Table 2.2:   Revenues of migration segments   46
Table 3.1:   Ranking of customers' problems with cruise operator   81
Table 5.1:   Switching reasons in 45 service industries   149
Table 5.2:   Reasons for innovations by German companies   168
Table 5.3:   Elimination reasons of financial service providers   183
Table 6.1:   Attributes and attribute levels of the recreation centre   202
Table 6.2:   Conjoint measurement results for the recreation centre   203
Table 7.1:   Characteristics of different service places   230
Table 7.2:   Differences between electronic delivery channels   252
Table 7.3:   Dimensions and attributes of call centre expectations   254
Table 7.4:   Channel preferences of bank customers   257
Table 8.1:   TOP 20 of Interbrand's brand equity ranking 2004   278
Table 8.2:   Results regarding the degree of integration in services advertising 295
Table 9.1:   Importance of hotel tangibles associated with cleanliness   323
Table 10.1: Examples of demand gaps and consequences of capacity gaps   348
Table 10.2: Typical long-term capacities in different service industries   353
Table 11.1: International service industries   386
Table 11.2: Steps of systematic service outsourcing   395

Preface

In both business and practice, *services* have become the most discussed goods category. Today, many services markets are extremely dynamic, for several reasons. The banking and airlines industries are heavily affected by the movement towards globalisation, for example. A second group of service industries are being liberalised, and are facing demanding customers for the first time. This includes utilities, telecommunications, postal services, and administrative services. A third group, which includes the retail industry, is characterised by strong competition. Whereas this group was originally dominated by smaller providers, there are now huge players involved.

From an academic perspective, *services are special* compared to manufactured goods since services are more intangible, necessitate the participation of the consumer and are more heterogeneous. These reasons are the starting point for many publications in the area of services marketing which deal with operational issues in this field.

Services Marketing: Managing the Service Value Chain complements this literature by providing a *more strategic approach* to services marketing. It takes into account the current challenges in business practices. In many service industries, the competitive tendencies mentioned above result in a stronger value orientation of service firms. The shareholders and top management ask for a value contribution of each activity of a service firm. In addition, marketing is supposed to create value by making sure that the service firm delivers value by itself to the customer. Our Service Value Chain delivers a framework for a systematic, value-oriented, services marketing.

Book concept

Services marketing is often approached from an operational standpoint, by starting with the specifics of services. Most services marketing texts do not cover the specifics comprehensively and are traditionally structured, often following the '4Ps' approach.

This book takes both a strategic view and innovatively applies the service specifics to the discipline. Value orientation as the central strategy is the starting point for our approach. We ask how a service provider's marketing activities help create value to the service firm. To conceptualise this idea, we tie in Porter's value chain which structures a firm's value processes. Next, we examine the most important point – how customer integration into the service process is used to adopt the value chain to services.

The result from this is the Service Value Chain – our book's basic concept. This chain structures the processes of a service provider that contribute to the value creation of the service firm by influencing the service profit chain, i.e. the cost of the service provider as well as its revenues, via the effects of services marketing activities on customer perceptions (for example, perceived service quality and customer satisfaction) and customer behaviour (for example, customer acquisition and customer retention). The main difference to the traditional value chain is the notion that, for services, there is no 'throughput' of a material product through the processes of a firm, but a customer 'throughput' through the processes between firm and customer.

Book overview

Part 1 presents and explains the concept of the Service Value Chain and illustrates the ways to create value by a service provider through integrating the Service Value Chain with the Service Profit Chain. The following parts treat the specific *value processes* in detail. *Part 2* deals with the primary processes (managing customer interactions and managing customer relationships) and describes the 'throughput' of a customer through the firm's processes which directly affects value. By managing interactions and relationships, value is created for the customer, thus resulting in value for the firm. *Part 3* explores the secondary value processes which support the primary value processes and encompass first the creation of service value by service product, price, and delivery, as well as branding and communications decisions. *Part 4* examines how managing service resources concerns the management of service employees, tangibles and technology, as well as capacity management decisions. Finally, *Part 5* elaborates on the internal and external environment of a value-oriented services marketing. Externally, service providers make decisions regarding marketing strategies, international services marketing, outsourcing and networks from a value perspective. We explain the implementation drivers of a value-oriented services marketing, the firm's organisation, its systems and its culture. Further, for controlling services marketing from a value perspective, we outline a value driver approach.

Target audience

The book is geared towards third and fourth year marketing students on marketing, management, or tourism courses. It is also ideal for MA students and service managers. It will also appeal to newcomers to Services Marketing as we present the basic concepts of the discipline. More experienced readers in the field will find this book appealing given the innovative, strategic, value-oriented perspective.

Orientations

The book is characterised by the following orientations:

- *Value orientation*: The book asks how services marketing activities contribute to a service firm's value creation.

- *Customer orientation*: Customer perceptions and behaviours, as proposed by the Service Profit Chain, are the starting point for value creation. They are used to explain how diverse services marketing activities create value.

- *Management orientation*: Value creation is the most important goal of the majority of managers. By applying a consistent value orientation, business needs are fully accomplished by the Service Value Chain.

- *Integrative orientation*: The Service Value Chain delivers a framework which connects all services marketing activities.

Unique features

The unique features of this book include:

- *Service Value Chain*: By developing and applying the Service Value Chain, we structure and present Services Marketing activities from a value perspective. This framework is used throughout the book.

- *Service Profit Chain*: One of the more strategic concepts in the services marketing literature, we elaborate on the Service Profit in order to explain the value effects of services marketing activities.

- *Services as processes*: Services as processes are a basic premise of our book.

- *Customer relationships*: We present our own concept of relationship marketing and present arguments of the crucial role it plays in services marketing.

- *'Hot topics' of services marketing*: We examine cutting-edge and innovative topics in areas such international services marketing, service networks, and technology use in services.

Additional resources

To access the Instructor's Manual, PowerPoint slides, and other teaching and learning resources visit www.pearsoned.co.uk/bruhn.

Acknowledgements

Developing and writing this innovative book would not have happened without the help of various organisations and individuals. We would like to thank them all. Involved in the review process were: Des Thwaites, Leeds University Business School; James Sallis, Uppsala University; Sue Vaux Halliday, University of Gloucestershire Business School; and Robert J. G. Connor, School of Hotel, Leisure and Tourism, University of Ulster.

We want to especially thank Manto Gotsi from the University of Aberdeen Business School and Gillian Lyons from the University of Wolverhampton, who were involved as 'super-reviewers' during the writing process. They provided us with valuable input at various stages during the creation of this text. In addition, we want to thank several colleagues from the Department of Marketing at the University of Basel. Marina Bogdanovic, Falko Eichen, Kerem Taskin and Nicole Tschanz were of significant help in researching, preparing illustrations, proof-reading and undertaking several administrative tasks.

Finally we would like to thank the team at Pearson Education for making this project a reality. Thanks to our Senior Acquisitions Editor, Thomas Sigel, for sign-ing and believing in this project and guiding us through the process. We also thank Peter Hooper, Editorial Assistant, for his support and assistance. We also thank Andrea Bannuscher, Designer, for her work on the cover and internal design. Last, but not least, we thank Sarah Wild, Senior Desk Editor, for her excel-lent and meticulous work and attention to detail during the production process.

By interpreting services marketing from a value-oriented perspective, our book delivers the grounds for services marketing that is strategically based. We would appreciate an intense discussion about the Service Value Chain concept and look forward to any comments or recommendations!

Manfred Bruhn
Dominik Georgi
Basel, Switzerland
October 2005

Guided tour

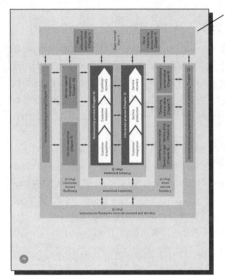

Part openers concisely introduce the themes and issues explored in each chapter so that you can assess the importance of the chapter at each specific point in your study. They also explain the interdependencies with the other parts, utilising the framework delivered by the Service Value Chain.

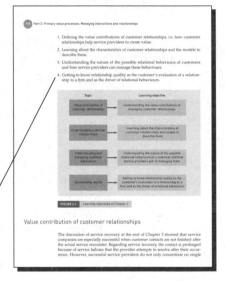

Learning objectives summarise the main points for you to refer to when studying or revising.

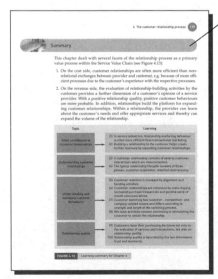

Summaries at the end of each chapter are directly linked to the learning objectives. They systematically show what has been learnt after reading the chapter.

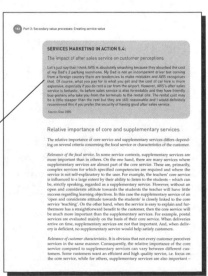

Services marketing in action boxes present stories, interviews and short case studies to improve your understanding by concentrating on specific real-world business examples.

CASE STUDY: TESCO'S CLUBCARD

Case studies at the end of each chapter provide real-life examples of popular international service organisations. The cases relate to a majority of the chapter's topics.

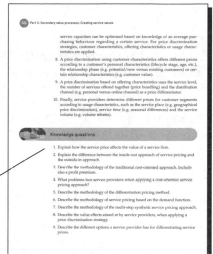

Knowledge questions directly test your understanding of the chapter's content.

Application and discussion questions

Application and discussion questions encourage you to apply your new knowledge to both fictitious and real-life scenarios.

Bibliography

The **Bibliography** at the end of the book provides a comprehensive list of additional readings to help gain further insight into Services Marketing.

Publisher's acknowledgements

We are grateful to the following for permission to reproduce copyright material:

Table 1.1 from 2002/03 *Student Income and Expenditure Survey: Students' Income, Expenditure and Debt in 2002/03 and Changes Since 1998/99*, Department for Education and Skills (Callender, C. 2004), © Crown Copyright, reproduced with the permission of the Controller of Her Majesty's Stationery Office; Figure 1.5 from The effect of retail customer loyalty schemes. Detailed measurement or transforming marketing? in *Journal of Targeting, Measurement and Analysis for Marketing*, Vol. 12 No. 3, OlvivyOne, (Stone, M. *et al.* 2004); Figure 2.3 reprinted by permission of *Harvard Business Review*, issue 72(2), from Heskett, J.L. *et al.* 1994, Putting the Service-Profit Chain to Work, copyright 1994 © by the Harvard Business School Publishing Corporation, all rights reserved; Figure 2.7 from Kundenorientiertes Rechnungswesen als Voraussetzung des Kundenbindungsmanagements by Bruhn, M. and Homburg, C. in *Handbuch Kundenbindungsmanagement, 5th Edition*, Gabler Verlag, (Kohler, R. 2005), with permission from Gabler Verlag; Figure 2.9 from Segmentation Based on Customer Profitability. Retrospective Analysis of Retail Bank Customer Bases in *Journal of Marketing Management*, Vol. 13 No. 5, Westburn Publishers Limited (Storbacka, K. 1997); Table 2.1 and Figures 2.15, 3.11, 4.4, 4.6 and 4.7 from *Relationship Marketing*, Pearson Education Limited, (Bruhn, M. 2002); Figure 2.10 from Financial Services Survey, www.credo-group.com/ftp/finserv_jan2003.pdf, (Moustfield, N. 2003); Table 2.2 reprinted with permission from *Marketing News*, published by the American Marketing Association, Sampathkumaran, S., 1994, Vol. 28, pp 18–19; Figure 2.12 reprinted with permission from *Journal of Marketing*, published by the American Marketing Association, Parasuraman, A. *et al.*, 1985, Vol. 49, S. 4–50; Figure 2.13 reprinted with permission from *Journal of Marketing*, published by the American Marketing Association, Brady, M.K. and Cronin, J.J., 2001, Vol. 65, pp. 24–49; Figure 2.14 from Alternative Scales for Measuring Service Quality: A Comparative Assessment Based on Psychometric and Diagnostic Criteria in *Journal of Retailing*, Vol. 70 No. 3, New York University, (Parasuraman, A. *et al.* 1994), copyright © New York University, Stern School of Business; Figure 2.19 from Linking actions to profits in strategic decision making, *MIT Sloan Management Review* Vol. 42 No. 3, Massachusetts Institute of Technology, (Epstein, M.J. and Westbrook, R.A. 2001); Figure 3.5 reprinted with permission from *Journal of Marketing*, published by the American Marketing Association, Bitner, M.J. *et al.*, 1990, Vol. 54, pp 71–84; Table 3.1 reprinted with permission from Add Value to your Service, Proceedings Series, published by the American Marketing Association, Lindqvist, L.J., 1987, pp. 17–20; Figure 3.7 from Designing Services That Deliver in *European Journal of Marketing*, Vol. 16 No. 1, Emerald, (Shostack, G.L. 1984), republished with permission, Emerald Group Publishing Limited; Figure 3.8 from *Qualitätsmanagement für Dienstleistungen* (Fig. 3.19), Springer-Verlag, (Bruhn, M. 2004), copyright © Springer-Verlag; Figure 3.12 from A Typology of Retail Failures and Recoveries in *Journal of Retailing*, Vol. 69 No. 4, New York University, (Kelley, S.W. *et al.* 1993), copyright © New York University, Stern School of Business; Figures 4.2 and 4.5 reprinted by permission of *Harvard Business Review,* Vol. 68 No. 5, from Reichheld, F.F. and Sasser,W.E., 1990, Zero Defections. Quality Comes to Services, copyright 1990 © by the Harvard Business School Publishing Corporation, all rights reserved; Figure 4.3 reprinted from

Advances in Services Marketing and Management. Research and Practice, Vol. 4, Liljander, V. and Strandvik, T., *The Nature of Customer Relationships in Services*, S. 141–167, Copyright © (1995), with permission from Elsevier; Figure 4.8 reprinted with permission from Diagnosing the Termation of Customer Relationship published by the American Marketing Association, Roos, I. and Strandvik, T., 1997, pp 617–631; Figure 4.9 from *Kundenabwanderungs- und Kundenrückgewinnung-sprozesse*, Gabler, (Michalski, S. 2002); Figure 4.10 from The Danger of Defection – A Comparative Study into Winning Back Lost Customers, www.lindsellmarketing.com, © copyright Lindsell Marketing (2004); Figure 4.12 from *Entwicklung von Kundenbeziehungen*, Gabler, (Georgi, D. 2000); Table 5.1 reprinted with permission from *Journal of Marketing*, published by the American Marketing Association, Keaveney, S.M., 1995, Vol. 59, No. 2, S. 71–82; Figures 5.5 and 8.13 from *Dienstleistungsmarketing (Services Marketing), 4th Edition*, Gabler Verlag, (Bruhn, M. and Meffert, H. 2003), with permission from Gabler Verlag; Figure 5.7 from www.sixt.com; Table 5.2 from Service Engineering. Ergebnisse einer empirischen Studie zum Stand der Dienstleistungsentwicklung in Deutschland, IRB, (Fähnrich, K.P. *et al.* 1999), copyright © Klaus-Peter Fähnrich; Figure 5.9 from A proposed model for new service development in *Journal of Services Marketing*, Vol. 3 No. 2, Emerald, (Scheuing, E.Z. and Johnson, E.M. 1989), republished with permission, Emerald Group Publishing Limited; Figure 5.10 from Markteinführung von Dienstleistungen. Vom Prototyp zum marktfähigen Produkt by Bruhn, M. in *Service Engineering. Entwicklung und Gestaltung innovativer Dienstleistungen* (Fig. 4, pp 235–258), Springer-Verlag, (edited by Bullinger, H.-J. and Scheer, A.-W. 2003), copyright © Springer-Verlag; Figure 5.11 from *Dienstleistungsmanagement (Service management)*, Oldenbourg, (Corsten, H. 2001); Figure 5.12 and Table 5.3 from The end stage of a financial service product in *Journal of Financial Services Marketing*, Vol. 7 Issue 3, pp 220–229 (Harness, D.R. 2003), first published by Henry Stuart Publications; Figure 6.2 from The pricing of bank payments services in *International Journal of Bank Marketing*, Vol. 13 No. 5, MCB University Press, (Drake, L. and Llewellyn, D.T. 1995), © MCB University Press, republished with permission, Emerald Group Publishing Limited; Figure 6.3 and Tables 6.1 and 6.2 from The use of conjoint analysis in the development of a new recreation facility in *Managing Leisure*, Vol. 8 No. 4, Routledge Taylor & Francis Group www.tandf.co.uk/journals, (Ross, S.D. *et al.* 2003); Figures 6.4 and 6.5 from Service pricing. A multi-step synthetic approach in *Journal of Services Marketing*, Vol. 11 No. 1, MCB University Press, (Tung, W. *et al.* 1997), © MCB University Press, republished with permission, Emerald Group Publishing Limited; Figure 6.7 from Application of Price Bundling Strategies in Retail Banking in Europe, Handelshögskolan vid Göteborgs Universitet, FE-rapport 2001–379, (Mankila, M. 2001); Figure 7.3 taken from Location evaluation, www.doubledaves.com, with permission from Chuck Thorp CEO, DoubleDave's Pizzaworks Systems, Inc.; Table 7.3 from Customer expectation dimensions of voice-to-voice service encounters: a scale-development study in *International Journal of Service Industry Management*, Vol. 11 No. 2, MCB University Press, (Burgers, A., *et al.* 2000), © MCB University Press, republished with permission, Emerald Group Publishing Limited; Table 7.4 from Improving satisfaction with bank service offerings: measuring the contribution of each delivery channel in *Managing Service Quality*, Vol. 13 No. 6, MCB University Press, (Patrício, L. *et al.* 2003), republished with permission, Emerald Group Publishing Limited; Figure 8.4 from The impact of different media channels on consumers and the wastage of potential advertising opportunities through existing customer communications in *Journal of Financial Services Marketing*, Vol. 8 Issue 3, pp 279–290, (Greenyer, A. 2004), first published by Henry Stuart Publications; Table 8.1 adapted from August 9–16, 2004 issue of *Business Week*, by special permission, copyright © 2004 by The McGraw-Hill Companies, Inc.; Figures 8.7 and 8.8 from Communicating a quality position in service delivery: an application in higher education in *Managing Service Quality*, Vol. 13 No. 2, MCB University Press, (Gutman, J. and Miaoulis, G. 2003), © Copyright MCB UP Limited, republished with permission, Emerald Group Publishing Limited;

Table 8.2 from Addressing services' intangibility through integrated marketing communication: an exploratory study in *Journal of Services Marketing*, Vol. 16 No. 5, MCB University Press (Grove, S.J. *et al.* 2002), © Copyright MCB UP Limited, republished with permission, Emerald Group Publishing Limited; Figure 8.13 from Dienetlelstungemarketing, 4 Auglage, Gabler Verlag Wiesbaden 2003 (Meffert and Bruhn 2003); Table 9.1 reprinted from *International Journal of Hospitality Management*, Vol. 22, Lockyer, T., Hotel cleanliness—how do guests view it? Let us get specific. A New Zealand study, pp. 297–305, Copyright (2003), with permission from Elsevier; Figure 10.8 from *Service Management for Competitive Advantage, New York*, McGraw-Hill College, (Fitzsimmons, J.A. and Fitzsimmons, M.J. 1994), reproduced with permission of The McGraw-Hill Companies; Table 11.1 from The internationalization of services: trends, obstacles and issues in *Journal of Services Marketing*, Vol. 13 No. 4/5, Emerald, (Samiee, S. 1999), © Copyright MCB UP, republished with permission, Emerald Group Publishing Limited; Figure 11.5 from Big Mac Index in *The Economist*, December 18 2004, © The Economist Newspaper Limited, London (2004); Table 11.2 used with permission from *Journal of Healthcare Management*, Vol. 46, No. 4, pp. 239–249, (Chicago: Health Administration Press, 2001); Figures 11.7 and 11.8 from Der Auslese der Fluggesellschaften folgt das Allianzsterben in *Frankfurter Allgemeine Zeitung*, 29, No. 226, FAZ, (Noack, H-C. 2003); Figure 11.10 reprinted from *Journal of Business Research*, Vol. 57, Wiertz, C., *et al.*, Cooperating for service excellence in multichannel service systems: An empirical assessment, pp. 424–436, Copyright (2004), with permission from Elsevier; Figure 12.2 from Reengineering versus Prozessmanagement. Der richtige Weg zur prozessorientierten Organisationsgestaltung in *Zeitschrift Führung und Organisation*, Vol. 64 No. 3, Schäfer-Pöschel Verlag, (Kamiske, G.F. and Füermann, T. 1995); Figure 12.4 from *Database Marketing und Computer Aided Selling*, Verlag Vahlen, (Link, J. and Hildebrand, V. 1993); Figure 12.6 reprinted with permission from *Journal of Marketing*, published by the American Marketing Association, Deshpandé, R. *et al.*, 1993, Vol. 57, pp. 23–37; Figure 12.8 from *Integrierte Kundenorientierung*, Gabler Verlag, (Bruhn, M. 2002).

Box 1.1, Banking section, from speech by Dr. A.H.E.M. Wellink at the launch of the Netherlands Society of Investment Professionals, *BIS Review* 107/1999; Box 1.1, Airline market section, from Economics Case Study. The European Airline Market, (Riley, G. 2003), copyright © www.tutor2u.net; Box 1.1, Tour operators section, from Collins, Verité Reily: All change for travel sector, *Eurograduate 2004*, 105–109, Setform Ltd; Chapter 1 case study adapted from König Kollege in *McK. Das Magazin von McKinsey*, Vol. 3, March, pp. 122–127 (Bendl. H. 2004); Chapter 2 case study: The service profit chain at a UK grocery store from Applying the service profit chain in a retail environment in *International Journal of Service Industry Management*, Vol. 11 No. 3, MCB University Press, (Silvestro, R. and Cross, S. 2000), © Copyright MCB University, republished with permission, Emerald Group Publishing Limited; Box 3.2, reprinted by permission of *Harvard Business Review*, Vol. 68 No. 4, from Hart, C.W.L. *et al.* 1990, The Profitable Art of Service Recovery, copyright © 1990 by the Harvard Business School Publishing Corporation, all rights reserved; Chapter 3 Case Study from Self-Service for Mobile Users Report, www.netonomy.com, (Fujitsu/Netonomy 2004); Box 4.3 from Building B-t-B e-loyalty in *CRM Today*, www.crm2day.com, (Reid Smith, E. 2004); Box 4.5 from Case Study: Retention plan builds card issuer's bottom line with integrated analytics and consulting, www.fairisaac.com, (Fair Isaac 2004) © copyright 2003–5 Fair Isaac Corporation, all rights reserved; Box 4.6 from The Danger of Defection – A Comparative Study into Winning Back Lost Customers, www.lindsellmarketing.com, Lindsell Marketing (2004); Chapter 4 Case Study from *Scoring points* by Hunt, Humby and Philips published by Kogan Page 2003 Isbn 074943578X; Box 5.2 from The company history, www.tetrapak.com, Tetra Pak (2004); Box 5.3 from 'Pizza Hut Puts Pie in the Sky with Rocket Logo', www.space.com, Space.Com (1999), with permission from Imaginova Corp.; Box 5.6 from 'Leading Hotels Extends Its Line' in *Hotels* magazine, a Reed Business Information publication,

Vol. 36 No. 9, (2002); Box 5.7 from FTSE case study, reproduced from www.thetimes100.co.uk (2004); Box 5.8 from E-mail works its way onto business-minded flights in *USA Today*, (Adams, M. 2003). From USA TODAY, a division of Gannett Co. Inc. Reprinted with permission; Box 5.9 from At your service!, excerpt reprinted with permission from the August 2004 issue of *Food Management*, copyright © 2004 by Penton Media Inc.; Box 5.10 from Onboard service – Easyjet kiosk, www.easyjet.com, Easyjet (2004); Chapter 5 Case Study from Der tollste Laden der Welt in *Textilwirtschaft*, No. 35, Textilwirtschaft (Zeitschrift)-Verlagsgruppe Deutscher Fachverlag, (Howe, U. 2003); Tables 6.1, 6.2 and Figure 6.3 from The use of conjoint analysis in the development of a new recreation facility, in *Managing Leisure*, Vol. 8 No. 4, pp. 227–44 (Taylor & Francis Ltd), www.tandf.co.uk/journals (Ross, S. D., Norman, W.C. and Dorsch, M. J. 2003); Box 6.1 from The pricing of bank payments services in *International Journal of Bank Marketing*, Vol. 13 No. 5, MCB University Press, (Drake, L. and Llewellyn, D.T. 1995), © MCB University Press, republished with permission, Emerald Group Publishing Limited; Box 6.3 from Service pricing. A multi-step synthetic approach in *Journal of Services Marketing*, Vol. 11 No. 1, Emerald, (Tung, W. *et al.* 1997), © MCB University Press, republished with permission, Emerald Group Publishing Limited; Box 6.4, Relationship pricing by The Body Shop section from Customer Club, www.uk.thebodyshop.com, Body Shop (2005) © copyright The Body Shop International Plc; Box 6.4, Membership programme of the Youth Hostels Association from Membership Discounts, www.yha.org.uk, Youth Hostels Association (England and Wales) (2005); Box 6.5 from Application of Price Bundling Strategies in Retail Banking in Europe, *Handelshögskolan vid Göteborgs Universitet*, FE-rapport 2001–379, (Mankila, M. 2001); Chapter 6 Case Study from Pricing a Sporting Club Membership Package in *Sport Marketing Quarterly*, Vol. 13 No. 2, Fitness Information Technology, a division of ICPE/WVU-PE, (Daniel, K. and Johnson, L.W. 2004); Box 7.1 from Arola launches home service in Barcelona in *Caterer & Hotelkeeper*, Vol. 193 No. 4352, www.caterer-online.com, (Stevens, T. 2005); Box 7.2 from Mobile Learning Gains Foothold, reproduced with permission from *The Korea Times* (2005); Box 7.6 from Cost-Effectiveness Evaluation of Hoosier Helper Freeway Service Patrol in *Journal of Transportation Engineering*, Vol. 125 No. 5, American Society of Civil Engineers, (Latoski, S.P. *et al.* 1999), reproduced by permission of ASCE; Box 7.7 from L.L. Berry, The Substance of Success, *Retailing Issues Letter*, Vol. 13 No. 4, July 2001, Center for Retailing Studies, Texas A&M University; Box 7.9, (1) Value effects of low channel integration (para 2) and (3) Dark (value) side of multi-channeling, and Box 7.10 from Multiple Channel Systems in Services: Pros, Cons and Issues in *The Service Industries Journal*, Vol. 24 No. 5, (Taylor & Francis Ltd), www.tandf.co.uk/journals (Coelho, F.J. and Easingwood, C. 2004); Chapter 7 Case Study from Umsatzsteigerungen mit Multichannel-Marketing bei der Mövenpick Wein AG, FHBB Case Study, (Scheidegger, N. and Taaks, G. 2004), copyright © Dr. Pascal Sieber & Partners AG and Nicole Scheidegger; Box 8.1 from McDonalds turns new leaf with salad sales boost in *The Independent*, (Griffiths, K. 2005), copyright © The Independent, 9 February 2005; Boxes 9.2 and 9.4 from McDonald's: Recruiting, selecting and training for success, www.thetimes100.co.uk, reproduced with the kind permission of The Times 100 (2005): For more case studies please see www.tt100.biz; Box 9.3 from Changes in Multiunit Restaurant Compensation Packages in *Cornell Hotel and Restaurant Administration Quarterly*, June 1998, pp. 45–53, Elsevier, (Patil, P. and Chung, B. 1998); Box 9.5 reprinted from *International Journal of Hospitality Management*, Vol. 22, Lockyer, T., Hotel cleanliness—how do guests view it? Let us get specific. A New Zealand study, pp. 297–305, Copyright © (2003), with permission from Elsevier; Box 9.6 from Conduit plc – Employee motivation builds productivity for directory services provider, www.performixtechnologies.com, Performix Technologies (2005); Box 9.7 from Implementing successful self-service technologies in *Academy of Management Executive*, Vol. 16 No. 4, (Bitner, M.J. *et al.* 2002), from USA TODAY, a division of Gannett Co., Inc. Reprinted with permission; Chapter 9 Case Study: Service orientation through employee commitment at Novotel London from Exceeding customer expectations at Novotel in *Strategic HR review*, Vol. 4 No. 2, Melcrum Publishing Ltd. (www.melcrum.com), (Angoujard, R. 2005); Chapter 9 Case Study: British Airways: Improving value through self-service kiosks from British Airways Teams Up With IBM to Roll-Out Self-service Kiosk Technology, www-1.ibm.com, reprint courtesy of International Business Machines Corporation copyright (1998) © International Business Machines Corporation; Box 10.1 from Frequently Asked Questions (FAQ's) – Customer Service, www.redding-electricutility.com, Redding Electric Utility (2005); Box 10.2 from Shopping Habits Likely to Be Affected by Euro 2004, www.prnewswire.co.uk, (PR Newswire 2004), copyright © Footfall Ltd; Box 10.3 from Consumer Foodservice in Germany – Executive Summary, June 2004, www.euromonitor.com, copyright Euromonitor International (2004); Box 10.4 from Ticket overview and Interview with Beckenbauer: Football will take pride of place, www.fifaworldcup.yahoo.com, FIFA (2005) and FIFA (2002); Box 10.5 from Germanwings: Profitable Growth in *Flug Revue*, No. 3, Vereinigte Motor-Verlage GmbH & Co.KG, Motor Presse International (Steinke, S. 2005); Chapter 10 Case Study reprinted from *Omega – The International Journal of Management Science*, Vol. 32, Hur, D. *et al.*, Real-time schedule adjustment decisions: a case study, pp. 333–344, Copyright © (2004), with permission from Elsevier; Box 11.2 from Lauwarmes Geschäft mit Kaffee in *Handelszeitung*, No. 43, Handelszeitung, (Büsser, B. 2003); Box 11.6 from Citibank recharts its technology course in *ABA Banking Journal*, May 1998, pp. 40–48, PARS International, (Levinsohn, A. 1998) Reprinted from May 1998 ABA Banking Journal © by the American Bankers Association. For more information about reprints from AARP The Magazine, contact PARS International Corp. at 212-221-9595; Box 11.7 from TBWA Worldwide named 2004 Global Agency Network of the Year by Advertising Age and Offices and contacts, www.tbwa.com, TBWA, (Miller, J. 2005); Box 11.8 from Der Auslese der Fluggesellschaften folgt das Allianzsterben in *Frankfurter Allgemeine Zeitung*, 29, September, No. 226, FAZ, (Noack, H.-C. 2003); Chapter 11 Case Study: Networking at Nexcom from Die Globalisierung der Netzwerkbildung von professionellen Dienstleistungsunternehmen: Fallbeispiele von drei Start-up-Unternehmen by Welge, M.K. and Borghoff, T. in *Dienstleistungsnetzwerke Dienstleistungsmanagement Jahrbuch 2003*, Gabler Verlag Wiesbaden 2003, (edited by Bruhn, M. and Stauss, B.); Box 12.5 from Wir haben an der falschen Stelle gespart in *Die Welt*, p. 12, Copyright © Die Welt, (Seidel, H. 2004); Chapter 12 Case Study reprinted with permission from *Journal of Marketing*, published by the American Marketing Association, Rust, R.T. *et al.*, 2004, Vol. 68, pp 109–127.

We are grateful to the Financial Times Limited for permission to reprint the following material:

Box 8.6, Amex expands net marketing, © *Financial Times*, 9 November 2004; Box 8.7, Advertisers go back to the future, FT.com, © *Financial Times*, 24 October 2004; Chapter 8 case study, Virgin Mobile's maiden numbers, © *Financial Times*, 19 November 2004, and Customer growth for Virgin Mobile, © *Financial Times*, 30 July 2004; Box 9.1, Barclays embarks on radical shake-up, © *Financial Times*, 7 June 2004; Box 11.1, Air France-KLM ahead on savings, FT.com, © *Financial Times*, 12 April 2005; Box 11.3, Foreign insurers gear up for push into China, © *Financial Times*, 1 December 2004; Box 11.4, Sir Terry's formula for foreign fortune: Tesco's international profits rise sharply, FT.com, © *Financial Times*, 13 April 2005, and Tesco's international empire, FT.com, © *Financial Times*, 12 April 2005; Chapter 11 case study: Ikea's Globalisation Strategy, Ikea continues to build on global success, © *Financial Times*, 28 September 2004; Box 12.2 Reuters to give managers profit responsibility, © *Financial Times*, 21 August 2004; Box 12.4 Money talks in culture of compensation, © *Financial Times*, 11 December 2004.

In some instances we have been unable to trace the owners of copyright material, and we would appreciate any information that would enable us to do so.

PART 1 Basic concept: The Service Value Chain

When investigating categories of consumer goods such as natural goods (e.g. forest, agriculture), industrial goods (e.g. shoes, cars, machines) and services (e.g. banking services, restaurants, management consultancies), services emerged as the most important category in the developed countries during the second half of the twentieth century. Subsequent and parallel to the increasing *importance of services* in the economies, **services marketing** has become a major discipline in marketing research and the lecture circuits during the last two decades.

Traditional marketing concepts were designed for consumer goods with limited suitability to the marketing of services. This is caused by the *characteristics of services* which make them unique compared to consumer goods. Most importantly, services cannot be produced in autonomous processes, i.e. processes which are conducted and fully controlled by the service provider (e.g. producing a car). In order to produce a service, the production process involves the customer. The customer is present when his hair is cut at the hair salon, the customer's money is involved when using the services of a bank and the customer's car is involved in a car wash service.

When defining marketing as all *activities of a service provider which are directed to the customer*, these service specifics imply that marketing cannot only be delimited to the communications activity of a service firm, but concerns many processes of the service firm. For example, when the employee 'produces' a service together with the customer, the employee's attitude and behaviour affects the customer. Thus, the employee delivering the service is an integral part of a service firm's marketing activities. Marketing activities in service firms are therefore *more comprehensive* than in consumer markets, and even employee training in order to increase employee motivation – traditionally an internal activity of a manufacturer – is to be interpreted as a marketing activity.

Due to the specifics of marketing in service firms, marketing processes are central drivers of company **value**. Therefore, it is crucial for a service provider's success to orient its marketing activities at the premise of creating value. From this perspective, the core of this book is the Service Value Chain which structures the value processes of a service firm. This concept is developed in Chapter 1 and serves as a framework for the subsequent chapters. The interconnections between the different elements of this framework are outlined specifically at the end of Chapter 1. Chapter 2 focuses on the value effects of the Service Value Chain by explaining the revenue and cost impact of services marketing activities. The Service Value Chain encompasses primary and secondary processes which are the subjects of Parts 2 to 4. As services marketing interacts with the internal and external environment of a service firm, Part 5 focuses on the relevance of the external markets for services marketing as well as the implementation and controlling of services marketing from a company-internal viewpoint.

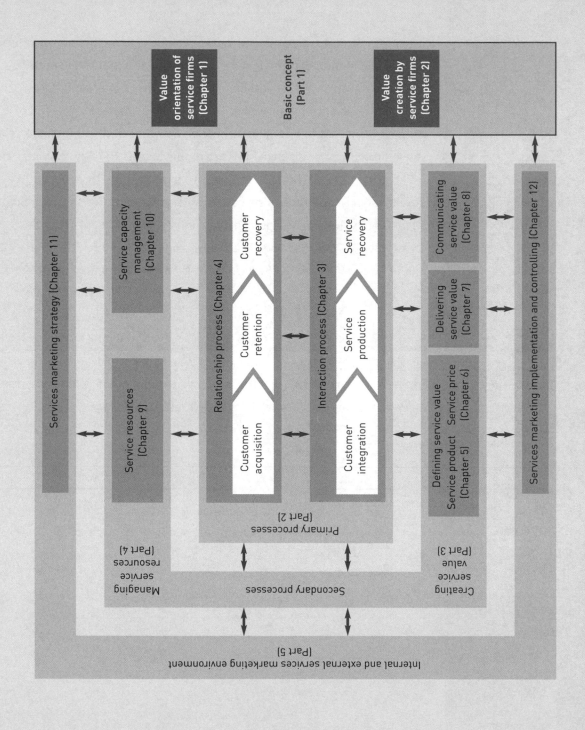

Value orientation of service firms (Chapter 1)

Basic concept (Part 1)

Value creation by service firms (Chapter 2)

Services marketing strategy (Chapter 11)

Service capacity management (Chapter 10)

Service resources (Chapter 9)

Relationship process (Chapter 4)

Customer acquisition

Customer retention

Customer recovery

Interaction process (Chapter 3)

Customer integration

Service production

Service recovery

Defining service value
Service product
Service price (Chapter 5)
(Chapter 6)

Delivering service value (Chapter 7)

Communicating service value (Chapter 8)

Services marketing implementation and controlling (Chapter 12)

Primary processes (Part 2)

Managing service resources (Part 4)

Secondary processes

Creating service value (Part 3)

Internal and external services marketing environment (Part 5)

1 Managing the service process by the Service Value Chain

Students spend – according to statistics – more than half of their monthly budget on services (see Table 1.1). Although some of their biggest spendings might have been for consumer goods (e.g. car, surf board or hi-fi-system), most of the spendings will be for services. And this spending behaviour is even more valid for working individuals who use further services that are not typically used by students (e.g. dry cleaning, ironing service, car rentals, tax accountants). Consequently, *services* account for the greatest part of the economies in developed countries. In economic statistics, services account for an important part of the so-called Third Sector, i.e. all economic activities that are not part of agriculture, fishing and forestry (First Sector) as well as industry (Second Sector). Even though the Third Sector is a residual category where all activities are allocated which cannot be attributed to the First or Second Sector, a major part of the activi-

TABLE 1.1	Students' expenditure on services in the UK 2002/2003		
Category of expenditure		**Percentage of total expenditure**	**Estimated percentage of services expenditure of total**
Living cost	Entertainment (sport, hobbies, cultural, activities, alcohol)	20%	15%
	Food	16%	0%
	Personal expenses	16%	5%
	Other expenses	15%	5%
Housing cost	Rent	19%	19%
Participation cost	Travel	7%	7%
	Books and equipment	5%	0%
	Personal contibution to tuition	2%	2%
Total		100%	53%

Source: Based on Callender 2004.

ties in the Third Sector are pure services. The importance of the different sectors is commonly expressed by the proportions of Gross Domestic Product and employment in the Third Sector. In 2002, the respective proportions of services were 72.6 per cent and 73.8 per cent in Great Britain (United Nations 2003), comparable values are known for other European countries or the US.

Due to the importance of services in the developed economies, in marketing academia, **services marketing** has developed into a specific field within the overall marketing research area during the last 20 to 30 years. In today's management practice as well as academia, the value creation by services marketing is emphasised. Consequently, this book follows a value-oriented approach which is presented in this chapter. Before presenting this approach at the end of this chapter, the fundamentals for value-oriented services marketing are outlined. Regarding management practice, we consider the current market situation in many service industries that disclose value creation as a major challenge for service corporations. From the services marketing academia's perspective, we trace the development of this marketing field during the last 50 years leading to current research topics that are also concerned with value. Then, the specific characteristics of services are explained which differentiate them from consumer goods, and it is outlined how these characteristics have an impact on the value creation by services. Based on these characteristics, we derive the processes of a service company that lead to value. These processes are integrated into the **Service Value Chain** – the basic concept of this book. Consequently, the learning objectives of Chapter 1 are as follows (see Figure 1.1):

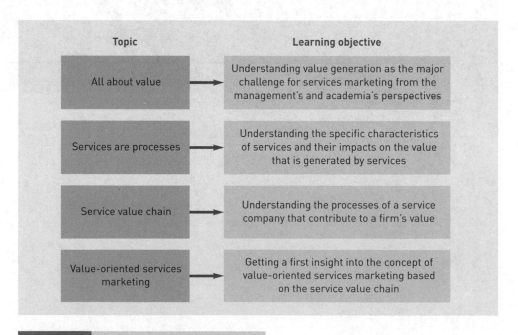

FIGURE 1.1   Learning objectives of Chapter 1

1. Understand value creation as the major challenge for services marketing from the management's and academia's perspectives.

2. Define the specific characteristics of services and their impacts on the value that is created by services.

3. Describe the processes of a service company that contribute to a firm's value and that are structured within the Service Value Chain.

4. Obtain a first insight into the concept of the Service Value Chain as well as an overview of the book.

It's all about value

The management's perspective: competition and value

From the middle until the end of the twentieth century, the services sector's relevance in the developed countries – measured by the services sector's portion of the total employment or the **value** creation – increased continuously. The emergence and development of the services marketing concept in practice and the services marketing discipline in marketing academia were driven by these figures. However, the services sector's relevance in economic statistics has stabilised and market saturation can be observed.

When interpreting this tendency from the demand-side, one can conclude that the demand for services is not growing any more. This general and overall tendency in the services sector consisting of very heterogeneous industries can also be observed in single industries within this sector (see Services marketing in action 1.1). For example, the airline industry has experienced tough price competition for several years. After years of steady growth during which flying

SERVICES MARKETING IN ACTION 1.1:

Strong competition in many service industries

Banking

The widely held view thus appears to be that European banks are heading for turbulent times. Several driving forces will lead to *intensified competition* not only among banks but also between banks and other, new financial intermediaries. This is generally expected to increase the need for a restructuring of the banking sector. The general tenor seems to be that banks are specialised in an economic activity that can, to a growing extent, be performed by non-specialist players. If so, the demand for bank loans will decline and the structure of the balance sheets of banks will alter.

▶

. . .

Looking at simple capacity indicators like the number of banks or branches per inhabitant, it can be expected that *consolidation will continue* in the French, German, and Italian banking sectors in particular.
Source: BIS 1999.

Airline market

History suggests that the low-cost airline sector will experience *market consolidation and increased market concentration* over the coming years. Because of the network economies of scale available to large-scale, low-cost airlines and other factors (including aggressive defence of existing profitable routes), the low-cost airline segment in the European market may eventually be dominated by just two carriers – easyJet and Ryanair. Numerous start-ups will come and go. Scale matters in the aviation industry. EU airlines and their customers are failing to benefit from the full potential of the EU single market. On a global level, many European players are of a sub-optimal size, compared to their major international rivals. Some traditional Flag Carriers are facing serious financial difficulties and need airline partners or new investment to improve their long-term commercial viability.
Source: Riley 2003.

Multiplex cinemas

Until recently a multiplex was often a monopoly supplier to its local catchment area. However as competition intensifies it is becoming increasingly common for multiplex operators to *compete directly against one another within a locality*. Some observers believe that as *market saturation* is reached cinemagoers will be swamped and operators forced to slash admission prices.
Source: McKosker 2001.

Multiplex operators are about to enter a period of *savage competition*, in which the big players will invest tens of millions of pounds into top of the range complexes on the doorstep of their competitors in a drive to kill or be killed.
Source: Newton 1998.

Tour operators

Europe's baseline has changed, especially in Germany where the 'new' Eastern Germans do not have their Western colleagues' *spending power*. Short coach tours are popular, or seven- or ten-day holidays, particularly if sport (cycling, riding, etc.) is in the package. For clients with money the world is their oyster and tour operators look for more exotic far-flung destinations. *Recession* in Germany probably prompted the giant tour operators to buy up British companies; Britain's Thomson is now part of 'the world of TUI', and Thomas Cook has become Thomas Cook AG (part owned by Lufthansa). The Swiss company, Kuoni, with its own British arm, continues to provide holidays for a clientele spread across Europe.
Source: Collins 2004.

transformed from an elite means of transportation to a common one, a further market increase is improbable. Political events like 11 September 2001 did their part to narrow the market. Another example is the private banking market. The rise of the financial markets attracted many new private banking customers or at least new private banking money. Recent statistics show that this part of the banking market is declining.[1]

Due to the shrinking or at least stable services markets, the competition within the respective industries becomes more severe, and service providers must ask themselves how they respond to these developments. For a long time it seemed to be enough for service providers to offer a certain range of services at a certain quality level for competitive prices in order to attract demand. In some industries, especially in service markets that were characterised by a monopoly or monopoly-like market structure (e.g. telecommunications, energy, postal services or airlines) the customers did not really have choices. As a consequence the providers in these markets did not have to concentrate on market shares, etc. In other markets, the customers were locally oriented, such as travel agents or retailers. In these areas, new distribution channels, like the internet, have led to new market dynamics.

Severe competition in these markets has resulted in greater difficulties for the service providers to ensure and increase their **firm value**. Put simply, firm value is composed of revenues on the one hand and cost on the other hand. All incidents that lead to revenues generated above the cost for the service provision, i.e. paid usage of the company's services by its customers, increase value. Thus, firms aim at concentrating upon activities that increase that value. These activities again lead to cost. For example, a direct mailing campaign of a bank that offers a new investment product to its customers, aims at increasing value by inviting customers to purchase the new product. However, these activities also generate cost, i.e. the cost of developing the campaign, printing the letters and brochures as well as sending them out. Activities only increase a firm's value when they generate more revenues than cost. Since revenue is generated by the customers' behaviour, i.e. the purchase of the new investment product, the value creation of an activity depends on its ability to induce positive customer behaviour. Customers only use a service when this usage promises to *create value for the customer*. In the banking example, the customer will only purchase the new product when it promises to increase his/her assets. The same condition is valid for other service industries: a customer only books a holiday when it promises to be interesting, fun or relaxing. These promises represent the value the customer perceives to receive from the provider and its services. Consequently, a service firm's value depends on the services' value perceived by the customer. These relationships will be explored in more detail in Chapter 2. For the time being, we emphasise the fact that service providers aim at delivering value to the customer in order to increase their firm's value. In the banking example, we outlined that the marketing activity 'direct mailing' affects the firm's value. Thus, service firms evaluate their activities according to their ability to create value. As we will explore later, these activities can be summarised to certain value processes that represent the value creation potential of a service firm.

In accordance with the development of services marketing in practice, a tendency towards a more value-oriented approach to services marketing can also be observed in academia and the literature.

The academic perspective: Developmental stages of the services marketing discipline towards value orientation

Today, many of the articles in the important journals in the marketing field as well as many presentations at marketing conferences are about services marketing. Twenty-five years ago, however, services marketing played only a minor role in marketing academia, even though initial works on services marketing appeared around 1960. In the following, we give a short overview of the emergence and development of services marketing in academia in order to outline the topics that are discussed in the field and make up part of this book, as well as to understand the research questions that are currently being addressed. It is possible to differentiate between five corresponding *developmental stages of services marketing* research chronologically (see Figure 1.2).

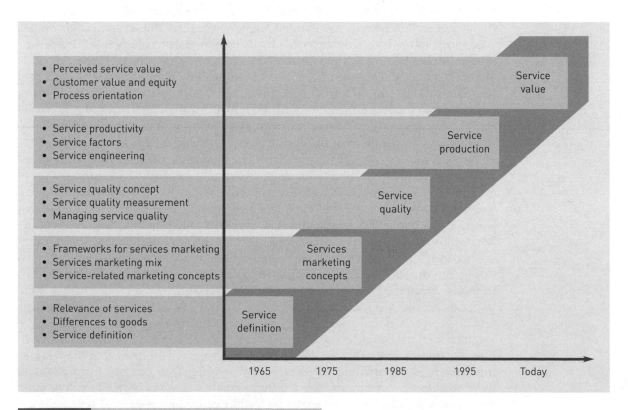

FIGURE 1.2   Developmental stages of services marketing

1960s: Service definition (definitional focus). The first publications in the field of services marketing dealt with the concept of a 'service'. Topics in this stage of academic research were focused upon the relevance of services, their differences to goods and the constitutional definition of services.[2] Regarding the relevance of services, authors discussed above all the increasing proportions of services within the economic statistics.[3] Often, this development was called the 'service revolution'.[4] Furthermore, the differences between services and goods were outlined. Although this topic has been discussed in later developmental stages as well, the foundations of the services-versus-goods discussion can be traced back to this first stage of services marketing research. Based on these differences, first definitions of a service were proposed.[5] An important characteristic of services is the process character of a service. The main benefit of a service is created through the service process when provider and customer meet (e.g. for food services, the restaurateur serves the customer at the restaurant; or the patient seeks medical services at the doctor's practice). This process character is a basic idea in services marketing and will be elaborated on later in this chapter.

1970s: Services marketing concepts (conceptual focus). In this stage of services marketing research the focus was shifted to developing concepts for services marketing. This stage reached its climax in the late 1970s and early 1980s. The research concentrated on translating the differences of services compared to goods into service-specific marketing concepts. It was argued that in service industries the marketing concept had not been established because 'marketing offers no guidance, terminology, or practical rules that are clearly relevant to services'.[6] This conceptual focus resulted in the definition of services marketing frameworks.[7] Furthermore, service typologies were used to derive strategic emphases depending on the service type. Another stream of research focused on the marketing mix of service corporations, either by applying the marketing mix concept to services comprehensively[8] or by specifying certain marketing mix elements for services, e.g. distribution channels for services.[9] Finally, in this stage 'new' marketing concepts arose based on the services marketing themes, such as relationship marketing.[10]

1980s: Service quality (measurement focus). In the following stage of services marketing development, the concept of **service quality** emerged as a major challenge for service companies. Because of the characteristics of services, especially the encounter of provider and customer in the service process, service quality is a more complex construct than product quality. The characteristics of service quality are not objective, but subjective for each customer. As a consequence, major efforts were undertaken to conceptualise service quality. The best-known model in this context is the so-called GAP model of service quality that explains the determination of service quality as the gap between service expectations and perceptions by four internal gaps.[11] Based on the conceptual considerations regarding service quality, further research put emphasis on the development of instruments to measure service quality. The widely known and discussed measurement instrument based on the GAP model is the SERVQUAL approach that measures service quality using 22 items that are associated with the five service quality dimensions: tangibles, reliability, responsiveness, assurance and empathy.[12] Other researchers stressed the service encounter as the focal source of service quality[13] – the so-called 'moments of truth'.[14] This philosophy resulted in the emergence of even more service-specific measurement approaches, such as the critical incident technique[15] or the **service blueprinting** approach.[16] A further area in this stream of research dealt with the management of service quality. Respective research emphases were the development of concepts for managing service quality and the identification of drivers of service quality.[17] The evaluation of service quality management from a controlling perspective, namely the determination of a return on quality was also taken into account.[18]

1990s: Service production (operational focus). The increasing profitability and cost orientation in the 1990s resulted in a more systematic look into service production. The starting point was the analysis of service productivity[19] by examining input–output relations of the service production process. Consequently this research involved an analysis of service factors and opportunities to improve productivity as well as the effectiveness of service production by managing these factors. Major topics in this area were service technology,[20] service employees and the internal marketing concept.[21] In addition, the concept of customer integration that dealt with the efficient and effective integration of the customer into the service production process (i.e. managing the customer participation) was part of academic research. This production-oriented approach was also applied to new services by developing concepts for service design and engineering.[22]

Today: Service value (process focus). In recent years – in accordance with the increasing relevance of value in general management – research in services marketing has been focusing on the value contribution of services. One area of research in this field of services marketing academia is the **perceived service value** concept, i.e. the analysis of the value that is created by a service company for the customer through the eyes of the customer.[23] While this research takes on the perspective of the customer, studies on customer value and customer equity analyse value creation from the firm's perspective.[24] **Customer value** is the value that is contributed to the overall firm's value by a single customer relationship, while customer equity is the value that is created by the whole customer base. Recently, research has questioned how these values can be managed actively by service firms by asking what service processes contribute to value creation. This process orientation is primarily a focus of current services research.[25]

Comparing the developments in management practice of service companies and research in services academia, we observe a recent tendency towards a value orientation. This orientation is the guideline for our value-oriented services marketing approach that we present later in this chapter. Before this, we will consider the nature of services because – as outlined above – the characteristics of services have an impact on the processes of a service firm.

Services are processes

In the services marketing literature, many differences between services and consumer goods are discussed. These differences are then interpreted as the 'characteristics of services'. Figure 1.3 shows a selection of typical differences or **service characteristics** respectively. We will see that all these characteristics can be ascribed to one central characteristic: *services are processes*. The service itself is predominantly a process: the flight on an aeroplane, consulting with an investment adviser, haircutting, attending a university, repairing a car. Of course, the customer also benefits from the service outcome, e.g. the arrival at the flight destination, the chosen portfolio strategy, the university degree or the repaired car. However, each of these services itself is a process.

The notion of the process outcome leads to one of the other service characteristics mentioned most often: *services are intangible*. Especially compared to the outcome of the production process in the consumer goods industry, i.e. the produced good, this difference becomes obvious. A car, a suit, a diamond or a

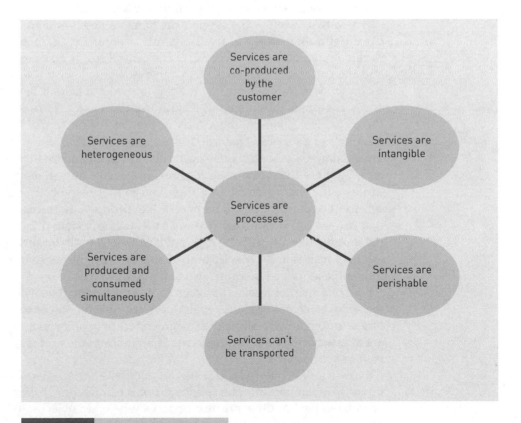

FIGURE 1.3   Services are processes

detergent are very tangible outcomes – although their benefit might often be intangible. However, the outcomes of service processes are in most cases intangible. Furthermore, in the service process itself, tangible rather than intangible elements are relevant, like competencies, know-how, etc. The intangibility of services results in the importance of employees and communications in the quality evaluation process of a customer.

Because of their intangibility, service capacities can decay, i.e. *services are perishable and cannot be stored*. The seats in an aeroplane, the cinema, the football stadium, the rooms in a hotel, etc. cannot be utilised at another point in time if they are not utilised at their scheduled time. Another consequence of the intangibility of services is that *services cannot be transported*. These characteristics of services especially influence the capacity management and the delivery systems.

Furthermore, *services are consumed and produced simultaneously*. In contrast to consumer goods, e.g. a can of beer, a customer cannot purchase a service, then go home and utilise it later. Quite the contrary, when a flight is over (i.e. after the production process of this flight) the service is already consumed.

In addition, *services are heterogeneous*, i.e. a service can be very different for each customer. A tennis coaching course for a customer who is very talented, engaged and willing to learn, will be very different from that for a customer who is the opposite.

These two factors – that services are heterogeneous and are consumed and produced simultaneously – are the result of another characteristic that will be covered in greater depth because of the central role it plays in services marketing and the concept of this book. A major characteristic of the service process is the *participation of the customer*, i.e. the service process cannot be conducted without some customer involvement. Therefore, the customer in services marketing theory is also called the *co-producer* or *prosumer of the service*. In other words, the customer of a service is regarded as an 'external factor'. In production theory, the production of goods is explained by the specific combination of production factors, i.e. how the work of employees, materials, etc. are combined in order to produce the end product that is then sold to the customer. In order to 'produce' a service the customer has to be part of the 'production process' (e.g. a visit to the hair-dresser). Therefore, the customer is called an **external factor**. The meeting of the internal (e.g. doctor) and external factors (e.g. patient) during the service 'production' results in the service outcome. Even though service outcomes are mostly intangible in nature, there are also material outcomes of service processes, e.g. the report of a market research project. In most services, the customer benefits from the service outcome, i.e. the repaired car, the new haircut or the revenues realised based on the growth strategy recommended by management consultants. There are also services where the customer benefits from the process itself, e.g. a theatre visit or sports event.

How can the external factor be characterised? The general view that the customer is integrated into the service process can be more differentiated when we acknowledge that there are also services where an 'object at the customer's disposal' is integrated into the process (e.g. car repair). Thus, the external factor can be the customer himself or objects (animals or in some cases people) which are at the customer's disposal or for which they are responsible.

What does this customer integration mean to provider and customer? From the *provider's perspective*, the customer and their objects are production factors that are necessary for the service delivery. In contrast to the internal factors, these external factors are not at the disposal of the service firm. For example, a car cannot be repaired when it is not at the garage. Or a hotel room cannot be used when the customer does not appear at the hotel. Therefore, this external factor is a source of uncertainty for the service provider. Furthermore, customers differ according to their characteristics that might be relevant for the quality of the service produced, thus the external factor is heterogeneous resulting in heterogeneous service processes and outcomes. For example, the outcome of a consulting service might differ considerably depending on the customer's openness and willingness to provide information that is needed in the process.

From the *customer's perspective*, the integration of the external factor means the abandonment of the external factor during the production of the service. In the case of the personal integration into the process, the customer spends time that could be used for other activities. In the case of a visit to a cinema, the customer for example cannot simultaneously eat in a restaurant or work. When an object is integrated into the process, the customer dispenses with this object – they cannot drive their car during a car repair nor can they spend their money when it is invested in some banking product. Furthermore, during the production process, the external factor might be affected by internal factors. Thus, the customer, too, experiences an uncertainty regarding possible damages of the external factor: at the hairdresser, the customer risks a bad haircut; when investing money, the customer risks the loss of the money, and at the dry cleaner, the customer risks damage to their clothes.

As we have outlined, all the service characteristics discussed above are connected with the notion that *services are processes* (see Figure 1.3):

- Services are intangible because of the intangible nature of the service process, its input (e.g. employees' abilities) and its outcome.

- Services are perishable because processes can only be conducted and not stored.

- As a consequence services are not transportable.

- Services are produced and consumed simultaneously within the service process.

- Services are heterogeneous because for different customers, service processes might differ.

- Services are co-produced by the customer because without the presence of the customer in the service process, a service cannot be produced and delivered.

The process characteristics of services lead us directly to the company processes aimed at creating value which will be discussed in the following section.

The Service Value Chain

Structuring value processes

In the previous section, we dealt with the process character of services and the fact that when service provider and customer meet a value is created for the customer. As process orientation means to manage a service provider's processes with the goal of creating value we must ask more specifically: What can a service provider do in order to create value? Keeping this objective at the back of our minds, we present the concept of the *Service Value Chain* that – based on the general value chain concept by Porter[26] – illustrates the company processes which create value.

Since the processes are aligned with their impact on value, we first have to outline what kind of value we are talking about. From the provider's perspective, value concerns the *value of the firm*. Simplifying this concept, value in services marketing can be explained by addressing revenues and cost in service processes. Revenues increase value and costs reduce value. All activities of a service provider lead to revenues and cost. Certain marketing activities such as a competitive price or a superior service quality try to attract customers to use the services. By attracting customers, revenues are generated. However, the marketing activities also affect cost. To illustrate this, take the efforts to ensure a high service quality at an airline check-in: when an airline appoints more employees at the check-in counters in order to reduce the waiting time of the customers (i.e. in order to increase service quality), these employee appointments will generate further personnel costs.

At this point, we will not discuss the value definition in more detail. All you need to remember at this stage is that value is determined by what remains after all costs have been deducted from the revenues. Initially, we are more interested in the service provider's processes that lead to value and, in order to consider these, we differentiate between two types of processes. There are primary value processes which have a direct impact on value creation, and there are secondary value processes that affect value via the primary processes.

Primary value processes

The **primary value processes** of a service provider are the provider's *activities that create a direct value*. The 'services are processes' notion explained above accentuates that in services value is created by the *'throughput' of the customer* or his objects in the service production process. This throughput creates a direct value for the customer as well as for the provider. During a hotel visit, stages of this throughput are the customer's arrival and entrance into the hotel, checking-in and entrance into the hotel room, etc. By this, the customer's need for a place to stay is satisfied and, thus, a value is created. The hotel is paid for letting the room to the customer, thereby also creating a value for the hotel.

A central characteristic of services is that the production of services is realised by means of interactions between the service provider and its customers, thus the customer participates in the service production. Consequently, in order to create value, the **service interaction process** (see Figure 1.4) starts by integrating the customer into the service production process, e.g. a patient visiting the doctor's practice, a motorist taking their car to the garage. Therefore a primary value activity of the service provider is to render possible **customer integration**, i.e. facilitate the customer's integration into the service production process. Through this integration, the customer 'meets' the internal production factors of the service provider. The central function of this 'meeting' is the production of the service, i.e. *service production* is a second primary value activity of a service provider. Particularly in services, production failures are common. This is also caused by the process characteristics of services. Even though **service employees** are prepared to interact with the customer, failures can occur. While in industrial production these failures can be resolved without the customer's perceiving the mistake, in services, the customer is directly affected by production failures. When a hairdresser uses the wrong colouring, the customer's hair ends up a different colour from what the customer expected. In many cases a recovery of the service outcome can be achieved by improving the service or by offering compensation. As a consequence, the customer might be eventually satisfied. Often, customers are even more satisfied after a successful **service recovery** than without failures. Thus, service recovery is an important **value driver** and therefore the third primary value activity of a service provider.

These processes of value creation concern single service processes, i.e. a single flight, a single hotel or restaurant visit or a single attendance at a language course. However, in many services, value for the provider is not necessarily created only by a single interaction. For example, a single counselling interview between a bank employee and a customer is not the major value driver for the

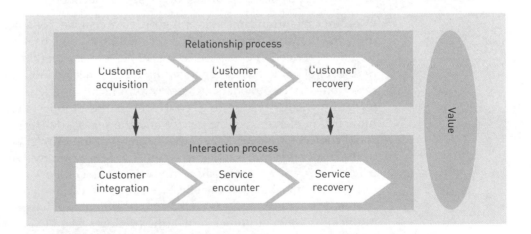

FIGURE 1.4   Primary value processes

bank, it is rather the sum of the various services the customer uses that creates value for the bank. For the bank the fact that it has direct access to the customer means that it can create value by offering and selling various bank products to the customer. In the case of an airline, the airline creates a direct value by the customer's purchase of a single flight. However, convincing the customer to come back and fly again with the airline is just as important as the purchase of the single flight in order to produce further revenues and ensure future value for the airline. This notion clarifies the differentiation of **interactions** and **relationships**. While an interaction describes the throughput of a customer via an individual service process, the relationship concerns the *customer's throughput through a relationship* with the provider.

This throughput creates value for the customer (e.g. efficiency because of experience with the provider's processes). For some services, especially for so-called membership services (e.g. banks, telecommunications), a relationship is even a prerequisite for service delivery. As for the customer, there is value created for the service firm as well because the number of customer relationships generally correlates in a positive way with sales and profits. Furthermore, the longer relationships last, the more profitable they are in many service industries.[27] On the relationship level, the value chain is made up of three stages of the *relationship process* (see Figure 1.4). Each stage affects the value creation differently and is operationalised by various activities in the fields of service product, service pricing, service delivery and service communications. The value processes on the relational level are as follows:

- **Customer acquisition** aims at recruiting new customers who have not yet used the services of the provider. In order to attract customers, service providers make use of communications (e.g. advertising, direct mail), the pricing system (e.g. first-user discount) or elements of the service and the service delivery system (e.g. physical appearance of the service location).

- **Customer retention** aims at keeping the customer, i.e. convincing them to stay in the relationship for membership services or to come back on a regular basis for other services. The major objective of customer retention is to keep the current level of value that is generated by a customer relationship. For customer retention, service providers also use communications (e.g. a customer newsletter), the pricing system (e.g. contracts in the mobile telecommunications industry) or elements of the service and the service delivery system (e.g. personal contact employee). The importance of customer retention is highlighted in the box Services marketing in action 1.2. Moreover, the customer retention process aims at a relationship enhancement, seeking to intensify the customer's relationship, and thereby increasing the volume and frequency of the customer's service usage as well as cross-selling. Service providers use communications (e.g. customer cards), the pricing system (e.g. volume discount) and service elements as well as the service delivery system (e.g. a special hotline for an airline's top customers).

- **Customer recovery** aims at regaining lost customers in order to renew the value potential for the provider. Respective marketing measures are winback calls (communications), regain offers (pricing system) or offering more convenient service delivery solutions (service elements and delivery system).

SERVICES MARKETING IN ACTION 1.2:

Grocery market share through customer retention

For several years, new differentiators of customers' buying behaviour have emerged in the UK grocery market. One of these differentiators is the use of customer loyalty cards as a tool to bond the customer to the firm. Figure 1.5 shows the results of a study regarding bonding/customer loyalty, to a grocery store and market share.

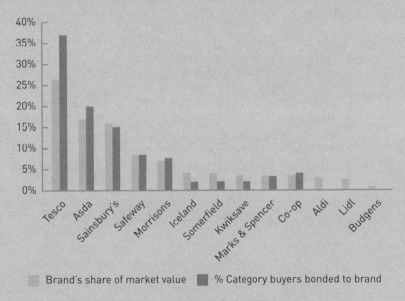

Brand's share of market value   % Category buyers bonded to brand

Figure 1.5 Relationship of bonding and market share for UK grocery stores
Source: OgilvyOne and Millward Brown, cited in Stone *et al.* 2004.

The results illustrate that the percentage of buyers who are bonded to a brand correlates with the market share of the grocery store. Tesco exhibits the highest bonding rate (37%) as well as the highest market share (26%), while the stores with low market shares (Aldi, Lidl, Budgens) have minimum bonding rates.

See Services marketing in action 1.3 for an illustration and application of the Service Value Chain idea in a concrete business context.

SERVICES MARKETING IN ACTION 1.3:

Service Value Chain in the tourism industry

The last few years were probably the most difficult experienced by the hotel industry in living memory. Sluggish economies around the world, the threat of war in Iraq followed by war, the advent of Severe Acute Respiratory Syndrome (SARS), etc. caused an unsatisfactory market situation. Consequently, many tourism service providers, like airlines or hotels, encountered major problems in terms of decreased revenues and profits. This was the reason for a (re)-structuring of the Service Value Chain in the tourism industry.

An important part of the redefinition of the Service Value Chain is the distinction of interactional processes on the one hand and relational processes on the other hand (see Figure 1.6). The interactional processes encompass the sales and marketing, reservation, capacity management and operations processes. Most differing from goods manufacturers, due to the participation of the customer in service production, tourism service providers first acquire customers by sales and marketing (e.g. by mass communications or via travel agencies); then by intensely managing demand and capacity in order to ensure an efficient use of their capacities (e.g. hotel rooms, aeroplane seats). Only 'at the end' of the value chain do they 'produce' the actual service by service operations, i.e. serving the customer, cleaning the room, etc. As in other service indutries, customer retention has become a major marketing goal of tourism service providers. Therefore, many providers installed relationship marketing approaches, like loyalty programmes, which are designed to build relationships with the customers which ensure that customers come back and recommend the services of the provider.

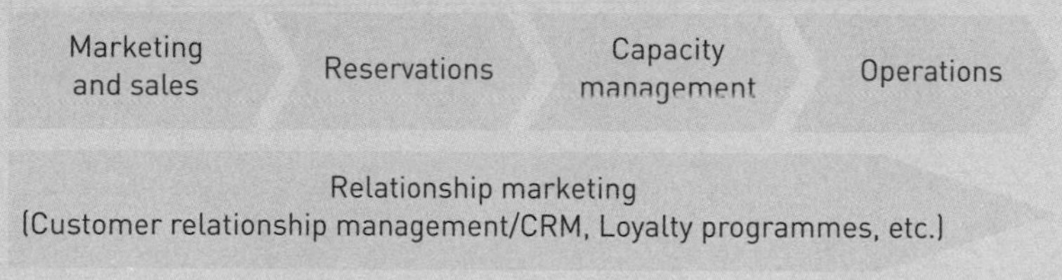

Marketing and sales	Reservations	Capacity management	Operations

Relationship marketing
(Customer relationship management/CRM, Loyalty programmes, etc.)

Figure 1.6 Typical Service Value Chain in the tourism industry

Secondary value processes

Primary processes that have a direct impact on value are influenced by **secondary value processes** that affect value indirectly, via the primary value processes. In the example of the airline, value is created by a passenger taking a flight and paying for that flight. In order to create that value, the customer has to know the airline and must be informed about the flight schedule, a price must be determined, the plane and pilot must attend the flight, etc. The value is not generated directly by the plane or pilot or because a manager determines a price that is profitable for the airline – the value is generated because the passenger takes the flight. Thus, all the other activities mentioned here are prerequisites for value creation and are therefore secondary value processes. We differentiate between two categories of secondary processes: creating service value and managing **service resource**s.

In order to conduct service processes, the customer must be presented with a *service concept* that can be purchased. This service concept might be the reason that the customer is attracted to the firm. Service excellence drives customer loyalty. Thus, the service concept ensures value creation in the relationship process. In addition, the service concept can support the primary interaction process. During the process, the customer chooses from a set of services that are bundled in the service concept of the firm. Service providers define and transfer the service concept to the customer. Regarding the definition of the service concept, the concrete services offered as well as the pricing system for these services are determined. Furthermore, the service concept can only support the value creation when it is transferred to the customer, i.e. when value is communicated before and during the service process and provided by the service delivery activities.

As outlined before, the value creation in the interaction process depends heavily on the customer's participation. Nevertheless, the service provider's input also determines the value creation by means of the company's internal resources that are involved in the service process. In order to create a service, there are specific service resources necessary. Service resources account for the ability of the service firm to provide the specific service. Typical service resources are for example the rooms of a hotel, the knowledge and competence of a management consultant or the aeroplanes of an airline. However, there are other so-called operating resources which do not represent service resources (e.g. food, writing paper and bedding in a hotel). Generally, the most important service resources are:

- *Employees*. Depending on the kind of service, employees are the most important and vital service resource. Their competencies and behaviour in contact with the customer account to a large extent for the perceived quality of the service offered. Examples are the product knowledge of a retailer's employees or the back-office employee's ability to understand the investment philosophy of a customer.

- **Tangibles**. In many service situations, the physical surroundings of the service delivery are an important driver of the service production and the service perception by customers. Examples are the design of a bank's hall, equipment in a university's classroom and the dress of retail employees.

- *Technology*. For many services, technology is an important potential resource. Examples are internet services or airlines' computer systems.

The degree and type of service resources the service firm must provide can differ. However, no service exists that can be delivered without applying the service resources of the firm.

Value-oriented services marketing based on the Service Value Chain

The Service Value Chain framework presented in the previous paragraphs presents the core of the value-oriented services marketing approach that is depicted in Figure 1.7. Simultaneously, this concept is the basis for the structure of the book. In this chapter, we have outlined and explained the foundations of the framework, identifying the challenges of services marketing, the process character of services, as well as the framework itself. In Chapter 2, we specify the idea of the Service Value Chain by looking more deeply into the value creation process. We will illustrate in detail how the processes of a firm affect the value creation. By doing so, we will have provided the basics to understanding the specific contributions of the different service processes on value in subsequent chapters.

In Part 2 we focus on the primary value processes and elaborate on provider activities within these processes. To do so we deal with the interaction process, i.e. the customer integration, the service production itself as well as service recovery in Chapter 3. In Chapter 4, the relationship process of a service provider is outlined, namely the activities required to recruit customers, keep customers as well as expand relationships and regain customers.

Parts 3 and 4 concentrate on the secondary value processes of services marketing. Part 3 deals with the service value and explains how it is defined for a specific service firm, delivered and communicated. Part 4 looks at the service resources, more specifically at human and tangible resources (including technology). In addition, capacity management activities that aim at the optimal provision and utilisation of service resources will be discussed.

Finally, Part 5 links value-oriented services marketing and its environment internally and externally to the service corporation. Externally, services marketing not only manages the relationships with the customers, but also the delivery to market in general as well as the relationships with other relevant market players, e.g. suppliers and competitors. In Chapter 11, the impact of concepts such as international services marketing, service networks and outsourcing on the value processes is explained. Internally, services marketing interacts with other parts of the organisation. Chapter 12 deals with the implementation and control of services marketing.

Summary

The learning objectives of Chapter 1 can be summarised thus (see Figure 1.8):

1. Service industries are characterised by highly competitive market situations that complicate service providers' efforts to gain and keep customers who use the services and eventually create value for the service firm. Therefore, service companies try to focus their business processes on value creation, by

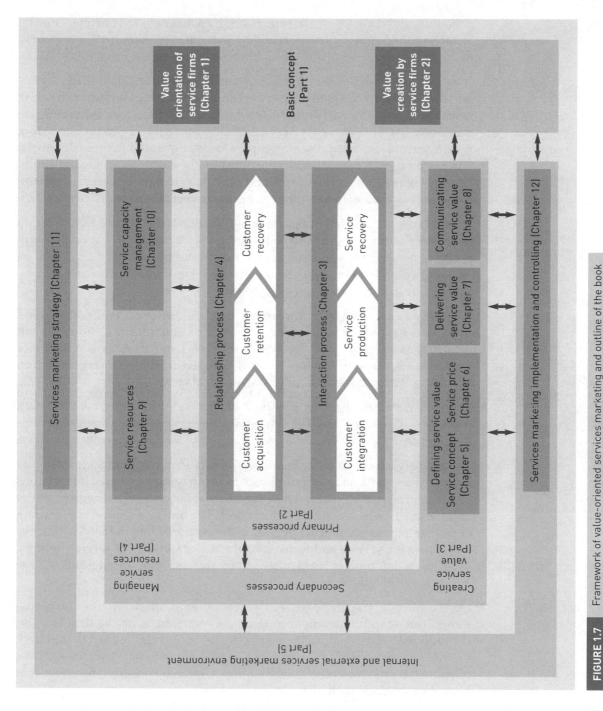

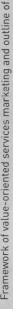

designing and conducting marketing activities that help to generate value by attracting and keeping customers and by inducing revenues that contribute to the firm's value.

2. In accordance with the development of services marketing in practice, a similar tendency towards value orientation can be observed in services marketing research. During the last 40 years, research in this field focused mainly on services marketing concepts, service quality and service production. More recently value-oriented research topics are at the core of research efforts. Studies on service value perceived by customers, customer value and equity that contribute to the firm's value and on value creation by services marketing processes dominate the current services marketing research.

3. How a firm's activities contribute to value creation is determined by the nature of services. Services differ from consumer goods according to various service-specific characteristics. Services are intangible and perishable, they cannot be transported and are produced and consumed simultaneously. Furthermore, services are heterogeneous and are co-produced by the customer.

4. All these factors can be summarised under the notion that services are processes. In contrast to consumer goods, the value for the customer is not created via a material good, but within a process. In that process, the service provider affects the customer, who takes part in the service production process and therefore is also called the 'external factor'.

5. These characteristics have an important impact on the nature of value-creating processes of service firms. The concept of the Service Value Chain structures these processes and illustrates the value impact of services marketing activities.

6. The primary processes of the Service Value Chain aim at managing customer interactions and customer relationships. Managing customer interactions results in the service process where the internal factors of the service provider and the customers as external factors meet. The business processes regarding customer interactions aim at integrating the customer into the service process, delivering the service and recovering the service in case of service failures. This interaction process is characterised by the customer 'throughput' via the interactions with the firm.

7. On the more aggregated level of the customer relationship, there is a customer 'throughput' not only through the interactions with the firm but also through the relationship with a firm. A customer relationship is initiated, maintained, expanded and recovered in case of customer defections. These relationship processes contribute to a firm's value by ensuring revenues that have their origin in customer relationships.

8. The two primary processes, i.e. the relationship and the interaction process, are influenced by the secondary processes of a service provider. These secondary processes principally concern the service value that is defined by the

service concept and the service price, that is delivered by the distribution systems of the service firm and that is communicated by branding and communication efforts.

9. A second group of secondary processes concerns the service resources. Service employees, tangibles and technologies facilitate customer interactions and relationships. The optimal level of these resources in terms of value contribution is defined and realised by a service firm's capacity management.

10. This basic idea of the Service Value Chain is the core of value-oriented services marketing that helps in managing the value creating processes of a service firm.

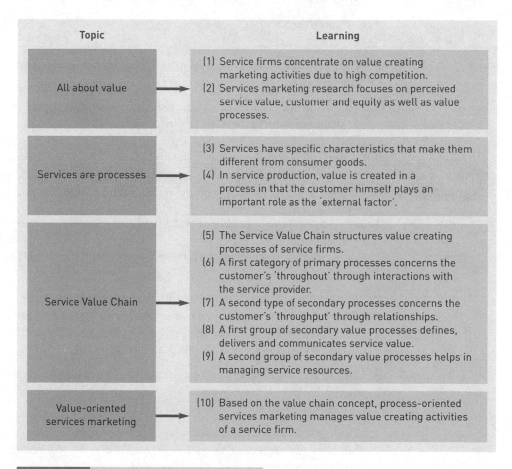

Topic	Learning
All about value	(1) Service firms concentrate on value creating marketing activities due to high competition. (2) Services marketing research focuses on perceived service value, customer and equity as well as value processes.
Services are processes	(3) Services have specific characteristics that make them different from consumer goods. (4) In service production, value is created in a process in that the customer himself plays an important role as the 'external factor'.
Service Value Chain	(5) The Service Value Chain structures value creating processes of service firms. (6) A first category of primary processes concerns the customer's 'throughout' through interactions with the service provider. (7) A second type of secondary processes concerns the customer's 'throughput' through relationships. (8) A first group of secondary value processes defines, delivers and communicates service value. (9) A second group of secondary value processes helps in managing service resources.
Value-oriented services marketing	(10) Based on the value chain concept, process-oriented services marketing manages value creating activities of a service firm.

FIGURE 1.8   Learning summary for Chapter 1

Knowledge questions

1. What are the reasons for the value orientation of services marketing in many service industries?

2. Describe the developmental stages of research in services marketing.

3. What are the specific characteristics of services that make them different from consumer goods?

4. What is meant by a service company's focus on value creation?

5. Explain the concept of 'customer throughput' within the Service Value Chain concept.

6. What primary value processes are conducted by service firms and how do they contribute to the firm's value?

7. What secondary value processes can be distinguished and how do they affect the primary value processes and thus value?

Application and discussion questions

1. Try to recap your monthly expenditure and identify the proportion of services in your budget. What percentage do services constitute in your total budget? Compare this percentage with the economic statistics and discuss the reasons for the difference.

2. Do some research on a certain industry (e.g. banking, insurance, hotel, restaurant, education, public transportation, airline) and find out what are the current challenges in these industries. Discuss how these challenges can be addressed by the Service Value Chain concept.

3. Choose a particular service (e.g. banking, insurance, hotel, restaurant, university, public transportation, airline) and explain how the specific characteristics of services apply to that service.

4. Think of one of your recent service utilisations and explain the process character of this service usage. What situations do you remember that illustrate the specific characteristics of services?

5. Discuss the concept of customer 'throughput' through the interaction and relationship process. Try to illustrate the concept with a practical example from your own experience.

6. Explore how a provider of a certain service (e.g. banking, insurance, hotel, restaurant, university, public transportation, airline) creates value in the interaction and relationship processes.

7. Think of your last visit to a cinema or supermarket. What secondary value processes did you perceive? Discuss the relevance of the various secondary processes for the chosen example.

CASE STUDY: CREATING VALUE AT RITZ-CARLTON

Since the beginning of the new century, the hotel market in the United States and Europe has been a stable one. Due to economic and political developments throughout recent years, the number of occupied rooms and the revenue per room were stable or even declined, while in 2004 an increase in these figures could be stated. In 2001 and 2002, even the profitability of European hotels decreased by a total of 14 per cent. In this highly competitive situation, Ritz-Carlton permanently strives to create value for its customers and thus, via customer loyalty, has created a high firm value. For Ritz-Carlton, value creation starts with a superior service quality. For the firm, high quality is not defined by little details such as heated bathroom mirrors, but by consistent and consequent high-class service. This strategy is documented by the service level Ritz-Carlton realises along the entire hotel value chain.

Within the *interaction process* of the value chain, everything is done to satisfy the customer. This includes all service options during the stay (service production stage in the value chain), starting with little services that are self-evident for a hotel of this class. For example, when the coffee is too cold, the guest gets a fresh cup at the hotel's expense. Also, a hotel can employ a technology assistant who helps guests to send data via a laptop. The Ritz-Carlton strives for extra service. This becomes obvious at the after-sales stage of the Service Value Chain, as the example reported by a managing director of one European Ritz-Carlton shows: 'Recently, we conveyed a guest to the train station, where he discovered that he had left important documents at the hotel.' The chauffeur took the fastest available car at the hotel, drove to the station at which the guest was due to arrive, getting there before the guest, and handed his case to him when he alighted from the train. Another employee went out and purchased essential medicine for a guest. Then there is the example of the employee who let a guest use his personal car because the rental car did not arrive at the hotel on time.

Not only at the interaction process level, but also at the *relationship level*, Ritz-Carlton aims at delivering value. A guideline for employees is 'Never lose a guest'. This demand corresponds to the organisation's philosophy, but also to a simple financial calculation: an average guest spends 100,000 euros within the group during his life. Next to this simple philosophy, a relationship system is implemented in order to collect information of guests, such as 'Mr X prefers to sleep on the left side of the bed', or 'Mrs Y likes bananas on the fruit plate'. One employee – without being asked to – recorded a Formula 1 race for a guest who had mentioned in passing during his last visit how annoying it was that he could not watch the race.

Regarding the secondary value processes of Ritz-Carlton's value chain, many of the services are individualised and – despite the assistance of information systems – require the full dedication of the hotel's employees. Therefore, Ritz-Carlton places a strong emphasis on *employee recruitment and motivation* activities.

With regard to *employee recruitment*, the opening of the Ritz-Carlton in Berlin, Germany is a good example. One year before the opening of the hotel, Ritz-Carlton started searching for candidates and training the selected ones, recruited from all over the world. For each position, there is an exact job description, says Sue Stephenson, the senior human resource manager of the chain. These were developed based on a worldwide internal benchmarking for each position and depict exact qualification requirements for each position.

Besides the training and personal development opportunities for each employee, the image as 'best hotel and locations all over the world' also attracts the best employees. However, Ritz-Carlton pays salaries that are only slightly higher than those of its competitors. At the same time, the working hours are no better than at other hotels, but Ritz-Carlton stands out from the crowd in terms of *employee motivation*. This starts with the philosophy that they are not only employees but hosts. In internal communications, employees are addressed as ladies and gentlemen and, for example, take their meals in the restaurant rather than in a cafeteria.

The most significant element of this philosophy is that, in contrast to the employees of other hotels, the employees of Ritz-Carlton have real decision-making authority. Not only are they allowed to act self-dependently – they have to do so. The philosophy says 'The employee should interrupt his actual work in order to attend to the guests' needs'. This often happens in day-to-day situations, but this **empowerment** approach can also be applied on a higher level. Every chambermaid is allowed to offer a room to a guest, every waiter is allowed to invite a guest to a meal – without asking the supervisor for permission. The employees utilise their authority only because they are not asked for justification in the event of mistakes. For Ritz-Carlton, standardised excuses are not enough – 'When you forget a wake-up call, it does not help the guest when you bring him a bottle of champagne'. The only thing that counts is solving the problem. As a consequence at Ritz-Carlton one does not consider problems as 'problems' but 'challenges' – freely adapted from César Ritz, the eponym of the hotel group: 'Never say no when a guest asks for something. Even when he would like you to obtain the moon for him. At least, we can try.'

The implementation of the firm's philosophy is a continuous process. *Internal communications* play an important role in ensuring the high-quality service level. For example, every employee carries a credit-card-like piece of paper stating 'We are ladies and gentlemen serving ladies and gentlemen'. In addition, for half an hour every day, employees discuss the principles of Ritz-Carlton as well as what challenges they encountered and how they could be solved.

For Ritz-Carlton the value-oriented strategy has brought about *superior results*. The firm was the first and only hotel company to win the Malcolm Baldrige National Quality Award – the American quality prize that is awarded to companies with superior quality management. Ritz-Carlton was the first and only service company to win the award twice, in 1992 and 1999. Ritz-Carlton's image as a high-class employer was documented by hundreds of applicants queuing up at the beginning of the application process for the new Ritz-Carlton at Berlin in order to hand in their application personally. Furthermore, according to a JD Power study, Ritz-Carlton is leading in every measure of guest satisfaction (which includes pre-arrival/arrival; rooms; food and beverage; hotel services; and departure). Thirty-six per cent of Ritz-Carlton guests say that their experience was above expectations, which is higher than for any other hotel brand in the segment. In terms of profitability, at the end of the 1990s Ritz-Carlton was more profitable than its direct competitor and than the average of the luxury hotels segment.

Sources: adapted from Bendl 2004; 4hoteliers 2004, Deloitte 2004, JD Power 2004, Ritz-Carlton 2004a, 2004b.

Notes

[1] See Reuters 2004.
[2] See Brown *et al.* 1994.
[3] See Blois 1974.
[4] See Regan 1963.
[5] See Judd 1964; Rathmell 1966.
[6] See Shostack 1977, p. 73.
[7] See Bateson *et al.* 1978.
[8] See e.g. Booms and Bitner 1981.
[9] See Donnelly 1976.
[10] See Berry 1983.
[11] See Parasuraman *et al.* 1985.
[12] See Parasuraman *et al.* 1988.
[13] See Czepiel *et al.* 1985.
[14] See Carlzon 1987.
[15] See Bitner *et al.* 1990.
[16] See Shostack 1984.
[17] See e.g. Parasuraman *et al.* 1985.
[18] See Rust *et al.* 1994.
[19] See Gummesson 1995.

[20] See Domegan 1996.
[21] See Greene 1994; Rafiq and Pervaiz 1993.
[22] See Pullman and Moore 1999.
[23] See McDougall and Levesque 2000; Sweeney and Soutar 2001.
[24] See Payne *et al*. 2001; Rust *et al*. 2004.
[25] See Van Looy *et al*. 1998; Flieβ and Kleinaltenkamp 2004.
[26] See Porter 1998.
[27] See Reichheld and Sasser 1990.

2 Value creation by services marketing: Service Value Chain and Service Profit Chain

The focus of the value-oriented services marketing concept is to manage the activities of the service provider, so that higher value can be realised. From a marketing perspective this means that service providers try to focus on marketing activities that help to increase customer value, which will eventually lead to a higher firm or shareholder value. Before dealing with the different marketing activities, i.e. the primary and secondary value processes, we need to have a closer look at how value is created by services marketing activities.

In contrast to other decisions made by a service provider (e.g. financing decisions) which focus on increasing the firm's value, the value contribution of marketing activities is realised by the *behaviour of the customers*. When the service provider is successful in attracting new customers or retaining existing customers, then the company will eventually realise increases in its value by increased revenues and/or reduced cost. Whether new customers can be attracted or not depends on the customer's evaluation of the provider. When the customer appreciates a provider, they are more likely to choose the company's services than if the customer is not convinced by the provider. These general relationships are basic principles of the so-called **Service Profit Chain**, which is closely linked to the Service Value Chain. The activities within the Service Value Chain outlined in Chapter 1 aim at initiating the Service Profit Chain in order to create value. The Service Value Chain encompasses a firm's activities or processes, while the Service Profit Chain structures the impacts of these processes on the customer. Thus explaining value creation through the Service Value Chain means *connecting the Service Value Chain and the Service Profit Chain* (see Figure 2.1).

Accordingly, the general objective of this chapter is to ensure you understand the various relationships within the Service Profit Chain as well as the analysis of the value creation within this chain. The following learning objectives are highlighted (see Figure 2.2):

1. Understanding how services marketing activities create value and how the activities' value contribution can be analysed.

2. Describing the concept of customer value, how it is composed and how it can be analysed.

3. Learning about the customer behaviours that create value and how the behaviour can be analysed.

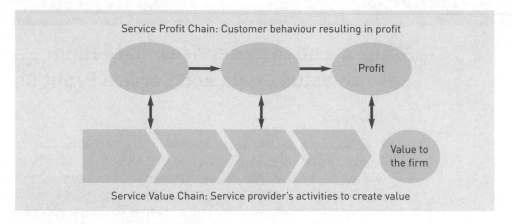

FIGURE 2.1   Service Value Chain and Service Profit Chain

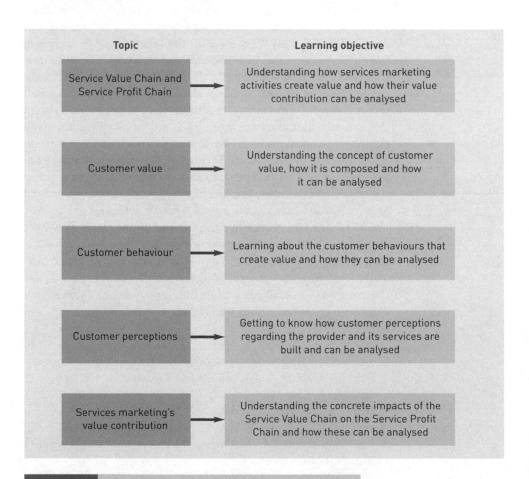

FIGURE 2.2   Learning objectives of Chapter 2

4. Getting to know how customer perceptions of the provider and its services are built and how they can be analysed.

5. Understanding the impact of the Service Value Chain on the Service Profit Chain and how these relationships can be analysed.

Integrating the Service Value Chain and the Service Profit Chain

As outlined in Chapter 1, the Service Value Chain structures the activities of a service provider that create value into primary value processes and secondary value processes. In contrast to the Service Value Chain, the *Service Profit Chain*[1] structures the impacts of a service provider's activities on the customer's perceptions and behaviour. Regarding the effects on the customer's side, the original version of the concept encompasses customer satisfaction and customer loyalty, which lead eventually to revenue growth and profitability for the service provider as the consequences of the delivered service value (see Figure 2.3). Revenue growth and profitability at the right end of the chain therefore represent the link to the firm's value as customer value is a major determinant of firm value: a company's value is created by revenue growth and the profitability of the firm's customer relationships. The chain elements to the left of these two outcome figures such as customer satisfaction and customer loyalty explain how the value of a customer relationship is generated, i.e. the more loyal a customer, the more valuable the relationship, the more satisfied a customer is, the more loyal the customer will be and finally the better the service value is perceived, the more satisfied the customer will be.

This basic idea of the Service Profit Chain can be generalised by defining a *generalised Service Profit Chain* that also explains how customer value is created (see Figure 2.4). However, the stages explaining the creation of customer value are interpreted on a more general level: services marketing activities are evaluated by the customer and will lead to certain customer behaviours such as customer loyalty when the evaluation is positive. Thus positive behaviour will ultimately lead to increased firm value. This kind of generalisation – the use of umbrella concepts such as customer behaviour which encompasses customer loyalty for example – has the advantage that customer behaviours that lead to customer value but are not part of customer loyalty can be integrated (e.g. the acquisition of a customer or the contribution of the customer within the service process). The service quality and customer satisfaction elements are also generalised, by defining a stage called customer evaluations. Here, the perceived service quality, as well as other relevant evaluations, such as price perception or perceived relationship quality can be integrated.

Services marketing activities aim to increase the consecutive values in the service profit chain, through realising more positive customer evaluations, resulting

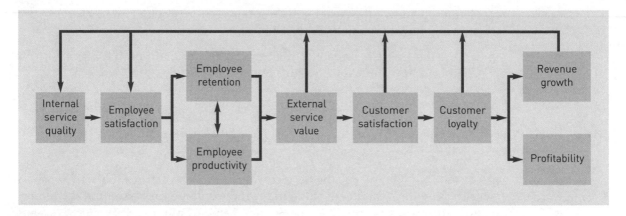

FIGURE 2.3 Original Service Profit Chain

Source: Reprinted by permission of *Harvard Business Review*, issue 72(2), from Heskett, J.L. *et al.* 1994, Putting the Service-Profit Chain to Work, copyright 1994 © by the Harvard Business School Publishing Corporation, all rights reserved.

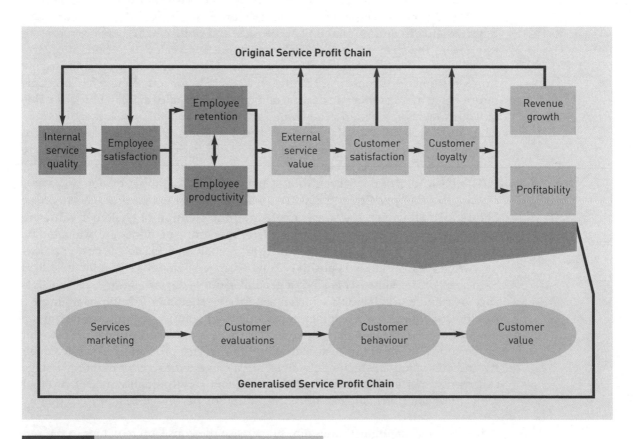

FIGURE 2.4 Original and generalised Service Profit Chain

in more positive customer behaviour and in higher customer value. Thus, service providers try to design and realise the *Service Value Chain* in order to manage the Service Profit Chain (see Figure 2.5). The service provider will focus on a sequence of services marketing activities that influence the customer evaluation and behaviour in such a way that at the end of the day value is created.

One can differentiate between marketing activities within the relationship process and activities within the interaction process. Marketing measures within the *relationship process* (e.g. loss-leader prices for customer acquisition) influence customer perceptions (e.g. interest, perceived attractiveness, image, preference) that eventually influence customer behaviour (e.g., in this case, the first choice of

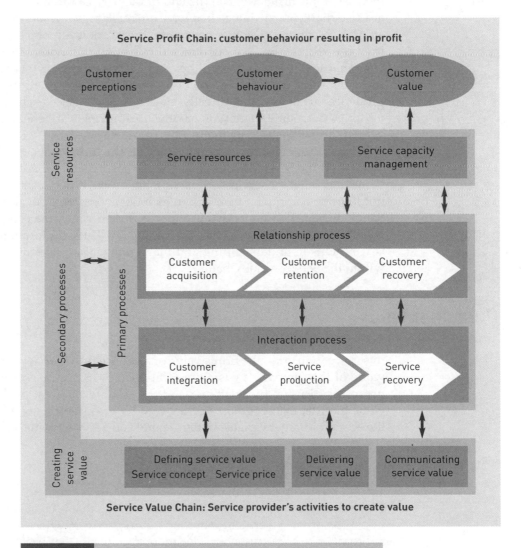

| FIGURE 2.5 | Integration of Service Value Chain and Service Profit Chain |

a provider by a customer, i.e. customer acquisition). The *interaction process* also influences customer perceptions and behaviour. The better the interactions with the customer are, i.e. the better the customer is integrated, the better the actual service delivery will be perceived to be. The better the service recovery activities work, the more positive are the customer's perceptions (e.g. perceived service quality or, in the case of further positive incidents, perceived relationship quality) and consequently the customer's value-relevant behaviour.

So far we have only outlined services marketing activities that are intended to influence customer perceptions in the initial phases of the relationship in the hope that this will lead to the desired customer behaviour and eventually to an increase in the firm's value at the end of the Service Profit Chain. However, there are also marketing activities that have *direct effects on customer behaviour and value creation*. Regarding customer behaviour, the relationship process marketing activities can directly induce customer purchasing behaviour (e.g. by promoting customer loyalty cards with direct purchasing incentives). Furthermore, measures regarding both the interaction process and the relationship process can influence customer value directly via cost effects. Since each of these measures involves personnel, materials or other resources that generate cost, customer value is also influenced by these.

Why are service providers interested in the links between the Service Value Chain and the Service Profit Chain? The reason is that these links explain how value is created by services marketing activities. When a service provider does not know what impact their activities have on customer evaluations, customer behaviour and consequently customer and firm value, the company will not be able to plan marketing activities systematically. Thus, exploring the Service Profit Chain helps in understanding and managing the services marketing processes within the Service Value Chain.

Customer value

In service industries, the firm's value of a service provider depends mainly on the value of the company's customer relationships. Since marketing activities and processes focus on the customer and thus (should) aim at increasing customer value in order to strengthen a firm's value, we concentrate on customer value as the economic target variable in the generalised Service Profit Chain.

Definition and types of customer value

Generally, customer value is defined as the value that is created by customer relationships from a service provider's perspective.[2] There are very different approaches to *define customer value* more specifically. For example, a very simple definition understands customer value as the current revenues generated by a customer. However, this definition neglects the cost a customer relationship generates. In many industries, the cost to service a customer may vary considerably. For example, the cost for an online banking transaction is only one-tenth of the cost of personal contact between customer and contact personnel. Furthermore, future potentials are neglected in this definition. Depending on the use of the customer value results (e.g. investment in the customer, retention of the customer), it is more important to know future potentials than current revenues. These simple examples show that there is a variety of different customer value components that can be subsumed into four generic types of customer value components. These differ according to the customer value component applied and to the underlying time perspective (see Figure 2.6):

- *Profitability* concerns the value component from a past-oriented time perspective. This figure states the value of a customer in terms of current revenues or contributions.

- *Potential* also concerns the value component, but from a future-oriented perspective, where the future profitability of a customer is taken into account.

- *Lifetime* means the current lifetime of a relationship, defined as the time period between the relationship's starting point and the current point in time.

- *Loyalty* represents a future-oriented interpretation of the relationship lifetime and is measured, for example, by the probability that the customer will stay or the estimated future lifetime of the relationship in question.

At first sight, it seems obvious that customer value should be defined in terms of future-orientation. When planning the investment potential of the customer base,

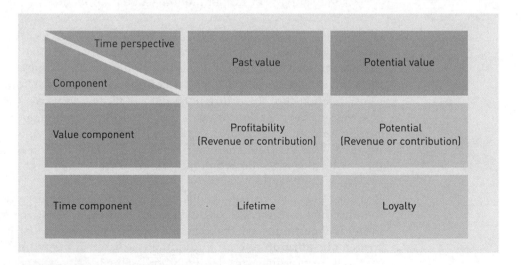

Time perspective / Component	Past value	Potential value
Value component	Profitability (Revenue or contribution)	Potential (Revenue or contribution)
Time component	Lifetime	Loyalty

FIGURE 2.6   Generic customer value components

a customer's future potential is more relevant than their past profitability. However, consider the following statement of an airline manager:

> We planned valuing our customers solely according to their potential. But, imagine this situation: at the check-in, there is the 63-year-old president of a huge company as well as his 32-year-old assistant. Purely because of their ages, our employee could estimate without any computer system which of the two has greater future potential for us . . . the assistant. But imagine what would happen if we were to upgrade the assistant to business class as a relationship measure and wouldn't do so with his boss because of his lack of potential.

This example illustrates that there is *no ideal definition of customer value*. The choice of customer value definition depends on various factors, among others on the prerequisites for customer value analyses in the firm, based on existing data and the purpose of the analyses applied (e.g. cross-selling versus retention). The following pairs of customer value orientations represent extreme forms of how customer value definitions can differ.

Time versus value orientation. A holistic definition of customer value encompasses both components of the customer value construct: time and value. However, in most cases companies only follow a value orientation for the valuation of their customers, where profitability and even future potential are analysed statically, which leads to the fact that the dynamics of customer relationships are neglected. In companies where a time perspective is applied, both orientations are often treated in a segregated manner. For example, customer loyalty analyses are undertaken within market research studies, while customer profitability is examined by the control or datamining departments. Occasionally a combined approach relating to customer lifetime value is applied.

Past versus future orientation. Past-oriented customer values are determined using data from the past, such as last year's revenues, that are often easier to determine than future-oriented data. Future-oriented data are, however, more useful for most investment decisions. When deciding whether a firm should invest in a customer relationship, the future potential is a more valid scale for orientation than past value. However, future value is always an estimation, and associated with a certain amount of measurement error. Furthermore, in many industries, if the revenue with a certain customer is relatively stable over a certain time period, then past value is an important indicator of future value.

Revenue versus contribution orientation. For many companies, attributing revenues to individual customers is already a major challenge. However, attributing cost to individual customers seems to be unrealistic for many industries. While product cost can be attributed to an individual customer in many industries, like credit cost, cost of products sold by a mail order business, other costs, like the cost of serving the customer or marketing cost, are difficult, if not impossible to allocate to a single customer relationship. For example, it is difficult to allocate the expenditures for an advertising campaign to a single customer. However, companies try to integrate cost as comprehensively as possible in their value calculations for a good reason: studies show that cost can differ a lot. Consequently, analysing only customer revenues produces misleading results. However, of course, there are also decisions that can be taken sensibly based only on revenue figures. For example, for a given response probability the revenue potential of a customer without taking into account the associated cost is a good indicator of the value of cross-selling activities.

The most important methods for a financial valuation of the customer relationship are customer profitability analysis and customer lifetime valuation which will be explained below.

Analysing customer profitability and potential

A *customer profitability and potential analysis* is designed either as a customer revenue analysis or a customer contribution analysis. *Customer revenue analysis* looks at the turnover of individual customers. In addition to the current revenues (current value) this could include factors such as the expected or maximum revenues for that customer, the potential value of future revenues. However, absolute sales levels often provide little information about a customer's relationship. Hence, a relative customer analysis should be conducted, for instance, to determine the following key figures:

- A customer's *proportion of sales* versus total corporate sales indicates the value of that customer for the particular firm.

- The *customer penetration rate* is based on the definition of the absolute market share and gives the customer's share of sales compared with their total expenses for that product.

- The *relative supplier position* is derived from the relative market share and designates the ratio of sales achieved by the respective seller with a customer to the biggest competitor's sales with the same customer.

When the profitability analysis is defined more comprehensively by taking into account not only the revenues but also the cost of a customer relationship, a *customer contribution analysis* is applied. This kind of analysis extends the customer revenue analysis by considering not only the costs but also the revenues involved in a relationship with a customer (see Figure 2.7). Determining the associated costs for serving customers is to some extent problematic, since ascertaining the customer contribution margin requires eliciting first which costs caused by the relationship apply to a particular customer, and secondly which costs would not apply if the relationship no longer existed.[3]

Customer gross sales revenue per period
–   Reduction of sales revenue

=   Customer net sales revenue per period
–   Costs of goods/services sold
    (direct costs per unit multiplied by sold units)

=   Customer contribution margin I
–   Customer-driven cost per order
    (e.g. cost of reservation)

=   Customer contribution margin II
–   Customer-driven costs per period
    (e.g. travel cost for customer calls)
–   Other direct costs of customer per period
    (e.g. salary of an account manager exclusively
    responsible for the customer, mailing expenses,
    interest on overdue accounts)

=   Customer contribution margin III

FIGURE 2.7   Calculation scheme for the customer contribution margin

Source: Köhler 2005.

Both customer revenue and customer contribution analysis can be used for customer segmentations that aim at identifying profitability differences between customer groups in order to weight customer segments in accordance with their value. A traditional and established segmentation approach is the *ABC analysis* that compares *key turnover levels between various customers*.[4] This analysis ranks the customers according to the sales level with the seller. The data are entered on an x–y plot with the axes 'cumulative share of customers' and 'cumulative turnover'. Starting with the largest customers on the basis of sales, the value is located on the y-axis and plotted against the sales contribution along the x-axis. This often demonstrates that a relatively small number of customers make up the largest proportion of sales. In this context, the so-called *20:80 rule* states that 20 per cent of the customers account for 80 per cent of sales. On the basis of the resulting curve the customers can be divided into A, B, or C customers. The A customers are the largest sales generators and should thus be the first ones to be invested in (see Figure 2.8).

How a service company conducts a profitability analysis depends on different company-specific factors, such as the research question under consideration or the availability of data. The box Services marketing in action 2.1 demonstrates how a Scandinavian bank analysed its customer base in terms of profitability.

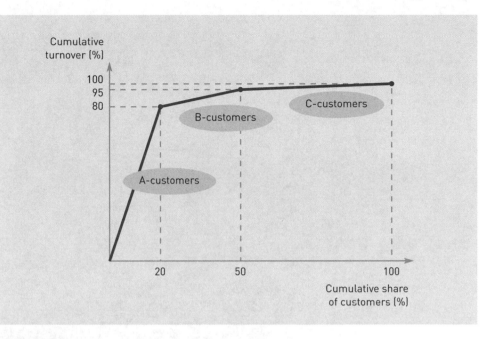

FIGURE 2.8   ABC-analysis based on customer sales

SERVICES MARKETING IN ACTION 2.1:

Customer segmentation based on customer profitability in a Scandinavian bank

Profitability problems caused senior managers of a Scandinavian bank to investigate the sources of profitability. One hypothesis was that there were huge differences between different customers in terms of profitability. Therefore, customers were grouped according to their profitability. A further hypothesis was that the more transactions a customer carried out, the more profitable they were. As a consequence, the transaction volume was applied as a second dimension. The grouping worked in the following way: due to a negative average profitability of the customers, the division value of 'low profitability' and 'high profitability' customers was also negative, −100. According to the transaction value four groups were established (see Figure 2.9).

The figure also presents the results of the profitability segmentation, with 48 per cent of the bank's customers in segments 1, 2, 3, which stood for only 4 per cent of the transaction volume. Segment 6 consisted of only 8 per cent of the customers and these customers accounted for 42 per cent of volume and 111 per cent of profitability. Segment 4 consisted of 14 per cent of the customers accounting for 29 per

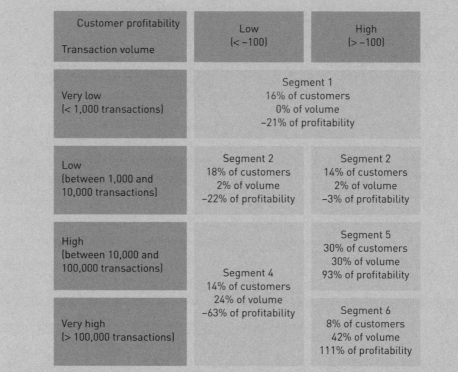

Figure 2.9 Customer segments for a particular Scandinavian bank based on customer profitability and transaction volume

Source: based on Storbacka 1997.

cent of transactions and a negative contribution to profitability, –63 per cent. A more detailed analysis of these customers showed that they accounted for a huge percentage, 47 per cent, of the total loans. Further analyses revealed that most of them were customers with loans that were tied to an unfavourable base rate. This example shows that a profitability analysis helps to identify differences in the customer base in terms of profitability and can act as the basis for recommendations on the management of customers and services.

Source: Storbacka 1997.

Analysing customer lifetime value

The **Customer Lifetime Value (CLV)** method is, simply put, a computation methodology that translates the principles of dynamic capital investment analysis to customer relationships. The CLV is usually defined as the *present CLV* determined by discounting the current and future payment stream to derive the present value of a customer. This approach is based on the principle that future payments are less valuable than current ones.[5]

A *sample calculation* of the CLV is presented in Table 2.1 (for more numerical examples refer to Berger & Nasr[6]). In this case, the customer relationship is evaluated over an average duration of eight years at a discount rate of 10 per cent. The customer specific acquisition (investment) costs of 50 units are deducted in the first year. Table 2.1 illustrates how the numbers are accumulated for each period. The value is calculated for a period of seven years. The first five rows show the determinants of the contribution margin of a customer. Sales and price result in revenues; on the cost side, product cost, marketing expenditure and acquisition costs are considered – the latter ones only for the first period. The resulting margin is then discounted as in traditional investment theory. Summing up the discounted margins for the seven periods leads to the customer lifetime value as a present value of the next seven years' margins.

TABLE 2.1	Sample CLV calculation								
	$t = 0$	$t = 1$	$t = 2$	$t = 3$	$t = 4$	$t = 5$	$t = 6$	$t = 7$	
Predicted sales	4	6	10	16	20	20	20	20	
Product price	10	10	10	10	10	10	10	10	
Piece costs	3	3	3	3	3	3	3	3	
Marketing expenditure	20	30	40	40	30	30	20	20	
Acquisition costs	50	–	–	–	–	–	–	–	
Margin	–42.00	12.00	30.00	72.00	110.00	110.00	120.0	120.0	
Discount factor ($r = 0.1$)	1.00	1.20	1.44	1.73	2.07	2.49	2.99	3.58	CLV
Margin (discounted)	–42.00	10.91	24.79	54.09	75.13	68.30	67.74	61.58	$\Sigma = 320.55$

Source: Bruhn 2002b, p. 212.

While Table 2.1 exhibits the calculation of the CLV in detail from a theoretical standpoint, organisations often face difficulties in practice when trying to implement the CLV method. However, when the calculation of a complete present CLV proves to be too cumbersome because of the lack of information, using statistical models and so forth, organisations often try to calculate an average customer's lifetime value in a rather simplified manner, often by customer segments.

Comparable to the profitability segmentation above, CLV can vary significantly between customer segments of a service firm. Furthermore, CLV varies across industries (see for example Figure 2.10). This variation implies the necessity of specific CLV analyses per industry, firm or even customer group.

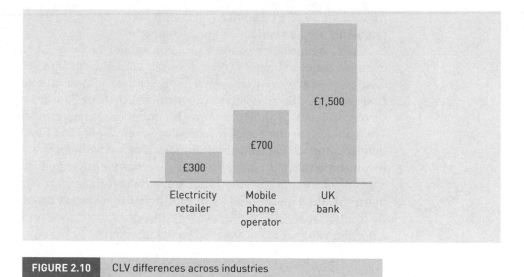

FIGURE 2.10   CLV differences across industries

Source: Moustfield 2003.

Value-driving customer behaviours

Types of customer behaviours

The value of an individual customer relationship as well as the total value of all customer relationships of a company strongly depends on the customers' behaviour regarding the firm and its services. Most obviously, the more services of a single service provider a customer uses the more value is created for the firm. This basic logic leads to the *customer behaviours* – specifically the customer purchasing behaviours – with different effects on value:

General service usage. First of all, whenever a customer uses a service of a firm, this behaviour has a value effect via the revenues this usage generates and the cost it induces. An important distinction regarding service usage is the difference between first usage by newly acquired customers and repeated usage by loyal customers. Why is that differentiation important? One could say that every sale of a plane ticket, every transaction concerning a banking account, etc. contributes to revenues and thus to value. However, to illustrate the difference, take car rental as an example. When you rent a car for the first time at a certain rental firm, they record your personal data and credit card information and this information is processed. This collection as well as the processing of your information requires time and effort, resulting in costs. Thus, your first car rental with that firm induces singular costs that will not occur on later rental occasions. These singular costs are not compensated by additional revenues. This is different to banks that charge fees for their accounts based upon money transactions.

Relationship termination. The opposite of general service usage is the termination of a relationship by a customer. Especially in membership-like services, such as insurance or banking, this relationship termination becomes obvious. In other cases, the relationship termination is less obvious, as is the case when a customer changes their hairdresser for example. Losing a customer affects value twofold. First of all, revenues that determined value in the past are lost and thus must be compensated by other revenues in order to realise an equal value. When this is done by the acquisition of new customers, there are further negative effects because of the cost of acquiring new customers. Secondly, revenue potentials within the terminated relationship are also lost. The respective customer might have had potentials in addition to current revenues (e.g. an airline customer who usually flies the airline in his job and might use it for vacational trips as well). With the customer terminating the relationship, these potentials cannot be realised.

Cross-buying. This potential is addressed when the **cross-buying** behaviour of a customer is considered. Cross-buying means that a customer starts using further services of the firm not used before. For example, a bank customer cross-buys when they had, thus far, only used investment products of the bank, and now raises a loan. Hotel guests cross-buy when they eat at the hotel's restaurant. Cross-buying directly results in higher revenues with a customer, often associated with lower cost. For example, when the hotel guest pays the restaurant bill with his total hotel bill, then the paying procedure is easier and shorter and thus produces less cost.

Increasing purchase volume. As in the case of cross-buying, the customer potentials are also concerned when firms target increases in the purchase volume. This is the case when, for example, an airline passenger uses the airline more often or a supermarket customer makes more expensive purchases at a certain supermarket than before. Comparable to cross-buying, there are both revenue as well as cost effects.

For service providers, in order to manage these behaviours, it is important to analyse them. Therefore, companies try to *track customer behaviours*. The possibilities of measuring these figures differ between service types. In many service industries, it is part of the business model to collect customer data (e.g. banks). In other service industries, even though it might not be necessary, it is nevertheless relatively easy to collect this data because of the direct contact with the customer (e.g. mail order business, telecommunications). Thus, in these businesses, it is relatively straightforward to measure the number of customers acquired, retained and lost. In other industries where the customer contact is less direct, such as fast food restaurants, service companies might develop sample measures that can be used to estimate the total numbers. If the amount of change within a relationship (e.g. through cross-buying) needs to be analysed, the regular customer data is, however, often not sufficient. In these cases, further data about the buying frequencies and amounts might need to be generated. As a consequence, the box Services marketing in action 2.2 illustrates how the tracking of customer behaviour is summarised in a customer migration analysis for an anonymous firm.

SERVICES MARKETING IN ACTION 2.2:

Customer migration analysis

By measuring customer actions at points in the past and comparing them to actions today, customers are separated into the following migration groups:

- upgraded (increased spending)
- downgraded (reduced spending)
- maintained (same level)
- lapsed (stopped spending)
- new/reactivated (started spending).

For example, Company A with 100,000 customers at the end of 2003 had 4% growth in its customer base during 2004 by adding 32,000 new customers, while 28,000 existing customers lapsed. Among the 72,000 retained customers, 22,000 upgraded, 24,000 maintained, and 26,000 downgraded.

Available data, such as transactions, corporate demographics, survey responses, etc. are used to understand these groups better. Using the example of Company A, the revenue generated by the migration groups is measured, as shown in Table 2.2.

TABLE 2.2   Revenues of migration segments

New/reactivated	£0	£12 million
Upgraded	£14 million	£35 million
Maintained	£42 million	£43 million
Downgraded	£36 million	£16 million
Lapsed	£9 million	£0
Total	**£101 million**	**£106 million**

Source: Sampathkumaran 1994.

The measurement of customer behaviour provides important insights into the situation and the development of the customer base. On a strategic level, these figures facilitate concrete guidelines for services marketing in terms of managing the customer base. In order to do so, service firms build groups of customers with similar behaviours, i.e. behavioural customer segments.

Behavioural customer segmentation

Customer behaviours are never equal for all customers. There are always customers that are acquired and always customers that are lost. That is why there are not many marketing activities that have the same impact on all customers' behaviours. Consequently, companies try to find out for what customers which activities are most appropriate to focus upon in terms of influencing their behaviour. This is done by means of behavioural segmentations, using segmentation approaches that deal with the differences in customers' behaviours.

There are various *criteria for behavioural segmentations*. First of all, the probability for certain customer behaviours is a relevant segmentation criterion. In simple terms, existing customers can be segmented into customers with a high and low retention probability. This simple segmentation already gives important indications for the marketing activities of the service provider. For customers with a high retention probability, cross selling activities might be relevant – if the customer has a potential. For customers with a low retention probability retention activities might be relevant – in this case the customer is profitable and is likely to react positively to retention activities. These examples show that such a simple segmentation approach gives initial indications for the directions of services marketing for the respective customer group (see Figure 2.11). However, in most cases, there are combinations of criteria necessary in order to derive the right marketing decisions.

The knowledge about the behavioural state of the customer base in total as well as single customer relationships gives first indications for services marketing on a strategic level, i.e. what customer behaviours are valuable for the firm and should be managed by the services provider. In order to get further insight regarding how to manage the behaviours concretely, we have to know more about the causes of certain customer behaviours. Across industries, the most important driver of customer behaviour is the customer's evaluation of the respective services.

Loyalty Potential	Not loyal	Loyal
Low potential	Disinvestment	Exploitation
High potential	Retention	Cross selling

FIGURE 2.11 Customer segmentation regarding customer behaviours

How customers evaluate services

Why did you choose your mobile telephone provider? A realistic scenario is that you somehow evaluated the provider, compared it against others and then decided to choose that company. Even though this decision process might have been relatively short, it is very probable that you undertook some kind of evaluation – even when it was only the evaluation of the advertising. Generally, service evaluation plays an important role as a driver of customer decisions. Therefore, in the generalised Service Profit Chain, service evaluations are the determinant of customer behaviour. A central construct regarding customers' service evaluations is the concept of perceived service value.

Perceived service value

As outlined in Chapter 1, the focus of value-oriented services marketing is the value of the firm and the contribution of marketing activities to this value. Regarding the determinants of a firm's value, there is a mirror-like relationship regarding the value concept: value to the customer leads to value for the firm. We discussed how different customer behaviours affect the value of a firm, and assessed the determinants of these behaviours, then, on an aggregate level, we came to the conclusion that it is the value the customer perceives to receive from the provider. Perceived service value is the link between services marketing and value creating customer behaviours. The more a customer values a service the more likely it is that they will use the service. Although this sounds straightforward, problems arise when we ask for *definitions of perceived value*, because there are four different interpretations:[7]

1. Customers can disregard the benefits and interpret *price* as the perceived value.

2. By overemphasising the benefit components, the perceived value can also be defined as a *benefit* derived from the output.

3. Alternatively, the perceived value is often viewed as the *benefit at a given price*.

4. Additionally, the perceived value could be inferred as a *cost–benefit relationship*.

The third and fourth interpretations above represent the most frequently encountered definitions of perceived value. The perceived value is generally defined as the *relationship between the customer's perceived benefit and effort*.[8]

In order to *measure perceived value* in practice, specific attributes questioned often do not relate to those of a particular object such as an output or a relationship, but rather to aspects by which the construct can be described. This could include the price–benefit ratio or the price sensitivity depending on the definition of perceived value. The following sample questionnaire formulations can be scaled to determine the perceived value:[9]

- Service X has a good price–benefit ratio

- Service X has a high quality for its price

- Service X is a good buy

- Service X is fairly priced.

With regard to the benefit part of perceived value and thus to a varied field of management levers, the perceived service quality plays an important role in managing perceived value.

Perceived service quality

How do you evaluate the quality of batteries? The value creation to the customer is one-dimensional and most people evaluate batteries according to their lifespan. Thus, when comparing a set of batteries, one can tell objectively which battery exhibits the best quality. However, when you turn to services, how objective can be an evaluation of a dentist, a theatre performance or even a flight – where at first sight in the last case the only relevant attribute is arrival on time at the scheduled destination? However, when evaluating airlines, customers also focus on the friendliness of the staff, the waiting times at the check-in, etc.

These are factors that are especially relevant for services, and they are attributed to the specific services characteristics discussed in Chapter 1. Because of the intangibility of services, customers look for quality indicators in order to evaluate a service, such as the modernity of an aeroplane. Secondly, the perishability and non-transportability imply possible bottlenecks regarding the service resources, i.e. a service might be evaluated according to dimensions that are less relevant for most consumer goods, like waiting times. Finally, because of the heterogeneity of services, each service process can exhibit a different quality. All these reasons can be attributed to the fact that services are processes and that the customer takes part in the service production. When customers are heterogeneous, then their participation in the service process as well as their evaluations of the service process can be quite different. The box Services marketing in action 2.3 visualises this fact for the evaluation of one and the same cinema by two visitors.

These considerations show that with regard to service quality, only the customer's evaluation is relevant and therefore the perceived service quality construct has been discussed intensely since the early 1980s. Even when conceptualising quality as perceived by the customer, the question is nevertheless 'How does the customer define quality?' An answer to this question gives the so-called *GAP model of service quality*[10] (see Figure 2.12). Within the GAP model, service quality is defined as the gap between customer perceptions and customer expectations. When customers' perceptions of a service exceed their expectations, they will perceive a high service quality. However, when a customer perceives that a service fails to meet expectations, the customer perceives bad service quality. This difference, called GAP

SERVICES MARKETING IN ACTION 2.3:

Different sides of the same coin

The services of cinemas, such as showing a movie, are standardised services, even though there is some differentiation in terms of seats. However, because of the heterogeneous opinions and tastes of individual customers, the evaluations of the same cinema visit can be quite different. Here are two opinions about one and the same cinema ('Küchlin 1' in Basel, Switzerland):

Positive	Negative
I never had the feeling that it was too hot. Sound system is great. And the atmosphere of an opera-like cinema gives it a special touch.	By far the most uncomfortable cinema in Basel. On the balcony seats, you definitely do not have enough space for your legs. And the climate in the cinema (especially for long movies or 'long movie nights' – remember 'Die Hard' parts 1 to 3 with Bruce Willis) is just too hot.

The two evaluations visualise that service evaluations can differ strongly because of heterogeneous customers in terms of expectations. The first visitor for example accentuates the sound system, while the second does not mention the sound system but emphasises the seating space. Furthermore, the two visitors evaluate the same characteristic differently – while the first person never had the impression that it was too hot, the second one finds the climate in the cinema 'just too hot'.

Source: Mybasel.com 2003.

5, is determined by four other gaps, GAP 1 to GAP 4: service quality is not reached when there is a GAP 1 between customer expectations and the management's perceptions of these expectations and/or a GAP 2 between the management's perceptions of customers' expectations and the defined service specifications and/or a GAP 3 between the defined service specifications and the delivered service and/or a GAP 4 between the communicated service and the delivered service. These gaps are the starting point for a service provider's quality management initiatives. By diminishing the four gaps, service quality will be maximised.

While the GAP model explains how the customer defines service quality, there can still be different interpretations of what is a high or low service quality. The reason for this lies in the **customers' expectations**. These expectations can concern different aspects of a service. There are airline customers who emphasise above all flexibility, whilst other customers evaluate a flight only according to its price. These two groups of customers can evaluate one and the same flight very differently. The different aspects of a service we address here, are called *service quality*

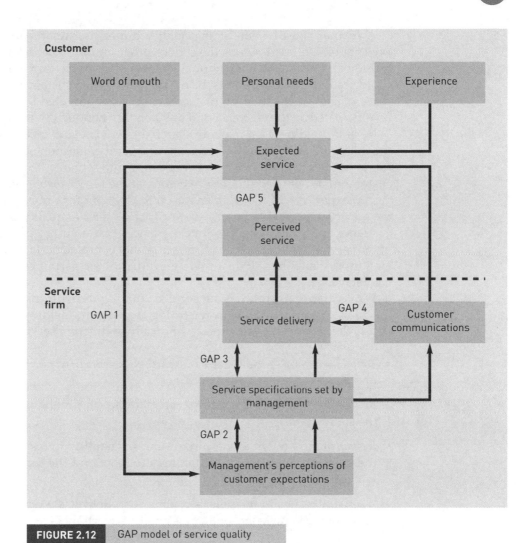

FIGURE 2.12   GAP model of service quality

Source: Parasuraman *et al.* 1985, p. 44.

dimensions. In this respect, the perception of various quality characteristics is taken as the quality dimension. Here, the focus in the marketing literature has been on a differentiation into the three dimensions based on the phases of service production – structure, process and outcome.[11] The *structure dimension* includes the seller's technical, organisational and personal output requirements. The *process dimension* is based on all processes during the provision of products and services, and the *outcome dimension* judges the final result.

A differentiation of the quality dimension is also possible within the scope and type of output provided.[12] In this sense, the *technical dimension* covers the scope of the service programme, and questions the 'what' of a service. In contrast, the *functional dimension* questions the 'how', the form in which the service is offered.

A further sub-division of the quality dimension relates to the customer's expectation attitude towards the service programme:[13] The *customary components* include all qualities that are normally a part of a service. Any negative variances could result in 'penalty points' being assigned by the customer. In contrast, *occasional components* include supplementary services provided by the seller that are unanticipated by the customer and are therefore honoured with 'bonus points'.

By sub-dividing a service into search, experience and credence components, the following three quality dimensions answer the question on how well the customer knows the service when making a judgement.[14] Supposing that the customer has not used the service before, at the *search quality* stage the customer has no experience of the seller and is on the lookout for prior indicators to assess the service. Opposed to this, *experience qualities* refer to quality characteristics the customer can evaluate because of experiences that occurred during or at the end of the service delivery process. *Credence quality* components encompass all output attributes that either elude a precise evaluation or permit estimation only at a later stage.

While these approaches of service quality dimensions are conceptually founded, within the research regarding the GAP model of service quality, *five quality dimensions* were identified empirically in different service industries:[15]

- *Tangibles* comprise the seller's outward appearance, in particular the room furnishings and appearance of personnel.

- *Reliability* designates the seller's capability to supply the promised outputs at the stated level.

- *Responsiveness* refers to the corporation's capability to respond to and satisfy the customer's wishes. A willingness to react and the reaction speed play a vital role here.

- *Assurance* relates to the seller's capability to deliver the output, specifically in terms of the knowledge, politeness and trustworthiness of the employees.

- *Empathy* characterises both the seller's willingness and capability to respond to individual customer desires.

Although the SERVQUAL dimensions were applied to various industries because of their simplicity and general conclusiveness, they are associated with several problems. Along with very specific statistical problems,[16] on a conceptual level, they only partly describe the level or form of quality dimensions and characteristics and not the features themselves.[17] For example, according to the critics, the quality dimension 'reliability' cannot be interpreted as a quality dimension because this attribute can concern several quality dimensions. When using a bank as an example, the employees or the teller machine can both be reliable. This thought leads to the opinion that service quality is a hierarchical construct that encompasses dimensions on various levels.[18] Consequently, one approach of a *hierarchy of service quality dimensions*[19] (see Figure 2.13) was developed.[20] On the

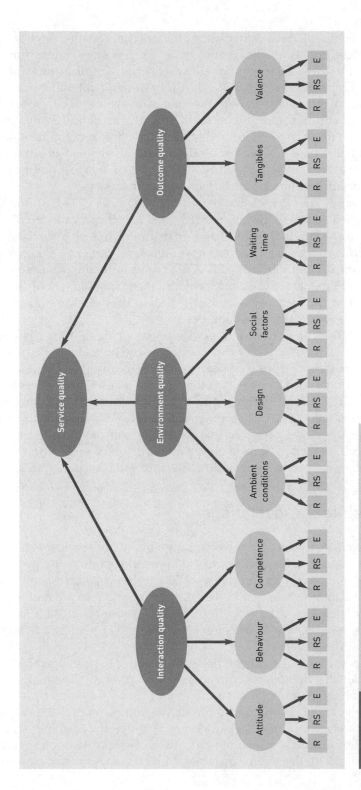

FIGURE 2.13 Hierarchical structure of service quality dimensions

Source: Brady and Cronin 2001, p. 37.

first level, the three dimensions of interaction quality, environment quality and outcome quality are differentiated. On a second level, these dimensions are specified by three factors that allow concrete implications for service quality management. The SERVQUAL dimensions of reliability, responsiveness and empathy are used to specify the main dimensions, i.e. for each dimension exists one reliability, responsiveness and empathy attribute. Evaluating this approach, one can draw the conclusion that the interaction, environment and outcome quality in this case are viewed as determinants instead of dimensions of service quality. However, it presents a structure of service quality aspects that give important conclusions for service quality managers.

Despite the criticisms regarding the SERVQUAL dimensions, the most accepted approach to *measure service quality* is the so-called SERVQUAL approach. While the original SERVQUAL instrument has been revised and refined, its length, structure and content have remained the same.[21] Figure 2.14 depicts the revised attributes from a SERVQUAL questionnaire for assessing *service quality*. The statements are to be answered by the respondents with simultaneous measurement for perception and expectation on a scale ranging from 'absolutely relevant' to 'totally irrelevant'.

In close connection with perceived service quality is **customer satisfaction**. Customer satisfaction is also defined as the balancing of customer expectations against the perception of services delivered by the company.[22] The difference between the two constructs is that service quality often refers to concrete quality attributes, like friendliness and assurance, whereas customer satisfaction often refers to the service of a provider as an entity.[23] Often, satisfaction is understood as the link between perceived service quality and customer loyalty. For the building of both, perceived service quality and customer satisfaction, customer expectations play an important role and therefore will be explored in detail below.

Customer expectations

When does a customer perceive a high quality of service? When does he perceive a low quality? The concept of customer expectations helps in answering these questions. According to the so-called *'disconfirmation paradigm'*, customers perceive a high service quality when their expectations are met by the provider and perceive a low service quality when the provider did not meet the customer's expectations. Thus customer expectations are an important variable 'on the way' to assessing value.

An individual's expectations represent a psychological state that relates to future behavioural consequences for that person.[24] The marketing literature has numerous interpretations of the *concept of customer expectations* (see Figure 2.15), which can be classified into predictive and normative expectations.[25] *Predictive expectations* have an anticipatory nature in that the customer states in advance the level of output foreseen which is taken for granted or considered likely to be delivered by the service provider. In contrast, *normative expectations* represent a

Reliability
1. Providing services as promised.
2. Dependability in handling customers' service problems.
3. Performing services right the first time.
4. Providing services at the promised time.
5. Maintaining error-free records.

Responsiveness
6. Keeping customers informed about when services will be performed.
7. Prompt service to customers.
8. Willingness to help customers.
9. Readiness to respond to customers' requests.

Assurance
10. Employees who instil confidence in customers.
11. Making customers feel safe in their transactions.
12. Employees who are consistently courteous.
13. Employees who have the knowledge to answer customer questions.

Empathy
14. Giving customers individual attention.
15. Employees who deal with customers in a caring fashion.
16. Having the customers' best interests at heart.
17. Employees who understand the needs of their customers.
18. Convenient business hours.

Tangibles
19. Modern equipment.
20. Visually appealing facilities.
21. Employees who have a neat, professional appearance.
22. Visually appealing materials associated with the service.

FIGURE 2.14   SERVQUAL item battery

Source: Parasuraman *et al.* 1994, p. 207.

demand for the service provider and characterise the output level required by the customer from the firm.

The *difference between the two expectations types* becomes obvious when you ask yourself how the word 'to expect' is used in day-to-day language. When a mother tells her child 'I expect you to be home at 6pm', then this 'expect' , represents a command, and is quite normative. However, when you say 'I didn't expect that England would make it through to the finals', then the respective 'expect' concerns your forecast, i.e. is quite predictive (although football fans also expect from their teams in a normative sense).

Schematically, the two types of expectations differ with respect to their classification on a scale of output levels and the reference item (see Figure 2.15). The

Types of Expectations			Affiliation to basic types	Classification on a scale	Reference object	
Authors[1]	Definition	Description		Given (High ⟷ Low) / Not given	broad, not company-focused	narrow, company-focused
Miller 1977; Tse and Wilton 1988	Perception of an ideal level which cannot be exceeded	Ideal level	Normative	Given (High)	X	
Parasuraman et al. 1988; Boulding et al. 1993	Level which is desired by customers or which should be provided through the organization	Desired level	Normative	Given		X
Cadotte et al. 1987	Customer perception of the product and service quality of the best provider in a single category	Best-Brand-Level	Normative	Given	X	
Cadotte et al. 1987	Perception of a typical and average quality of all products or services known to the customer in one category	Product-Type-Level	Normative	Given	X	
Zeitham et al. 1993	Minimum level which is accepted by customers	Moderate level	Normative	Given	X	
Miller 1977	Level which is just tolerated by customers	Minimum tolerable level	Normative	Given (Low)	X	
Miller 1977; Boulding et al. 1993	Perception of the level that the customer feels to be deserved	Deserved level	Normative	Given		X
Olson and Dover 1979; Oliver 1980; Cadotte et al. 1987; Boulding et al. 1993	Perception of the product and service quality of a specific provider	Predicted level	Predictive	Not given		X
Miller 1977	Likelihood of the occurrence of an event	Most likely level	Predictive	Not given		X

1 These authors provide an introduction into each type of expectation in the literature. An overview of more types can be found at Lijander and Strandvik 1993; Ngobo 1997.

FIGURE 2.15   Overview of expectation types

Source: Bruhn 2002b, p. 61.

criterion *type of classification on an output scale* represents a specific, objectively comprehensible output level in terms of the expectation type. This classification is given for normative expectations. Hence, an ideal expectation is always at a high output level whereas the minimal acceptable level is relatively low. Predictive expectations, on the contrary, are not bound to any specific level.[26] In relevance to a firm's offer, customers can foresee or probably envision either a relatively high or low output level. This state of affairs becomes clear on examination of different types of *reference items* anticipated. Normative expectations do not relate to any specific seller, whereas predictive expectations always do.

Customer expectations and the other evaluative concepts of services marketing play an important role by 'translating' the services marketing activities into value-creating processes and thus are an important part of the value impact of the Service Value Chain.

Value contribution of the Service Value Chain

Value-oriented services marketing aims at managing service processes such that the Service Profit Chain is influenced positively, positive customer evaluations are induced, resulting in positive customer behaviours, and so that these evaluations and behaviours lead to more customer value resulting in more value to the firm. Now that we know the relevant customer evaluations, behaviours and dimensions of customer value, the integration of the Service Value Chain and the Service Profit Chain that was denoted in Chapter 1 can be specified.

The *relationship process* is illustrated by a service provider's activities regarding customer acquisition, customer retention, relationship enhancement and customer recovery, and influences customer perceptions, behaviours and value. For example, a restaurant presenting its daily menu on a blackboard outside the restaurant (customer acquisition) gives the customer a first impression of the quality he can expect from the restaurant (evaluation). When a mobile telecommunications provider calls customers whose contracts are close to expiry in order to convince them to renew the contract, via a new mobile handset as a gift (customer retention), it will probably keep the majority of its customers (customer behaviour). The airmiles programmes of airlines (relationship enhancement) provoke many customers to fly as often as possible with a certain airline (customer behaviour) and a concentration of winback activities (customer regain) for profitable customers, will lead to a higher average customer profitability (customer value).

Next to the business processes on the level of the customer relationship, the marketing activities aimed at the customer interaction also affect the Service Profit Chain. Regarding the *interaction process*, evaluations, behaviours and value are influenced by customer integration, service production and service recovery. A well-designed customer integration system, such as systematic reservations, will enhance the customers' perception of a high service quality because of short waiting times. Customer value will be affected via cost, because fewer waiting facilities are necessary. The service production where the basic benefit is delivered to the customer, who is often in direct contact with the provider, directly influences service evaluations. Finally, service recovery can be an important determinant of customer loyalty, i.e. customer behaviour.

While the *secondary value processes* determine value by influencing the primary value processes, their impact can also be retraced in a direct way. The service offering itself and how it is communicated and transported to the customer strongly influences customers' evaluations. Most of the dimensions of service quality concern these aspects. And since the service resources are perceived as an important part of a service – especially within the interaction process – they also directly influence customer evaluations and, in part, customer behaviour, too. For example, private banking customers often follow their advisers when those advisers change jobs and work for another private bank.

Summary

In this chapter we had a closer look at how the value processes of a service provider affect the value of a firm. Since marketing processes focus on the customer and the value contribution of these processes is via customer behaviour, the Service Profit Chain is an appropriate concept to explore these value effects. The respective learnings are summarised in Figure 2.16:

1. This chapter is about the integration of the Service Value Chain and the Service Profit Chain. While the Service Value Chain structures the value activities of a service provider, the Service Profit Chain depicts the value effects of these activities.

2. The value processes within the Service Value Chain affect customer evaluations, customer behaviours and customer value.

3. There are a variety of definitions of customer value that can be classified according to the value and time dimensions of customer value. Regarding the value dimension, customer value can be understood as revenue-oriented or profitability-oriented. The first option neglects the cost of a customer relationship which, in some industries, can vary heavily and thus can be a determining factor for services marketing decisions and service value. The time dimension varies according to whether value is understood as past- or future-oriented. The latter option is more valid for decision making, but difficult to implement, because of data problems.

4. Two important concepts in the field of customer value analysis are customer contribution analysis and customer lifetime value analysis. They differ above all with regard to the time dimension. While customer contribution analysis is past-oriented and determines the current contributions of a customer, customer lifetime value analysis aims at measuring the value of a customer over the entire span of the relationship with that customer.

5. Customer value depends on customer behaviours, the behaviour of a customer determines the value that the customer contributes to a firm's value. Based on this logic, different customer behaviours can be differentiated according to their value contributions: general service usage describes whether a customer uses a firm's services at all or whether the company can expect a regular income stream. Furthermore, it is only with existing relationships that further potentials might be exploited. The contrary behaviour is relationship termination which has a negative impact on a firm's value. In existing relationships, value-relevant customer behaviours are cross-selling and increasing the purchasing volume.

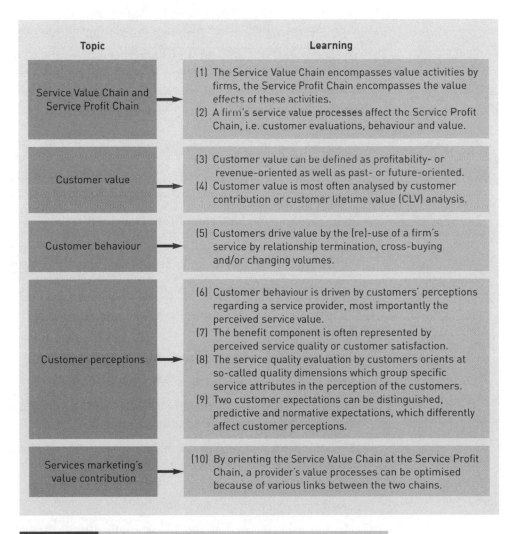

Topic	Learning
Service Value Chain and Service Profit Chain	(1) The Service Value Chain encompasses value activities by firms, the Service Profit Chain encompasses the value effects of these activities. (2) A firm's service value processes affect the Service Profit Chain, i.e. customer evaluations, behaviour and value.
Customer value	(3) Customer value can be defined as profitability- or revenue-oriented as well as past- or future-oriented. (4) Customer value is most often analysed by customer contribution or customer lifetime value (CLV) analysis.
Customer behaviour	(5) Customers drive value by the (re)-use of a firm's service by relationship termination, cross-buying and/or changing volumes.
Customer perceptions	(6) Customer behaviour is driven by customers' perceptions regarding a service provider, most importantly the perceived service value. (7) The benefit component is often represented by perceived service quality or customer satisfaction. (8) The service quality evaluation by customers orients at so-called quality dimensions which group specific service attributes in the perception of the customers. (9) Two customer expectations can be distinguished, predictive and normative expectations, which differently affect customer perceptions.
Services marketing's value contribution	(10) By orienting the Service Value Chain at the Service Profit Chain, a provider's value processes can be optimised because of various links between the two chains.

FIGURE 2.16 Learning summary for Chapter 2

6. The better customers evaluate a service provider and its services, the more beneficially they behave for the organisation. The concept of perceived service value mostly consists of a benefit component and an effort component. The latter is often represented by the price the customer has to pay, the former is best mirrored by the perceived service quality.

7. The benefit which is perceived by the customer is often represented by the perceived service quality or customer satisfaction. Both constructs are the result of a customer's comparison of the delivered service and customer expectations.

8. The service quality evaluation by customers is focused upon quality dimensions which group specific service attributes in the perception of the customers.

9. Two customer expectations can be distinguished, predictive and normative expectations, which affect customer perceptions differently.

10. The stages of the Service Profit Chain, customer evaluations, customer behaviours and customer value combine to build the objectives and effects of services marketing activities. Thus, the more the Service Value Chain is oriented at the Service Profit Chain the more probable is it that value will be created.

Knowledge questions

1. What is the difference between the Service Value Chain and the Service Profit Chain and how are both concepts linked together?

2. What are the customer-related value effects that are structured by the Service Profit Chain? How can the links within the chain be explained?

3. Explain the different types of customer value.

4. What are the differences between a customer revenue and a customer contribution analysis?

5. Compare a customer contribution and a customer lifetime value analysis.

6. Describe the methodology of an ABC analysis.

7. Which value-driving customer behaviours can be distinguished and how do they contribute to value generation?

8. How can 'perceived service value' be interpreted and what are the differences between the different interpretations?

9. How is service quality defined and what role do customer expectations play regarding the perceived service quality?

10. What types of customer expectations can be distinguished?

11. Explain how the different processes of the Service Value Chain affect the Service Profit Chain.

Application and discussion questions

1. Discuss which customer value definition applies for which marketing decisions.

2. Why is it important to integrate cost into customer value calculations? And in which industries is it more/less important ?

3. A service firm has ten customers with the following contributions: A = 120, B = 170, C = 80, D = 250, E = 110, F = 150, G = 20, H = 210, I = 10, J = 10. The firm plans to shift down its capacity by 50 per cent and asks you which customers should not be served any more (assuming that every customer takes the same amount of capacity). Prepare a decision based on the ABC analysis.

4. The most profitable customers of the firm from question (3) are D, B and F. Now the firm wants to calculate customer (lifetime) values over the next five years with these customers. They assume that the customers' behaviour will develop as in the past: D does not change its behaviour, B purchases 20 per cent more each year and F 10 per cent less each year. Prices will increase by 10 per cent over the whole period and the discount factor is 5 per cent. What is the total customer lifetime value for the three customers?

5. In which service industries are cross-buying and increasing purchase volume most relevant as value driving behaviours? Try to identify service attributes that influence the importance.

6. Collect service quality attributes of a theatre based on the SERVQUAL approach. Do the SERVQUAL dimensions seem applicable for the services of a theatre?

CASE STUDY: THE SERVICE PROFIT CHAIN AT A UK GROCERY STORE

The UK grocery retail sector was dominated by a small number of major players and high competition with low margins in the 1990s. In this situation, the chief executive of a major UK grocery retailer set the strategy of his firm in order to ensure growth and profit by stating that the 'real drivers' of his company's growth and profit were customer satisfaction and customer loyalty. Within the last years on the input side of the Service Profit Chain, i.e. the Service Value Chain, the company had increased selling space and had experienced significant sales growth over the previous three years.

Applying the Service Profit Chain, the company wanted to find out whether this growth was a result of the customer-centred strategy in order to learn for further strategy renewals and customer-oriented behaviours. Therefore, the firm collected data from five stores within the chain in order to quantify the Service Profit Chain and to establish the links between customer evaluations (service value and customer satisfaction), customer behaviour (customer retention) and value (profits). Two sources of data were used: a customer survey and company reports.

Regarding the customer survey, 30 customers each from the 15 stores were interviewed when leaving the store. These surveys were principally used in order to measure customer satisfaction with 18 quality attributes perceived by the customers. But customer behaviour indicators, such as the customer's likelihood of recommending the respective store to friends, were also taken into account in the interviews. Other criteria were measured by researching the company reports delivered on a store level, for example information about profits on a store level and average basket size were collected. See Figure 2.17 for a summary of the measures taken.

Next to the absolute values of the variables within the Service Profit Chain, the company analysed the links between the stages of the chain (see Figure 2.18) in order to find out whether their success was retraceable via the Service Value Chain.

Regarding the link between customer behaviour and value in the Service Profit Chain, a strong correlation between mean customer loyalty (over the three meas-

Profit chain variable	Indicators	Data source
Service value	Customer perception of service value	Customer survey
Customer loyalty	Average basket size	Customer survey
	Referral of the store as place to shop	Customer survey
	Share of grocery budget spent in store	Customer survey
Store profitability	Store profit margin	Store report

FIGURE 2.17 Operationalisation of profit chain variables

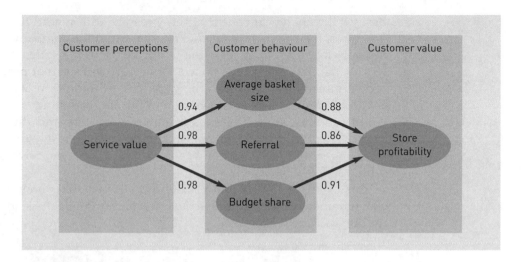

Customer perceptions   Customer behaviour   Customer value

Average basket
size

0.94   0.88

Service value   0.98   Referral   0.86   Store
profitability

0.98   0.91

Budget share

FIGURE 2.18   Relationships within the Service Profit Chain

ured indicators) and store profit margin could be observed. On an indicator level, for example, the store's profit margin was linked positively to the share of customers' grocery budgets indicating that stores with loyal customers were more profitable than those with less loyal ones. This suggests that customers who spent a high proportion of their grocery budget within the store were likely to purchase items with high levels of profitability, thereby increasing the overall margin. Furthermore, the larger basket size increased sales volume, resulting in scale economies and cost reduction.

The next link in the Service Profit Chain analysed by the company was the connection between customer perceptions and customer behaviour, with customer perceptions measured as the service value perceived by customers. Here again, a positive correlation could be observed for the relationships to all three loyalty indicators.

Regarding the link of services marketing activities and the service value perceived by customers, the company analysed further the connection between the customers' satisfaction with eighteen specific service characteristics of the stores and the perceived service value. This analysis resulted in the following characteristics that had a significant influence on perceived value:

- prices;
- checkout speed;
- staff competence;
- product availability;
- queues.

Besides the analytical benefit of these results with regard to future marketing measures, the results explained to a large extent the company's success. A core measure had been to increase the selling space in the stores. When you have a look at the five criteria mentioned above you will see that product availability is determined directly by the selling space. Furthermore, other criteria are influenced indirectly by the selling space. With larger selling space, the company could purchase more volumes from the suppliers and thus achieve better prices. In addition, checkout speed and queues are closely linked to the selling space – assuming that the number of cash desks and employees is linear to the selling space.

This example of a UK grocery store chain visualises how the Service Profit Chain framework can be used in order to analyse the value-generating impacts of the Service Value Chain.

Source: Silvestro and Cross 2000.

CASE STUDY: THE SERVICE PROFIT CHAIN AT CANADIAN IMPERIAL BANK OF COMMERCE (CIBC)

In 1996, Canadian Imperial Bank of Commerce (CIBC), a national bank with 6 million customers and $250 billion in assets, was facing increased competition from deregulation. Its customer defection rate, i.e. the proportion of customers leaving the bank, was approaching 10 per cent, with another 15 per cent of its customers estimated to be on the fence or close to defection. Being seriously concerned, senior managers pondered how to re-establish the bank's market position. A first step would be to articulate the drivers of business success. In order to identify these drivers, they developed a model for a company specific Service Profit Chain (Figure 2.19).

CIBC's model asserts that profit is driven by customer behaviour which is influenced by certain categories of loyalty drivers concerning service value from the customer's perspective. CIBC created parallel models for four customer groups: personal groups (consumers), small businesses, large businesses and insurance groups. The bank used surveys to gather the information needed to analyse the links. It also invested in a customer-information warehouse with more than 1,000 data attributes per customer and 25 rolling months of data.

From that information, CIBC was able to define customer-loyalty variables. Variables included customers' intentions – to continue using the banking services, to purchase additional products, to recommend the bank to other customers, to purchase more of the bank's services and to use the bank's services exclusively. CIBC then linked those loyalty variables to their drivers: what customers thought about core service, non-core services, banking fees, the bank's image and barriers to switching banks. Finally, it elaborated each loyalty dimension for its own drivers. For example, it found out that core services loyalty was

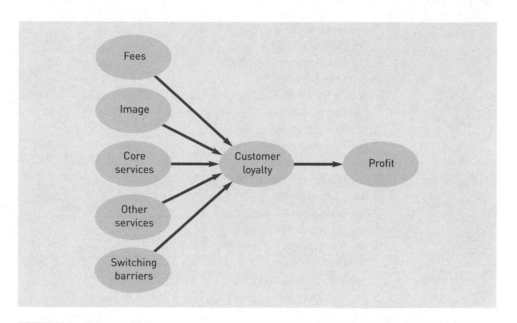

FIGURE 2.19   Service Profit Chain of Canadian Imperial Bank of Commerce (CIBC) (extract)

Source: Epstein and Westbrook 2001

linked to factors such as customers' evaluation of the local branch and the bank's efficiency in resolving problems.

The model helped CIBC managers to identify key relationships. For example, they worked out that a 1-point increase in any of the loyalty-behaviour elements increased profits by $0.60 per month and per customer. They also discovered that a 5 per cent increase in employee commitment yielded a 2 per cent increase in customer loyalty which increased profitability by $72 million annually. Using that information, future marketing activities could be planned based on information regarding the probable effectiveness of these activities.

Source: Epstein and Westbrook 2001.

Notes

[1] See Heskett *et al.* 1994; Storbacka 1997.
[2] See Blattberg and Deighton 1996; Dwyer 1997.
[3] See Berger and Nasr 1998.
[4] See Peck *et al.* 1999, p. 412.
[5] See Berger and Nasr 1998.
[6] See Berger and Nasr 1998.
[7] See Zeithaml 1988, p. 13.

[8] See Monroe 1991; Zeithaml 1988.

[9] See Zeithaml 1988.

[10] See Parasuraman *et al*. 1985.

[11] See Donabedian 1980.

[12] See Grönroos 2000b.

[13] See Berry 1986.

[14] See Zeithaml 1981, p. 186.

[15] See Parasuraman *et al*. 1988.

[16] See Cronin and Taylor 1992.

[17] See Brady and Cronin 2001, p. 36.

[18] See Carman 1990.

[19] See Brady and Cronin 2001.

[20] See Churchill 1979.

[21] See Parasuraman *et al*. 1988.

[22] See Oliver 1996, pp. 11–12.

[23] See Bruhn and Grund 2000.

[24] See van Raaij 1991, pp. 401–2.

[25] See Liljander 1994.

[26] See Oliver 1996, pp. 71–2.

PART 2　Primary value processes: Managing interactions and relationships

Only a small portion or partly less important part of service processes are autonomous because of the integration of the customer into service production. Consequently, autonomous processes in most cases do not create value by themselves. For example, the preparation of a salad by a restaurant's chef itself does not create value for the firm. The definition of a well-designed investment product of a bank and intensive communications to market this product do not create value for the bank. In contrast, these activities could even be said to destroy value because they induce cost exclusively. Only when the customer is involved, i.e. when the customer pays for and eats the salad and when bank customers purchase the investment product, do revenues occur and the service providers create value.

Therefore, the so-called primary processes of the Service Value Chain – as the processes that directly create value – concern processes where the customer is involved. As indicated by the restaurant and banking examples above, value for the firm is created when the customer purchases a service, pays a price and consequently the service is produced by more or less intensive customer interactions, such as ordering the salad, being served, getting the bill. In these interactions, there is a 'throughput' of the customer which creates value for the customer and for the firm. Consequently, one group of primary processes is combined within the *interaction process* between service provider and customer.

In most service industries, interaction processes vary with increasing relationship duration between provider and customer. When the customer hasn't used a service before, the service provider first must entice this customer to use the service. The first contacts are affected by little customer knowledge about the provider and vice versa. The customer does not know the provider's services, e.g.

the menu of the restaurant, and processes: how long it takes to get the bill after asking for it. Vice versa, the provider does not know the specific customer needs yet (which dressing the customer likes for the salad). This situation changes with further interactions between service customer and provider. When a regular guest of a restaurant orders a salad, the waiter or chef possibly knows which dressing the guest likes. Also, the customer knows the provider, its employees as well as services and becomes an expert in using the provider's services. Moreover, the customer possibly tries further services of the provider not used yet, resulting in further revenues for the provider. These examples show that value for the customer and for the firm is not only created by the single interaction but also by the linkages between more than one interaction, which when combined constitute a customer relationship. In consequence, next to the interaction process a second group of primary processes concerns the relationship process.

Based on these considerations, the interaction and the relationship process as primary processes of the Service Value Chain are presented in Chapters 3 and 4.

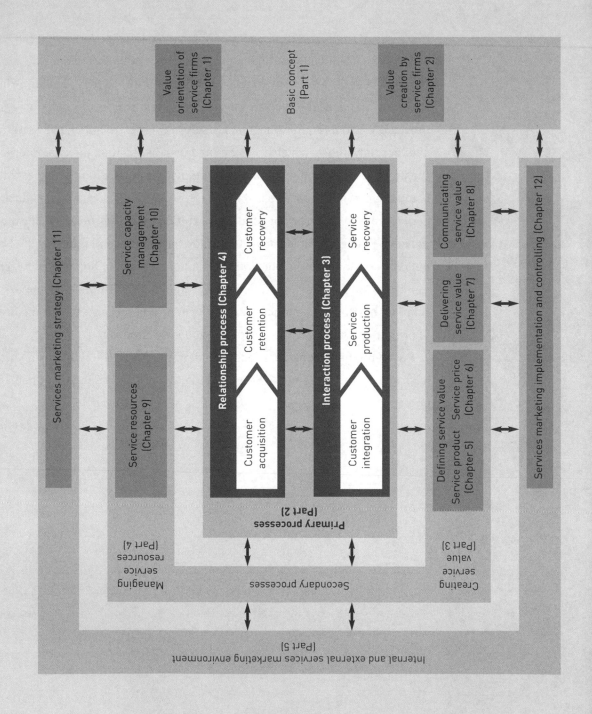

Value orientation of service firms (Chapter 1)

Basic concept (Part 1)

Value creation by service firms (Chapter 2)

Services marketing strategy (Chapter 11)

Service capacity management (Chapter 10)

Service resources (Chapter 9)

Relationship process (Chapter 4)

Customer recovery

Customer retention

Customer acquisition

Interaction process (Chapter 3)

Service recovery

Service production

Customer integration

Communicating service value (Chapter 8)

Delivering service value (Chapter 7)

Defining service value Service product Service price (Chapter 5) (Chapter 6)

Services marketing implementation and controlling (Chapter 12)

Primary processes (Part 2)

Managing service resources (Part 4)

Secondary processes

Creating service value (Part 3)

Internal and external services marketing environment (Part 5)

3 The customer interaction process: Managing customer integration, the service encounter and service recovery

Think of any recent contacts you have had with a service provider, buying a sandwich at a kiosk, a drink in your favourite café, drawing money at an ATM or visiting the cinema. What are the things you remember of these service contacts? Maybe the vendor of the sandwich was especially friendly; the café was crowded which you enjoyed in terms of atmosphere but not that you were unable to get a seat; the ATM did not work in the first place and you had to insert your credit card twice in order to get the money; you enjoyed the film very much – however, right in front of you were a bunch of girls giggling most of the time. Many of the contacts you probably remember concern what is called the interaction with the service provider and/or other participants of the service process.

Thus, service interactions are important to the customer – in many cases even more important than the core service, like the film seen or the fact that you eventually got money from the ATM.

Therefore, the Service Value Chain puts the service interactions at the centre of value considerations. Service interactions are – next to customer relationships (see Chapter 4) – one of the two primary value processes of a service provider. Due to the fact that in service situations value is created via the throughput of the customer through the service production process, and this throughput is realised in service interactions, these interactions are one of the major value drivers of a service firm's value.

As outlined in Chapter 1, the interaction process can be divided into three sub-processes: customer integration, service production and service recovery. First, since a service can only be produced when the service provider and the customer meet, the interaction process needs to be initiated, the customer must bring the car to the garage, the mechanic has to put the car into the right position in order to start the inspection, or, the bank customer needs to come to the bank branch, to the ATM or visit the internet banking website of the bank. In other cases, the service provider comes to the customer, e.g. the ambulance arriving at an accident site or the babysitter coming to a family's house.

Once the customer has been integrated and the interaction process has been initiated, the actual *service production* can take place during the so-called **service encounter** during which, in most cases, the service provider conducts activities involving the customer or their objects, e.g. cutting hair, transporting the customer to the holiday destination, giving the customer a bed during an overnight stay in a hotel. However, the production of many services also necessitates activities of the customer, such as delivering information to the provider. For example, in many cases a doctor needs a first indication by the patient in order to be able to give a diagnosis.

Furthermore, because of the simultaneity of service production and consumption during a service encounter, there is a high potential for failure. In contrast to goods manufacturing where a failure is clearly defined by not meeting very specific and concrete product specifications, the specifications and requirements for a service encounter are very subjective and can change between customers or between provider and customer. For example, a customer might find the behaviour of a contact employee friendly or not. Because services are ambiguous, customers' perceptions of service mistakes are less obvious than failures of tangible goods. Furthermore, in comparison to goods manufacturing, service failures are directly perceived by the customer in many cases, while failures in the production process of goods are often detected before the product is sold to the customer and before failure is perceived. Therefore, service failures can influence a customer's behaviour more directly. When a customer perceives poor quality because of mistakes and does not repurchase the services of the focal provider, the firm's value will be affected by the service failures. Thus, when accepting that – to a certain extent – failures are inevitable for services, e.g. because of the human element in service production, then the reactions of a service provider to the failures are of major importance. These reactions are summarised under the concept of **service recovery**. Because of the relevance of failures in service production, service recovery is defined as a separate process of the Service Value Chain.

Based on these considerations regarding the interaction process, the following are the learning objectives of this chapter (see Figure 3.1):

1. Recognising how service interactions contribute to a firm's value by understanding the value effects of initiating interactions, service production and service recovery.

2. Learning what problems occur when the customer is integrated into service interactions and what options service providers have to overcome these problems in order to start the actual service production.

3. Acknowledging the challenges of service production that arise from the meeting of customer and provider in the service production process. These challenges concern for example the customers' roles in service production and the provider's approaches to managing service production.

4. Realising how service failures occur, what value effects they have and how service recovery activities can help diminish the negative consequences of service failures.

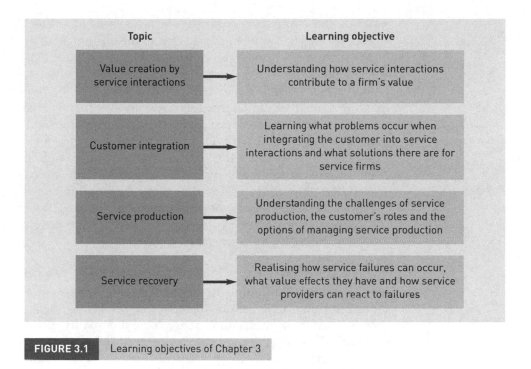

FIGURE 3.1   Learning objectives of Chapter 3

Value creation by service interactions

The three processes customer integration, service production and service recovery *create value within a service process*:

- The production of a service is represented by a customer's throughput through the production process. Without the customer's throughput, and therefore without *integrating the external factor* first, a service cannot be delivered and thus, value cannot be created.

- In contrast to goods manufacturing, customers perceive many parts of the *service production process*. At the hairdresser, the customer can watch the stylist cutting their hair, at a restaurant the customer directly perceives the processes of order taking, serving and billing. And during a flight, customers experience good or bad service, but also 'production outcomes' such as turbulence. Since customers' perceptions influence their behaviour and consequently the value to the firm, a firm's value is affected by these perceptions.

- The *value consequences regarding failures* are twofold. First, failures themselves destroy value, because of lost revenues when customers defect because of the failures. Secondly, service recovery creates value by reacting to the failure, by compensation or – more indirectly – by using the information generated by the failure analysis to improve future interactions and thus improve value.

- While these impacts concern the revenue side of value, the *cost side* is also affected by service interactions. Due to the customers' participation in service production, their behaviour strongly influences the cost of the interactions. Customers who are experienced with a certain provider and its services, who tend to solve problems by themselves without asking too many questions or who are not that critical, are less cost-intensive than customers who use a service for the first time, who prefer to ask a lot of questions or who find fault everywhere. The first group of customers demands less attention from the service provider than the second. The latter demands more of the service employees' time for answering the customer's questions and redoing faulty activities. Since the working time of service employees is the most important cost component in many service industries, these examples illustrate that service interactions can vary significantly according to the customer's behaviour which eventually influences the interaction cost.

The described direct value affects customer integration, service production and service recovery and represents primary value processes of a service firm. Many of the respective activities are dependent on secondary value activities, for example, the quality of interactions depends on the quality of the service personnel, and the primary value process 'service production' depends on the secondary value process 'managing human resources'. However, the primary value processes directly affect value. Therefore, we explore a service provider's options for managing these processes.

Customer integration

In Chapter 1, we pointed out that the integration of the external factor is a central differentiating characteristic of services compared to manufactured goods. From a process-oriented view, customer integration is the process of *integrating the external factor into the service process* – a process that takes place prior to the actual service production. The service production process can only be conducted when the external factor has been integrated into the process. The integration process therefore encompasses all activities that provide the basis for the actual service production. In the case of ensuring that a language course student arrives at the language school, activities such as opening the school's facilities, giving directions, letting the customer park their car; or a locksmith travelling to the home of a customer who has locked hinself out.

The prerequisites regarding the integration of the external factor necessary for service production vary depending on the following two dimensions (see Figure 3.2). The first dimension, as the examples above illustrate, concerns the **service location**, i.e. the place where the service is produced and the customer is integrated. One can differentiate whether the service is produced at the customer's place or the provider's place. In the examples above, the language school's services are provided at the provider's place, while the locksmith's service is produced at the customer's place. The second dimension varies according to the type of external factor. The integration process differs significantly depending on whether the external factor is a human being or an object. According to these two dimensions, implications for services marketing can be drawn.

The **service location** (see also Chapter 7), defined as the place where the service is produced, has an impact on the requirements regarding the *characteristics of the provider's place*. In cases where the service is produced at the provider's premises the design of the provider's premises determines how the external factor can be integrated into the service process. By providing elevators in a department store with several floors the service provider ensures that disabled customers or clients with buggies can use all the services of the store. When the service encounter takes place at the customer's place, such as repair services for washing machines, the distance of the provider's place to the customer's place determines the external factor's integration by the time needed until a service can be produced and therefore the respective cost as well as the quality of the service delivered, especially in the case of an emergency.

The service location influences the *service resources* necessary for initiating the interaction. However, this does not concern the service resources that are necessary for the actual service production itself. For example, independent of whether the doctor consults at the practice or the patient's home, the doctor and the diagnostic materials are the predominant service resource. However, the service location determines the service resources needed for initiating the service interaction. When the service is produced at the doctor's practice, in most cases, this employs a receptionist and provides further facilities such as a waiting room.

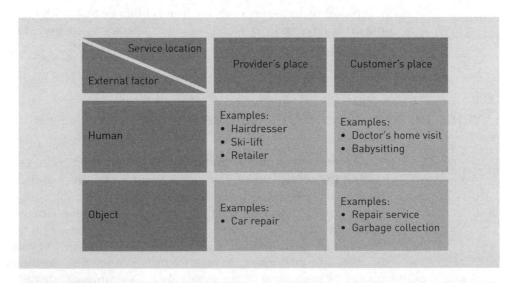

FIGURE 3.2   Examples of services with different challenges for initiating a service interaction

When the doctor visits the patient at their home, the doctor will use a car in order to drive from the surgery to the patient's home.

On the other hand, the service location influences the *customer's efforts* for preparing the service process. When the service is produced at the provider's place, the customer must come to the provider's place. For example, the customer drives to a restaurant they plan to visit, or flies to the holiday destination where the hotel has been booked. When the service is produced at the customer's place, the customer often has to prepare the service location, perhaps clear a bathroom that is to be renovated or make arrangements to use the neighbours' bathroom during the renovation process. The service provider can react to the customer's efforts by services marketing activities. Providing value-added services can help reduce the customer's efforts. The restaurant could provide a collection service for its guests and the plumber could provide a mobile showering system during the renovation period.

Next to the two specifications of the place dimension, a service can also be produced at a *third-party place*, e.g. a wrecking service. However, the implications for services marketing are not different, just a combination of the two extreme implications. For example, the customer as well as the service resources must be transported to the service location.

The second dimension depicted in Figure 3.2 concerns the *type of external factor* that has to be integrated into the service process. Depending on the type of external factor, emphasis is upon *service timing* (see also Chapter 7). In this sense, service timing means the period until the service production starts. When an object is integrated, it is done more easily in that the customer does not necessarily perceive any waiting time, as in the case of a car repair. For example, when the car mechanic asks the customer to bring the car in the morning and promises that he can pick it up in the evening, the firm is quite flexible with regard to when exactly the car will be repaired. However, when a person is integrated into the service production, waiting times are a quality characteristic, such as waiting at the hairdresser or the dentist.

Producing a service in the service encounter

The **service encounter** is the heart of the service process. A service is produced during the service encounter where service resources and customers meet.[1] In this section we will explore various aspects regarding service encounters (see Figure 3.3) starting with different types of services encounters in order to understand different implications for services marketing based on these different types. The characteristics of a service encounter also affect the way these encounters are perceived by customers. As an encounter is a process, customers perceive it as a row of incidents and notice especially the significantly positive or negative critical incidents. Furthermore, we will structure the determinants of a service

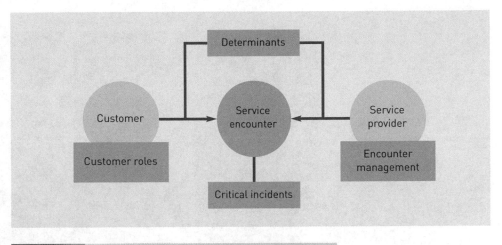

| FIGURE 3.3 | Service encounter elements in service production |

encounter leading us to the customer's roles in service encounters as well as the provider's management options.

Types of service encounters

A service encounter is defined as the situation where customer and service provider or specific resources of the service provider meet. In these situations, the actual service is produced. Service encounters can differ significantly and these differences determine the implications for services marketing. Service encounters differ according to two dimensions, the type of service resource and the type of external factor that meet in the service encounter (see Figure 3.4).

The first dimension, the *type of service resource*, indicates what kind of service resources are primarily utilised for service production. We differentiate between the two extreme forms: human resources, bank staff versus automated resources, the ATM at a bank. The type of resources influences the management requirements of the service provider. Automated resources are more standardised than human resources, and the challenges of ensuring a high service quality are more difficult to resolve by service companies for human resources. Note that human resources and automated resources are extreme forms and that there are many variations/combinations possible within these two extremes. Often, service encounters are divided into face-to-face, voice-to-voice and bit-to-bit encounters with voice-to-voice as a combined type with human parts (e.g. the telephonist) and automated parts (e.g. the telephone system).[2]

As with customer integration, the *type of external factor* is a valuable differentiator of service encounters. Human beings as external factors are often more heterogeneous and more active within the service process. They often influence

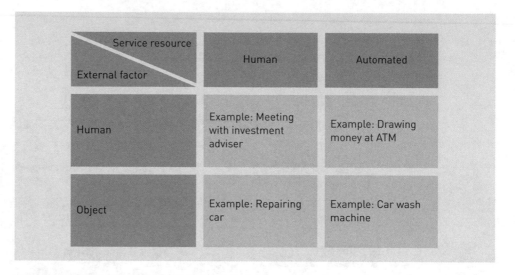

Service resource / External factor	Human	Automated
Human	Example: Meeting with investment adviser	Example: Drawing money at ATM
Object	Example: Repairing car	Example: Car wash machine

FIGURE 3.4   Types of service encounters

the service process in a stronger way than does an object as external factor. Therefore, when a human being is the external factor, the service process is much more dependent upon the external factor than in the case of objects as external factors. In addition, when human beings are integrated into the service process, the customer perceives the service process which results in there being more service dimensions that the service provider must address.

This perception of the customer is also an important facet when understanding service encounters as a series of (critical) incidents.

Critical incidents

Customers often do not perceive and evaluate service encounters such that they go through a systematic list of service characteristics. Because of the process- and experience-oriented character of a service situation, customers often evaluate these in the sense of a *'pars pro totis'* by evaluating the total service based on their perception of more or less specific individual characteristics or events. These specific situations are called **critical incidents**. Critical incidents are specific service situations that are perceived by the customers as being especially positive or negative.[3] Figure 3.5 illustrates the idea of critical incidents by some examples in several categories.

Since service interactions have a high experiential factor for the customer, the identification of **critical incidents** *from the customers' perspective* is important for designing and improving services. When a large number of customers state that the waiting time or the friendliness of the employees are critical for their evalua-

Incident	Satisfactory Response	Unsatisfactory Response
	Group 1 Sample Incidents: Employee Response to Service Delivery Failures	
Response to Unavailable Service	They lost my room reservation but the manager gave me the VIP suite for the same price.	We had made advance reservations at the hotel. When we arrived we found we had no room – no explanation, no apologies, and no assistance in finding another hotel.
Response to Unreasonably Slow Service	Even though I didn't make any complaint about the hour and a half wait, the waitress kept apologising and said that the bill was on the house.	The airline employees continually gave us erroneous information; a one-hour delay turned into a six-hour wait.
Response to Other Core Service Failures	My shrimp cocktail was half frozen. The waitress apologised, and didn't charge me for any of my dinner.	One of my suitcases was all dented and looked as though it had been dropped from 30,000 feet. When I tried to make a claim for my damaged luggage, the employee insinuated that I was lying and trying to rip them off.
	Group 2 Sample Incidents: Employee Response to Customer Needs and Requests	
Response to 'Special Needs' Customers	The flight attendant helped me calm and care for my airsick child.	My young son, flying alone, was to be assisted by the stewardess from start to finish. At the Albany airport she left him alone in the airport with no one to escort him to his connecting flight.
Response to Customer Preferences	The front desk clerk called around and found me tickets to the Mariner's opening game. It was snowing outside – car broke down. I checked 10 hotels and there were no rooms. Finally, one understood my situation and offered to rent me a bed and set it up in one of their small banquet rooms.	The waitress refused to move me from a window table on a hot day, because there was nothing left in her section. The airline wouldn't let me bring my scuba gear on board coming back from Hawaii even though I brought it over as carry-on luggage.
Response to Admitted Customer Error	I lost my glasses on the plane; the stewardess found them and they were delivered to my hotel free of charge.	We missed our flight because of car trouble. The service clerk wouldn't help us find a flight on an alternative airline.
Response to Potentially Disruptive Others	The manager kept his eye on an obnoxious guy at the bar, to make sure that he didn't bother us.	The hotel staff wouldn't deal with the noisy people partying in the hall at 3 a.m.
	Group 3 Sample Incidents: Unprompted and Unsolicited Employee Actions	
Attention Paid to Customer	The waiter treated me like royalty. He really showed he cared about me.	The lady at the front desk acted as if we were bothering her. She was watching TV and paying more attention to the TV than the hotel guests.
Truly Out-of-the-Ordinary Employee Behaviour	We always travel with our teddy bears. When we got back to our room at the hotel we saw that the maid had arranged our bears very comfortably in a chair. The bears were holding hands.	I needed a few more minutes to decide on a dinner. The waitress said, 'If you would read the menu and not the road map, you would know what you want to order.'
Employee Behaviours in the Context of Cultural Norms	The busboy ran after us to return a $50 bill my boyfriend had dropped under the table.	The waiter at this expensive restaurant treated us like dirt because we were only high school kids on a prom date.
Gestalt Evaluation	The whole experience was so pleasant ... everything went smoothly and perfectly.	The flight was a nightmare. A one-hour layover went to 3½ hours. The air conditioning didn't work. The pilots and stewardesses were fighting because of an impending flight attendant strike. The landing was extremely rough. To top it all off, when the plane stopped, the pilots and stewardesses were the first ones off.
Performance Under Adverse Circumstances	The counter agent was obviously under stress, but kept his cool and acted very professionally.	

FIGURE 3.5 Examples of positive and negative critical incidents

Source: Bitner *et al.* 1990, pp. 77–78.

tion of the service, the service provider knows that it is crucial to improve these characteristics. As a consequence, these critical incidents are important for services marketing due to customers' tendency to use single specific elements of a service provider as quality indicators. Even when a critical incident might seem to be very particular in the eyes of the service provider, this evaluation by the customer might be crucial for a firm's success.

Since the critical incidents are on a very situational, disaggregated level, they give very *specific guidelines for service improvements*. Take the critical incident analysis of an airline. One of the findings might be that customers are dissatisfied repeatedly with the airline employees not being able to give any information regarding the means of transportation at Paris airport. In this case the airline can very easily improve that level of information. Compare this example with a possible result of an aggregate, quantitative analysis of quality dimensions. The service provider would find out that a certain percentage of customers are dissatisfied with the employees' level of information, but, the provider would not know what information content is relevant. Consequently, it would be very difficult to react to this result. Analyses on an aggregate level have their advantages – thus, a combined use of quantitative and qualitative analyses, such as the *Critical Incident Technique*, is preferable.

When analysing critical incidents, service providers try to find critical facets of a service that can be generalised. Therefore, even if the critical incident analysis starts with single situations, the use of this method also implies building categories of ciritical incidents in order to manage service encounters in a systematic way. More specifically, the Critical Incident Technique identifies these critical service situations by asking the following questions:[4]

- Do you remember an especially (un)satisfying contact with an employee of the service firm XY?

- When did that occur?

- What specific circumstances resulted in this situation?

- What did the employee do or say exactly?

- What did happen exactly so that you were (un)satisfied with the service situation?

Based on these questions, service providers can collect various critical incidents perceived in service encounters. In order to analyse these incidents more systematically, certain categories of positive and negative incidents can be built in order to derive emphases of services marketing activities to address the incidents. A slightly varied application of the Critical Incident Technique is presented in Services marketing in action 3.1.

In order to derive implications for services marketing, it is not only necessary to understand the nature of service encounters and identify critical incidents, but also to know the determinants of service encounters.

SERVICES MARKETING IN ACTION 3.1:

Critical incidents of a cruise operator

Jack Simmons, the manager of a medium-sized cruise operator, was disappointed about the repeated bad results from the firm's customer satisfaction surveys. However, even though three of his assistants had looked at the study results back and forth and had already spent several weeks on the project, they did not provide him with concrete suggestions for improving the situation. One day, he read an article about the 'Critical Incident Technique' as a method used to identify quality problems in service interactions that is both standardised and at the same time capable of generating results on an actionable level. He immediately initiated the application of this technique by his company.

This study revealed 81 problem areas that were evaluated by a problem score:

$$\text{Problem score} = \frac{\sum_{i=1}^{n} (a_i + b_i)}{n}$$

with

- a_i: degree of subjects perceiving a problem
- b_i: importance of the problem's elimination from the subject's perspective
- n: number of subjects

Based on these calculations, Simmons ranked the problems according to the problem score (see Table 3.1).

TABLE 3.1 Ranking of customers' problems with cruise operator

Rank	Interaction problems	Problem score
1	'There is no storage room for the luggage after exiting the cabin.'	6.182
2	'It is uncomfortable to leave the cabin two hours before arrival.'	5.892
3	'It is bad that all facilities close on arrival.'	5.833
4	'It is impossible to make conversation during dinner when sitting close to the band.'	5.625
5	'In the cabins, there is a lack of information regarding the activities on board.'	5.485
⋮	⋮	⋮
79	'The personnel in the sales office are unfriendly.'	2.929
80	'The personnel at the terminal are unfriendly.'	2.814
81	'In the cocktail bar, it is boring without disco music.'	2.749

Source: Lindqvist 1987, p. 18.

According to this ranking, the two most important problems concern the last two hours of the whole cruise. Obviously, the customers keep those aspects in mind and associate a high importance to them. Therefore, the conduct of this period of the cruise was addressed by the quality team and rectified immediately.

Source: Based on Lindqvist 1987.

Determinants of the service encounter

The determinants of service encounters are the starting point for services marketing activities used to manage service encounters. Most of the service encounter determinants can be found either in the area of the service resources or in the area of the customer.

A first determinant of a service encounter are the *service resources* that are responsible for the course of the encounter and the outcome.[5] An important resource in a service encounter that repeatedly and strongly influences the perception of the encounter by the customers is the customer contact employee. Especially for individual services, service encounters depend to a large extent on the employees' behaviour (e.g. consulting services). But also in other areas where the employee is not the major element of the service, employee's behaviour is also an important driver of encounter perceptions. For example, the most important resources of airlines are the aeroplanes. However the service encounter is strongly influenced by the employees' behaviour. Unfriendly employees who are not willing to understand the interests of the customer negatively affect the perception of the service encounter. Other service resources as determinants of the service encounter are tangibles and/or technology (see Chapter 9).

A second important determinant of service encounters is the *customer's contribution* to the service encounter. Due to the customer integration into the service process, the customer has certain functions within the service process. An insurance customer must give certain information, the openness of the customer determines the quality of a visit to the doctor, the ability of the customer to describe ideas regarding the required hairstyle will influence the experience during and after a haircut. Not only the respective customer influences his perception of a service encounter. For many services, the *behaviour of other customers* who are present during the service encounter also determines the experience, either positively or negatively. There are services where third-party behaviour is a central quality dimension, as in discotheques. However, third-party behaviour might also have an impact in a negative sense in the case of misbehaviour. All the different facets of customers' contributions to the service encounter become more obvious when looking at the different possible roles a customer might possess in a service encounter.

Customers' roles in service interactions

The external factor's integration into the service process as a central service characteristic and the important role of the customer in the service production have already been stressed, although so far they have only been considered as a general notion. However, this 'important role' of the customer can have very different facets, and very different *customer roles* in the service process can be distinguished. In order to consume the services of a cinema or theatre the customer has to go to the cinema complex or theatre. To have a car repaired, the customer has to take the car to the garage; at a hair salon, the customer attempts to articulate the desired hairstyle before and during the service process; and when parking a car in a car park, the customer 'produces' the service. The roles imply necessary activities of the service provider. Thus, the knowledge of the possible roles is important for services marketing.

The examples mentioned above clarify that there are diverse roles that a customer can have in service interactions that differ according to several characteristics. These are differentiated according to the following five *customer roles in service interactions*:

- the specifier;
- the transferer;
- the abandoner;
- the co-producer;
- the co-user.

Each of these roles contributes differently to the value creation of the service provider. Generally, service providers analyse the customer roles in order to derive the correct and value-enhancing services marketing activities. In the following, the five roles, their value contribution and possible misbehaviours as well as services marketing activities are explored.

The specifier

In order to initiate a service process, the customer must often specify the purchase order and communicate individual needs regarding the desired service. Even for the use of standardised services, the service provider often depends on the customer in order to specify the service. For example, insurance services are often standardised in the sense that the service is pre-structured by the provider. However, in order to conclude an insurance policy, customers have to provide much information in terms of filling out a questionnaire. Other examples where the information that the customer provides is even more individual are medical services and haircutting. From a value perspective, the customer's specification activities are necessary in order to deliver the desired service. Without these specifications, the service would be of no value to the customer. Since the customers' perceived value influences their behaviour and consequently the firm's value, customers' specifications are a driver of the revenue side of value. Furthermore, without the specifications, service production would be uneconomic from the provider's perspective. For example, insurance companies calculate individual rates based on various criteria, like gender, smoking habits and medical history. Using these criteria, insurers differentiate the rates for their customers. Defining rates without these specifications might be uneconomic when the customers with negative characteristics become unprofitable and the customers with positive characteristics do not take out insurance because the premiums are too high. In order to obtain the customer's specifications in a systematic manner, many service providers prepare standard questionnaires that the customer fills out at the beginning of the service encounter. Misbehaviour such as customer non-compliance will lead to negative value effects for the provider. In the insurance example this would be the case if the customer concealed a smoking habit, which would affect the risk factors attributed to a contract. A defensive measure to prevent this misbehaviour is that the terms of the insurance company state that the company will not pay out in the event of incorrect information supplied by the customer.

The transferer

In several service contexts, the customer is *responsible for certain preparation activities* before the actual service process takes place, all of which concern the transfer of persons or objects. For many services where the customer is personally integrated, they come to the service provider's premises. Of course, a doctor, hairstylist, gardener, mechanic or others can come to the customer, but the standard business model reflects that in the majority of cases, the service is 'produced' at the provider's location. In these cases, the customer is responsible for transfer to the provider's premises and back. In addition, when objects belonging to the customer or other persons for whom the customer is responsible need to be integrated into a service process, the customer has to organise the integration of this object or person, for example, taking the children to their swimming lesson, taking the car to the garage, collecting a parcel from the post office or posting letters into the mailbox. In these cases, there are *options for providers* to add value by adopting the customer's role in the transfer process, for example by collecting the car for servicing and then delivering the car back to the customer's location. The value effect of transferring activities of the customer is comparable to that of the specifying activities. If the customer did not transfer the 'external factor' to the service location, the service could not be performed and thus no value could be generated, either for the customer or for the provider. The provider might even encounter negative value effects when resources are available and prepared for the customer, but the customer does not transfer the service object to the service location as promised. This is the case when a patient does not show up for a medical examination or a hotel guest cancels a booked room at short notice. A proactive measure of service providers is giving directions to the customer in order to support transfer activities. A defensive measure is the charging of cancellation fees. For example, when booking a journey at Britannia Travel, a tour operator for vacation travels, the cancellation fee is scaled according to the duration between cancellation date and travel date: it is between 10 per cent when cancelling 30–45 days prior to departure and 100 per cent when cancelling within six days of departure.[6]

The abandoner

During every service interaction the customer dispenses with something. During the participation activities, the customer dispenses with *time*. If the customer did not use the service they could use this time for other activities. For example, by driving the car to the garage and then leaving work by other means of transportation the customer loses working time. Instead of the visit to the doctor, the customer could have lunch with his partner or friends. Generally, the customer abandons degrees of freedom. At IKEA, they provide children's facilities where children can play under observation while their parents are shopping. During a flight, a customer can dispose of time but is restricted regarding the activities that can be conducted. For example, a customer cannot meet a business partner in the office and is forbidden to smoke. When an *object* of the customer or another person is integrated into the service process, the customer has to dispense with these. During the car repair, the customer cannot use the car and must use alternative means of transportation, during the children's swimming lesson, the customer cannot go shopping for the groceries. Again, the positive value effect of the abandonment by the customer is that the service can be delivered and thus value can be created. Misbehaviour, such as incorrect information being provided by the customer, might result in service mistakes and thus affect costs or result in a lower perceived value for money. A proactive *measure* of a service provider is to communicate the positive service outcome to be expected. A defensive measure against customer misbehaviour could be punishments, such as a fine for fare-dodging on the Underground.

The co-producer

This role is often interpreted as a synonym for customer integration. As a co-producer the customer inherits central parts of the service process. In contrast to the three roles discussed previously, in this case the customer takes on an *active role in the service production*. A patient who is prescribed ten lessons of physiotherapy will contribute heavily to the outcome of the service through their involvement in the exercises. An individual who uses the services of a tax firm for tax submissions influences the service production significantly by the documents that are prepared for the tax firm. A tennis player contributes to the service provided by a tennis coach, through the customer's mood, talent and form. The co-producing activities of the customer can increase the value of the service when the customer fulfils the requirements with regard to appropriate behaviour. When the customer 'delivers high quality input' the overall quality of the interaction will be higher. In the tennis coaching example, the tennis experience will be better if the customer is fit and wants to learn. An important proactive *measure* to manage customer behaviour is customer education in order to increase the customer's quality as a determinant of the interaction quality. Misbehaviour on the part of the customer might lead to a bad interaction quality or even an interaction without the desired outcome. For example, when a patient should diet after an operation and does not, the increased weight may slow the healing process and the operation may be ineffective and have to be repeated, enforcing new costs and evoking the dissatisfaction of the customer. Defensive measures in these cases are the denial of service guarantees in the case of customer misbehaviour or non-compliance.

The co-user

The expression co-user describes certain service interactions where several customers take part in the service interaction simultaneously. This is the case during flights, in a restaurant, at a discotheque, in a sports stadium, in the waiting room at the doctor's, in the fitness club, etc. During the delivery of these services there are other customers in addition to the focal customer present, yet some of the services necessitate the *attendance of other customers*. When we simplify the functions of the co-users, we have two *types of co-users*:

- *Co-users with explicit value to the customer*: This is the case when the value of the service to the consumer depends on the existence and behaviour of the other customer, and the customer benefits explicitly from the co-usage. The evaluation of restaurant, discotheque and sports stadium visits directly depends on the attendance and behaviour of other people. In these cases, service providers try to manage the behaviour of the co-users so that it improves the perceived quality of the interaction from the other customers' point of view.

- *Co-users without an explicit value to the customer*: There are other service situations where customers co-use a service but the co-usage does not contribute in a positive way to the value perception of the customers. In many (too many) cases other customers are not appreciated by the customer, as in the case of many patients in a doctor's waiting room. Fitness clubs illustrate that there is a difference between quantity and quality of co-users as well as that there is no linear relationship between number of co-users and perceived value. Many members of fitness clubs enjoy the attendance of other members to a certain degree. But when the attendance results in longer waiting times to use the equipment and facilities, then the impact of the co-usage inverts to the opposite. Regarding the negative effects of co-users, there is the special group of 'problem customers' who misbehave during a service interaction. The reason for the co-usage by several customers is not under the control of the customer and does not add value to the customer. This may be due to economic reasons (e.g.

airlines) or organisational reasons (e.g. doctor). In these circumstance s, the service provider needs to ensure that the behaviour of co-users does not negatively affect the other users' quality perception.

The *value effects* of co-usage are twofold. In the case of positive co-usage behaviour, the perceived value of the other customers might increase and thus also add value to the firm. In a language course, the active behaviour of a student who asks intelligent questions can help improve the learning outcomes for the whole class. Misbehaviour regarding co-usage can have negative effects on the behaviour of the remaining customer and eventually on a firm's value. A bar where the guests behave badly and do not contribute to an attractive atmosphere will have difficulties attracting further guests. A proactive *measure* to influence the co-usage quality is customer selection for the services of the company, as done by holiday clubs that offer special facilities for families, seniors or singles. Defensive measures include punishments, such as no longer being allowed to enter the bar.

The five customer roles discussed above describe *typical activities by customers* in the service production process. These five roles are not exclusive. They can, but do not have to, happen together. For example, an airline passenger determines the flight date and destination (specifying), comes to the airport (transferring), cannot be at other places during the flight (abandonment). The co-producing part is low during a flight and the passenger is co-using the service for economic reasons and not in order to increase the value for himself or the other customers.

The customer roles are used by service providers in order to *modify a service*. Depending on the service level that is delivered by the provider and the level that is conducted by the customer, a service can be very different. For example, in a self-service restaurant, the co-producing part of the customer is extensive compared to a traditional restaurant where the customer only orders the meal.

There are also customer activities that are *exceptional* only for a certain service. For example, before a flight in an aeroplane, customers are taught how to behave in case of an emergency situation. The instructed behaviour is not expected of the customer when the service delivery runs as normal. Only in an emergency situation would the customer have to 'co-produce' the service 'flying'.

How a customer role is conducted by a customer can differ according to several criteria. There are *customer characteristics* that can influence the performance of customers' roles. For example, the personality of a customer can influence his role performance. Whether a customer is open and active in service interactions depends on their general openness and activeness. However, the overall determinant of the relevance, form and also variation of customer roles is the type of business a firm is dealing with, i.e. the *service type*. For example, for providing insurance services, the customer's roles are limited, while they are more extensive at a customer's restaurant visit.

The analysis of the customer roles is important for service providers in order to derive activities used to *manage the customers' activities in the service process*. For the five customer roles, respective marketing measures were discussed. These can be structured into the areas of proactive measures, defensive measures and substitute measures. Proactive measures help the customer in conducting their role ('customer as employee'), defensive measures aim at preventing customer misbehaviour ('prevention') and substitute measures ('internalisation') help to standardise a service by the provider conducting the original customer role as well as offering value-added services to the customer. These measures are summarised in Figure 3.6 for the five customer roles.

Service blueprinting for planning service interactions

Service interactions are very subjective and heterogeneous. Therefore, they are difficult to plan. In the case of consumer goods, there exist instructions for the production that describe concretely how the goods are to be produced. For service interactions, this kind of instruction cannot be realised. However, a method that can help planning service interactions systematically is the so-called service blueprinting. Blueprinting is linked directly to the concept of the Service Value

Customer role	Proactive measures	Defensive measures	Substitute measures
	Customer as employee	Prevention	Internalisation
The specifier	• Standard questionnaire • Employee openness	• Denial of a service in case of wrong specification • Self-selection	• Standardised service packages
The transferer	• Giving directions • Delivery systems	• Cancellation fee	• Transfer services
The abandoner	• Reservation systems • Communicating the positive outcome to be expected	• Punishments	• Time-saving measures
The co-producer	• Customer education	• Denial of service guarantees	• Internalisation
The co-user	• Customer selection	• Punishments	• Substitute for co-users

FIGURE 3.6   Measures for managing the customer roles

Chain and the value-oriented perspective of services marketing. A service blueprint depicts the different steps of the primary process 'interaction process'. Furthermore, a service blueprint indicates what facilitating products or services are needed in order to produce the service. These are linked together with the secondary value processes of the value chain concept. In addition, an important question of the blueprinting method is how the processes deliver a benefit to the customer and what effects the processes have on profitability. Thus, the blueprinting approach incorporates the value chain principle of processes' value creation. This discussion shows that the blueprinting approach is a valid instrument for planning service interactions based on the value chain idea. We present a service blueprinting approach introduced by Shostack[7] and illustrate it in parallel using the example of a basic service (see Figure 3.7). The methodology of service blueprinting follows a three-step approach: identifying service processes, identifying benefits and identifying standards and tolerances.

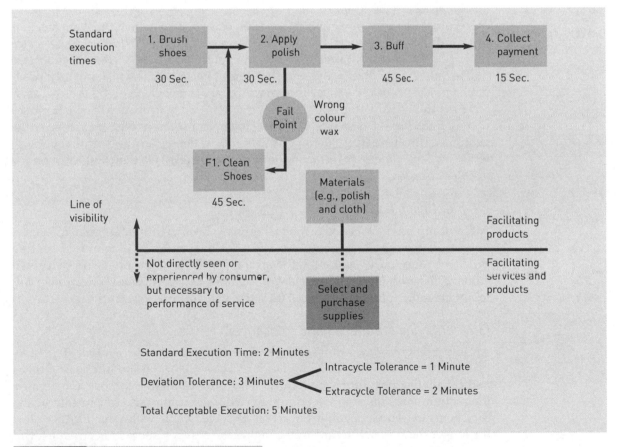

FIGURE 3.7   Blueprint for a corner shoeshine

Source: Shostack 1982, p. 59.

(1) Identifying service processes

The various consecutive *processes* (symbol in Figure 3.7: rectangular with numbered process labels) that are part of the service interactions are identified. To do so, the processes of the Service Value Chain (interaction process) can be a starting point for a company–individual determination of the service processes. Interviews with employees, managers or other experts, who know the respective service, help the specification of the identified service processes. Each process is a limited entity of activities that is linked together with other activities of the overall service process.

When all processes have been identified, possible *fail points* (symbol: circle) are detected. Fail points designate possible mistakes – weak points – in the service process. By identifying the fail points the probability of service failures can begin to be decreased in the planning phase.

Next to the primary value processes, for each service interaction there are *facilitating products and processes* (symbol: rectangular with unnumbered process labels) necessary to support the primary value processes. While all the primary value processes are – by definition – perceived by the customer, there are facilitating products and services that are not perceived by the customer. In a service blueprint, products and processes that are perceived by the customer and those that are not are divided by the so-called 'line of visibility'. The visibility of a product or process is of relevance since processes that are perceived by the customer have distinguished value effects compared to invisible processes. The latter ones merely influence the cost side of value. However, processes that are visible to the customer directly affect customer evaluations, behaviour and thus revenues, while invisible processes influence these only indirectly via their influence on the visible processes.

(2) Identifying benefits

After all processes of a service interaction have been identified, service managers determine the *benefits* of these processes for the customer. The more benefit a process brings to the customer, the stronger will be its influence on perceived value. This information, together with the links between processes can help differentiate more valuable processes from less valuable processes.

(3) Identifying standards and tolerances

An important *cost factor* of a service interaction is the *interaction time*. The blueprinting approach takes this into account by modelling to-be interaction times and calculating deviations from those. Each service interaction has a maximum interaction time that is tolerated by the customer. In the case of this interaction time being exceeded, negative effects on perceived value will occur. Furthermore, the longer the interaction time is, the higher the cost per interaction and the lower the value of the service process. It may occur that the target duration of the interaction is not achieved due to intra-cycle or extra-cycle deviations. Intra-cycle deviations are part of the actual service interaction, e.g. rework during the contact with the customer, like the re-completion of a questionnaire because of an error. Extra-cycle deviations do not concern the direct service encounter, but periods before and after the service encounter, i.e. integrating the external factor. A typical example for such a deviation is the waiting time. While both types of deviation affect the value perceived by the customer, only the intra-cycle deviations influence directly the cost of the interaction.

As a consequence, a blueprint helps service managers to plan a service interaction systematically. In detail, the following *uses of a service blueprint* can be distinguished:

- The blueprint visualises the process as a whole and the single processes that occur within a service interaction, i.e. it helps to operationalise the service interaction.

- Possible failures and deviations can be identified and, consequently, failures can be avoided. By that, both effects on perceived value and cost help to increase value.

- The service provider can identify the internal processes or secondary activities that are necessary to facilitate the interaction processes. Thus, service blueprinting helps to plan the management of human resources, technology and capacities in general.

Figure 3.8 shows the blueprint of a flight that visualises the phases of service delivery by an airline. The dark blue boxes encompass prerequisites for a quality service delivery at the respective stages of the process. Next to identifying quality pitfalls, this blueprint could also be used by the management of the airline in order to change interaction. For example, when the firm realises that the stage 'refreshments and food service' is not valued by the customer significantly, this service could be questioned, as has been done especially by low-cost carriers.

Due to the heterogeneity of services, the participation of the customer as co-producer and the simultaneity of service production and consumption, service failures often cannot be prevented despite good planning. Nevertheless, service providers can react to the failures through service recovery activities.

Service recovery

Failures

Failures of products or services can generally cause negative value effects on both the cost side, because of redoing activities, and the revenue side, via customer dissatisfaction. Therefore, marketing as well as production theory stress the relevance of *quality management* in order to avoid mistakes in the first place. This fact is stressed by principles such as the 1:10 rule explaining that at each production stage the cost

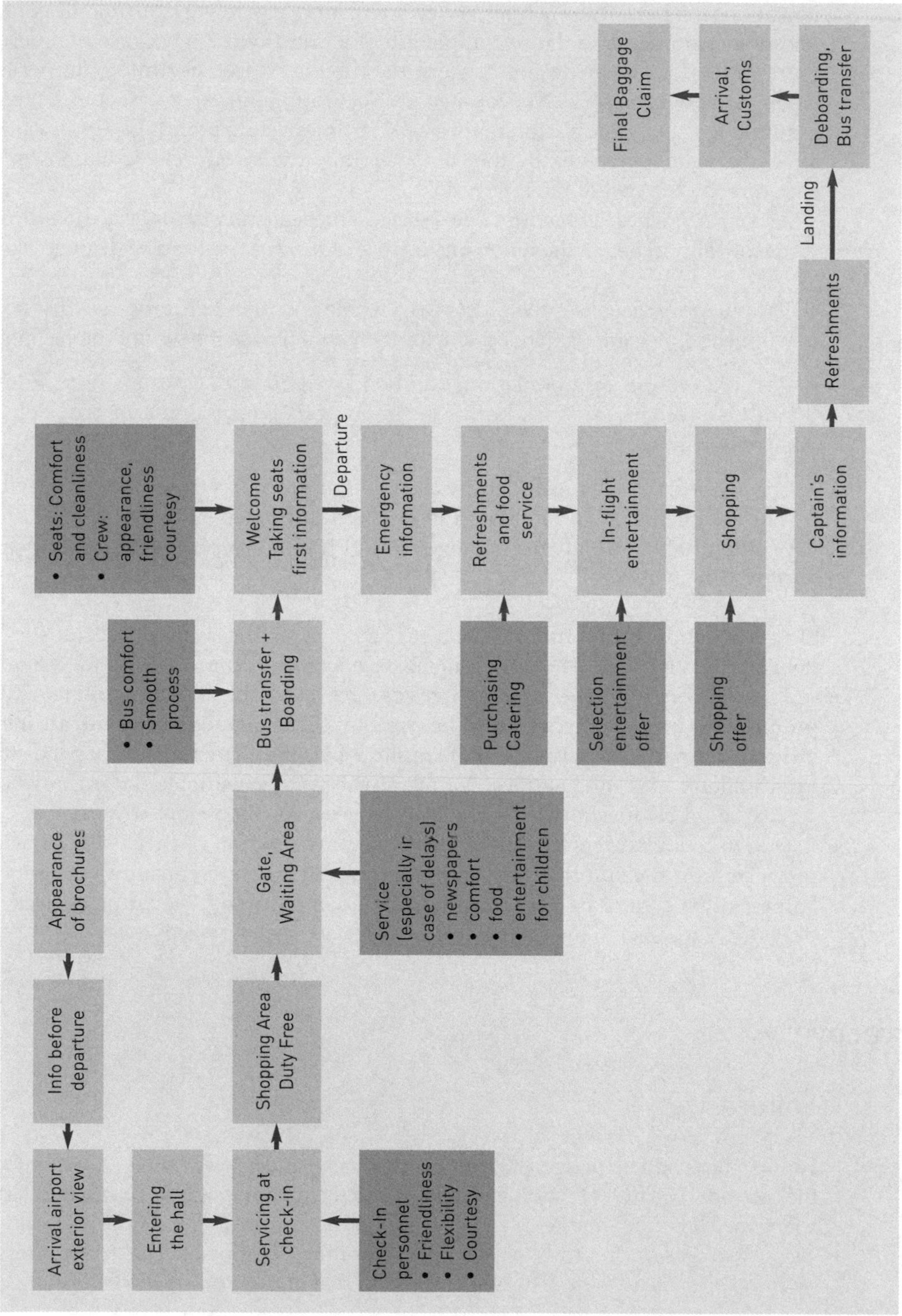

FIGURE 3.8 Blueprint of a flight with an airline

Source: Bruhn 2004.

of failure is 10 times higher than correcting the failure one stage earlier. For example, repairing a systems failure in a machine that produces parts is 10 times cheaper than repairing the failure of each individual part afterwards. This thinking initiated the 'zero defections'[8] and the 'do it right the first time' philosophies.

Although this logic is very reasonable and should be followed by every company to a profitable extent, services marketing theory has accepted that 'zero defections' is an unrealistic strategy for services. The various differences of services compared to goods increase the *probability of failures during service production and delivery*. Since a service is produced and consumed simultaneously, in processes with customer participation there is no rework possible without the customer's realising the rework. Additionally, the customer's participation can cause mistakes that are precipitated by the customer and therefore not manageable in the first instance by the firm.

Because of the unavoidability of failures in services, alongside the prevention of service failures there emerged in services marketing the service recovery strategy, i.e. 'doing the service right the second time'.[9] *Service recovery* encompasses all activities of a service provider that aim at reacting to service failures.

Service failures are a critical element within value-oriented services marketing because of various *negative value effects* (see Figure 3.9). These effects differ according to whether a mistake is perceived by the customer or not. As outlined before, *internal failures* are not perceived by the customer but only by an employee

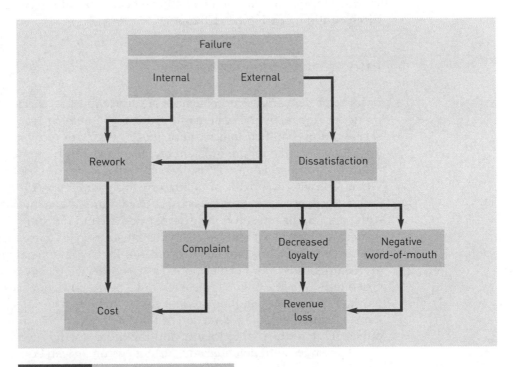

FIGURE 3.9   Effects of service failures

or a company system. The failure can result in consecutive failures and might initiate a chain of failures. That chain of failures is a catalyst for the failure consequences described below and the resulting cost to recover the service.

External failures are perceived by the customer and consequently affect the customer's perception and behaviour and thus the value of the customer to the firm. A common reaction to service failures is dissatisfaction that can lead to three possible customer reactions: complaints, decreased loyalty and negative word-of-mouth. Complaining is a customer behaviour that is aimed at informing the service provider about service failures. Complaints are a typical reaction to service failures or customer dissatisfaction in general, although studies indicate that in many situations only a small proportion of dissatisfied customers make use of complaining. However, compared to other possible customer reactions, complaints are the most favoured reaction at least from the service provider's point of view. Not only might single or repeated failures result in decreased loyalty in terms of a decreased purchasing level of the customer, less buying frequency, using fewer services of the provider or even quitting the relationship with the provider; service failures can lead to negative word-of-mouth. Independent from changes in the purchasing behaviour, customers might talk about service failures with friends, colleagues, etc. By doing so, the customer keeps potential customers from choosing the focal firm or might even inspire current customers to leave the provider. The reactions regarding loyalty and word-of-mouth are part of the relational behaviour of the customer and thus are discussed in more depth in Chapter 4.

Effects of service recovery

Because of the various consequences of service failures, service providers implement service recovery systems in order to be able to react systematically to service failures and customer complaints. The service recovery activities aim not only to resolve the failure problem but also to avoid the consequences of service failures described above. Thus, the *effects of service recovery* can be understood when following the paths of failure impacts (see Figure 3.10). While successful service recovery helps to avoid consecutive failures at the internal path of the failure diagram, the effects on the external side are more distinguishable. Generally, a successful recovery leads to customer satisfaction.[10] Consequently, the impacts of service failures on complaints, decreased loyalty and negative word-of-mouth are compensated for. Furthermore, an early service recovery leads to minimal cost effects. When a failure is resolved quickly, the consequences such as repeated work or complaint handling are less costly than after various consecutive problems. Furthermore, the redirection of the customers' behaviour leads to revenue effects. Due to the higher loyalty and the more positive word-of-mouth, additional revenues with potential and current customers can be expected.

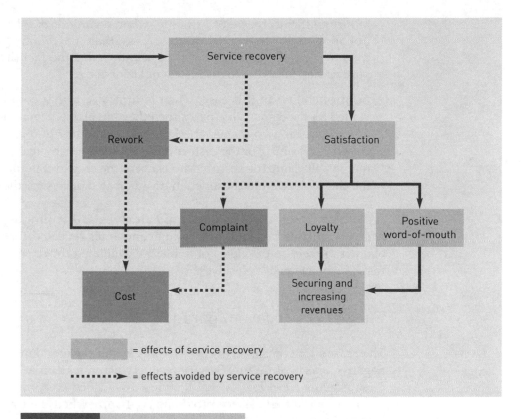

FIGURE 3.10   Effects of service recovery

Service recovery and attribution

The strength of the impact on satisfaction differs strongly according to various criteria. One important factor is the *attribution* of the failure by the customer. There are three dimensions used in order to describe the attribution:[11]

- Locus: The question is who is made responsible by the customer for the service failure. There are at least three important alternatives: either the customer blames themselves or the service provider as an entity or employees of the service provider.

- Stability: Next to the locus the customer questions whether the failure will occur repeatedly. In case of affirmation, the attribution towards the responsible company will be stronger. Although service customers might tend to attribute service failures to the provider, it is also possible that the customer attributes a failure to themselves. For example, when a student in a language school is unhappy with personal learning success, they may blame themselves more than the lecturer, especially if they acknowledge the fact that they have not participated fully due to disinterest or laziness.

- Controllability: In this case, when failures occur that could have been prevented by the responsible party, then they are blamed even more; for example when there are two cashier checkout points and one of the checkout points is closed for cleaning or the cashier has gone for a lunch break. Customers in the queue will blame the cashier who is not at the checkout point, as the closure of the checkout point has resulted in unanticipated delays for the shoppers.

A study including 354 customers of hair stylists, discount department stores, legal consultants and film processing companies revealed that customers who blamed the service provider for a mistake evaluated the service worse than customers who blamed themselves.[12]

The service recovery paradox

The reason for service recovery activities lies in the avoidance of the described negative effects of failure. Service recovery activities aim at avoiding customer dissatisfaction or at least at re-satisfying dissatisfied customers. It sounds obvious and logical that service providers are happy when their recovery activities lead to a satisfaction level that is comparable with the satisfaction level of those customers who did not encounter any mistakes and thus were more or less satisfied in the first place. However, there exist various studies that show a result that is called the *service recovery paradox*.[13] In these studies it was discovered that service recovery activities did not make the customers who encountered mistakes only as satisfied as customers who were satisfied right from the beginning – these customers were even more satisfied than the second group of customers. This result, which of course delighted companies that already invested a lot in their service recovery activities, is surprising only at first sight. In customer satisfaction surveys, there are many customers who are satisfied at a 'normal' or 'standard' level and often fewer customers who are 'very satisfied' or 'excited' or 'delighted'. When a provider conducts a satisfying service recovery, then it adds a further and surprising quality dimension to the quality of the service that might lead to a satisfaction higher than that of only 'satisfied' customers. From this perspective, studies also show that customers with positive recovery experiences are seldom more satisfied than 'very satisfied' or 'delighted' customers. A practical example of the service recovery paradox is given in Services marketing in action 3.2.

SERVICES MARKETING IN ACTION 3.2:

Service recovery at Club Med Cancun

An excellent example of the service recovery paradox is the story of Club Med Cancun that 'recovered from a service nightmare and as a consequence won the loyalty of one group of vacationers'.

'The vacationers had nothing but trouble getting from New York to their Mexican destination. The flight took off six hours late, made two unexpected stops and circled for 30 minutes before it could land. Because of all the delays and mishaps, the plane was en route for 10 hours more than planned and ran out of food and drinks. It finally arrived at 2 o'clock in the morning, with a landing so rough that oxygen masks and luggage dropped from overhead. By the time the plane pulled up to the gate, the angry passengers were faint with hunger and convinced that their vacation was ruined before it had even started. One lawyer on board was already collecting names and addresses for a class-action lawsuit.

Silvio de Bortoli, the general manager of the Cancun resort and a legend throughout the organisation for his ability to satisfy customers, received word of the horrendous flight and immediately created a solution. He took half the staff to the airport, where they laid out a table of snacks and drinks and set up a stereo system to play music. As the guests filed through the gate, they received personal greetings, help with their bags, a sympathetic ear, and a chauffeured ride to the resort. Waiting for them at Club Med was a lavish banquet, complete with mariachi band and champagne. Moreover, the staff had rallied other guests to wait up and greet the newcomers and the partying continued until sunrise. Many guests said it was the most fun they had had since college.

In the end, the vacationers had a better experience than if their flight from New York had gone like clockwork' and became loyal Club Med customers.

Managing service recovery

In order to avoid service failures systematically and to satisfy the first unsatisfied customers as well as to use the information gathered by service recovery, companies conduct several service recovery-related activities aimed at identifying service failures and suitable service recovery measures.

Identifying service failures

An important step within service recovery is identifying possible service failures as the prerequisite to service recovery. The most critical service failures are those perceived by the customer as they have a negative impact on customer behaviour and thus value. Therefore, a measure aimed at identifying possible failures in advance is stimulating complaints. Complaints are customers' expressions of service failures they have perceived during the contact with the provider and its services. When *stimulating complaints* companies review three dimensions:

- Companies give *complaint incentives* to the customer, i.e. customers are rewarded for complaining – in addition to the actual outcome of the service recovery. An example of stimulating customer complaints is the Maine Savings Bank, which pays its customers $1 for each complaint.[14]

- Service providers install *complaint channels* that are easy to reach. There are various different complaint channels possible: personal complaints, passive written complaints, such as comment cards in hotel rooms, or active written complaints, letters, faxes or emails to a bank's customer service team, and complaints by telephone via toll-free numbers. It depends on the service type and also partly on the customer type what channels seem best for a company. For example, personal complaints are more sensible or even possible for services with an intense customer contact. In order to initiate customer complaints, British Airways installed 'Video Point' booths at Heathrow Airport in London so that travellers could record their reactions on arrival. Customer service representatives view the tapes and respond.[15]

- Furthermore, the expected *complaint result* is an important driver of the customer's complaining behaviour. When the customer perceives a complaint as worthless, it is less probable that they will articulate the complaint.

While the knowledge about these aspects helps service providers to initiate customer complaints systematically, there are other sources for identifying service failures. Most crucial are *service employees* who are in direct contact with the customers within service interactions and as a consequence perceive service failures more or less automatically, either by their own perception or by customers' remarks. In order to make this information available for systematic service recovery management, service providers implement systems that let the employees transfer the respective information to the right place in the company. There, the information is integrated in the existing recovery processes.

After service failures have been identified, service providers emphasise that complaints are processed systematically in the firm. This means above all that the complaint information is forwarded to the right person or the right department: the so-called *'complaint owner'* is defined, the person or organisational unit responsible for the complaint until it is resolved.

Service recovery measures

One important consequence of an identified service failure is to react to this failure by responding to the customer who has perceived the mistake. These *reactions* aim at preventing the customer's dissatisfaction due to the service failure and to change perceptions in such a way as to ultimately achieve a perception of high value. Service recovery measures can concern error rectification or compensation. Error rectification means correcting the service, while by compensation the service provider offers a benefit to the customer that substitutes for the defective service. These two functions can be realised by measures in all four areas of the four Ps namely product, promotion, pricing or place (see Figure 3.11):[16]

- Because of the process character of services, they often cannot be improved after their occurrence – a popular measure in consumer goods complaint management – but only repeated. However, as a *product-related recovery measure* some elements of the service process or outcome might be corrected afterwards. For example, when a customer is dissatisfied with a new haircut, the stylist might improve the haircut by altering the outcome of the initial service process. Additionally, compensation is possible regarding some elements of the service process. When a customer is unhappy with a rented car, the firm rental can provide him with another one, sometimes with more features than the original model.

- *Communication measures* aimed at error rectification are especially suitable when the failure is caused by customers having difficulties in operating specific service facilities, ATMs, electronic ticketing machines, etc. Errors can be rectified or even prevented here by explaining the use of the machines to the customer. For compensation, gifts or apologies can support service recovery.

- Regarding *pricing measures*, price reductions can help recovery of a service via error rectification and compensation. An error rectification by price reduction is possible when the customer does not necessarily benefit from certain aspects of the service, but from the value of the price–performance ratio. This is the case when a bank repays a customer's money lost due to failure by the bank; or when a restaurant guest is unsatisfied with their meal and the restaurant waives the bill. Often, it depends on the customer's perception as to whether the price reduction is perceived as a rectification or compensation. Therefore, we do not differentiate between these two fields for price-related measures of service recovery.

- Also *place-related measures* can be utilised for service recovery. An error rectification is conducted by improving the service delivery, such as lost luggage delivered directly to the home of the owner. Other forms of service recovery techniques include compensation such as a gift or the free return of books by amazon.com.

Services marketing in action 3.3 shows an example of which measures work and which do not.

Instrument \ Task	Error rectification	Compensation
Product	Output improvement Example: Improved haircut	Substitute output Example: Making a new rental car available
Promotion	Customer training Example: Training on a self-service machine	Gift/Apology Example: Meal ticket for a flight delay
Pricing	Price reductions Examples: Bank repaying a customer's lost money Restaurant waiving a guest's bill in the case of dissatisfaction	
Place	Improved distribution Example: Package search by the post office	Gifts Example: Free returns by amazon.com

FIGURE 3.11   Service recovery measures

Source: Bruhn 2002b, p. 155.

SERVICES MARKETING IN ACTION 3.3:

Successful and unsuccessful recovery strategies in retailing

A retailing study revealed different service recovery strategies by retailers and analysed the strategies' impact on customer retention. Overall, 661 critical incident reports were used to identify the strategies, 335 of which were positive, and 326 of which were negative.

Figure 3.12 shows how often the respective strategies were encountered, their evaluation by customers on a scale from 1 (very poor) to 10 (very good) and their impact on customer retention. There were seven strategies observed that could be interpreted as *successful strategies* by being evaluated with values between 6.48 and 8.86, resulting in high to very high retention rates (between 81 and 96 per cent). For example, correction as recovery type 2 was evaluated at 8.81, with 96 per cent of the respective customers being retained. The correction plus strategy (type 4) is a correction combined with some other type of compensation. From theory, this strategy should outperform corrections or discounts. The reason why correction plus was evaluated worse than the first two strategies lies in the severeness of a failure. Many of the failures that were recovered from, by means of discounts or corrections, were less severe failures. Therefore, customers were already satisfied with 'only' discounts or corrections.

Next to the seven successful recovery strategies, the study identified five *unsuccessful strategies*. These were associated with a worse evaluation by the customer (worse than 4) and lower retention rates (between 62 per cent and 31 per cent). Examples are customer-initiated corrections, store credits, unsatisfactory corrections, failure escalations and no reaction. The latter was evaluated worst with the lowest retention rates.

Although some recovery types of the study were associated with small samples, it nevertheless revealed significant differences between successful and unsuccessful recovery strategies.

	Recovery strategy	Number of cases	Evaluation (1=very poor, 10=very good)	Retention rate %
Successful strategies	1. Discount	22	8.86	86.4
	2. Correction	81	8.81	96.3
	3. Manager/employee intervention	12	8.42	75.0
	4. Correction plus	21	8.24	90.5
	5. Replacement	173	7.91	87.8
	6. Apology	53	6.75	77.4
	7. Refund	81	6.48	81.5
Unsuccessful strategies	8. Customer-initiated correction	6	3.83	50.0
	9. Store credit	11	3.36	36.4
	10. Unsatisfactory correction	37	2.57	62.2
	11. Failure escalation	50	2.36	42.0
	12 Nothing	114	1.55	31.0

Figure 3.12 Evaluation of service recovery strategies
Source: Kelley *et al*. 1993, p. 439.

In most cases, service recovery measures are only valuable when the provider conducts them rapidly. However, an error rectification is only possible when the value the customer expected from the service can be delivered despite the failure, and often this is not possible immediately. When a train passenger is going to miss an appointment because of a delayed train, there are few, if any, options for the train company to act fast enough in order to rectify the mistake. Another reason for quick recovery reactions is the prevention of negative word-of-mouth communications by the customer. Many unsatisfied customers tell their friends about their problems with a provider. In many cases the customers' reactions right after or during an unsatisfying service interaction, a customer's railing against the service provider or its employees when leaving a bank branch, for example, is a form of indirect word-of-mouth, noticed by other customers standing around. An employee can react the fastest to ensure damage control, and a service recovery system can be best organised by using *systematic rules*. For example, the employees of German Railway (Deutsche Bahn) were allowed to hand out vouchers worth 10 euros to customers if they complained of delays longer than 30 minutes. However, there might be situations when the determined rules do not apply. In these cases, the more responsibility the employees have in order to *make their own decisions spontaneously* and intervene appropriately, the more effective is the service recovery. This delegation of responsibility is discussed in theory as empowerment of service employees: the service provider's empowering of employees to act independently to a certain extent. At Ritz-Carlton, service employees are allowed to spend more than US$2,000 in order to correct customers' problems, such as driving a customer to a destination when the guest has missed the train.

Summary

This chapter can be summarised as follows (see Figure 3.13 on p. 104):

1. As one of a service provider's primary value processes, the interaction process aims at managing the service interactions by integrating the customer, providing the service in the service encounter and a recovery service in case of service failures.

2. These three main value-enhancing sub-processes contribute differently to a service firm's value by influencing both revenues and cost. Revenues are created first by the customer's throughput through the service process, and secondly by preventing customer defections as a consequence of service failures. Cost effects of service interactions are caused by the different degrees of customers' participation in the service process. While some customers are cost intensive due to their behaviour during interactions, others are not.

3. Customer participation is inherent in the service production to a greater ot lesser degree of intensity. Accordingly, integrating the customer into the service process is a major task for services marketing.

4. Two dimensions are critical for service providers when planning customer integration. First, the service location, generally the provider's premises versus the customer's home, influences the challenges for services marketing. Secondly, the type of 'external factor' (human being versus object) affects the necessities of services marketing.

5. The service itself is produced in the so-called service encounter, the situation where customer and the service provider's resources meet. There are different service types, dependent upon the service resources and the types of 'external factors' participating in the service encounter. The process character of services and thus the service encounter, result in the fact that customers do not perceive service as an entity – as it might be for consumer goods – but as a series of incidents. Most important from the customer's perspective and therefore also from the provider's perspective are the so-called critical incidents that decide whether a customer perceives value or not. Service providers can detect these critical incidents by the so-called Critical Incident Technique that explores the critical incidents from the customers' perspective.

6. In order to manage these incidents and thus service interactions, service providers must first know what influences service interactions. These are, on the one hand, service resources, employees, technology and other facilities, and on the other hand – and most important for service production – the customer's behaviour.

7. Generally, a customer can assume different roles in service encounters, namely specifying the service, transferring the external factor, co-producing the service, dispensing with time and for many services co-using the service with other customers. One approach to planning a service, and especially an interaction with the customer considering the aspects discussed in this chapter, is the blueprinting approach.

8. The nature of services implies that failures happen in service encounters. Because of the simultaneous production and consumption of services as well as the customer's participation it is almost impossible to realise 'zero defects' in services delivery. Therefore, service recovery is the third primary value process within the service interaction process value chain.

9. Interestingly, according to the recovery paradox, customers are often more satisfied after a successful recovery than they are without experiencing any failures (unless they are very satisfied).

10. In order to manage service recovery, service providers therefore aim at identifying service failures in order to react to the service failures by correcting the failure or compensating the customer.

As the Service Value Chain proposes, service providers not only create value by providing services in the service process but also by managing customer relationships as a second primary value process, which will be the topic of Chapter 4.

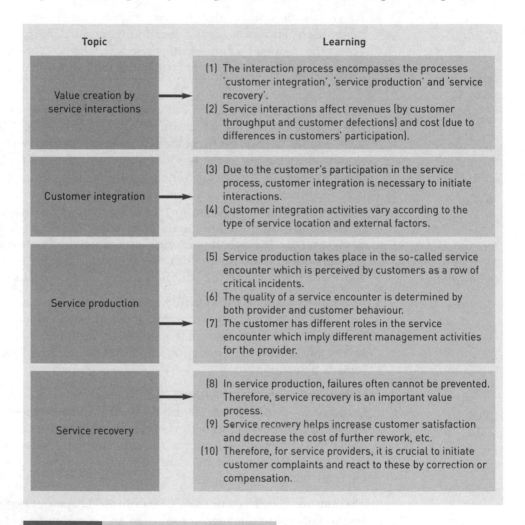

Topic	Learning
Value creation by service interactions	(1) The interaction process encompasses the processes 'customer integration', 'service production' and 'service recovery'. (2) Service interactions affect revenues (by customer throughput and customer defections) and cost (due to differences in customers' participation).
Customer integration	(3) Due to the customer's participation in the service process, customer integration is necessary to initiate interactions. (4) Customer integration activities vary according to the type of service location and external factors.
Service production	(5) Service production takes place in the so-called service encounter which is perceived by customers as a row of critical incidents. (6) The quality of a service encounter is determined by both provider and customer behaviour. (7) The customer has different roles in the service encounter which imply different management activities for the provider.
Service recovery	(8) In service production, failures often cannot be prevented. Therefore, service recovery is an important value process. (9) Service recovery helps increase customer satisfaction and decrease the cost of further rework, etc. (10) Therefore, for service providers, it is crucial to initiate customer complaints and react to these by correction or compensation.

FIGURE 3.13   Learning summary for Chapter 3

Knowledge questions

1. What value effects are associated with integrating the customer, producing a service and offering service recovery as primary interaction value processes for the service provider?

2. Explain the different ways of integrating the customer into the service process.

3. What are critical incidents and how can they be detected?

4. How can a problem score for negative critical incidents be calculated and how can it be used?

5. What are the two most important areas of determinants of a service encounter?

6. What are the possible roles of a customer in service encounters? What misbehaviours can occur? What marketing activities can be derived from the customer roles?

7. What is service blueprinting, how does it work and how can it be used in order to plan and manage interactions?

8. What types of service failures can be differentiated and how do they affect value?

9. Explain how service recovery affects value.

10. Explain the service recovery paradox.

11. How do service providers conduct service recovery systematically?

Application and discussion questions

1. Discuss the differences in the importance of integrating the customer, producing the service and service recovery as determinants of value between different industries.

2. Collect for each type of customer integration one example and explain the characteristics of the respective type using the example.

3. Collect typical examples of service encounters.

4. Think of your latest restaurant/café visit, flight, train journey or supermarket visit and collect positive and negative critical incidents. What measures could the respective service provider derive from them?

5. With what do you estimate are the customers of your favourite cinema most dissatisfied? Develop a short questionnaire in order to collect problems and calculate a problem score. Use this questionnaire by interviewing friends or other visitors to the cinema and evaluate them by the problem score. What appears to be the most important problem?

6. In what industries is the customer contribution especially important for the quality of the service encounter? And why?

7. Take a sample service (e.g. banking, insurance, hotel, restaurant, university, public transportation, airline) and collect the different roles of the customer. Also, consider what activities the respective providers apply for managing the customer roles.

8. Develop a service blueprint for a sample service (e.g. banking, insurance, hotel, restaurant, university, public transportation) and derive possible marketing activities based on the blueprint.

9. Think of one of your latest service interactions. Describe failures that you perceived. What effects did they have regarding your behaviour concerning the respective service provider?

10. Consider service situations that you have experienced. Do you remember situations when the service recovery paradox has applied to you?

11. Discuss why the service recovery paradox applied to the Club Med customers in Services marketing in action 3.2 'Service recovery at Club Med Cancun'.

CASE STUDY: FUJITSU CONSULTING: MOBILE OPERATORS CREATING VALUE BY SERVICE INTERACTIONS

John Lacey[17], Director of Marketing at Fujitsu Consulting (Telecoms) has considerable experience with consulting projects in the UK telecommunications industry. Recently, his shareholders asked him repeatedly what would be the solution in the competitive world of the telecommunications industry. Shareholders would ask for increasing firm value and customers demand more value for less money. But all that customer orientation, such as building call centres, cost a lot of money on the one hand. On the other hand, it is neither obvious nor quantifiable whether these investments would be converted into profits.

At one of the dinners with his director colleagues, Lacey discussed the airline industry with reference to new business initiatives and recent projects. He was impressed with the mention of the introduction of self-service. Customers were purchasing tickets and even ordering special menus via the web. Travelling home he considered whether these innovations could be applied to his telecommunications customers.

He listed the value effects that online self-service for telecommunications customers might create for the providers. On the cost side, online self-service should be less expensive than call centres. That was already an important factor for his customers. However, he expected even more value potential on the revenue side. He realised that in telecommunications customers only interact with the technology, the invisible network of the telecommunications provider. Only in the case of problems was there any interaction with the company – then the customer phoned the call centre. The other contact between the company and the customers was one-directional, predominantly bill mailings and direct mailing campaigns. However, there was no customer interaction within the standard value creation processes. He planned to initiate a study regarding his assumptions the next morning and assigned his two best senior consultants to the task. Three days later the first results were on his desk.

The research showed that nearly half of all UK mobile users would prefer to handle their own customer service online, rather than by means of a call centre. The result confirmed that the company could be missing out on a significant opportunity to reduce the cost of call centres, improve customer satisfaction and increase revenues.

Lacey's next assumption, the cost-saving element of self-service, was illustrated by the fact that respondents said that they were most likely to use self-service in the evening (80%) and weekends (55%) – times when call centres are most expensive to run. Furthermore, his senior consultants found out that industry experts estimated that each customer enquiry handled via self-service would cost less than a tenth of one handled via a call centre. Research by Datamonitor/ContactBabel estimated the cost of handling a customer in a call centre to be between £2.30 and £8.40 as opposed to between £0.10 and £0.65 for a web-based self-service customer enquiry. He calculated quickly that operators can save approximately £100,000 per million customers for every 1% of customer service enquiries handled via the web rather than through a call centre. That meant that the cost effects estimation exceeded even his expectations.

On the revenue side, customer satisfaction could be improved by giving consumers a self-service option. Self-service turned out to be the preferred means of communication with an operator (with contacting a call centre and visiting a retail store following) for:

- viewing your bill (42%);
- checking minutes (44%);
- checking/changing a talkplan/package (37%);
- subscribing to services (38%);
- topping up pre-pay cards (31%).

Contract customers were particularly interested in using self-service.

According to the study results, self-service also provided marketing opportunities. Thirty-nine per cent of those interested in self-service said they would visit the site at least once a week – offering operators a fourfold increase in interactions compared to a typical user who only hears from the operator when he or she receives a monthly bill.

Self-service is particularly popular amongst those who are likely to spend more money on their mobile: notably those who spend over £20 a month on mobile services (48% against 34% overall); respondents under 25 (55% expressed interest in self-service compared to 27% of those aged between 35 and 54); those who banked or shopped online (43% and 44% respectively against 34% overall); and those who had WAP/GPRS (50% against 34%).

The survey findings also suggested that mobile dealers would increasingly be asked to provide online customer support in the store. While the overwhelming preference for customer support was a well-informed sales assistant (64%), 16% preferred the concept of an in-store self-service facility that they could use independently (this ratio rose to 1 in 5 with contract customers).

Reading these results, John Lacey immediately called one of his telco customers and arranged a meeting to discuss the opportunities for a project aimed at improving the service interactions of the customer firm.

Source: Based on Netonomy (2004).

Notes

1 See Shostack 1982.
2 See Burgers *et al.* 2000.
3 See Bitner *et al.* 1990.
4 See Bitner *et al.* 1990.
5 See Farrell *et al.* 2001.
6 See Britannia Travel 2004.
7 See Shostack 1984.
8 See Reichheld and Sasser 1990.
9 See Berry and Parasuraman 1991.
10 See Bitner *et al.* 1990.
11 See Bebko 2001.
12 See Bebko 2001.
13 See Goodwin and Ross 1990.
14 See Hart *et al.* 1990.
15 See Hart *et al.* 1990.
16 See Bruhn 2002b.
17 Names are fictitious.

4 The customer relationship process: Managing customer acquisition, retention and recovery

In many service industries (e.g. banks, insurance companies, telephone companies), firms are valued based on the size of their customer base, a certain number of customers that are considered the 'current customers' of that firm. These current customer relationships of a provider represent revenue and profit potential for the provider. As a consequence they try to prevent the loss of these customers and strive for customer retention. In some service industries, companies try to win back recent customers who have abandoned the provider. Both customer retention and recovery are based on the belief that acquiring new customers is more expensive than retaining current customers or winning back lost customers. These examples show that there are marketing activities that do not directly influence the service itself, but do influence the relationship with the customer, and that these activities can influence value, which will be outlined in detail in this chapter.

Apart from service providers aiming at managing customer relationships towards value, customers also evaluate the provider's relational behaviours. While in the Service Profit Chain, service quality is the main driver of perceived value, from a relational perspective there arise further dimensions of the customers' perceptions of a provider and its services. Airline passengers value airlines based on their frequent flyer programmes, a private banking customer appreciates a permanent contact person instead of talking to different customer contact personnel, insurance companies are not only chosen by customers because of the best price or the best service description or the most eloquent insurance agent, but also based upon the trust of the customer who believes that the insurance company will help the customer in the event of disaster. All these are aspects that can be important drivers of customers' behaviour, but are not part of single interactions and are not covered by service quality dimensions. Consequently, there are aspects in the context of the **customer relationship** next to service quality that influence the Service Profit Chain (see Chapter 2). In line with the service quality conceptualisation, these aspects are subsumed under the concept of relationship quality, i.e. the perceived quality of a customer relationship from the customer's perspective.

Consequently, relational aspects of services marketing are both relevant from a provider's and a customer's perspective. This logic is the basis for this chapter which addresses the following *learning objectives* (see Figure 4.1):

1. Defining the value contributions of customer relationships, i.e. how customer relationships help service providers to create value.

2. Learning about the characteristics of customer relationships and the models to describe them.

3. Understanding the nature of the possible relational behaviours of customers and how service providers can manage these behaviours.

4. Getting to know relationship quality as the customer's evaluation of a relationship to a firm and as the driver of relational behaviours.

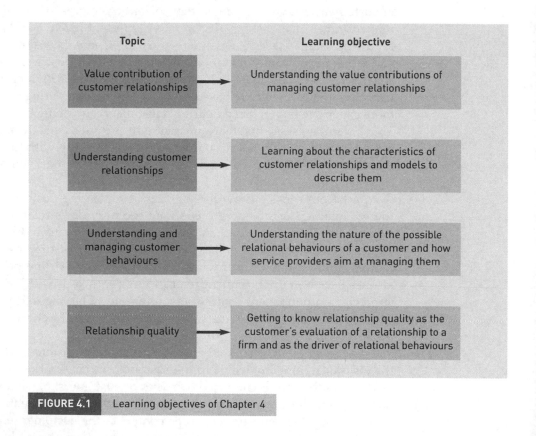

FIGURE 4.1   Learning objectives of Chapter 4

Value contribution of customer relationships

The discussion of service recovery at the end of Chapter 3 showed that service companies are especially successful when customer contacts are not finished after the actual service encounter. Regarding service recovery, the contact is prolonged because of service failures that the provider attempts to resolve after their occurrence. However, successful service providers do not only concentrate on single encounters but on customer relationships as a whole, they not only correct mistakes but also improve the value to the customer and the value they create for the firm. Customer relationships and thus managing them contribute to the perceived value from the customer's perspective which eventually increases the value of the service provider in financial terms. But how are these values increased?

In many industries the *value of a customer relationship* develops during the course of the relationship. With *longer relationship duration* various financial figures can be improved:

- The cost of serving a customer decreases during a relationship because of the customer's experience with the service and thus there is less need for information, explanation, etc.

- Not only service providers, but also customers can perceive value in the existence of a relationship to a provider. Possible reasons are the convenience of not having to choose a new provider for every service usage (e.g. for every telephone call) or the risk of receiving a worse service by another provider, especially for services that are difficult to evaluate (e.g. medical services). Because of the customers' appreciation of a relationship in these cases they are willing to pay a price premium due to increased price tolerance, customers are willing to pay for the value a relationship gives them – next to the value realised by the single service.

- With increasing experience with a certain provider, customers are willing to shift more of their budget in the respective service category to that provider. That means that customers increase their purchase frequency or volume with that provider and/or engage in cross-buying, purchasing other services of the provider's programme they have not purchased previously. Airline passengers who are members of a frequent flyer programme tend to try to use that airline for as many flights as possible in order to collect enough miles to get on a certain level in the programme.

- There are also indirect effects of customer relationships on customer value and firm profitability as in the case of positive word-of-mouth behaviour of committed customers. They tend to recommend their provider more often than customers who are less committed and thus help the provider recruit new customers.

The described value effects can be verified in various industries[1] (see Figure 4.2).

Despite the plausibility of this logic, there is various *criticism* against the validity and linearity of the described effects. For example, customers with a longer relationship duration might demand price reductions instead of being willing to pay price premiums because of their loyalty to the firm. This logic is followed by customer card programmes by retailers who give discounts to customers with certain purchase volumes. Also, 'established' customers do not always generate less cost than 'newer' customers. Customers are aware of their importance to the

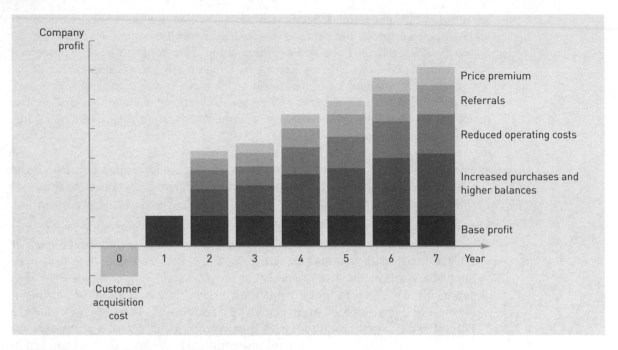

FIGURE 4.2   Value effects of a customer relationship

provider as a loyal customer, they expect superior service and for example use the service hotline at every opportunity. Here, the logic of the increasing experience is valid, too. With more experience, the customers know the company systems better and might utilise their knowledge to their own advantage.

Despite this criticism regarding the logic of value effects of a customer relationship the basic notion of *increasing profitability with longer customer relationships* is valid for many industries, even though not all value effects are relevant in every industry. For example, the value effect of increased purchases is less relevant for firms with few services because then there is no cross-selling possible. However, the criticism and the contrary results of other studies demonstrate that service providers should not blindly believe in the value of relationships. Instead they should analyse their customer relationships, their value contribution and how the relationships can be utilised best for the service provider's benefit.

Although the value impacts of customer relationships discussed above can be realised in many industries, even in non-service industries, many of the effects are particular to service providers. The main reason for this is the direct contact between the customer and the provider. For example, the direct contact facilitates cross-selling activities (e.g. by direct mailings). Furthermore, the continuous relationship learning is much more obvious when there is a direct contact between provider and customer.

Understanding customer relationships

A *customer relationship* consists of several, non-accidental customer interactions. This definition stresses the fact that a customer relationship does not necessarily start with the second interaction between a customer and a service provider. The initial and second interactions must be linked together somehow in order to develop a customer relationship. This *linkage* means that there must be a reason within the relationship for the consecutive interactions. The reason can be a conscious repeated choosing of the provider by the customer because of satisfaction with the service provider or because of repeated efforts of the service provider to keep in contact with the customer (e.g. direct mailings, personal communication). In Figure 4.3, a relationship between the Hotel Grand and a hotel guest is presented in diagram form. Three episodes, i.e. hotel visits, including several interactions have taken place. The respective interactions concern the different stages of the hotel service process, such as check-in, room occupation, visiting the restaurant, etc. This diagram also shows the linkages between interactions (or in this case episodes as series of interactions) within a customer relationship. Earlier interactions have an influence on later interactions. At the second visit, the customer already knows the processes and facilities in the hotel, possibly resulting in cost reductions for the hotel (e.g. fewer customer requests regarding how things work) and increased well-being of the customer.

Not every series of interactions necessarily develops a customer relationship. Take the example of the relationship between a car driver and a motorway petrol station. In scenario 1, the driver uses the petrol station only twice in five years although passing the station more often. The two times the driver used the petrol station were due to necessity, not choice. In this case, one obviously would not allude to a relationship. In scenario 2, the driver uses the petrol station a first time and is very satisfied with the service personnel, cleanliness and availability of fuel pumps and therefore plans refuelling for the next journey so as to use the petrol station again. This is the start of a relationship because of the conscious choice of the petrol station by the customer. In scenario 3, the driver uses the petrol station once and fills out a customer information card that was offered by

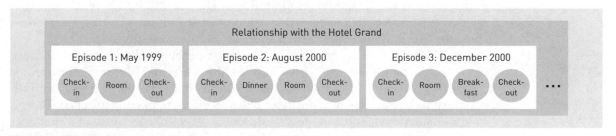

FIGURE 4.3   Relationships and episodes of interactions

Source: adapted from Liljander and Strandvik 1995, p. 149.

the service station employee. Based on this address information the petrol company sends the customer a voucher for a 5 per cent discount at the company's petrol stations. In this case, the petrol station company initiates the relationship by contacting the customer after the first interaction. As these examples clarify, a relationship consists of several interactions between provider and company that are somehow linked together.

This linkage is not an abstract concept, and is illustrated by the following example: John Deynard cancelled his relationship with his bank and thereby automatically his contract with its credit card firm. On the same day, he opened a new account at another bank and, also on the same day, applied for a credit card from its credit card company. One week later, John received a letter from his former credit card company stating that they regretted his cancelling the relationship and hoping that he would choose them again one day – obviously not 'knowing' that John had already signed a new credit card contract. Although John's behaviour seems like an everyday procedure (switching bank accounts), the credit card company could not manage these incidents on a relationship level. The customer himself knows the linkage between the several interactions in the relationship. When the provider misses making this connection by itself, the customer will not perceive the provider as being relationship-oriented. Moreover, this non-relationship behaviour is inefficient for the provider. In the credit card example, the letter by the original company would not have been necessary.

For every customer relationship, the sequence of interactions between service provider and customer and thus the development of the relationship takes on an individual form. However, there is a general pattern that seems to apply to every customer relationship and that is described and shown in the so-called **customer relationship lifecycle**. According to this concept, the development of every customer relationship can be described based on the time period, i.e. in dependence of relationship duration. Following this concept, customer relationships are characterised differently at the beginning of the relationship compared to later stages.

The relationship lifecycle is depicted in a two-dimensional diagram (see Figure 4.4). The diagram represents the customer relationship duration and the ordinate reflects the relationship intensity. *Relationship intensity* can be measured with both pre-economic measures – customer satisfaction and customer loyalty, and economic measures – customer profitability, customer value. A typical customer relationship starts with a lower relationship intensity. In the course of the relationship, the intensity increases and at some stage, most relationships become less intensive for various reasons, for example the tendency of individuals to seek variety, by searching for alternatives because of habituation and boredom. The average course of customer relationships for several industries was analysed in an empirical study, the results of which are described in Services marketing in action 4.1.

The customer relationship lifecycle describes a typical concourse of a customer relationship. Service providers can draw specific *conclusions for the relationship management* from this model. The lower relationship intensity in the beginning indicates that at this stage investments into the relationship are necessary which

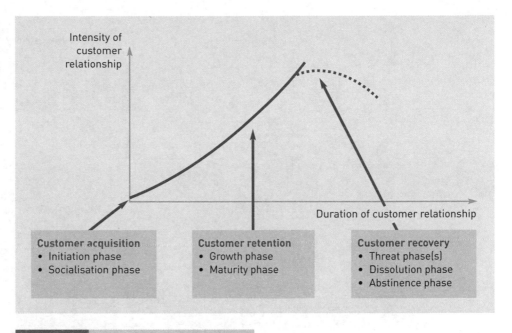

FIGURE 4.4   Customer relationship lifecycle

Source: Bruhn 2002b, p. 46.

are justifiable by the possibility of higher relationship intensities in later stages. The possible growth of a customer relationship in the retention phase emphasises that service providers only utilise the full potential of a relationship when succeeding in bringing the relationship to a higher level. Also, the possible fall of relationship intensity demonstrates that it is important to observe customer relationships even when they are at a high intensity level.

The notion that the lifecycle describes a typical course further indicates that the lifecycle is an *'average' model*. The lifecycles of individual customers differ. There are short and long relationship lifecycles, there are lifecycles with strong or weak variations of relationship intensity, and there are lifecycles with more or fewer

SERVICES MARKETING IN ACTION 4.1:

Customer relationship lifecycle

In connection with the growing economic relationship trend, one of the studies most often quoted is that by Reichheld and Sasser.[2] Figure 4.5 illustrates examples of the profit made per customer as a function of the relationship length by credit card organisations, laundries, wholesalers and automobile servicing companies.

▶

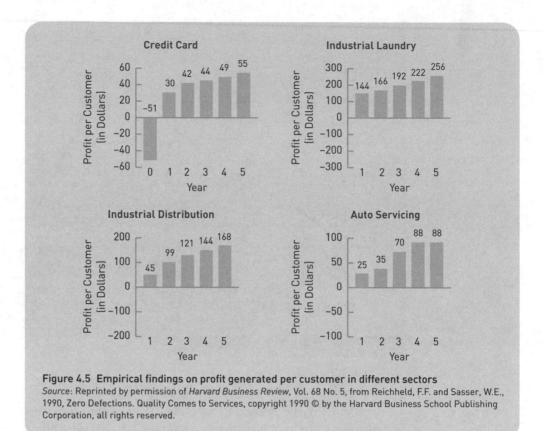

Figure 4.5 Empirical findings on profit generated per customer in different sectors
Source: Reprinted by permission of *Harvard Business Review*, Vol. 68 No. 5, from Reichheld, F.F. and Sasser, W.E., 1990, Zero Defections. Quality Comes to Services, copyright 1990 © by the Harvard Business School Publishing Corporation, all rights reserved.

problem phases. Therefore, service providers analyse individual lifecycles in order to derive specific measures for a single customer.

On the level of the entire customer base, the lifecycle approach still allows general implications for services marketing. In order to do so, the lifecycle concept distinguishes a number of phases that customer relationships typically comprise over time. There are three *core phases* every customer relationship passes through (see Figure 4.4):

(a) Customer acquisition;

(b) Customer retention;

(c) Customer recovery.

These three customer relationship lifecycle phases can be characterised in greater detail in terms of certain relationship attributes and *implications for services marketing activities*. The *customer acquisition phase* is comprised of the initiation and socialisation phases. The initiation phase is the precursor to interactions involving an information exchange between the provider and the customer. The customers have their first interaction with the provider, who undertakes measures such as promotion to acquire the (potential) customer. This phase ends with the first exchange, thereby initiating the socialisation phase in which the seller and buyer become familiar with each other. The customer gains preliminary experience with the seller's offering, which enables the seller to collect data about the customer for subsequent preparation of customised service outputs. Since both customer initiation and socialisation entail start-up costs, this acquisition phase is often uneconomic for the company.

If there is a positive development the customer relationship grows during the *customer retention phase*, which can be separated into the growth and maturity phases. The growth phase is characterised by full exploitation of the customer's potential. Efforts are made to broaden the relationship through increased service use by the customer and to increase cross-buying. In the maturity phase, since the respective customer's potential has been almost fully exploited the goal is now to maintain the sales level reached.

The *customer recovery phase* is concerned with the termination of the relationship by the customer and covers the threat, dissolution and abstinence phases. In the threat phase, as a result of certain events, such as unsatisfying interactions with service employees, the customer begins to mull over the idea of no longer using the seller's products and services. A decision is then reached in the dissolution phase to stop using the seller and the customer openly cancels the relationship especially in case of a membership (e.g. as in the case of banking services), or just gives it up quietly, and uses other providers (e.g. hotels). This leads to the abstinence phase where the customer refrains from using any of the provider's services. The relationship could commence again, because of either customer-originated reasoning or due to recovery measures undertaken by the provider.

The design of the *relationship process within the Service Value Chain* is based on the customer relationship lifecycle. Here, we distinguish between customer acquisition, customer retention and customer recovery as the primary value processes. These processes encompass all activities supplied by service providers that aim to manage the relationship lifecycle for value. In each phase specific measures are utilised to create value for the customer and the firm.

This 'thinking in relationships' is more relevant in some industries than in others. One concept for explaining the relevance of a relationship-oriented perspective of services marketing in different industries is the differentiation of 'always-a-share' and 'lost-for-good'[3] markets. In *'always-a-share' markets* customers can easily switch provider without incurring high switching costs and as such have a lower state of dependence. On the one side, buyers can rely on a mix of suppliers without incurring significant variation in performance. On the other hand, multiple suppliers have a share of a customer's business either now or in the future. Examples of 'always-a-share' markets are cinemas, restaurants or copy shops. For these markets, there are no genuine relationships between provider and customer.[4] In *'lost-for-good' markets* customers are confronted with high switching costs (e.g. specific investments, economic penalties, cost of finding a new supplier) and have a high state of dependence. In these markets, relationship marketing is highly significant.[5] If treated badly and lost, the chance of winning a 'lost-for-good' customer back is very low. Examples of 'lost-for-goods' markets are tax accountants, health insurance companies or dentists.

Understanding and managing relational behaviours

In traditional, transaction-oriented marketing, the focus of marketing activities is on initiating single transactions, i.e. single purchases, neglecting the individual customer in focus, above all whether a certain customer has already bought the firm's products. The transactional marketing instruments are structured according to the 4Ps approach: product, price, promotions and place[6] (see also Part 3). Relationship marketing theory suggests that managing relationships is at least a complement to transaction marketing. Systematic management of customer relationships focuses upon the customer lifecycle by managing customer acquisition, retention and recovery.

Customer acquisition

Managing relationships starts with *initiating customer relationships*. At this stage, the service provider focuses on potential customers who have not yet been in contact with the provider and have not yet purchased its services. Consequently, these potential customers have no experience of the provider and its services and often are more willing to compare offers of different providers than are customers who are loyal to a certain provider. At this stage marketing aims at convincing customers to choose the focal provider, or more specifically to:

- *Reduce uncertainty*: Due to service characteristics, the potential customer perceives uncertainty because in many service industries it is difficult to evaluate the services beforehand. For example, in the case of a hotel information retrieved from websites or presented in brochures cannot give the customer a 100 per cent correct picture of the service facilities, not to mention the interactions with the provider. One example of a measure for reducing uncertainty is service guarantees. By installing and communicating service guarantees, service providers indicate that they are willing to deliver a service at a specified quality level. Should they fail to do so, the customer is rewarded. See Figure 4.6 for sample service guarantees from different industries.

- *Differentiate from competitors*: Taking on the potential customer's perspective, they are, at this stage, potentially looking for a service provider in a specific industry. Therefore, the consumer is collecting information about different providers by reviewing TV adverts, reading service tests or asking friends

Segment	Corporation	Guarantee
Parcel services	FedEx	Next day delivery, absolutely, positively by 10:30am
Office equipment	XEROX	If a customer is dissatisfied with any Xerox equipment, it is replaced free of charge
Hotel	Hampton Inn Motels	Unconditional 100% Satisfaction Guarantee, that is, if a customer is not completely satisfied with his stay at a Hampton Inn motel, he does not have to pay
Food services	Domino's Pizza	Guaranteed 30-minute delivery on telephone orders for pizza, late-arriving pizzas are free (later amended to $3 off the order)
Insurance	Delta Dental Plan	Seven separate guarantees are given covering accessibility of personnel, problem-free billing, punctuality of reimbursements, etc.

FIGURE 4.6 Examples of service guarantees

Source: Bruhn 2002b, p. 135.

about their experiences in order to form a decision for one of the optional providers. Further, if the potential customer is currently a customer of another provider, the service firm aims at convincing them to switch providers. Therefore, in order to attract these potential customers, providers aim at differentiating from competitors in the eyes of the potential customers, for example by establishing a differentiated image or by price advantages.

- *Enhance word-of-mouth communications*: Due to the uncertainty of potential customers regarding new providers and services not yet used, they prefer information from credible sources. One of these sources constitutes recommendations from friends or colleagues regarding service providers. These recommendations represent significant purchase decision factors in many industries. In consequence, service providers strive for initiating so-called **word-of-mouth communications**, recommendations by existing customers. This is realised by direct measures, offering incentives for current customers when recommending the provider and indirect measures by setting the stage for good rankings in consumer tests and reports.

- *Stimulate customers*: Often it is not sufficient to deliver the reasons (e.g. better quality) for current customers of other providers to switch, concrete inducements to switch are also required. These can be short-term measures, such as direct mailings, price reductions or other special activities, but also long-term decisions, such as the choice of a service location or the transparency of the service and pricing system.

When a customer is acquired, the relationship building begins from the provider's perspective. In the customer retention phase, existing relationships are not only to be sustained but also to be expanded.

Customer retention

According to the Service Profit Chain (see Chapter 2), an important customer behaviour is repeat purchases. Only when a customer keeps buying the services of a company, can the latter profit from that customer relationship. This is especially obvious for so-called membership relationships by banks, insurance companies or telephone companies. In membership relationships, a customer only purchases services of the respective firm when the customer is a 'member' of the firm, and there is a contract regarding the usage of the firm's services (e.g. bank account).

In order to manage customer retention, it is important for service providers to identify what promotes customer retention. Although the Service Profit Chain and many other marketing studies propose service quality and customer satisfaction as the main drivers of customer retention – and these clearly are important drivers – in many service industries, we find various levers for customer retention. Overall, the determinants of customer retention can be divided into two groups:[7]

- alignment;

- bonding.

Alignment concerns a voluntary, emotional connection between the customer and the provider that can be explained by the psychological appreciation of the provider by the customer. Retention determinants in this category are several psychological constructs whose influence on retention behaviour was shown for several industries. These determinants include customer satisfaction,[8] trust or commitment.[9]

Bonding represents not an emotional but a formal connection between customer and provider that implements switching barriers for the customer, such as for membership-like relationships. There are four types of switching barriers:[10]

- Contractual switching barriers cause contractual bonds by contracts between provider and customer. This is the case in the mobile telephone industry. Typical offers encompass free mobile phones, free minutes and sms texts when a contract is initiated.

- Economic switching barriers cause bonds based on financial reasons, e.g. discounts for theatre performances in a theatre subscription.

- Functional switching barriers allow the use of certain services only in connection with other services, e.g. purchase of shares via a bank only with an account at that bank.

- Situational switching barriers concern factors that bring the customer into a situation that allows customer retention. In comparison with the other three categories, situational switching barriers are often less manageable by the focal provider. Examples are monopolies in certain industries or the physician providing night and holiday emergency cover.

The *effects of alignment and bonding* are diverse. While alignment causes a voluntary retention, bonding is often associated with so-called lock-in effects. The customer is locked into the focal relationship for contractual, economic, functional or situational reasons. Furthermore, there are interconnections between alignment and bonding, especially when a dynamic perspective is applied. In most cases, a provider can only realise a bonding with an existing alignment. When a customer of a mobile telephone company is dissatisfied with the company, they will not renew the contract with the company. Furthermore, bonding can have a negative impact on alignment. When the customer is annoyed with the contract or the monopolistic situation, they will switch providers as soon as the switching barrier diminishes. However, bonding can also help to build alignment. By a theatre subscription, the theatre gets the opportunity to build a relationship and alignment with the customer.

Possible *measures* in order to manage customer retention are geared to these two categories of retention causes. Alignment measures strive for customer retention by means of psychological determinants such as relationship quality and customer satisfaction, whereas a bonding measure sets up switching barriers to achieve customer retention. Furthermore, retention measures differ according to the time horizon of their use. We can differentiate between short-term and long-term bonding measures as well as short-term and long-term alignment measures (Figure 4.7):[11]

- Short-term bonding measures, like short-term agreements with customers, 1-month contract from cell-phone companies.

- Long-term bonding measures, like long-term agreements with customers, 2-year contracts from cell-phone companies.

- Short-term alignment measures, like low-price offers over a short period to build up trust by demonstrating fairness towards the customer.

- Long-term alignment measures, like securing a high level of employee retention by having the same customer representatives for familiarity development.

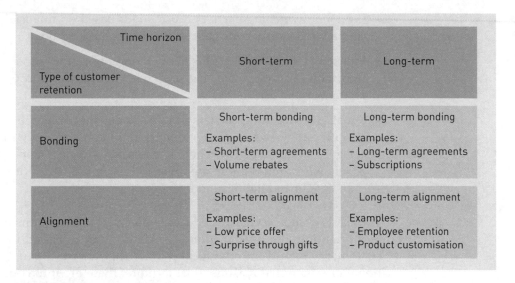

Type of customer retention \ Time horizon	Short-term	Long-term
Bonding	Short-term bonding Examples: – Short-term agreements – Volume rebates	Long-term bonding Examples: – Long-term agreements – Subscriptions
Alignment	Short-term alignment Examples: – Low price offer – Surprise through gifts	Long-term alignment Examples: – Employee retention – Product customisation

FIGURE 4.7   Customer retention activities

Source: Bruhn 2002b, p. 109.

In *relationship marketing practice*, there are marketing measures applied that are known from other contexts but can also be interpreted from a relational view. For example, subscriptions for theatre tickets are instruments to increase the sales with a certain customer, to expand the relationship with that customer. In addition to those measures, specific instruments have been developed with the aim of managing the customer relationships by increasing the alignment or bonding of the customers. These so-called *loyalty programmes* are often not isolated single marketing measures but combine several measures and differentiate their offer for different customer segments. One example of loyalty programmes is the mileage programmes of airlines. The passengers collect points (or 'miles') for each flight with the respective airline. With accumulated air miles, they get a certain customer status that is associated with certain privileges, express check-in, lounges, free flights. The idea of these programmes is to make customers prefer the focal airline. To a certain degree, the pioneers of the mileage programmes probably realised these goals. However, today, these programmes are mandatory – outside the low-fare market segment – because customers take the bonuses or extra flights provided by the mileage programmes for granted. Next to the airline market, loyalty programmes are widely used in the retailing sector. See Services marketing in action 4.2 for an example of a very successful loyalty programme in the UK.

In most markets, firms cannot differentiate via loyalty programmes because these are deemed a basic requirement by consumers. Moreover, the arguments from academics as well as the experiences of service firms indicate some criticisms of loyalty programmes. Conceptually, it is said that these programmes often do not create customer loyalty but attract customers who are seeking bargains. Analytically, loyalty programmes are often used to collect customer data,

SERVICES MARKETING IN ACTION 4.2:

Tesco's Clubcard

Tesco's Clubcard's success is part of a wider success (see also the Case Study at the end of this chapter). Launched in 1995, it has been part of a steady transformation of Tesco's marketing that has extended beyond its traditional retail product range into personal financial services (2.5 million customers and £40m annual profit) and internet ordering. Tesco.com is one of the few grocery e-tailers to make an operating profit and is the world's largest. The Clubcard has also paved the way for Tesco's market share growth in non-food items. Managing such a card involves very large numbers of people (e.g. 500 manning a hotline). Tesco mails its members every three months with their discount vouchers and coupons, and the call centre gets thousands of calls from customers who want to know when they will get their mailing. The analysis that provides the insight to enable the targeting of promotions is outsourced to DunnHumby, the design of mailings to EHS Brann, and the mailing to Polestar. The Clubcard Magazine has a run of nearly 9 million four times a year. Forward Publishing, a specialist in customer magazines and contract publishing, produces it. The general verdict of retail commentators is that Tesco's Clubcard is one of the most successful retail loyalty schemes in the world precisely because of the extent to which it has formed part of a retail transformation, and the reason so many of its competitors are trying to follow in its footsteps.

Source: Stone *et al.* 2004.

which may be used systematically for services marketing. Therefore, the design and implementation of a loyalty programme necessitates *profound planning*. Regarding this, see Services marketing in action 4.3 for a discussion on the success factors of loyalty programmes from the business perspective. Regarding the differentiation of retention causes, it is not explicit whether loyalty programmes focus on bonding or alignment, and that depends on the definition of the programme. In conclusion, loyalty programmes generally are an important tool in the customer retention phase, although their concrete effects are determined by a firm's specific programme design.

Service providers not only strive to keep their customers at the current revenue and profit level, they also aim at *increasing the relationship intensity* in order to exploit the customer relationships to the maximum. While the goal of customer retention is to keep the current level of revenues with the current customers, relationship enhancement aims at exploiting the potentials of the current relationships with loyal customers. As a consequence, service providers engage in activities to increase the loyalty of current customers, that means to increase the relationship intensity. Here, relationship intensity encompasses several behavioural dimensions that lead to value for the firm. The most important and most accepted behaviours of loyal customers are the following:

SERVICES MARKETING IN ACTION 4.3:

Who has the best loyalty programme?

by Ellen Reid Smith, President, Reid Smith & Associates

Since I perform industry reviews of loyalty programs for my clients, I'm always being asked, 'Who has the BEST loyalty program?'. We all like to gravitate to the best . . . the best car, the best wine, the best store. But who decides what's the best? In the case of Stanley Marcus, he decided what was the best the world had to offer and he developed a customer loyalty program that could parlay this 'best of the best' brand strategy. During his 75-year management of Neiman-Marcus, he integrated branding, customer service, product selection and a creative best-customer program to build the best customer loyalty strategy ever launched.

Stanley Marcus engendered customer loyalty to Neiman-Marcus around the world, though his store locations only included Texas at one time. He not only made customers loyal, but made shopping at Neiman-Marcus aspirational. His original Dallas store was as famous a Texas landmark as the Alamo. The genius of Mr. Marcus is that he knew how to integrate branding, customer service and promotions into a customer loyalty strategy that retained customers as well as it acquired them ... the true stamp of a successful loyalty strategy. While the Neiman-Marcus InCircle loyalty program launched in 1984 served to formalize many of Mr. Marcus's programs, it was merely the icing on the cake of a company-wide, customer loyalty strategy.

Below are ten of the most important loyalty strategy components and how Mr. Marcus and his sons aced each of them:

1. **Loyalty marketing resources are limited to best customers.**
   - Program participation requires a spending threshold (initially credit card spending was evaluated and in 1984 InCircle formalized membership with a $3000 spending threshold).
   - Limited membership has two advantages: it makes membership aspirational and ensures loyalty monies are spent where there is the highest return.

2. **The rewards are primarily soft rewards in the form of exclusive parties and unmatched personal services. These soft rewards are effective because they:**
   - Generate a personal and emotional attachment through local events;
   - Are very difficult for competitors to match (competitors haven't matched the uniqueness of the parties and details of personal services aren't made public);
   - Increase sales with store visits rather than cannibalising profits through discounts;
   - Provide flexibility to add/change rewards and requirements;
   - Generate an unmatched amount of free publicity.

3. **Hard rewards (1 point per $ redeemed for rewards) are used to bump incremental spending, but aren't the cornerstone of the loyalty strategy.**
   - Soft rewards include exclusive items and one-of-a-kind experiences which increase the value/exclusivity of the rewards as well as membership.
   - Competitors have matched the reward currency using cash back rewards, but they haven't matched the value and exclusivity rendered by InCircle.

4. **Program events drive extensive publicity and awareness, making the program as effective at acquiring customers as retaining them.**
   - The member-only unveiling of the Christmas catalog and the 'his and her' gifts draws press from around the world.
   - The annual member-only Fortnight parties and designer shows are covered in publications around the globe as a 'who's who' list of invitees.
   - Member-only receptions at operas, symphonies and other cultural events are staged to generate awareness of the elite 'access' privileges members receive.

5. **The program creates 'access' and 'exclusivity' to make membership aspirational.**
   - Access to parties, advance designer showings and other events create membership value.
   - The value of member 'access' and 'exclusivity' is never diluted by granting non-members the same privileges.
   - All communications 'speak with one voice' – special access and exclusivity.

6. **Customer service is the bedrock of its customer loyalty strategy.**
   - Employees are empowered to recognize members with on-the-spot services.
   - Employees are rewarded for providing exceptional, if not 'extreme' customer service (Neiman's employees have been known to fit fur coats on the beach, fly two stuffed animals abroad for a special event and cater to schedules of the rich and famous).
   - InCircle members are given coupons to recognize exceptional employees.

7. **InCircle generates incremental sales and defends against competitive offers.**
   - Member communications feature creative ways to earn enough points for his AND her rewards.
   - Special events increase store visits/purchases.
   - The annual membership spending threshold generates incremental spending.
   - When its main competitor, Saks Fifth Avenue, implemented a point program, customers didn't defect because the program's access privileges and customer service provided holding power. Only when service and product quality slipped, was Sak's point program able to successfully win over Neiman's customers.

8. **The program generates member referral.**
   - Redeemed rewards can be sent as gifts.
   - Members can bring a guest to a member-only party.

9. **Program managers do an exceptional job of managing partners.**
   - The program enjoys a 'halo effect' from its partners by only partnering with the most exclusive providers of products, travel, entertainment and services.
   - The program incorporates self-funding tactics through wise partner management.
   - Partners pay to participate in member-only parties and catalogs.

10. **The program defends against lapses in service and product quality.**
    - Complaints are responded to quickly and personally.
    - Customers believe poor customer service is the exception and not the rule; therefore, one bad experience doesn't cause defection.

The customer loyalty Neiman-Marcus generated over the years is so strong that many customers remain loyal even though the store ownership has changed, much of its exclusivity has evaporated and a steady degradation of customer service has evolved. A good loyalty program can help a company limp through several months of poor service and quality, but only a great loyalty program can have customers ignoring the present reality because they want to believe the past. Such is the case with Neiman-Marcus.

Source: Reid Smith 2004.

- *Increasing purchase frequency* means prompting the customer to use the services currently used more often. For example, in the airline industry, business customers often switch providers depending on flight timetables and price. Now, an airline might try to increase the number of flights booked by a certain segment by adding flights to the timetable or changing the flight times. The concept behind increasing purchase frequencies is the 'share of wallet', i.e. the proportion of a customer's budget in a certain service category used for purchasing the services of a certain provider. For example, the German airline Lufthansa regularly lets market researchers interview their passengers when waiting for departure. Questions asked concern, for example, how often the respective passenger uses Lufthansa in comparison with other carriers. Using the collected data, Lufthansa calculates the share of wallet of the respondents. Based on further information collected, like socio-demographics information, flight reason, etc., Lufthansa is able to determine average shares of wallet for distinctive customer segments.

- *Cross-buying* is another customer behaviour that directly leads to higher revenues and profits with a certain customer. Cross-buying means that the customer purchases services of a provider not used before, although they have used other services of that provider. This is the case when a banking customer who only previously had cheque accounts and some investments at a bank, now also obtains their mortgage from the same bank in order to build or purchase a new house.

- While increasing the purchase frequency and cross-buying concern potentials of the focal customer relationship, a customer's behaviour can also influence the exploitation of other customer relationships. The most important behaviour to do so is word-of-mouth communications. Loyal customers tend to recommend their provider to other current or potential customers. These recommendations often result in positive buying behaviours on the part of the other customers. By this, loyal customers help to attract new customers through word-of-mouth communications.

When managing relationship enhancement behaviours, service providers are geared to and focused on the causes of customer loyalty. Customer loyalty behaviour is determined on two levels. On the underlying level, an important condition of customer loyalty is the *alignment of the customers.* On a more operational level, service providers try to *stimulate relationship-enhancing behaviour.* Cross-selling is activated by direct mailings to certain target groups with probable needs of certain services, the purchase frequency is increased by discounts or service bundles and recommendations are stimulated by customer-attracting programmes.

Customer recovery

The opposite of retention behaviour is customer switching from a certain provider to another service company. At first sight, switching is the other end of the same continuum of customer behaviours, a customer either stays with a provider or switches. However, the reasons for switching are varied and not necessarily the exact opposites of the retention reasons, for instance, regarding bonding as one cause of retention, the opposite of bonding does not lead to switching. Also, the role of competitors is much more important for the customers' switching behaviour and less important for customer retention. When a competitor makes an attractive offer to the customers, they might switch providers.

Customer switching means that the customer terminates the relationship with the provider. Other expressions used in this context are customer defection or relationship termination. There are various nuances of switching behaviour: a customer can initially stop purchasing and/or using certain services, but only quits the relationship officially later in time. For example, the customer of a bank originally does all their banking with one particular bank. At a certain point, another bank offers an attractive stock funds option and the customer opens an account at the other bank in order to buy these funds. As a consequence, the customer is now a customer at two banks. Later on, the customer might encounter certain problems with the original bank which prompt a full switch to the other bank. This example clarifies also that there are various *categories of switching reasons*, which can be divided into three:

- customer-related switching reasons;
- provider-related switching reasons;
- competition-related switching reasons.

Customer-related switching reasons concern primarily customer characteristics with a more or less direct connection to the service provider. These characteristics concern the customer's age, sex, preferences, lifestyle, etc., and are directly connected with the customer's needs regarding the services of the focal provider. Individual needs directly influence the customer's potential from the provider's perspective.

For example, when a customer does not need an automotive service any more because the car is sold, the customer is no longer a potential for the provider. Or, when the customer moves to a new town, they will probably switch banks to a local or regional bank. The customer-related switching reasons cannot be managed by the provider. The firm can only accept the situation, it cannot change it.

The closest connection to the causes of customer retention are the *provider-related switching reasons*. These frequently feature aspects of the alignment of the customer to the provider and concern the perceived service quality and customer satisfaction. The tendency of a customer to switch providers is higher when the customer is not satisfied with the current provider and its services. Depending on the service industry, there can be different reasons for this dissatisfaction relevant to the switching providers. In the mobile telephone industry, an important switching reason is price, while in banking or restaurants, employee behaviour is an important factor. This category of switching reasons is the one most easily managed by service providers and thus the most important source for avoiding customer defection.

As a third category, *competition-related switching reasons* can lead to customer defection. In most service industries, providers of services are in competitive situations. Customers' behaviour seldom depends only on the focal provider and its services but also on the competitors. Competitor factors that can influence switching behaviour are all aspects of service quality that are also relevant for the provider itself. For example, when a mobile telephone customer's basic buying criterion is price, then they compare the price system of their current provider and other providers. There are further factors without a complement in the category of company-related switching reasons, in particular switching offers by service providers. Like the customer-related switching reasons, this category of reasons is less manageable by the provider and therefore the provider merely takes it into account. Nevertheless, service providers have the opportunity to react to the competitor's behaviour. For example, when one provider starts a switching campaign, the affected provider can react with an equivalent campaign, by offering gifts to the customers, to stay with the existing provider.

Switching or relationship termination as the end of the customer relationship lifecycle is modelled in more detail in the *relationship termination process*. The typical termination process starts with a trigger, a first event that causes serious switching considerations. In the negative case, a certain period of time follows within which other events occur that strengthen the switching considerations of the customer. At some point, the customer finally switches. Services marketing in action 4.4 depicts the termination process from the perspective of a specific bank customer.

Switching processes can differ tremendously depending on customer characteristics, such as the tendency to seek variety and industry specifics, switching barriers. In addition, the switching reasons partly influence the dynamic of the switching process: in the banking example on the previous page the banking cus-

SERVICES MARKETING IN ACTION 4.4:

Switching processes of bank customers

The switching process of bank customers was the object of a qualitative study of approximately eighty Swiss and German bank customers who had switched banks recently. Customers were interviewed about their switching process.

One of the interviewed persons was a female, 25-year-old, commercial clerk with a salary of between 7,500 and 10,000 Swiss Francs, and the bank was her main bank. Read her recollection regarding her switching process:

"When I opened my bank account, I applied for a banking card that could be used for withdrawals, etc. After 3 weeks, I had not received any card, and therefore contacted my bank branch to find out what was going on. They told me they were quite busy, but I should receive the card soon. However, I never received a card, and a month later, I again enquired at the bank branch regarding the status of my order. They then informed me that there was no application registered in my name, so I re-applied in February 1998. In August 1998, I married, and therefore re-applied for a new card because of my name change. Again, the card did not arrive. Once again, I applied for a new card. When the card arrived, it was issued with the incorrect name. I thought "That's enough", destroyed the new card and still used the old one when I was shopping. But then, at the shop, my card was seized. When I went to my branch in order to cancel my account, they asked me to give back my card. "One card is in the ATM, the other one is destroyed." – "Then, you cannot close your account.""

Source: Michalski 2002.

tomer first shifted some money to another bank and then cancelled her account later. In contrast, a customer who moves to another city where their current bank is not present, will switch rapidly. Overall, there are four *types of switching process* that can be differentiated according to the length of the termination process and the strength of the reaction by the customer towards the provider[12] (see Figure 4.8).

A relationship termination of *type 1* is quick and complete as well as conclusive. In the banking example, the customer would shift money to another bank suddenly and at once. This termination type is even more relevant in industries with lower or no switching barriers, and we often find them in the banking sector, not visiting a restaurant or not using a specific airline any more. This type is often connected with serious switching reasons that do offer the customer an alternative to switching. For the service provider, there is barely time to prevent the termination and the probability of winning the customer back is low.

Comparable to type 1 a termination of *type 2* does not provide the possibility to reinstate the relationship. However, the process between the trigger incident and final termination takes longer. For example, the client of a lawyer is disappointed by the service because of receiving incorrect advice on several occasions. At the beginning, the client considers switching counsellors, but is convinced that these mistakes were exceptions and gives the counsellor a second chance to improve the service. However, bad advice eventually leads to a great financial loss on the part of the customer, leading to the client terminating the relationship, and not being prepared to re-establish it, regardless of what might happen, and even though, should the service provider realise the negative perceptions of the customer, there would be enough time to react to the switching considerations of the customer in order to restore the relationship to its original level of intensity.

A relationship termination of *type 3* is comparable to type 1 regarding the length of the termination process. As in type 1, there is a short termination process. However, it is a weak termination, and the customer does not switch completely or can possibly be won back. When a person's mobile telephone contract approaches expiration, the customer will gather information about other providers and deals. Just before converting to the new provider the consumer's existing provider entices him with a comparable retention offer. For convenience reasons, the customer might stay with the provider and not switch to the alternative provider. As the example illustrates, type 3 terminations give the provider the chance to react to the relationship termination. However, such a reaction has to happen quickly, because once the customer signs a new contract with another provider they cannot be won back before the end of the new contract.

A *type 4* relationship termination is characterised by a weak and long relationship termination. The termination process proceeds over a longer period of time and still will not be complete or conclusive at the end of the process. Take a person who regularly attends the matches of their favourite football team. At the beginning of his studies in London, he is in the stadium every week to support his team. In the course of his studies he gets involved with his future wife. The two of them often spend time together and with friends on Sundays, therefore the supporter only goes to matches every third week. After university he starts working in a consultancy firm, and moves to the country. Now he only sees two or three matches per season. In this case, the customer does not switch completely, although it will be difficult for the club to make him go to the matches more often in the short term. Type 4 termination gives the provider the greatest chances to continue using the potentials of the focal customer relationship. Since the supporter is still a member of the club, the club can contact him easily and can offer him other products and services that are more suitable to his current needs, e.g. a subscription to the club's pay TV channel or merchandising articles for the children.

Based on the termination processes outlined above, in every service industry and for every service provider, specific termination processes can exist that have an impact on possible reactions of the service provider. For example, resigning from a church indicates a different termination process than airline switching. A methodology for service firms to detect different termination processes as well as different termination reasons is the *critical path analysis*. The method dynamically analyses the critical incidents within a customer relationship, and the termination process in connection with these critical incidents is examined.

Length of termination process / Strength of reaction	Short	Long
Strong	Type 1 The relationship is terminated quickly and completely	Type 2 The relationship termination process is long but leads to a complete termination. No return intentions
Weak	Type 3 The relationship is terminated quickly but not completely (shift of patronage pattern)	Type 4 The relationship is terminated gradually and not completely or with return possibilities.

FIGURE 4.8 Types of defection processes

Source: adapted from Roos and Strandvik 1997.

Qualitative in-depth interviews with former customers of the focal service provider are used in order to collect the relevant information. The interviews are structured by certain questions regarding the termination process, for example in the following categories:[13]

- Termination decision: When did you first think of terminating the relationship with provider XY?

- Termination process: How long did it take you to reach your decision to terminate the relationship with provider XY?

- Trigger: Did a certain event initiate the process of terminating the relationship with provider XY?

- Former state of relationship: How would you describe your relationship with provider XY before that event?

- Firm's reaction to termination: How did provider XY react to your relationship termination?

- Reasons for choosing a new provider: What were the reasons for you choosing a new provider?

- Comparison between former and new relationship: How do you evaluate the current relationship compared to the former one?

Based on these questions, the *critical path* of a customer relationship can be depicted, as in Figure 4.9. The diagram illustrates that the relationship has been at a loyalty level of 80 out of 100 for a long time. At a certain point in time, a trigger occurs, like an unsatisfying interaction, and the customer thinks about terminating the relationship with the provider for the first time. Then, loyalty levels decrease. Nevertheless, at the occurrence of a further problem, the customer complains. A negative reaction from the provider and the loyalty level deteriorates further until the customer quits the relationship. An empirical study in the Swiss banking sector revealed that the critical paths take between six months and three years (Michalski 2002).

The analysis of switching processes and reasons helps service providers to plan *win back activities* for customers who have defected. There are two major directions of win back activities of service providers:

- Since customers defect for different reasons, a solid and long-term win back is only possible when these reasons can be resolved. Of course, an active elimination of the reasons by the provider is only possible for provider-related switching reasons. For example when an airline realises that it is losing bookings because it does not offer London–Washington flights, it might extend its destinations by a further connection. Provided with the elimination of the switching reasons, service providers then engage in *persuading the customer* to re-establish the relationship with the provider. Persuasion is possible by creating extra value in the area of the switching reasons of one or several customers.

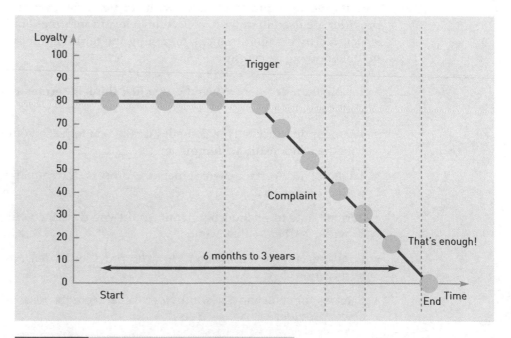

| FIGURE 4.9 | Critical path of a customer relationship |

Source: Michalski 2002, p. 141.

- Another operative way to win back lost customers is by *stimulating customers* by win back offers. In these cases the customer is offered a certain benefit that is not necessarily connected with the switching reason. This offer is often aimed at compensating the minor value due to the switching reason. Win back offers can be product-related, such as a free flight by airline, pricing-related, discount on certain services or channel-related, a personal adviser for the customer.

Next to these win back activities, the analysis of switching reasons and processes is used in the area of customer retention. Based on the analysis results, service providers develop early-warning systems that help to detect unstable customer relationships, i.e. customers who are more likely to switch to another provider, than others. Services marketing in action 4.5 visualises how to measure and manage customer defections using an example from the credit card industry.

SERVICES MARKETING IN ACTION 4.5:

Reducing customer defection in the credit card industry

Report of a consultant of the analytical solutions provider Fair Isaac about one of their customers:

A defection rate of 20% may be the industry average for credit card issuers, but this particular issuer refused to settle for average. The behaviour exhibited by their customer base demonstrates a problem experienced throughout the industry: customers used their new cards routinely during a special introductory offer period, but drastically reduced card usage or cancelled altogether when the special offer expired. Knowing that it can cost four to ten times more to acquire a new customer than it does to retain an existing one, the issuer realised that it needed to quickly strengthen its relationship with each customer before the customer became inactive. Otherwise, ballooning acquisition costs combined with dwindling account balances would continue to squeeze profits. The issuer also realised that retaining and growing profitable, long-term relationships would take more than traditional account-level tracking. It would require a new level of customer understanding coupled with timely, targeted strategies that would use this knowledge to reach potential defectors with the right offer at the right time. To meet this challenge, the issuer turned to us.

. . . Based on various data, Fair Isaac built a defection model that rank-ordered the likelihood of a customer cancelling their card or paying off their balance within 12 months. A complementary revenue model provided scores that indicated which customers were likely to be most profitable. . . . Together, these scores and information were used to determine a customer segmentation scheme. Different promotional offers were developed to effectively target each segment for the best response. Consequently, new customers with the potential to generate higher-than-average revenue who were also more likely to stop using their card could be pursued more aggressively than customers with lower revenue scores.

After implementing this solution, the issuer experienced a 10% overall reduction in its defection rate, equalling a potential revenue impact of $20.4 million. By testing

▶

and refining its promotions based on continuous feedback, the company achieved a 24% average balance increase among one segment that was offered a reduced annual percentage rate. The continuous testing and evaluation of results has enabled the issuer to refine its decision strategy over time and quickly deploy appropriate customer incentive campaigns. The full-relationship view of each customer has also facilitated an increase in cross-selling activity across all areas of the enterprise, further strengthening customer relationships.

Source: © 2003–2005 Fair Isaac Corporation. All rights reserved.

Continuous value creation in customer relationships

Service providers cannot learn only from relationship terminations as outlined above, but from their customer relationships in general. They can initiate a *self-enforcing value spiral* by learning from customer relationships. This can be implemented when service providers not only manage customer relationships with the goal of realising revenues and profits but also try to learn from their customer relationships. With the respective systems, a service provider can utilise the existing customer relationships in order to stimulate this value logic. When service providers use the information they can gain from their customer relationships, they will be able to conduct better relational measures. First, in an individual relationship, providers can generate specific knowledge about the individual customer from the interactions with that customer. When this knowledge is stored appropriately, it can be used in order to improve the interactions with the customer. Remember the Ritz-Carlton example (see Case Study in Chapter 1) where an employee recorded a Formula 1 race for a customer who could not watch the race and had mentioned on an earlier occasion that he loved Formula 1. Secondly, on a more aggregated level, the knowledge generated from existing customer relationships can be used in order to improve other customer relationships. For example, in the Interdiscount department store in Basel/Switzerland, many customers complained because the stairways were organised in such a way that one could not go directly upstairs, but had to walk to the other side of the stairway on each floor in order to continue going upwards. (This system was probably introduced to make the customers see more offers when ascending the store.) Activated by these complaints, the management decided to reconstruct the stairways and thereby improved the service not only for the customers complaining but also for customers encountering the same problem without complaining. Thus, companies can utilise customer relationships in two ways: either in order to improve the relationships to direct targets of relational measures or to improve the relationships with others, such as future customers, and thus to increase the value of these relationships for the firm.

Summing up the value effects of managing customers' behaviours in their relationships to service providers, Services marketing in action 4.6 visualises the differences between industries regarding the efforts and success in managing customer relationships.

SERVICES MARKETING IN ACTION 4.6:

Experiences with managing relationships across industries

A survey of about 150 senior managers of the UK Top 1000 firms revealed the following knowledge regarding analysing and managing customer relationships:

- Simple defection rates are not sufficient to understand, and counter, the commercial threat posed by customer defection. The defection rates need to be combined with the relative ease (or difficulty) that each sector experiences with winning customers back, along with each sector's ability to mount effective responsive marketing campaigns.

- There is a wide variation in the ability of different sectors to win back lost customers, with banking least able, and retail most able (see Figure 4.10).

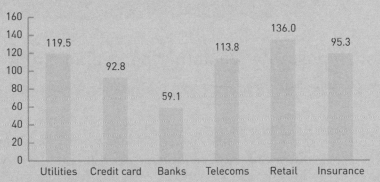

Figure 4.10 Index of the ability to win back lost customers by UK companies
Source: Lindsell Marketing 2004.

- There are three categories of service industry which differ regarding the opportunities for a regain management:
  - Low churn industries that nevertheless find it very difficult to entice customers to return once they have defected.
  - High churn industries that still find it difficult to win back lost customers.
  - Medium to high churn industries that have mastered the art of winning back defectors.

- Retail banking experiences low customer turnover (<10% per annum), but once customers have decided to leave, it is very difficult to persuade them to return.

- Credit Card issuers and general insurance companies/resellers experience high customer turnover (21–25% per annum), as their responsive campaign standards are not sufficiently supporting the process of winning back lost (or indeed new) customers. This leaves these sectors doubly exposed. It seems that both sectors need to pay more focused attention to customer retention strategies, making better integrated use of targeted marketing communications through existing customer channels (statements, customer correspondence, customer service calls) and external media (direct mail, email, telephone) (see also Services marketing in action 4.5).

- Telecoms, retail and utilities are the sectors that, although experiencing annual customer turnover rates of between 13% and 18%, seem to be able to combine high standards of lost customer recapture with generally high campaign response rates across existing and external channels. These sectors are the stars of this study. We believe this to be not just the result of higher targeted marketing standards, but also astute brand development. Mobile phone operators have managed to develop their products to fashion and lifestyle brands. Utilities are effectively exploring brand stretch into other product and service areas (also with the advantage of a blank sheet starting point at deregulation). And retailers have combined their rich data from loyalty schemes with their existing strengths in brand development, location strategies and early entry into internet trading.

Source: Lindsell Marketing 2004

Relationship quality: Customer perceptions of their relationships to service providers

The discussed relationship behaviours of customers in the course of the relationship lifecycle affect the value to the firm. Consequently, service providers aim at influencing these behaviours. According to the Service Profit Chain, drivers of this behaviour are service quality and customer satisfaction. Thus, so far we have concentrated on these drivers, supplemented by short-term stimulating offers, like win back offers or cross-buying stimulations. However, it is not only the provider who evaluates a customer relationship by measuring the value of its customers in terms of the relational behaviours of the customer. The customer also evaluates the relationship with the provider, whereby the customer not only evaluates the service quality of a provider, but also the *relationship quality*, and this relationship quality is also an important driver of the customer's behaviour.

By incorporating the construct of relationship quality into the customer behaviour considerations, the Service Profit Chain (see Chapter 2) is expanded by a relationship element leading to a *relationship profit chain*. Next to service quality, relationship quality becomes an important driver of perceived value and customer satisfaction (see Figure 4.11). Service quality and relationship quality interact with one another. As the services used are an important characteristic of a provider from the customer's perspective, consecutive positive experiences with the services cumulate to a positive perception of the relationship quality. Conversely, a high perceived relationship quality facilitates customer interactions. The better the provider and the customer know and value each other, the more open and constructive are the interactions between them.[14]

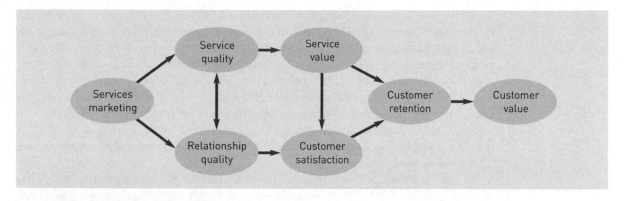

FIGURE 4.11   Relationship value chain

Relationship quality stands for the customer's perception of the relationship to the provider and is defined as the ability of the provider to fulfil the customer's relational needs. Relationship quality is not just the sum of the qualities of all the interactions within a customer relationship, but also concerns aspects that are central to the concept of the relationship. Consequently, relationship quality consists of dimensions that are different to those of service quality. In two studies, two central dimensions of relationship quality could be identified:[15]

1. Customer's trust in the corporation.
2. Familiarity between the customer and corporation.

Trust is defined as the customer's willingness to forgo any additional investigation and just rely on the corporation's behaviour in the future. Various processes for the emergence of trust can be identified in the context of the *trust-building process*:[16]

- In a *calculated process*, one relationship party assumes trustworthy behaviour of the other if the benefit of non-trustworthy behaviour is lower than the costs incurred when recruited.

- For *predictive processes*, trust is dependent on one's capability to anticipate the other party's behaviour.

- The *capability process* relates to an estimation of the relationship party's ability to accomplish its job.

- According to the *intent process*, trust is based on the goals and intentions of the other party.

- As per the *transferring process*, trust building is subject to an estimation of the relationship party by an outsider.

The customer's *familiarity* with the corporation is another dimension of relationship quality. Familiarity is closely related to trust and is based on the past. It encompasses the degree of familiarity with an object (e.g. situation) or subject. In the context of a corporate–customer relationship, familiarity characterises the *degree of convergence* with the respective relationship party in terms of its attitudes and modes of behaviour.

On the basis of *reciprocal dependence* of the parties in a relationship,[17] customer familiarity comprises not only their familiarity with a corporation but also the familiarity of the corporation with the customer as perceived by the customer. On the one hand, it is important for the customer to be aware of the corporate processes as long as the customer is involved in the provision of products or services. On the other hand, the customer is possibly very conscious of whether the company is familiar with, and understands their needs. Knowing the customer's name is a sample indicator of a corporation's familiarity with a customer, but awareness of specific requirements such as a non-smoking room in a hotel is more meaningful.

Consequently, a central task of relationship marketing lies in *building-up familiarity and trust*. In cases where familiarity appears partly and to a certain degree without action on the part of the company, the company can support the emergence of familiarity by means of appropriate familiarity-building measures. The higher the relationship quality is perceived to be by the customer, the less critical they will be of individual interactions and the sooner positive psychological consequences can be reached with the customer. Possible measures to increase familiarity are permanent contact personnel, personalised call centre interactions or stable service outfits at different service locations. Figure 4.12 depicts some examples for measures to manage trust and familiarity.

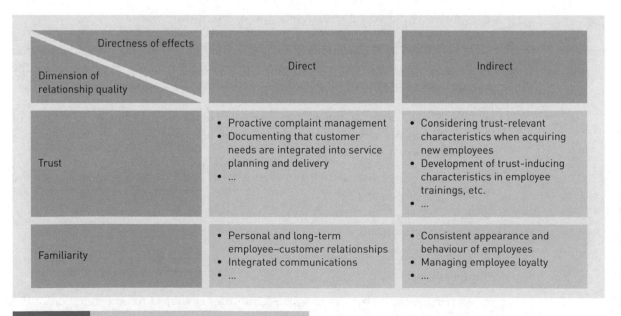

Directness of effects / Dimension of relationship quality	Direct	Indirect
Trust	• Proactive complaint management • Documenting that customer needs are integrated into service planning and delivery • ...	• Considering trust-relevant characteristics when acquiring new employees • Development of trust-inducing characteristics in employee trainings, etc. • ...
Familiarity	• Personal and long-term employee–customer relationships • Integrated communications • ...	• Consistent appearance and behaviour of employees • Managing employee loyalty • ...

FIGURE 4.12   Measures to manage trust and familiarity

Source: Georgi 2000, p. 191.

Summary

This chapter dealt with several facets of the relationship process as a primary value process within the Service Value Chain (see Figure 4.13):

1. On the cost side, customer relationships are often more efficient than non-relational exchanges between provider and customer, e.g. because of more efficient processes due to the customer's experience with the respective processes.

2. On the revenue side, the evaluation of relationship-building activities by the customer provides a further dimension of a customer's opinion of a service provider. With a positive relationship quality, positive customer behaviours are more probable. In addition, relationships build the platform for expanding customer relationships. Within a relationship, the provider can learn about the customer's needs and offer appropriate services and thereby can expand the volume of the relationship.

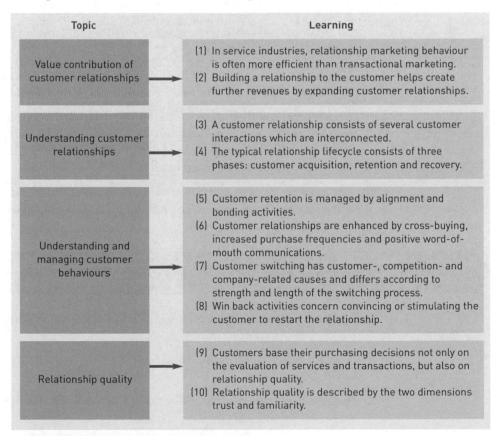

Topic	Learning
Value contribution of customer relationships	(1) In service industries, relationship marketing behaviour is often more efficient than transactional marketing. (2) Building a relationship to the customer helps create further revenues by expanding customer relationships.
Understanding customer relationships	(3) A customer relationship consists of several customer interactions which are interconnected. (4) The typical relationship lifecycle consists of three phases: customer acquisition, retention and recovery.
Understanding and managing customer behaviours	(5) Customer retention is managed by alignment and bonding activities. (6) Customer relationships are enhanced by cross-buying, increased purchase frequencies and positive word-of-mouth communications. (7) Customer switching has customer-, competition- and company-related causes and differs according to strength and length of the switching process. (8) Win back activities concern convincing or stimulating the customer to restart the relationship.
Relationship quality	(9) Customers base their purchasing decisions not only on the evaluation of services and transactions, but also on relationship quality. (10) Relationship quality is described by the two dimensions trust and familiarity.

FIGURE 4.13 Learning summary for Chapter 4

3. A customer relationship consists of several interactions between provider and customer that are connected somehow with one another.

4. The typical course of a customer relationship is depicted by the so-called customer relationship lifecycle that describes the development of the relationship intensity in dependence on relationship duration. The concept distinguishes three stages of a customer relationship: customer acquisition, customer retention and customer recovery that build the basis for the relationship processes in the Service Value Chain. The customer retention stage can be further divided into customer retention and relationship enhancement.

5. Customer retention is caused by either alignment or bonding. Accordingly, service providers employ alignment and bonding activities to strengthen customer retention. Loyalty programmes integrate the two types of retention activities.

6. Relationship enhancement is an important goal in the retention phase, and is realised by cross-buying, increasing purchase frequencies and positive word-of-mouth communications.

7. Customer switching behaviour can have customer-related, company-related and competition-related reasons and differs according to the strength and length of the switching process.

8. Win back activities aim at either convincing the customer to restart the relationship with the provider or at stimulating them to do so.

9. Customers base their decision regarding relational behaviours towards a certain service provider not only on their evaluation of the provider's services but also on their perception of the provider's relational behaviour, rendered by the perceived relationship quality.

10. Relationship quality consists of two dimensions, trust and familiarity, both of which are levers for the service provider in order to manage relationship quality.

Knowledge questions

1. Explain the importance of customer relationships regarding the value creation of a service provider.

2. How is a relationship defined and how does this concept interact with specific service interactions?

3. Describe the concept of the relationship lifecycle. What is the idea? Which phases are distinguished?

4. Explain the two groups of customer retention determinants.

5. Which are the value effects of customer enhancement?

6. Describe the possible reasons for customer switching.

7. Outline the typical course of the customer switching process and the four types of customer switching processes.

8. Which categories of regain activities exist in service industries?

9. Define relationship quality and explain the dimensions of this construct.

Application and discussion questions

1. Apply the value effects of customer relationships to concrete service industries. In which industries are these effects more relevant, in which less so? Discuss the reasons for these differences.

2. Analyse your 'relationship' with your mobile operator (or your bank, favourite book or record shop or others) and recap the development of the relationship using the concept of the relationship lifecycle.

3. Choose a certain service industry (mobile operator, airline, bank, café, department store, supermarket, university) and collect typical relational measures in the phases of the relationship lifecycle in these industries.

4. Loyalty programmes are specific relationship-oriented measures of service providers. How do these programmes influence customer retention via alignment and bonding?

5. Choose a certain service industry (mobile operator, airline, bank, café, department store, supermarket, university) and collect typical activities for enhancing customer relationships.

6. Do you remember your latest switching from a specific service provider? Try to reconstruct the reasons for your switching and the course of the switching process by applying the critical path analysis to yourself.

7. Which regain activities in a certain service industry do you know from your own experience? Otherwise, try to find specific regain activities/offers by means of internet research.

CASE STUDY: TESCO'S CLUBCARD

For many service providers, loyalty programmes are still a further marketing instrument. However, for Tesco, its loyalty programme 'Clubcard' that was introduced on 13 February 1995 meant a complete restructuring of the firm's business. It changed the way of taking decisions, developing products and markets, but above all of serving customers.

Before Clubcard was launched, Tesco was the UK's second ranking supermarket chain. The introduction of the Clubcard was the kick-off point for strategy change. The basic concept of Tesco's Clubcard is that customers collect points which can be used for purchases at Tesco. The success of the programme started right from the beginning. In March 1995, Tesco surpassed Sainsbury's for the first time ever in terms of UK supermarket market share (19.3 per cent compared to 19.1 per cent).

In today's programme, collected points can not only be used to purchase at Tesco but also to buy products and services at many partner firms. Early in the programme, Tesco initiated a partnership with Airmiles. Then, in 1999, the programme was expanded in order to be even more attractive for the highest spending customers. The campaign 'A million cheap tickets' introduced many more partners where Clubcard points could be used, like KLM, Disney, Eurostar or Virgin Trains.

In terms of expanding customer relationships, Tesco for example entered the UK non-food market and realised increasing market share there. The Clubcard fuelled this growth by identifying possible customers and communicating with them using a new medium – the Clubcard quarterly mailing. Further activities were the realisation of an internet supermarket as well as the opening of the Tesco bank.

The card was also utilised as a relationship learning tool in other contexts. Tesco's marketing director Tim Mason recalled: 'When a competitor opened up against one of our stores, we were able to see those customers that stopped shopping and were able to do something about that. We knew the names and the addresses of the couple of thousand people whose behaviour changed. If you were being aggressive about defending your store, previously you would have taken out advertisements in the local paper which said that you could get 2 pounds off every 20 pounds that you spend and 5 pounds off every 50 pounds that you spend, come on down! All those newspapers went through the doors of people who hadn't changed their behaviour at all and the costs were so exorbitant that actually you couldn't really afford to defend yourself very effectively. This completely changed the whole way in which we were able to defend ourselves from people opening new space against us.'

From a profitability perspective, loyalty schemes are not a minor marketing expense, as McKinsey found out in 2000: '16 major European retailers had a total of some $1.2 billion tied up in annual discounts to customers, with several supermarket chains devoting some $150 million. Given large sales volumes, even programmes with modest rebates (up to 1 per cent) can cost a great deal of money'. For Tesco, this logic has resulted in a £1 billion rebate to customers since 1995. For a larger retailer, the set-up cost of $30 million must be calculated, followed by annual maintenance costs amounting to between $5 million and $10 million. A loyalty programme also necessitates an investment of personnel and IT resources. At Tesco, about 100 people are connected directly with the Clubcard process. A further 500 people handle the calls for the Clubcard programme in Tesco's call centre. Further human resources budgets were needed for training and processing time invested in thousands of stores and checkouts.

On the growth side, Tesco today is not only the UK's largest grocer, but also the world's most successful internet supermarket and one of Europe's fastest-growing financial services companies.

Source: Humby *et al.* 2003.

Notes

1 See Reichheld and Sasser 1990.
2 See Reichheld and Sasser 1990.
3 See Jackson 1985.
4 See Jackson 1985, p. 122.
5 See Jackson 1985, p. 123.
6 In the services marketing literature, often, instead of the 4Ps of marketing, 7Ps of services marketing are distinguished (4Ps plus processes, people, physical facilities). The Service Value Chain approach structures the three further Ps differently. Processes are the core element of the value chain, people and physical facilities are service resources, while the activities explored in this part which are based on the 4Ps define service value.
7 See Bruhn 2002b.
8 See e.g. Bolton 1998.
9 See Morgan and Hunt 1994.
10 See Bruhn 2002b.
11 See Bruhn 2002b.
12 See Bruhn 2002b.
13 See Roos and Strandvik 1997; Michalski 2002.
14 See Georgi 2000.
15 See Bruhn 2002b.
16 See Doney and Canon 1997, p. 37.
17 See Håkansson and Snehota 1993, p. 2.

PART 3 Secondary value processes: Creating service value

Customer interactions and relationships consist of contacts between the service provider and the customer. The customer, or specific objects belonging to them, takes part in the interactions or relationships with the 'service provider', who represents an abstract entity. The customer does not interact with this entity itself but with specific tangible and intangible elements of the service provider.

One specific part concerns the concrete service that the customer purchases and uses, e.g. the flight, a banking account, a movie performance in a cinema, a dinner in a restaurant. According to the Service Profit Chain (see Chapter 2), the customer perceives and evaluates a service in terms of the *perceived service value* as the benefits and cost that occur for the customer when using a service. The central benefit component is the *service product* as it is defined by the provider. In a certain service category, a high profile service promises a higher benefit and consequently greater value for the customer than a low profile service. For example, a train seat in first class tends to be perceived as superior to a train seat in 'coach' class. The customer evaluates a service's value not only according to the benefits they perceive but also based on the cost they incur. The most important cost factor is the *service price* the customer has to pay for using a service.

The services are used and thus the service value is perceived by the customer in the service interactions. For example, the customer purchases a flight ticket (service product) and pays a certain service price for it. The actual interaction is the flight itself. The interaction is the process in which *service value is delivered* to the customer and the provider sets the stage for the conduct of the service by installing certain **service delivery** systems, like a hotline for ordering flight tickets or a bank branch system for serving the customer.

However, these service delivery systems come into play only when the customer approaches the service provider – respectively the very delivery systems. Beforehand, service providers *transport a picture of the service value to the customer* in order to convince the customer to use its services. This is realised by service branding and communications. The service brand is an abstract picture of the service value the customer is to receive. This brand is transferred to the customer via diverse communications instruments, such as TV adverts. Service communications also transfer information to the customer about the service value, i.e. service product and service price, as well as about the service delivery systems.

Summing up, comparable to the 4P (product, price, promotion, place) approach in traditional consumer goods marketing, there are four *activities concerning perceived service value* which are applied by service providers:

- defining the service product;
- determining the service price;
- providing service delivery systems;
- service branding and communications.

These activities of defining, delivering and communicating service value to the customer represent prerequisites for the initiation of customer interactions and relationships, i.e. the primary value activities of a service provider. Consequently, they are one group of so-called *secondary value processes* – next to a second group, the service resources which are the interaction partners of the customer and are covered in Part 4.

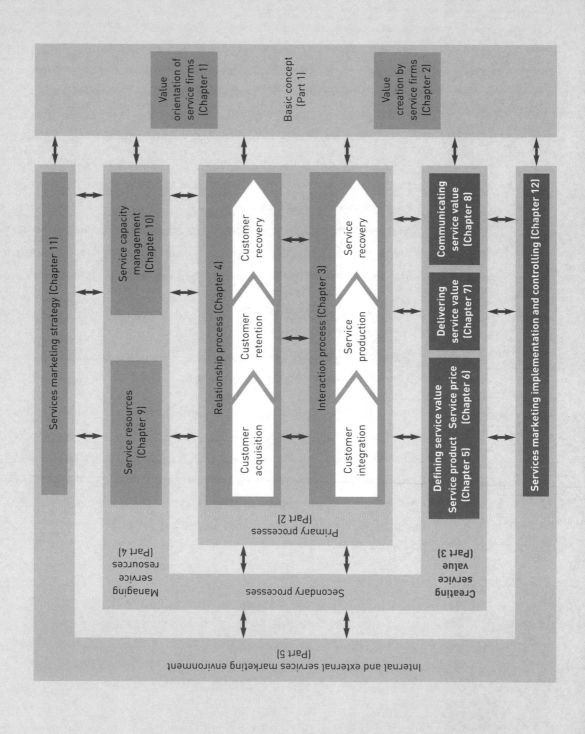

5 Defining the benefit part of service value: The service product

Service customers compare the benefits they receive from a service with the cost that is incurred when using the service, in order to evaluate a service's value (see Chapter 2). While Chapter 6 deals with the price as the major part of the costs that occur when using a service, this chapter concentrates on the counterpart – namely the benefits. The basic determinant of the benefit a customer receives from the service is the *service product*, the defined service itself. In contrast to consumer goods, the service product is often less tangible. Due to the process character of services, many service products involve a process dimension, like the service products 'showing films', 'styling hair', 'consulting regarding legal issues', 'providing credit', etc. The service product strongly determines other elements of the Service Value Chain. The service process varies depending on the characteristics of the service, whether a service is defined as an exclusive or a mass service or whether it is delivered with a broad range of value-added services. The service product comprises three separate elements (see Figure 5.1):

- core service;
- supplementary services (and goods);[1]
- integration of the service into the service programme.

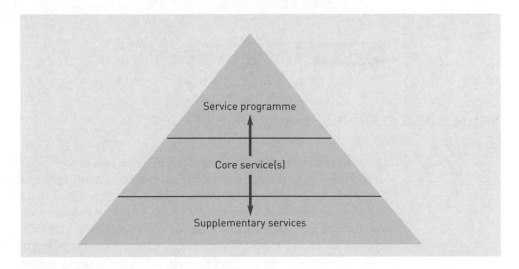

FIGURE 5.1 The service product pyramid

This distinction between these elements of the service product is a basic concept and will be discussed in this chapter in further detail. The *learning objectives* are as follows (see Figure 5.2):

1. Understanding the value contribution of the service product elements, i.e. the core service, supplementary services and the service programme.

2. Learning about the options of a service provider regarding the definition of the core service, supplementary services and the service programme.

3. Comprehending the decisions of a service provider regarding the service product which can be divided according to the service product lifecycle into service innovation, service modification and service elimination.

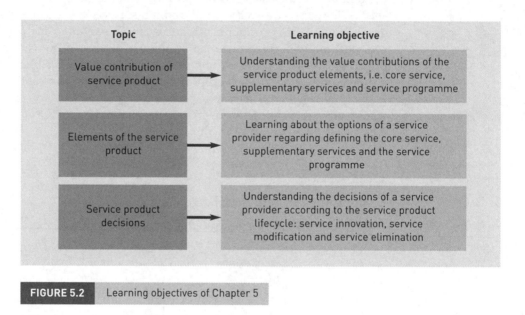

FIGURE 5.2 Learning objectives of Chapter 5

Value contribution of the service product

As outlined in the previous chapters, the value of a service provider depends on the customers' behaviour, for example on the customers' cross-buying activities (see Chapter 2). As the perceived service value is an important determinant of customer behaviours and the service product is an important element of the customer's perception of service value, the service product is a central driver of customer behaviour and consequently eventually influences the value of a service provider. The value contribution differs with regard to the three elements of the service product, the core service, supplementary services and the service programme.

The **core service** not only determines the customer's experiences with a service, but also their perception of the service without experiencing it (as with potential customers), and therefore determines the decision of potential and current customers for or against the provider. Where the firm is providing a service product that generally is able to fulfil the customer's needs and expectations, the customer is more likely to choose the respective service. Services marketing in action 5.1 reveals that the core service is not only a driver of customer behaviour in the positive sense, but also determines customers' switching behaviour.

While the evaluation of the core service is central in the purchasing decision of the consumers, **supplementary services** are a catalyst concerning this decision. In many markets, core services of service providers in one industry differ only slightly. For example, there are around ten flights from Frankfurt to New York every day. The core service of these flights – to transport passengers from Frankfurt to New York – differs little. In this case other marketing instruments such as price or supplementary services drive customers' decisions. As a catalyst, supplementary services therefore help to enhance customer relationships.

SERVICES MARKETING IN ACTION 5.1:

Core service drives customer switching

In a study concerning customers' switching behaviour,[2] more than 500 service users and switchers were asked about their switching behaviour in 45 different service industries. The collected switching reasons were grouped into eight categories, in which the core service was the most important switching reason. 24.8 per cent of the switchers reported failures connected to the core service as the primary reason for their switching behaviour (see Table 5.1).

TABLE 5.1	Switching reasons in 45 service industries

Switching reason	% of respondents
Core service failures	24.8
Failed service encounters	19.1
Pricing	16.7
Inconvenience	11.6
Response to failed services	9.7
Competition	5.7
Ethical problems	4.2
Involunatry switching	3.5
Other	4.7

Source: Keaveney 1995, p. 75.

Additionally, they influence customer loyalty, e.g. by representing bonds to the customer, and might increase customer sales via cross-selling.

Finally, the *service programme* also represents a central driver of customer behaviour. In many markets, customers expect a one-stop-shopping or full-service-offer (being able to purchase various, potentially connected services at one place, such as booking flight and hotel at a travel agency). In these cases, the breadth of the service programme is a competitive factor and directly influences the purchasing decisions of the customers. Furthermore, a broad service programme facilitates cross-selling and thus an intensive management of the relationship process and the expansion of customer relationships. Services marketing in action 5.2 presents an example of a value-oriented service programme definition. Although Tetra Pak is operating in the business-to-business sector, the example demonstrates the options of service programme variations, in this case, programme extensions.

We see that the service product consists of a service programme encompassing one or more core services as well as supplementary services which have distinctive effects on the value of a service provider. Thus, before discussing the decisions a service provider has to take regarding the service product, we shall consider these three descriptive elements of the service product.

SERVICES MARKETING IN ACTION 5.2:

Tetra Pak: Designing the service programme according to the customer's value chain

Tetra Pak started in the early 1950s as one of the first packaging companies for liquid milk. Today, the firm is one of the world's largest suppliers of packaging systems for milk, fruit juices and drinks, and many other products. The value creation by Tetra Pak can be understood best using the concept of the value chain (of the client firm) (see Figure 5.3 for the value chain of a food manufacturer).

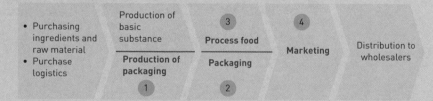

Figure 5.3 Value chain of a food manufacturer

Following the value chain of a beverage manufacturer, Tetra Pak increases the customer benefit according to the stages of this chain:

1. By producing packagings, it supports the stage 'production of packaging'.

2. Tetra Pak not only produces packages but also sells packaging machines. For example, in 1961, the first packaging facility for aseptic filling of milk was presented. By doing so, Tetra Pak also serves the 'filling' stage of the value chain. Further, the packaging system of Tetra Pak could be adapted to the customer's needs.

3. In the 1990s, Tetra Pak evolved into a full service provider by purchasing Alfa Laval, market leader in the production of facilities for the food industry. Now, it also provides its customers with equipment needed to process food.

4. One step further in the value chain, Tetra Pak serves the 'marketing' stage of the manufacturer's chain. The characteristics of Tetra Pak's packaging materials allow an effective and distinctive design of the packaging. Furthermore, the current marketing campaign stresses the ecological superiority of Tetra Pak packages and integrates the brands of Tetra Pak's customers.

Thus, by orienting itself towards the customer's value chain, Tetra Pak offers a diverse service programme to its customers.

Source: Tetra Pak 2004.

Elements of the service product

The core service: Delivering basic benefit to the customer

Which are the basic customer needs and expectations a service provider aims to fulfil? The answer to this question depicts the **core service**. Although, in many markets, supplementary services are needed in order to be successful in competition, a service provider cannot survive without a well-defined core service.

Depending on the market, the core service can (but does not have to) be the basis for a *USP (Unique Selling Proposition) definition*. In this case the core service is the main driver for differentiation and the customers' expectations and behaviours. If the core service of a provider represents a major benefit to the customer, the customer will choose that provider instead of its competitors. Therefore, in some business sectors, those providers with a clear and differentiated core service or those who invented and therefore stand for the core service (e.g. amazon, American express, Fedex) have success in the market.

However, in other industries, the core service is relatively static and basic and therefore does not offer a lot of space for *differentiation*. Most providers offer a core service of the same complexity and quality, as seen in the airline example with the Frankfurt–New York flight. Thus, this core service is a basic but not distinctive requirement in that industry. A differentiation is only possible via supplementary services or other marketing instruments.

The core service and the Service Value Chain

The core service is not only important because of its effects on customer perceptions and behaviours but also because it defines to a large extent the tasks of *other services marketing areas*. A well-defined core service is the starting point for systematic and successful services marketing. This is because the core service predetermines many of the other elements of the services marketing concept. Above all, the *interaction process* essentially depends on the core service. For example, a convenience-oriented service differs very much from a cost-oriented, self-service offer. Or take the example of a pizzeria versus a pizza delivery service. The core services of the pizzeria and a pizza delivery service, of course, have some similarities: especially, the major production factor, the pizza itself, is needed for both services. However, when you have a look at the service processes, you will notice that they differ dramatically. While the main part of the pizzeria service process is the consumption of the pizza by the customer, the pizza delivery process consists mostly of the ordering and delivery of the pizza.

Take this example, and you see that the core service determines other services marketing elements by means of the service process. In a pizzeria, there are more employee–customer interactions than is the case in the delivery service. Therefore, employee behaviour and internal marketing are more crucial in the pizzeria (see Chapter 8). Furthermore, the pizzeria location is an important quality characteristic of the pizzeria service. Therefore, the characteristics of the pizzeria and the delivery service exhibit different challenges for the service delivery system (see Chapter 7). Also, since there are different core services in both examples, communications will differ, regarding the communications' message. In addition the logistical processes are determined by the core service, as Services marketing in action 5.3 demonstrates.

As we have seen, the core service predetermines other services marketing elements. Nevertheless, the core service itself is often not enough for differentiation in today's customer-driven markets. Therefore, supplementary services have gained importance during the last decades.

Supplementary services and goods

Almost every service provider offers not only a core service, but also additional services (and goods) which supplement the core service. Those services are therefore called **supplementary services**. In many industries, these supplementary services are key success drivers. For example, in the transportation (airlines, railway) industry, supplementary services have gained importance during the last decade.

How can we structure the wide range of possible supplementary services in order to choose and manage them systematically? There are three dimensions to describe and derive different types of supplementary services (see Figure 5.4):[3]

SERVICES MARKETING IN ACTION 5.3:

Pizza Hut celebrates successful delivery to space

Although the nascent space tourism industry still has some big questions to answer, including transport and lodgings, one of the details has been safely resolved: you can now get a pizza delivered into orbit.

Pizza Hut announced Tuesday that 'the world's first space-consumable pizza' had safely arrived on the International Space Station (ISS), where it was eaten by the astronauts living onboard. 'Wherever there is life, there will be Pizza Hut pizza', the Dallas-based pizza chain's chief marketing officer Randy Gier said in a statement. 'If space tourism is going to be a reality, Pizza Hut pizza will make the trip even better.'

Despite the unusual delivery address, the pizza, called 'the culmination of nearly a year of collaboration' between the company and Russian nutritionists, largely conformed to the familiar recipe served up by some 12,000 Pizza Hut restaurants worldwide – crust, tomato sauce and cheese. However, the vacuum-sealed space pizza was topped with salami rather than the traditional pepperoni. 'Researchers found that pepperoni did not withstand the 60-day testing process,' a company release rather cryptically stated. After delivery, the station crew baked the 6-inch ('personal pan') pizza themselves in the ISS oven.

Pizza Hut, a division of Tricon Global Restaurants, pioneered the commercialisation of space in July by paying to have its logo placed on a Russian Proton rocket.

Source: Space.com 1999

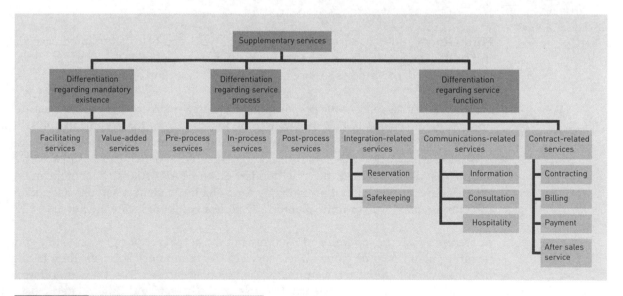

FIGURE 5.4   Types of supplementary services

- Depending on whether a service is mandatory or not, the supplementary service is either a facilitating service or a value-added service.

- Depending on the stage in the service process, there are pre-process, in-process and post-process supplementary services.

- Depending on the function of the service, it can be differentiated between integration-related, communications-related and contract-related supplementary services.

Facilitating and value-added services

Facilitating services are services which are mandatory, i.e. necessary in order to ensure the production and delivery of the core service. For example, in a hotel where the core service is 'providing a bedroom', it is absolutely necessary to hand over the keys to the clients. Of course, it is not necessary to provide a luxury reception, but the step of 'handing over the room keys' is mandatory in order to deliver the service.

Value-added services are unsolicited from the provider's perspective. They are not necessary in order to deliver the service. They are often provided in order to differentiate the offer from the competitors'. Accordingly, in many industries, there is strong competition over the value-added services offered to the consumer. What is a mandatory service and what is not depends on the service category. While a reception area is necessary in a hotel, a helpdesk at airports or railway stations is a value-added service.

Pre-process, in-process and post-process services

Furthermore, different supplementary service types can be differentiated according to the stage *in the buying process* where they are applied. Three service types can be defined: pre-process services, in-process services and after-process services.

Pre-process services concern the preparation of the service process. These services are applied before customer and provider come together in order to conduct the service process. Thinking of diverse services, you will find that in most cases, there are several needs which customers satisfy by themselves – or which are satisfied by supplementary services of the provider. For example, directions to a hotel can be provided by the hotel. If not provided by the hotel the customer will use telephone directories, maps and/or route planning systems in order to locate the hotel.

In-process services are offered and used during the actual service process. They can be either mandatory or value-added services. As mandatory services, they facilitate the ongoing of the service process. As value-added services, they are offered to improve the service experience. Because of the object- and time-related closeness to the actual service process, the in-process services are often difficult to separate from the core service – from the provider's perspective regarding the planning of the service production and delivery as well as from the customer's perspective when evaluating the service. Often, the in-service processes mean changes in the internal or external factors. For example, the service of minding the children of the customer visiting a furniture store concerns the external factor because the customer can concentrate more on the shopping experience in the store. But of course, the store has to provide personnel to watch over the children. Thus, internal factors are also involved.

Post-process services are services which are applied after the core service process has taken place. Like mandatory services, they are often needed in order to terminate the service process, such as the payment process, or to make the service process result applicable (e.g. training for the customer's employees by consultants regarding tools using during a consulting project). As value-added services, such as non-mandatory services, they make the service result easier to use for the customer, or deal with service delivery problems, as with the generous and compensatory behaviour of a restaurant offering a price reduction or extra drink, to compensate for inferior service delivery.

Integration-related, communications-related and contract-related services

Integration-related services

The integration-related services arise from the need to integrate the customer into the service process (see Chapter 1). Typical integration-related services are, for example, reservation and safekeeping services.

Reservation. For services where service resources are scarce, reservation services are applied. In this case, customers can purchase the right to use the service, i.e. to occupy the service resources of the provider. Generally, every service provider has scarce resources. But there are some services where it is rare that the resources cannot be used by customers because of over-usage. A reason for this can be the flexibility of the service resources, the flexibility of the customers or the relative low cost of the respective resources. For example, in a restaurant a seating place is more important for the customer than in an underground train. Considering the relevant service resources, there are two reasons for reservation systems. First, there can be human resources making a reservation system necessary, e.g. medical, consulting or teaching services. Secondly, there are services where service facilities or equipment are the major service resource. Examples are transportation services or event-like services, such as cinemas or sports events. In both cases, reservations help both the provider and the customer. They are not mandatory theoretically, but demanded by the provider for capacity management reasons. From the customer's perspective, reservation systems ensure access to the service resources booked. Furthermore, reservations can help minimise waiting times. Thus, meeting the agreed service time is an essential services marketing task for the provider. This becomes obvious when one has to wait at a service location, e.g. the hair salon, in spite of a reservation.

Safekeeping. In many service situations, especially those in which the customer is not personally involved in the service process as the external factor, the provider can help the customer by caring for other persons, e.g. the customer's children, or possessions. Examples of the safekeeping of objects are car park lots at airports, restaurants or shopping malls; an example of the safekeeping of people is babysitting. IKEA facilities include, for example, a playground where parents can leave their children to play under the supervision of IKEA personnel. In most cases, this service is a value-added service which is offered in order to simplify the service process for the customer. Car park lots, for example, allow easier and/or faster customer access to the service facilities. Looking after the customers' children by a department store allows the customer to concentrate more on the purchase process. There are also core services where safekeeping is mandatory. Examples are kindergartens, schools, car parks or banks providing safes.

Communications-related services

Communications-related services concern communications from the provider to the customer. However, these are not communications such as promotion or sponsoring, but communications which enable or improve the service process. Communications-related services are information, consultation and hospitality.

Information. In many service settings, information helps to facilitate or enhance the service experience. Thus, information can be, either a mandatory or value-added service. Information is mandatory especially for the use of complex or new services. For example, for many internet services an explanation of the service is necessary before the first use. For these services in particular, information is required by customers and often perceived as the firm's own quality dimension of the service. An example of information as a value-added service is giving the customer directions to the service location. Both kinds of information services can be an essential driver of the customer's perceived quality and buying decision. Consequently, informing the customer is of strategic relevance for a service provider in many service settings. However, information is only of value when it is accurate and useful for the customers' purposes. A negative example regarding information services is the approach of many mobile telecommunications providers whose websites mainly focus on potential and not current customers. For current customers, it is often very difficult to find information regarding the service already bought, e.g. when looking for the telephone number for the use of the mailbox service abroad. In some service industries, there are even legal requirements to consult the customer regarding the use of the service. For example, in the case of dangerous services such as bungee jumping, the service provider explains to the customer how to behave when jumping.

Consultation. In order to improve a service process, service providers often offer consulting services to the customer. While information services make the service easier to use for the customer, the consultation helps to improve the service decision and usage of the service by the customer. There are three different types of consultation:

- *Consultation regarding the service choice.* Here providers help the customer to choose a certain service, either from the whole market or from the service spectrum of the provider. One example is the approach of financial service providers to present a comparison of their own services with the competitors' for the customer (e.g. comparison of credit terms). In many situations, including relatively simple decision situations, the customer requires advice from the provider regarding the services to use. For example, it is often difficult for insurance customers to know precisely which policy specifications are applicable to their situation and consequently they expect the insurance agent to advise them accordingly. Or in a theatre, visitors want advice regarding the best seats available within their budget. Partly, it is also important for the provider to advise the customer to choose the right service. This is especially the case in service situations where several customers use the service simultaneously. For example, ski schools ask their customers to state their experience level or even conduct tests in order to set up homogeneous groups.

- *Consultation regarding the use of the service.* This kind of consultation service is especially relevant for more complex services. For example, before surgery, patients are consulted concerning optional anaesthetic techniques, the operation technique, etc.

- *Consultation regarding the service environment.* There are also consultation services in the broader context of the core service. For example, in fitness centres, customers are often offered a nutrition consultation. In this case, the core service is providing fitness equipment and classes in order to keep in shape. But in general terms, most of the customers join a fitness centre for health reasons. Therefore, they might also be interested in a nutrition consultation.

Consultation services can be *mandatory as well as value-added service*s. For example, supplementary services in the broader context of the core service, e.g. the nutrition consultation, are seldom mandatory. In most cases, these are value-added services that are offered based on the interests and needs of the customers. In contrast to value-added consultation services, mandatory consultation services are necessary in order to use the service. Take for example safekeeping services such as babysitting, management and tax consultancy or marriage counselling – in many cases, consultation is the core service.

Hospitality. Hospitality services take place during the actual service process, e.g. offering coffee at a consultancy meeting or at a hairdresser's. In most cases, hospitality is a value-added service which aims to ensure a harmonious atmosphere for the service experience. It is obvious that a hospitable environment leads to a positive customer perception – no essential failures of the core service provided. However, there are also services which are hospitality services in nature, e.g. hotels or restaurants. In these cases, hospitality is part of the core service not the supplementary service, even though providers can offer varying degrees of hospitality.

Contract-related services

As the name implies, contract-related services are related to the contract between provider and customer. They concern the contract itself (contracting), the customer's paying a price in return for service (billing, payment) or the use of services after the core service process has taken place (after sales service).

Contracting. In order to initiate the service process, it is often necessary to place a contract with the customer. In a broader sense, this is the legal agreement under which the provider delivers the service to the customer and the customer pays for the service. That might sound like an exaggerated view. But, depending on the service in focus, there is a more or less intense contracting process. The length and complexity of this process varies strongly with the *degree of service standardisation*. For highly individualised services, this process is complex and might take a long time, for example in the management consulting, architecture or plant construction industries. For more standardised services, this process is short and – theoretically – not very complex, for example buying a ticket for the cinema. But even in these cases, the relevance of contracting for the customers' perception must not be underestimated. Notably negative incidences in the contracting stage can lead to a bad perception or even a decision against the provider. Probably everyone has at some point felt anger about queues, etc. In many industries, the contracting process is simplified by *information technology*, automated teller machines to buy train, aeroplane or cinema tickets.

Billing. Billing refers to the process of explaining to the customer what they have to pay for the service used and the conditions and methods of payment. Obviously, there are considerable differences between the billing process in the different service industries. For example, at the cinema kiosk the billing is limited to the simple information to the customer about the price for the visit. So, for standardised services which can be easily divided into single units, no complicated billing procedure is necessary. But, for less standardised services or services with individual usage rates, such as consulting projects or telecommunication services, billing is more complex and, thus, an essential quality factor. The transparency of the billing is of particular relevance for the customer in these cases. Considering these differences, billing is mandatory in all industries. But the manner of billing can be a value-added service. For example, the itemised list of costs provided by telecommunication companies represents a value-added service. The Royal Bank of Scotland offers an e-billing-service to its business clients. Services that are offered by this bank include online viewing of documents in a choice of formats or data downloads to reduce the need for manual data entry and facilitate invoice analysis.[4]

Payment. Paying the price for a service represents the quid pro quo of the customer for the service received. Thus, payment itself is not a supplementary service, but the organisation of the payment process can be used as a supplementary service. This becomes obvious in situations when the payment process causes a deterioration in the service experience. A good example of this phenomenon is the example of having to wait for the bill in a restaurant for 30 minutes. For payment, a provider can offer different methods, such as cash, credit card or electronic payment. Furthermore, single or package payment, such as, for example, subscriptions, can be offered to the customer. Then, regarding payment time, pre- or after-service payment or combinations of both can be agreed on. For example, in industries where the service is comprised of large projects, parts of the payment are demanded before the beginning of the project, others during the project and again others on completion of the project. Finally, the structure of the payment can differ, e.g. total versus payment by installments. Note also that – in contrast to the consumer goods sector – payment often is required before the service usage (e.g. cinema or airline tickets, management consulting fees). Thus, payment-related supplementary services can also be pre-process services.

After sales service. After sales services were invented in the industrial goods area where companies wanted to expand their traditional offer by applying a service orientation and utilising the expertise from service providers. However, in many service industries, different kinds of after sales services are also applied. The most important ones are maintenance services which are especially relevant in the technical services area, e.g. heating installations or software implementation. But in a broad sense, all efforts in the area of complaint management (see Chapter 3) can be regarded as after sales services. After sales services are mostly voluntary and thus value-added services. From the customer's perspective, after sales services contribute to risk reduction. When a service firm succeeds in establishing an image as a provider with a strong after sales service (e.g. by offering service guarantees), it reduces the risk associated with using the service as perceived by customers and by this increases the customer's probability of choosing the service. A good example of an after sales service is the story of an AVIS customer described in Services marketing in action 5.4.

In spite of their significance for customers' perception and behaviour, supplementary services *cannot substitute for the core service for the customer*. The warmth and friendliness of a doctor as well as an electronic appointments system cannot compensate for a lack of know-how regarding health questions. The patient appreciates supplementary services, but would not choose a doctor with a weak core service in spite of excellent supplementary services.[5] This example can easily be adapted to other contexts and industries.

SERVICES MARKETING IN ACTION 5.4:

The impact of after sales service on customer perceptions

Let's just say that I think AVIS is absolutely smashing because they absorbed the cost of my Dad's 2 parking summons. My Dad is not an incompetent driver but coming from a foreign country there are tendencies to make mistakes and AVIS recognises that. Of course, what you pay for is what you get and the cost of car hire is more expensive, especially if you do rent a car from the airport. However, AVIS's after sales service is fantastic, its before sales service is also formidable and they have friendly bus-porters who take you from the terminals to the rental site. The rental cost may be a little steeper than the rest but they are still reasonable and I would definitely recommend this if you prefer the security of having good after sales service.

Source: Ciao 2000.

Relative importance of core and supplementary services

The relative importance of core service and supplementary services differs depending on several criteria concerning the focal service or characteristics of the customer.

Relevance of the focal service. In some service contexts, supplementary services are more important than in others. On the one hand, there are many services where supplementary services are almost part of the core service. These are, primarily, complex services for which specified competencies are required and where the service is not self-explanatory to the user. For example, the teachers' core service is influenced to a large extent by their ability to listen to the students – which can be, strictly speaking, regarded as a supplementary service. However, without an open and considerate attitute towards the students the teacher will have little success regarding learning objectives. In this case the supplementary service of an 'open and considerate attitude towards the students' is closely linked to the core service 'teaching'. On the other hand, when the service is easy to explain and furthermore has a straightforward benefit to the customer, then the core service will be much more important than the supplementary services. For example, postal services are evaluated mainly on the basis of their core service. When deliveries arrive on time, supplementary services are not that important. And, when delivery is deficient, no supplementary service would help satisfy customers.

Relevance of customer characteristics. It is obvious that not every customer perceives services in the same manner. Consequently, the relative importance of the core service compared to supplementary services can vary between different customers. Some customers want an efficient and high quality service, i.e. focus on the core service, while for others, supplementary services are also important –

sometimes even more important than the core service. Services marketing in action 5.5 shows that, on a general level, gender is a differentiator regarding the relevance of core and supplementary services.

SERVICES MARKETING IN ACTION 5.5:

Importance of core and relational service aspects differ according to gender

In an American study the customer's gender as a moderator was analysed, a criterion which can be easily determined and thus used for services marketing activities. Almost every provider with direct contact to the customers has a structured (database) or unstructured (knowledge of the service employees) knowledge about the gender of its customers. The question is whether gender is also a discriminating factor regarding the relative importance of core and supplementary services. In the study, an experimental design analysed how women and men evaluate waiters and attorneys regarding certain core and relational aspects. The core attributes measured comprise, for example, the promptness, efficiency, accuracy and experience of the service provider, while the relational attributes include the politeness, friendliness, trustworthiness and helpfulness of the provider. The results show that for women, the relational aspects are more important than the core attributes, and vice versa.

Source: Iacobucci and Ostrom 1993.

E-services: The role of technology for the service product

In recent years, due to technological developments so-called e-services have gained increased importance. The rise of e-services is closely connected to the development of the internet as a marketplace and the concept of e-commerce. Today, purchasing books via the internet, booking flights and online banking are far beyond being a speciality for web enthusiasts. Even though the discussion about e-services emerged partly due to the internet revolution, there are many other e-services that are independent of the internet. Examples are bank ATMs, electronic check-in machines at airports or ticket machines.

E-services are defined as services where the customer or external factor interacts with an interface (electronic service encounter). Compared to 'classical' services, e-services exhibit the following characteristics (see Figure 5.5):

- The resources needed and used for e-services are mostly automated and non-human. Examples are webservers, teller machines, a telephone system. However, many e-services also use human resources together with a technical component, e.g. call centre agents.

- Furthermore, direct contact between service customer and provider is not necessary for many e-services, especially for internet services. For other e-services, such as ATMs, there is still the necessity of contact between the customer and some kind of standardised resources, in this case the ATM, of the provider.

- Services are generally intangible. For web-services though, the degree of visualisation is higher than for 'classical' services due to the high degree of automated, material elements of an e-service.

- Another characteristic of 'classical' services is their perishability that causes a limited disposability of services. Compared to 'classical' services, e-services exhibit a less limited disposability.

- Regarding the interactions between the customer and a provider's resources, it is typical for service encounters to be 'high touch' due to the importance of service employees. In contrast, e-services utilise mostly material resources and can therefore be labelled as 'high tech'.

An important difference between classical services and e-services concerns the service resources used for service production, which will be discussed in depth in Chapter 9.

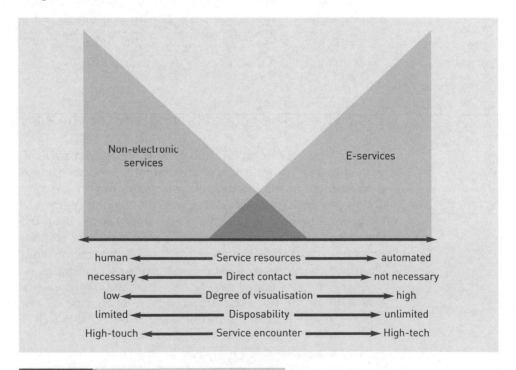

FIGURE 5.5   E-services versus classical services

Source: Meffert and Bruhn 2003, p. 418.

Designing the service programme

Next to the core service and the supplementary services a service provider has to define a service programme. Although there are providers which offer only a single service, most providers provide a full set of services which add up to a so-called service programme (see Figure 5.6). For a bank, for example, diverse core services (or 'products') and supplementary services can be differentiated. The range of core services includes accounts, loans, credits, investment products. Typical supplementary services are phone and online banking, advice in money issues, software for organising private finances, etc.

So far, we have talked about single services as well as supplementary services. But many providers offer a wide range of services, i.e. a set of services called the *service programme*. For example, banks offer accounts, investment facilities and loans. In many cases, it is difficult to decide whether a certain service is an additional service or a modification of the focal service. For example, it could be argued that airlines offer flights as the only core service. On the other hand national flights and international flights can be regarded as two separate core services. You might ask: What's the matter with that differentiation? However, it is important to acknowledge that the range of the service programme can have a significant impact on customers' evaluations and behaviour. A major influence of the service programme concerns the cross-buying behaviour of customers. One goal of services marketing is to enhance customer relationships, i.e. making cus-

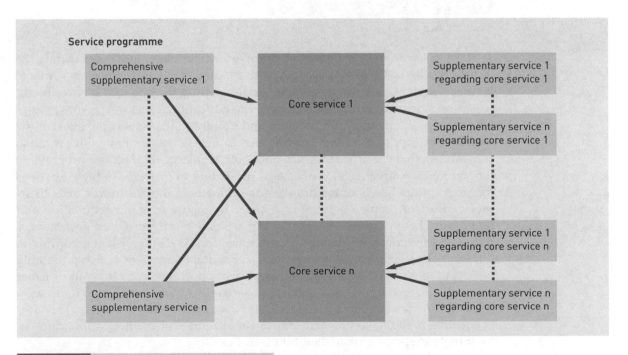

FIGURE 5.6   Structure of a service programme

tomers buy more of the provider's services. Of course, service companies can only realise this objective when they offer more than one service. But, not every service programme leads to intensive cross-buying behaviour. To achieve this, a provider must offer a synergetic service programme to enhance its relationships. One example for the relationship enhancement strategy via enlarging the service programme is the approach of banks to offer insurance services and vice versa. The car rental company Sixt also tries to realise more of its potential with its current customers by selling cars in addition to renting cars (see Figure 5.7).

| **FIGURE 5.7** | The Sixt service programme |

Source: Sixt 2004.

The service programme has gained importance in many industries during the last decade. In order to *make customers more loyal and profitable*, providers enlarge their service ranges. Examples of these industries are the financial services sector (e.g. banks offering insurance services), the educational sector (e.g. universities offering senior university programmes and training courses for companies) or the tourism industry (e.g. airlines offering cars to rent in cooperation with car rental companies). In the tourism industry hotels often enlarge their service programme for competitive advantage. See Services marketing in action 5.6 which describes the plans of the hotels consortium Leading Hotels of the World that extends its service line for its member hotels in order to ensure member acquisition and retention. These examples show that the existing service programmes are very different. More precisely, service programmes can be distinguished according to different criteria, as can single services: car rental companies which often only offer cars to rent as a single core service versus hotels which often offer further services, like restaurant or conference services next to the traditional hotel service, or the degree of target group focus, such as airlines offering car rental services in addition to flights for their customers versus universities offering programmes for target groups other than their traditional ones.

SERVICES MARKETING IN ACTION 5.6:

Leading Hotels extends its line

In today's information age, independent hotels need even more proactive market-ing help to compete with the broadshouldered chains. Consortia such as Leading Hotels of the World have recognised this fact of life in what has become a global universe and is extending its line of services beyond traditional reservation pro-grammes. At Leading Hotels' June 2002 annual convention held in Los Angeles, several line extensions were announced, ranging from financial management and consulting services to comprehensive educational programmes.

Perhaps the announcement made with the most fanfare was the plan to form a joint venture with the Hotelschool The Hague to be known as The Leading Hotel Schools of the World. The organisation is designed to provide the most advanced, luxury-focused education in the hospitality industry. The curriculum will be targeted at both students seeking a career in the industry as well as experienced managers.

Source: Hotels 2002.

Overall, a service programme not only contains several core services but also the *supplementary services* a provider offers. Regarding supplementary services, the provider has to decide which supplementary services are offered for which core services. On the one hand, services can be offered independently from the core service, while, on the other hand, there are supplementary services which are only offered in connection with specific core services (see Figure 5.6). Looking at a hotel for example, business services are often offered to regular guests as well as to conference guests (even when they are not staying in the hotel). However, room service is only offered to guests of the hotel.

Why might service providers design a comprehensive service programme? What are the *advantages* of a broad service programme?

Risk distribution. A full service programme helps to minimise risk because the risk associated with the different services is distributed. When one service fails, another might compensate for the losses. This logic could be observed in the European bank market at the turn of the twenty-first century. During the new economy hype, banks focused strongly on wealthy private clients, while espe-cially non-wealthy private clients as well as SME (small and medium enterprises) were neglected. Some banks even tried to 'outsource' their commercial banking organisation. But then, after the stock exchange crash, the preferred segment of wealthy clients suddenly was not as profitable as before because the services which had made them profitable previously, investments, were less lucrative. Consequently, banks were lucky that the other two segments which predomi-nantly used the account and credit services helped to compensate for the lower performance of the previously more valuable segment of wealthy private clients.

Cost synergies. Offering a wide range of similar services helps to realise synergies on the cost side. This is especially the case when all services of a programme can be offered with the same production factors. When for two services, more or less the same qualifications are needed, then spare capacities of the employees can be used for offering similar services. For example, when a bank is additionally offering insurance services, the bank employee is taught about these in order to be able to sell and manage the new services. But when the implementation of the strategy by means of technology systems is required, other employees (e.g. programmers and database experts) are needed.

Cross-selling potentials. If a service provider knows that its customers need other services which fit into the service strategy of the provider, an opportunity to realise cross-selling potentials exists for the service provider. One example of this is the tendency in the financial services sector to offer a full service programme. Banks offer insurance, while insurance companies offer bank products. By this strategy, banks and insurance companies try to use their competencies in order to offer other financial products. The intention is to realise the full potential of the existing customer relationships.

Switching barriers. The more services a customer purchases from a certain provider, the more the customer will become accustomed to that provider and so too the tougher and more elaborate it will be to dissolve the relationship with the provider, especially by competitors. In the financial services example, a customer who has not only to change their bank account but also insurance contracts when switching to another financial services provider will perceive higher switching barriers than in the case of a customer who only has to change his bank account.

Loyalty effect. When customers use a broad service programme, this will lead to better customer relationships. From the company point of view, they will gain more knowledge about the customers. Every interaction with the customer represents the opportunity to gain information about the customer. The more services a customer uses, the more interactions take place and therefore the more information can be gained which can be used to improve the relationship, e.g. by offering customised services. From the customer's point of view, the more services used, the more the customer will get to know the company, its services and employees. Providing that the customer associates positive perceptions with the company, services and employees, then more contacts because of the higher number of services used should result in a closer relationship with the customer being realised, which will eventually lead to the higher loyalty of the customer.

There are many reasons for broad service programmes. However, there are also *disadvantages of broad service programmes* that might prevent a service provider from offering them.

Higher complexity. The more services a company offers, the more complex is the management of these services. On the individual level, providing several services leads to higher requirements with regard to the service personnel. On the organisational level, a broader service programme leads to more complex structures and processes. For example, controlling the success of several services is more complex than controlling just a single service.

Negative side effects. In the event that one service of the whole service programme has certain quality or image problems, these might easily be transferred over the whole service programme in the customer's perception. While in the other direction, i.e. with positive side effects, there can also be synergies regarding customer perceptions, a provider with a broad service programme might have problems with negative side effects.

Image adulteration. The more services a provider offers, the more difficult it will be for the service provider to realise a precise and clear image in the market. This will be especially the case if the services offered are not very similar. However, in the case that the company intends to offer a broad range of similar services image adulteration is not a problem.

Decisions regarding the service product

Regarding the service product there are several decisions to be taken which can be associated with the different stages of a service product lifecycle. Comparable to the customer relationship lifecycle (see Chapter 4), the service product lifecycle interprets service products as 'creatures' and depicts the course of their 'life' in the market. The *service product lifecycle* has the following stages:

- service innovation, such as the development of new services;
- service modification, differentiation of services, e.g. for different customer segments;
- elimination of services, e.g. reducing the service programme.

In these three areas, decisions have to be taken by service managers. The three areas apply to core services, value-added services and the whole service programme.

Service innovation

An important decision regarding the service product of a provider is to invent new services. Why are successful service providers looking for innovations on a regular basis? There are several reasons for **service innovation** (see Table 5.2). Summarising these reasons, we find external and internal reasons for innovations.

TABLE 5.2	Reasons for innovations by German companies

Trigger for service innovations	Mean
Completion of existing service programme	4.0
Customer request	3.8
Developing new business segments	3.7
Change of general conditions	3.5
New technical options	3.4
Stress of competition	3.4
Ideas of own employees	3.3
Ideas from cooperation partners	2.9

Source: Fähnrich *et al.* 1999.

What is an innovation? There are intensive discussions in the marketing literature about the definition of service innovations. These discussions have led to the distinction of several types of **service innovations**. One typology which is derived from an empirical study distinguishes ten types of service innovations according to five differentiating factors (see Figure 5.8).[6]

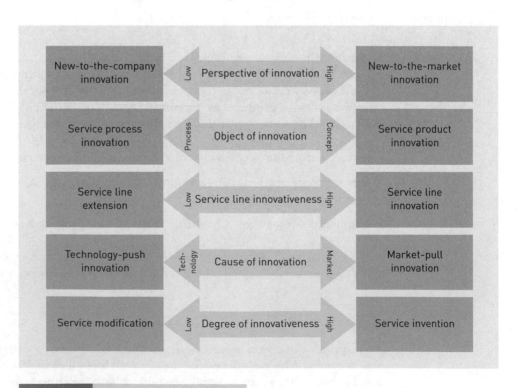

FIGURE 5.8	Types of service innovations

New-to-the-market versus new-to-the-company innovations. Regarding the perspective of the innovation new-to-the-market innovations are substantive innovations which are not yet offered by any provider. For example, eBay's invention was a new-to-the-market innovation because eBay was the first provider to offer an online auction service. Consequently, from the perspective of eBay's competitors, their market entry was involved with new-to-the-company innovations. Introducing new-to-the market innovations, i.e. being first in the market, can help to assure a long-term position in the market. However, new-to-the-company innovations are less risky because the provider can learn from the experience of the inventor.

New service product versus new service processes. Service innovations do not have to concern only the service product, as there are also process innovations possible. For example, the services of amazon.com are process innovations because the genuine service of delivering books to the consumer is an old service in itself. However, giving the customer the chance to order books on the internet and delivering them to their home was an innovation of the ordering and delivery process. Of course, sometimes there is a smooth transition between new service products versus new service processes. Next to the services of amazon.com, the invention of e-universities or eBay are strictly electronic forms of existing services but are often perceived as new service concepts because they were not used by the target groups of the new services before.

Service line innovations versus service line extensions. Service innovations can differ regarding the innovativeness of the service line in focus. For example the offer of insurances by banks in order to realise a holistic finance strategy for their customers, represents a service line innovation because the insurances are a new service category for the bank. In contrast, the offering of a new fund, for example, represents a service line extension. The service line 'funds' is extended by the new service.

Technology-push versus market-pull innovations. What is the cause of the innovation? Is the innovation more technology-driven, i.e. a technology-push innovation? Or is it a market-pull innovation, where consumers long for the new service actively? A typical example of a technology-push innovation are the offers of internet providers. These services supported the dispersion of the internet as a mass communication channel. Other examples are online ordering systems in industrial markets as well as online shipment status checking services offered by package delivery companies. On the other hand, in several industries of the consumer durables sector, such as electronics, cars, white goods, a trend recently observed is to offer financing instruments to their customers: a service which has developed due to the increasing financial long-term planning needs of the customers and their willingness to take out loans. Another example of a market-pull innovation is the FTSE4Good index for socially responsible investment which is described in Services marketing in action 5.7.

SERVICES MARKETING IN ACTION 5.7:

Service innovation at FTSE: The FTSE4Good Index for socially responsible investment

FTSE Group is a world-leader in the creation and management of equity indices and associated data services. It manages and develops globally recognised indices ranging from the FTSE All-World Index to the recently launched FTSE4Good Index Series. FTSE is owned by The Financial Times and the London Stock Exchange. FTSE became a limited company in 1995, although it has calculated indices since the 1930s. FTSE rose to global prominence in 1985 when it created the FTSE All-World Index to provide an index of prominent shares from across the globe.

By providing independent indices for clients in nearly 80 countries, FTSE offers the means by which pension providers, investment banks, brokers, stock exchanges and fund managers can monitor financial products relative to particular indices. This enables customers to measure the performance of their investments against an independently measured index. For example, individuals who contribute to a pension plan which is invested in a portfolio of shares in the FTSE 100 Index can keep a regular eye on how their future pension is performing by examining the FTSE 100 Index in their daily newspapers, TV or the internet.

In February 2001, FTSE launched a new family of indices named FTSE4Good. These are designed to help create a global standard enabling investors to identify and measure the performance of companies who practise a recognised, acceptable standard and social behaviour. Investment in ethical and socially responsible funds has grown rapidly. FTSE has responded to this investor interest by creating the FTSE4Good Index. Additionally, in July 2000 the UK government set out a new requirement that occupational pension funds must state in their investment policies the extent to which they take account of ethical, social and environmental issues in investment.

Today, it is particularly important that companies operate in a socially responsible way. Investors and other key stakeholders in companies are increasingly concerned that the companies in which they are involved behave in an ethical way. To be included in the FTSE4Good Index, a company must meet a number of important criteria. Research indicates that over 50% of the companies in the four regions (UK, Europe, US and Global) to which the FTSE4Good Index applies do not today meet the criteria. The creation of the new indices indirectly puts pressure on companies excluded from the index to change their ways in order to become eligible for consideration for inclusion in the index.

Source: The Times 100 2004.

Service inventions versus service modifications. Finally, many innovations are more service modifications than real service inventions. For example the offer of internet access by airlines during flights (see Services marketing in action 5.8) is a typical **service modification** by means of a value-added service (see also paragraph about service modifications in this chapter).

SERVICES MARKETING IN ACTION 5.8:

Online in air

The days of using your flight as an excuse for ignoring e-mail may be numbered. Eager to lure business fliers eager for Web access, several domestic and international airlines are testing and installing equipment that will provide two-way e-mail or full Internet surfing.

United Airlines announced last week that it will become the first U.S. carrier to offer two-way e-mail on its domestic fleet this year through a Verizon program. Continental Airlines followed with its own announcement. In May, Lufthansa announced much more ambitious plans to become the world's first airline with high-speed broadband Internet access on international flights through a Boeing program.

Today, travellers are largely cut off from clients, family and colleagues during flights. Some planes have phones, but the rates make long business calls impractical. No U.S. airline currently offers laptop users the ability to send and receive e-mail and attachments during flights. Federal safety rules also ban cell phone use in flight, although the government is about to re-examine that restriction.

Before the terrorist attacks, several major U.S. and international airlines had formed partnerships with Boeing on its new satellite-based program, Connexion, to provide passengers broadband Internet access.

But after September 11, amid the collapse of business travel and airlines' struggle to survive, most plans were shelved. The program requires installation of two antennas for each jet, a huge investment of time and capital. Lufthansa would not reveal the cost.

United's program presents little risk. United, which is in bankruptcy reorganisation, has offered Verizon's JetConnect service, with outbound e-mail, on some Boeing 767s since December. United and Verizon call two-way e-mail a boon to the business travelers United is fighting to keep.

'The availability of e-mail is critical to business fliers', says Verizon Airfone President Bill Pallone. 'Users have said access to JetConnect will determine which airline they'll choose.'

Verizon, which has 138 stations nationwide in its network, is providing and installing the equipment on planes. Passengers will access the service by plugging laptops into a jack in seatback Airfones. An onboard file server will provide regularly updated news, stocks, weather, sports and city information.

Users will swipe a credit card to pay $15.98 a flight – there will be an extra charge for big downloads – for e-mail using Microsoft Exchange or one of two other popular e-mail programs. Revenue will be split between United and Verizon. But the service will be limited to flights within North America.

Lufthansa's 'FlyNet' program will be more costly to the airline and passengers but will offer much greater capabilities: full access to the Internet during international flights, including corporate sites via virtual private network. Boeing's satellite-based program is designed to handle big downloads such as streaming video or big PowerPoint files. Passengers will use power plug-ins to access it.

▶

However, the service will not be available for a while. Installation of the antennas on the fleet could take two years. Lufthansa says the service will cost passengers $30 or $35 a flight paid with a credit card, miles or some other method.

Lufthansa offered this spring a free test of the service on Washington-to-Frankfurt flights. Onboard 'FlyNet assistants' gave instructions and even laptops to passengers interested in the service. Dozens of passengers on each flight have made use of the offer. Once implemented, 'We hope business travellers will switch carriers', says spokeswoman Jennifer Urbaniak. During the test, 'We had people coming up to our ticket counter in Washington asking, "Is this the Internet plane?"'

No one questions the novelty of in-flight e-mail or Web access, but whether Lufthansa can recoup its capital investment is unknown. The Verizon system is less of a gamble, but it only offers domestic e-mail.

'Putting business extras on planes might make sense for long international flights, but it adds weight', which increases fuel consumption, says Blaylock & Partners analyst Ray Neidl. 'I think the jury's still out.'

Source: E-mail works its way onto business-minded flights in *USA Today*, (Adams, M. 2003). From USA TODAY, a division of Gannett Co. Inc. Reprinted with permission.

Several of the described *types of service innovations* have been applied by the Robert Wood Johnson University Hospital in New Brunswick, NJ/USA, during the last decade, as outlined in Services marketing in action 5.9.

SERVICES MARKETING IN ACTION 5.9:

Service innovation in hospital foodservice

In the USA, you know a nutrition services department in a hospital is doing something right when it is highlighted in the hospital's annual report for two years in a row. At Robert Wood Johnson University Hospital (RWJUH) in New Brunswick, NJ, a computer-monitored patient room service program and a new 12,000 sq. ft. dining room have helped foodservice director Tony Almeida achieve that distinction. The glossy annual reports tout his department's medical innovations as examples of a commitment to quality patient care.

RWJUH has only emerged as a major academic medical center since the 1980s, but its roots as a community hospital in the region go back more than 100 years. In particular, though, it has been growing and building continuously since the 1990s. In contrast to most acute care facilities, its bed count has grown – from 415 to 567 beds – with another 32 beds slated to open next year in two new floors under construction at its attached Bristol-Myers Squibb Children's Hospital. And, like healthcare facilities everywhere, it has watched as outpatient services expanded at an exponential rate in the same period.

As you would expect, that growth has translated into significant additional food-service demand – and change – for Almeida's department. Today it delivers patient meals to 46 different locations on the seven-building campus, ranging from a typical floor with 32 patients to a critical care unit that holds ten. All those points of service make for a demanding patient meal program, one that has evolved with available technologies since the early 1990s.

'We've always been on the cutting edge', says Almeida, the hospital's director of food and nutrition/environmental/host services. 'Our administration has consistently made the patient and employee dining experience, and customer satisfaction, top priorities here.' That has meant a lot of change and evolution of the patient feeding program. Almeida's department has had food production and menu management software in place for over 15 years. 'We shifted from a select to non-select menu in the early 90s', he says, 'After that, we were one of the first hospitals to offer a spoken menu, using hand-held digital assistants to place the orders.'

Most recently, that drive to implement technology solutions to produce quality results led RWJUH to introduce a room service program that is among the largest and most sophisticated in the country. 'I don't want to seem immodest, but our philosophy is to find ways to make things work and work cost-effectively', says RWJUH Senior Vice President of Operations Stephen Jones. 'Simply put, we do not like to fail. When Harvey Holzberg, our president and CEO, said "Let's do room service!" we set out to do it and do it well.'

'If you look at our Press Ganey peer group scores for patient satisfaction with meal quality, we are in the 98th percentile', adds Herman Lindenbaum, vice president of support services. 'That's a great indication of the impact that move has had on how our patients perceive our service.'

Source: Lawn 2004.

For systematic service innovations, service companies organise their innovation activities according to an *innovation process*.[7] This process depicts several steps which help assure the success of service innovations. The 15 steps of this innovation process can be associated with three stages (see Figure 5.9):

- In the idea generation stage (steps 1 and 2), objectives and strategies for the new service are defined. Based on this, ideas regarding a new service definition are collected.

- The idea evaluation stage (steps 3 to 7) encompasses the assessment of several pre-selected ideas and the identification of one or a few service ideas which are to be followed up.

- Finally, the idea realisation stage (steps 8 to 15) comprises the design of the selected new service(s), its test and launch.

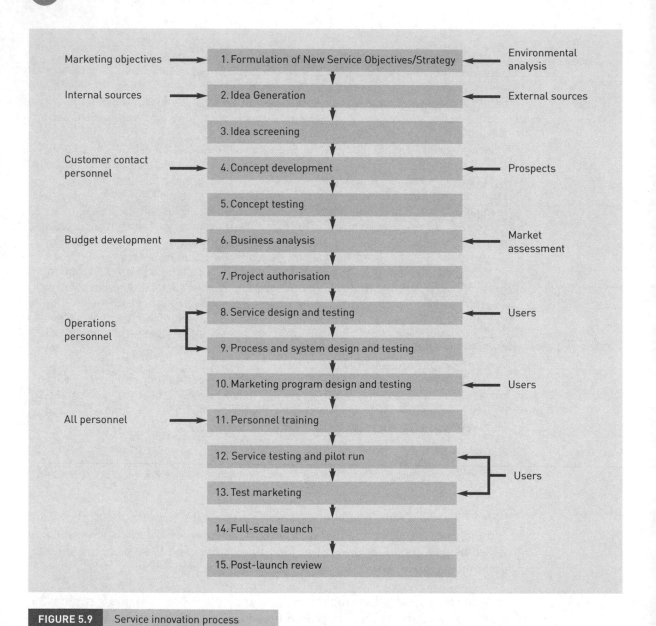

FIGURE 5.9   Service innovation process

Source: Scheuing and Johnson 1989, p. 30.

In general, this process describes many tasks which are also conducted in a consumer goods environment. So what is special about these tasks in a service environment? The integration of the external factor in service process results in some specialities of the innovation process in service companies. Some tasks are more difficult because of the integration, for others, more opportunities are available. Important specialities due to customer integration concern service blue-printing, prick-eared market research and service prototypes.

Blueprinting the service. Because of the process character of services and the inte-gration of the customer, in all stages of the innovation process blueprinting the service helps to document the respective process.[8] A service blueprint is a scheme which describes the different steps of the service process (see Chapter 3). This scheme can also be used for several tasks in the innovation process. For idea generation, employees and/or customers can be asked to identify potential modi-fications of an existing service. For cost-benefit-analysis, the blueprint can be used in order to associate cost with the process steps and to calculate the total cost of the service. Finally, blueprints can be used for the planning of the quality level. To sum up, the blueprint is the basis for finding possible quality problems within the service process, thus reducing existing waiting times for the customer.

Prick-eared market research. As opposed to product innovations, in services the oppor-tunity for some kind of passive market research exists which can be used in the idea generation stage. Because of the direct contact between customers and service employees, customer reactions and recommendations regarding existing or non-exis-tent services can be used in order to collect ideas for innovations. For example, when airline passengers mention to flight personnel that internet access during the flight would be of great advantage airline employees should tell their managers about the customers' wishes. And those again should realise that there are an increasing number of customers who expect internet access during flights. Yet the problem is that managers often do not get this kind of information from their front personnel or if they do, they often do not react to it. This problem is also described by gap 2 of the service quality gap model (see Chapter 2), i.e. the gap between customer expectations and the management's perceptions of these customer expectations.

Service prototypes. Especially in the idea evaluation and realisation stages, service prototypes are important in order to test the new service prior to going live with it. In contrast to prototyping in the consumer goods sector, for services it is often dif-ficult to prototype all the characteristics of the service idea. The service process elements are particularly difficult to prototype because of the customer's integra-tion. On the other hand, the service elements are easier to prototype, above all the material elements, like bank tellers, hotel rooms, aeroplane cabins or cinema spaces. Branding can also be prototyped, as well as, in part, the appearance and behaviour of the employees. For services with a high proportion of material ele-ments and a low variation in the quality level for each customer, prototyping is almost comparable to prototyping in the consumer goods industries. For example, the quality of a cinema is relatively independent from the single user. Thus, in this case relatively objective prototyping is possible. However, for services with a strong customer integration and less standardised processes, e.g. a doctor's visit or management consulting experience, prototyping is difficult. In these cases the service differs markedly depending on the single customer regarding service quality, but also regarding length and complexity of the service process. Because of the individuality of customer behaviour the service process also cannot be standardised in such a manner that an objective prototype could be designed.

Because of the heterogeneity of services the use of prototypes in the service sector is heterogeneous, too. Therefore, different *forms of prototypes* can be distinguished. The type of service determines the type of prototype which is adequate and might be applied for service testing. Four forms of service prototype can be differentiated according to the degree of service realisation and the integration of customers in the prototyping[9] (see Figure 5.10).

Prototype 1 is the realisation of the service process and the integration of real customers, i.e. the real conducting of an initial batch. Not only are the material service components constructed, but the whole process is conducted. One example is the recording and broadcasting of the first echelon of a TV series, partly including a viewer poll regarding the continuation of the series. Another example is a free first finance consultation.

Prototype 2 also integrates real customers, but the service process is only simulated. Simulation means that there is no real service result, only the designed processes are simulated. This prototype is applied in industries with high individualised services and high investments in the service factors (e.g. buildings or highly qualified employees), for example insurance services.

Prototype 3 realises an initial batch, but without real customers. This is often the case for automated or at least standardised services with low process variations with regard to the customer. Examples are the development of teller machines,

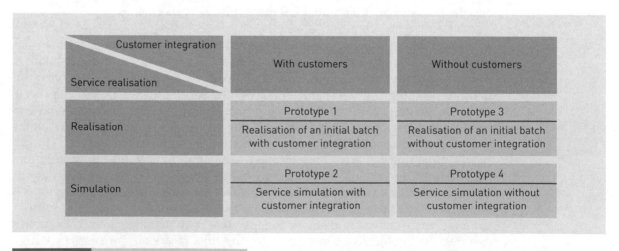

Customer integration Service realisation	With customers	Without customers
Realisation	**Prototype 1** Realisation of an initial batch with customer integration	**Prototype 3** Realisation of an initial batch without customer integration
Simulation	**Prototype 2** Service simulation with customer integration	**Prototype 4** Service simulation without customer integration

FIGURE 5.10   Forms of service prototyping

Source: adapted from Bruhn 2003, p. 251.

online-banking software or the outfitting of a new fast food chain. Although these prototypes are often applied without real customers it might make sense to include customers in the testing at a certain stage, because of the relevance of the customer's perception with regard to the success of the new service.

Prototype 4 simulates service processes without real customers. This type is adequate for services with a high proportion of autonomous processes and high mandatory investments in the service factors. For example, a logistic or transportation provider cannot prototype the whole car pool and route system. But that is not necessary. The 100th truck would load as much and drive as fast as the first one. And with the respective software, different routes can be simulated. Especially in the case of the logistics provider, the customer requirements concern speed and security – factors which are relatively objective and therefore can be tested without real customers.

Regarding the *success of service innovations* Martin and Horne[10] asked service providers from several service industries for the main success drivers for service innovations. From the perspective of the respondents there are two major success drivers:

- *Degree of formality*. This factor concerns the methods used when planning an innovation. Is there a systematic approach regarding the development of new services? Unsurprisingly, a high degree of formalisation results in more successful innovations. However, on the other end of the scale, no formalisation at all also leads to successful new services. This can be interpreted in two ways: first, the reason for the success might be the creativity of the service inventors which is not affected by rules and processes. Secondly, with no formalisation there are probably no assessments of the success of the new services. Consequently, the subjective view of the respondents might be a wrong self-assessment.

- *Relation to the core service*. New services which have a close relation to the core service, e.g. service modifications or service line extensions, are more likely to be successful. Of course the greatest innovations are new-to-the-market innovations, but for those there is also a high failure rate. In contrast, for new services with relations to the core service, internally there are fewer investments in new facilities and competencies necessary, and, externally the customer knows the competencies of the provider and trusts in the transfer of the provider's knowledge to the new services.

Service modification

Why would a service provider intend to modify its services? The reasons for a **service modification** are numerous:

- One reason might be that market research identified changes in consumer behaviour which indicate necessary changes in the services.

- Furthermore, complaints by customers can indicate that certain changes in a service – maybe at least for certain customer groups – are essential for future success.

- These research results might indicate that the provider serves different customer groups with different needs resulting in the definition of several customer segments and a respective service differentiation. For example, a restaurant might discover that certain customers stay at home when a sports event is on television. Consequently, it will also offer home deliveries.

How to vary a service? There are several *options for a service modification*, such as offering value-added services, service bundling, externalisation/internalisation as well as automation.

Offering (removing) value-added services. One way to vary an existing service or service package is to add (or remove) value-added services. There can be several reasons for a service modification by means of value-added services. First, it might be that certain segments have higher requirements, e.g. regarding the convenience of the service. Or other segments are not willing to pay for existing value-added services. Then certain services should be added or removed. Secondly, value-added services can be used as a competitive advantage. For example, the invention of the frequent traveller and business lounges by Lufthansa modified their service by embellishing the waiting time of its passengers before or between flights. From the perspective of the inventor's competitors, in many cases, they have to follow the inventor in order to keep their position in the market. Thus, from their perspective, the introduction of a value-added service by a competitor is a reason for their own intention also to introduce the value-added service. Thirdly, in some cases, certain services are offered implicitly. By defining them as value-added services the service provider can price them and thus increase the service's profitability. One example of this procedure is the invention of call centres by banks. Before the invention of call centres, the customer called the bank adviser at standard cost. By inventing a call centre and labelling it as a value-added service, some banks charge their customers for using this service via the telecommunications provider. How should a provider proceed when looking for value-added services in order to vary the existing service? In the paragraph about supplementary services we discussed several potential value-added services. Depending on the industry and the current definition of the service, a provider can go through the list of potential value-added services. Then, the provider should check at which stages of the service process the service should tie in with. Finally, it has to be decided whether the service should be chargeable or not.

Service bundling. Another way to vary a service is to bundle the focal service with one or more other core services or value-added services. Examples for service bundles are the breakfast which is included in the price of a hotel stay, a conference package which includes attendance, materials and hotel stay or also a theatre subscription. Thus, several services are linked together in a service package which is often marketed as a package (e.g. package holiday). Often, service bundling is closely linked to price bundling (see Chapter 6), especially in the communication towards the customer. Why do service providers bundle their services? One of the main reasons for service bundling is to realise customer potentials, i.e. to cross-sell services to existing customers. For example, in the case of the hotel breakfast, without the bundling customers might breakfast at another place. Even though bundling often goes hand in hand with a price reduction, in most cases it is profitable for the provider because of the volume effect. Regarding bundling there are three types of offer:

- *Unbundling* means marketing the core service including mandatory services and the value-added service separately. This strategy is especially valid when the value-added services have a good market position and can create a demand on their own.

- In the case of *pure bundling*, all value-added services are included in the offer. A typical example of this strategy are all-inclusive offers by restaurants or tour operators.

- Finally, *mixed bundling* means giving the customer the opportunity to choose between core service and certain service bundles. In this case, the customer can decide whether to purchase the core service only or the bundle. Here, the danger exists that only those customers who are interested in the value-added services purchase the bundle. In some cases, this effect would be realised with an unbundled offer, but without the price discount to the value-added service buyers.

Externalisation and internalisation. For all services, we know that the integration of the external factor, i.e. the customer or objects connected with the customer are necessary to produce the service. But why should the degree of integration be fixed for any service? When we think about restaurants, we automatically think of a place where we go, take a seat, order, get served, etc. But one day, someone questioned why people had to be served. When they serve themselves, they can be offered a cheaper price. The service idea of cafeterias was born. This simple restaurant example explains the internalisation and externalisation strategies to modify a services (see Figure 5.11).

Internalisation means that the provider inherits activities that are normally conducted by the customer.[11] One example is a garage picking-up the car to be repaired so that the customer does not have to take the car to the garage. We see that internalisation is connected with higher convenience for the customer – the use of the service is easier for them. This strategy can result in higher loyalty as well as higher sales and profits.

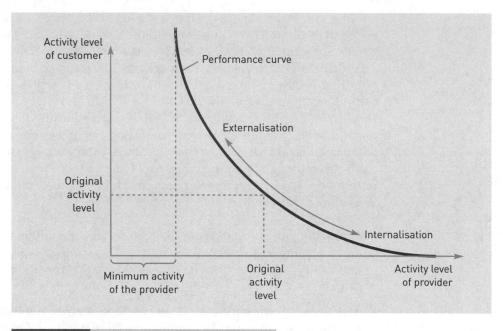

| FIGURE 5.11 | Externalisation and internalisation |

Source: Corsten 2001.

Externalisation is the process of reducing the activities of the provider and increasing the tasks of the customer within the service process.[12] One objective of externalisation might be cost and price reduction, like in the case of cafeterias or low-budget airlines which externalise the catering services by not offering food and refreshments by themselves. Services marketing in action 5.10 illustrates how the low-budget airline easyJet applies this strategy. However, externalisation is also the basis for individualising services. By involving the customer more strongly in the service production, and giving the customer a more active role as co-producer and/or prosumer, a customisation of the service is realised. An externalisation in this sense is for example the development of structured refinancing instruments in the investment banking sector where client companies define exactly their needs regarding financing, and the banks develop the respective instrument.

Automation. We cannot vary a service only by changing the role of the external factor but also by modifying the part of internal factors. A major means for this approach is technology (see also Chapter 8) in order to automate certain service processes. A classic example of service automation are bank teller machines. Certain activities of human beings, in this case activities of the bank employees are substituted by machine activities, i.e. activities of the teller machine. Automation can be applied when the external factor is a human being (e.g. electronic directory assistance) or an object (e.g. car washing machine). It is important

SERVICES MARKETING IN ACTION 5.10:

easyJet: Focus on price via externalisation

At easyJet, our philosophy is that 'there's no such thing as a free lunch' – so we don't offer one! 'Free' onboard meals add to the overall cost of a seat – and we believe that our passengers would prefer to forgo a tray of plastic airline food in order to save money on their fare.

Instead, passengers who want a drink or snack can purchase refreshments through our onboard easyKiosk from a selection of hot and cold drinks, alcoholic beverages, snacks and confectionery.

We also offer a wide selection of top fragrances and cosmetics, as well as an exciting range of gifts and gadgets – all at great value prices. You can pay in cash in pounds sterling, euros (minimum denomination of one euro) or Swiss francs (minimum denomination of one franc). Credit cards are also accepted onboard.

To help our cabin crew serve you quickly and efficiently, please try to have the correct change available for your purchase.

Source: easyJet 2004.

to notice that the decision is not between automated or unautomated. There are rather several stages of automation depending on the focal service. For the car washing example, note that using a sprinkler instead of a bucket and sponge is already a first step of automation, while the full automated washing and drying of the car might be the last step of automation.

Service elimination

As the lifecycle idea in this chapter indicates, it might make sense for service providers to eliminate certain services from the service programme, by not offering them any more to the market. There can be situations where *eliminating a service* from the programme is the best, i.e. most economic, decision to take. What might be reasons for eliminating a service?

There are generally two groups of reasons. The first group are *quantitative reasons*. When the service no longer pays, i.e. is not profitable, it might be the right decision to take it out of the programme. Quantitative indicators for a service elimination are decreasing sales, low or decreasing sales proportionate to the total sales or decreasing cash flows or contribution margins. The second group of criteria are *qualitative criteria*, like a negative influence of the service on the overall image of the firm, a change in the legal situation, changes in the customer's need structure or introduction of better new services by competitors. Regarding the general market situation, Singapore Airlines (SIA) needed to decide whether to cancel the implementation of its lie-flat seats in business class after the effects of the global recession on the travel industry in September 2001. SIA was considered the gold standard for its innovative customer service, and the US $100 million new seats project was planned to bolster that reputation. But with increased competition in the airline industry and the dramatic drop in travel after the 11 September terrorist attacks in the United States, the main agenda item for the airline was how to cut costs.[13] In addition, Services marketing in action 5.11 shows how financial service providers proceed with product eliminations.

SERVICES MARKETING IN ACTION 5.11:

Product elimination by financial service providers

In the financial services industry, there are different elimination strategies for financial service products[14] which can be grouped into two categories: partial elimination where only certain service components are eliminated and full elimination where a core service is eliminated completely (see Figure 5.12).

Financial service elimination strategies		
Partial elimination	Make a product a closed issue	Cease sales to new customers, maintain unchanged for existing users
	Withdraw features	As above plus remove product features, e.g. credit interest on a current account
	Drop product from sales; use name for new offering	Remove existing version from sales (leaving current user unaffected), launch new offering with same name but different features
	Amalgamate similar products under new name or existing name	Identify products with similar terms and conditions that can be easily amalgamated to simplify management effort, reduce operating cost, e.g. basic savings accounts
Full elimination	Core product elimination	Close down a whole product line, e.g. motor cycle insurance either by non-renewal or by selling to competitor
	Customer elimination	Cease relationship with customers by non-renewal or offering at end of consumption period, or terminating production

Figure 5.12 Financial service elimination strategies
Source: Harness 2003.

Generally, the activities needed in order to eliminate a financial service can be structured according to a four-stage process. The four stages are:[15]

1. Identification stage

In this stage, there is an initiating event which is the starting point of the elimination process. There are several event categories of which product performance-led and strategic-led events are the most important (see Table 5.3).

TABLE 5.3   Elimination reasons of financial service providers

Elimination reasons	% of respondents
Product performance led (poor sales performance, product becoming obsolete)	25
Strategic led (implementing strategic change, merging organisations together)	18
Customer led (poor fit to customer's need, large-scale account dormancy)	14
Cost control led (product unprofitable due to high cost base, too many products in portfolio)	10
Information technology led (inability to adapt to new IT system, incompatibility of new delivery systems)	9
Operational led (entry into new markets, rationalisation of existing delivery systems)	9
Personnel led (product too complex to sell, regulatory controls on who can sell)	8
Externally led (change in regulatory controlled industries, new players enter the market)	7

N = 101 retail banks, building societies and retail insurance organisations

Source: based on Harness 2003.

▶

2. Decision stage

After the decision for an elimination has been made, it must be checked whether there exist elimination barriers. For example, how might the customer react to the elimination? Depending on the existence of barriers, there are three possible decisions: first, in the case of no barriers, a full elimination strategy can be followed. Secondly, if the company cares about satisfaction, loyalty or image and in the event that the elimination of a service might affect these constructs, then a partial elimination in the sense of a gradual removal is recommended. Thirdly, if there are long-term barriers for an elimination, a partial elimination in the sense of maintaining production and support liability is the best alternative.

3. Implementation stage

Once the decision regarding the elimination strategy has been taken and possible barriers detected, the strategy must be realised, and a possible way to operationalise the respective strategy must be selected.

4. Post-elimination evaluation stage

The success of the elimination strategy should be examined. First, it should be tested whether the determined elimination objectives, such as timescale, financial budget, customers kept, have been realised. Secondly, it should be examined whether the elimination improved the performance of other services, segments and/or the whole organisation.

Source: Harness 2003.

But even if one of these reasons might call for an elimination of a service there might be some barriers against an elimination. For example, the service elimination might have negative image effects, or there might be synergy or cross-selling effects of the existing service. Furthermore, the service might be necessary for providing other services in the programme or there might be social reasons.

Summarising the decisions of a service provider within the service product lifecycle, Services marketing in action 5.12 visualises different stages of satellite telephones within the service product lifecycle.

SERVICES MARKETING IN ACTION 5.12:

Time-lapse of the Iridium story

Iridium is a consortium that produces and offers satellite telephones. These telephones can be used anywhere in the world. Respectively, the prices of the instruments are enormous. Consequently, the attempt of Irridium to market its product as a mass product did not succeed. Read the following Irridium headlines that trace the ups and downs of Irridium through the service product lifecycle.

08/11/1997: New satellites to revolutionise communications
A new chapter in the telecommunications revolution comes closer on Saturday, with the launch of five satellites from California.

13/08/1999 Phones firm files for bankruptcy
Troubled phones firm Iridium has turned to bankruptcy laws after defaulting on huge loans.

14/10/1999: New satellite phone launched
Despite the failure of Iridium, another global telecommunications company is set to launch its satellite phone service, as Richard Quest reports from Geneva.

18/03/2000: Flaming end for satellites
Bankrupt US phone firm Iridium is to send 66 satellites worth $6bn out of orbit to burn up in the Earth's atmosphere.

28/03/2001: Iridium satellite phone relaunch
The infamous US satellite phone company relaunches as a niche operator after new owners saved its satellites from destruction.

Source: BBC 2004.

Summary

Summing up this chapter, the following conclusions can be drawn (see Figure 5.13):

1. Customers' decisions regarding the use of services of a certain provider depend on the perceived value they attribute to the service. This service value is composed of a benefit and a cost component. The direct benefit component represents the service product, i.e. the services that are actually delivered by the provider.

2. The service product consists of three levels: the core service, supplementary services and the integration of these into an overall service programme. All three levels have different impacts on value creation by a service provider. The core service is a major driver of customer's buying decisions, yet it often represents the USP of a provider. When the core service is unsatisfactory and deficient, customers will choose another provider. The supplementary services are discriminating factors in markets with intense competition, and the breadth of a service programme influences, for example, the possibility of realising cross-selling opportunities.

3. The core service of a service affects many other Service Value Chain elements, e.g. the service process.

4. There are different types of supplementary services: regarding their mandatory existence, there are mandatory and value-added services; regarding the stages of the service process, there are pre-process, in-process and post-process services; and regarding the service function there are integration-related, communicative and contract-related services.

5. A special type of core and supplementary services are e-services that represent complementary services in many industries.

6. The service programme structures core and supplementary services. A distinctive element of a service programme is its comprehensiveness. There are advantages (risk distribution, cost synergies, etc.) and disadvantages (higher complexity, negative side effects, etc.) of comprehensive service programmes.

7. Core services as well as supplementary services run through a so-called service product lifecycle. According to this concept, three service product decisions are differentiated: service innovations, modifications and eliminations.

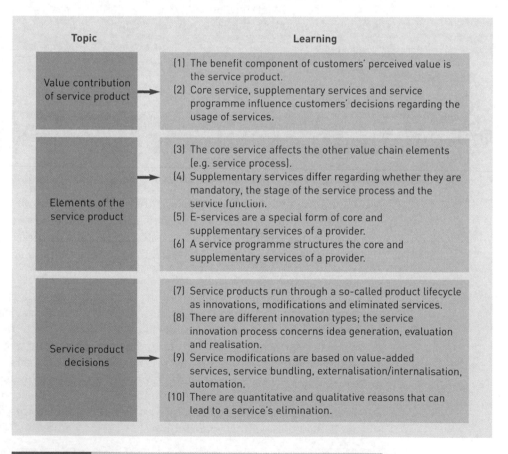

Topic	Learning
Value contribution of service product	(1) The benefit component of customers' perceived value is the service product. (2) Core service, supplementary services and service programme influence customers' decisions regarding the usage of services.
Elements of the service product	(3) The core service affects the other value chain elements (e.g. service process). (4) Supplementary services differ regarding whether they are mandatory, the stage of the service process and the service function. (5) E-services are a special form of core and supplementary services of a provider. (6) A service programme structures the core and supplementary services of a provider.
Service product decisions	(7) Service products run through a so-called product lifecycle as innovations, modifications and eliminated services. (8) There are different innovation types; the service innovation process concerns idea generation, evaluation and realisation. (9) Service modifications are based on value-added services, service bundling, externalisation/internalisation, automation. (10) There are quantitative and qualitative reasons that can lead to a service's elimination.

FIGURE 5.13   Learning summary for Chapter 5

8. There are new-to-the-market versus new-to-the-firm innovations, service process versus service product innovations, service line extensions versus service line innovations, technology-push innovations versus market-pull innovations and service modifications versus service inventions. Service innovations should be planned according to an innovation process which consists of idea generation, evaluation and realisation activities. The service innovation process can be improved by service blueprinting, involving the employees' knowledge in the innovation process as well as using service prototypes.

9. Service modifications are conducted by offering value-added services, service bundling, externalisation/internalisation and automation.

10. Finally, for certain reasons (e.g. a service becomes unprofitable), services are eliminated from the service programme.

Knowledge questions

1. What are the value contributions of the service product? Differentiate the contribution effects according to the core service, supplementary services and the service programme.

2. Define what is the core service and explain its relevance for the Service Value Chain.

3. How are supplementary services defined and what types of supplementary services can be differentiated?

4. Explain the reasons for the different relevance of core and supplementary services.

5. How can e-services be distinguished from 'traditional' services?

6. How is a service programme generally structured?

7. What are the reasons for and against a broad service programme?

8. What types of service innovations can be distinguished? What types promise to be most successful and why?

9. Explain the stages of the service innovation process. Which activities are special due to the characteristics of a service?

10. How can a service be modified?

11. What are the reasons for eliminating a service?

Application and discussion questions

1. What are the core services of a bank, a bakery, a copy shop, a cinema, a football club or a café?

2. What supplementary services are offered by a bank, a bakery, a copy shop, a cinema, a football club and a café? Use examples from your own experience. How do these supplementary services contribute to the value creation of these firms?

3. Imagine you opened a bookshop at your university's campus. Which supplementary services would you offer and why?

4. Collect examples for facilitating and value-added services for a car repair.

5. Collect examples for pre-, in- and post-process services of a hotel.

6. In what situations can you imagine supplementary services being more important for you than the core service and vice versa? Try to derive the underlying reasons for that.

7. List examples of e-services you frequently use.

8. How is the service programme of your mobile operator defined? What are the underlying reasons for the definition of the service programme?

9. Describe the service programme of a fitness club you know of. How could the service programme be changed to enhance value?

10. Which service innovations have you used recently? Classify these into types of service innovations.

11. Recall service modifications you perceived recently and classify them into the options of service modifications.

12. Which services you have used in the past have been eliminated? Can you imagine why?

CASE STUDY: RECREATIONAL EQUIPMENT (REI): THE GREATEST SHOP IN THE WORLD

The REI flagship store in Denver/Colorado (USA) is not comparable to normal sports retailing stores. Sunny daylight, gentle music, splashing water and everywhere the murmuring of impressed customers. REI was founded as a co-operative 65 years ago by Lloyd and Mary Anderson in order to sell mountain and hiking equipment of high quality at low prices. Today, REI has 2 million members, a multiply-awarded website as well as 63 stores worldwide.

The core service of REI, according to Bob Voltz, store manager at the flagship store in Denver, is to 'sell our customers exactly the product that they really need. For example, we want to assure that the shoes really fit and do not hurt the wearer, either at the ascent or at the descent. We want to ensure that the sleeping bag fulfils the requirements and the tent is the right size.'

In order to deliver that core service, REI offers uncommon value-added services. First of all, clients are invited to test every product before they decide to purchase something. At the REI stores, there are hiking trails of different lengths with ascents and descents. 'Some people walk around here for half an hour. And that's good because they are not supposed to get blisters.' Tents are presented set up. Where a client is interested in a different model, it is set up quickly. 'The people are supposed to know exactly how it feels inside the tent.' Also, the sleeping bags are tested at the store, directly in the tent. And when a journey in colder climes is planned, customers can test the outfit in the cold room that is adjusted to −17 degrees celsius, mostly, but can be turned down to −30 degrees. 'Who knows anyhow how 17 degrees feels?' Voltz asks rhetorically. 'Only in the cold room can inexperienced customers decide which article is suitable for them.' And what are the sandbags in the backpack department good for? Voltz grins: 'Most people don't take an empty backpack on their tour. We deliver pounds here. What feels comfortable in the store can press heavily when loaded.'

A second group of value-added services concerns consulting. At the 'Outdoor Resources Center', there are experienced employees who answer the customers questions regarding the planning of outdoor trips. These employees know the terrain in the environment very well, have ready maps of trails, and in this way can give some good tips. A third field of value-added services is the organisation of journeys by REI themselves, principally the more exotic journeys, e.g. to South America or Asia.

Next to these relatively standardised services, REI has the philosophy of standing by their customers in any situation. 'I remember a group of young people who went for a biking trip', Voltz says, 'at some point, they changed plans and switched to a car. Shortly later, they changed to an airplane. There was only one problem: for this part of the trip, the group needed a camping stove. They called the next REI store, and the manager sent an employee with the desired equipment to the next airport.'

Inevitably, these service offers demand the respective service resources. The heart of the store in Denver is a 15-metre climbing wall with four different climbing routes of different degrees of difficulty. This 'Climbing Pinnacle' is directly under the glass roof of the store and is astonishingly authentic during daylight. At night, when it becomes darker outside, an electronically operated light machine inconspicuously compensates for the declining daylight. On the other side of the hall, there is a waterfall with stones that is used to test water filters just as in 'the great outdoors.'

Also, the core service determines the service process. At REI, customers are more involved than in other sports equipment stores. 'Our customers can touch, lift and test everything.' It is normal for teenagers to drive past on 900-dollar mountain bikes in order to do some testing on the test track. 'When something breaks, we repair it. But in most cases, nothing happens. Our customers mostly treat the products with the greatest respect, and during short test rides, not even the tires become dirty.'

REI's strategy is not only successful in terms of growth, their success can also be perceived from the statements from satisfied customers, such as 'That is the greatest store in the world.' Meanwhile, the flagship store has become a tourist attraction – even travel groups from Australia visit.

Source: Howe 2003.

Notes

1. In the literature, a categorisation into 'core', 'supplementary', 'peripheral' and 'augumented' services is often made. In this text, we make the central distinction between core and supplementary services by merging all non-core services under the expression of supplementary services. We leave it with this more aggregated distinction because it depends on service type, situation and other factors whether a certain service is, for example, a supplementary or peripheral service according to the categories mentioned above. Later in the chapter, we present several types of supplementary services when, for example, value-added services will also be discussed.

2. See Keaveney 1995.

3. There are various categorisations of supplementary services in the literature. Lovelock and Wirtz (2004) for example differentiate facilitating services (information, order taking, billing, payment) and enhancing services (e.g. consultation, hospitality, safekeeping, exceptions).

4. See Royal Bank of Scotland 2004.

5. See Iacobucci and Ostrom 1993.

6. See Avlonitis *et al.* 2001.

7. See Scheuing and Johnson 1989; Alam and Perry 2002.

8. See Shostack 1984.

9. See Bruhn 2003.

10. See Martin and Horne 1993.

11. See Corsten 2001.

12. See Corsten 2001.

13. See Harvard Business School 2004.

14. See Harness 2003.

15. See Harness 2003.

6 Defining the cost part of service value: Service pricing

While the service product represents the benefit part of service value perceived by the customer, the price paid for usage is the cost part. As customers balance the service received and the price paid, in most cases the value delivered by a service decreases with the price paid.[1] A restaurant that sets high menu prices is measured against this price level.

From a service firm's perspective, price is – next to sales – the second revenue component, i.e. a direct factor influencing value. For developing and providing a service, costs arise for the service provider which are supposed to be compensated for by the price paid by the customer. However, service providers cannot set prices based solely on their cost. Excessively high prices reduce the perceived value, customers may decide against using the services of the respective provider. Therefore the customer's willingness to pay is often a further determinant of a firm's price setting.

In many service industries, the willingness to pay is not equal for all customers. There are always customers who are willing to pay a higher price and customers who are willing only to pay a lower price.[2] This fact complicates service pricing, it gives the service provider the opportunity to exploit the willingness to pay on different levels. For example, by differentiating a first, business and coach class, airlines exploit the higher willingness to pay by first and business class passengers.

Based on these considerations, this chapter focuses on the following learning objectives (see Figure 6.1):

1. Understanding the value effects of service price, i.e. how the service price leads to economic success for the provider.

2. Learning different approaches of how service prices are determined.

3. Getting to know the strategic pricing options of a service provider applying a price discrimination, i.e. applying different prices according to various criteria, such as the age of the customer or the year's season.

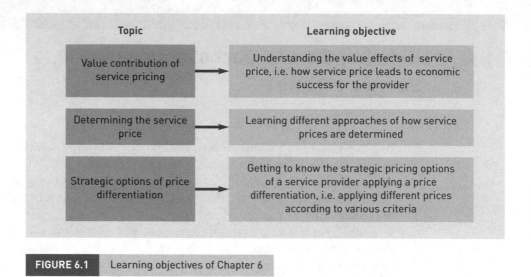

Topic	Learning objective
Value contribution of service pricing	Understanding the value effects of service price, i.e. how service price leads to economic success for the provider
Determining the service price	Learning different approaches of how service prices are determined
Strategic options of price differentiation	Getting to know the strategic pricing options of a service provider applying a price differentiation, i.e. applying different prices according to various criteria

FIGURE 6.1   Learning objectives of Chapter 6

Value contribution of pricing

Since the price for a service is a component of a service provider's revenues (with revenues being a major component of value; see Chapters 1 and 2), it, first, has a *direct effect* on the value of the service provider. Assuming constant sales, which is often not realistic, a higher price results in increased revenues. Take a football club that sells tickets for £10 each and has a full stadium of 30,000 visitors per match; the revenue would then amount to £300,000 per match. Imagine that the club increases the price by 50 per cent to £15. Nevertheless, the club can keep the stadium full. Even though there are some people who would not purchase a ticket for £15, there are still 30,000 tickets sold resulting in increased revenue of £450,000 per match because there were many people before who did not get tickets due to the high demand. Raising the price yielded a 50 per cent revenue increase, thus the price directly increased value. However, in this case the assumption existed that the sales were not affected by the price. In many situations, however, there is – according to the demand function – a negative correlation between price and sales. For example, many airline passengers would only purchase airline tickets at a low-fare level. Regarding the direct value effect of pricing it was shown in an empirical study with more than 2,000 firms that a price change of 1 per cent induces a profit change of 11.1 per cent.[3]

Next to this direct effect, service price has a second, *indirect effect* on value. This is effective via the price's influences on customer behaviour and thereby on value. More specifically, there are three functions the price can take as a determinant of customer behaviour:

- First, price can have the role of a *quality indicator*. For the customer, price is a signal for the quality level of the service. A high price signals a high quality level, while a low price signals a low quality level. For example, a package holiday for £3,000 promises to include better hotels, etc. than a package holiday of the same length to the same destination for a price of £300. Also, low-fare flights are often perceived as less secure than flights at a higher fare. Although price can be a quality signal in consumer goods markets, such as fashion, its role as a quality indicator for services is especially important. Services, due to their intangibility and heterogeneity, are more difficult to evaluate than many tangible products, and therefore customers are looking for quality indicators such as price, in order to estimate the quality level of a service.

- Secondly, the price can represent a *purchasing trigger*. This is almost valid only for low prices, and especially for prices which are low for a certain period of time, such as special offers. For the period of the special offer, new demand can be generated because of the attractive price. For example, the German railway company Deutsche Bahn offered for one month trips through Germany for 29 euros (instead of up to about 100 euros at the standard price) during its 'November–Summer' – campaign. Other examples are the acquisition offers by internet providers, with the offer of a free modem. In these cases, the price directly influences purchases by the potential or current customers.

- Thirdly, as mentioned above, there is a *reciprocal relationship between price and sales*. The higher the price, the lower the sales and vice versa. This logic according to the demand function is a generalisation of the price's role as a purchasing trigger, without a time period specification. Together with the direct effect on revenues, there is an ambiguous effect of price on revenue with respect to value. Therefore, one task of service pricing is to determine 'optimal' prices where the resulting revenues are highest. Interestingly, optimal prices vary in different market segments. In every market, there are niches of customers who have special expectations and requirements but may also have a higher willingness to pay, e.g. private banking customers, first-class aeroplane passengers. On the other hand, there are customers with lower expectations who consequently demand lower cost service processes. However, these customers also have a lower willingness to pay. An example of a low-cost niche segment, is the low-fare airline carrier. By dividing the markets according to the consumer segments' optimal prices, service providers are able to exploit the respective segment's willingness to pay.

These value effects can be specified when analysing the connections between service pricing and *other elements of the Service Value Chain*. Regarding the two primary processes, there is primarily a connection with the *interaction process*. Interactions with the customer generate cost and therefore are one determinant of service price. The role of internal cost for the determination of service is presented in the section 'Determining service price', the 'inside-out approach'.

However, the price is not only influenced by the interaction process via cost but also affects the interaction process. The price – as a quality signal – influences the customers' expectations regarding the interaction process and consequently the customers' evaluation of the entire interaction process.

In contrast to the inside-out approach, the outside-in approach (see 'Determining service price', the 'outside-in approach') reviews the external conditions, especially the customers' willingness to pay which is influenced by the customer's evaluation of the service. Behind this logic is the price's role as the *return for the service product* the customer receives, and – as per the customer's perspective – the value the customer attributes to the service received. Depending on the type of service received and the respective interaction process, the customer is willing to pay more or less for a service.

Reflecting upon the two primary processes, the service price is also connected to the *relationship process*. The relationship process aims at managing the customers' behaviour within the relationship to the provider. As explained above, the service price is an important driver of the customer's behaviour. More specifically, in order to recruit and retain customers, the price either takes on the role as a quality signal or a purchasing trigger. To expand the relationship, strategies used to increase the customer's purchasing frequency or 'share of wallet', pricing might be relevant in the form of volume rebates (see the section 'price discrimination'). The price is often used as a regain offer. For example, the German mobile operator Cellway offers customers who do not renew their contract a 20 per cent discount on all rates when they re-sign the contract.

Furthermore, the *service resources*, employees and technology, are important drivers of the cost for producing a service. Therefore, they play a crucial role for a cost-oriented view on service pricing (see section 'Determining service price'/' inside-out approach'). As far as resources are concerned, service price is an important driver for managing service capacities (see Chapter 10). In the football example at the beginning of this section there was greater demand than capacity. Therefore, the club could raise the price and still have the stadium full. However, often there are under-utilised resources, such as flights at certain times that the airlines attempt to fill via pricing strategies.

In order to realise the value contribution options of service pricing via the Service Value Chain, service providers take various decisions regarding the service price. There are several options available in the determination of the price for a service.

Determining service price

When service providers decide on the prices for their services, they consider certain factors that lead to higher or lower prices.[4] These factors can be inside the firm, costs for producing a service, or outside the firm, the customer's willingness to pay. Accordingly, two general categories of methods to determine service prices can be differentiated: inside-out approaches as well as outside-in approaches. Both have their advantages, furthermore there are approaches that combine both methodologies.

Inside-out approach

From an inside-out perspective, the firm's expectations of what payment it should receive from the customers for its services determines the prices that are fixed by the company. Companies are profit-oriented, and the price is an important element of the revenues that face the cost of producing and delivering a service. Consequently, these costs are an important factor within the inside-out approach of price determination.

The *traditional cost-oriented approach* calculates the price by adding a targeted profit premium to the measured cost.[5] An important component of price according to this approach is the cost of a service. In order to calculate these costs, based upon total costing, a firm would divide its total cost by the service units produced. Typically, using this procedure, some costs are allocated randomly over the different units, such as the cost for senior management that is responsible for all products. On a more detailed level, there are several service-specific problems that can be observed for this method.

The first category of problems concerns the *cost association* to specific service units. When a service provider offers a range, and maybe a diverse variety of single services, then an *association of the total cost across services* is problematic. Take the client adviser at a bank that offers a variety of services, among others loans and investments. The adviser spends more time with the loan product than with the investment product. To produce and deliver the loan, the adviser must evaluate the customer's solvency, determine the interest rate, work in co-operation with a central loan unit within the bank and control the customer's payments during the loan duration. In contrast, with the investment product, the adviser invests almost no time or effort apart from the initial detailing of the aspects of the investment, such as the interest rate and associated benefits. Consequently, the service charges associated with the selling of the loan product cannot be valued with the same average cost as the investment product. A solution for this problem is that banks or service providers generally calculate the typical cost of a product category, based on the expenditure of time, and divide the total cost according to various distribution methodologies to determine an average cost.

Another problem regarding the cost association methodology is that many parts of the service providers' costs do not directly concern service production and delivery, for example the advertising costs for customer acquisition or the cost of the customer loyalty programmes. These costs concern the *customer relationship* – and are caused by activities of the relationship process within the Service Value Chain – and therefore only indirectly the product, especially the sales of the service products. However, these costs do not vary with the number of service units produced and sold but vary with the number of customers of the firm. Even for service production and delivery cost it is difficult in some cases to attribute a cost component to single services. An example are the sunk costs that are incurred in some service industries. These costs, such as research and development costs, would have to be attributed over an indeterminable number of service units over an indeterminable number of years, e.g. the cost of new tracks for the railway system of a railway provider or for the development of a network for a telecommunications provider.

Furthermore, *service production costs vary across customers*. Due to the customer's integration into the service production process and because of the heterogeneity of customers in many service industries, one unit of the same service can vary greatly. In a restaurant, servicing a customer with special wishes who returns half of the meals because of problems is more expensive than servicing an uncomplicated guest. For medical services, treating a patient who can express problems and is willing to co-operate generates less cost than treating a patient who is difficult to diagnose and who is not willing to adhere to advice. Costs can also vary for the same customer and the same service. Especially for services where the customer's involvement is important to produce the service, the mood or motivation of the customer can influence the cost of delivering a service. But, there are also criteria that affect the service cost for one and the same customer and that can be generalised. One of these criteria is the stage of the customer relationship lifecycle. At the beginning of a customer relationship, the customer has less experience with the service provider, its services and its employees, resulting in longer and more expensive interactions with new customers.

Next to the cost association, another problem concerns the *determination of a single service unit*. For many services, a *service unit* is difficult to define because of the heterogeneous and ambiguous character of the respective service. A service that is easy to define is a bank transaction or an airline flight. In these cases, the outcome of the service can be defined and thus the service itself is defined by this outcome. However, for a language course, the outcome is not clearly defined. Therefore, for language courses, time is the unit of measure used to define the service cost.

Many services are not produced in such a way that the *number of service units* can be counted or at least forecast. One reason is that service providers do not supply a certain quantity but provide service potentials, and the service itself is produced together with the customer. For example, a hotel provides a certain number of rooms. However, whether the service is produced depends on whether a customer reserves a hotel room or not. For an airline, the service unit is also difficult to determine. Is it the flight itself? If so its these costs cannot be used to determine the price of a single aeroplane ticket. Is it the number of seats in the plane? Or is it the number of seats sold for a certain flight? The first option would not cover costs, especially if all tickets were not sold, and the second option is difficult to forecast. However, in the case of the airline, as for other services, at least there are experiences that can be used for price determination. This is done by price discrimination (see later in this chapter) where the same service is offered at different prices according to certain criteria, e.g. season.

Determining service units as well as associating cost with these service units has two major problems when calculating the service cost as a basis for price determination. Looking at the second component of the price formula, the *profit premium*, further problems arise. Service providers aim at making profits and therefore do not ask for a price that covers the cost but charge a price that generates profits. Therefore, a profit premium is added to the calculated cost. Here, the question is what premium should be added because this premium decides upon the survival of the firm against its competition. When the profit premium is too high, then the firm might not attract enough customers to ensure profitability. When the price and profit premium are too low it might be difficult to be profitable.

A good example of the difficulties of a cost-oriented pricing approach is the price determination for bank transfers, as can be seen in Services marketing in action 6.1. Interestingly, despite the problems of cost-oriented pricing, in services marketing practice this approach is relatively common.[6]

SERVICES MARKETING IN ACTION 6.1:

UK banks' pricing practices for current account and payments services

Previously, banks implicitly charged their current account users for overdrafts and loans, service charges via the adjustment of the interest rates that the customer was paid for deposits. Today, account charges and service payments are charged explicitly, individually and directly. The implicit and explicit forms of pricing apply to three general pricing strategies in banking:

1. 'Disneyworld pricing', i.e. the imposition of a flat (e.g. quarterly) charge irrespective of the use of the account with no additional transaction charges;

2. single transactions charges which cover fixed and variable costs;

3. two-part tariffs with a fixed flat charge (irrespective of the use of the account) plus transaction charges.

All three strategies can take an explicit or implicit form (see Figure 6.2).

Although British banks apply a wide range of charges, since 1985 the norm has been for no explicit transactional charges on current accounts provided that they remain in credit. In addition, competitive pressures have forced banks to pay interest on a larger proportion of deposits (including current accounts) and the general policy is for a tiered structure of interest rates to be applied. Thus, small balances carry a higher rate of interest. This is a form of implicit charging for current account services. In particular, many current account services are offered free of

▶

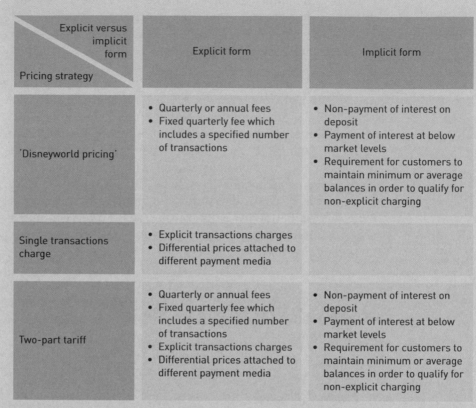

Explicit versus implicit form / Pricing strategy	Explicit form	Implicit form
'Disneyworld pricing'	• Quarterly or annual fees • Fixed quarterly fee which includes a specified number of transactions	• Non-payment of interest on deposit • Payment of interest at below market levels • Requirement for customers to maintain minimum or average balances in order to qualify for non-explicit charging
Single transactions charge	• Explicit transactions charges • Differential prices attached to different payment media	
Two-part tariff	• Quarterly or annual fees • Fixed quarterly fee which includes a specified number of transactions • Explicit transactions charges • Differential prices attached to different payment media	• Non-payment of interest on deposit • Payment of interest at below market levels • Requirement for customers to maintain minimum or average balances in order to qualify for non-explicit charging

Figure 6.2 Forms of charges for current account and payments services
Source: adapted from Drake and Llewellyn 1995, p. 4.

charge provided that the account remains in credit: cheque-books are issued without charge, statements are issued without charge, cheque guarantee cards are issued free; there are no explicit payments for cheques, cash withdrawals, standing orders, debit orders, online transactions, etc. However, some services are explicitly charged even when the account is maintained in credit. For instance, stopped cheques are almost invariably charged, as are returned cheques and the request for intermediate statements.

Source: Drake and Llewellyn 1995.

Outside-in approach

The inside-out approach of service costing only covers the costs that are generated by a certain service of the provider. This can be suboptimal in two ways. Either consumers are not willing to pay the prices charged and consequently the sales are too low to be profitable or consumers may be willing to pay a higher price and in this case, the service provider would give away a profit premium without generating more sales.

There are two general options for an *outside-in approach*: the differentiation premium pricing method and methods based on the demand function.

The *differentiation pricing method*[7] is based on the assumption that consumers are willing to pay a higher price for a service when it is clearly differentiated from the competitors' services. When consumers perceive the firm is different to its competitors with regard to specific characteristics, such as price, and evaluate the service better than the competitors' services, then the consumer will be willing to pay higher prices for the services. A hotel that differentiates itself from its competitor – a four-star hotel compared to a competitor with three stars – can demand higher rates. In contrast to the traditional cost approach, the base price is not derived from the service cost but from the competitor's price. Then the service provider that has a differentiation advantage compared to its competitors adds to the competitors' price a differentiation premium, so that its price is higher by the amount that the consumers are willing to pay in excess of the competitors' price because of the competitive advantages of the service. In theory, that sounds straightforward. However, in practice the question is how to calculate the differentiation premium. The basic idea here is that a firm must identify the factors that influence the price premium, what will influence the consumers' willingness to pay a higher price than for the competitors' services. Then these factors can be used in order to calculate the premium.

A second group of methods for an outside-in-pricing method is *based on the demand function* that is known from economics. The demand function explains the relationship between price and sales volume. Normally, these two are correlated negatively. Thus, the demand function explains the phenomenon that when a price is too high, sales might be too low in order to be profitable, and when the price is too low, it is possible to lose profit margins. In economics, the demand function is used in order to derive an optimal price theoretically. For service providers' pricing, an empirical measurement of the demand function can be used in order to determine the services' prices. There are four *approaches* for determining demand function-based service prices:

- expert opinions;
- historical data;
- direct customer survey;
- conjoint measurement.

Expert opinions. Experts evaluate how many service units are sold for alternative prices. The validity of the results depends on the knowledge of the experts regarding the customer needs and willingness to pay as well as the service type.[8] Especially for innovative services where there is no previous experience regarding the price–sales relationship, it will be difficult for experts to estimate the demand function. While this approach is easy to conduct and associated with relatively low cost, the results are subjective. Furthermore, even though the experts are asked to take on the customers' perspective or at least to evaluate the customers' probable behaviour from their own perspective, only an indirect customer perspective is applied.

Historical data. Furthermore, historical data can be used in order to estimate the demand function and determine an optimal service price.[9] Using regression analysis, the relationship between price and sales volume is estimated for a service and can then be used in order to find the price that leads to highest profits. This method has the disadvantage that for new services there is no reliable data regarding the customers' willingness to pay. Further, many service providers keep their prices stable or at least change prices only marginally over the years. Therefore, there are not enough price–sales combinations in order to estimate a demand function.

Direct customer survey. Another option is to ask potential customers directly what price they are willing to pay for a service. By counting how many respondents are willing to purchase a service for a certain price, the demand function can be derived. This method is easy to conduct and low cost. However, for many services, especially with a large proportion of experience and credence qualities, such as medical and legal services, it is difficult for the consumer to estimate the true value of a service and therefore to declare their willingness to pay. The customer might be prepared to hide their true willingness to pay, and by indicating a lower willingness to pay, the respondent might hope to contribute to a lower price for the service.

Conjoint measurement. Service pricing based on conjoint measurement takes into account that the customer's willingness to pay might not be driven by a service as an entity but by the single components or characteristics of the service.[10] For example, when a restaurant customer is primarily interested in quick service regarding his lunch, then a restaurant with quick service is able to charge a higher price than a restaurant with slow service. More specifically, given that the customer really primarily focuses on speed, then the quick service restaurant might be able to ask for a higher price even when its service and food quality may be worse. The conjoint measurement method aims at identifying the service characteristics that drive the customers' willingness to pay. To do so, the respondents are confronted with different combinations of service characteristics, and asked what combination they would prefer. The customers' evaluation and indirectly the customers' willingness to pay regarding specific service characteristics are calculated. Knowing these specific 'values' per characteristic, the price for a certain combination of characteristics that is chosen for the service offered can be calculated. The conjoint measurement method has the advantage that it is able to identify the reasons for the customers' willingness to pay in terms of the service characteristics that drive a service's evaluation and consequently the customers' willingness to pay regarding the service. The example in Services marketing in action 6.2 illustrates how this approach combines evaluations of price and service respectively.

SERVICES MARKETING IN ACTION 6.2:

Pricing for a new recreational centre

The Ashepoo, Combahee and Edisto (ACE) River Basin National Estuarine Research Reserve is one of the largest undeveloped freshwater systems on the east coast of the USA. It covers approximately 450,000 acres and 1,500 species of plants and animals, including several endangered species. In order to increase visitor understanding of the ACE Basin, an interpretative centre is planned. In order to develop the centre, the institution aimed at identifying the key attributes for such a centre and the most preferred feature combinations from the perspective of the visitors as well as determining the optimal admission price. These questions were the object of a conjoint analysis that contained the following three steps:

1. *Attribute identification*. The attributes of the centre were identified by research and review of interpretation literature as well as interviews with state agency representatives associated with the project who provided information regarding public opinion of the proposed facility. The final attribute list included seven attributes with several levels each (see Table 6.1).

2. *Data collection*. Based on the seven attributes, 32 profiles, i.e. combinations of attributes, were developed. The respondents were then asked to evaluate the different profiles on a scale from 1 ('definitely don't prefer') to 7 ('definitely prefer') (see Figure 6.3). A total of 162 subjects were selected at random; 111 answers could be used for the conjoint analysis.

Recreational Opportunities:	Canoe/Kayak Rentals
On-site Information Source:	Available staff
Price:	$1.00
Exhibits:	Fish Tanks
Educational Opportunities:	Self-Guided Walking Tour
Length of Stay:	2 Hours
Payment Type:	Per Person

Would you prefer to visit this nature centre?

1	2	3	4	5	6	7
Definitely Don't Prefer						Definitely Prefer

Figure 6.3 Sample profile
Source: Ross *et al.* 2003, p. 233.

▶

3. *Data analysis.* Data was analysed with the objective of finding out which profile and consequently which individual attributes influence the 'preference for visiting of the centre' most.

TABLE 6.1	Attributes and attribute levels of the recreation centre
Attributes	**Attribute level**
Price	$1.00 $2.00 $3.00 $5.00
Length of stay	1 hour 2 hours Half day Full day
Exhibits	Computer touch screens Fish tanks Photographs Live animal touch tanks
Educational opportunities	Self-guided walking tours Educational boat trips Wildlife observation deck Guided walking tour
On-site information source	Brochures Computer touch system Available staff Information desk
Recreational opportunities	Canoe/kayak rentals Walking trails Picnic areas Fishing pier
Payment type	Per car Per person Per family

Source: Ross *et al.* 2003, p. 232.

TABLE 6.2	Conjoint measurement results for the recreation centre		
Attribute levels	Part-worth estimate	Part-worth range	Importance rank
Price $1.00 $2.00 $3.00 $5.00	0.098 −0.163 0.037 0.028	0.261	1
Length of stay 1 hour 2 hours Half day Full day	−0.095 0.080 0.014 0.001	0.175	2
Exhibits Live animal touch tanks Computer touch screens Fish tanks Photographs	0.072 −0.011 0.002 −0.063	0.135	3
Educational opportunities Educational boat trips Self-guided walking tours Wildlife observation deck Guided walking tour	0.059 −0.017 −0.012 −0.030	0.089	4
On-site information source Information desk Brochures Computer touch system Available staff	0.038 −0.010 −0.034 0.006	0.072	5
Recreational opportunities Picnic areas Canoe/kayak rentals Walking trails Fishing pier	0.030 −0.029 −0.027 0.026	0.059	6
Type of payment Per car Per person Per family	0.010 −0.006 −0.004	0.016	7

Source: Ross *et al.* 2003, p. 235.

The results of the study reveal the importance of the several criteria for the total of the respondents. The average respondent was 38.6 years of age, married and with an income level of between $40,000 and $59,999. They were also well educated, receiving at least a 4-year college degree. The average preferences for centre attributes are depicted in Table 6.2. In the first column, the attribute levels are shown. The second column indicates the so called part-worth, a value for what an individual attribute is worth to the respondents. The third column indicates the part-worth of a whole attribute and the fourth column the resulting importance ranking of the attributes. It can be seen that price is the most important criterion. The best profile from the respondents' perspective was a combination of a $1 entrance fee, a two-hour stay and live animal touch tanks.

Source: Ross *et al.* 2003.

However, there are also some *disadvantages*. First, the aspects that were mentioned for the direct customer surveys are also partly valid. Especially for services with a high proportion of experience and credence qualities, it is difficult for consumers to evaluate fictive services. Secondly, the conjoint measurement design might be critical. It is only possible to analyse a limited number of attributes and attribute levels. Otherwise the number of combinations would become too high to be able to ask respondents to evaluate the alternative combinations. Therefore, often not all possible combinations are used. Then, the selection of the combinations analysed is crucial. A wrong decision regarding the combinations might lead to totally wrong results and consequently suboptimal prices.

Overall, the outside-in approach allows the integration of the consumers' willingness to pay into the considerations for the service pricing decisions. The problems of the various approaches as well as the need to be profitable prevent a complete focus upon the consumers' willingness to pay. Imagine that the consumers would not be willing to pay the price that is necessary for a service firm to be profitable. In this case, the service would be unprofitable when sold at the outside-in-based price. Therefore, service providers try to combine inside-out and outside-in approaches.

Combined approaches

The combined approaches integrate the cost-oriented and customer-oriented methods to determine a service price. One proposal for a combined method is the *multi-step synthetic service pricing approach*.[11] It combines several of the methods presented earlier in this chapter. By this, the approach takes into account the different perspectives that can influence the service price, such as market competitiveness, cost structure, profit goals, price/demand sensitivity and unique service characteristics. The pricing process contains the following steps (see Figure 6.4):

- *Step 1* concerns the competition and is about determining the service positioning and identifying the competitors. This step focuses upon the differentiation pricing method and aims at building the basis price based on the competition. One option here is to define the average competitors' price as the base price.

- Knowing the competition-driven base price, the market premium service price (MPP) is determined (*step 2*). As in the differentiating pricing method, a service differentiation premium (SDP) is developed that can lead to higher or lower prices than the competition.

- Then, following the inside-out approach, a cost-plus price (CPP) is calculated by adding a profit premium – based on the profit goals of the service provider – to the costs that are generated by producing the service (*step 3*). While the MPP represents a competition-oriented price, the CPP serves the role of internal control. Since it is only an internal planning result, it must be balanced with the outside perspective.

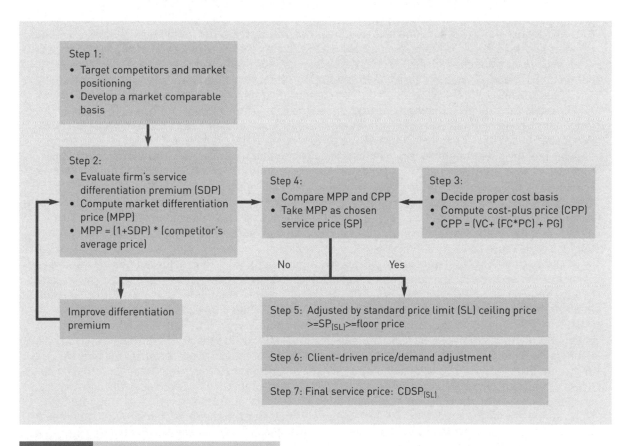

FIGURE 6.4   Multi-step synthetic service pricing

Source: Tung *et al.* 1997, p. 58.

- Therefore, MPP and CPP are compared (*step 4 plus steps 5 to 7*). When MPP is greater than or equal to CPP, then MPP is determined as service price. When MPP is smaller than CPP, the service provider has two options: the first is to set MPP as the service price. CPP is an internal goal only and when it is not reachable, it still is not reasonable to set the respective price. The second option concerns the service differentiation premium (SDP) from *step 2*. The provider could try to increase this premium by marketing efforts or service improvements until it can be justified to set this price in the context of the competitive situation.

In Services marketing in action 6.3, a sample calculation based on the method is presented.

SERVICES MARKETING IN ACTION 6.3:

Multi-step synthetic pricing for a hotel

Hotel A, part of a hotel chain, has selected business and upscale personal travel segments as its target market. To set room rates for Hotel A (see Figure 6.5 for an illustration of the hotel's multi-step synthetic pricing process), the pricing/marketing manager first needs to identify its competitors. Hotel A's competitors would consist of Hilton, Hyatt and Marriott, and similar hotels. The rates of these hotels would be used for comparative purposes. The pricing approach these hotels use is most likely a bundled-package price. The room rate includes breakfast, free cable television and free local telephone, plus other amenities such as providing fax and conference facilities. For the purposes of our example, the average price of these hotels is $145 per night.

After identifying competitors' prices, the pricing/marketing manager can formulate a market premium price by using the results of its customer surveys (hotels conduct customer satisfaction surveys regularly) to evaluate if one or more of the differentiation premium factors can be used for SDP (service differentiation premium). For example, if, from its surveys, the marketing manager found that Hotel A has an excellent reputation in providing the salient services (copying and fax, etc.) to its customers and its hotels are conveniently located, he could then add a 0.15 SDP (SDP = [Ap + Rtp + Clp + Psp] / 4) to its room rate.

In computing CPP (cost-plus price), capacity utilisation should be considered because services cannot be stored like manufactured products, and unused capacities are revenues forgone. As a result of this characteristic, CPP should be based on the occupancy rate of different seasons. This could result in different CPPs for different seasons. For Hotel A the CPP for this example is $112 {CPP = VC + (FC*PC) + PG}. The MPC derived from step two is then compared with CPP. If MPP is greater than or equal to CCP, then MPP is the chosen service price (SP). If MPP is less than CPP, the differentiation premium must be improved. The original service differentiation premium model provides the direction for improving SDP. Increasing availability of the service, enhancing the hotel's reputation, offering incentives to stimulate repeat business and customer loyalty, and attempting to desensitise the consumer to price through service attributes not easily emulated in the short term are among ways to improve SDP.

As suggested in the model, the SP has its upper and lower limits. The upper limit is the highest price that consumers are willing the pay. Therefore, this upper SL is analogous to the reservation price that was popularised in marketing and retailing literature. The lower limit would be the cost of keeping the hotel operational. In this example, the upper and lower SL would be $195 and $92 respectively.

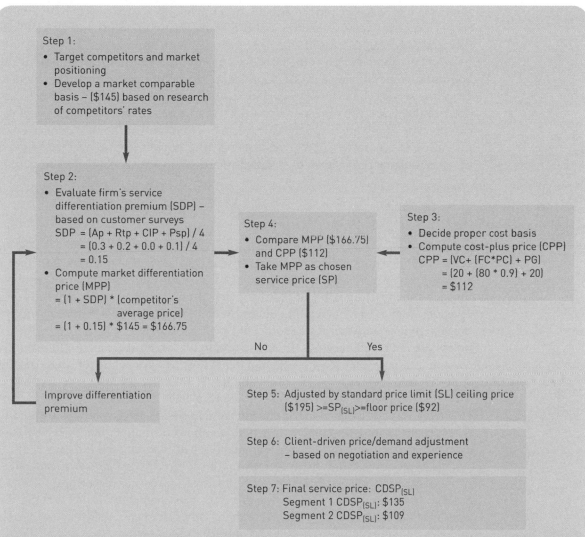

Figure 6.5 Multi-step synthetic service pricing for a hotel
Source: Tung *et al.* 1997, p. 61.

The final step is to determine the client-driven service price (CDSP). Negotiation with clients and pricing experience would be the basis for determining CDSP. This CDSP may result in different prices for different segments. For example, Hotel A could offer a corporate rate for the large corporations and a regular rate for the general public. Further, for the price sensitive travellers, Hotel A could offer special rates for weekends and during slack seasons. For the corporate clients, Hotel A could charge $135, which is below the regular rate of $166.75, in order to build long-term relationships. Furthermore, Hotel A could charge a weekend rate of $109 to entice some price conscious travellers.

Source: Tung *et al.* 1997.

A second means to combine inside-out and outside-in approaches is based on the conjoint measurement, a method that originally focused on the external view and therefore has been discussed as one of the outside-in approaches. However, integrating cost information into the 'conjoint' method can help complement this approach by introducing a profit component, instead of a sole revenue component. Thus, the service characteristics that are valued from the customers' perspective by determining a specific price per characteristic are also valued from a cost-oriented perspective. For every characteristic, costs are determined that are generated by providing the characteristic. In consequence, the 'conjoint' approach is applied to the generation of profits per characteristic instead of price per characteristic.

Strategic options of price discrimination

When a student goes to the cinema or museum or theatre, they will pay less for the entrance than working people. That is not because the owners of cinemas or museums or theatres might be philanthropists but as a measure to maximise the revenues. Many students would not be able or willing to pay the standard price for these activities and therefore would not visit the cinema or museum or theatre unless offered the discounted entrance price. In the long-term, the providers' initiatives might have relationship-oriented behaviour as a consequence. By attracting students into their service locations at a lower rate, the students may develop a love for the theatre and might keep coming back later, also at higher rates. However, this approach also has short-term reasons, excess capacity is utilised by the students visiting the cinema or exhibition and contribute to the fixed cost, even though their contribution is lower than that of visitors paying the full rate.

This approach is called **price discrimination**. *Price discrimination*[12] means that a service provider charges different prices for the same service according to certain criteria. In our example, the criterion is a customer characteristic, i.e. whether the customer is a student or not. There are many other characteristics that are used in order to differentiate prices and that will be discussed below.

The student price example further enlightens the *goals of* price discrimination from the perspective of the service provider. Price discrimination has a strategic importance for service providers.[13] From a value perspective, price discrimination contributes to value via revenues. In most markets, there are customer segments with different willingness to pay. In our example, students have a lower willingness and sometimes lower ability to pay than other visitors. By differentiating prices, a provider can *skim the different willingness to pay*.[14] Looking at the student price settings from the lower price limit for the student, the provider would lose revenues because other visitors are willing to pay more for the service. In this case, revenues would be lower because of a lower average price. When there would not be a student price and students would have to pay the standard price, most students would not purchase an entrance ticket. Consequently, sales would be lower, possibly resulting in lower revenues. The characteristics of services allow the setting of different prices. Because of the intangibility of services, their value is often difficult to judge. Consequently, it is difficult for a customer to estimate the true value of a service. Therefore, the customer's willingness to pay often depends more on their ability to pay (e.g. income), instead of the 'objective' estimation of a service. Furthermore, services are often regionally structured. Due to the integration of the customer, for many services, a customer does not know the prices other customers pay (e.g. attorney fees). If that is the case, this might lead to envy by the unprivileged customer. When a mobile operator offers low rates to new customers on its website and current customers see that offer, they might feel treated inequitably and be driven to cancelling their contract to realise an equal advantage with the same or other providers.

The objective of skimming the willingness to pay in order to increase revenues becomes even more important when service capacities are not fully used. In this case the first goal goes hand in hand with the goal of *exploiting free capacities*. In the theatre example, the cinema or theatre would probably not be full if the seats were not taken by students. Because service capacities degenerate when not used it is better for a service provider to sell capacities at a lower price than not to sell the capacities. Empty theatre seats cannot be used in another performance when more people want to see the play.

As mentioned, being a student or not as a customer characteristic is one possible criterion for price discrimination. There are many other criteria in the areas of customer characteristics, offering characteristics and usage characteristics (for an overview see Figure 6.6).

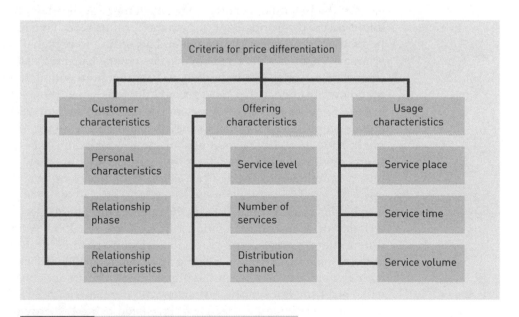

FIGURE 6.6 Criteria for service price discrimination

Price discrimination according to customer characteristics

Personal characteristics. This group of discrimination criteria has already been mentioned in the example of student prices. In the example, the customer's 'lifecycle phase' was used to set different prices. A human being's lifecycle phase is a good indicator of an individual's willingness and ability to pay. It rises from childhood and student life to working life and might decrease in retirement age. By differentiating price according to the lifecycle phase, prices are oriented at the willingness and ability to pay of the different customer segments and therefore help exploit the willingness to pay of these segments. A similar criterion is the age of the customer. Compared to the lifecycle phase age is easier to implement as a differentiation criterion because it is enough to check any document that confirms the customer's age and not a specific identity card, like the student card. Other personal characteristics used for price discrimination are marital status, gender or income.

Relationship phase. Next to the personal lifecycle phase of the customers, the customer relationship lifecycle phase (see Chapter 4) is used for price discrimination. Many mobile operators apply special acquisition offers in order to recruit new customers. Further, retention offers are made to current customers as an incentive to renew a mobile contract, e.g. 20 per cent lower rates. Also, providers try to win back lost customers by communicating win back offers including better prices. In this case, the price discrimination aims at increasing revenues by managing the customers' behaviour in respect of the relationship lifecycle phase. The reason for differentiating the price is to make the relationship to the provider more attractive for the potential, current or lost customers. A disadvantage of this strategy might be the disgruntlement of customer groups who have to pay higher prices. In contrast to price discrimination and according to personal characteristics, this approach might be less acceptable to customers. Current customers will not perceive themselves as less important and are therefore willing to pay a higher price than new customers. This is especially the case when the respective acquisition prices are not stable and at a certain point in time current customers had paid a higher acquisition price than the newly acquired customers. Although customers might have no ability to react at short notice, for example because of an existing contract with a mobile provider, privileges for potential/new customers result in lower commitment of current customers in the long term.

Relationship characteristics. Besides the relationship phase, there are further characteristics of a customer relationship that are used by service providers for differentiating prices. One criterion is customer value. Providers that pursue a professional relationship marketing approach focus their marketing activities and their customer treatment on the premise that a customer contributes to the total value of a firm. Put simply, customers who purchase more of a service or – from a long-term relational perspective – have been using the provider's services for a long time, are more valuable to the provider. Consequently, the provider gives part of this value added back to the customers themselves by offering lower prices. One example is that many high-profile banking customers do not have to pay account or transfer rates because these would constitute a small proportion of the total revenues of the respective customers. Next to customer value, memberships of customer clubs, etc. are often used to differentiate prices. For example, the Academy of Marketing (AM) offers its seminars and conferences at a member fee and a non-member fee. Moreover, Services marketing in action 6.4 exemplifies relationship-oriented approaches of price discrimination by showing the 'loyalty programmes' of The Body Shop and the Youth Hostels Association which offer price reductions for various services – with and without direct connection to the core service – to members.

SERVICES MARKETING IN ACTION 6.4:

Examples of membership-related price discrimination

Relationship pricing by The Body Shop

The Body Shop International plc, a cosmetics and toiletries high street retailer, offers membership to its 'Love Your Body' customer club. The features of the club in the UK contain several price elements. Overall, the features offered are (for a club fee of £5):

- 10% off all purchases from The Body Shop for one year
- Rewards with fourth and eighth qualifying purchase*
  - After the fourth qualifying purchase ** choose a free product (s)
  - After the eighth qualifying purchase ** choose a free product (s)
- A birthday gift for customers coming in during their birthday month (retail value up to £5)
- Exclusive updates on what's happening in the shops
- Special offers by e-mail
- Exclusive member events

* One stamp for each qualifying purchase of at least £10.
** If product value exceeds £5 or £10, member pays difference at full retail.

Source: The Body Shop 2005.

Membership programme of the Youth Hostels Association

The Youth Hostels Association (England + Wales) (YHA) operates a network of 227 Youth Hostels across England and Wales for over 310,000 members. The YHA also offers a membership programme that realises price discrimination indirectly by offering rebates for many other products and services of YHA's partners. These rebates include offers of the following organisations:

▶

- YHA Credit Card – Donation to YHA for every £100 spent.
- Trail Cyclists Association – 20% off membership.
- The National Trust – 3 months additional free membership.
- Alton Towers – 20% Off Pre-booked Visit Prices.
- The American Adventure – 2 for 1 Offer: One child or adult ticket free when accompanied by a full paying adult.
- Blackpool Pleasure Beach – 3 for 2 Offer: 1 Show & Ride Wristband free when 2 Show & Ride Wristbands at full retail price purchased.
- Chessington World of Adventures – 20% Discount Off Pre-booked Visit Prices.
- Columbus – 10% Off Travel Insurance.
- YHA Global Phonecard – Reductions of up to 70% on international calls from over 80 countries, plus a £6 free online bonus.
- LEGOLAND Windsor – Reductions of 25% for admission prices.
- The London Pass – £5 Discount off Multi-day London Pass.
- Lonely Planet – £2 off any Lonely Planet guidebooks costing £9.99 or more.
- Madame Tussauds & Tussauds London Planetarium – 20% Discount Off Pre-booked Visit Prices.
- National Express – £2 Off any journey booked online a www.nationalexpress.com
- Planet Hollywood – 15% off a Food & Beverage Bill and in the Merchandise Store.
- SeaFrance – 15% off lowest fares.
- Shakespeare's Globe Exhibition & Tour – 2 Exhibition Tickets for the Price of One.

Source: Youth Hostels Association 2005.

Price discrimination according to offering characteristics

Service providers differentiate their prices according to certain characteristics of the offered services. Different customer needs and expectations result in different levels of the willingness to pay, different variants of the same service are offered. The factor for the price differences can be a quality difference and/or a cost advantage that is transferred to the customer.

Service level. An important offering characteristic that is used for price discrimination is the service level offered. Here, the quality-side of the value perceived by the customer is addressed (see Chapter 2 for a definition of value as perceived by consumers). When a service is divided by nature or can be divided into variants of different service or quality levels, the price often varies with the quality level. Due to the lower quality level, customers are willing to pay only lower prices. In theatres, prices for seats are often strongly differentiated. Additionally, the service level-based price discrimination helps attract customer segments that potentially would not use the service at a higher price level. Regarding the theatre, certain customer segments could not afford a visit at a higher price. A good example is the Royal Albert Hall that offers 'seats' on its balcony at cheap prices that are often occupied by students.

Number of services ('price bundling'). The strategy when service providers apply different prices depending on the number of different services or service elements (not number of units of one specific service – see below 'service volume') used, is also called **price bundling**.[15] In some industries, price bundling is applied systematically, as in the banking industry. See Figure 6.7 for the points of time when different banks introduced their bundling concepts. In addition, Services marketing in action 6.5 illustrates the concept of one of the banks. Restaurants often offer menus that combine several dishes. When the dishes are purchased individually, the total price would be higher than the price for the menu. Package holidays are also a form of price bundling. Price bundling helps service providers realise cross-selling potentials. Customers thus purchase some of the services in the package that they may not have purchased separately. The differences in demand levels can be outweighed by price bundling. When marketed in a bundle together with services being associated with a high demand level, services with a lower

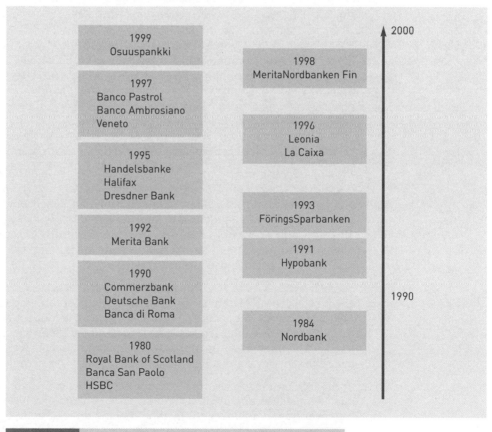

| **FIGURE 6.7** | Points of time of banks introducing service bundling |

Source: Mankila 2001, p. 17.

demand level are sold more often than if they were marketed individually. As an entity, service bundles are often perceived by customers as being convenient mechanisms to reduce the purchasing decision efforts in the selection of single services, and therefore represent a purchase decision factor. Internally, cost synergies can be realised and service resources utilised.

SERVICES MARKETING IN ACTION 6.5:

Price bundling at Royal Bank of Scotland

Price bundling plays an important role in the services marketing mix of Royal Bank of Scotland. Due to its total market focus in the consumer market, it targets highly differentiated customer groups. Accordingly, its pricing targets these different customer segments. In 2001 the bank offered four main price bundles to its customers, combined with respective service and product bundles:

1. *Royalties Account*: The basic bundle is the 'Royalties Account' that includes a current account, chequebook, and a choice of credit cards, 24-hour-telephone banking and direct banking by PC and Royalties newsletter. In addition, the account gives the customer several other benefits: holiday and travel discounts of various kinds, overdraft and borrowing at preferential rates, investment and savings bonuses, cash discounts (telephone calls, £500 off the cost of a new car, 20 per cent discount on CDs, videos, etc.) and extra protection and insurance cover. The customer is charged £5 per month for this account.

2. *Royalties Gold Account*: The second price bundle is an upgraded version of the 'Royalties Account', the so-called 'Royalties Gold Account'. It costs £9 per month and those benefits in addition to the 'Royalties Account' benefits involve family travel insurance, a slightly better interest rate on personal loans, Gold Visa or Master Card, preferential terms on agreed overdrafts, additional savings bonuses on the savings account and time deposits, more alternatives to cash discounts and enhanced insurance cover.

3. *Student Royalties Account:* This account is a current account with instant access via chequebook and ATM or debit card. Students are offered an interest-free overdraft limit which varies depending on how many years the student has been studying. Other benefits free of charge are credit card, student mortgages, cash discounts, holiday and travel discounts, career development loans, personal possessions insurance and extra protection and insurance cover. This account is free of charge.

4. *Graduate Royalties Account*: This bundle includes the basic banking services such as cheques and debit card, telephone banking and Internet. An interest-free overdraft is offered until the end of June after graduation year as well as beneficial graduate mortgages, holiday and travel discounts, and extra protection and insurance cover. This account is also free of charge for about a year after graduation.

Summing up, Royal Bank of Scotland combines service bundling with price discrimination. The four packages bundle certain services, which is the idea of price bundling. Further, the prices for the packages are differentiated, for example according to the life status (student or not).

Source: Mankila 2001.

Distribution channel. In contrast to the example above, lower prices can also be realised without lowering the quality level. This is the case with the use of the distribution channel as a criterion for differentiation. In several service industries, the distribution channel is an important cost driver. Especially with the introduction of internet distribution, dramatic cost differences between distribution channels can be observed. These cost advantages are (partly) handed over to the customer by the providers. For example, banking transactions are cheaper when conducted via the web. Also, airline tickets are less expensive when purchased via the web. Interestingly, the lower prices are not connected with a lower level of quality, neither concerning the service itself nor regarding the distribution channel. When used to the internet channel, purchasing services via the internet can be even more convenient for the customer than purchasing the service in a physical facility (e.g. bank branch, travel agency).

Price discrimination according to usage characteristics

Next to customer and offering characteristics, service prices are differentiated dependent on the usage of the service. Here, the service place, the service time as well as the service volume used by the customer are applied for price discrimination.

Service place. In terms of the service location, a regional price discrimination is an important option of service pricing. These price differences are mostly caused by the differences of the general price level in different regions. For example, for many services, the price level is higher in cities than in the country. These price differences in most cases are accepted by the customers. Due to the direct contact between customer and provider, in many service situations the customer would not travel from a city to the country in order to pay a lower price for a service. (In most cases this would be uneconomic, too, because of the travel cost.) Another criterion in this category is the differentiation between the service delivery at the provider's or the customer's place. Depending on the cost generated by the service place (or the change of the service place), prices are differentiated (e.g. higher prices for a doctor's home visit).

Service time. Timing of the purchasing and usage process is also an important factor in price discrimination. Many service prices differ according to the time when a service is used (e.g. time of day, season). See Services marketing in action 6.6 for an example where service timing is an important price determinant. In contrast to this example, the basis for the price differences most often are differences in the demand. In winter time, demand for ski lifts is higher than in summer time. Consequently, ski lift providers demand higher prices during winter time. For the same reason, tickets for cinemas are more expensive at prime time than in the afternoon. Furthermore, order time is used as a price differentiator. In the airline industry, early bookings and last minute tickets are less expensive than the standard ticket price. These price discriminations are important tools of service capacity management, especially in the form of so-called **yield management** (see Chapter 10).

SERVICES MARKETING IN ACTION 6.6:

Last-minute birthday package

Jim Hamming once again found the right birthday present for Anne, his girlfriend, one day before her birthday itself. The problem however was that she was studying in Madrid/Spain – actually he was already too late to get the present to her on time. When he talked to his father about his problem, his father suggested using a courier service to deliver the present.

Jim quickly went online and visited the DHL website in order to find out the price for the parcel delivery, but the search was not that straightforward. After having indicated that he was going to ship a package and not a document, he was asked to indicate destination country, weight and dimensions of the package. The weight was asked for in kg, so he put in '1 kg' without knowing the exact weight of the final package. But his idea was to get an estimate of what the price for this last-minute action might be. He was not sure about the dimensions, so he left them out. For the country, a drop-down alphabetical list was shown. As an experiment he investigated the cost of sending the parcel to Afghanistan – the result was '£60.98' with the remark 'call for details' for shipping time. He then began the search for Spain. The result surprised him: the figure appearing was approximately £60.00 and there were different prices. The reason for the differentiation was very relevant to him – they concerned the transit time. There were three categories but at least all of them indicated a one-day shipping time. The three categories were labelled 'European Union Express', 'Pre-12 noon (MidDay Express)' and 'Pre-9 am (StartDay Express)' and they were the reasons for the big price differences: £42.99, £56.00 and £82.30. He decided that the cheapest category would be fine – with the added advantage of surprising Anne later in the day when she would probably no longer anticipate a present from him. When he clicked down further on the page, the header 'Frequent User Discount' appeared. If he was a frequent user and sent between 41 and 60 packages a year by DHL, he would realise a discount of £10 . . . Well, he had spent enough time with the price calculator – and still needed time to organise the parcel shipment.

Source: based on information of DHL UK 2005.

Service volume. Finally, the service volume purchased by the customer is used as a factor for price discrimination. Generally, the price decreases with increasing service volume. In order to implement a volume-oriented price discrimination, the central service must be divided into units, like theatre performances visited, kilometres flown, hours being taught skiing. Volume-based price discrimination can be described as a non-linear price determination. A linear price determination means that the total price is a linear function of the service units consumed. When a customer consumes five service units, the consumer pays five times as much as when one service unit is consumed. When one visits the hairdresser ten times a year, one pays ten times the rate for a haircut. In contrast, with volume-based price discrimination the price per unit decreases with increasing numbers of units. When the hair stylist offers a haircut subscription with 10 per cent discount per haircut when one purchases ten haircuts, then it applies a non-linear price determination. There are four *types of volume-based price discrimination*:

1. *Volume discounts* are the typical form of volume-based price discrimination. When a consumer purchases a certain number of service units, the total price for all units is lower than the total price for all service units purchased individually. Volume discounts can be found in many service industries. Cinemas and theatres sell season subscriptions with a certain number of performances sold as a package. Ironing services sell ten ironed shirts as a package for a lower unit price. Volume discounts encourage customers to purchase several service units at once. Next to generally increasing sales, service providers gain more planning reliability regarding sales and resource utilisation.

2. *Incentive plans* reward the customer after a certain number of service units are purchased. In contrast to volume discounts, the customer pays the original service unit price. When the customer has purchased a certain number of units, the customer is rewarded by receiving money, free service units, other services or goods, etc. In contrast to volume discounts, the customer is not committed to purchasing a certain number of service units and the 'discount' is received after purchasing/using all service units. A typical example would be the reward programmes of airlines. A customer can collect points or miles for each flight. With a certain number of points or miles, free flights, upgrades to better seats or other services from hotels or rental car firms can be received. Next to these more complex forms, there are also simple versions of incentive plans, like the fast food restaurant where the tenth fish and chips portion is free. The rewards function as incentives for the customer to purchase more units of a service. The main purpose of the incentive plans is to increase sales. Unlike for volume discounts, planning reliability of the service firm changes only slightly.

3. *Multi-level pricing* describes a pricing approach whereby the service price is divided into two parts. Mostly, one part is a base fee, and a second part is comprised of usage fees. Mobile operators often ask for a basic fee per month and a usage fee per minute that the service is used. The basic fee gives the provider a minimum revenue. Therefore, multi-level pricing is often used in industries

with high sunk costs, the basic fee then compensates for the sunk cost, like the cost for the mobile network. Often, the basic fee and unit price are interdependent. Mobile operators offer different tariff plans: the higher the basic fee the lower the unit price. This logic also is applied by railway firms that sell customer cards that allow card holders to purchase tickets at lower prices.

4. *Flat rate pricing* is an extreme form of multi-level pricing where customers only pay a basic fee. Actually, a flat rate only means that a different unit definition is applied than is common in an industry. For example, an internet flat rate is calculated based on the calendar time the service resources are available to the consumer. A traditional tariff applies the usage time as unit definition. The longer the service resources are used by the customer, the more the customer pays.

The various forms of price discrimination are not exclusive and many service providers apply *combined forms of price discrimination*. Cinemas that show children's films in the afternoon at lower prices than other films at night, combine service time (afternoon versus night) and customer characteristics (age) as criteria for differentiation. Airlines combine age (children's rebates), booking time (early booking, normal price, last-minute), volume (length of flight, rebates for firms purchasing flight regularly, incentive plan), service level (first, business and coach class), etc. A further example of multi-criteria price discrimination are the pricing systems for football match tickets, as you can see from Services marketing in action 6.7.

Problems associated with price discrimination

Price discrimination is a common strategy in many service industries because of the positive value effects achieved via skimming consumer surplus respectively utilising service resources that would otherwise have remained unused. However, there are also some pitfalls associated with price discrimination that can be divided into external and internal problems.

Regarding external problems of price discrimination, most importantly *effects of enviousness* can have an impact on customer perceptions and behaviour. Certain customers or customer groups are given an advantage by the price discrimination measure. Consequently, other customers or customer groups are discriminated against. When they perceive this discrimination, dissatisfaction and decreased loyalty can be the consequences. In some industries, such as in mobile communications, there are special offers for potential customers that are heavily advertised. These advertisements are also perceived by current customers. For example, on many mobile providers' websites current customers must struggle through a jungle of new customer offers before finding relevant information for themselves. This problem is less relevant in industries where customer acquisition is mostly done by personal communications, such as in consultancy services.

SERVICES MARKETING IN ACTION 6.7

Price discrimination at Werder Bremen

Football supporters come from all social strata – that is probably one of the reasons why football clubs apply various criteria for differentiating the ticket prices of their team's matches. For example, the German football champion club Werder Bremen, uses various criteria for price discrimination:

- Within the stands, there is a two-level discrimination. On the first level, there are business class seats, standard seats and standing room (still common in Germany). On the second level, there is a traditional discrimination comparable to the Manchester United Club stand. The cheapest standing room ticket is 6.50 euros, and the cheapest business class ticket is 7.50 euros.

- Furthermore, prices differ according to the team that Werder Bremen is playing against. For the Bundesliga matches (for Champions League, there are special prices), the price for a standard ticket against Bayern Munich is around 15 euros, which is more expensive than a ticket for a match against SC Freiburg.

- Children up to the age of 14 years receive a rebate of 50% on all tickets.

- Senior citizens and disabled persons receive a rebate of 30%.

- The prices for season tickets vary between 80 euros and 2,600 euros (VIP stand Platin).

Compared to the price discrimination systems of other football clubs which primarily take into account stand and personal characteristics, Werder Bremen's system considers further criteria that are supposed to influence the willingness to pay of the supporters, i.e. the club against which the team is playing.

Sources: based on information from Werder Bremen 2005.

Furthermore, neither capacity usage nor the customers' willingness to pay are stable, but have *dynamic developments*. These dynamics concern both cyclical developments, e.g. seasonal changes of demand, as well as a continuous development, e.g. structural changes in willingness to pay of customers, because of changes in the market situation or the customers' way of life, such as when changing from student life to work life. The price discrimination system of a service firm is only useful when it takes into account these dynamics. The cyclical developments can be planned, and the best price discrimination systems have integrated these developments. The booking systems of airlines adapt on demand changes on a daily basis. The more flexibly it is designed, the better a pricing system can react continuously to current developments.

Internal problems concern problems and risks regarding the implementation of a price discrimination system. The more complex the pricing system is, the higher the requirements for the company's accounting and billing systems. The more price options exist the less likely it is that employees will know the pricing. While a cinema employee might know the cinema's prices even though there is a differentiation regarding age and maybe weekday, it is impossible for employees to determine a price manually when a dynamic pricing system is applied, as it is for airlines. In this case, the price for a flight can change by the minute. Therefore, airlines need sophisticated systems in order to determine real-time prices. Otherwise, and this is a second, associated, problem, the failure probability of price determination increases with complex price systems. These failures can have various consequences. When too high a price is communicated to the customer and the customer does not complain and the price error is not realised, missing business opportunities might result. When a customer looks for a flight on an airline's website and a wrong price is communicated, the customer will simply not purchase the flight and 'click' to another provider. The communicated price may be too low and as it is impossible to correct the price after the communication, resulting revenues are lower than projected.

These problems reveal that it is important for service providers to consider a systematic implementation of a price discrimination strategy. Otherwise the price discrimination might have the converse effects than those aimed at.

 ## Summary

Summarising this chapter, the following lessons about service pricing can be learnt (see Figure 6.8):

1. A service's price has a direct value effect by representing one component of the revenues with a certain service.

2. In addition, service price indirectly influences value, as a quality indicator, purchasing trigger, and with a negative effect on sales.

3. For determining a service's price, a (mostly cost-oriented) inside-out-approach and a (mostly customer-oriented) outside-in approach can be differentiated. Furthermore, there exist combined approaches based on the two extreme versions.

4. Within the inside-out approach, the cost for producing a service is the basic standard for determining a price (with the addition of a defined profit premium). This approach is connected with several problems, such as the cost association to a single service (because of the high proportion of fixed cost) and determining single service units.

5. The outside-in approach integrates the customer's perceptions of a service into the price determination. According to the different methods, the customer's perception of the firm's differentiation from competitors is integrated into the relation between price and function. These methods aim at determining an optimal price, taking into consideration the customers' willingness to pay. The major challenge is measuring the demand function for a certain service.

6. The combined service pricing approaches apply principles from both the inside-out as well as the outside-in perspective. The customers' willingness to pay and the cost of producing a service are considered when determining a service's price.

7. Price discrimination is an important strategic option for service providers from a value perspective. Applying price discrimination, the willingness of differing customer segments to pay are considered. In addition, usage of

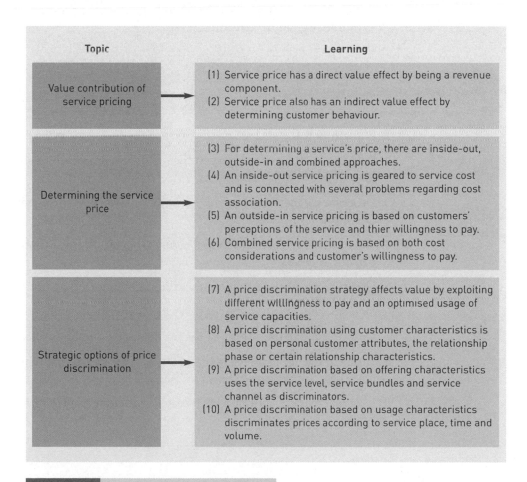

Topic	Learning
Value contribution of service pricing	(1) Service price has a direct value effect by being a revenue component. (2) Service price also has an indirect value effect by determining customer behaviour.
Determining the service price	(3) For determining a service's price, there are inside-out, outside-in and combined approaches. (4) An inside-out service pricing is geared to service cost and is connected with several problems regarding cost association. (5) An outside-in service pricing is based on customers' perceptions of the service and thier willingness to pay. (6) Combined service pricing is based on both cost considerations and customer's willingness to pay.
Strategic options of price discrimination	(7) A price discrimination strategy affects value by exploiting different willingness to pay and an optimised usage of service capacities. (8) A price discrimination using customer characteristics is based on personal customer attributes, the relationship phase or certain relationship characteristics. (9) A price discrimination based on offering characteristics uses the service level, service bundles and service channel as discriminators. (10) A price discrimination based on usage characteristics discriminates prices according to service place, time and volume.

FIGURE 6.8 Learning summary for Chapter 6

service capacities can be optimised based on knowledge of an average purchasing behaviour regarding a certain service. For price discrimination strategies, customer characteristics, offering characteristics or usage characteristics are applied.

8. A price discrimination using customer characteristics offers different prices according to a customer's personal characteristics (lifecycle stage, age, etc.), the relationship phase (e.g. potential/new versus existing customers) or certain relationship characteristics (e.g. customer value).

9. A price discrimination based on offering characteristics uses the service level, the number of services offered together (price bundling) and the distribution channel (e.g. personal versus online channel) as a price differentiator.

10. Finally, service providers determine different prices for customer segments according to usage characteristics, such as the service place (e.g. geographical price discrimination), service time (e.g. seasonal differences) and the service volume (e.g. volume rebates).

Knowledge questions

1. Explain how the service price affects the value of a service firm.

2. Explain the difference between the inside-out approach of service pricing and the outside-in approach.

3. Describe the methodology of the traditional cost-oriented approach. Include also a profit premium.

4. What problems face service providers when applying a cost-oriented service pricing approach?

5. Describe the methodology of the differentiation pricing method.

6. Describe the methodology of service pricing based on the demand function.

7. Describe the methodology of the multi-step synthetic service pricing approach.

8. Describe the value effects aimed at by service providers, when applying a price discrimination strategy.

9. Describe the different options a service provider has for differentiating service prices.

Application and discussion questions

1. Chose various service providers and explore which value contribution they emphasise with their pricing policies. Explain how they aim at increasing value by their pricing approach.

2. Discuss the advantages of the inside-out approach of service pricing and the outside-in approach.

3. Apply the traditional cost-oriented approach of service pricing including a profit premium for copying your services marketing script.

4. Explain the concrete problems an airline would face when applying a cost-oriented approach to price a flight from London to New York.

5. Design and conduct a survey with some of your friends in order to determine their willingness to pay for a one-day car rental. Compare your results with the typical fares of existing car rental companies and discuss potential differences.

6. Design a conjoint measurement-based approach for pricing a laundry service.

7. Apply the multi-step synthetic service pricing approach for a standard meal in your favourite restaurant.

8. Discuss which options for differentiating service providers apply in which industries and why.

9. Imagine you are the marketing manager of a telephone company. Which service differentiation options would you apply and why? Would you apply different approaches for fixed or mobile phones? Which and why? Do you suggest options which are not applied by telephone companies today? Discuss why they are not applied.

10. Discuss the problems associated with service differentiation.

11. Evaluate the price discrimination approaches of airlines, banks and cinemas.

CASE STUDY: RESTRUCTURING THE PRICING STRATEGY OF AN AUSTRALIAN FOOTBALL CLUB

In mid-1998 the Sydney Swans, the only Sydney team in the Australian Football League (AFL) faced a pricing decision concerning its various membership packages. A tenant of the Sydney Cricket Ground (SCG), a famous old stadium, the Sydney Swans had a maximum number of 26,000 seats for membership sales. Management budgeted for membership sales to provide revenue growth.

In the past, the club could never sell all available membership packages. However, at the start of the 1998 season, all membership packages were sold. Therefore, the Swans were thinking about raising the prices for the membership tickets. However, price might also negatively affect customer loyalty. Sydney is a relatively competitive sports market with four competing professional football codes (soccer, rugby league, rugby union and Australian rules football).

Therefore, the Swans initiated a thorough analysis with regard to the pricing options. They applied conjoint analysis in order to analyse the willingness to pay of different customer segments and to find out the potential effects of a price increase. It was also an objective to find out how upgrades between three membership groups can be achieved, i.e. how 'Standard Members' and 'Full Club Members – Concourse seating' could be shifted one category higher respectively to the final stage 'Full Club Members – Grandstand seating'. Three membership packages were designed with different kinds of benefits for members and at different price levels. The following (additional) benefit attributes constituted the packages:

- grand final ticket preference (if Swans playing);
- ticket resale programme;
- an official 'glossy' yearbook;
- discount on public transport on presentation of membership card for travel to/from game;
- entry to 'new improved' social club facilities after each home game at SCG.

The conjoint analysis revealed that 'Standard Members' were the most price sensitive group but in general they were prepared to move to a higher price level towards the 'Full Club Members – Concourse seating' level. As membership programme characteristics, this group prefers above all discounted travel opportunities. It was decided on the basis of these results to raise the Standard Member price by 25 per cent.

The 'Full Club Members – Concourse seating' found access to the grand final tickets very important. There was a sub-segment of respondents, who were also very interested in expanded social club facilities. The Swans management decided on a price increase of 19 per cent. Regarding price, they seemed prepared for a medium price increase. 'Full Club Members – Grandstand seating' were the least price sensitive. Regarding benefits, they were most interested in final tickets and the ticket resale programme. Despite the low price sensitivity, for this group, the price was increased by 20 per cent and was thus comparable to the other groups.

Regarding benefits, in the 'Full Club Membership' packages, a ticket resale scheme, grand final ticket preference, a discount travel offer and access to a new improved social club facility at the stadium, were included. The 'Standard Members' were only offered the added benefit of the ticket resale scheme in order to initiate a willingness to upgrade.

In terms of results, 18 per cent of existing members upgraded to the next level. In 1998, the overall membership renewal rate was 81 per cent. The club was now interested in whether the price increase resulted in lower loyalty. However, in 1999, the renewal rate was better, at 82 per cent. The only reactions to management were '2 letters and another 10 verbal complaints'.

Source: Daniel and Johnson 2004.

Notes

[1] See Matanovich 2003.

[2] See Docters *et al*. 2004.

[3] See Marn and Rosiello 1992.

[4] For an overview of pricing methods for services see Waters and Hussey 2004.

[5] See Beard and Hoyle 1976.

[6] See Avlonitis and Indounas 2005.

[7] See Arnold *et al*. 1989.

[8] See Simon and Damian 1999.

[9] See Ratza 1993.

[10] See Simon and Damian 1999.

[11] See Tung *et al*. 1997.

[12] See Yelkur and Herbig 1997; Varian 2002.

[13] See Avlonitis and Indounas 2004.

[14] See Yelkur and Herbig 1997.

[15] See Guiltinan 1987; Ng *et al*. 1999.

7 Delivering service value: Managing service delivery

Francis, a 75-year-old retired banker, does business the old-fashioned way. Whenever he wants to make a bank transfer, he writes a letter to his bank indicating the amount and transfer information. One day, when checking his account statement, he realised that the bank had started to charge a fee for his transfers – a fee almost as high as the transfer amount itself. He cannot believe it and immediately calls his bank adviser, whom he has not called for some time, in order to ask him how this can be. However, on dialling the number, an automated voice thanks him for calling the service centre of the bank and says he will have to wait some seconds. But, he hangs up and is extremely frustrated.

Instead, he calls Jeffrey, his grandson who lives in London and studies Business and Marketing at London Business School. He tells him what has happened to him and expresses his anger about the bank. Jeffrey laughs and explains that he has never talked to a bank employee face-to-face so far, and narrates how happy he is about this and about his doing his banking business via online banking. Francis moans 'Leave me alone with this …'. But Jeffrey insists on demonstrating to his grandfather at the next occasion how convenient and easy internet banking is. Jeffrey immediately surfs to the homepage of his internet provider and opens an account for his grandfather in order to be able to demonstrate the process to him.

The anecdote of grandfather and grandson points out various aspects regarding the delivery and distribution of services. **Service delivery** has generally been defined as 'the process of making a [product or] service available for consumption or use'.[1] The main aspects which are addressed in the example are the different service delivery and distribution channels, e.g. personal contact, telephone or internet channels. Closely connected with the channels are the place and time where and when a service is delivered. A customer can use online banking almost all the time and from everywhere, and connect to the internet. Utilising the bank's services through direct contact in a bank branch implies more restriction regarding the service usage options for the customer. Furthermore, the different channels as well as place and time of service delivery have very different value effects for the service provider. For example, the grandfather in the anecdote must pay for his bank transfers by letter because this process involves much more cost for the bank than an online bank transfer. Consequently, this chapter deals with the following learning objectives (see Figure 7.1):

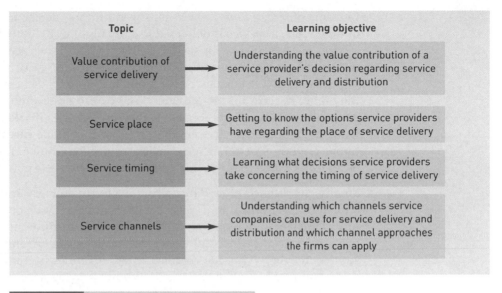

Topic	Learning objective
Value contribution of service delivery	Understanding the value contribution of a service provider's decision regarding service delivery and distribution
Service place	Getting to know the options service providers have regarding the place of service delivery
Service timing	Learning what decisions service providers take concerning the timing of service delivery
Service channels	Understanding which channels service companies can use for service delivery and distribution and which channel approaches the firms can apply

FIGURE 7.1   Learning objectives of Chapter 7

1. Understanding the value contribution of a service provider's decisions regarding service delivery and distribution.

2. Getting to know the options service providers have regarding the place of service delivery.

3. Learning what decisions service providers take concerning the timing of service delivery.

4. Understanding which channels service companies can use for service delivery and distribution and which channel approaches the firms can apply.

Value contribution of service delivery

Where service delivery and distribution are concerned, service providers take a variety of decisions in the areas of situational service delivery and time of service delivery as well as channels of service delivery. These decisions have various *impacts on value*:

• Regarding the *service location*, there are three possibilities: a service delivery can take place at the provider's location, at the customer's location and at a third party's location. Each service location has different impacts on value. When a service is delivered at the customer's location, a main part of a provider's cost relates to the transfer to the customer's location, while a service delivery at the provider's place implies higher cost for maintaining the service location.

- In terms of *service timing*, there are several timing decisions, such as the point of time when a service is delivered (e.g. by night or by day), but also how long a customer has to wait for service delivery (e.g. in the case of pizza deliveries or the ordering of furniture). Examples of relevant value considerations are: the more flexible a customer is in terms of choosing the service delivery time, the higher the cost for the provider. When a provider offers permanent service availability (24-hour), its cost are higher, but so is its market availability. Also, value is influenced by the length of a service. In some cases, value to the customer (and thus price) increases with service length (e.g. hotel stay), while in other cases, value to the customer and price decrease (e.g. train trip).

- Finally, the *channels* offered by a firm for service delivery and distribution have a major impact on value. Typical channels are personal contact, telephone and internet channel, which first imply extreme cost differences. In some industries, a personal service delivery is ten times more expensive than an online service delivery. Also, the channels affect revenues by representing a quality dimension from the customer's viewpoint and by a determinant of market availability.

Place of service delivery

Provider's place vs. customer's place

The story of Sergi Arola in Services marketing in action 7.1 illustrates that an important decision service firms have to take when designing the delivery system for their services is the **service place** or the location where the service is supposed to be produced, delivered and consumed. As discussed in the example, there are two *general options* for the service place: at the provider's location, e.g. cinema or at the customer's place, e.g. cleaning service. This is a fundamental difference from goods production. Consumer goods in particular are generally produced at the provider's place and then transported via intermediaries to the customer's place (industrial goods, especially immovable properties such as production plants are, in most cases, produced at the client firm's location). Along with these two general options, there is a third option for the service place: a third-party's location, such as with a breakdown service.

When comparing the three options of service place, the provider's place, the customer's place or a third party's place, there are some characteristics of *service types* that determine the usual service place for a concrete service. It is primarily the kind of production factors on the provider's and/or the customer's side which predefine the service place. Services which necessitate immovable internal factors, such as space in the case of a cinema, a restaurant or a club, can only be produced at the *provider's place*. As the immovable factors could not be moved to another place, e.g. the place of an individual customer, it is not possible for the

SERVICES MARKETING IN ACTION 7.1:

Food de luxe at home in Barcelona

Sergi Arola, head chef at the critically acclaimed La Broche in Madrid, last week launched a new catering division from his eponymous restaurant Arola, at the Hotel Arts, Barcelona. Arola's latest restaurant venture goes back to basics by rejuvenating the Catalan tradition for pica-pica (small snacks to share among friends) with modern twists on established traditions. The new catering arm is its mirror image, meaning that Barcelona residents can now get the full Arola experience without leaving home. Five distinct menus are on offer, from new-wave finger food such as roast chanterelle mushrooms and smoked sardines for cocktail parties, to a more formal several-course menu showcasing the year's best dishes from the restaurant. As well as the food and drinks, the service also provides waiters, tableware, flowers, and even the music. 'I wanted to do something relevant to the people of Barcelona', said Arola. 'Something fun and informal that reflects the spirit of the restaurant. I thought it was the best business card I could leave.' A basic 10-course tapas menu costs €85 (£59) per head, while the full menu costs up to €160 (£110) per head before tax. Both include dessert, petits fours, a bottle of Champagne, a white wine and a red wine.

Source: Stevens 2005.

respective service to be produced at the customer's place. These 'immovable' services can be transformed into services which can also be produced at the customer's place. However, in these cases, the determining character of the service is changed. This is the case in Services marketing in action 7.1 where the restaurant service is changed fundamentally into a home service. On the other hand, there are also services where the external factors are immovable, in which case the service can only be produced at the *customer's place*. For example, a cleaning service which is supposed to clean the customer's house can only be delivered at the customer's house.

Service characteristics which determine the necessity of delivering a service at a *third party's place* concern the service needs of the consumer. Especially when a customer has situational needs which have to be fulfilled immediately and/or the customer is situated at a third party's location and is immovable, only a service delivery at the third party's place is possible. A typical example of this are all kinds of emergency services, e.g. medical emergency services, a key service when the key for one's car has been lost or a breakdown service.

The first two lines in Table 7.1 compare the three types of service locations for service delivery according to the service types for which the respective type is relevant and lists examples of those.

TABLE 7.1	Characteristics of different service places

Characteristics	Service delivery at		
	customer's place	provider's place	third party's place
Service types	• Services with immovable external factors	• Services with immovable internal factors • Services with high process standardisation	• Services with immovable external factor at third party's place • Services where third party determines place
Examples	• House clearing service • House-keeping service • Home surveillance • Elderly care • Gardening services	• Hairdresser • Bank • Restaurant • Hotel • Airlines (part of service delivery on board)	• Medical emergency service • Automobile roadway repair service • Legal services before a court • Airlines (part of service delivery at airport)
Specific quality dimensions	• Reliability • Timeliness • Appearance of employees • Empathy and thoughtfulness of employees	• Tangibles of the service place • Availability of service personnel • Organisation of service place • Orientation at service place	• Speed of reaching service place • Timeliness

So far, in our examples, there are predominant services for delivery at certain service locations: the provider's place, customer's place or third party's place, are the most usual or most logical service locations. However, there are also services where several places are involved when a service is delivered. This is often given when immaterial service resources are involved, either internal factors (e.g. information as an internal factor, as for a route planner on the internet) or external factors (e.g. money as the external factor of a bank's services). In these cases, a *service place splitting* is applied. Part of the service delivery takes place at the provider's location and part of the delivery takes place at the customer's location. One example of a service place splitting with immaterial internal factors is that of telecasts. Parts of the service are delivered (produced) at the broadcasting company's studios, and other parts of the service are received at the customer's place. An example with immaterial external factors is online banking where the service is also produced at both the customer's and the provider's place. The relevant external factor is the customer's money that is transferred, for example. The examples highlight the fact that technology plays an important role in service place splitting.

Service place strategies

There are also service industries or service types where the service place is not predetermined by the service itself. When the immovability of service factors often was an argument for the service type–service place compatibility discussed above, the possibility of moving service factors gives service providers strategic options. A customer can usually move himself, for example a language course can take place at the customer's place or at the provider's place. When there are different service places possible, then the service places chosen and offered become *strategic options*. Two typical strategic decisions with a connection to the service place are:

- service place-related service innovations;
- multi-option service place strategies.

From a strategic perspective, the service place can be used to develop *service innovations*. In many industries, the service place is given and both providers and customers are used to the service location. However, in many cases the same service can be delivered at a different service location. Then, the change in service place can be the source of service innovations by creating a new service by determining the new service place. This is also the case in the example of the Arola restaurant introduced in Services marketing in action 7.1. Coming from a traditional restaurant, a home delivery service can be interpreted as an innovation. Today, there are many service innovations in this category which are based on new technologies. One example is given in Services marketing in action 7.2. While the 'traditional' e-university, which is also still an innovation, necessitates a fixed service place in the sense that students must have access to the internet, the u-university (u for 'ubiquitous') facilitates learning everywhere by providing lectures to download on to PDAs. Also, Services marketing in action 7.3 on 'Groundbreaking new service delivers museum-quality high resolution art and photography into the home on flat panel TVs and PCs' accentuates how fundamental changes in the service place or fundamental innovations based on service place changes can be supported by information technologies. In the case described, a totally new service is developed by combining the traditional service 'museum' with the traditional (electronic) service 'television' as well as new information technologies, resulting in the delivery of museum-like arts at home – with the difference that they are dynamic and change the object of utility 'TV' into an art object – and consequently create an entirely new benefit which is delivered by the new service.

SERVICES MARKETING IN ACTION 7.2:

Mobile learning gains foothold

Taking courses while on the go, such as on the subway or bus, is not an unusual practice for people who want to study anytime and anywhere. A mobile classroom will be accessible by a personal digital assistant (PDA), notebook computer or mobile phone handsets and will provide lectures with animations from a cyber university. Kyunghee Cyber University (www.khcu.ac.kr) will offer course lectures on mobile devices next semester for busy working students. Mobile lectures can be downloaded on a PDA or portable PC so that students can learn on the subway or bus as well as outdoors at their leisure.

Cyber university official Chae Su-jin said mobile lectures are offered to help students with jobs. 'Other cyber universities have e-learning systems, such as internet lectures, but in this situation, students have to have access to computer sites for lessons. But mobile lessons allow students to take lessons whenever and wherever they want', she said.

Mobile education is not only popular with cyber university students but also for those who are preparing for civil service examinations. The online education provider Ubion Corp. has also joined the wave of launching new media education content through ubiquitous learning (u-learning), upgraded from electronic learning (e-learning), on its own website for its member examination takers. The website has been providing lecture content for students preparing for civil service examinations since last May, which were available only via the internet, to make them more accessible to students using animated pictures and MP3 players. The mobile contents include lectures for public official examinations and other information updated in real time from news, notices and other resources relevant to the examinations posted on the website.

Ubion Corp. official Moon Seong-hoon said mobile lectures are in the initial stages as supplementary tools to be used in conjunction with the main lectures being displayed on the internet, because gadgets like PDAs have yet to become mainstream. 'But mobile lectures are becoming effective tools for studying as students can take summarised lectures with them, wherever they may go', he said. Ahn So-yeong, 26, is studying for the civil service exam and makes good use of mobile lectures through her mobile phone to listen to English grammar lectures. 'They are very effective when I review what I learned at school at home', she said. 'Now I am using my MP3 players and mobile phone, but if PDAs become widely available, I want to use it for other subjects, such as Korean language and law, necessary for the civil service exam because students need to see what lecturers write on the board', she said.

Learning outdoor sports does not necessarily mean learning outdoors if people have a mobile phone. Yahoh Communication has been delivering snowboard lectures composed of 11 sections and displayed over mobile handsets through the wireless network. The lectures have been providing basic knowledge about the winter sport, such as putting on snowboots and jumping down hills, for beginner snowboarders. In particular, it was devised to help beginners start snowboarding right after acquiring the basic poses and theories through animations from mobile handsets. It displayed basic techniques for the 'regular' style for right-handed riders and the 'goofy' style for left-handed riders as well as advanced techniques.

In line with the move, the Ministry of Education and Human Resources Development has also pushed for the u-learning policy. Ministry official Kim Il-soo said the authorities have already devised educational policies to connect cyber technology with national human resources development. 'The ministry is planning to introduce u-learning or mobile education services as pilot programmes in six high schools nationwide in two years', he said. 'The pilot project will include TV lectures aired on Educational Broadcasting System (EBS) on the College Scholastic Ability Test (CSAT) and other useful educational programmes', he added. However, another official said the u-learning service will be prudently adopted after closely reviewing the effects of the pilot programmes for two years given the cost burdens of students' parents.

Source: Korea Times 2005.

SERVICES MARKETING IN ACTION 7.3

Groundbreaking new service delivers museum-quality high resolution art and photography into the home on flat panel TVs and PCs

Beon Media today announced availability of GalleryPlayer, a groundbreaking new service that allows consumers to view museum-quality art and photography right in their homes, including content from *Life Magazine*, *National Geographic*, *Corbis*, The Andy Warhol Foundation, George Eastman House, Eaglemont Press and others, in extremely high definition on any display.

GalleryPlayer transforms any display into a digital canvas for museum-quality art and photography, giving everyone the chance to experience truly incredible content that has never before been available to a mass consumer market.

'With the proliferation of flat panel TVs, there is a growing demand for unique content to place on them', said Rob Enderle, President and Principal Analyst for the Enderle Group. 'A good example of a device that fills this need is GalleryPlayer which enables a flat panel TV to become the centerpiece for a party and turn a device that would otherwise be a distraction into an asset. It is this added utility that makes these new TVs so much more than the products they replaced. Products like GalleryPlayer are extremely important for the future of these new televisions.'

▶

'Dynamic digital imagery presents a new and unique opportunity to differentiate a space and control an environment, including tone, time of day, etc., all tailored to meet consumer decor objectives. From sports to travel, from black & white vintage photography to fine art, GalleryPlayer can be used to entertain and educate its audience' said Alexis Gerard, president and publisher, *The Future Image Report*.

At launch it will be available to consumers as a 7-day free trial. Following the free trial, subscription pricing will be offered from $4.95 per month and up for individual galleries. Individual image pricing starts at $0.99, and permanent collections are priced from $8.95 for 15 images, depending on the number of images in the collection, the perceived value of the collection, and the costs of the underlying image license rights. High-margin, limited-edition private collections will be offered at premium prices.

'GalleryPlayer is the Holy Grail for content owners such as publishers, institutions, brands artists, collections and museums, because we make dormant content suddenly mainstream by ushering in what has previously been a completely untapped consumer market', said Scott Lipsky, Beon Media Founder and CEO.

Source: Market Wire Incorporated 2005.

Furthermore, when observing the behaviours in many service industries, the service place is often not 'fixed', with many service providers offering service delivery at various places. We call this *multi-option service place strategies* when service providers do not predetermine the service place that has to be accepted by the customer but let the customer decide regarding the place of service delivery. This is the case for the Arola restaurant example cited in Services marketing in action 7.1. In this example, the restaurant offers its services both at its own location, as it is a traditional restaurant characteristic, and then, recently, as a home service, i.e. part of the service is delivered at the customer's place. Also, computers can be repaired at the customer's and the provider's place. From a *value perspective*, such a multi-service place strategy has several implications. On the revenue side, the needs of more customer groups can be served. Both customers who do and do not request a home delivery can be served. Consequently, revenues can be increased by attracting more customers than when only one service place option is offered. On the cost side, this offering results in increased fixed costs, because more and different service resources, such as personnel at the restaurant's place as well as delivery personnel, must be provided.

Above we considered different forms of service places and several variations of their application in service offerings. Now, focusing on the three basic forms, service delivery at the provider's place, at the customer's place and at a third party's place, we explore more specific differences between these forms that are of relevance for services managers. These differences concern the relevance of quality characteristics in evaluating the service place, the customer's integration into the service process as well as the service place's role as a purchase decision criterion.

The effect of the service location on customer behaviour

The service place is not only a quality characteristic itself – the design and convenience of a restaurant's place – but also determines the *relevance of quality characteristics* in the customers' perception. Emphasising the SERVQUAL dimensions: tangibles, reliability, responsiveness, assurance, empathy (see Chapter 2) helps to clarify the differences between the three types of service place (see also Table 7.1). When a service is delivered at the provider's place, the most striking quality dimension which is influenced by this fact, are the tangibles regarding equipment and employees. When a service is delivered at the customer's place, the firm has less influence on the service environment. However, the customer might be sensitive regarding the persons who intrude into his home. Consequently, the employee-related tangibles as well as the employees' empathy regarding the customer's sensitivities might be important. When the service is delivered at a third party's place, the customer will usually expect quick service. As a result, responsiveness in terms of the firm's ability to react to the customer's order is crucial to the customer's perception.

Furthermore, the location of a service delivery is related to the *customer's integration* into the service process. When the service is delivered at the provider's place, the customer is often 'integrated into the provider's processes'. On the other hand, the provider is partly integrated into the customer's processes when service delivery is at the customer's place. In the latter situation, the provider is less able to influence the service delivery and this service delivery varies more strongly between different customers.

Additionally, the factors for *customers' purchasing decisions* vary according to the service delivery place. When the service is delivered at the provider's place, then the place's characteristics influence the customers' perceptions and buying decisions significantly. The location of the service place, especially for day-to-day services, plays an important role for customer acquisition, especially walk-in customers. For example, retailers located in the centre of a city are more likely to attract (walk-in) customers than retailers located outside the centre – other than those who offer other USPs, such as a price advantage, that attracts customers to their disadvantageous location. Services marketing in action 7.4, 'Customer "run" on Mediamarkt due to marketing tricks', describes how many customers were lured into the shops of the electronic product retailer by partly dishonest marketing statements. Next to the location of the service place, its design can have an important impact on buying decisions. Restaurants with well-designed interiors and exteriors are likely to attract more, or at least more suitable, customers than other restaurants. See more on the design of the service place in Chapter 9 'Service resources' on tangibles.

SERVICES MARKETING IN ACTION 7.4:

Customer 'run' on Mediamarkt due to marketing tricks

The German Mediamarkt, a retailer chain for electronic articles, has followed a price-leadership strategy for years. This strategy is implemented by various marketing campaigns which often go to extremes.

One example is the 'tax paradise' campaign in January 2005 when Mediamarkt offered all its products 'reduced by 16 per cent' (the percentage of the German value added tax) on a specific day. The campaign resulted in customers 'flooding' their shops – regardless of how far away they lived. Traffic jams were even reported due to the campaign.

For the sake of completeness, we should mention that the campaign was accompanied by several criticisms and legal actions. Not only competitors but consumer lobbyists opposed the campaign. The reason for this was the campaign itself, which was perceived as aggressive, and also price 'corrections' directly before the campaign. For one shop, it was reported that a digicam was offered for 300 euros at the end of December 2004 and then for circa 350 euros on the campaign day. The shop manager justfied this by saying that the old price was based on a Christmas campaign which ended right before the campaign day.

Sources: Lawchannel (2005); dpa (2005); Balci (2005).

Deciding on the service location

Consequently, a service firm's decisions regarding the *location of the service place* are particularly important. There are various criteria that play a role in that decision and these can be classified into three categories (see Figure 7.2). Two of them, the market-related criteria as well as the position-related criteria, are of an external nature in the sense that they concern the customers' perceptions and decisions or more generally the demand. The third category, profitability-related criteria, is of an internal character and concerns the efficiency of service delivery.

The *market-related criteria* are relevant because the service location influences the market potential for the service firm. Especially for day-to-day services the location strongly influences the potential number and quality of customers. More specifically, the following criteria affect the market of a service firm and thus are important when evaluating a service location:

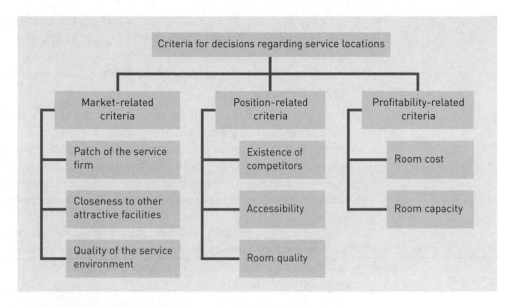

FIGURE 7.2 Criteria for decisions regarding service locations

- The *patch* of the service firm influences the number of customers that potentially walk in or become attentive regarding a certain provider.

- The *closeness to other attractive facilities* also influences the number of potential customers. For example, service businesses located close to a train station can attract the attention of many walk-in customers.

- The *quality of the service environment* directly influences the calibre of the customers attracted. In areas which are less prestigious than others, the potential clientele is, too.

Next to the market-related criteria, there are *position-related factors* that influence the decision regarding the service place. These factors concern the current or possible market position of the provider compared to competitors which is partly influenced by the service place. The following aspects can be classified as position-related factors:

- The *existence of competitors* is the first aspect which affects the market position of a provider at certain locations. For example, when competitors are located close to the provider, as is often the case in the fast-food sector, then the competition is higher and it is more difficult for a certain provider to realise a good market position.

- *Accessibility* also influences the market position of a service provider. In many service industries, accessibility is a relevant quality criterion for customer perceptions. That concerns both the location of a service, e.g. closeness to public transport, as well as the specifics of the service place, such as parking space or opening hours.

- This is also valid for the *quality of the rooms* of the service location, which is an important element of the tangible resources of a service (see Chapter 9). Note, however, that good room quality might also have negative consequences on customer perceptions. For example, the prestigious (non-customer-contact) outfits of banks sometimes make customers suspicious regarding the cost structure of banks and consequently the reasons for the fees they have to pay.

While the market-related and position-related criteria concern the service place's effects on customers' decisions and consequently on revenues of the service provider, the *profitability-related* criteria concern more the internal effects on efficiency and profitability:

- The *room costs* affect the profitability of a service provider. The costs are related to other criteria, e.g. the area where the service place is located. Service providers aim to outweigh their cost, including the service place cost, by the revenues they can realise. Consequently, a service provider must trade off whether certain room costs are overcompensated by the positive value effects of the room quality and other relevant location characteristics.

- Also, the *room capacity* has profitability-oriented effects. Generally, other costs increase on a diminishing scale with increasing room capacity. For example, both a hotel with ten rooms and a hotel with twenty rooms can probably be managed with the same number of receptionists. Next to these cost-oriented effects of room capacity, there are also revenue-related aspects: the more capacity a service provider can deal with, the more customers can be served, resulting in higher revenues. For the value effects and the management of service capacities in general see Chapter 10.

The *relevance of the evaluation criteria* strongly varies with whether a service is delivered at the provider's or the customer's location or at a third party's location. The criteria that concern customer perceptions are especially relevant for services that are delivered at the provider's location (from a marketing perspective; of course these criteria also concern internal aspects such as employee motivation etc., see Chapter 9). When a service is delivered at the customer's place or a third party's place, then the service location of the provider especially determines the cost of reaching the customer and other quality characteristics in the customers' perceptions, such as the speed of service delivery. For some criteria, the nature of the relevance as location criteria differs between evaluations for service deliveries at providers' places and customers' places. For example, the area of a service firm becomes a cost-relevant criteria, especially when a service is delivered to the customer's location. The greater the 'reach' of a firm, the shorter the distance to the customer and from customer to customer, clearly illustrated by the example of home food delivery services.

In addition, the *service type* influences the relevance of the evaluation criteria. There are several service type-related aspects which determine the importance of the discussed criteria for evaluating service locations. First, the frequency of service demand affects the criteria relevance. For day-to-day services the market-related criteria are especially relevant. In contrast, for services that are used by customers less frequently, the proximity to the service location and its accessibility are less relevant to the customer. Secondly, the number of customers affects the relevance of some of the criteria. For service deliveries at the customer's place, from a cost-oriented perspective, the patch of a service location is less important for a provider's decision on the service location.

As became obvious in the discussion on service place decisions, these are connected closely with *other services marketing decisions*. For example, the quality of the service place is strongly dependent on the tangibles and the facilities of the service place and other service resources (see Chapter 9). Furthermore, the service place might be connected with the offer of value-added services (see Chapter 5). For example, collection services at garages are more important to customers who live further from the provider. However, the further away a customer lives, the more expensive becomes the delivery of this value-added service to the provider.

Services marketing in action 7.5 on the 'Evaluation of service locations by a pizza restaurant chain' presents an example of how different criteria are used to evaluate a service location.

SERVICES MARKETING IN ACTION 7.5:

Evaluation of service locations by a pizza restaurant chain

DoubleDave's is a Texas-based franchising chain of pizza restaurants with about 40 branches in the US, especially Texas. The firm sees the location of its branches as the main success factor in the fast food business. Consequently, when a potential franchisee aims at opening a DoubleDave's restaurant, an important part of the application is the evaluation of the potential location for the restaurant. For the purpose of evaluating a location, DoubleDave's provides the evaluation form depicted in Figure 7.3 (overleaf).

The 11 factors indicated for an evaluation of a potential restaurant location partly cover the criteria discussed in this chapter and even become very industry-specific (e.g. factor 9 regarding a speed limit).

Source: DoubleDaves 2005.

▶

LOCATION EVALUATION

SITE ADRESS: _____

LANDLORD: _____ PHONE: _____

RESTAURANT SIZE (SQ. FT.): _____ DIMENSIONS (L X W): _____

The Real Estate industry recognizes three major factors when estimating the potential of a business property. The first is location, the second is location, and the third is location. DoubleDave's Pizzaworks puts the same emphasis on locating your franchise location. As you begin to look at and evaluate potential locations for your franchise, consider the following:

FACTORS	ANSWER
1. Is the site located on a high traffic street? (30,000 + cars; 20–30,000 cars; 10–20,000 cars)	_____
2. What is the population within a 3-mile radius of the site? (100,000 +; 50,000 +; 25,000 +)	_____
3. Is the site in a middle or middle-upper income area? ($60,000 +; $50,000 +; $40,000 + household income)	_____
4. Is the site in a growing or stable area? (growing, stable, declining)	_____
5. How do you rate the other stores in your center or vicinity? (excellent, good, fair, poor)	_____
6. Will the site allow illuminated signs? (on site, near site, shared sign, none)	_____
7. Is the site located at or near an intersection? (at, near, no)	_____
8. Is the site accessible/visible from several directions? (three ways, two ways, one way)	_____
9. Is the speed limit by the site appropriate? (25–35 mph; 35–45 mph; over 45 mph)	_____
10. How far is the site set back from the street frontage? (25–50 ft. back; 50–75 ft. back; 75–100 ft. back)	_____
11. How far away is nearest competitor? (2+ miles; 1–2 miles; less than 1 mile)	_____

OTHER CONSIDERATIONS:

College_____ High School _____ Church/Synagogue _____ Hospital _____ Office Bldgs. _____

McDonald's _____ Burger King _____ Other Fast Foods _____ Restaurants _____ Lg Employers _____

(Make additional copies of this form if you are evaluating several locations.)

Figure 7.3 Location evaluation form by DoubleDave's pizza restaurant chain

Source: DoubleDaves 2005.

Timing of service delivery

Service delivery varies not only according to service place; service providers also determine *timing aspects of service delivery*. Time aspects regarding service delivery are the length of service delivery, the time flexibility, the permanence of service availability and the time-lag between order and delivery (see Figure 7.4).

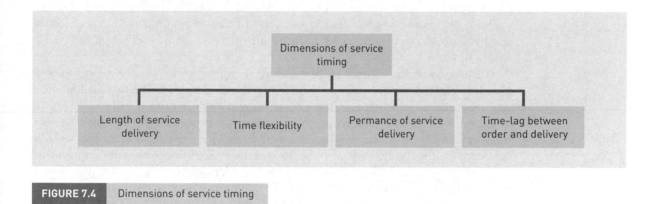

FIGURE 7.4 Dimensions of service timing

Length of service delivery

Services vary significantly in terms of *length of their delivery*. Compare for example the service of selling chewing gum at a kiosk with the service of presenting an art performance or the service of flying from the UK to the USA. Service delivery times are very different for these services. However, service length differences are also possible for the same service. Take the flight example again. The service of flying from London to Glasgow is much shorter than flying from London to Los Angeles.

The length of service delivery is *dependent upon various criteria*. In some cases the customer's specific needs determine the length of service delivery, such as a hotel stay. The customer or external factor also affects the service delivery length via the complexity of the customer problem, e.g. in the case of a car repair. Furthermore, other service characteristics have an influence on the length of a service, the distance between two cities as a determinant for the flight length, for example.

Next to these exogenous factors, the length of service delivery is also a *strategic means* of a service provider. By varying the service delivery length, service firms can develop new business segments. A classical example is fast food service versus the traditional restaurant service. A major difference between the two foodservice types is length of service delivery. From a value perspective, the two service types can be compared from both the customers' and the firm's perspective. From the customer's view point, shorter delivery time can accomplish a service need. When the customer only has a little time for lunch and still prefers to eat a hot meal, than a fast food service fulfils this need more than a traditional restaurant. From the firm's perspective, different service lengths affect both cost and revenue. The shorter the service delivery, the more customers can be served in a given time within a given capacity. Consequently, sales and possibly revenue increase. However, this is only valid when demand is higher than capacity. In other cases, it might be more feasible to extend service delivery times from an isolated profitability perspective. This logic is applied by hospitals varying the 'lengths of stay' for patients, according to given bed capacities and treatment. Of course, the objective quality and the customer's perception will often be associated negatively with this behaviour.

Different service lengths imply different *requirements for services marketing*. Shorter targeted service delivery times might imply more sophisticated logistical and operational processes, while longer service delivery times put more importance on the customer's perception of the service processes. With longer service delivery times the customer has more and/or longer contact with the service resources, thus the quality of these resources and of the process become more important compared to services with short service delivery times where only the service outome might be important to the customer. Furthermore, other service characteristics and services marketing decisions are linked with the delivery length, such as service design and pricing. For example, a fast food restaurant often offers standard dishes at low prices. In other industries, service delivery times and price correlate negatively; the shorter the service delivery, the higher the service price. This is the case for mail express services whose prices vary according to the guaranteed delivery times.

Time flexibility

A further time aspect of service delivery is the *customer's flexibility* regarding the point of time when the service is delivered. Generally, services differ according to whether provider and customer agree on a certain delivery time or not. The necessity for agreeing on a service delivery time is determined by the dependence on specific service resources which are scarce and often can only be used by one customer (or a certain number of customers) at a time. For example, a flight can only be conducted when a plane is available, a pilot is present and a departure time determined by the capacity 'airspace' is given. More specifically, for a given service time flexibility can vary depending on the customer's willingness to pay. For example, customers' flexibility is low for scheduled flights, while it is higher for private flights. This gain in flexibility is compensated for by significantly higher prices for private flights.

The degree of the customer's flexibility becomes especially obvious by whether appointments are made for service delivery or not. Using this criterion, the following *levels of the customer's flexibility* can be differentiated:

- *Predetermined delivery times without choice*: In these cases the customer has no choice regarding the delivery time. A fixed 'appointment' is given. An example of this are predetermined times by heating companies for reading the meter. This case also illustrates that time flexibility depends on a customer's willingness to pay. Often, when the customer is not present at the given time, the heating company representative returns on another day, for the customer is paying a fee.

- *Predetermined delivery times with choice*: This form of service timing is typical for all means of transports. An airline offers different flights at different times and the customer can choose a flight (up to a certain capacity of seats). As mentioned above, when the customer is willing to pay, flight scheduling can be more flexible, as is the case for private flights.

- *Undetermined delivery times*: For many services, there are no fixed delivery times. Generally, it is open to customers to choose delivery times. However, as services are perishable and service resources and capacities often limited, this can result in restrictions of a service's usage, e.g. traffic jams at certain times, queues in supermarkets or problems getting a seat on the train at certain travel times. In many industries, providers and customers agree on delivery times voluntarily or as a marketing instrument: appointments at the hairdresser, reservations at a hotel. These measures of so-called capacity management are discussed in more detail in Chapter 10. Also, other factors, such as legal conditions, can restrict the freedom of delivery time choice. In many countries, there are more or less rigorous laws on shopping hours determining a range of service delivery times for retailers.

Permanence of service availability

The preceding example of shopping times leads to a further time dimension of service delivery, the *permanence of service availability*. This dimension describes the time phases when the service resources are usable by the customer. Opening hours of service facilities e.g. supermarkets, fitness centres, car wash machines, are a typical indicator for the service availability. At the extreme, service facilities are available permanently. In many industries, there are limited availability hours. Often, there are standard availability hours in certain industries, e.g. opening times of retailers. In some cases, opening times depend on exogenous factors such as laws for retailing hours, availability of emergency services or the position of the sun for operating hours for ski lifts. In other cases, service availability is subject to the business strategy, '24 hours, 7 days a week'.

The firm's chosen position regarding the permanence of service availability has a major *influence on other services marketing instruments*. A permanent service availability necessitates the permanent provision of the respective service resources. For example, retail shops which are open 24 hours must be staffed by employees for that time. In many industries, there is the problem that the usage of capacities varies. Many retailers are used less frequently at night than during the day.

Consequently, it is not generally profitable to offer a 24-hour service. Profitability analyses must show whether such a service is effective in a particular case.[2] Services marketing in action 7.6 on 'Effectiveness of a 24-hour freeway patrol service' illustrates an example where a 24-hour service resulted in increased effectiveness.

Time-lag between order and delivery

A final dimension of service timing is the *time-lag between order and delivery*. Although there are service industries where services are used when purchased, e.g. restaurants, or the customer decides on the time-lag, e.g. purchase of a flight ticket when the departure date is known even if it is some time ahead, there are also services where it is in the nature of the service that there is a time-lag between the customer's ordering the service and service delivery. This is the case when a customer orders a physical good, such as furniture, books or a car, from a retailer and the delivery of the service includes taking the order, organising the transfer of

SERVICES MARKETING IN ACTION 7.6:

Effectiveness of a 24-hour freeway patrol service

The Hoosier Helper program is a roving freeway service patrol program in northwest Indiana. The program began operating between 6:00 am and 8:30 pm on 30 August 1991. The service was expanded and started providing 24-hour operations 7 days a week during the 1996 Memorial Day weekend. The program maintains a total of six vehicles, with a minimum of two used in the 24-hour service.

Hoosier Helper patrols 26 km of the Borman Expressway (I-80/94) near Gary, Indiana. Also, the program patrols a 13 km section of the Interstate Freeway I-65. The program provides support during incidents, and assists drivers free of charge by changing flat tyres, supplying fuel, and calling tow trucks.

A study estimates that during daytime operations the total annual benefit of the program is $1,937,800 ($1,241,300 from nonrecurring delay, $618,200 from secondary crash reduction, and $78,300 from vehicle operating cost savings). Total annual costs for these operations are $411,200, yielding a benefit to cost ratio of 4.7:1 for daytime operations.

The study also estimates that for the 24-hour operations the total benefit for a seven-month study period is $5,496,600 ($3,708,100 for non-recurring delays, $1,539,100 for secondary crash reductions, and $249,400 for vehicle operating cost savings). The cost of operations for the same study period were $413,900, yielding a benefit to cost ratio of 13.3:1 for 24-hour operations.

Source: Cost-Effectiveness Evaluation of Hoosier Helper Freeway Service Patrol in *Journal of Transporation Engineering*, Vol. 125 No. 5, American Society of Civil Engineers, (Latoski, S.P. *et al.* 1999), reproduced by permission of ASCE.

the ordered products from the producer and finally transferring the product to the customer. Furthermore, repair services, such as shoe, car or washing machine repairs, are typical services with a time-lag between order and delivery.

The existence and length of a time-lag is *caused by two time periods*: the time for conducting the core service and the time for preparing and organising the associated service execution, including waiting or storage times in case of a non-just-in-time service fulfilment, as is usual for car repairs, for example. These times are also determined when certain inputs are necessary. For example, the car retailer can only deliver a car when it has already been produced by the car manufacturer.

In the context of these time-lags, the major challenge for service managers is *service standardisation*. The more standardised a service in general, the more the specific elements of the service are standardised, resulting in a shorter time-lag between order and delivery. For example, in a traditional restaurant – compared to a fast-food restaurant – there are more processes and elements of the service in the delivery of the meal because the core elements of the service are standardised. Consequently, the time-lag between order and delivery is usually shorter in fast food restaurants. When service providers succeed in standardising as many elements as possible, a reduced time-lag between order and delivery can become a competitive advantage. This strategy was followed by Houston-based Gallery Furniture (see Services marketing in action 7.7).

SERVICES MARKETING IN ACTION 7.7:

Delivering furniture: A race with the customer

In the furniture retailing industry, it is generally accepted by customers that they have to wait for their furniture for some time. In that market situation, Gallery Furniture, Houston/USA identified the time between order and delivery as a potential competitive advantage and organised its processes in a such a manner that it delivers furniture to customers the same day they buy it.

When purchasing furniture, customers often take a long time to make a decision. They monitor furniture throughout the store. As purchasing furniture is often a 'long-term investment', they balance alternatives, think of special offers and luxury pieces. All in all, purchasing processes regarding furniture are often extensive and take a long time. But, when a decision is taken, there is often disillusion, because when one has decided on a certain piece of furniture, one wants to have it immediately. However, in many cases, one has to wait for the delivery of the piece for days or even weeks.

Not at Gallery Furniture. Customers who decide on a certain piece of furniture in the store will have it in their homes within hours. Storeowner Jim 'Mattress Mac' McIngvale loves telling stories about the delivery truck beating the customer home with the recently purchased furniture.

Source: based on Berry 2001.

Channels of service distribution and delivery

The integration of the customer into the service process and the *need for direct contact between service provider and customer* for service delivery, result in requirements regarding the channels which can be used for service distribution and delivery. When you recapitulate the standard delivery in consumer goods markets, these service specifics become even more obvious. In consumer goods industries, most often the actual producer of a consumer good never has contact with the customer. The producing firm delivers the good to the end consumer through different channels via mail or via a distributor. However in service industries, a contact between service firm and customer is necessary. The consumer goods markets actually demonstrates this difference: the postal company which delivers a consumer good from the producing firm to the customer is a service provider which conveys the product to the customer, via the letter box as an external factor.

For these reasons, direct distribution and delivery is essential for services. For a start, let us consider single service providers rather than huge service corporations. Here, the natural form of service distribution and delivery is a *'one-to-one'* distribution. The service provider is a single person who distributes and delivers services to several customers (see Figure 7.5). While this form of service was predominant within 'service industries' before the industrial revolution, even in today's global and concentrated society there are still many examples of such one-to-one service deliveries: independent tax accounts without employees, photo machines, kiosks. The resources which are necessary to deliver the service are provided by the 'one-man' service firm. In cases where the service provider serves more than one customer, then in most cases (apart from in the case of services which are delivered to several customers simultaneously) service deliveries for more than one customer proceed sequentially. The tax accountant meets with his clients one after another and customers use a photo machine one after another.

Although there are many examples for these one-to-one service delivery situations, their proportion on the services market in terms of customers, employees, sales or revenue is low. Comparable to goods industries, service providers aim at providing greater amounts of service deliveries than is possible via one-to-one deliveries. They aim at a **multiplication of service deliveries** which is more difficult than the multiplication of goods production due to the integration of the customer. There are different types of service delivery multiplication (see Figure 7.6) which can be differentiated on a first level according to whether the multipli-

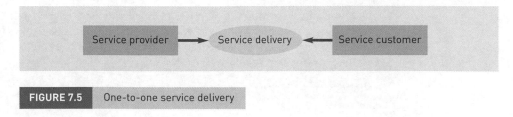

FIGURE 7.5 One-to-one service delivery

cation is conducted via a direct or indirect service delivery. An indirect service delivery means that a distributor transfers the service from provider to customer, like retailers for consumer goods. Due to the necessity of a direct contact between provider and customer to produce a service, this form of service delivery is an exception for services.

There is only one exception to this rule, and this concerns a *divided service delivery*. In this case, two steps of the service delivery can be differentiated. In the first step, the customer is sold a voucher which records the customer's right to receive a specific service. Examples of these vouchers are train or airline tickets, tickets for rock concerts, etc. In these cases, the vouchers can be distributed like consumer goods, thus an indirect distribution is then possible too, as is the case for travel agencies or ticket agencies.

For most services, a *direct service delivery* is predominant. In most service industries, the customer has contact with the service provider. This is possible via two types of **service channels** (see Figure 7.6):

- personal channels (as in bank branches or fast food restaurants);
- electronic channels (e.g. telephone or internet).

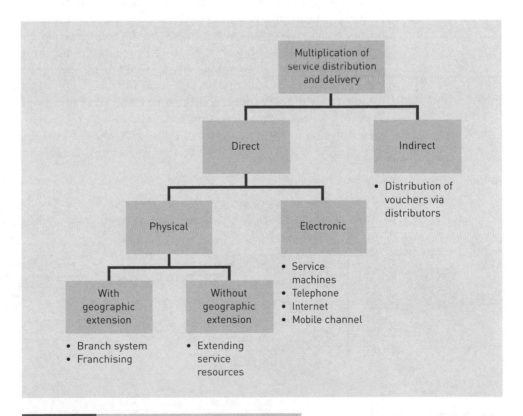

FIGURE 7.6 Types of service delivery multiplication

Personal service delivery

Before the technological developments in the last decade, especially the internet, personal channels were almost the only service delivery channels. The multiplication options within *personal service delivery* can be conducted in two forms: with or without geographical extension. *Without a geographical extension*, service deliveries are multiplied via an extension of service resources (see Figure 7.7). Starting from a one-to-one service delivery, the number of those resources which are necessary for service delivery is increased, as in the case of the kiosk owner who employs an assistant. As a consequence, the two can conduct two service deliveries at a time. This model of service delivery multiplication is found frequently and applies to many small businesses, such as restaurants, shops, hairdressers or dental clinics. Multiplication of services, without a geographical extension, can be conducted not only via a multiplication of the human resources, as in the examples mentioned, but also via a multiplication of physical resources. Take a hotel which extends its facilities by adding more bedrooms, resulting in the ability to serve more customers at a time. The advantage of this form of extension is that in most cases not all resources have to be multiplied in order to realise the delivery multiplication. Often, administrative or supervising resources can still handle the extended service deliveries. However, the overall potential of these extensions in terms of increasing sales significantly is low. New market segments are seldom attracted.

An important reason for the restricted potential of multiplication without geographical extension is customer integration. For most services, customers are not willing to travel too far to a service location. Consequently, for a certain service location only the consumers living within a certain range are potential customers. Therefore, other forms of multiplication have emerged over the decades which take into account the necessity of being close to the customer. These forms are

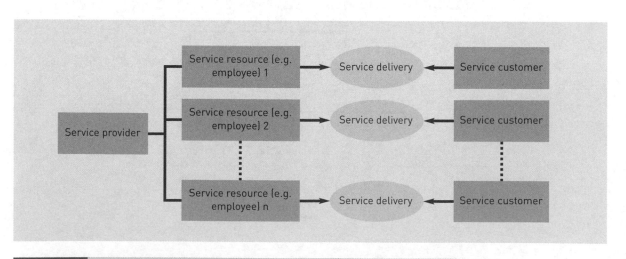

FIGURE 7.7 Multiplication of personal service delivery without geographical extension

summed up under the label of *multiplication with a geographical extension*. This extension is often realised by extending the number of service locations by establishing new service locations at other marketplaces (see Figure 7.8). This is the case when Starbucks opens a new café in an area where they are not yet located or for the branch system of many banks. There are two forms of such multiplication which are quite common and intensely discussed in the literature:

- multiplication by a branch system;

- multiplication by franchising.

In both cases, an *existing concept* for a service location is reproduced at different places. In contrast to the multiplication without geographical extension, in this case the whole bundle of service resources, and not only specific resources, are multiplied. In every new bank branch, a new lobby is needed, new counters, new employees and new teller machines. Furthermore, some kind of administrative or supervising organisation is mostly also established, because the geographical distance results in inefficiencies when these tasks continue to be conducted by headquarters.

The traditional form of such a multiplication is via a *branch system* as it is known in banks and classically for supermarkets. The service firm's delivery system then consists of more than one service outfit. The service outfits are managed more or less

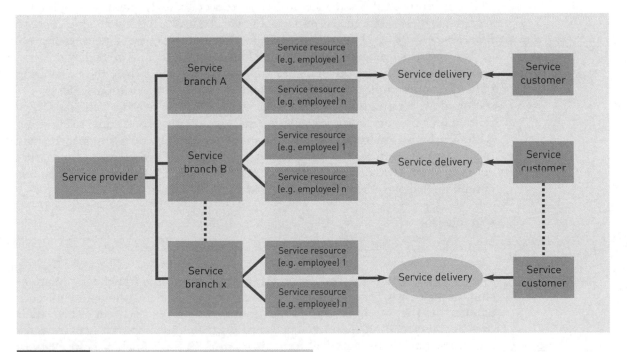

FIGURE 7.8 Multiplication with geographical extension

independently and are, to some extent, directed by the headquarters of the service provider. To what extent the headquarters are involved in the management of a branch depends on several factors, but most importantly the degree of customisation which is usual for the respective service affects the *power distribution between headquarters and branch*. The degree of customisation is a component of customer integration and concerns how a specific service unit is influenced by individual customer characteristics. The more customised a service is, the less powerful the headquarters often are. A highly customised service is that of a consultancy firm which develops the service strongly focusing on the needs of a specific, regional customer base. The 'branches' of consultancy firms are invariably autonomous and powerful, when compared to the headquarters. Regional consultancies can best take into account specific customer needs when the branch can take all decisions regarding a customer or certain project instead of having to have every decision confirmed by headquarters. This is very different to the situation with supermarkets. Here, we have a relatively standardised service, few strategic decisions have to be taken on a day-to-day basis and, most strategic decisions, e.g. listing the products of a certain producer, approaching new customer segments, are realised without the customer. For conducting a media campaign or taking decisions regarding the range of services, the customer is not involved. Consequently, these are preparatory tasks of the service provider and can be realised without customer contact. However, establishing a branch system also involves certain risks, especially because of the significant investments associated with establishing such a system.

For the purpose of risk reduction, another concept of a geographical extension of service businesses has gained importance over the years: the **franchising** concept. Franchising is a quasi branch system with a different legal model in terms of property and ownership rights. While the standard branch system is owned by the focal service firm and the single branches are part of the whole firm, the franchising model is more complex. Franchising is defined as 'a business form essentially consisting of an organisation (the franchisor) with a market-tested business package centred on a product or service, entering into a continuing contractual relationship with franchisees, typically self-financed and independently owner-managed small firms, operating under the franchisor's trade name to produce and/or market goods or services according to a format specified by the franchisor'.[3] Based on this definition, two players in a franchising system can be identified:

- franchisor;

- franchisee.

The *franchisor* brings its whole marketing concept into the franchising relationship. In this sense, franchising is a combination of a branch system and a licence agreement. The *franchisee* is an independent entrepreneur who invests in their own business within the franchising chain. Regarding the importance of franchising, in Britain there were 569 franchisors and 29,100 franchisees in 2000. In Europe, only in Germany are there more active franchise partners.[4]

Compared to a standard branch system, *franchising defers risk from the service firm* (the franchisor) because the franchisee invests into its franchising business, and assumes some of the business risk. Furthermore, franchisees might be more easily motivated for that very reason. They are often locals and know the specific market situation. On the negative side, most importantly, the service firm has less influence and control over the franchisees than is the case with a standard branch system. Therefore, it is especially difficult to achieve a standardised quality and expertise level. Consequently, franchising is mostly found in sectors where material resources are predominant compared to immaterial, interaction-related resources, and where processes are more standardised compared to other industries, e.g. in the hotel, restaurant, fast food or retailing industries.

Electronic service delivery

Next to the service delivery via personal channels, an alternative becoming more and more important are *electronic delivery channels* (see Figure 7.9 and Table 7.2). While the internet is the first choice in this field, there are other electronic channels, such as the telephone. More specifically, we differentiate four types of electronic delivery channels:

- service machines;
- telephone;
- internet;
- mobile channel.

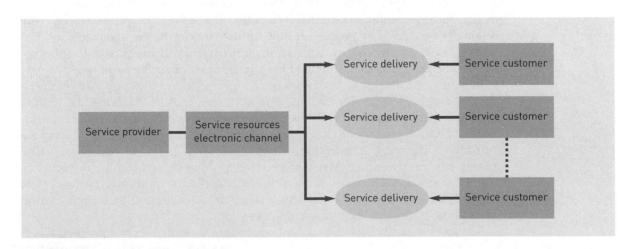

FIGURE 7.9 Electronic service delivery

| TABLE 7.2 | Differences between electronic delivery channels |

Characteristics	Electronic delivery channels			
	Service machine	Telephone	Internet	Mobile channel
Customer's location flexibility	Low	High	Medium	High
Breadth of modalities	Medium (Visual)	Medium (Voice)	Medium (Visual)	High (Voice, Visual)
Interactivity	High	High	Medium	High
Responsiveness	Low	High	Medium	High

(1) Service machines

Service machines – or interactive kiosks[5] – are technical installations which conduct certain service processes for the customer. Classical examples are underground ticket machines, ATMs or automated check-ins at the airport. The service process does not change dramatically when using service machines. As with non-automated services, the customer (as the external factor) comes to the provider's place in order for the service to be conducted, and it is still necessary for there to be *direct contact between customer and provider*. The main difference between this and the classical personal service delivery is that the service processes which were originally conducted by people, are now fulfilled by computers and machines. The ATM inherits the employees' actions, the photo machine the actions of the photographer and the check-in machines at the airport those of airline employees.

In terms of *value*, these machines have an impact on efficiency. Although the development of the service machines involves some costs (which are higher than the cost of acquiring new employees), the long-term cost of running the automated service processes are lower than for personal service processes due to the employees' salaries. In addition, service machines result in perceived value effects for the customer. Many automated processes can imply convenience effects, such as reduced waiting times. Overall, the perceived value effect depends on the customers' technology acceptance levels, and their appreciation of personal contacts with service employees.

Service machines, however, are not applicable for every service process, this is especially true of service processes where service characteristics play an important role and there is a high degree of customer integration into the service process resulting in a high heterogeneity of service processes. These services are difficult to automate. In contrast, more standardised processes which are quite autonomous and therefore homogeneous for every customer can be automated easily.

(2) Telephone

A second, powerful service technology which modifies the traditional service process is service via *telephone*. The installation of call centres and telephone computers emerged increasingly at the end of the twentieth century. In service interactions via telephone, a direct, physical closeness between customer and service provider is no longer necessary. The customer can be located anywhere where there is a telephone. In contrast to service machines, so called *voice-to-voice encounters* where service employees talk to the customer necessitate service employees who must be available for service delivery – as with traditional personal service deliveries.

The *value effects* of service delivery via telephone also concern cost elements. Even though call centres involve some costs such as for the call centre agents as well as the service technology, it is much more efficient for a service provider than maintaining a set of service outfits. It also becomes easier to react to changes in demand. To illustrate, assume that a bank's call centre substitutes for two branches. With the two branches in place, it can happen that in branch A clients have to wait for service delivery while in branch B there are unused service resources. When the two branches (and in reality even more branches) are pooled together to form a call centre, then these differences in the usage of service resources can be compensated through economies of scale. On the customer's side, telephone service deliveries have implications for perceived value. The technology makes a service provision possible which does not necessitate the customer's presence at the service provider's location. Thus, for the customers too the use of telephones in the service delivery offers efficiency advantages. Regarding whether a telephone service encounter delivers value to the customer and the customer's evaluation of voice-to-voice service encounters, customers have *expectations regarding four dimensions* (see Table 7.3):[6]

- *Adaptability* of the call centre agent. The customer evaluates whether the agent is able to handle and cope with different questions, to adapt to each and every situation, taking the customer's level of knowledge into account, etc.

- *Assurance* of the call centre agent. Regarding this dimension, the customer expects the agent to explain where service problems come from, what steps are taken to resolve the problem and the reasons for possible transfers to other agents, etc.

- *Empathy* of the call centre agent. Here the customer is interested in the agent's understanding of what the customer is going through, making the customer feel special and treating the customer's questions as important.

- *Authority* of the call centre agent. In this regard, the customer expects the agent to be empowered to handle the problem effectively and to have the authority to effect the appropriate changes.

TABLE 7.3	Dimensions and attributes of call centre expectations
Adaptability	Treatment of different questions Ability to adapt to each and every situation Taking my level of knowledge into account Ability to remain calm and friendly Helping me to define my problem more specifically Ability to help me with each and every question
Assurance	Explanation of the reason for a complaint Explanation of each and every step for answering my question Explanation for the reason to be transferred Giving me the feeling that my information is used confidentially Inform me about the use of my information
Empathy	Imagining what I am going through with a complaint Ability to give me the feeling of being a special customer Treatment of my question as an important one
Authority	Leaving my questions unanswered disturbs me Calls being returned, because the agent is not allowed to answer my questions

Source: Burgers *et al.* 2000, p. 153.

(3) Internet

Even though based on telephone technology, service deliveries via the internet channel exhibit some important differences from traditional voice-to-voice encounters. The fact that modalities other than 'voice' are applicable means that there are extended possibilities for the internet channel based upon the design of various service interactions. Telephone service interactions can only include contents which are presentable verbally. If the customer is not able to explain their problem verbally, a voice-to-voice encounter is impossible. For example, when documents, etc. are necessary, a service delivery via telephone is not possible. In many cases, it is difficult for the service provider to present the features of its services via the telephone. For example, travel agency offers would be difficult to make very clear via telephone conversation.

These disadvantages of telephone encounters are overcome by *internet service interactions*. In these interactions, more modalities can be used than via the telephone.

The notion that internet encounters lack the interactive aspect of telephone encounters can be overruled when the former include the option to email service operations – and the respective answering system is efficient.

Regarding *value effects*, internet interactions are even more efficient for the service provider as in most cases the problem of unavailable service resources is not evident. Internet interactions are still connected with cost to some extent. This concerns not only the investment in the installation of the technological systems, but also the cost of running internet operations. Further, assuming the customer's acceptance of the internet channel, it involves several advantages in terms of value for the customer: Often, the customer can choose the service time, and in many cases, internet interactions are cheaper than other interactions because service providers pass the cost advantages to the customers. However, the acceptance of some of the problems still associated with the internet channel prohibits 100 per cent of the service processes being conducted via the internet.

(4) Mobile channel

For traditional internet services, the customer must still be at a certain place, although it need not be the provider's location or a place which is determined by the service's objects, but a place where internet access is available. This restriction is overcome by so called *m-commerce*, mobile commerce via mobile phones and PDAs. Today, for technological reasons, it is not possible to use the same applications in mobile commerce as in e-commerce. But in the future, this will be possible, and the advantages of internet interactions will be combined with the advantages of geographical independence and flexibility.

As mobile commerce is relatively new, there are even more obstacles regarding its acceptance by consumers. For wireless financial services, five *determinants of the attitude and usage intentions* concerning the new form of service interactions were found:[7]

- perceived usefulness (e.g. faster accomplishment of tasks);

- perceived ease of use (e.g. WAP applications not being cumbersome to use);

- perceived costs (e.g. reasonableness of the price charged for WAP-enabled mobile phones);

- perceived system quality (e.g. speed of connection between WAP phones and the internet);

- social influence (e.g. friends and relatives encouraging the customer to use WAP applications).

The discussion of the options of self-service technologies illustrates the possibilities of technologies in service interactions. The use of the technologies contributes to a change in the service interaction, leading to a weakening of the restrictions associated with the service characteristics. Direct contact between provider and customer is now partly unnecessary, and the customer becomes more flexible in terms of the service location. However, technological versions of service processes are only feasible for certain service processes. Processes with a high proportion of personal qualities, such as consulting or medical services, or processes which concern the customer's body (e.g. medical services) or the customer's physical objects (e.g. car repair) need some contact between provider and customer at some time.

Multi-channelling in service industries

With the increasing number of channels which are available to service providers for distributing and delivering their services, the number of *differences between these channels* rises. The differences concern several internal and external aspects, such as cost differences or differences regarding the consumers' preferences. Some customers prefer the use of the internet, which is often involved with lower cost, while others insist on the traditional personal contact with the service provider and its employees (which is often more expensive than electronic channels). Services marketing in action 7.8 illustrates for the Portuguese banking sector how different the functions can be which customers associate with the different channels.

Because of the differences between the channels, service providers systematically plan the combined offer of the channels to the customers. The question is, what channels are offered to which customers and at what price? The respective decisions are summarised under the concept of **multi-channelling**. From a more differentiated view on the multi-channelling concept, the channelling approach of a service firm can be described by three *dimensions*:[8]

- number of channels offered;
- degree of channel integration, as in the degree to which a firm conducts channel activities itself or lets them be conducted by other firms;
- degree of personal contact with the customer.

The three dimensions of a service firm's channel concept enlighten the *value impacts of a multi-channelling approach*. Generally, multi-channelling aims at compensating the advantages and disadvantages of the different channels. This objective can be analysed more specifically from a value-oriented perspective. First, service providers take *profitability-oriented decisions* when determining their channel offers. For example, many banks turned to offering only telephone interactions to certain, low-profit customer groups recently. Secondly, the channel decision can be evaluated from a *sales- or revenue-oriented view*.[9] The number of channels has an impact on market availability and further on the ability to meet customer needs. The more channels a firm offers, the more it is able to satisfy the differentiated needs of different customer groups resulting in higher satisfaction, loyalty and value. Market availability is also determined by the degree of integra-

SERVICES MARKETING IN ACTION 7.8:

Channel preferences of bank customers

For researching the differences of bank channels perceived by customers, 36 customers of Portuguese banks were interviewed regarding the reasons why they use certain banking channels. From the interviewees' perspective, internet banking has the advantages of accessibility, time saving and ease of use. Bank branches are associated with mutual knowledge, individual attention as well as professional knowledge. The benefits of telephone banking include human contact, convenience and accessibility. ATMs are associated with usefulness of available options, accessibility and time saving. Table 7.4 summarises the study results.

TABLE 7.4   Channel preferences of bank customers

Internet banking	Percentage of customers	Bank branch	Percentage of customers	Telephone banking	Percentage of customers	ATM	Percentage of customers
Advantages of each service delivery system							
Accesability	67	Mutual knowledge	75	Human contact	19	Usefulness of available operations	39
Time saving	64	Individual attention	72	Convenience	14	Accessibility	39
Ease of use	61	Professional knowledge	56	Accessibility	11	Time saving	31
Information capabilities	53	Empathy and courtesy	44	Ability to answer questions	11	Convenience	14
Feed-back control	53	Ability to solve, clarify and decide	44	Courtesy	11	Feed-back control	14
Usefullness	47	Completeness of functionalities	44				
Convenience	44						
Autonomy	36						
Disadvantages of each service delivery system							
Security concerns	64	Time loss	72	Lack of feedback control	25	Security concerns	39
Unavailability of operations	53	Lack of accessibility	42	Lack of mutual knowledge	22	Technical features	36
Lack of information quality	47	Lack of convenience	22	Lack of personalisation	22	Unavailability of operations	22
Lack of personalisation	28			Lack of value added	17	Lack of back-office response	19

Source: Patrício *et al.* 2003.

tion. The lower the channel integration into the provider itself, the lower the fixed cost. Furthermore, the lower the channel integration, the higher the market availability of the firm's services, as the first section of Services marketing in action 7.9 demonstrates. However, higher channel integration results in higher control and a more direct contact with the customers – aspects which might also affect sales and revenues. Thirdly, there are cost-related effects which can be attributed to the channelling approach of a service provider. Multi-channelling aims at a cost reduction by substituting high-cost channels with low-cost channels, for example with substituting personal channels with electronic channels (see the second section in Services marketing in action 7.9). However, this is often not realised. The channel system of the service provider often becomes more complex through multi-channelling resulting in a higher cost for the channel system. The third section in Services marketing in action 7.9 visualises that problem.

SERVICES MARKETING IN ACTION 7.9:

Value effects of multi-channelling

(1) Value effects of low channel integration

Bank of Scotland and Royal Bank of Scotland (RBS) have teamed up with Sainsbury's and Tesco, respectively, to expand their market coverage. Tesco's Clubcard Plus was originally set up with NatWest, but this arrangement broke up as the retailer wanted to increase its range of financial services. The two former ventures have provided the two banks with a very cost-effective channel. Tesco and RBS claimed to have acquired 400,000 new customers, and Sainsbury's an extra 600,000 customers and an extra £1.3bn on deposits.

Source: Feuchtwanger 1997.

Hence, teaming up with other organisations and forgoing some control over distribution can produce attractive benefits. Therefore, a company's sales volume and degree of control over channel activities is strongly influenced by the extent to which it has integrated its distribution channels.

Source: Coelho and Easingwood 2003.

(2) Cost advantages of electronic channels

It costs £100,000 a year to keep a sales person in the field, but £60,000 to employ and equip a teleoperative resulting in a cost-saving of 40 per cent. Likewise, if a company has an over-the-counter unit sales cost of £1.90, a direct mail sales cost of 97p and a phone cost of 63p, that opportunity to be 66 per cent more cost-effective is appealing.

Source: Reed 1997.

(3) Dark (value) side of multi-channelling

As one manager put it, 'The activities of the call centre so far have been primarily service banking, anticipating a reduction in customer branch traffic and hopefully saving money. But it just added extra costs. The call centre lacks selling skills. We have very confident people on the phone, but we must take salesmanship to the telephone.'

Source: Coelho and Easingwood 2003.

Next to the positive value effects that are expected from introducing a multi-channel approach, there are also some *problems* which service providers encounter when introducing such an approach.[10] There is the danger of customer confusion. When the attributes of the channelling approach are not clearly communicated to the customer, it might be confusing, for example the customer might not understand why they pay different prices according to channel usage. Channel conflicts can arise, namely internal or external channel conflicts. Internal channel conflicts concern compartmentalised thinking on the part of the different departments of a firm. For example, in banks, call centres and personal contact organisations are attached to different departments and there is an inherent potential for conflict, especially regarding the responsibilities of the different departments. External channel conflicts emerge when there is competition between internal and external channels, as Services marketing in action 7.10 shows.

SERVICES MARKETING IN ACTION 7.10:

External channel conflicts in the life insurance industry

Life insurance companies in the UK have also been precluded from introducing, or at least have been delaying the introduction of other channels, because of the effect on their direct sales forces: 'If we were going to adopt direct channels in a more committed fashion, we would have other concerns, because we would set the direct channels in direct competition with brokers and intermediaries. It can be seen as a hostile move and damage these relationships. We don't want to jeopardise the relationships with intermediaries. Multiple channels can create conflict with intermediaries if you are not careful with the way you market to different channels. The classic example might be that the insurance company markets directly to a client who is also a client of a financial adviser. The adviser would be straight on the phone demanding to know why the company had contacted the adviser's clients directly. You have to be very careful, and conflicts tend to arise. It is a possibility, but it's something that has not happened frequently because we are trying to be very careful about making sure that we do not upset existing channels.'

Source: Coelho and Easingwood 2004.

Summary

The learning objectives of this chapter can be summarised as follows (see Figure 7.10):

1. Service delivery decisions imply various value effects. Both delivery costs as well as revenue implications vary according to whether a service is produced at the provider's or the customer's location, the service timing (e.g. permanent service availability) and the service channels (e.g. personal versus electronic channels).

2. There are services for which the place of service delivery is predetermined to take place at the provider's, the customer's or a third party's location. When the service place is not predetermined, there are greater options for strategic decisions, like developing service innovations based on the service location or applying a multi-option service place strategy.

3. The place of service delivery affects the quality characteristics relevant to the customer, as well as the process of integrating the customer and the customer's purchasing decisions.

4. Service providers apply market-related, position-related and profitability-related criteria in order to evaluate different service locations.

5. Service providers take several decisions regarding service timing which concern the length and time flexibility of service delivery, the permanence of service availability as well as the time-lag between order and delivery.

6. In today's service industries, various types of service delivery channels can be observed. However, the classic delivery channel for a service is personal delivery due to the necessity of direct contact between provider and customer.

7. In order to increase value, service providers apply strategies of service multiplication which is possible via personal and electronic channels.

8. A multiplication via personal delivery channels can be realised with or without a geographical extension. For conducting a geographical extension, branch systems and franchising are common concepts.

9. An electronic service delivery can be realised via four channels: service machines, telephone, internet and the mobile channel.

10. Many service providers apply multi-channelling approaches which can be specified according to the number of channels offered, the degree of channel integration as well as the degree of personal contact with the customer.

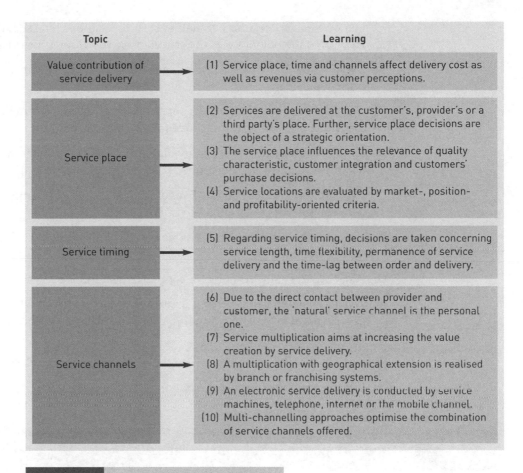

Topic	Learning
Value contribution of service delivery	(1) Service place, time and channels affect delivery cost as well as revenues via customer perceptions.
Service place	(2) Services are delivered at the customer's, provider's or a third party's place. Further, service place decisions are the object of a strategic orientation. (3) The service place influences the relevance of quality characteristic, customer integration and customers' purchase decisions. (4) Service locations are evaluated by market-, position- and profitability-oriented criteria.
Service timing	(5) Regarding service timing, decisions are taken concerning service length, time flexibility, permanence of service delivery and the time-lag between order and delivery.
Service channels	(6) Due to the direct contact between provider and customer, the 'natural' service channel is the personal one. (7) Service multiplication aims at increasing the value creation by service delivery. (8) A multiplication with geographical extension is realised by branch or franchising systems. (9) An electronic service delivery is conducted by service machines, telephone, internet or the mobile channel. (10) Multi-channelling approaches optimise the combination of service channels offered.

FIGURE 7.10   Learning summary for Chapter 7

Knowledge questions

1. Explain how service costs vary between service delivery at the customer's and at the provider's place.

2. How can the delivery channel affect cost and revenue?

3. Explain why the service location affects the quality characteristics relevant to the customer. List sample quality characteristics for the three possible service places.

4. Describe the differences in consumers' purchasing decisions depending on the service place.

5. List possible criteria for evaluating service locations by a service provider. How does the relevance of the criteria vary for different service types?

6. Explain how the service length can be used as a strategic means by service providers.

7. Describe the different levels of service delivery's time flexibility and the different consequences they have for customer behaviour.

8. How does permanent service availability affect the management of service resources (e.g. service personnel)?

9. Explain how service standardisation can be used for minimising the time-lag between service order and delivery.

10. Explain why a personal one-to-one service delivery is the 'natural' form of service delivery.

11. What are the value reasons for service firms' multiplication strategies?

12. What are the value impacts of a multiplication via personal channels with a geographical extension compared to a multiplication without geographical extension?

13. Describe the differences between the different electronic channels.

14. Explain the value impact of applying a multi-channelling approach.

Application and discussion questions

1. Collect examples of services for which the service place is predetermined to be the provider's, the customer's or a third party's place. Explore the reasons for this predetermination.

2. Describe an example of a firm which offers multiple service locations for the customer to choose from. What are the reasons for this multi-option offering?

3. Compare your evaluations of a restaurant visit and a pizza delivery service. How do the quality characteristics you use for your evaluation differ?

4. Imagine you were opening a café. Which criteria would you choose to evaluate different service locations? Select three possible locations and compare them according to the criteria. What decision would you take?

5. List examples of services for which you prefer a longer delivery time and those for which you prefer a short delivery time. Try to find the reasons for the differences in your delivery time preferences.

6. Find an example of a service provider who offers restricted times of service availability and discuss the feasibility of this strategy.

7. Discuss why being served takes longer in some restaurants than in others.

8. List examples from your personal experience where you are served in a personal one-to-one service delivery situation.

9. Explore the reasons why banks do not apply a franchising-type of service multiplication.

10. What are the advantages to a McDonald's franchisee in contrast to their opening their own independent restaurant?

11. Select two services: one service you usually use via personal channels and one service you usually use via electronic channels. What are the reasons for you using the different channels?

12. In which service industry do you use various service channels? What are your reasons for using, and the firm's reasons for offering, multiple channels?

CASE STUDY: MULTI-CHANNELLING AT MÖVENPICK WEIN CORPORATION

The MPW Mövenpick Wein Corporation, an independent business segment of the Swiss Mövenpick Holding, is a leading importer and retailer of international quality wines. The firm sells premium wines to end consumers and the restaurant trade, and delivers to selected retailers. In 2003, 7 million bottles were sold, revenues were 112 million Swiss francs. Within the product range of Mövenpick, there are quality wines, especially from North and South America, but also selected wines from France, Spain, Italy and other world regions.

However, Mövenpick Wein operates within a *difficult market situation*. Especially for medium and upmarket wines, demand is stagnating, and competitors like food retailers follow a low-price strategy. Therefore, Mövenpick Wein has had to *refine its strategy* in recent years. This strategic change encompassed two important elements. First, broadening the product range by also including low-priced wines, and secondly, distinguishing itself in the private customer segment with the principle 'Closer to the customer!' An important strategic tool in realising the latter principle was the implementation of a *multi-channelling approach*.

Traditionally, Mövenpick Wein offers its wines via three *personal channels*:

- Wine cellars: there are twelve Mövenpick wine cellars where the customer can test more than 1,000 wines and take part in wine tastings.

- Caveau wine bar: the wine bars are a mixture of wine cellar and restaurant.

- Caveau restaurant: these are classic restaurants with a wide selection of wines.

Mövenpick Wein Switzerland employs 135 staff to ensure the delivery of a quality service for its quality wines. In order not only to sell wines to the customers who are central to the firm's philosophy, Mövenpick Wein started applying further channels in order to contact the customer, like traditional direct marketing and the online channel. The *different channels* in the multi-channelling approach of Mövenpick diversify marketing *tasks*.

New customers are recruited via the wine cellars, the online shop and through cooperation with partner firms.

The direct marketing channel is used in order to *send professional monthly wine-related information* to the customers. Each year, about 1.2 million customers are contacted via direct mailing. The mailings further point out the online shop which is used by many customers right after reading the mailing. During a year, eleven *promotions with special offers* are conducted which reach the customer via letter or email. For ordering the special offers, the customer can use five order channels:

- mail (with order form);

- telephone;

- fax;

- wine cellar;

- online shop.

The mailings *affect revenues* significantly and are based on long-term planning. Here, the customer can choose which channel is used. Mövenpick Wein does not try to shift the customer to one channel or the other via incentives. Many customers contact Mövenpick via different channels – depending on their situation. Some customers order by telephone initiated by a mailing, others visit the next wine tasting or order from the online shop. Similarly, many recipients of the email newsletter visit the wine cellars after receiving the newsletter.

The percentage of online orders is between 5 and 10 per cent – depending on season and campaign. This is not aimed at replacing the personal channel by the online channel, but a reasonable *integration of the different channels*. Many customers attracted via the online channel will visit a wine cellar sooner or later to get further information in a personal dialogue. More than 30 per cent of the online orders are collected personally. Conversely, traditional wine cellar customers appreciate the opening hours and efficiency of the online shop.

The multi-channelling is also used for the *generation of customer information*, like the customer's address. Each year, Mövenpick Wein conducts campaigns whereby customers are asked to provide their email address and to subscribe to the email newsletter. These campaigns are supported by wine competitions that further increase interest and customer response rates.

In addition to the email newsletter, the electronic channel is used for specific *email campaigns* in order to generate further revenue from a customer. These campaigns are customised in order to address the customers according to their wine interests. Furthermore, only customers whose purchasing behaviour corresponds with the wines in the campaign are selected as recipients. Thus, communication costs are reduced to a minimum and customers who are not interested in certain wines or in the newsletter are not approached. Using the respective technologies and software, the mailing can be sent out by automated formats and the feedback from the customers is registered by an order form and processed efficiently. Diverse studies as well as the experiences by Mövenpick Wein show increased customer orders. The demanding customer wants to be served round the clock via their preferred channels.

This results in higher pressure for the firm to *integrate the different channels* and requires investments in respective marketing concepts and integrated technical solutions. Customers' acceptance regarding receiving messages from Mövenpick is restricted. Furthermore, Mövenpick Wein aims at avoiding too many contacts which are not integrated.

In recent years, multi-channelling has become a core element of Mövenpick's wine marketing strategy so as to realise a sustained customer loyalty by achieving a consistent perception of Mövenpick Wine World and the implicit quality promise. The physical shops support the online activities and profit from increased customer visits and additional revenue.

The multi-channelling approach resulted in a significant increase of private customers from 2003 to 2004. While total revenue decreased by 2 per cent, revenue from private customers increased by 8.7 per cent and revenue via the internet channel increased by 80 per cent. The e-shop further impressed the Swiss technology magazine 'anthrazit' which appoints the 100 best Swiss e-shops every year. In 2004, Mövenpick Wein was awarded third place in this competition. Finally, despite the difficult market situation, Mövenpick opened several new wine shops.

In conclusion, Mövenpick Wein's multi-channelling strategy helped the firm to resist the difficult market situation, especially in the private customer segment where revenue increased significantly above market level.

Sources: Scheidegger and Taaks 2004; Mövenpick 2004.

Notes

[1] See Stern *et al.* 1996, p. 1.

[2] See Perkins 2005.

[3] See Curran and Stanworth 1983, p. 11.

[4] See Schulz 2001.

[5] See Meuter *et al.* 2000.

[6] See Burgers *et al.* 2000.

[7] See Kleijnen *et al.* 2004.

[8] See Coelho and Easingwood 2003.

[9] See Ennew *et al.* 1989; Coelho and Easingwood 2003.

[10] See Cespedes and Corey 1990; Coelho and Easingwood 2004.

8 Communicating service value: Service communications and branding

Rethink your typical actions in service encounters: you are talking to a bank employee or reading an ATM messages whilst punching in information for the ATM. When you have a doctor's appointment you tell the doctor your problem and the doctor diagnoses the problem. In class, you listen to the professor and discuss business topics with him and the other students. At the cinema, you watch and listen to the film being shown. All these actions are or concern some form of communication.

Since *services are processes*, communications play an important role within service production and delivery. Many service interactions representing a service process are represented by communications. Moreover, communications have *relational functions* in customer relationships. When a bank customer has to talk to a different bank employee at every encounter, communications are more difficult, and there is no stable bank employee relationship. This type of communication concerns the individual customer relationships and is very important in service production and delivery, due to the service specifics. However, *brand communications* by mass media in order to develop a certain brand image are extremely expensive. Consequently, *three types of communication* are important for services marketing: interactional communications, relational communications and brand communications. Based on these considerations, this chapter about service communications follows specific learning objectives (see Figure 8.1):

1. Comprehending the value contribution of service communications.

2. Understanding the functions which interactional, relational and brand communications have for services marketing.

3. Learning about a service brand and how it can be developed.

4. Getting to know the different types of communication instruments a service provider can choose from and which functions they fulfil.

5. Learning how a service provider can integrate the different communication instruments in order to realise synergies when applying different types of communication.

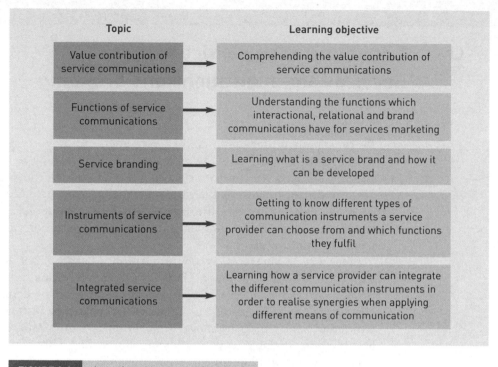

Topic	Learning objective
Value contribution of service communications	Comprehending the value contribution of service communications
Functions of service communications	Understanding the functions which interactional, relational and brand communications have for services marketing
Service branding	Learning what is a service brand and how it can be developed
Instruments of service communications	Getting to know different types of communication instruments a service provider can choose from and which functions they fulfil
Integrated service communications	Learning how a service provider can integrate the different communication instruments in order to realise synergies when applying different means of communication

FIGURE 8.1   Learning objectives of Chapter 8

Value contribution of branding and communications

Service communications affect the value of a service firm in various ways. Considering the Service Profit Chain, the following *value contributions* can be identified for service communications (see Figure 8.2):

- Service communications are a *driver of customers' perceptions* for the service interactions and service usages. In service production and delivery, communications within these interactions are an important element in the customer's perception. Consequently, communications are a driver of service quality[1] and thereby indirectly influence value.

- On a perceptual level, service communications influence the customers' general attitudes of a provider.[2] The *brand image* of a provider is strongly influenced by service communications. As brand image is an important behaviour driver of both prospective and current customers, service communications indirectly affect value.

- Finally service communications also affect customer behaviour as a direct determinant of revenue and value directly. Communications on websites or in direct mail are supposed to stimulate purchases directly, e.g. by presenting special offers or providing the customer with a coupon.

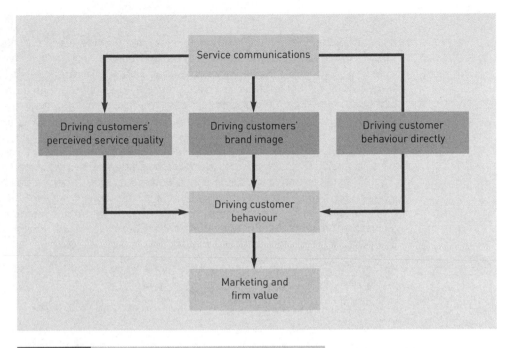

FIGURE 8.2 Value contribution of service communications

Services marketing in action 8.1 about McDonald's visualises how service communications directly affect value.

SERVICES MARKETING IN ACTION 8.1:

McDonald's recovery

McDonald's showed signs yesterday that the world's largest restaurant chain was back in favour in Europe, thanks to a massive campaign to distribute discount coupons and to promote the nutritional content of its fast food. The upturn was a welcome development for the burger giant, which has suffered from a barrage of bad publicity including Morgan Spurlock's film *Super Size Me*, which attacked fast food companies' marketing tactics and products.

Europe, McDonald's second-biggest market after the US, had been a particularly problematic area, with health concerns damaging sales in the UK and high unemployment contributing to a downturn in demand in Germany. Sales in European stores open for more than a year rose 5.4 per cent in January compared with last year, McDonald's said. The company, whose headquarters are in Illinois, distributed booklets with coupons and nutritional information last month to 20 million British

▶

households. In Germany, McDonald's increased advertising of 11 items including a dark-meat chicken sandwich that sells for 1 euro.

Jim Skinner, the chief executive, said: 'While I am encouraged by January's results, we must continue to make progress to strengthen our European business. We are focused on enhancing our performance across the region through relevant menu offerings, targeted marketing and improved operations, with emphasis on service.' Overall, sales rose 5.2 per cent last month, with growth in the US rising at its lowest rate since April 2003. However, it managed to sell a larger number of its more expensive menu items, which include salads. The performance in the US was also against already strong growth in its core market, where it has been recovering from a health consciousness-related dip for some months. Sales in the region encompassing Asia, the Pacific, the Middle East and Africa increased 7.1 per cent after improvements in menu variety and value, McDonald's said. It was the region's biggest gain in four months.

Source: McDonalds turns new leaf salad boost in *The Independent*, (Griffiths, K. 2005), copyright © The Independent, 9 February 2005.

Interactional, relational and brand communications

As described in the previous section, service communications have several direct and indirect influences on the Service Value Chain. According to the Service Value Chain, services are delivered through a sequence of service interactions with the customer and some elements of the service firm lead to the development of relationships between service provider and customer. Within service interactions as well as service relationships, communications have a crucial role. Interactions, for example between a service employee and a service customer, consist primarily of communications between the two of them. A relationship exists when the interactions between service provider and employee are connected with each other and are not isolated events without a textual connection. This connection between interactions is often realised by communications. Furthermore, next to these direct value functions of service communications there is also an indirect value. Due to the intangibility of services, customers' perception of a service brand outshines – or overshadows – service interactions and relationships. Following this logic, service communications have three functions in value-oriented services marketing resulting in three *types of service communications* (see Figure 8.3):

- interactional communications;
- relational communications;
- brand communications.

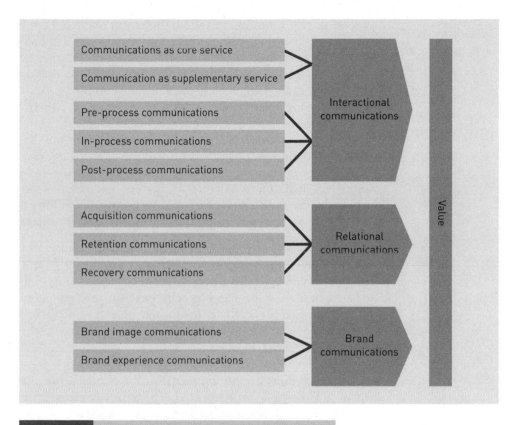

FIGURE 8.3 Value-oriented types of service communication

Interactional communications

The customer plays an important role in service production and delivery. In most cases, services can only be produced and delivered when the customer is integrated into the service process and participates in producing and delivering the service. Service interactions are contacts between the customer and certain service resources. Generally, in these service interactions the service is produced and delivered. A central characteristic of service interactions is that there is a contact between the customer and the respective service resource, i.e. the service employee or a service technology. Communications are an important means for contact between service resources and the customer. According to the *importance of the respective communications for the interactions,* two types of interactional communications can be differentiated (see Figure 8.3):

- *Communications as core service*: In many service processes, communications play an important role. Many elements of the service processes are communicative. For example, in an interaction between a doctor and a patient, the doctor first needs to collect information about the health of the patient in order to be able to make a diagnosis. The diagnosis itself in most cases is made autonomously by the service resource, e.g. the doctor himself or some research institute (e.g. in the case of a blood analysis). Then, the result of the diagnosis is transferred to the customer by some means of communications (e.g. personally by the doctor or by sending a report via mail). This description illustrates that a service is often not a single act but a sequence of acts. Depending on the definition of the core service, communications are either part of it or not. In the doctor example, a narrow definition of the service would see the diagnosis as the core service. Then the production of the core service is autonomous. However, a broader and more accepted definition of the service process includes the doctor's interrogating the patient and communicating the test results to the patient. Consequently, many parts of core service processes concern communications.

- *Communications as supplementary services*: Following the distinction of core services and supplementary services, communications can also take on a supplementary role within a service process.[3] For example, the small talk before, during or after a service interaction can be seen as a communicative 'value-added service', as in the case of a hairdresser. But there are also supportive functions of communications, such as informing the customer about the directions to the service location.

Service interactions are not only part of the actual service process but also prepare or represent a follow-up of the actual service process. Consequently, according to the *phases of the service process*, three types of interactional communications can be identified (see Figure 8.3):

- *Pre-process communications* take place before the actual core service process. They help to prepare the actual service production and delivery. Typical tasks before the service process itself are informing the customer about details of the service process (e.g. security advice by airline personnel before a flight departure), collecting information from the customer about their needs regarding the service process (e.g. asking the passenger if they have menu preferences) or 'just' 'entertaining' the customer (e.g. small-talk between airline employee and customer when awaiting boarding).

- *In-process communications are communications* during the actual service production and delivery. Typical communicative acts within a service process are collecting information from the customer which is needed for service production (e.g. workshop with a firm's employees during a consulting project) or explaining a service outcome, such as the explanation of investment advice.

- *Post-process communications* are communications that occur after the service process. They can take place directly after the service process (e.g. the customer leaves) or some period of time after the service process (e.g. complaining by the customer regarding an unsuccessful investment strategy advised by a bank employee).

Relational communications

Relational communications concern the relationship between the service provider and the customer. A characteristic of relational communications therefore is that they do not concern one single interaction but the connection between interactions. The individually directed sales emails generated by amazon.com are typical relational communications. They use information from earlier interactions, the type of products a customer purchased at earlier occasions, in order to initiate further interactions, by offering products which seem to fit the customer's interests with price reduction. Customer relationship communications between the relationship partners drive mutual learning about the other.[4] The connected interactions are represented by the customer relationship and more specifically by the *phases of the customer relationship lifecycle*. Accordingly, there are three types of relational communications (see Figure 8.3):[5]

- *Acquisition communications* aim at recruiting new customers by converting non-users of a service to using the service. Consequently, acquisition communications have the task of transmitting the value of a service for the customer to the customer. A major challenge for communications regarding acquisition communications is that services cannot be presented before their production and delivery. Therefore, communications have the function of creating a picture of the service value in the customer's mind. Communications often transmit stimuli for using a service to the customer, as when communicating price reductions.

- *Retention communications* concern all communications to existing customers. Two main functions of this type of communications are stabilising the customer relationship as well as extending the relationship. Several aspects of service communications influence the stability of a relationship. These aspects concern personal communications between customer and employee: regular communication can stabilise a relationship; automated communications, such as a frequently changing website design can irritate the consumer and destabilise the relationship with the provider. The overall concept of communications is that of an integrated communications approach that increases the stability of the customer's perception of a service firm. Next to the relationship stabilisation, service providers aim at extending the relationships with existing customers. As a result, retention communications also concern a relationship extension. Typical examples of this type of communications are cross-selling activities and individualisation of the communications to the customer, like the amazon.com example. The financial impact of unused communication potentials by service providers is emphasised by Services marketing in action 8.2.

- *Recovery communications* are directed to lost customers and aim at regaining those that are valuable. Recovery communications have some parallels with acquisition communications by convincing the customer to choose the service provider again. However, in addition to acquisition communications, recovery communications tie in with the customer's switching reason. When the customer has exited the relationship because of dissatisfaction with the provider and its services, communications play a defensive part. When the customer is lost because of variety seeking, it is up to communications to lift the customer's picture of the provider and its services.

SERVICES MARKETING IN ACTION 8.2

Wasted communications opportunities by UK banks

UK banks (five important banks were analysed in the study) send out an average number of 15.9 bills, statements or letters regarding the customer's account. However, they waste potential advertising opportunities, compared to other industries, by not using these communications for additional marketing purposes (see Figure 8.4). For example, they use only 12.5 per cent of the communications for cross-selling.

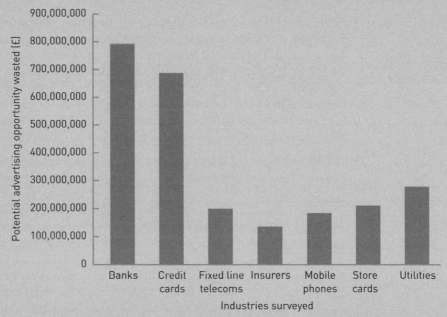

Figure 8.4 Potential advertising opportunity wasted by banks each year compared to other industries

Source: Greenyer 2004, p. 287.

This result is especially astonishing since banks obviously have many opportunities to communicate with their customers. In addition, banks dispose of a large volume of customer information. They 'automatically' collect customer data not only regarding the customer's financial situation but also regarding shopping interests, and information obtained from movements in the customer's account. This information is valuable for developing individualised communications to the customer.

Source: Greenyer 2004.

Brand communications

Next to the perceptions of a service or a relationship from the customer's perspective, customer behaviour – as a major objective and managing lever of services marketing – is influenced by the image a service provider has in the eyes of a customer.[6] While interactional and relational communications play an integrated role within the service and the relationship process, building and maintaining a certain image is a central task of service communications or more specifically service brand communications. These communications do not directly concern a certain service, service process or the customer relationship, but they do concern the service brand and ultimately influence the image of a service firm.

Compared to managing relationships and interactions which come within the focus of the whole services marketing concept, branding is a specific communications-related task. Therefore, we explore service branding in more detail in the next section.

Service branding and communications

Although branding is a traditional marketing instrument in consumer goods markets (see 'Coca-Cola' or 'BMW'), there are many service firms that have created well-known service brands: British Airways, Hilton, Merryl Lynch, Ryanair, Vodafone, McDonald's – to name but a few. Regarding the brand object, the firm's element that the brand is associated with, in service industries there are *firm-level brands*. The brand does not concern a single service – as is often found in traditional consumer markets (e.g. Procter & Gamble as a manufacturer and 'Head and Shoulders' as a product-level brand) – but the entire service provider, as an organisation; even though service providers brand certain service elements, too, like the 'Royal TS' by McDonald's or the Royalties accounts by Royal Bank of Scotland. However, the strongest association of the customer is with the firm or company brand.

In many service industries, brands are an important asset of firms and the source for competitive advantage and firm value.[7] Brands drive customer behaviour: in many purchasing decisions the customer decides on the 'best brand'. When we discuss brands, we mean more than the narrow definition of brands, i.e. a brand's name or logo. What is important regarding a brand's evaluation is the consumers' perception and evaluation of the **brand image**. The brand image is a cluster of attributes and associations that consumers connect to a brand name.[8] The totality of these attributes determines the value that is delivered to the consumer by a brand. Here, not only functional values play a role, but also symbolic ones.[9] For example, customers incorporate themselves into brands. Take for example the BMW driver, who reflects the attributes of the BMW brand. Airlines utilise these coherences when they provide their top customers with name tags indicating that they are members of the airline's top customers' club.

Following the Service Profit Chain (see Chapter 2), brand image is one part of the customer's evaluations regarding a service provider and its services (see Figure 8.5). According to the chain's principle, brand image affects the *purchasing behaviour* of the customers. When customers perceive a positive brand image, they are more likely to use the provider's services.

The relevance of the brand image as a behaviour driver can be partly explained by the specific characteristics that are inherent to services (see Chapter 1). One of the specifics of services is that they are *more difficult to evaluate* for customers than physical objects.[10] Services are processes and therefore do not provide a material outcome as do physical goods. There are only some service elements which are tangible and can easily be perceived by the customer, such as the employees' outfit or the design of service location. Many, and often central service elements are intangible by nature, e.g. the competence of a bank adviser. From an information theory perspective, services consist of only a small proportion of so-called search qualities, compared to experience and credence qualites, which are perceivable before using the service in order to evaluate the service. In the absence of search qualities consumers utilise other aspects in order to evaluate a service beforehand. These aspects are called *quality indicators* as they indicate the quality level of a service provider to the customer. One of these quality indicators is the brand image.[11] Consumers set their perceived brand image as the expected quality level of the firm and take their puchasing decision based on this.

The relevance of quality indicators is caused by the lack of search qualities. Services that are comprised predominantly of *experience qualities*, characteristics that are perceivable and easy to evaluate during or after the service experience, can be better evaluated by the customer when the service is purchased and used at least once. Following the customer relationship lifecycle concept (see Chapter 4), potential customers in the acquisition phase are more dependable on search qualities than are current customers in the customer retention phase. Current customers have experience with the provider and its services. Consequently quality indicators become less important. Translating this into the brand context, the brand image becomes less important as a behaviour driver. In the brand literature, brand image transforms to *brand experience*,[12] a construct which is similar to the perceived service quality.

Brands are not only evaluated on a single customer relationship level where the brand image of a certain customer influences specific behaviour and in consequence the success of a service provider. Also on a firm-level, brands are evaluated due to their strategic relevance. In this context, the **brand equity** is seen as a major determinant of shareholder value, next to the customer relationship value (see Figure 8.5).[13] Following a present value argumentation, brand equity can be defined as the future income streams which can be attributed to a brand. There are a variety of approaches in order to determine brand equity. One approach which is widely accepted and published on a yearly basis is the brand value ranking by the advertising agency 'Interbrand'.[14] Interbrand defines brand value – understood as a synonym of brand equity – based on a multiplier model in which the profit of a firm is weighted by a brand-related multiplier. This multiplier is calculated based

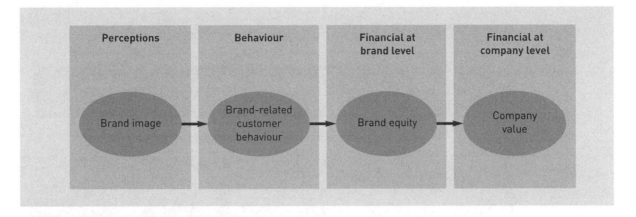

| Perceptions | Behaviour | Financial at brand level | Financial at company level |

FIGURE 8.5   Brand-related profit chain

on factors such as market leadership, brand stability, internationality, continuous marketing support or legal protection of the brand. The better these factors are for a certain brand, the higher the multiplier and the higher the equity of the respective brand. Services marketing in action 8.3 on 'Interbrand's brand value ranking' describes the methodology and presents the 2004 TOP 20 world brands.

SERVICES MARKETING IN ACTION 8.3:

Interbrand's brand value ranking

The advertising agency Interbrand regularly measures the brand value of the world's TOP 100 brands. To qualify for the list, each brand must have a value greater than $1 billion, derive about a third of its earnings outside its home country and have publicly available marketing and financial data. One or more of these criteria eliminates brands such as Visa, Wal-Mart or CNN. The brand value is evaluated on the basis on how much they are likely to earn in the future. Then the projected profits are discounted to a present value, based on the likelihood that those earnings will actually materialise. The first step is figuring out what percentage of a company's revenues can be credited to a brand. Based on analyst reports, Interbrand projects five years of earnings and sales for the brand. Finally, the brand's strength is assessed to determine the risk profile of those earnings forecasts. Considerations include market leadership, stability and global reach. That generates a discount rate which is applied to brand earnings to get a net present value. Table 8.1 shows the 2004 TOP 20 brands and indicates that most of them are consumer good brands. Under the TOP 20, the only service providers are Disney (rank 6) McDonald's (7), Citibank (13) and American Express (14).

Source: adapted from Brady 2004.

▶

TABLE 8.1	TOP 20 of Interbrand's brand equity ranking 2004

Rank	Brand	2004 Brand Value	2003 Brand Value	Per cent Change	Country of Ownership
1	Coca-Cola	67.394	70.453	–4%	US
2	Microsoft	61.372	65.174	–6%	US
3	IBM	53.791	51.767	+4%	US
4	GE	44.111	42.340	+4%	US
5	Intel	33.499	31.112	+8%	US
6	Disney	27.113	28.036	–3%	US
7	McDonald's	25.001	24.699	+1%	US
8	Nokia	24.041	29.440	–18%	Finland
9	Toyota	22.673	20.784	+9%	Japan
10	Marlboro	22.128	22.183	0%	US
11	Mercedes	21.331	21.371	0%	Germany
12	Hewlett-Packard	20.978	19.860	+6%	US
13	Citibank	19.971	18.571	+8%	US
14	American Express	17.683	16.833	+5%	US
15	Gillette	16.723	15.978	+5%	US
16	Cisco	15.947	15.789	+1%	US
17	BMW	15.886	15.106	+5%	Germany
18	Honda	14.874	15.625	–5%	Japan
19	Ford	14.475	17.066	–15%	US
20	Sony	12.759	13.153	–3%	Japan

Firms in highlighted lines are service companies. Value figure in $ millions.

Source: adapted from August 9–16, 2004 issue of *Business Week*, by special permission, copyright © 2004 by The McGraw-Hill Companies, Inc.

A brand's image is an intangible asset whose creation is complex to plan because it is built upon the customers' perceptions. Therefore, it is feasible to explore these perceptions when planning to implement a certain brand image. Following the brand image definition, this variable represents the values which consumers associate with a service provider and its services. Consequently, service providers aim to identify the values that are relevant to consumers in a certain service category in order to try to associate these values with their own service brand by *developing a brand image*. A method which can be utilised to do this is the so-called 'Means–end chain' approach.[15]

The *conceptual basis of the 'Means–end chain' approach* is that consumer actions have consequences and consumers learn to associate particular consequences with aspects of a certain product. When a hotel guest cannot sleep well in the hotel and is tired in the morning, the customer will associate the consequence of 'being tired' with the hotel. Therefore, when the guest needs a hotel again and there are alternatives, they would probably not choose that hotel again. This is because consumers choose certain products in order to realise discrete values or needs. The need for 'being rested' is to be achieved by choosing the right hotel. In the language of the means–end chain, choosing certain service providers, in this case the hotel, is a means in order to realise certain 'end states' or the values which are derived from these ends, in this case being rested. The consequences of consumers' behaviour can be located on several levels of abstraction (see Figure 8.6):

- *Attributes*: There are concrete and abstract attributes which are perceived by the consumer. Concrete attributes are physical characteristics like the interior design of a hotel or the number of service employees and can be defined more or less objectively. Abstract attributes are on a lower level of abstraction and can mostly only be evaluated subjectively, such as the luxury and ambiance of the hotel.

- *Benefits*: Benefits are divided into functional and psychosocial benefits. An example for a functional benefit in the hotel context is 'getting rest', while 'feeling comfortable' is a psychosocial benefit.

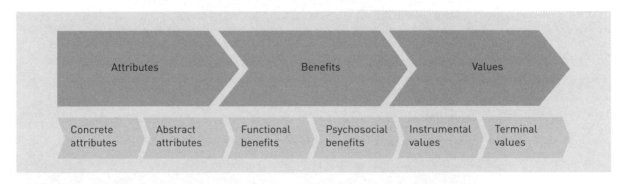

FIGURE 8.6   Consequences of consumers' behaviour according to the means–end approach

- *Values*: Attributes and benefits lead to instrumental and terminal values which are associated on a very low level of abstraction and are far apart from concrete service perceptions in the mind of the consumer. Instrumental values concern preferred modes of behaviour (e.g. ambitious), while terminal values concern preferred end states of being (e.g. security, self-esteem).

These three categories of behaviour consequences manifest a goal hierarchy with the values representing the consumers' final goals and thus being the underlying reasons of consumers' purchasing decisions. While the means–end chain approach might be used in service planning in order to define concrete service elements which are connected to the consumers' desired end states, it plays another important role for *brand communications*. For brand communications, the means–end chain approach helps identify the values the customer aims at by purchasing a certain service. The knowledge about these values can then be used in order to define the communication messages of the service firm. Services marketing in action 8.4 on 'Brand image messages of US universities' lists examples of communication messages based on brand attributes.

How can service firms identify these values and even better the value hierarchies that map the consumers' associations with a brand? Based on the 'means–end chain' approach, a specific technique has been developed which can be used in order to identify these value hierarchies. This method is the so-called *'laddering'* approach. The approach applies qualitative interviews and uses the respondents' own words in order to identify each respondent's value hierarchy. The respondent is asked 'why' they would choose a certain service brand. In

SERVICES MARKETING IN ACTION 8.4:

Brand image messages of US universities

US universities are in strong competition with each other. Consequently, branding and brand image messages are used in order to position each university in the market. The brand image messages of a selection of US universities are as follows:

- University of Miami: 'a major research university set in a tropical garden'.

- University of Iowa: 'as the smallest of the big ten public universities, Iowa offers the best of both worlds: a large variety of resources in a comfortable, close-knit community'.

- Pomona College: 'the finest liberal arts college in the west'.

- Rice University: 'named the best value in private education'.

Source: Gutman and Miaoulis 2003.

most cases, respondents would then mention concrete attributes. Starting from those, the interviewer 'climbs' the 'ladder' of the consumer's values by asking a series of 'why' questions. Finally, by integrating a respondent's value hierarchies as well as the hierarchies of all respondents, an aggregated value hierarchy can be determined. Services marketing in action 8.5 shows how the laddering technique was applied with students at one university and the resulting value hierarchy.

SERVICES MARKETING IN ACTION 8.5:

Means–end chain of students at the University of New Hampshire

In order to identify the value hierarchy of its students, an empirical study based on the means–end approach using the laddering technique was applied. Respondents were first-year college students. The interviews started with a mid-level goals question with subsequent 'Why' questions in order to identify the individual goals on higher levels of abstraction.

The interviews resulted in 203 ladders from 86 respondents, with some respondents providing only one ladder and others up to five ladders. Most ladders contained five elements, while some contained more than eight elements. Figure 8.7 shows some example ladders.

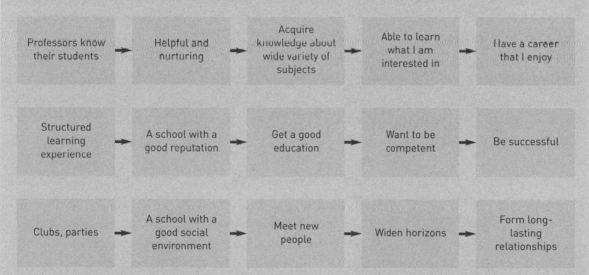

Figure 8.7 Exemplar individual ladders
Source: Gutman and Miaoulis 2003, p. 109.

The analysis of the ladder started with a coding of the content of the ladders. Each ladder element was associated with one of the categories consisting of two types of attributes, two types of benefits and two types of values (see description of the means–end approach in this section). Then, similar elements were combined resulting in 48 separate elements. Subsequently, a matrix was built that displayed the links between the elements, e.g. one element preceding another element of the set. Based on these linkages, the hierarchy of the students' perceptions was constructed using specific software. This analysis resulted in the value hierarchy depicted in Figure 8.8.

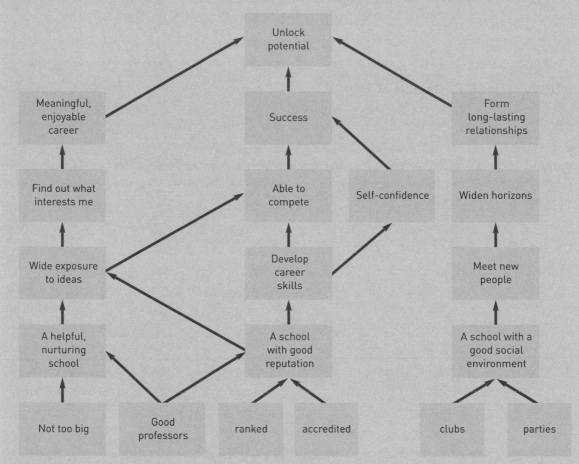

Figure 8.8 Means–end ladder of the University of New Hampshire
Source: Gutman and Miaoulis 2003, p. 109.

The hierarchy in Figure 8.8 presents the goals or value hierarchy as indicated by the respondents. The overall goal of students deciding to go to the University of New Hampshire is to 'unlock potential'. This goal is influenced by lower-level goals according to several ladders. For example, the ladder on the left side of Figure 8.8 explains that students believe they can realise the overall goal by realising 'a meaningful, enjoyable career' by 'finding out what interests me' by having a 'wide exposure to ideas' because the university is 'a helpful, nurturing school' and because it is 'not too big'.

Source: Gutman and Miaoulis 2003.

Instruments of service communications

In service industries, there are many means of communications a provider has to manage. This is because of the direct contact between customers and employees in the service encounter. Next to the traditional communications instruments, an important part of a service provider's communications is the communication between employee and customer. However, the other communications instruments also contribute to a service firm's value. The *variety of communications instruments* can be distinguished regarding the manner of communications which is explained by the kind of contact between customer and service firm as well as the degree of standardisation of the communication.

The *kind of contact* ties up with the important characteristic of services mentioned above, the direct contact between service employees and customers. Consequently, there are face-to-face communications where a direct contact is given and there are media communications where the provider (or customer) uses some media channel (TV, mail, email, internet, etc.) to communicate with the other. Actually, this dimension addresses the differentiation between 'high touch' and 'high tech' communications (although there are also media which are not 'high tech'). The kind of contact has various consequences for the provider and the customer. Media communications are more able to be controlled by the service provider and in many countries less expensive than face-to-face communications. Further, for face-to-face communications, capacity problems can occur. However, many consumers do prefer the 'high touch' contact with the provider and therefore show reactions towards 'high tech' communications.

The *degree of standardisation* refers to the extent that the provider's communication is standardised for all recipients. With standardised communications, there is only one communication format defined by the service firm, while individualised communications go hand in hand with different communication formats for different customers. That differentiation does not mean that an individualised communication refers to unplanned communications. There are for example communication guidelines for employees with customer contact. However, the resulting communications are not equal for all customers. Individualised communications tend to result in higher cost, but they allow a service provider's communications to focus upon the customer's communications needs.

Using these two criteria, three *types of service communication instruments* can be specified (see Figure 8.9):

- personal communications as individualised face-to-face communications, e.g. employee communicating with a customer in a service encounter;

- customised communications as individualised media communications, e.g. direct mail;

- mass communications as standardised media communications, e.g. TV spots, sponsoring.

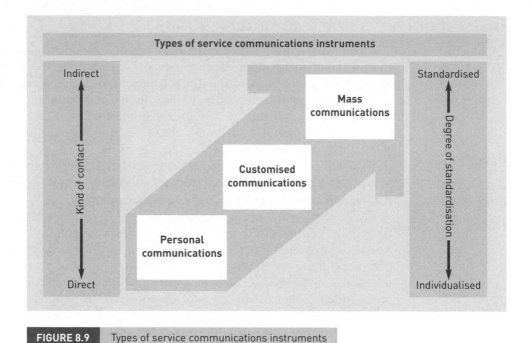

FIGURE 8.9 Types of service communications instruments

Personal communications

Personal communications take place between service employee and customer. Although there are means for service providers to quasi-standardise these communications, because of the nature of personal communications, every communicative act remains individual. Service employees are not machines and might react heterogeneously to the behaviour of the customer. Regarding their function for the service provider, two *forms of personal communications* are distinguishable:

- *Personal communications as a selling activity.* This form of personal communications concerns the traditional function of firm communications: attracting consumers' interest for a provider's services and in the end selling the services to the consumers.

- *Personal communications as a service delivery activity.* When services are produced and delivered in interactions between service employees and customers, personal communications are an important element in these interactions. In this case, the communication does not have a selling character. In contrast to a selling-oriented communication, delivery communication is often reactive, which means that the customer initiates the communication, e.g. by visiting a bank branch.

In most service interactions there is a *strong inter-dependability* between the two functions of personal communications. Often, they cannot be separated. In a counselling meeting between a bank adviser and customer delivery communications certainly take place. However, in most cases the adviser is also there to sell the bank's services. This does not mean that the adviser exhibits an exaggerated selling orientation, but – ideally from the firm's perspective – that they have the bank's interests in mind. Given the time-, place- and content-related interdependence between the two functions of personal communications, the customer often does not separate these as two different acts of communication. Therefore, a separate treatment by a service provider is not sensible.

The customer's evaluation of the personal communication with bank employees is presented by the customer's *perceived communication quality*[16] which describes a service employee's ability to fulfil the communication needs of a customer. Employees' communicative behaviour is evaluated according to two *dimensions of communication quality* (see Figure 8.10):

- The *professional communication quality* concerns the reliability, e.g. giving sufficient as well as correct information, and the competence of the service employee, e.g. adequate explanation of pros and cons, in the interactions with the customer.

- The *interpersonal quality* refers to the empathy, e.g. honesty and openness of conversation and listening to the customer (appearance and poise of the contact employee) and the familiarity of the service employee, e.g. the existence of a personal relationship.

The two dimensions address two very different aspects of the communications between employee and customer. The first dimension 'professional communication quality' concerns the 'service product' which is delivered by the employee. The second dimension 'interpersonal quality' concerns the interaction between the two communication partners.

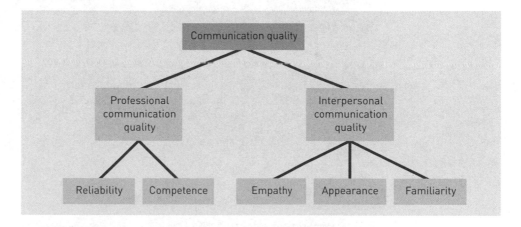

FIGURE 8.10 Dimensions of personal communication quality

Source: Bruhn and Frommeyer 2005.

While communications often address explicitly or implicitly verbal communications in the interactions between employee and customer, service research indicates that **non-verbal communications** also have a vital effect on customer's perceptions of a service contact.[17] It might make a huge difference whether a service employee smiles openly at the customer or grumbles while avoiding eye contact. This example visualises that there are many modes of non-verbal communications which can be grouped into four categories (see Figure 8.11):[18]

- Kinesics are body movements, the general demeanour of the person (relaxed and open posture) eye contact, nodding, hand shaking, smiling.

- Paralanguage concerns vocal pitches, vocal loudness or amplitude, pitch variation, pauses, fluency.

- Proxemics refers to the distance and relative postures of the interaction partners. Touch plays an important role here.

- Physical appearance is also an important element of non-verbal communication and probably the most easily managed compared to the other modes. For example, Disney requires its male employees to remove facial hair and its female employees to use cosmetics sparingly.

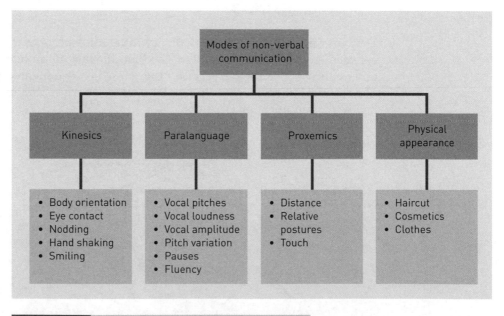

FIGURE 8.11   Modes of non-verbal communication

Source: based on Sundaram and Webster 2000.

Customised communications

Customised communications have much in common with personal communications, in so far as they are individualised to a certain extent. However, they differ from them regarding the kind of contact. In this case, media channels are used for the communication between provider and customer. Therefore customised communications are more readily controllable by the provider and can still be differentiated between customers. There are two groups of *instruments within customised communications*:

- direct communications;
- internet communications.

Direct communications

This category describes communication activities which address service customers via mail, email or telephone. Thus, every recipient receives their own letter, email or phone call. Although these are partly standardised, they are able to be customised in the sense that individual customers or certain groups of customers receive individualised messages. For direct mail, customers can be selected individually for a campaign, which is not possible with TV advertising. Then, recipients are addressed personally in a letter or telephone call. More sophisticated, differentiated offers can be the content of a differentiated direct mailing. Direct marketing activities have several advantages over other forms of communication. On the one hand, they are more readily controllable than personal communication. On the other hand, they provide several interactional opportunities which are not given for standardised types of communication. Next to the possibility of differentiation and exclusion, there is the opportunity for a direct response by the recipient. Thus, direct marketing gives the opportunity to start a dialogue with the customer[19] and to establish a relationship.

Internet communications

A second media channel which can be used for customised communications is internet marketing. Internet marketing encompasses diverse communications options, via a service provider's own website, ad banners on another website, webforums, etc. Internet communications are or can be *customised* in four aspects (see Figure 8.12):

- *Permission marketing*. In contrast to traditional media communications like TV spots, recipients themselves determine if, when and for how long they receive a certain communications activity. For example, a web banner is perceived when visiting the website and not at the time when the banner is 'broadcast'.

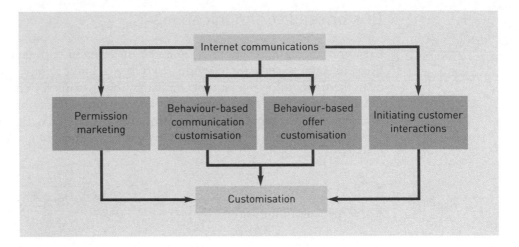

FIGURE 8.12   Options for customising internet communications

Furthermore, recipients can decide whether to process a certain web message or even to intensify their attention, by clicking on a web banner in order to be linked to another website which specifies the message of the banner. The duration of attention is also determined by the recipient. This does not necessarily mean that it has negative effects on the viewers' perception of the communication. This point is illustrated in Services marketing in action 8.6.

- *Behaviour-based communication customisation*. The provider can customise the communications messages according to the recipient's web behaviour. The customer's web behaviour discloses interests, value and needs. Thus, having prepared a set of differentiated web messages, a service provider can react to pre-defined recipient characteristics. Search engines as internet service providers utilise this possibility by programming communications messages according to the search expressions of a recipient. When one looks for a flight offer, the websites of airlines are advertised.

- *Behaviour-based offer customisation*. Service providers – especially those with selling functions on the internet – can customise their websites according to the purchasing behaviour of website users. As the purchasing process on the internet is an electronic one, a customer's purchasing behaviour on the internet can be traced more systematically than the purchasing behaviour of a customer at a physical service location. The key for these analyses, for example by internet booksellers such as amazon.com, is that they let their customers register in order to first be able to track the behaviour of an individual customer. Secondly, this allows the provider automatically to programme individual websites for these customers. Regarding offers communicated to customers, the respective website consists of a standardised part and a placeholder which is customised according to the recent purchasing behaviour of a customer.

SERVICES MARKETING IN ACTION 8.6:

Permission marketing by Amex

American Express said yesterday it was expanding its internet marketing experiments to include a website offering entertainment content from performers such as Ellen DeGeneres, a US television talk show host.

The financial services company's internet strategy has been closely watched in the advertising industry since it unveiled a four-minute 'webisode' this year starring comedian Jerry Seinfeld and cartoon character Superman. The short internet film represented an attempt to respond to the central challenge posed by the rise of digital media – how to reach consumers at a time when technology is giving people a greater ability to avoid commercials.

Amex experimented with a strategy known to advertisers as 'permission marketing', which attempts to engage consumers rather than interrupt them – the typical tactic of the network TV era. Amex said yesterday the webisode featuring Mr Seinfeld was so successful it was setting up a website, called www.mylifemycard.com, as part of its new global ad campaign. 'We have learned that to sell to people today you have to engage them, and the only way to engage them is with content', said John Hayes, chief marketing officer at Amex. Mr Hayes said the company's webisode attracted millions of people to the Amex site. More importantly, he said the visitors spent an average of 10 minutes per visit – more than twice the time spent at the webisode starring Mr Seinfeld. 'It has convinced us that we have to continue to engage in that medium', Mr Hayes said.

The new campaign, which will also include TV advertisements, will include internet options such as giving consumers a chance to look through Ms DeGeneres's handbag. There, consumers will find other entertainment options. Other performers in the ad campaign include actor Robert DeNiro, golfer Tiger Woods and surfer Laird Hamilton. The TV ads were unveiled yesterday in the US. They will start in the coming days in the UK, Australia, Japan, Germany, France, Italy, Puerto Rico, Mexico and Canada.

Source: Silverman 2004a. Reproduced with permission from Financial Times Limited.

- *Initiating interactions*. Moreover, interactions between the provider and the recipient as well as between recipients can be initiated by internet communications, as Services marketing in action 8.7 illustrates.

Internet communications exhibit several characteristics which are appropriate to designing a service-related communication in a sense that the *specific characteristics of services* can be considered. Due to their process character, services can only be perceived when they are produced and used. The internet allows not only the presentation of specific service attributes but also the stimulation of whole service processes. Also, the dependency on a certain location is partly abolished. When a

SERVICES MARKETING IN ACTION 8.7:

Car race at Times Square

For several weeks over the spring, the character of New York's Times Square underwent a dramatic change. The bustling section of Manhattan that once symbolised the grim realities of urban life became the venue for a video game. To promote its motoring page, Yahoo, the internet portal, staged a car race on the 22-storey-high Reuters screen that dominates the south-west corner of Seventh Avenue and 43rd Street. People on the street could play by dialling a toll-free number and using the buttons on their mobile phones to manoeuvre virtual vehicles on a digital screen looking down on the area known to many people as the 'crossroads of the world'.

The screen is a technological marvel. R/GA, a subsidiary of US marketing group Interpublic, designed the software using special effects developed for films such as *Braveheart* and *Zelig*. But for all the sophistication of the production, the intent of the Yahoo promotion was decidedly old-fashioned. Yahoo says every April about 1m people attend New York's car show. It timed its promotion to coincide with the event, trading its customary perch in cyberspace for a chance to reach potential car buyers on the street.

'We wanted to take a very targeted approach and catch consumers who were actually in the process of buying a new car', said Brett Gardner, marketing director for Yahoo Autos. 'You would be surprised at how many people are attending auto shows to look at all the models.'

Yahoo's pursuit of the Times Square crowd – it even dispatched 'street teams' to recruit players for its video game – illustrates one of the ironies of modern marketing. Amid rapid technological change, many advertisers are returning to the industry's roots, looking for new ways to use traditional venues for marketing messages: the street, the store or anywhere people interact socially.

Source: Silverman 2004b. Reproduced with permission from Financial Times Limited.

---

recipient has become aware of a certain service provider, say by a web banner, the customer can directly visit its homepage which represents the whole 'service location' in the case of internet services or at least parts of the 'service location' (e.g. an airline booking opportunity on the homepage is comparable to a travel agency or airline ticket shop).

In terms of the *value effects*, customised communications have efficiency advantages compared to other communication instruments. Due to the adaptation of the communications according to recipient characteristics, spreading losses can be prevented. The proportion of recipients who are interested in a certain communication or even react to it therefore is higher than for standardised communications. This is because of the ability of customised communications to consider a recipient's needs when designing and/or delivering a communication message.

Mass communications

Though the described categories of communication instruments are valuable for services and applicable in service industries due to the direct contact with the customer, mass communications still have a high importance in service industries. Take the financial service industries or airlines – they dominate the mass communications market together with traditional consumer goods manufacturers such as Coca-Cola or Procter & Gamble. The *relevance of mass communications in service industries* can be explained from various perspectives:

- The direct contact between service employees and customers which facilitates personal and customised communications is mostly only given to current customers or prospects of a service provider. However, most of the *prospects* are not personally known to a service provider. To reach these people, personal or customised communications are much more expensive than for current customers because it is difficult to collect relevant customer information such as address and segmentation criteria. Mass communications help to address these potential customers on a segment level by developing and conducting segment-specific mass communications, e.g. advertisements in business magazines.

- Furthermore, some service industries are characterised as *mass markets* comparable to traditional consumer goods markets. In these markets, the advantages of personal or customised communications are often outweighed by the mass factor. For example, for an airline to make sure that sporadic flyers remember the airline when they next fly, it might not be feasible to send them as many direct mails as are sent to frequent flyers.

- From a value perspective, *brand image* is another important driver of service purchasing behaviour next to personal interactions. And mass communications are a significant lever for building a brand image. Consequently, mass communications also have a value function in service industries.

An important *task of mass communications* is to make the intangible tangible. Due to their process character, services are intangible and therefore cannot be examined physically or be touched. Therefore, mass communications use certain *means to make services tangible*[20] which refer to one of two functions: materialisation and personification. The *materialisation* strategy aims at presenting physical elements of the service resources, process or outcome. The *personification* function establishes an association between the recipient and other persons in order to make the service tangible. Both strategies can be realised using internal or external factors resulting in four options for making services tangible (see Figure 8.13):[21]

- *Materialisation with external factors* means presenting the customer or their associated objects, for example, on a television advertisement. The tangibility in this case, is often reached by visualising the service outcome. This strategy is realised by 'before and after' images generated by hair stylists. Another possibility is presenting the need satisfaction by depicting the customer's house as a service outcome of a building society's mortgage services.

- *Personification with external factors* is conducted by presenting 'customers' in the communications. Typically, customers are presented through testimonials, by using anonymous typical customers, celebrities or reference customers. These 'customers' are shown during the service process or when formulating a statement regarding the service provider, which is to be advertised.

- *Materialisation with internal factors* presents material elements that are provided by the service firm and are utilised to perform the service. Examples are as hotel facilities, a service sample, e.g. a film trailer, or use of symbols representing characteristics to be associated with the service firm, such as the bull used by Merrill Lynch.

- *Personification with internal factors* presents employees of the service firm in order to create an association with the service. These can be managers of the firm documenting the quality and customer orientation of the firm, service employees as testimonials of the service process, or specific employees in the case of high-profile employees, for example using a famous investment banker, musician, sportsman, actor, journalist, etc. or a typical service process can be illustrated with the use of an advert on TV showing the different steps of the delivery service.

Service providers can utilise a variety of communications instruments with very different characteristics and functions. Due to the direct contact with the customer associated with services marketing organisations, there are considerably

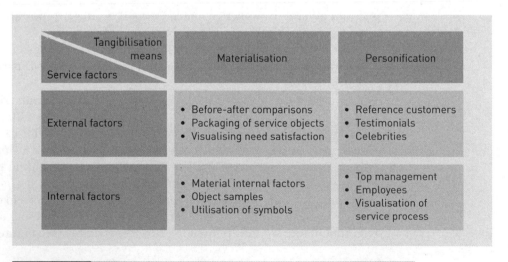

Tangibilisation means / Service factors	Materialisation	Personification
External factors	• Before-after comparisons • Packaging of service objects • Visualising need satisfaction	• Reference customers • Testimonials • Celebrities
Internal factors	• Material internal factors • Object samples • Utilisation of symbols	• Top management • Employees • Visualisation of service process

FIGURE 8.13   Options of service communications for making services tangible

Source: Meffert and Bruhn 2003, p. 458.

more opportunities for communication than for consumer product manufacturers. However, this diversity also increases the need for integration of the different instruments.

Integrated communications

A service provider can choose between a variety of communication instruments. Most service providers utilise a set of communication instruments. This strategy has the advantage that there are multiple channels which can be used to communicate with the customer and thereby, for example, consider the different communication needs between customers. However, this wide use of communication instruments – combined with information overload on the consumers' side – might result in ambiguous perceptions by the consumer of a service provider, its services and its brand. In order to prevent this, service providers aim at applying what is called *Integrated Marketing Communications (IMC)*. Integrated marketing communications refers to the coordination of different communication tools for the development of a brand.[22]

More specifically, integrated marketing communications aim to deliver a *clear brand message and image* to the consumer. Due to the brand image's relevance for the purchasing decision of service users, integrated marketing communications affects value indirectly. Moreover, one task of service communications is to make the intangible service more tangible in the mind of the consumers (see earlier on in this chapter). Obviously, a clear brand image helps to create a clear image of a service provider and its services in the eyes of the consumer.[23] Consequently, integrated communications are a means of *making a service more tangible* in the consumers' perception.

At first sight, integrating communication instruments sounds more straightforward than it is in reality. Integrated communications are not only about sending the same communications message via different communication channels. In contrast, it is easy to observe *integration problems in service communications* to different extents, such as:

- In services, due to the direct contact between employee and customer, it happens that the *communications of the service employee may be in conflict with the mass communications* of the provider. For example, when the German railway organisation Deutsche Bahn introduced a new pricing system, it frequently happened that travellers received different information from the website or mass communications from that they received from the service employees.

- Furthermore, service providers often forget that they already communicate to the customer without specific marketing communications, e.g. bank statements. These *delivery-related communication means* are often not integrated with other communication messages and formats used by the provider. Moreover, they are not utilised for realising potentials in the existing customer relationships.[24]

- Mass communications sometimes exaggerate the attributes of the service provider and even its location, resulting in *exaggerated expectations*. This results in unmet customer expectations and dissatisfied customers.

How can a service provider integrate its marketing communications? How can the different communication tools be coordinated with the goal of building and maintaining a clear brand image? Most importantly, service providers aim at integrating their communications according to four *dimensions of integration*:

- *Formal integration* means standardising the design of the different communications, in the sense of a corporate design.

- *Time integration* refers to the coordination of communications means in terms of their time relevance. These instruments which affect the success of other instruments are implemented earlier. For example, existing customers are informed of important changes (e.g. a merger) before the public is informed.

- *Content integration* aims at aligning the messages of the different communications instruments applied. This is to avoid any inconsistency between the different messages.

- *Hierarchical integration* concerns the interdependence between different communications instruments. Some instruments are strong drivers of other instruments (so-called lead instruments), while yet other instruments are more affected by others (so-called following instruments). For example, mass communications are often a lead instrument defining the brand message of the service firm, while personal communications aim at supporting this message by experiences in the service interactions. There are many criteria which indicate an instrument's role as a leading instrument, one of which is the customer's awareness of the instrument.

Services marketing in action 8.8 on 'Integrated advertisements by service firms' shows the diffusion of integrated marketing communications in service industries using the example of service advertisements.

SERVICES MARKETING IN ACTION 8.8:

Integrated advertisements by service firms

A US study examined the diffusion of integrated marketing communications in service industries. The study analysed 100 advertisements of service firms from various industries (e.g. airline, broadcast, financial services). The advertisements included in the study were published in the magazines *Cosmopolitan*, *Fortune*,

Business Week, Men's Health, Maxim, People, Southern Living, Sports Illustrated, Road & Truck, Time. The main purpose of the study was to analyse how many advertisements were integrated. The integration of an advertisement was defined by whether other communication tools were addressed in the advertisement. Further, the 'orientations' (e.g. image-oriented versus behaviour-oriented) of the tools addressed were taken into consideration. In order to do this, communication tools were classified into four categories: public relations, brand advertising (both image-oriented) as well as consumer sales promotion and direct response advertising (both behaviour-oriented).

According to this definition, 63 per cent of the advertisements were classified as integrated (see Table 8.2). However, 76 per cent of those (48 per cent of the total sample) conducted integration at the lowest level. The most common form of integration (67 per cent; 42 per cent of the total sample) utilised two different communication tools, i.e. an image-oriented (brand advertising) and a behaviour-oriented (direct response) tool. The second most common form utilised three different communication tools, mostly one image-oriented and two behaviour-oriented tools (direct response and sales promotion). None of the advertisements addressed all four communication tools.

TABLE 8.2	Results regarding the degree of integration in services advertising		
Degree of integration in services advertising	Non-integrated advertisements	One communication tool	32%
		Two communication tools: same orientation	5%
	Integrated advertisments	Two communications tools: different orientations	48%
		Three commuincation tools	5%
		Four communication tools	0%

Source: adapted from Grove *et al.* 2002, p. 403

Source: Grove *et al.* 2002.

Summary

The lessons about service communications in this chapter can be summarised as follows (see Figure 8.14) :

1. Service communications affect value-relevant customer behaviour, both directly and indirectly. A direct influence can be realised by stimulating purchases through communications, while the indirect influence is due to the communications' role on customers' perceptions of the provider and its services.

2. Service providers employ interactional, relational and brand communications which concern different levels of the usage of the communications as well as the customers' perceptions.

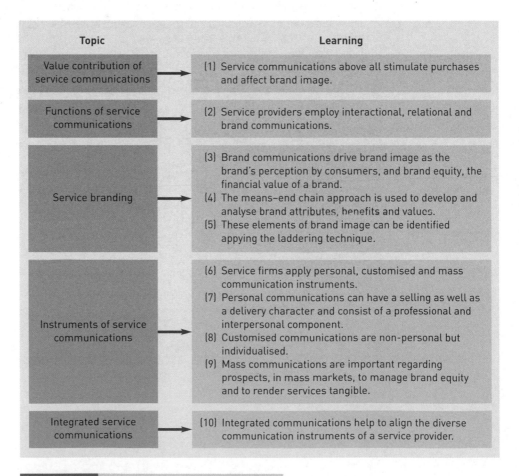

Topic	Learning
Value contribution of service communications	(1) Service communications above all stimulate purchases and affect brand image.
Functions of service communications	(2) Service providers employ interactional, relational and brand communications.
Service branding	(3) Brand communications drive brand image as the brand's perception by consumers, and brand equity, the financial value of a brand. (4) The means–end chain approach is used to develop and analyse brand attributes, benefits and values. (5) These elements of brand image can be identified appying the laddering technique.
Instruments of service communications	(6) Service firms apply personal, customised and mass communication instruments. (7) Personal communications can have a selling as well as a delivery character and consist of a professional and interpersonal component. (8) Customised communications are non-personal but individualised. (9) Mass communications are important regarding prospects, in mass markets, to manage brand equity and to render services tangible.
Integrated service communications	(10) Integrated communications help to align the diverse communication instruments of a service provider.

FIGURE 8.14　Learning summary for Chapter 8

3. Brand communications aim at driving brand image which describes the consumers' perceptions regarding a certain brand and is an important influencing factor of brand equity, the financial value of a brand.

4. In order to develop a brand image the means–end chain approach can be used which structures the customer's attribution regarding a brand into attributes, benefits and values.

5. The attributes, benefits and values which a customer attributes to a brand, can be identified by the so-called 'laddering technique' which applies subsequent 'why' questions in order to explore the effects of the brand on the recipient.

6. There are three distinct types of service communication instruments: personal communications, customised communications and mass communications.

7. Personal communications can be a selling or delivery activity and consist of a professional and an interpersonal component in the view of the customers.

8. In customised communications, service providers communicate impersonally with the recipients (instead of the employees). They use direct and internet communications in order to realise a differentiated communication on a segment-specific basis.

9. As in other industries, mass communications also strongly affect value in service industries, especially for addressing prospects, communicating in mass markets, in order to manage brand equity and to make the intangible service tangible by means of materialisation and personification.

10. Due to the diversity of communications instruments in the service industry, an integrated communication is crucial for a service provider to convey a consistent communication message.

Knowledge questions

1. Explain the value impact of service branding and communications.

2. How do the different types of services communications (interactional, relational, brand) differ?

3. What impact do communications have on brand image?

4. Explain the relationship between brand image and brand experience.

5. Describe the importance of the brand experience in service industries.

6. Define brand equity and explain its importance for the management of a service provider.

7. How is brand equity structured by the means–end approach? How is the laddering technique used in this context?

8. Describe the differences between the types of service communications.

9. What are the functions of personal communications of a service provider?

10. Define the dimensions of personal communications quality.

11. Explain the role of non-verbal communications in service interactions.

12. Explain how a differentiated communication can be realised through direct and internet communications.

13. Why are mass communications in services important, despite the high relevance of direct customer contact and personal communications?

14. How do service providers use mass communications in order to 'tangibilise' services?

15. Describe the reasons for the importance of an integrated marketing communication.

16. Explain the different forms of an integrated marketing communication.

 ## Application and discussion questions

1. Do you remember the last time communication activities of a service provider affected your behaviour? Which activity was it? And how was your behaviour changed?

2. Take your university as an example: compile its communication activities and assign them to the types of interactional, relational and brand communications.

3. Choose a certain service provider and try to describe its brand image (either by your own judgement, by asking friends about their image of a certain brand or by researching the web). Then explore how the firm's communications in recent years have contributed to the development of that image.

4. Do you remember a situation where the image of a brand in your eyes was destroyed by the brand experience? Explain how this happened. What role did the firm's communications play?

5. Apply the laddering technique to determine your own brand equity hierarchy for a certain service (e.g. holiday location, café, supermarket, mobile communications provider).

6. Find examples of the two dimensions of personal communication quality for a chosen industry.

7. Remember a recent service situation. Which aspects of non-verbal communication did you perceive in this situation?

8. Try to find the latest personalised mail you received from a provider (e.g. telephone bill). Explore which elements of the communication are customised and which are not.

9. Go through a magazine and/or watch some TV spots and collect examples of service communications. Analyse them in terms of the following aspects:

   - Which means are used in order to make a service tangible?
   - Which factors are used in order to make a service tangible?
   - Does the provider integrate several communication instruments in the ad?

CASE STUDY: VIRGIN MOBILE: GROWTH THROUGH BRANDING AND COMMUNICATIONS IN A SATURATED MARKET

The UK mobile communications market is a highly saturated market which implies difficulties for providers to realise profitable growth. Within this market, Virgin Mobile has continued its strong run in customer growth with its total number of users rising 7.2 per cent to 4.25 million in the first quarter of 2004 and increased revenues with an 18 per cent rise in the six months until September 2004. When searching for the success factors of Virgin Mobile in this difficult market situation, the firm's branding appears to be one important aspect.

Some of the key planks that differentiate Virgin Mobile's brand from its competitors were conceived on the back of a paper napkin at Nice airport following 1999's GSM mobile show in Cannes. While waiting for their flight back to London, Joe Steel, then marketing director, and Tom Alexander, Virgin Mobile's chief executive, came up with what were then unique ideas in the mobile market: daily discounting voice tariffs and call vouchers with no set expiry dates.

Unlike other operators, Virgin Mobile does not own its own network but uses that of T-Mobile. When it was launched, there were many who questioned whether the UK needed another mobile provider. The company's growth, however, has been built on a strong brand targeted at fashion-conscious youth – next to a broad, high street distribution spanning 5,000 UK outlets, and a drive to offer customers simple tariffs.

Tom Alexander says it is Virgin Mobile's attention to detail with its brand and image that has engendered a strong loyalty among its customers. While around a quarter of customers at some of its rivals switch operators each year, Virgin Mobile's annual 'churn' is a relatively impressive 14 per cent. 'It's tweaking all these quirky things that make the difference', he says. 'This even comes down to the way we write the words in our catalogue. We very much keep that at the heart of the business. That's how we keep our customers. We take all that very seriously internally.'

Virgin Mobile was the first mobile operator in the UK to avoid putting mobile handsets on its packaging in shops. Instead it plastered its boxes with alluring pictures of the young and attractive. Vodafone followed suit. Virgin Mobile's insurance contract – normally the last thing any consumer wants to read when they buy a new phone – is wrapped inside a condom package.

The approach is typical of the Virgin Group which has sought to shake up other markets such as financial services with simple products and lively marketing campaigns. 'You've got to have a bit of an edge. You've got to challenge convention. It's part of what we do as a brand', says Alexander. But he says the high profile of the Virgin name means Virgin Mobile has also been able to spend far less on advertising than other operators such as O_2, which rebranded from BT Cellnet in 2002. Virgin Mobile uses ad agency Rainey Kelly Campbell Roalfe/ Y&R and spends around £37m a year on marketing, ploughing some of its budget into often controversial and high-profile TV commercials such as its recent ad featuring singer Christina Aguilera simulating sex.

The approach has given it a strong following among its core 18- to 34-year-old target market. It has also meant that Virgin scores well on text messaging. Around a third of its revenues come from texts, compared with less than 20 per cent for most of the other operators. Virgin believes this will stand it in good stead for the roll-out of next-generation services such as picture messaging and video and music downloads. 'There is a reasonably strong correlation between someone who is into texting and someone who will be into new services such as downloading content', says Steel, now the company's commercial director. 'We see the emergence of new services as an exciting area but one that will take place in a measured way.'

In the summer, Virgin Mobile will launch Virgin 'bites', video-based services aimed at its youthful customer base. Earlier this year, the mobile operator signed a new network contract with carrier T-Mobile which will enable it to offer a wide range of data services in an attempt to compete with the already established service offerings of operators such as Vodafone and Orange.

Sources: Budden 2004a; 2004b; Budden and Pesola 2004. Reproduced with permission from Financial Times Limited.

 Notes

1 E.g. Sharma and Patterson (1999) show that communication effectiveness affects functional quality, technical quality, trust and – indirectly– relationship commitment.
2 Meenaghan and Shipley (1999) show how sponsoring affects the values which a customer associates with a brand.
3 See the section on 'supplementary services' in Chapter 5.
4 See Grönroos 2000a.
5 See Bruhn 2002b for service providers directing their marketing activities in general including their communications to the relationship lifecycle.
6 See Fornell *et al*. (1996) and Grönroos 2000b for the role of a firm's image in service purchasing decisions.
7 See O'Loughlin *et al*. 2004.
8 See Biel 1992.
9 See Keller 2003.
10 Hartman and Lindgren (1993) identified the difficulty of judgement – next to the degree of customisation and the waiting time for a product/service – as a major difference between services and consumer goods.
11 See Hite and Hite 1991.
12 See Berry 2000.
13 See Rust *et al*. 2000.
14 See Brady 2004.
15 See Gutman 1982; Olson and Reynolds 1983.
16 See Bruhn and Frommeyer 2005.
17 See Sundaram and Webster 2000.
18 See Sundaram and Webster 2000.
19 See Shannon 2002.
20 See e.g. Stafford 1996; Mittal and Baker 2002; Meffert and Bruhn 2003.
21 See Meffert and Bruhn 2003.
22 See Krugman *et al*. 1994.
23 See Grove *et al*. 2002.
24 See Greenyer 2004.

PART 4 Secondary value processes: Managing service resources for value

The customer or objects and possessions of the customer, the 'external factors', play a vital role in service production, though they are equally as important as the 'internal factors' of the service provider.

Part of the internal factors is what we call service resources. These are the provider's resources used to produce and deliver a service. These resources – which consist of human resources, e.g. service employee, and material resources, e.g. service machines, such as an ATM – are the contact points between the customer and the service firm. From the contact with these resources, the customer forms an image of the provider and its services. These resources are a major driver of customer behaviour and thus of value creation.

While secondary processes regarding service value (Part 3) set the framework for customer interactions and relationships, by defining what services can be purchased and via which channels these can be purchased and utilised, managing service resources are secondary processes which provide the resources for customer interactions and relationships.

The direct contact between these resources and the customer implies that a service cannot be conducted when the amount of resources available, e.g. the number of employees, does not match the existing demand. These so-called capacity problems occur because a service provider cannot plan its resources independently. Therefore, for planning the usage of service resources, service providers apply measures of service capacity management.

Based on these considerations, Part 4 presents how the service resources are managed by a service provider (Chapter 9) and proceeds to show how these resource capacities can be planned and managed (Chapter 10).

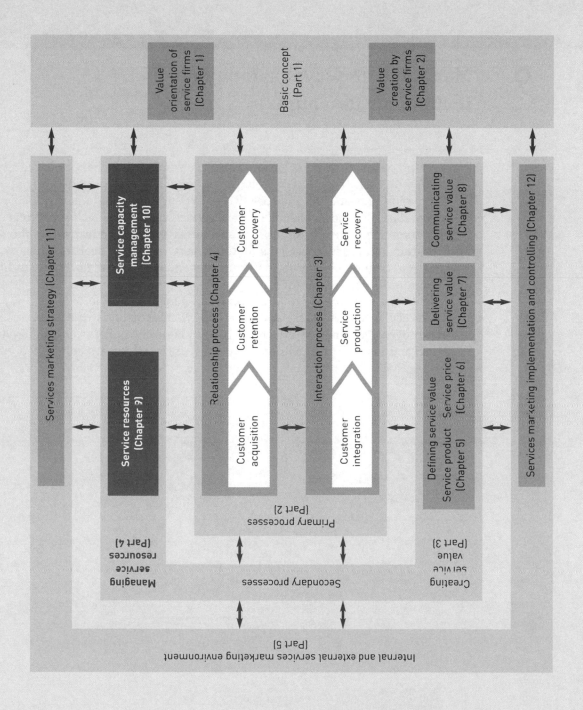

Value orientation of service firms [Chapter 1]

Basic concept (Part 1)

Value creation by service firms [Chapter 2]

Services marketing strategy [Chapter 11]

Service capacity management [Chapter 10]

Service resources (Chapter 9)

Communicating service value [Chapter 8]

Delivering service value [Chapter 7]

Defining service value
Service product
[Chapter 5]

Service price
[Chapter 6]

Services marketing implementation and controlling [Chapter 12]

Relationship process [Chapter 4]

Customer recovery

Customer retention

Customer acquisition

Interaction process [Chapter 3]

Service recovery

Service production

Customer integration

Primary processes (Part 2)

Managing service resources (Part 4)

Secondary processes

Creating service value (Part 3)

Internal and external services marketing environment (Part 5)

9 Managing employees, tangibles and technology for value

The preceding chapters reviewed various elements of the Service Value Chain on different levels. The primary value activities of a service provider are the interaction and the relationship process. These are supported and made possible by the secondary activities which all concern service value as the value which is created by a service to the customer. The secondary activities encapsulate the service product and pricing decisions (defining service value), decisions regarding the service channels (delivering service value) and decisions regarding branding and communications (communicating service value). We have implicitly addressed the service resources a provider utilises for generating value.

Every service necessitates more or less three groups of service resources: employees, tangibles and technology (see Figure 9.1). Services are delivered in interactions with the customer and these interactions are conducted by these

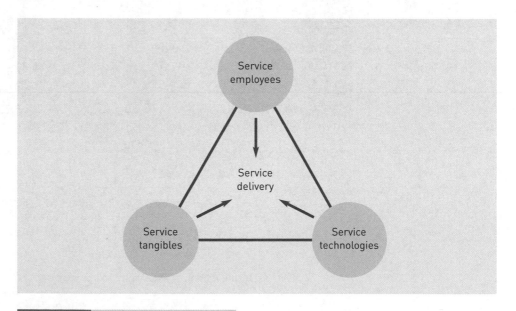

FIGURE 9.1 Types of service resources

three service resources. Often, the three resources are utilised in combination. A hotel receptionist (employee) is standing behind a desk (tangible) and uses a computer with the reservation system of the hotel (tangible and technology). However, each of the three resources is associated with distinctive tasks for value-oriented services marketing. The three groups of service resources are explored so as to understand these distinct circumstances. This chapter ensures the following learning objectives (see Figure 9.2):

1. Defining the role of service employees as value drivers, the determinants of employee behaviour as well as exploring the need to manage employee behaviour by the service provider.

2. Understanding the value effects and types of service tangibles as well as the tangible quality dimensions perceived by customers which build the levers for managing the tangibles.

3. Learning about the role of technology within the Service Value Chain and as a value driver, the types of service technologies as well as the implementation issues to consider when managing service technologies.

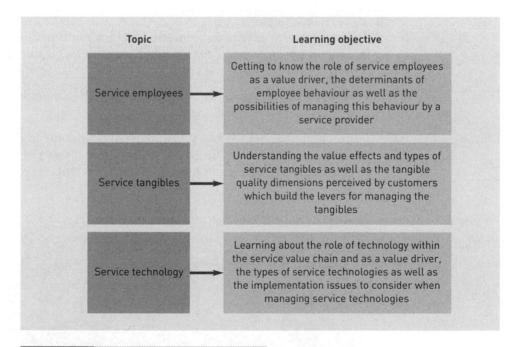

Topic	Learning objective
Service employees	Getting to know the role of service employees as a value driver, the determinants of employee behaviour as well as the possibilities of managing this behaviour by a service provider
Service tangibles	Understanding the value effects and types of service tangibles as well as the tangible quality dimensions perceived by customers which build the levers for managing the tangibles
Service technology	Learning about the role of technology within the service value chain and as a value driver, the types of service technologies as well as the implementation issues to consider when managing service technologies

FIGURE 9.2   Learning objectives of Chapter 9

Managing the behaviour of service employees

Value effects of service employee behaviour and managing service employees

The value contribution of human resources arises from service employees' behaviour. Their behaviour has consequences which have a direct or indirect impact on revenues or costs and consequently affect the value of the service firm. The value consequences of employee behaviour as well as its determination by service resources can be depicted in analogy to the customer-oriented Service Profit Chain (see Chapter 2). The *internal Service Profit Chain* structures the consequences of managing human resources into perceptual consequences (internal service quality), psychological consequences (internal customer satisfaction) and behavioural consequences (internal customer loyalty).[1] There are links between the external and the internal profit chain (see Figure 9.3) which explain various ways of managing service resources so as to create value. Some of the respective arguments regarding the *value consequences of managing human resources* are:

- Human resources activities help increase employee satisfaction.[2]

- Satisfied employees are more motivated and more willing to act in a firm's interest in the customer interaction. This increases customer satisfaction and consequently organisational value.

- The higher motivation of satisfied employees also strengthens their efficiency in the service process resulting in cost reductions.

- Loyal employees help to keep customers loyal. In some industries (e.g. private banking), customers are linked to the employee instead of to the service firm. In consequence, making employees loyal helps retain these customers.

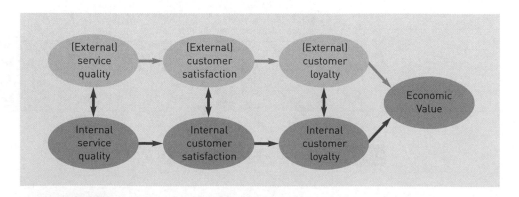

| FIGURE 9.3 | Internal and external Service Profit Chain |

- Employee loyalty reduces costs as high employee turnover means increased recruiting and training costs for the service provider.

The different value implications of service employees are illustrated in Services marketing in action 9.1.

Dimensions of employee behaviour

Central to the internal Service Profit Chain and crucial for the service employees as a service resource is their behaviour in the service process. Employee behaviour in this context is a complex phenomenon. There are various aspects of their behaviour which are important for services marketing. The various aspects can be associated with two *behavioural dimensions*, to internally and externally oriented behaviour.

SERVICES MARKETING IN ACTION 9.1:

Restructuring at Barclays

The strategic importance of service employees for a firm's success was the reason for a significant restructuring plan at Barclays, Britain's third biggest bank. At the centre of the restructuring was the reformation of the weightings of non-customer contact middle management compared to customer contact employees. The bank was going to 'cut 800 middle management and support jobs as part of a radical shake-up of its UK operations that will also see it recruit 1,000 branch staff in an effort to improve customer service'.

The move has been masterminded by Roger Davis, chief executive of the UK banking division, which accounts for half of Barclays' group profits. As part of the restructuring, Barclays will strip layers of relatively well-paid middle managers in areas such as human resources, IT, strategy and finance. It will also reduce support staff and cut duplication. Mr Davis has also decided to raise the salaries of bank cashiers and is considering ploughing more money into the bank's 2,000 branches to improve them. Local branch managers will decide how the 1,000 new staff will be deployed.

'We all felt we needed to do more to get customers back in the focus of the business', Mr Davis said. 'Customer satisfaction in the banking industry generally has not been as high as we would like and customers have pointed to a lack of personal attention and a lack of feeling valued.' Barclays recently admitted that in an experiment, not a single passer-by called into its Croydon branch to collect a free £5 note because they did not trust the bank enough to believe the offer was genuine.

'The plans are the biggest restructuring of Barclays' UK operations in years. They are likely to be welcomed by analysts who want Barclays to cut its cost base.'

Source: Croft 2004. Reproduced with permission from Financial Times Limited.

Internally oriented customer behaviour contains behaviour which directly influences the service organisation or other members of the organisation.

Productivity is defined as the amount of output which is delivered by an employee (e.g. number of customers served) divided by the amount of input (e.g. number of working hours). It is a measure of the efficient utilisation of human resources and affects the efficiency of the service firm. As human resources are an important part of the resources of a service firm, the firm's overall productivity and efficiency is determined strongly by the employees' productivity. An employee's productivity generally is represented by the number of output units they 'produce' and consequently by their working speed, absences and breaks. Whether service employees are productive or not is influenced by, and thus can be managed via, the service firm's ability to motivate employees and to ensure employee commitment towards the customer and the firm. The more motivated and committed the employees are, the more productive behaviour will occur.

Another internally oriented behavioural dimension is *internal customer orientation*. When understanding internal working relationships such as internal customer relationships (see previous section), the single employee has to serve a number of stakeholders. Viewing them all as customers, internally customer-oriented employees aim to fulfil the expectations and needs of these internal customers. An example of the securing of an internal relationship is the service level agreement between two divisions of a service provider which represents a treaty defining the quality and quantity of service units which are delivered from one division to another. The relationship between supervisor and employee is also defined in a firm's organisation, although it is not interpreted as a customer relationship. However, the duties of both supervisor and employee can be interpreted as requirements derived from internal customer expectations. Less formalised are the relationships between employees working together in teams. Their common output strongly depends on their co-operation and their willingness and ability to behave in a customer-oriented manner towards each other. An important prerequisite for internal customer orientation is the understanding of internal customer relationships. This construct is not obvious and in many cases, even supervisors – despite being role models for their employees – do not behave in a customer-oriented manner. Consequently, the company culture of a service firm plays an important role for the internal customer orientation demonstrated by employees.

Internally, the customer-oriented behaviour of employees which is not directed towards specific members or departments of the service organisation, but concerns their behaviour with respect to the firm in general, is the so-called *organisational citizenship behaviour*, an 'individual behaviour that is discretionary, not directly or indirectly recognised by the formal reward system, and which, in general, promotes the effective functioning of the organisation'.[3] Organisational citizenship behaviour is especially important in the service industries because service processes are heterogeneous and not entirely predictable due to the integration of the customer into this process. Organisational citizenship behaviour can be described by various behavioural facets, for example 'help' (i.e. helping colleagues) or 'voice' (i.e. making suggestions for innovations or improvements).[4] These kinds of behaviours are strong indicators of the commitment of an employee. Moreover, just commitment of the employee is not enough. The systems and culture of a service provider are prerequisites of the organisational citizenship behaviour of employees. For example, implementing empowerment and allowing the employee to have responsibility and to make their own decisions supports the responsible behaviour of the employees and their security regarding taking decisions.[5]

Externally oriented employee behaviours concern the employee–customer relationship and the service employee's behaviour within this relationship and in the interactions with the customer. There are two important dimensions of the externally oriented behaviour of a service employee: customer orientation and firm orientation.

The employee's *customer orientation* is a relevant driver to ensuring a customer-oriented value orientation of a service provider. As for the customer orientation of the service firm, an employee's customer orientation means that the employee must focus attention on meeting the needs and expectations of the customers. This starts with analysing customer expectations. In services, employees play an important role in identifying customer expectations. Through direct contact with the customer, employees can perceive many behaviours and reactions of the customers from which customer expectations could be derived. Furthermore, due to the direct contact between employee and customer, the employees are representatives of the service firm and therefore their customer-oriented behaviour is a reflection of the firm's customer orientation in the view of the customers. The employees' customer orientation is influenced by the internal customer orientation of the service firm and by the support given by the organisation, such as by providing relevant customer information in the customer information system in order to be able to serve the customer individually.

The role of an employee's customer orientation is often misunderstood. It is not meant that an employee should focus on customer expectations as an end in itself. Rather, being customer-oriented is – following the Service Profit Chain – a means for creating value for the firm. So, in the end, from the provider's perspective, the primary goal is the employee's *firm orientation*. As customer-oriented behaviour helps to increase the value of the firm, it drives firm orientation. The difference between customer and firm orientation is obvious in service settings with a strong relationship between customer and employee. This might be the case in the high-profile private banking sector where a bank adviser has only a limited number of customers who are advised by the employee, who simultaneously develops the customer/client relationship. Logically, a personal relationship between adviser and client evolves, and the adviser might even perceive a dilemma between the firm's and the customer's interests. It is optimal for service providers to reach a combination of customer and firm orientation by strengthening the employee's commitment towards both the customer and the firm.

Instruments of managing service employee behaviour

In order to ensure that the employees of a service firm behave in a way the service provider aims for, there are various levers with very different intentions and effects. Four groups of *employee-oriented measures* can be differentiated: employee role management, evaluation and feedback, recruiting and qualifying employees and motivating employees (see Figure 9.4).

Employee role management

Every individual performs several roles in everyday life. These multiple roles include being a son/daughter, partner, friend, employee, etc. to different persons. A role concerns behaviour patterns of an individual (in contrast to single behavioural acts).[6] Within each of these roles there are again subroles to perform. For the *employee roles* the subroles are derived from the different tasks and the different stakeholders an employee has to deal with. Regarding different tasks, an airline employee has tasks at the check-in, boarding, internal processes, etc. For each of these tasks, the employee takes on different roles. Regarding different stakeholders, the service employee is an employee in relation to their supervisor and service provider, complaint manager or even a punching bag for the customer. Depending on the customer's stress resistance, this role variety can cause negative emotions, misunderstandings and misbehaviour on the part of the customer.[7]

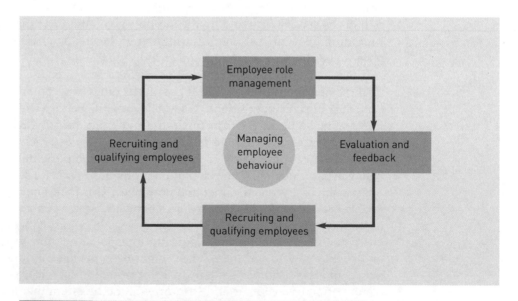

FIGURE 9.4   Instruments of managing service employee behaviour

In order to prevent these negative consequences, service providers often enforce a *systematic role management* for employees which aims at designing roles for employees by defining specific sets of behaviours which are expected by employees according to their positions, communicating these roles to the employees, selecting, training and motivating employees in order to support them in fulfilling the roles and giving feedback to the employees regarding their performance against the requirements of these roles.[8]

When defining employee roles, it is important for service providers to ensure *role clarity* by designing and communicating unambiguous behavioural sets. The contrast of role clarity is *role conflict* which is defined as the incompatibility between one or more roles. In this case, fulfilling one role makes fulfilling the others difficult for the employee.[9] A typical example of a role conflict is the bank adviser example mentioned above. Other examples concern favouritism when some customers are treated better than other customers, such as a restaurant's employee giving free drinks to friends visiting the restaurant or a bank employee bestowing interest reductions on friends who are clients of the bank. Role conflicts can also be caused internally. When a service provider's organisation consists of both a classic hierarchical organisation as well as a parallel project organisation, an employee might have a direct supervisor as well as part-time supervisors, i.e. project leaders. When the employee has to fulfil tasks in both roles, role conflicts may occur when there are conflicting deadlines. The organisation's ability to minimise role conflict, helps to achieve job satisfaction for the employees.[10]

A tool for defining clear roles for employees is by using *behavioural repertoires*. A behavioural repertoire[11] represents a specific combination of behaviours which make up an employee's role. These behaviours need to be conducted by the employee in order to perform their role. By describing customer roles by a set of criteria, types of behavioural repertoires can be distinguished. For example, behavioural repertoires can be distinguished according to whether the employee is supposed to derive their own solutions for customer requests, in the case of a bank adviser, or to just choose from a set of given solutions or providing a specific service that the customer chooses (e.g. handing out meals at a fast-food restaurant).

A further personnel-oriented and role-related instrument is **empowerment**. Empowerment means giving the employee the discretion to take day-to-day decisions about job-related activities.[12] When employees are empowered their behavioural repertoires are less restricted and they do not need to consult the supervisor on every decision. The general role of the employee is clearly defined, however within this role the employee has certain tolerances regarding their decisions. A typical example of an empowered employee is the Ritz-Carlton employee who is allowed to compensate customer problems with services for up to US $2,000. Although empowering employees means lowering the control over the employees' behaviours, various positive consequences are accredited to this instrument. Through the opportunity to react directly in a customer interaction and the employee's responsibility perceived by the customer, the interaction quality as perceived by the customer is affected positively. Further, employees are motivated to think about their behaviour and therefore are more involved in their jobs, e.g. resulting in suggestions for improving their work or the service in general. Furthermore, empowerment's positive influence on job satisfaction is widely accepted.

Evaluation and feedback

Whether an employee fulfils their role as intended or not is important for both the management of the service provider as well as the employee. The management learns from *employee evaluations* how the respective employees contribute to the firm's goals and consequently to the firm's value creation. Based on this information, further human resources activities, such as training, can be decided on. For the employee, this information helps to improve individual knowledge or abilities. A useful *feedback* by the supervisor is a determinant to do so.

There are generally two approaches for *evaluating employees* depending on the criteria used for this evaluation: outcome-related and behaviour-related evaluations.

Outcome-related evaluations use the outcomes of employee behaviours for valuing them. According to the internal Service Profit Chain, pre-economic and economic outcomes can be differentiated. An evaluation based on economic criteria uses, e.g. sales or profits in order to evaluate employees. Possible pre-economic criteria are customer satisfaction or customer retention. Using outcome-related criteria is straightforward as it aims at making the employees responsible for realising the firm's objectives. However, it is often complex for employees to link their own behaviour to the outcomes specified by the management.

In contrast to an outcome-related evaluation, a *behaviour-based evaluation* controls employee behaviours themselves, rather than the results of these behaviours.[13] Service managers identify the behaviours that are believed to determine the objectives and then reward employees when they behave in this way, e.g. advising customers regarding the right decision. That means, when managers ask for customer-oriented behaviours and when customer-oriented behaviour does not lead to sales, the manager and not the employee must take responsibility. By this evaluation approach, it is made easier for employees to know how to behave and role conflicts are decreased. Certain behaviours can have conflicting impacts on goals, e.g. helping customers has no direct revenue effect, but a direct cost effect. For a behaviour-based evaluation, the service firm predefines what behaviours are interpreted as goal-oriented behaviours for the firm. The employee is relieved from their own analyses of which behaviours are best for realising the desired outcomes and can concentrate on realising the behaviours predefined by the firm.

For *managing employee behaviour* directly, the evaluation results can be used to inform the employee about the evaluation and to discuss steps to improve performance as well as define respective objectives. This *feedback* to employees is as important as the evaluation itself.

Recruiting and qualifying employees

An important tool for providing employees with the abilities to perform adequately in the sense of the firm's objectives is termed, *'qualifying employees'*. Depending on the complexity of the contents regarding which employees are to be qualified, guidelines or training can be used as qualification instruments. *Employee guidelines* can be used in a less complex context. Certain behavioural rules which are straightforward to understand and apply, may be communicated via this instrument.

However, many aspects which are to be taught to the employees of a service firm cannot be explained or conveyed via such guidelines. In this case, service firms use *training employees* to ensure that the learning objectives and desired outcomes are achieved. The more 'abstract' behaviours such as 'being customer-oriented' are typical contents of employee training. Generally, training aims to influence the employees' competence. There are *four types of competences* which are regularly trained:

- Professional competence concerns the knowledge and abilities of the employee, specifically applicable to their task (e.g. knowledge of the biotech market of a biotech consultant).

- Methodological competence concerns the knowledge of concepts and methods which are needed for conducting a job (e.g. knowledge of statistical methods by a market researcher).

- Social competence is about the employee's capacity regarding dealing with other persons, like customers, colleagues, supervisors (e.g. capacity for teamwork).

- Psychological competence pertains to the employee's psychological state with relevance to individual behaviour in the job (e.g. employee motivation).

All of these *types of competence* consist of parts, some of which are easier to influence than others. For example, some parts of professional competence can be learned quickly, competitor knowledge is essential and can easily be taught, while other competences are only acquired through experience, such as the knowledge of market key opinion leaders, like a bank manager knowing the head of the central bank. The same is valid for social competence. Some rules for behaviours in customer interactions can be learned in a short period of time, while a generic employee empathy is acquired over years, if not inherent. See Services marketing in action 9.2 on McDonald's for insights into the training practices of the fast-food company.

SERVICES MARKETING IN ACTION 9.2:

The McDonald's training programme

McDonald's success is built on the highest standards of quality, service and cleanliness delivered to customers in each of its restaurants. Well-trained crew and managers are the first step to achieving these standards. It is company policy to provide career opportunities that allow employees to develop their full potential. This includes a comprehensive training programme for crew and operations management and career progression that enables a 'first job' employee to progress through to a senior management position via merit-based promotions.

The first stage of training is at the Welcome Meetings. These set out the company's standards and expectations. This is followed by a structured development programme that provides training in all areas of business. Crew trainers work shoulder-to-shoulder with trainees while they learn the operations skills necessary for running each of the 11 workstations in each restaurant, from the front counter to the grill area. All employees learn to operate state-of-the-art foodservice equipment, gaining knowledge of McDonald's operational procedures. The majority of training is floor based, or 'on-the-job' training because people learn more and are more likely to retain information if they are able to practise as they learn. All new employees have an initial training period. Here they are shown the basics and allowed to develop their skills to a level where they are competent in each area within the restaurant. The timescale for this depends on their status i.e. full or part time. They will also attend classroom-based training sessions where they will complete workbooks for quality, service and cleanliness.

After the initial training period all employees receive ongoing training. This is done using 'Observation Checklists' for the station they are working at. The rating will go towards their appraisal grading.

The restaurants do promote crew members to hourly-paid management positions that carry accountability for areas within the restaurant, or responsibility for a shift. Training and development is given in the restaurant and in addition the participants will attend regular development days. On successful completion of a management entrance exam, employees will attend a training course held by the training department at the regional office before returning to the restaurant in a management position.

The McDonald's Management Development Curriculum takes new recruits from trainee manager to Restaurant Manager. The Management Development Curriculum is divided into four key programmes:

- Shift Management: developing trainee managers in the skills and techniques required to become effective in all aspects of running a shift.

- Systems Management: targeting second assistant and newly promoted first assistant managers. This programme covers all areas of McDonald's systems, increasing the manager's business knowledge. It also develops individual techniques.

- Restaurant Leadership: introducing managers to the key skills needed to become effective restaurant leaders e.g. team building, communication, decision making.

- Business Leadership: Focusing restaurant/general managers on the need to develop a business strategy that encompasses both internal and external factors.

Most departments in the regional offices offer restaurant managers opportunities to be seconded to work in the regional office. This gives an experienced manager the opportunity to develop and learn new skills, to see a different side of the business and to experience how each department's strategies have a role in achieving the company's goals.

Source: The Times 100 2005.

Training focuses above all on those competences which can be influenced in the short term. Service providers aim at acquiring other competences by *recruiting employees* who already have other competences. Employee recruitment is an activity which focuses on the job market, whilst in customer-directed services marketing, a firm aims at marketing its offering towards the consumers in a market. For recruiting employees, the provider aims to attract the appropriate skills, marketing its employee-relevant offerings, position, pay, perspectives, etc. to the job market. In the service industry, there are a wide range of jobs, requiring different sets of skills ranging from general to highly specialised niche jobs, such as investment banking.

In any given market, there is also a wide range of employees in terms of qualification and other competence-relevant characteristics. Service providers aim at recruiting those employees who fit the firm's requirements regarding the different competence types best. In order to find these employees, service providers employ activities of *human resources marketing* which consists of two important tasks: personnel attracting and personnel selection.

For *personnel attracting* – comparable to a service provider's attempts to recruiting customers – a *competitive advantage* in the view of potential and current employees supports the attraction of the best potential employees. A competitive advantage can be built based on the image a service firm has as an employer. Relevant dimensions which build the image perceived by the employees are the payment package, i.e. the fixed and variable parts of the salary, the material (e.g. office equipment) and immaterial characteristics (e.g. responsibility) of the job, but also aspects which are not closely connected with the respective job, such as career opportunities and the culture of the organisation. Services marketing in action 9.3 shows how compensation affects the attraction and retention of restaurant managers.

SERVICES MARKETING IN ACTION 9.3:

Compensation drives attraction and retention of restaurant managers

The role of compensation as a tool for attracting and retaining managers in the restaurant industry was the object of an empirical study. Forty-nine US restaurants were examined regarding their changes made to compensation and incentive packages, the reasons for and perceived consequences of those changes.

In general, 42 of the 49 restaurants had changed their packages within the past five years; 39 had effected the changes within the last two years. Between the elements of a compensation and incentive package, the following aspects were subject to change in the companies analysed:

- 24 restaurants increased the general salary level.

- 12 restaurants changed their policy to now offer newly hired managers a choice of geographic locations.

- There were almost no changes regarding vacation days.

- 15 restaurants enacted retirement plans.

- 12 restaurants offered either stock options or partnership opportunities to their managers.

- Further changes include: providing company cars, increasing bonuses, providing insurance and performance-based compensation.

The most important reasons for these changes were the desire to attract new managers and the desire to retain managers, indicating the important role of compensation packages as levers of employee recruitment and retention in the restaurant industry.

Source: Patil and Chung 1998.

Next to defining such a competitive advantage, service providers stimulate potential employees' attention by conducting direct and indirect *communicative measures* towards the labour market.[14] When employing direct measures, the provider itself communicates to the target group. *Direct communication* is conducted via non-specific mass image communications, specific job advertisements or actively contacting potential employees. An active contact is often made to competitors' employees, supplier firms (e.g. a bank recruiting a management consultant from a firm consulting to the bank) or customers (e.g. former students employed as lecturers at a university). An *indirect communication* is accomplished via intermediaries such as an employment service, a temping agency or a human resources consultancy. After having attracted employees, an *evaluation and selection of employees* is conducted. Various tests regarding the competences mentioned above are applied in order to evaluate the candidates. How McDonald's proceeds in order to attract and select new employees, is shown in Services marketing in action 9.4.

Motivating employees

The – mostly cognitive – competences of future or current employees targeted by activities to recruit and qualify employees are not the only prerequisites an employee needs to demonstrate, to be valuable for the service firm. Of equal importance is the *motivation of employees* which is closely connected with employees' attitude towards the job and their employer. Motivation is a central driver for employees' performance.

Some of the activities mentioned in the previous sections also affect employee motivation even though that is not the primary goal. Employees feel appreciated when they have the opportunity to develop further, even though the primary goal of qualifying employees is to improve their ability to perform in their job.

SERVICES MARKETING IN ACTION 9.4:

Attracting and selecting new employees at McDonald's

A recruitment exercise at McDonald's often generates more applications than there are positions available. The manager will select the applicants to be interviewed and will conduct the interviews.

A well-run interview will identify an applicant's potential to be a successful McDonald's employee. To find people who will be committed to delivering outstanding service, McDonald's scripts an interview guide that helps the company predict how an applicant's past behaviour is likely to influence future performance. It uses a fact-based decision-making process. The questions look for actual events or situations rather than allowing applicants to give a general or theoretical response. Interviewers look for behavioural evidence in the applicant's life history that fits with the requirements of the job. The interviewer rates candidates on their responses and offers jobs to those who earn the highest ratings.

The selection process includes an initial online psychometric test. This test produces an initial score. The applicant then attends a first stage interview and is offered 'On Job Experience' (OJE). This is a 2-day assessment in a restaurant. Successful completion at OJE will lead to a final interview, after which the manager decides whether or not to hire the applicant.

After the final interview the manager will rate the applicant's responses. A successful applicant will have demonstrated skills and behaviours that have been identified as key to the position.

Source: The Times 100 2005.

However, it is essential that service firms plan specific measures which aim at motivating employees. There are plenty of options for such measures and the levers via which they affect motivation are incentives. *Incentives* differ according to two dimensions:

- The *degree of individuality* concerns whether the incentive is directed towards a specific employee (individual incentive) or a group of or all employees (collective incentive). Individual incentives are defined in a general form but applied for each employee individually. For example, a firm has general compensation schemes. Which bonus or which specific pay rise an employee receives can be differentiated. Collective incentives are applied to a group or all employees simultaneously and cannot be utilised by individual employees alone (e.g. a cafeteria).

- According to the *degree of materiality*, material and immaterial incentives are distinguished. Material incentives concern tangible elements of the working place (e.g. equipment at workplace) or financial elements (e.g. bonus). Immaterial incentives are of intangible nature, such as career opportunities or company culture.

Matching these two differentiation criteria results in four *types of incentives* which are applied by service firms in order to motivate employees (see Figure 9.5). Most of these incentives are closely connected with the company structure (e.g. career oppor-

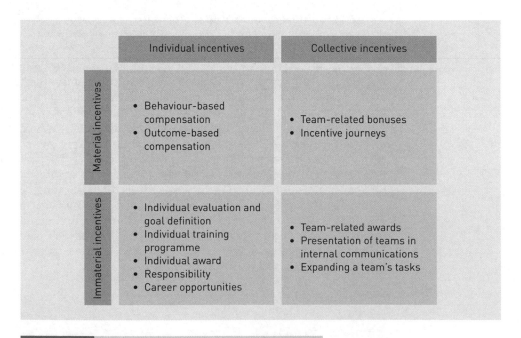

FIGURE 9.5   Incentives for motivating service employees

tunities), systems (e.g. reward system) and culture. These are important drivers of services marketing implementation which are treated in more detail in Chapter 12.

Managing the tangibles of a service

A further resource which is relevant in most service interactions involves the tangible aspects of a service. Tangibles are all aspects of a service which can – in contrast to a service in general, or specifically the process part of a service – be perceived physically, such as the appearance of physical facilities, equipment, personnel and communication materials,[15] as well as the atmosphere at the service location.[16]

Value effects of service tangibles

Due to the process character of services, the interactional elements of a service, i.e. the process itself, constitute an important driver of customer perceptions. Therefore, and partly because of studies indicating a low relevance of tangibles as a service dimension,[17] service research concentrates on customer perceptions of this process and somehow neglects the tangibles of a service. However, there is also empirical evidence that tangibles play an important role in *influencing customer perceptions and decisions* (see Figure 9.6).[18] This is at least valid in certain industries. The design of a restaurant's menu often says a lot about the quality

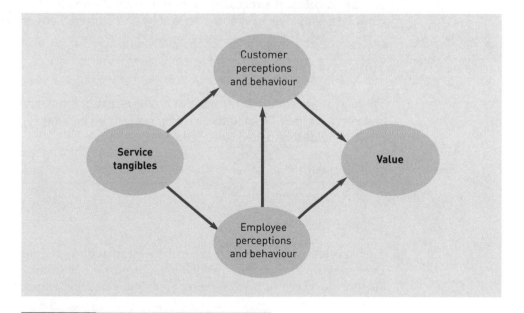

FIGURE 9.6   Value effects of service tangibles

level. Or many bank customers probably judge a well-dressed bank employee differently to an unshaven employee wearing jeans and a well-worn sweatshirt. These examples illustrate that service tangibles play an important role as so-called *quality signals*. The quality of a tangible factor signals a certain quality level of the whole service to the consumer. The consumer simplifies the evaluation process in this manner in order to reduce uncertainty about the quality level of the service: damaged equipment in an airplane is interpreted as a negative quality indicator. This uncertainty is caused by the fact that many other service characteristics are more difficult to evaluate, especially the competence of employees.

The consumer's uncertainty is even more relevant for *potential customers* compared to existing customers. Potential customers have no experience with a service provider and its services and therefore lack evaluative criteria. A potential customer cannot evaluate the service process and all factors which are relevant in the service process, such as employee behaviour. Therefore, potential customers in particular utilise quality indicators consciously or unconsciously in order to estimate the quality level of a service before purchasing.

Next to this external effect of service tangibles on consumer perceptions and decisions, there is also an internal effect of service tangibles on *employees* (see Figure 9.6).[19] As employees are part of the service interaction, they perceive the service tangibles as do the customers, and, as employees are also human beings, they also appreciate an appropriate service environment.[20] Besides the customer facilities where service interactions take place, there are facilities which are offered to and evaluated by employees, such as the cafeteria, restrooms, dressing room. The tangible attributes of the working environment influence the employees' psychological processes. A well-designed and clean office motivates and stimulates employees more than a shabby and cluttered environment.

Types of service tangibles

There are service tangibles which vary in terms of existence, design, relevance and service types. Despite these differences, three general types of service tangibles can be distinguished (see Figure 9.7):

1. servicescape;

2. service environment;

3. service materials.

The **servicescape**[21] is the physical location where the service is delivered. Examples are the counter area of a bank or post office or the different parts of an airport: the check-in area, security area, lounges, etc. The *servicescape* consists of three elements:

- The *design of the servicescape* is the most important part of service tangibles. The attributes of the furniture or the technical equipment (see also the section on 'managing service technology' later in this chapter), such as the computers at the check-in counters of an airport, are part of the design of the servicescape.

- Although they are an important process factor, *employees in the servicescape* reflect several tangible attributes, such as their dress or physical appearance. In many service industries, these factors are taken as a quality indicator by the consumer.

- Finally, the *ambiance of the servicescape* or the 'atmospherics'[22] of the service interaction strongly affect the service process in the perception of the customer. The ambiance consists of visual elements, (colour, brightness), aural elements, whether there is background music (volume, pitch), olfactory elements (scent, freshness) and tactile elements (softness, smoothness, temperature).

The *service environment* represents the overall surroundings of a service location. It concerns the attributes of the servicescape and includes the neighbourhood where a service branch is located, the exterior design and quality of a service location and the appropriateness of the service location in terms of accessibility by the consumer.

Finally, *service materials* are used in the service encounter and mostly have a supportive function in the encounter for the employee or the customer. The menu in the restaurant illustrates the options for the consumer to choose from, the laptop of the management consultant helps present concepts and methodologies, the canteen in restaurants and airports are used by the consumer. Although service materials have only a supportive function, they can play an important role as a 'hygiene

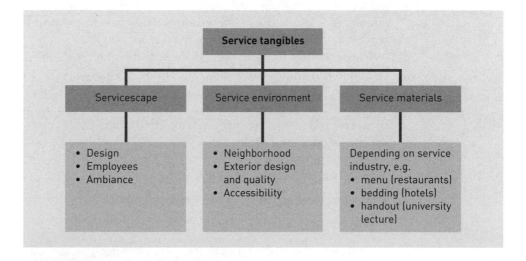

FIGURE 9.7   Types of service tangibles

factor': when they irritate the customer, they have a negative effect on perception, often these hygiene factors are taken for granted by the customer. A dirty eating area in a top restaurant is perceived negatively by demanding guests.

Across the three groups of service tangibles, these can be either *mobile* (e.g. laptop) or *immobile* (e.g. furniture) according to whether they can be transported easily to a service location. This differentiation is important when considering that there are services which are delivered at the customer's location and those which are delivered at the provider's location. For the latter, a restricted number of service tangibles – manageable by the service firm – are of relevance because the service employees travelling to the customer's location can bring only mobile tangibles. In this case, the employee and mobile equipment (as parts of the servicescape) as well as service materials are perceived by the customer.

Depending on the service category, different tangibles can be *core or supplementary services*. Tangibles as core services are absolutely necessary to deliver the service. A hotel without rooms cannot provide the customers with space to rest and sleep. The equipment of a cinema is the prerequisite to showing a film. Supplementary services are tangible elements which enhance or improve a service but are not necessary to perform the service. A restaurant can abandon a menu and the waiter can recite the dishes offered. In some cases this strategy is used as a speciality attribute of a restaurant.

Quality dimensions of service tangibles

Service tangibles are relevant to the consumers' perceptions in two ways. Consumers perceive and evaluate whether a tangible exists at all and perceives missing tangibles negatively: no hand towels in the restroom. Here, the consumer asks WHAT tangibles are present at the service location. In addition, the consumer asks HOW the existing tangibles are arranged and how this affects the consumers' quality perception of the service tangibles.

Consequently, the question is what are the quality dimensions which are used in order to evaluate the different service tangibles? This question has to be answered for the specific service and the specific service tangible. However, there are some general ideas about how customers perceive and evaluate service tangibles. The following list concerns quality dimensions which can be attributed to specific service tangibles:

- being up-to-date (equipment);
- being appealing (physical facilities);
- being well-dressed (employees);
- neat and well groomed appearance (employees);
- cleanliness (rooms);

- usability (materials, equipment);
- being organised (equipment).

As one example, the results of a study regarding the importance of the quality dimension 'cleanliness of hotel tangibles' are presented in Services marketing in action 9.5.

SERVICES MARKETING IN ACTION 9.5:

Cleanliness as a tangible quality dimension in hotels

The differences in importance of specific quality dimensions for different tangibles is emphasised by a study of hotel guest requirements and evaluations of the cleanliness in hotels in New Zealand. A survey was conducted in three cities in New Zealand: Auckland (New Zealand's largest city, population approximately 1.3 million), Hamilton (New Zealand's fourth largest city, 125km south of Auckland, population 113,000) and Wellington (New Zealand's second largest city, 530 km south of Hamilton, population 160,000). The statements of 412 hotel guests were included in the study.

They were asked to consider the importance and perception ratings concerning the cleanliness of 31 tangible items in hotels. These items were broken down into specific areas of 'The Outside of the Hotel or Motel', 'The room or unit', 'The kitchen', 'The Bathroom/Toilet', 'Reception and staff'. The study revealed that the highest importance was associated by respondents to bathroom items, more specifically the 'Toilet pan/seat' (mean 6.78), followed by Bathroom/Toilet 'Smell or odour' (mean 6.76), 'Shower cubicle' (see Table 9.1 below).

Source: Lockyer 2003.

TABLE 9.1 Importance of hotel tangibles associated with cleanliness

Tangible items	Importance
The outside of the hotel or motel	
Garden and driveway	4.89
Building exterior	5.00
Age of building	4.29
The room or unit	
Paintwork or wallpaper	5.40
Furniture	5.36
Overall decor	5.31
Smell or odour	6.55
Windows	5.37

▶

TABLE 9.1	Continued

Tangible items	Importance
The room or unit	
Bed linen	6.63
Windowsills	5.37
Curtains	5.41
Carpet and floor coverings	5.68
Upholstery	5.57
Cushions	5.41
Bedspreads	6.13
The kitchen (if available)	
Kitchen floor/walls	6.22
Smell or odour	6.68
Kitchen utensils	6.43
Plates and cutlery	6.46
Sink and stove	6.45
Decoration	5.17
Bathroom/toilet	
Walls	6.08
Floor	6.29
Shower cubicle	6.64
Toilet pan/seat	6.78
Smell or odour	6.76
Basin or sink	6.56
Towels	6.62
Reception	
Staff overall appearance	5.61
Staff hair and hands	5.90
Reception area	5.53

Legend: Respondents were asked to 'indicate in this column how important the factor is in determining Hotel or Motel cleanliness' using a scale from 1 = Extremely Unimportant to 7 = Extremely Important.

Source: adapted from Lockyer 2003, p. 301.

Managing service technology

Technology and the Service Value Chain

In different fields of services marketing, technologies play an important role. Consequently, in different parts, chapters and sections of this book the use of technologies has already been stressed. Following the Service Value Chain framework, technology affects the two *primary value processes*. In the *relationship process*, information technologies are used to collect customer data and to analyse customer relationships. Most customer cards work only through their linkage to complex information systems which collect the purchasing information of the customers, and other technologies, e.g. statistical software, are used in order to analyse the value of different customer relationships. In the *interaction process*, technology has an impact on customer interactions by providing information (e.g. website), supporting employees (e.g. customer information systems at the check-in counter at an airport) or even delivering the service itself (e.g. ATM of a bank or literature databases on the internet).

Consequently, the service product technologies take on the role of a core service or supplementary services. The 'e-service' is a service which is entirely delivered by technologies. For example, e-services in the travel industry such as expedia.com are a full replacement of a travel agency in the eyes of many consumers in this market. But also the other instruments for *defining, delivering and communicating service value* are influenced by technologies. Technologies help to conduct real-time pricing, which sets prices in accordance with various situational factors. In the airline industry, the same flight can vary in price significantly from one day to another, depending on the current booking numbers. Furthermore, technology has created brand new distribution channels which are used to sell and deliver a service and to communicate with consumers, e.g. by telephone, kiosks or the internet.

While technology is a service resource by itself, it interacts with the other two groups of *service resources*. *Employees' work* is supported by technology. Customer information systems provide employees with individual customer information and help them effectively to fulfil customers' needs. When customers call the service hotline of a bank, they are asked to enter their account number. The number is then used by the call centre system to retrieve the specific customer's information on the screen of the customer contact system containing information such as account balance, movements, etc. which are needed by the employee to serve the customer during the telephone interaction. Moreover, the employee is provided with information on the service which is used in the customer interaction. The employee at the information desk of a railway company does not have to page through a book containing the train connections but retrieves this information from the company's online connection system. The relevance of technologies for service employees' behaviour is shown in Services marketing in action 9.6. Regarding the second group of service resources, there is a close relationship between *tangibles and technology*. Technologies are sometimes part of the tangibles. The quick check-in counters at an airport determine the appearance of an airport's lobby. Technology is also used to design the tangibles. Starting from ambient elements, such as light, music or temperature, which are controlled by technology, real-time changes of these tangibles become possible through technology. For example, the outside colour of the Grand Casino Basel (Switzerland) can be varied using phosphoric technology.

SERVICES MARKETING IN ACTION 9.6:

Customer motivation and productivity through technology in Conduit call centres

Conduit is one of the fastest growing information services companies in Europe. Providing directory services in four countries, it competes aggressively in an increasingly deregulated marketplace characterised by tight margins and exacting quality demands.

In order to manage the call centre agents' objectives, the firm implemented the product 'Emvolve Performance Manager' by Performix Technologies. By implementing a performance-related pay structure that focuses the agents' attention on key productivity and service metrics, it has delivered significant cost savings, boosted service quality and dramatically improved employee motivation.

The system is used to drive Conduit's performance-related pay programme, so agents can constantly review the impact of their performance on their pocket. By motivating employees in this practical way the company has focused agents on key objectives: improving service, reducing call times and increasing revenues by up-selling direct customer connections. Conduit has seen dramatic improvements in each of these areas. 'The success of our call centres is highly dependent upon individual performance. To get the right numbers at the top you have to get the right numbers at an individual level', says Katherine Whidden, Call Centre Director at Conduit.

Because agents can see how they're performing – and the impact that has on the business and their pockets – motivation has improved. Absenteeism and attrition, common problems in high-pressure environments such as directory enquires, have dramatically reduced. By improving accuracy and reducing call time, agents have delivered a 60% cost saving to the business.

Source: Performix Technologies 2005.

Value effects of technology

The type of value creation through technology influencing the primary and secondary value processes is generally twofold. Following the definition of value, technology helps increase revenues by improved value to the customer and decreasing cost of the internal processes (see Figure 9.8).[23]

The *cost effects* of technology primarily concern an increase in process efficiency. Technology permits many processes to be conducted faster and at a lower variable cost than processes which require activities of service employees. An empirical study in the USA revealed that a call is handled by interactive voice response (IVR) at a cost of 45 cents, while a telephone call involving an employee generates cost of $7.60.[24] Also, for standard processes the failure probability is lower when the process is conducted by technology instead of an employee,

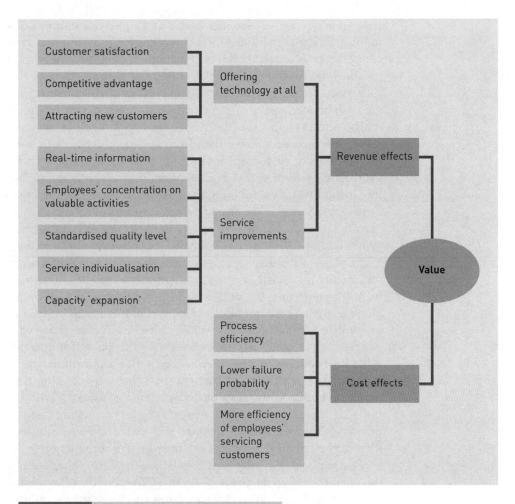

FIGURE 9.8   Value effects of service technologies

resulting in lower cost for rework or failure compensation. Furthermore, the supportive use of technology by employees helps them to serve the customers more efficiently. The call centre agent who does not have to ask the customer for account numbers in order to get the customer information on the screen can deliver a faster service.

Although cost reduction is the obvious goal of technology use in service delivery, it implies a series of *revenue effects*. First, *offering technology-based services* at all has become a customer requirement in some industries. By fulfilling these expectations, service providers realise customer satisfaction by those customers who require the technology.[25] Providing technology-based services can be the basis for a competitive advantage as long as the e-service is not standard in an industry.[26] By offering e-services, a service provider might even succeed in attracting new customer segments.[27] Smaller hotels at a holiday location utilise the tendency of many tourists to compose their travel package by internet research, by this they can attract customers who were reached only by huge hotel chains' mass communications before the internet age.

Service providers realise *service improvements* through technology. As technologies can be managed in a standardised manner, a defined quality level is easier to realise and to control. Supportive technologies used by service employees in customer interactions release them from non-productive activities such as searching in price lists or customer files in filing cabinets and allow them to concentrate on productive activities in the sense of activities which are valued by the customer, like a travel agent's advising the customer to choose the best flight connection. Furthermore, the information which an employee can provide the customer is conducted in real-time due to technology usage. Without the airlines' booking systems, the travel agent could not guarantee a certain flight to the customer. Technology also adds service elements, such as the opportunity to make a reservation for a specific seat in an airplane when booking the flight. Moreover, technology permits the individualisation of services. Although employees generally can treat a customer individually, too, this is difficult for mass services, such as mobile communications, hotels, airlines, etc. In these cases, the systematic processing of customer information is the basis for providing the customer with individualised offers. A best-practice example is the internet bookshop amazon.com which individualises its website by offering the customer specific products based on the customer's purchasing history. Several of the aspects mentioned above allow the service process to be conducted faster which is perceived positively by the customer in many service settings. Finally, technology has a positive capacity effect. A service can only be delivered when there are the necessary service capacities available. If this is not the case, there are negative impacts for the customer, such as queues (see also Chapter 10). When the service is delivered based on technology, service capacities can be managed more easily and are less restricted than human resource capacities for example.

How the Wells Fargo Bank and Cisco Systems create value through service technologies is described in Services marketing in action 9.7.

Types of technologies in services marketing

The discussion of technology's value effects has made it obvious that service firms utilise various types of technologies that they can select for their marketing activities. A *value-oriented typology of technologies* by differentiating technologies according to their usage for services marketing activities gives insight into how service providers can utilise technologies in order to manage and improve services, interactions and customer relationships as well as the internal processes of the service firm.

On an aggregate level, technologies can be distinguished according to the *locus of their utilisation*. Customer contact technologies are applied at the interface

SERVICES MARKETING IN ACTION 9.7:

Driving value through technology

There are various aspects which make technology a competitive weapon. In some cases, customers demand the technology-based alternative and will demonstrate their displeasure by going to a competitor if it is not provided. If the new technology solution is viewed as better in some way than the previous interpersonal alternative, customer satisfaction can actually increase. This is what has happened for Wells Fargo Bank. Wells Fargo was the first bank to offer online banking in the US, and its overarching positioning strategy is one of providing 'alternative delivery channels' for banking services in a variety of forms from ATMs to telephone banking, to in-store bank branches to PC-based and wireless services. Their research showed that their online customers were their most satisfied and most loyal group. But, in order to see these positive results in terms of satisfaction and loyalty, the bank needed to provide excellent service as well as benefits not readily available to consumers via traditional bank branching alternatives.

In some cases, as with Cisco Systems' customer service applications, companies achieve multiple objectives with self-service technologies. Cisco was growing so fast that there was no way it could find enough people, let alone technically savvy people, to provide personal customer service over the telephone. Thus, the company introduced its highly successful online customer service systems. Not only did the company reduce its costs by doing this, but it also found that customer satisfaction increased as the usage of the automated service systems increased.

Source: Bitner *et al.* 2002.

between the service provider and the customer, while internal technologies modify and support the internal processes of a service provider (see Figure 9.9).

Customer contact technologies are a resource in the interactions with the customer. According to the *relative importance as a service resource* compared to other service resources, above all employees, technologies differ according to their role in the customer interaction. *Support technologies* have a lower relative importance compared to employees; they are only used by employees in order to serve the customer. Examples for support technologies are front-end applications (e.g. customer information systems) which provide employees with information needed in the customer contact; reservation systems which harmonise service capacities as well as customers' usage times and indicate whether there are service capacities available for a specific customer request in terms of usage time; service product information software which provides the employee with a structured presentation of the service characteristics they can offer to the customer (e.g. insurance agents' laptops loaded with data in order to tailor an individualised insurance policy for a customer); appliances for collecting customer information

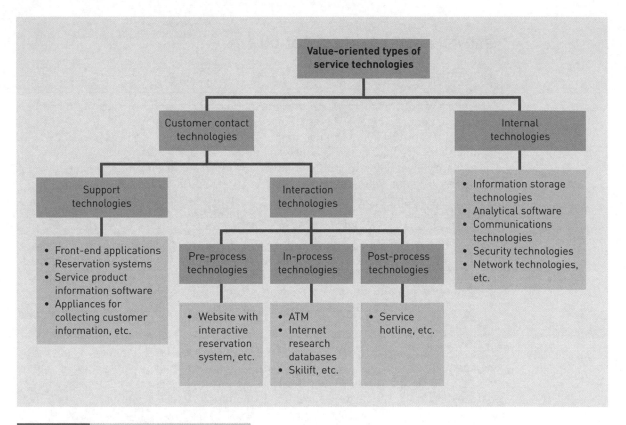

FIGURE 9.9 Types of service technologies

needed for service delivery (e.g. handhelds used by restaurant waiters in order to take customers' orders).

When technologies are the predominant service resource, they take on the role as *interaction technologies* and are the main interaction partner of the customer in order to produce the service. Service interactions consist of several phases (see Chapter 3), the pre-process, in-process and post-process phases. Technologies used in service interactions differ according to which of the phases they are utilised in. Technologies which are employed in the in-process phase are called *in-process technologies* as they actually deliver the service. Then, the respective technologies are the most important service resources without which the service cannot be delivered. Examples are ATMs, internet research databases and equipment such as ski lifts, aeroplanes, trains. The latter ones exhibit both elements of a tangible resource – as they are perceived physically by the service user – and elements of a technological resource – as they work based on relatively complex technologies.

According to the phase concept of service interactions, as well as the in-process technologies there are *pre-process and post-process technologies*. The main service process is conducted by other resources which are used to prepare the actual service process or to handle necessary activities after the actual service process. Examples are a service firm's website with information about the service offering or the possibility of making a reservation for the service (pre-process) or the service hotline for customer complaints (post-process).

There are also technologies which are not connected with the customer–firm interface but concern internal processes. These *internal technologies* fulfil several tasks within services marketing, such as storing information (e.g. customer databases), analysing information (e.g. statistical software packages), internal communications (e.g. intranet, email, video conferencing systems), security (e.g. alarm equipment) or networking with other providers (e.g. reservation systems of airlines).

Customer contact technologies are those technologies which induce the most radical *changes of service interactions* and therefore are of crucial relevance for services marketing. The changes regarding service interactions become obvious when examining the degree of activity between provider, employee and customer respectively. A classic service interaction is between a service employee and a consumer. Both interaction partners perform certain activities in order to make the service happen. In a restaurant, the customer chooses dishes from a menu, the waiter takes the order and transfers it to the kitchen, etc. In the classic service interaction, there are *transfers of activities* in both directions. A transfer from employee to customer is, for example, when the customer orders directly at a one-man diner. Contrarily, the customer transfers activities to the employee when ordering a home delivery meal. Then, the customer's coming to the restaurant is absorbed by the employee.

The introduction of service technologies results in a network of activity transfers. Within the triangle technology–employee–customer various transfers of service activities are possible. *Service technologies* in particular inherit activities from both employees and customers. In the restaurant example, handhelds are used by employees in order to transfer the customer's orders to the kitchen. Payment technologies such as credit card transmitters facilitate the payment process for the customer by not forcing them to carry enough cash to pay the bill.

Issues of service technology implementation

Although technologies themselves are easier to manage and control by the service firm than, for example, employee behaviour, there still arise implementation problems when applying service technologies.[28] This is because technologies are not applied in isolation but are connected with other aspects inside or outside the service firm. More specifically, there are five areas where *implementation issues* regarding service technologies arise frequently (see Figure 9.10 and Services marketing in action 9.8 'Questions for the implementation of service technologies'):

- service category;
- market;
- customer;
- environment;
- firm.

Service-category-related implementation issues are caused by a varying applicability of technologies in different service categories. These differences are due to technology usage that is appropriate for different service processes. The most important criterion for evaluating the appropriateness of a process for technology usage is the degree of standardisation of a service. When a service is standardised, designed to proceed in the same or similar manner for all customers (e.g. drawing money, watching a film at the cinema, booking a flight), it is more feasible to apply technology. However, when a service is individualised (e.g. consulting service, medical examination), technology can only be used as a supportive function.

Furthermore, *market-related implementation issues* concern aspects which are associated with the market situation the service provider is in. Here, service providers evaluate the manner in which technologies are used by the relevant competitors. The analysis of competitors' using or not using a technology either argues for the firm's own technology usage (e.g. aiming at a competitive advantage when the competitors do not use a certain technology) or against it (e.g. bad experiences of competitors regarding the technology usage). Furthermore, it is to question whether the application of a technology might build an entry barrier

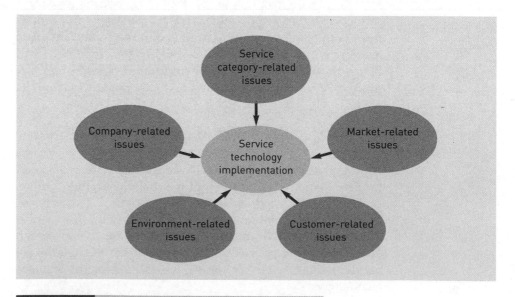

FIGURE 9.10   Issues of service technology implementation

SERVICES MARKETING IN ACTION 9.8:

Questions for the implementation of service technologies

When service providers aim at implementing new service technologies, they ask several questions in the areas where implementation problems might occur. The answers to these questions help prepare a systematic implementation process.

Questions regarding service type

- Does the service offered involve a good proportion of standardised processes?
- Are the service processes quite stable or changing in character over time regularly?

Questions regarding the market situation

- Do the customers perhaps want the technology?
- Are there customer segments which can be attracted by applying technology-based services?
- Is technology a possible switching barrier?

Questions regarding the service company

- Is the organisation ready for the new technology?
- Do employees demonstrate the abilities which are necessary to use the technology?
- Are employees willing to use the technology?
- How can high-tech and high-touch be combined?
- How can time be gained by technology usage?
- How can USPs be generated in other areas by technology usage?

Questions regarding customers

- Are your customers ready to use the technology?
- Do they have to be taught how to use the technology?
- Is there the option to teach them how to use the technology?
- Does the technology keep new customers away?

(e.g. in the case of non-compatibility with customer's hardware). Finally, it is important to analyse whether the respective technology is appropriate for attracting new market segments. This criterion strongly influences profitability analyses of a certain technology.

Service providers consider not only general market aspects but also *customer-related implementation issues* which concern the acceptance of a technology by the customer. The growth of online banking has slowed recently. In the USA, only 4 per cent of internet users who do not yet use online banking are planning to use it in the future. Half of those who do not use online banking have heard about phishing – i.e. false emails directing respondents to false online banking sites in order to retrieve respondents' online banking information – and since then 41 per cent feel even more insecure about online banking (Barber 2004).

Moreover, *environment-related implementation issues* are connected with requirements of other external stakeholders besides the consumers. One important stakeholder here is legislation. There are many legal issues regarding the usage of different technologies (e.g. data protection rules).

As well as the diverse, externally oriented implementation issues there are also internal, *firm-related implementation issues*. Problems with technology implementation arise when service firms introduce isolated technologies in different areas of the firm. Often, at some point in time, the need for integrating different technologies becomes obvious, but is difficult to realise depending on the compatibility of the different technologies. Moreover, technology implementation is threatened when the firm's employees do not accept the technology or are not able and/or willing to use it. Finally, projects of technology implementation often fail owing to insufficient profitability analyses. Due to the long-term character of, and the huge investment amounts involved in, many technology investments, it is often difficult to evaluate a technology's profitability effects properly. The mobile providers' investments in the UMTS technology, whose long-term profitability is unclear today, illustrate how risky technology investments are.

Summary

Regarding service resources the following lessons are summarised (see Figure 9.11):

1. Service providers utilise three groups of service resources which are connected to each other: service employees, tangibles and technology.

2. Service employees affect the value of a service firm by influencing costs directly and revenues indirectly via customer behaviour which is determined by employee behaviour.

3. The behaviour of employees consists of three internal dimensions (productivity, internal customer orientation, organisational citizenship behaviour) and two external dimensions (customer orientation, firm orientation).

4. Service providers manage employee behaviour by defining employee roles, evaluating and giving feedback to employees, recruiting and qualifying employees as well as motivating employees.

5. Service tangibles affect value above all by being a quality indicator in the eyes of the consumers.

6. Service tangibles exist in the categories servicescape (design, employees, ambiance), service environment and service materials.

7. The tangibles of a service provider are evaluated by consumers according to various quality dimensions, like cleanliness or functionality.

8. Service technologies are an integral part of the Service Value Chain and affect all other elements of the chain. Regarding concrete value effects, technology has diverse impacts on the revenue side of value, although its cost effects are the most obvious.

9. There are internal process and external customer contact technologies. The latter ones induce changes in the degree of activities of service employees and customers and are further divided into interaction (in-process as well as pre- and post-process technologies) and support technologies.

10. When implementing service technologies, it is crucial to consider various factors regarding the service category, the market, the customer, the environment and the firm itself.

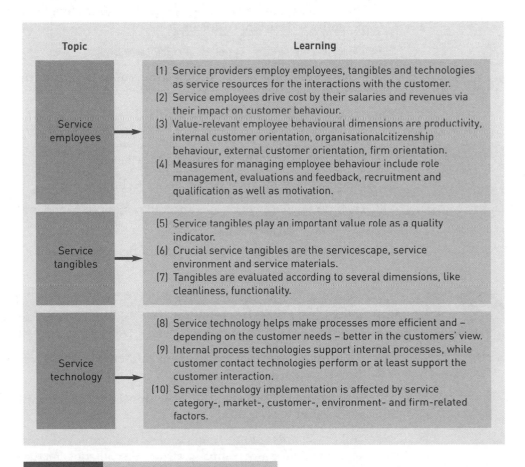

Topic	Learning
Service employees	(1) Service providers employ employees, tangibles and technologies as service resources for the interactions with the customer. (2) Service employees drive cost by their salaries and revenues via their impact on customer behaviour. (3) Value-relevant employee behavioural dimensions are productivity, internal customer orientation, organisationalcitizenship behaviour, external customer orientation, firm orientation. (4) Measures for managing employee behaviour include role management, evaluations and feedback, recruitment and qualification as well as motivation.
Service tangibles	(5) Service tangibles play an important value role as a quality indicator. (6) Crucial service tangibles are the servicescape, service environment and service materials. (7) Tangibles are evaluated according to several dimensions, like cleanliness, functionality.
Service technology	(8) Service technology helps make processes more efficient and – depending on the customer needs – better in the customers' view. (9) Internal process technologies support internal processes, while customer contact technologies perform or at least support the customer interaction. (10) Service technology implementation is affected by service category-, market-, customer-, environment- and firm-related factors.

FIGURE 9.11   Learning summary for Chapter 9

Knowledge questions

1. Explain the value effects of service employees' behaviour.

2. What are the dimensions of employee behaviour?

3. Why is it important to define roles for employees and how can they be used for managing employee behaviour?

4. How do evaluation and feedback influence employee behaviour?

5. What competences should service providers consider when recruiting and training employees?

6. Explain the different possibilities a service provider has to motivate its employees.

7. What is meant by service tangibles representing a quality indicator for potential and current customers?

8. Describe the several types of service tangibles.

9. What are the typical quality dimensions used by customers to evaluate service tangibles?

10. How interactive are service technologies with the other elements of the Service Value Chain?

11. Explain the value effects of using service technologies.

12. Describe the different types of service technologies.

13. How do service technologies affect the employees' and customers' activities in the service process?

14. Explain the different factors which affect service technology implementation.

Application and discussion questions

1. Show for a chosen service (e.g. bank, airline, restaurant, cinema) how the three service resources interact with each other.

2. Simulate typical behaviours of a waitress in a café and explain how they affect value.

3. Collect examples of role conflicts of service employees in several industries (e.g. bank, insurance company, airline, discotheque, medical services, public administration, police, university).

4. Think of one of your own work experiences (e.g. during a student job or an internship). What factors drive or have driven your motivation positively or negatively? And what are or have been the consequences in your own behaviour?

5. Discuss the differences regarding the manageability of the different types of employee competences.

6. Go through some service purchasing decisions you have taken in recent months and identify how service tangibles influenced both your original purchasing decision and then your evaluation of the service and consequent purchasing decisions in the respective service category.

7. Take a specific service provider (e.g. bank branch, airport, railway station, bakery, restaurant, supermarket) and describe the tangibles of this service provider. Discuss which ones are more and which are less important and why.

8. Take the list of tangibles you have generated in question 7 and discuss which is the most important quality dimension for each of them. What can the provider do in order to improve the respective quality dimension?

9. What service technology do you use frequently? Discuss the value effects of this technology from the provider's perspective.

10. How has your own and the service employees' behaviour changed in using the service technology described in the preceding question?

11. Surf the website of British Airways and identify as many different functions of the website as possible.

12. Are there service technologies you do not use? If so, why?

CASE STUDY: SERVICE ORIENTATION THROUGH EMPLOYEE COMMITMENT AT NOVOTEL LONDON

Any significant change, whether to the structure, strategy or goals of a business must be supported by its people, if it is to succeed. This message was embraced by the Novotel London West when, in 2001, significant investment was made to help the hotel make the transition from a 'high-volume tourism' hotel to a convention hotel. They increased the number of meeting rooms tenfold giving them the capacity to hold meetings for up to 3,000 people. The previous model was based on getting people in and out quickly. In the convention and business market, they needed to serve a different type of customer: people more likely to stay for longer than one night, have business needs, who are well travelled and know what they want. Having made the investment in the hardware, they needed to concentrate on the software – the service employees.

The hotel started by getting feedback from staff, guests and clients. The management decided to review everything from uniforms to recruitment to help them reach their vision: to be the best hotel in London and the best Novotel in the world. 'Service Extraordinaire' is the programme that was enabled to realise this service orientation. It's concerned with customer service at all levels. At its foundation are four simple standards that all employees should live by every day in the hotel:

1. Look professional – be professional. If people look good and have a high-quality uniform they feel good about themselves.

2. Greet every guest and colleague. It's a big hotel and people aren't used to acknowledging everyone, but we want it to feel like a village. If you smile at someone, they smile back and everyone feels better.

3. Look after your hotel. Take responsibility. Don't leave things for someone else. The staff area has been redecorated to the same standard as the guest rooms – the investment in employees is highly visible.

4. Be positive. A positive attitude and behaviour will create positivity around you.

Each employee agreed to adhere to these four standards, and their importance and meaning are communicated via meetings and training sessions where employees have the chance to be involved and ask questions. Awareness of the four standards has also been raised using newsletters and posters.

A key part of Novotel's strategy is to drive success at all levels of the business. They recognised early on that people respond better to their peers than to those in authority. Among the employees, 10 coaches have been selected based on their passion, attitude and behaviour. The coaches were trained to coach their colleagues and went through a formal observation and evaluation. The coaches support management and employees to ensure that events, activities and actions across the hotel are of the agreed standard. They can provide coaching for other employees, regardless of department or function. Every day coaches do a 'quality walk' round the hotel and note behaviours compared to the standards. Their report is sent by e-mail to everyone in the hotel – it's not, however, an exercise in 'pointing the finger'. It's about working together to overcome obstacles to excellent performance. For example, if a person appears to have shoes that aren't very well polished, they are helped by a shoe shiner being installed in the staff room.

All employees and regular agency staff attend a three-hour Service Extraordinaire training session which is lively, fun and activity-based. It has also become an important part of the hotel's induction process, so all new staff are able to deliver excellent customer service from their first day. The purpose of the session is to ensure all employees have the tools they need to deliver the four standards. The training session addresses ten service behaviours:

1. Give customer assurance – first time, every time.

2. Be well mannered and always be gracious.

3. Always repeat key information.

4. Be open minded, jump the obstacles.

5. Cushion the blow.

6. Give time, all the time, on time, every time, at the right time!

7. Don't hold it, pass it to the right player.

8. Be thankful.

9. Keep the guest informed.

10. Apply the finishing touch!

The standards and behaviours are a cornerstone of employees' three-monthly appraisals. The hotel asks employees to gather examples to demonstrate that they are living the standards and behaving in accordance with the 10 elements listed above. Another key part to maintaining momentum around customer service excellence is that every manager must be on the floor. In a hotel business this is where you make money – managers in offices studying figures and trying to save money by cutting costs are still losing money outside.

As well as rewards based on the standards and behaviours, the management encourages internal recognition and a strong focus on training. They try to encourage teamwork and a sense of community by rewarding to a group more than individuals. In terms of external recognition the hotel has won five awards within 18 months including 'Customer Service Strategy of the Year' in the National Business Awards.

Customer complaints have reduced by 92 per cent since Service Extraordinaire was implemented – 99 per cent of customers report that they are delighted with the hotel's service. Employee retention, in an industry that is notorious for high staff attrition levels, has increased dramatically. Staff turnover levels have dropped from 78.1 per cent to 34.2 per cent. The results have also been impressive in terms of bottom-line impact. Sales growth for 2004 is 9.11 per cent and repeat bookings stand at 70 per cent. Before Service Extraordinaire, people were almost coming to the hotel by default when other alternatives were full. Clearly, the investment is paying off. They have also received letters of thanks from CEOs of major companies who have held events at the hotel, demonstrating that the shift to the convention market has been a success. At one of the events in the hotel recently a company president told her 500 employees that the service they experienced in the hotel during their conference was the level of service they were aiming for.

Source: Angoujard 2005.

CASE STUDY: BRITISH AIRWAYS: IMPROVING VALUE THROUGH SELF-SERVICE KIOSKS

In today's highly competitive travel environment, increasing customer satisfaction is a key to future success. Customer loyalty has always been a top objective at British Airways. That's why it teamed up with IBM to implement self-service kiosk technology which is being rolled out internationally. Maintaining and increasing customer satisfaction was a key objective behind this effort. British Airways is also looking for a faster, more efficient way to provide better service to its customers while maintaining a competitive edge. Self-service kiosk technology and electronic ticketing are helping it to achieve these goals.

Electronic ticketing replaces the paper ticket with a virtual 'electronic' ticket. All the information that's traditionally printed on a paper ticket is stored electronically on a computer database. Once the passenger makes a reservation and pays for the ticket, there's no need for British Airways or a travel agent to issue a paper ticket.

Self-service kiosks enable passengers (with hand baggage only) to access their electronic record by using their Frequent Flyer card or credit card of payment, select their seat from an optional seat map, print a receipt and their boarding pass, all in one of six languages of choice. The process is very similar to using an Automated Teller Machine (ATM) at a bank. The kiosk confirms the customer's selection and then dispenses the boarding pass, all in a matter of seconds. 'We're delighted with customer reaction', says Adam Daniels, British Airways Self-service Project Manager. Customer benefits include choice of check-in (kiosk or counter), speedier, more convenient service from the kiosk, even seat selection and staff support at the kiosk.

The new technology is a definite winner with British Airways' customers. Over 70 per cent of the transactions at the kiosk are electronic tickets. It's a powerful combination – self-service technology coupled with electronic ticketing – that improves customer service, reduces costs and provides faster and more efficient passenger processing.

According to Kieron Gavan, British Airways Head of Distribution, 'Our research shows that passengers using electronic ticketing on our domestic flights have found it easy to use. It handles check-in more quickly, plus it's flexible and convenient.'

When the self-service kiosk technology was rolled out, a number of elements were key to the project's success:

- involvement of all airport staff at all times;
- a skilled and dedicated application development team from British Airways;
- careful attention to customer detail through all project phases;

- targeting self-service product to specific customer segments;
- concentration on all aspects of the Operational Support processes;
- a very reliable self-service product from IBM;
- implementation of the kiosk network so that it works with the same reliability and availability as an ATM network.

It has been and continues to be a team effort. Regular meetings are held between the British Airways development team and the IBM development laboratory. 'We've worked very closely with British Airways and the project has consistently beaten the targets set for it', says John Howes, IBM Travel and Transportation Self-service Solutions Manager. 'We quickly achieved acceptance of the new kiosks by installing and testing them first with British Airways staff.'

Once proven reliable, British Airways then moved on to the next project phase which involved passenger trials for ATB-2 check-in in London's Heathrow Terminal One. British Airways handles over 9 million passengers a year at London Heathrow Terminal One, so congestion is a problem. Trial testing in Terminal One was a great success, especially when passengers were given the opportunity to complete their own seat selection. The functional benefits of self-service kiosks were enhanced with the launch of Electronic Ticketing as a domestic product in March 1997. The product roll-out has proceeded at a rapid pace since then.

British Airways is firmly committed to self-service technology as a key component of its customer service within the airport. 'Self-service kiosks are not just a technology for us, they are now part of our mainstream business', says Peter Stanton, British Airways Senior Project Manager.

Source: IBM 1998.

Notes

[1] For the concept of the Service Profit Chain see Heskett *et al*. 1997.
[2] For example, Hartline and Ferrell (1996) found that the employee management tools empowerment, management commitment to service quality and behaviour-based evaluation affect the employees' job satisfaction.
[3] See Organ 1988, p. 35.
[4] See Stamper and van Dyne 2003.
[5] See Gist and Mitchell 1992.
[6] See Naylor *et al*. 1980.
[7] Rogers *et al*. 1994 found that role conflict negatively affects role clarity. Both impact job tension and consequently job satisfaction.
[8] See Dobni *et al*. 1997.

9 See Weatherly and Tansik 1993.
10 See Rogers *et al*. 1994; Hartline and Ferrell 1996.
11 See Dobni *et al*. 1997.
12 See Bowen and Lawler 1992.
13 See Hartline and Ferrell 1996.
14 See Meffert and Bruhn 2003.
15 See Parasuraman *et al*. 1988.
16 See Hoffman and Turley 2002.
17 See Parasuraman *et al*. 1988.
18 See Lentell 2000, p. 7; Hightower *et al*. 2002, p. 697ff.
19 See Bitner 1992, p. 60.
20 See Mangold and Babakus 1991.
21 See Bitner 1992.
22 See Kotler 1973; Hoffman and Turley 2002.
23 Some authors, e.g. Agnihothri *et al*. 2002, elaborate isolated aspects of value, like service productivity and customer satisfaction which are part of the effects on the revenue and cost side of value, as discussed here.
24 See Nickell 2001.
25 See Bitner *et al*. 2002.
26 See Lewis 2002.
27 See Bitner *et al*. 2002.
28 See Griffith *et al*. 1999; Edmondson 2003.

Service capacity management

Why is it that in the travel industry prices for the same flight, the same hotel room, the same rental car, differ so extremely at times? For example a request for a British Airways flight from London to New York made on 21 March resulted in prices of between £78 and £199 to fly between 28 March and 11 April. For the same service, the price varies by a multiplier of almost 3. Why do some restaurants or bars offer drinks for half price or less at 'happy hours'?

These practices can be interpreted from various perspectives. From a pricing perspective, price discrimination is utilised in order to skim different willingness to pay. Sometimes, they may only be a 'marketing gag' in order to attract new customer segments. But most often, the main or at least the underlying reason for such practices is the objective of service providers to balance service capacity and demand. This is the objective of what is called *service capacity management*.

For producing and delivering a specific service unit, say the hotel stay of a guest, certain service resources are necessary: the hotel room, receptionists, etc. The **service capacity** describes the amount of service resources (e.g. number of hotel rooms, number of receptionists) which are available for service production and delivery. Due to the direct contact between these service resources and the customer (or their objects), which are integrated into the service process, a service provider can only deliver as many service units as service capacities are available. In an aeroline with 300 seats, a maximum of 300 people can fly. In a hotel with 100 double rooms, a maximum of 200 people can stay.

However, in every service setting there are often situations where there is a *gap between demand and capacity*, meaning the gap between the number of potential users of the service and the amount of service resources available. Trains are sometimes overcrowded so that many commuters do not get a seat and at other times a few passengers are seated in empty carriages. Museum visitors often have lots of space in which to view the works of art, but sometimes (e.g. at weekends or right after the opening of a famous exhibition), people have to wait for hours in order to enter the museum and then are navigated through the museum by the crowd of visitors. At certain times it is difficult to book flights to certain destinations, at other times flights are cancelled due to insufficient passengers.

The examples describe situations where service demand and capacity do not match. Actually, for most services it is unlikely that demand and capacity will match exactly. The underlying reason for this is that the *characteristics of services* are derived from the customer integration into the service process. This main characteristic results in a so-called perishability of service capacity.[1] Empty seats on a flight at a certain time can never be filled at this same time. Furthermore, there is an uncertainty of demand patterns;[2] a service provider can never predict exactly how many prospects will demand a certain service at a certain point in time.

From the service provider's perspective, gaps between demand and capacity result in *value deficits*. When there is not enough demand for the given capacity, a service is not profitable. When there is not enough capacity to serve a given demand, potential revenues are wasted. Consequently, service providers aim at optimising – so as to minimise – the gap between demand and capacity. This is done by service capacity management, which strives to balance demand and capacity by managing both.[3]

To explore service capacity management in more depth is the topic of this chapter. More specifically, based on the precedent considerations, the chapter addresses the following *learning objectives* (see Figure 10.1):

1. Gaining insight into the value consequences of the service capacity problem and consequently of service capacity management.

2. Understanding the emergence of gaps between demand and capacity in service industries and thereby understanding the fields of activity of service capacity management.

3. Exploring the reasons for the gaps between demand and capacity.

4. Getting to know the various options of a service provider to manage demand and capacity by service capacity management.

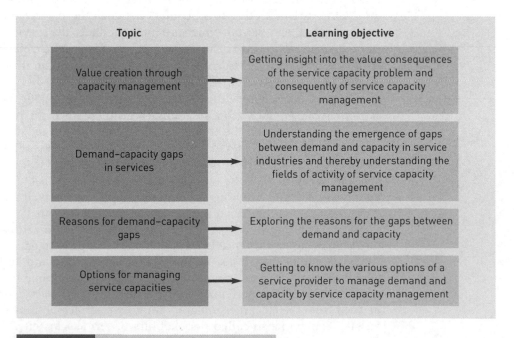

FIGURE 10.1 Learning objectives of Chapter 10

Value contribution of capacity management

Service capacity management has various significant effects on value (see Figure 10.2):

- When service capacities are not used, certain parts of fixed costs are not covered. A hotel potentially pays interest on loans financing the hotel facilities and rooms. When rooms are not used, a portion of these costs are not covered by the revenues generated by stays at the hotel.

- Vice versa, when a service provider's capacity is not enough to satisfy the existing demand, the firm 'realises' lost sales and revenues. When a hotel has enquiries for 200 stays, but can only offer beds to 150 guests, the potential revenues of the 50 inquiries are lost.

- Moreover, not being able to provide a room possibly results in dissatisfaction of these potential customers and this negative experience thus prevents them from approaching the hotel in future.

- Customers currently using a service might perceive a bad service quality when there are not enough service resources available. Typical examples are waiting times or waiting for the waitress to bring the bill, which directly affect perceived service quality and customer (dis)satisfaction.[4]

According to this comprehensive value relevance of service capacity management there are many *links to other elements of the Service Value Chain*. Regarding the *primary value processes*, the interaction process where the customer meets the service

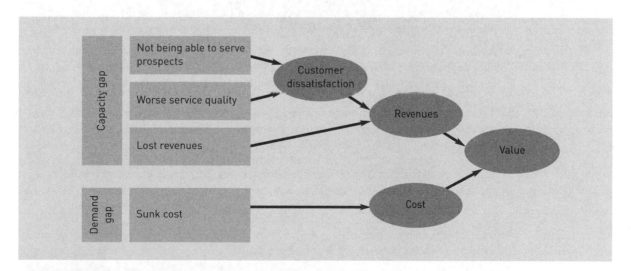

| FIGURE 10.2 | Value effects of service capacity management |

resources in order to produce and deliver a service is negatively affected when the service capacities are overcrowded or overused during periods of high demand. In consequence, a bad service quality is perceived by the customer. In an extreme situation, an interaction with a specific customer cannot take place at all. On the level of the customer relationship, this can lead to an impeded customer acquisition when a prospective customer planned to try a service for the first time and was not able to use it because of capacity constraints. Also, customer retention can be affected when a customer is annoyed because of not receiving a service due to capacity constraints.

While the service capacity and consequently capacity management affect the primary value processes of a service provider, conversely, the *secondary value processes* are utilised by service capacity management. Regarding the service product, service providers apply value-added services in order to facilitate reservations or waiting times. Service pricing and communications are used in order to manage service demands according to existing patterns of demand (see Services marketing in action 10.1). The utilisation of the secondary value processes for capacity management will be treated in more depth later in this chapter (see section on 'Options for managing service capacity').

SERVICES MARKETING IN ACTION 10.1:

Managing service capacity by service communications

Redding Electric Utility
Frequently Asked Questions (FAQs)
– Customer Service –

Question: What is the best time to contact a Customer Service Representative about my bill or services if I am in a hurry?

Answer: The most convenient times to call the Utility Customer Service Center are Tuesdays through Thursdays between 8:00 a.m. and 10:00 a.m., and from 1:30 p.m. to 3:30 p.m. Typically, Monday and Friday afternoons and the day following a holiday are our busiest days. Our voice mail system is available 24-hours a day, seven days a week for non-emergency calls. A Customer Service Representative will return your call by the end of the next business day. If you are planning to come into our Customer Service Center at 777 Cypress Avenue and wish to avoid a long wait in line, the best times are also Tuesdays through to Thursdays. If you leave a voice mail, please do so only once, we will return the call. It is very confusing if you have more than one call in the message queue.

You may contact us by facsimile 24 hours a day at (530) 339-7299; visit our website at ci.redding.ca.us; click on Utility Customer Service to set, close, or transfer your utility service or click on ASK PAT if you have a general question that you would like to ask and we will respond promptly.

Source: Redding Electric Utility 2005.

Finally, *service resources* compose a service provider's capacity. Depending on the service, this capacity is constrained by the number of employees or the tangible or technological resources of a provider. Consequently, managing the amount of these resources is the object of service capacity management (see section below 'Options for managing service capacity').

Gaps between service demand and capacity

Service capacity problems are determined by the existing service capacity on the one hand and the current service demand on the other hand. By contrasting these two variables, two generic *forms of capacity gaps* can be described which have different causes as well as different consequences for customer and provider. These forms are:

- demand gap;
- capacity gap.

When there are more capacities than are requested by consumers, the service capacity exceeds the demand and a **demand gap** results. The consequences are vacant service facilities (e.g. empty hotel rooms) or non-occupied service employees (e.g. train conductor waiting for more people to enter the train at the next stop). Vacant facilities result in fixed costs which are sunk without a respective revenue. Moreover, variable costs are generated because the service facility possibly still has to be maintained. An aeroplane has to be checked for technical problems regardless of whether the plane is fully booked or not. A hotel room which was not in use for several days probably is cleaned more than it is used. Unoccupied employees tend to feel underutilised, resulting in lower employee motivation, satisfaction and productivity.

Conversely, a **capacity gap** is the result of demand exceeding the service capacity available. In this case, there are more prospects for a specific service delivery at a certain time than can be served by the provider. A capacity gap has consequences on two levels. On the level of core service, a capacity gap leads to the inability of the respective customers to use the service. When a flight is booked on a certain day and at a certain time, then prospects who would like to use this flight cannot be served. Either this results in lost revenues because the prospect then books the flight with another airline or – given a certain time flexibility of the prospect – the customer reorganises their time schedule with dissatisfaction: as a consequence at the need for schedule reorganisation or at least the effort to do it. On the level of a partial process within the whole core service process, a capacity gap results in waiting times for the customer (e.g. waiting to order drinks in a crowded bar) and possibly also customer dissatisfaction. Table 10.1 lists examples of typical demand gaps as well as the consequences of capacity gaps for several service industries.

TABLE 10.1	Examples of demand gaps and consequences of capacity gaps

Industry	Typical demand gaps	Typical consequences of capacity gaps
Hospital	• Empty beds • Unoccupied nurses	• Waiting times • Long-term appointments • Less thorough examinations • Over-worked doctors and nurses
Hotel	• Empty hotel rooms • Empty restaurant • Unused business areas • Unoccupied receptionists, clerks	• Refused guests • Need for early reservations
Ski lift	• Unoccupied seats • Unoccupied 'lift boy'	• Long queues
Restaurant	• Unused kitchen • Unused materials (e.g. food) • Unoccupied waiters	• Need for reservations • Refused guests • Long waiting times • Stressed employees
Car park	• Unused parking spaces	• Refused customers
Airline	• Empty seats • Under-worked stewards	• Refused customers • Stress situations for employees and passengers
Football stadium	• Empty seats (resulting moreover in poor atmosphere)	• Refused customers
Language course	• Under-booked course	• Refused customers
Car rental company	• Unused cars	• Refused customers
Post-office	• Under-worked employees	• Waiting times • Stress situations for employees and customers

The tricky thing for service providers with these gaps is that they are dynamic. For any service, there might not always be a capacity gap or a demand gap. Unfortunately, the dynamics are often unpredictable. Consequently, the *optimal service level* is a central objective of service managers. The service level describes the percentage of capacity utilised compared to the capacity available. Because of the profit relevance of the service level – both from a cost and a revenue perspective – service firms aim at realising a high utilisation of service resources. For example, for the call centre channel it was found that an aggregation of demand (e.g. concentrating demand in a few, large call centres) and the absolute staff number, positively affect service levels.[5]

More specifically, service providers aim at managing the dynamics of the gaps between service demand and capacity. The starting point for doing this is the knowledge of the factors which influence these gaps.

Determinants of service capacity management

There are several reasons behind the general capacity problem in services, as has been discussed earlier in this chapter. Based on the general reasons for the capacity problem, like the perishability of capacities and the heterogeneity of service demand, the determinants of service capacity management, the factors which influence the opportunities and decisions of capacity management, can be identified. There are demand-related and capacity-related determinants (see Figure 10.3).[6]

Regarding the *demand-related determinants*, it is principally the *demand level* that influences capacity management decisions. Knowing the demand level or at least having some knowledge of the demand level is a basic requirement in order to be able to determine service capacities. As service demand is uncertain in services, providers define the optimal service capacity satisfying the service demand to be lower than the maximum capacity. This is because, if a service location is too busy, service quality is perceived as being poor, but if it is too slow, often the atmosphere suffers.[7]

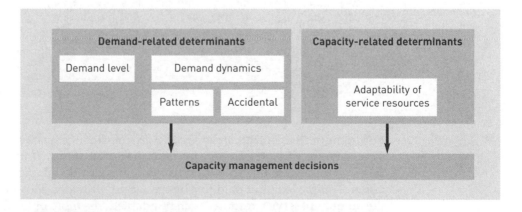

FIGURE 10.3 Determinants of service capacity management decisions

For the most part, service demand is not constant over time. In contrast there can be strong *demand dynamics* due to seasonal, daytime-related or weekday-related differences between demand levels. There are various reasons for these variations in time, such as habits and culture (e.g. lunch at noon as a determinant for restaurants) or external influencing factors: patients contracting more colds in winter, as a determinant for doctors. When there are specific reasons for the demand dynamics, so-called *demand patterns* are identifiable and are utilised by capacity management (see Services marketing in action 10.2 for a forecast of a change in shopping habits). However, there still remains a relatively distinct degree of *accidental demand dynamics*.

SERVICES MARKETING IN ACTION 10.2:

Shopping habits affected by football event
Birmingham, 2004 June 10

FootFall, the world leader in the provision of retail business information, predicts that Euro 2004 will impact retailers in the coming weeks as people change their normal shopping habits and make the most of the opportunity to support England. John Gallagher, MD of FootFall, comments: 'The build up to Euro 2004 has been much more evident this time around than in 2000 and England-fever will no doubt grow if we do well in the tournament. This is likely to impact retailers – especially regional and out-of-town shopping centres – as people stay closer to home to give them time to make preparations to watch the matches with family and friends, but we predict that it's likely to be a moderate change rather than a significant swing.

'During the Rugby World Cup final we saw a 9.6% drop in the number of shoppers out and about – a clear indication of the impact a sporting event can have on our normal habits.

'On a positive note I'm sure that the sales of beer, BBQ food, widescreen TVs, branded England goods and clothing, and, of course, flags will be on the up – especially if England does well and the heat wave continues. Who knows, if we get to the final it could have a significant effect – a real "feel good" factor could affect optimism and spending in the high street, but we'll have to wait and see on that one!'

Source: PR Newswire 2004.

Furthermore, the central *capacity-related determinant* of capacity management decisions is the *adaptability of service resources* in respect of how fast and to what extent service employees, tangibles and technologies can be adapted in terms of their amount employed (and paid for) by the service provider. The more and the faster the amount of service resources can be adapted, the more options service capacity management has.

Options for managing service capacity

As the capacity problem in service production and delivery is determined by the two factors demand and capacity, these represent the levers for managing service capacities systematically by managing demand and/or capacity.[8] Managing demand means applying measures in order to influence the customers' perceptions and behaviours, while managing capacity concerns changes in the amount of service resources available.

A further fundamental differentiation of capacity management activities is the *point in time* when the measure is applied compared to the time of the service usage. Following the concept of the interaction process, capacity management activities can be applied in two of the three phases: before the service interaction starts (*pre-process*; e.g. reservation system) and during or at the beginning of the service interaction (*in-process*; e.g. providing a waiting room). Crossing the time dimension with the object of the measures (i.e. demand versus capacity) results in four *types of service capacity management activities* (see Figure 10.4):

- determining the capacity level;
- short-term capacity adjustments;
- demand adjustments;
- waiting time management.

An *integrated instrument for capacity management* which concerns several of these categories is *yield management*.

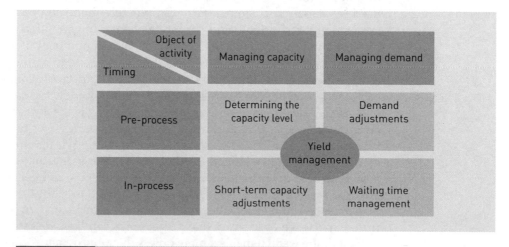

FIGURE 10.4 Options for managing service capacity

Determining the capacity level

A service provider's long-term capacity management defines the quantity and the quality of service capacities to be employed by the service firm. This decision concerns the number of employees employed, the dimension of the service facilities, etc. and concerns especially capacities which can only slowly be modified, extended or downsized, such as hotel building, or the general level of the workforce. Examples for typical long-term capacities in different service industries are shown in Table 10.2. The determination of the long-term capacity is affected by the following influence factors:

- expected demand level;
- expected demand dynamics.

The *expected demand level* plays a role in determining the long-term capacity because the capacities are established in order to satisfy the demand. The relevant demand level is composed of the number of customers as well as the expected service usage of these customers (e.g. number of flights per year, number of nights in a hotel, level of utility usage). Services marketing in action 10.3 about the food-service industry exemplifies an analysis of the demand level for a whole market. Furthermore, the *expected number of customers* is affected by the customer segments targeted by the service provider and their own expected market share. Consequently, the market structure affects the ability to assess the expected number of customers. In a monopoly (e.g. state utility provider), the demand level is much easier to determine than in a highly competitive market with a lot of customer churn (e.g. mobile communications, airlines). Furthermore, the expected service usage is a component of the expected demand level. Independent of the number of customers, the expected demand varies with the amount of services used by a specific customer. For example, telephone companies target two customer segments, private and corporate clients. In general, a telephone provider serves more private clients than corporate ones in number but the single corporate customer generates more revenues than the single private customer. Overall, often, it is easier and more valid to forecast the expected demand by many small customers compared to forecasting the demand by a few big customers.

A further determinant of the long-term capacity is the *expected demand dynamics*. For most services, demand is heterogeneous and varies over time according to certain patterns. Ski lifts are used frequently in the winter time, flower demand increases on days like Valentine's day and Mother's day, many entertainment and leisure services are used more frequently at weekends, and generally, most services are used more frequently in the daytime compared to night-time. Because there are many reasons influencing demand dynamics which are known by service providers from experience or logic, demand dynamics can be forecast to a certain extent. Although there still remains a more or less dynamic demand which can not be foreseen, service providers have some indicators of the probable demand patterns.

Industry	Long-term determined capacities
Hospital	• Facilities • Number of operating rooms • Number of rooms • Number of beds • Number of doctors • Number of nurses
Hotel	• Facilities • Number of rooms • Number of restaurants • Size of reception and lobby • Number of receptionists and other employees
Ski lift	• Lift facility • Number of seats
Restaurant	• Dining room size • Size and design of kitchen • Restrooms
Car park	• Size • Number of parking spaces
Airline	• Number of aeroplanes • Number of seats • Number of pilots and stewards overall
Football stadium	• Size of stadium • Number of seats
Language course	• Teacher
Car rental company	• Number of cars • Number of customer contact employees
Post office	• Size and design of post office • Number of employees

TABLE 10.2 Typical long-term capacities in different service industries

Next to these external, demand-related influence factors, there are also *internal determinants* which arise from financial criteria. First, the *financial resources* of a service firm determine the capacity which is built and maintained in the long term. To build a hotel with 200 rooms is more expensive than building a hotel

SERVICES MARKETING IN ACTION 10.3

Demand level analysis for the foodservice industry

Low consumer confidence and consumer dissatisfaction with perceived and real price increases following the introduction of the euro in 2002 resulted in two extremely negative years for consumer foodservice in 2002 and 2003. Consumer demand patterns continued to shift away from large main meals towards snacks and smaller dishes. Further, greater health consciousness also led to greater demand for healthy food. Salads and wraps were the main winners from this trend, whilst white meat products also enjoyed an increase in popularity at the expense of red meat.

The number of units sold declined by 5.5% over the review period due to the closure of loss-making independent outlets. Consumer foodservice units stood at some 175,000 in 2003. There were just over 2.5 billion consumer foodservice transactions in 2003, a decline of 2.2% on 1999. This was brought about by a decline in transactions in 2002, which continued in 2003. In current consumer price terms, sales were worth some 26 billion euros in 2003, equivalent to a fall in current value terms of 9.4% on 1999. Lower consumer confidence and the switch to lower-priced products were the two main reasons behind this trend.

Regarding sub-industry importance, the single most important area in unit terms in 2003 was full service restaurant (FSR), which took a share of more than 40% of units in 2003. This consists of both stand-alone and hotel restaurants. In transaction terms, the single most important in 2003 was fast food, with a 50% share. This share was up from 47% in 1999 driven by greater demand for fast food offerings. FSR took the single highest share in consumer value terms, with 50% in 2003. This was down from 54% in 1999 as a result of less consumer demand for main meals, which is the core competency of FSR outlets. Home delivery/takeaway was the fastest growing in unit, transactions and value terms due to fast growth in the first half of the review period. However, this was also affected by the slump in spending in 2002 and 2003 and suffered a decline in sales in those years.

The most significant international new entries over the review period were Subway and Starbucks. Subway entered in 1999 but expansion really took off only in 2002. Starbucks entered in 2002 in a joint venture with department store chain Karstadt.

Regarding an outlook, Euromonitor predicts that over the forecast period, consumer foodservice will decline by 7% in unit terms, increase by 1% in transaction terms and decrease by 3% in constant consumer value terms. Unit growth will be held back by the displacement of small outlets by chains, whilst the decline in transaction growth and value sales will be underpinned by changes in lifestyles and eating habits, favouring fast food outlets with lower prices than FSR outlets.

Source: Euromonitor 2004.

with 100 rooms, and being certain of being able to pay employees is not only difficult for small firms, but also for huge corporations. From time to time, this is made obvious by dramatic bankruptcies of big corporations, furthermore, the cost of capacities affects the decisions about the capacity to be made available. In the case of cost-effective resources such as hotel buildings, aeroplanes and specialist employees, it is especially important that these resources are working to full capacity as often as possible.

These criteria are considered when determining the long-term capacity level but also capacity patterns over time. In order to do so, service providers aim to balance demand and capacity. Four *strategies* for the long-term capacity determination can be distinguished (see Figure 10.5):[9]

- In general, service providers wish to *match the demand exactly* with their capacities. However, in most service situations this is not possible due to the demand dynamics and the inflexibility of service resources.

- The provider can make the *maximum capacity* available by providing as many service resources as are necessary to satisfy the maximum possible demand. This strategy is uneconomic in most situations because it results in unused capacities at many times.

- In contrast, the provider might provide a *minimum capacity* which is sufficient to satisfy the minimum possible demand. Then, there will be many times at which customers cannot be served, at least not directly. This leads to negative value effects by prospects not using the service in order not to wait or by customer dissatisfaction resulting in customer migration and negative word-of-mouth in the long run.

- In most real service situations, service providers aim to provide an *average capacity* by considering demand dynamics and resource flexibility. Then, the provider accepts that at some times, some customers cannot be served directly

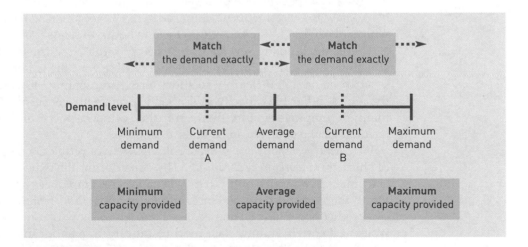

FIGURE 10.5   Strategies for long-term capacity determination

(but more than with a minimum capacity strategy), and at other times there are unused resources (but less than with a maximum capacity strategy). By balancing demand and resources, these service providers aim to provide an optimal capacity in terms of value.

For *changing the service capacity*, service providers use several measures which concern the service resources, especially human and tangible (including technological) resources:

- The *amount of human resources* is changed by hiring new employees or by releasing employees. Further measures are the systematic use of overtime or a shift system.[10]

- The *amount of tangible resources* is changed by adding new tangibles (e.g. a hotel building more rooms) or decreasing the number of tangibles (e.g. closing a track of hotel rooms and utilising it for other tangibles, e.g. a swimming pool, or leasing part of the building). Furthermore, tangibles can be divided (e.g. splitting hotel rooms).

By these measures, the service provider plans and determines the long-term service capacities which build the framework for further capacity management activities.

Short-term capacity adjustments

Even if a service provider estimates the probable demand and demand dynamics, it is unrealistic in most service industries to expect that the exact demand and demand dynamics can be foreseen. A bank cannot forecast exactly how many clients will visit a branch at a specific time on a specific day for every single day. And even if the bank knew the customer behaviour exactly, it cannot hire new employees for hours with a lot of client traffic and release them in hours with less traffic.

Therefore, in many service industries, providers realise short-term capacity adjustments. By installing capacities in a flexible way, the generally given capacities can be adjusted flexibly to short-term, predictable or accidental demand dynamics. A flexible capacity utilisation is principally concerned with the assignment of employees, but there are also other aspects of how tangible or technological resources can be utilised flexibly.

For *predictable short-term demand patterns*, service providers employ approaches of short-term *workforce scheduling*.[11] By considering the expected appearance of customers in a service outfit, the tasks of service employees are planned according to the demand pattern. For example, in a fast food restaurant, the manager can predict how many customers are expected to show up on a certain day of the week at a certain hour. A fast food restaurant in a shopping area is more frequented during shopping hours than when shops are closed and the area is less busy. About noon, more customers visit a restaurant than in mid-morning, etc.

Based on this information, the restaurant manager plans how many employees are to be present in the restaurant at a certain point of time. This flexible short-term workforce scheduling requires *flexible working hours* instead of a working time from 9 to 5.

It is obvious that there are still deviations from the expected customer frequency which leave space for adjustments of the planned workforce schedule. Here, a service provider has several options for *short-term capacity adjustments* (see Figure 10.6):

- *Short-term changes of working schedule* means that real-time adjustments are made to the working schedule. For example, employees quit work earlier than planned in order to work the hours on another day when there is more customer traffic.

- *Employing a flexible workforce* is realised by using not only salaried employees but also freelancers who are only employed and paid when there is work to do. Freelancers are often used for services with project character (e.g. consultancy).

- *Utilising capacities for other activities* is applied by appointing employees to other tasks than the original planned ones. At times when a bank branch is not frequented, bank employees in customer contact have back-office work to do. Also employees' time can be utilised for relationship marketing activities.[12] For example, the bank employee serves a client more intensely and effectively when there is a low customer frequency. In call centres, call centre agents assume direct marketing activities (e.g. conducting sales calls) when they are under-worked with customer requests. In order to let employees conduct non-customer contact tasks when there is time available requires first that employees are qualified (e.g. trained) for other activities and second defining a reasonable set of such activities in order to allow employees to recognise their task at times of low customer frequency.

- *Reservation systems.* In some service industries where service capacities are restricted, service providers apply reservation systems (e.g. hotels, rental car firms, restaurants, theatres, cinemas, airlines, railway companies). Customers

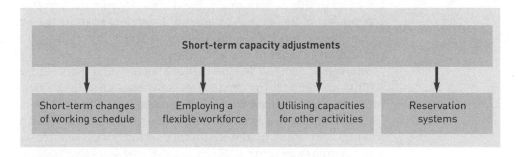

Short-term capacity adjustments

| Short-term changes of working schedule | Employing a flexible workforce | Utilising capacities for other activities | Reservation systems |

FIGURE 10.6   Options for short-term capacity adjustments

are given the opportunity to book a certain unit of a service (e.g. one flight). The booking information is then stored, and with each booking, less capacity is left to be offered. Note that reservation systems do not change the given (maximum) capacity but change the capacity which is offered to the customer. Then, customers asking for a service unit can be informed beforehand whether there are service capacities available. Both provider and customers gain security: the provider gains the security of the capacities which are sold and the customer's security is the guaranteed accommodation. In most of these cases, customers do not necessarily have to make a reservation, but can 'walk-into' the service location. However, the service capacities for these walk-in customers are restricted to the maximum capacity minus the already booked capacity.

As mentioned, the tangible and technological resources are difficult to adjust to short-term demand behaviour. However, a flexible usage of such capacities can be considered by an appropriate development of facilities and/or appliances. Then, comparable to human resources, a *multi-usage of tangible and technological resources* can be applied. Some banks have separate statement printers and ATMs installed. By installing two appliances which integrate the two functions, variations in demand can be compensated. Imagine the situation with two separate machines and two customers who would like to print their statements. Then one of the two has to wait until the statement printer is available after the other customer has completed their transaction. In the case of integrated machines, both customers can be served at the same time.

Demand adjustments

Even when a service provider plans expected demand thoroughly and prepares for short-term capacity adjustments, in many cases gaps will remain between demand and capacity in both directions. This is relevant when service resources are fixed in relatively unflexible units. An airline cannot purchase aeroplanes for every possible passenger number but chooses from standard types of aircraft. Further, the capacity of an aeroplane cannot be reduced in the short term. The only possibility for reducing the demand–capacity gap then is via the second component of this gap, i.e. demand. Providers in industries with a high number of unflexible service resources (e.g. airlines, hotels) use the option of *demand adjustments* in order to minimise the gaps.

Managing demand is a pivotal goal of services marketing activities in general. Adjusting demand for capacity reasons uses specific services marketing instruments out of the *secondary value processes* in the Service Value Chain which are utilised in order to adjust demand to the given capacity. Instruments from the following four areas of the secondary value processes are applied for demand adjustments (see Figure 10.7):

- service product decisions;

- service price decisions;

- service delivery decisions;

- service communications.

The definition of the *service product,* the core and the supplementary services, pre-determine the service resources needed. Consequently, changing the service product can influence the demand for the services. A first option is *service bundles* which – combined with service pricing – offer at least two service units of a provider linked with a price reduction. The bundle can be a combination of different services or a certain number of service units. A *combination of different services* is realised by offering package holidays or set menus in restaurants. By these packages, the attractiveness for services with a higher demand is utilised in order to sell services and capacities for which demand is lower. For a package holiday, both airline and hotel aim at utilising the demand for the other provider in order to increase their own demand. *Service bundling regarding the number of service units* is connected with the pricing tool of quantity discount in order to fill capacities. An example are group discounts in the entertainment industry. While service bundles partly concern differences in demand between different services, there can also occur (systematic) demand differences between segments with different service needs. For example, guests of a bar during the day have different service needs (e.g. having lunch) compared to guests at night (e.g. having drinks

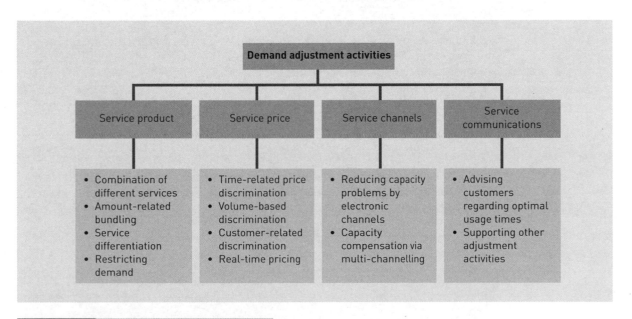

FIGURE 10.7   Options for demand adjustments

and partying). This pattern can be utilised by *segment-specific service differentiations*. In the bar example, the bar has to be designed with enough flexibility in order to adapt the service situation for day and night users. A further example is cinemas which present children's films during the daytime, thus, segment-specific demand is directed towards times with available capacities. Moreover, a special form of a service product measure in case of a capacity gap is *restricting demand* for a certain number of service units per individual customer. For example, the rules of the Football World Championship 2006 ticketing process restrict demand in the first ticketing round to seven matches per person (see Services marketing in action 10.4). By this measure, the organisers aim at satisfying more customers than if everybody could purchase as many tickets as they wanted, on a first come–first served basis.

SERVICES MARKETING IN ACTION 10.4:

Ticketing procedure for Football World Championship 2006

Various aspects of capacity management can be observed at the ticketing procedure for the Football World Championship 2006 which is outlined on FIFAworldcup.com, the official website of the event.

First, ticket prices vary according to the predicted demand for matches. 'Single tickets are on offer in four price categories. The cheapest tickets for group stage matches cost 35 euros. The most expensive seats at the group stage cost 100 euros. The cheapest ticket for the Final costs 120 euros and the most expensive 600 euros.'

For the Organising Committee, capacity management plays an important role, as Franz Beckenbauer, President of the Organising Committee states: 'Obviously, we are principally counting on revenues from ticket sales. We are assuming that we will sell all of the 3.2 or 3.3 million tickets, because that is our main source of revenue, alongside the national suppliers, who are also supporting us financially.'

Capacity management logic is even used for communication with the ticket applicants. 'To ensure a fair and open process even if demand exceeds supply, and to guarantee as many interested parties as possible receive tickets, ticket sales will take place in five periods. Applications cannot be accepted in between sales periods.'

In order to ensure security for the organisers as well as for the supporters, ticketing started about 16 months before the tournament itself. 'The first sales period begins on 1 February 2005 and ends on 31 March 2005. At the end of this application phase, should the number of applications exceed the number of available tickets for this phase, the tickets will be allocated via ballot on 15 April 2005.'

Further, demand is restricted on a per-customer basis. 'Individual tickets are on offer in four price categories. Per household, you may apply for a maximum of four individual tickets for up to seven matches in categories 1–3. In category 4, the cheapest category, the maximum is two individual tickets for up to three matches per household.

Sources: FIFA 2002; FIFA 2005.

In many service markets, price is a crucial decision criterion. Consequently *pricing decisions* play an important role in demand adjustments. Several variations of price discrimination are utilised intensely in order to adapt demand to the given capacities. Since demand dynamics over time are an important influencing factor in a service provider's capacity problems, *time-related price discrimination* is a first option for adjusting demand by pricing. Then, according to typical demand patterns, prices are reduced for times at which demand is generally lower. The rule for the price differentiation is caused by the nature of the demand pattern. Ski lift prices are differentiated by season (summer versus winter) and fitness centres offer daytime subscriptions at significantly lower rates than all-day subscriptions. A second option is *volume-based price discrimination* which is closely related to service bundling (see above). Third, service providers apply a *customer-related price discrimination*. For example, students pay lower prices in museums in order to attract them to the museum. More straightforward is the approach of a squash centre which leases squash courts at student prices – however only until 5 pm when demand for the squash courts starts to increase. While the first three options of using price differentiation for capacity management define a fixed price system based on experiences regarding demand patterns, the fourth approach is directly pegged to actual demand. This approach is called *real-time pricing or dynamic pricing* and the price is continuously determined based on current demand. This approach is also labelled 'yield management' which is a holistic capacity management concept and is discussed later in this chapter. Several aspects of price-related capacity management are presented in Services marketing in action 10.5.

Moreover, *service delivery and channel decisions* are taken with regard to capacity effects. By handling certain standardised processes via *standard electronic channels* (e.g. the internet), capacity problems can be reduced. Also, by applying a *multi-channelling* approach, capacity problems within certain channels can be compensated by other channels. This is the case when a bank customer calling his bank branch is redirected to a call centre when the contact personnel in the branch are busy.

SERVICES MARKETING IN ACTION 10.5:

Price-related capacity management at Germanwings

As in the case of virtually all the low-fare airlines, the business model used by Germanwings is to offer only a limited number of the cheapest fares advertised, which must be claimed a considerable time in advance of the travel date, with prices for bookings made at shorter notice significantly more expensive. Due to the greater demand for flights early and late in the day and at the start and end of weekends, these flights are usually more expensive than mid-day flights or mid-week flights. For example, under this model the spectrum of prices for a one-way flight from Cologne to Paris ranges from 19–250 euros, plus taxes and airport charges. It is this 'yield management' approach that makes all the difference between profit and loss for the low-cost airlines. At Germanwings, the department in charge of pricing is therefore located directly next-door to the directors. The airline needs to achieve an average ticket price of 60–80 euros per route segment in order to make a profit at 80 per cent seat utilisation. Whereas passengers do not receive any money back for their unused tickets, bookings can be changed up to two hours before departure for a fee of 25 euros.

Source: Steinke 2005.

As a further services marketing instrument, *service communications* are utilised in order to adjust demand to given capacities. First, communications are applied in order to explain to the customer the origin of capacity gaps, with the aim of convincing them to use the service at times with free capacities. In a ski resort in the Rocky Mountains it could be shown that an information system indicating the waiting times at the various lifts results in customers' avoiding lifts with the longest queues and switching to lifts with shorter queues.[13] However, as it is often more difficult to determine the real effect of service communications on customer behaviour, service communications primarily play an important role in capacity management by transferring other capacity management measures to the customer, such as by communicating the price differences to the customer and letting the customer decide.

Waiting time management

Despite all the measures already mentioned, for some services demand and capacity will still not balance exactly at certain stages. This is especially true for so-called 'walk-in' services, services where the customer just walks into the service outfit in order to be served. Examples of these services are fast food restaurants, cafés, post offices, standard services of banks, underground services, etc. For these services, there are often situations where the customer has the need for the specific service but cannot be served immediately. The result is that in most cases the customer has to wait. Although waiting times in most cases are not unreasonably long – meaning that any form of reservation system, etc. would be neither reasonable nor economic – customers dislike waiting because waiting for a service is perceived as being unfair or at least a waste of time.[14]

In order to avoid customer dissatisfaction and its negative consequences in terms of customer behaviour and value, service providers employ specific activities to *manage waiting times*. Waiting time management encompasses the following elements:

- *Reducing waiting time.* Comprehensive waiting time management aims to minimise waiting time using measures which were discussed for the other three types of capacity management, and aims not only to reduce waiting times, but also to minimise demand–capacity gaps, in general.

- *Organising waiting lines.* When customers have to wait for only one specific service resource, such as a doctor, then patients' waiting is organised based on a first come–first served basis. Patients who arrive first are treated first. In many walk-in service situations, there are several comparable service resources, e.g. counters in a post office or ticket counters at the train station. Then, customers' waiting is often organised. There are various waiting line systems, such as a simple line system, a multiple line system, or a number system, which differ in several ways, such as the perceived movement of the line, or the situation in general, which reduces the perceived waiting time, or the perceived injustice (see Figure 10.8).[15]

- *Waiting time communications.* Communications about the expected waiting time and explaining the reasons for the delays are important determinants of customers' waiting time perceptions. The communicated waiting time, by signs indicating approximate waiting time in lines in, say, amusement parks, influences customers' expectations. When the customer has to wait longer than communicated and expected, the customer will be even more dissatisfied. Therefore, it is sensible to communicate a waiting time which can be complied with.

- *Waiting time services.* These are services offered by the provider in order to make the waiting situation for the customer more agreeable. Examples are offering a drink, offering magazines, playing background music or providing TV entertainment.

- *Waiting time compensation.* These are measures to compensate the customer for disproportionate waiting times. One Dutch supermarket guaranteed its customers that they would not to have to wait long when checking out and that they would not have to pay for the goods purchased when more than two people were ahead of them in the queue.

- *Involving customers in service processes.* This tool uses the general characteristic of a service, customer integration: the patient completes a medical history questionnaire whilst waiting to see the doctor.

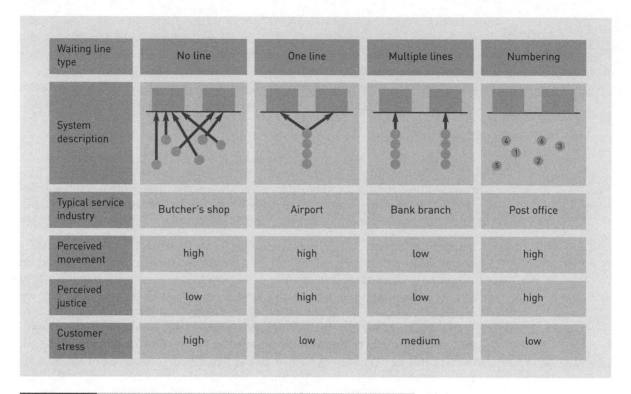

Waiting line type	No line	One line	Multiple lines	Numbering
System description				
Typical service industry	Butcher's shop	Airport	Bank branch	Post office
Perceived movement	high	high	low	high
Perceived justice	low	high	low	high
Customer stress	high	low	medium	low

FIGURE 10.8 Types of waiting lines and their advantages and disadvantages

Source: *Service Management for Competitive Advantage*, New York, McGraw-Hill College, (Fitzsimmons, J.A. and Fitzsimmons, M.J. 1994), reproduced with permission of The McGraw-Hill Companies.

Yield management for integrated capacity management

In some industries where capacity problems are very significant and relevant for value creation (e.g. airline industry, travel industry, hotel industry), capacity-oriented and demand-oriented approaches of capacity management are combined using the concept of **yield management**. 'Yield' expresses that this management approach aims at balancing capacity and demand according to profitability criteria. Remembering the approaches which have been discussed so far, yield management realises an *integration of price discrimination and reservation systems*. Moreover, the prices vary according to the remaining time between booking time and service delivery time.

In the *basic model of yield management* without price discrimination, it is assumed that customers' willingness to pay varies with the distance to the time of service delivery. For the purpose of simplicity, three periods before the time of service delivery are distinguished:

- At a time *'long before' the delivery time*, many capacities are available. Customers who decide on a specific service delivery time (e.g. a flight on a specific day at a specific hour) lose flexibility when booking the service. In contrast, the service provider gains security that at least a portion of the capacity is booked. At this stage, the customer pays a relatively low price; they are compensated for the loss of flexibility.

- With a *'normal' distance to the time of service delivery*, prices are relatively high (or 'normal'). This is the time when most customers book the service. The higher demand results in higher prices which the provider is able to ask for.

- At a time *'shortly before' the delivery time*, the service provider risks unused capacity (e.g. empty seats), the demand is lower than with a 'normal' time distance. Consequently, the capacities available are offered at lower prices, in order to fill them through, e.g. 'last-minute offers'.

The exact point in time and length of the three periods vary according to the demand patterns in the specific service industry and market. When customers tend to book immediately before the actual delivery time, the 'last-minute' period is significantly shorter in comparison with those customers who tend to book earlier. The three phases are an over-simplification of the situation; in fact, modern yield management systems change real-time prices according to the current demand in respect of the current number of bookings and capacities available.

Furthermore, in reality, the *willingness to pay* of customers not only varies depending on the time distance between booking and delivery but also *varies between customer segments*. Some customers are more price-sensitive than others, depending on the customers' budget for the service or their need for the service. Therefore a more sophisticated form of yield management is conducted when *taking into account differences in price sensitivity*. In this case, yield management contains two basic steps:[16]

- defining customer segments according to price sensitivity;

- assigning capacity to the customer segments.

The fact is that each customer probably has a different price sensitivity. However, it would be impossible and uneconomical to determine the exact price sensitivity for every single current and potential customer. Therefore, the service provider builds broad *segments of customers with comparable price sensitivities*. There are groups of customers with comparable price-demand curves and the service provider aims to identify the groups which are significantly distinct from each other. In order to do this, those criteria are identified which determine the price sensitivity of the customers. One such criterion is the geographical region where a customer comes from. Airlines further segment customers according to their demand for business or economy class. The class the customer chooses is a means of self-selection. The customer chooses the class which corresponds to their willingness to pay.

After establishing the price sensitivity segments, the available capacities are assigned to these segments. The criterion for the assignment is the marginal revenue which is expected when the capacity offered to a specific segment is increased (e.g. the expected further revenue when one more row in business class is offered). The firm first assigns capacity to the most valuable customer segment, i.e. the segment with the lowest price sensitivity, e.g. business class, when considering only business and economy class seats, because one more customer in this segment pays a higher price than one more customer in a segment with higher price sensitivity and lower revenue generation. However, the probability of filling this capacity decreases with each unit of capacity which is assigned to the most valuable segment. Consequently, at some point in time, the marginal revenue, the price under consideration of the booking probability, of a capacity assigned to the most valuable class decreases under the marginal revenue of the next, less valuable segment.

The service provider optimises this system even more by *varying the described procedure* further. First, applying the concept of *threshold curves*,[17] the decision of capacity assignment to segments varies according to the real-time bookings. Within a certain corridor, the marginal revenue where the provider switches capacity assignment from one segment to the other is dependent on the current booking numbers. When there is a higher demand from business class passengers than expected (e.g. because of a group booking in business class), then more capacities are assigned to the business class segment. Secondly, service firms apply the concept of *nesting* which means that the capacities reserved for one segment are made available to other segments, for example the upgrading of customers of a lower class or extending the business class, which is technically possible in smaller airplanes where the divide between the two classes is movable. Thirdly, independent from the price segment, there is always a certain proportion of customers who do not use the assigned capacity, resulting in further free capacities. Therefore, service providers tend to *overbook*, and allow more bookings than available capacity, based on standard cancellation rates.

The various determinants of yield management decisions and their variations are too complex to allow yield management to be calculated in a simple way. Service providers apply several systems in order to implement a yield management approach:

- *Booking databases* store the information which is needed in order to take the yield management decisions. Information stored covers historical information regarding demand patterns, typical capacity utilisation per segment or the number of 'no shows'.

- *Optimisation programmes* calculate the optimal capacity assignment and price depending on the information in the reservation database.

- The *reservation system* records the current bookings in real time. These are adjusted with the information in the booking database and the results of the optimisation process, and used for real-time adjustments of the yield management decisions.

Yield management promises a value-oriented balancing of demand and capacity for firms which are concerned with significant capacity problems. However, not every firm can apply this concept due to several requirements:

- It must be possible to book the services under consideration.

- The investments in a yield management system are only profitable when there are significant variations of demand.

- A firm only can sustain the investments when a certain company size is given.

- The firm must be active in a price sensitive market. Only when customers react to price variations, does a yield management process make sense.

Services marketing in action 10.6 describes the yield management approach and history of one of the pioneers in this field.

SERVICES MARKETING IN ACTION 10.6:

Yield management at American Airlines

American Airlines were the pioneers in automated reservation systems. In the 1960s, they developed the first online reservation system. Later on, they became so specialised that they formed the SABRE Group originating from the software they first implemented called SABRE (Semi-Automated Business Research Environment) that dealt with centralising and controlling reservation activity. Even today, the SABRE Group is the leader in terms of methodology and technology in their field. They react quickly to any change in the industry. For quite a while now, they have been selling access to their reservation systems to other airlines for huge fees.

At American Airlines, almost everything is automated because the yield management decision-making process is too large and therefore too complex to be processed manually. It is the SABRE Group that first decided to split this problem into three smaller ones: overbooking, discount allocation, traffic management. Today, the module aggregating these three issues dealing with yield management at American Airlines is called DINAMO (Dynamic Inventory and Maintenance Optimizer). It was fully implemented in 1988; this was the latest step in a development process that spans the past 25 years. Using this system, it was calculated that spoilage was only 3%; which means that only 3% of the seats were empty on sold-out flights.

We said that almost everything is automated because a small part is still done manually. When a flight is critical, that is it does not meet yield management control parameters (because of the Superbowl or an input error), it is manually reviewed by yield management analysts. After the implementation of DINAMO, the productivity of these specialists has increased by 30%. This was due to the fact that

▶

these people could make better revenue decisions because the job changed from spotting problems and solving them quickly, to having the machine identify the problem and have the analyst fix it with the help of another American Airlines' software that allows for flight specific analysis and re-optimisation.

Since 1987, American Airlines Decision Technologies has applied yield management techniques to other industries. The first non-airline applications were with passenger rail transport applications, with the major difference being that the railway system was not a hub-and-spoke network. It was then expanded to the hotel industry, car rental companies, the broadcasting industry, etc. Management estimates their benefits from their automated yield management program at half a billion dollars per year.

Source: Voneche 2005.

When a firm meets these requirements, service capacity management is an essential element of profitable and consequently value-oriented services marketing. Applying systematic capacity management, service resources are not only utilised for creating value through a high quality service but also managed for profit in terms of capacity–demand gaps.

Summary

The following lessons have emerged from this chapter (see Figure 10.9):

1. Service firms potentially experience capacity problems which affect value via revenue effects (lost revenues when demand cannot be met) and cost effects (under-recovered fixed costs when capacities are not filled).

2. Service capacity problems are defined by gaps between capacity and demand, when demand cannot be met by the available capacity (capacity gap) and when the capacity is not filled by the given demand (demand gap).

3. Capacity problems and consequently service capacity management are determined by the demand level, demand dynamics and the adaptability of service resources.

4. There are four types of capacity management measures which differ according to whether capacity or demand is managed as well as according to whether measures are applied before or during a service interaction: long-term capacity determination, flexible capacity utilisation, demand adjustments and waiting time management.

5. Long-term capacity determination is influenced by internal (financial possibilities) and external factors (anticipated demand level and dynamics).

6. Short-term capacity adjustments of the determined capacity are realised by a flexible capacity utilisation by real-time workforce scheduling, employing a flexible workforce, utilising capacities for other activities and applying reservation systems.

7. Demand adjustments are used in order to manage short-term demand by measures of service product, pricing, delivery channels and communications.

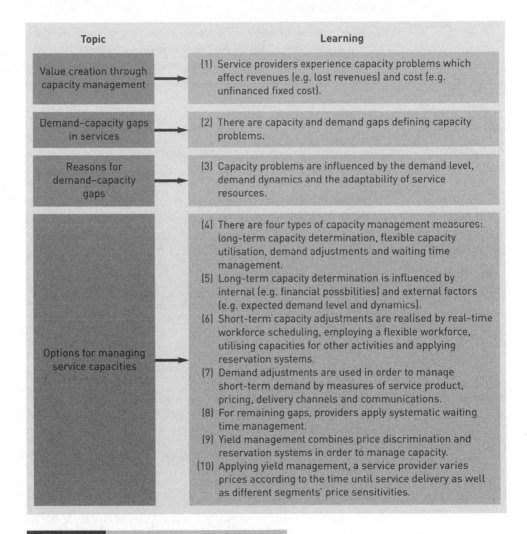

FIGURE 10.9 Learning summary for Chapter 10

8. Even though a firm applies systematic capacity management there will still remain capacity gaps at some time resulting in waiting times for customers. At this point waiting time management helps to prevent negative consequences of this waiting time by introducing measures for reducing waiting time, organising waiting lines, waiting time communications, services and compensation as well as involving customers in service processes.

9. Yield management is an integrated concept of service capacity management which combines the measures of price discrimination and reservation systems. Industries typically applying yield management are the airline industry or hotel industry.

10. Yield management varies prices according to the time distance between booking and service delivery. Furthermore, customer segments are established using the criterion of price sensitivity. Service capacities are assigned using a multi-layer method, beginning with the least price sensitive segment.

Knowledge questions

1. Explain the different methods of value creation using service capacity management. Outline first the possible service capacity problems and then describe the value effects of capacity management.

2. How can the optimal service level be defined?

3. Explain the factors responsible for demand and capacity gaps.

4. Define the four groups of capacity management measures and explain their importance for capacity management.

5. Explain how a firm can proceed in order to determine long-term service capacity.

6. Which possibilities exist for long-term demand extension and demand reduction? Discuss the value effects and risks for each option.

7. Explain the options of a service provider for short-term adjustments of service capacity.

8. Which groups of measures for adjusting demand in the short term do you know? Explain how they affect capacity–demand gaps.

9. Explain the various effects of different measures of waiting time management.

10. Explain the basic idea of yield management. Include both dynamic pricing and capacity assignment.

11. Why is it not reasonable to reserve all seats for the best paying customer segment?

Application and discussion questions

1. Choose a certain service provider (e.g. café, doctor) and describe situations of a demand and a capacity gap.

2. Discuss why it is not possible for most services to achieve a 100 per cent capacity utilisation.

3. List examples of industries where demand is very dynamic. Also discuss possible reasons for the respective dynamics.

4. List one industry for each capacity management measure where the respective measure is widely used. Discuss why.

5. Do you know a service where they <u>always</u> have the same capacity problem (e.g. capacity gap)? Did the management plan incorrect long-term capacity?

6. Reservation systems are widely used capacity management activities. What are the reservation systems' benefits for both provider and customer?

7. Find an example of a service industry where reservation systems are not common. Why are reservations not used in this industry?

8. Discuss the concept of short-term demand adjustments.

9. Remember your last long waiting time in a service situation. How did you feel? What did the provider do in terms of managing the waiting time? If you were a waiting time consultant, what actions would you suggest taking?

10. Sometimes, in restaurants, guests have to wait for their bill. Discuss this situation from a value perspective.

11. Go to the website of an airline and calculate prices for the same flight on different days, in different classes and so on. Try to rebuild the yield management model of the airline.

CASE STUDY: CAPACITY ADJUSTMENTS AT MCDONALD'S

A typical industry with varying demand levels and capacity problems is the fast food industry. Consequently, the McDonald's franchise consisting of six restaurants located in Bloomington, Indiana, also faces these problems, and therefore applies respective capacity management activities. The weekly work schedule development, along with real-time adjustments to this work schedule, are conducted at the centre.

The average annual sales of the restaurants under discussion range from $2 to $2.5 million per store, higher than the national average per restaurant ($1.5 million in 2000). Average daily sales per store vary from $4,500 to $7,025, while average 'cheque value' per day (= daily sales revenue divided by total daily transactions) are between $3.60 and $4.20. Drive-thru sales account for approximately 62–65% of total sales revenue at each store.

The scheduling manager of each store prepares the weekly work schedule with the help of a computerised scheduling system. This process starts with the generation of an hourly sales projection for the upcoming week using a modified five-period moving average model. The unit manager modifies the computer-generated sales projection by reflecting upcoming events associated with the community – schools, sports, weather, and so forth. Hourly projected sales are translated into hourly staffing requirements for specific workstations by the sales-to-staff conversion table, which is designed with a service target that has the average customer experiencing 3.5 minutes in the system (queue time plus service). Updates are made to the workforce size (new hirings and resignations), work time availability windows for employees, and skill ratings. Next, the computer system produces the 'crew daily schedule report' for the planning horizon; rest (meal) breaks are inserted if employees qualify. Tour scheduling aims to minimise the sum of absolute deviations between scheduled labour hours and target staffing requirements while satisfying employees' preferences for work times. Finally, the scheduling manager edits the computer-generated schedule for any changes and it is then posted. It takes a scheduler an average of 2–6 hours per week, per store to develop the forthcoming weekly tour schedule.

The need for real-time schedule adjustment during the day arises mainly from uncertain customer demand and unexpected worker absence or lateness. The adjustment process can be broken into two phases. First, in the *monitoring and detection phase*, managers carefully monitor discrepancies between the available and required capacity every hour throughout the day, and revise forecast and staffing requirements for the rest of the day. In the adjustment phase, the managers need to identify available capacity alternatives by ensuring both service and profit goals. 'The crew schedule is a starting point. Scheduling does not end until the service day is over', one seasoned store manager with more than 20 years of experience in this industry stated.

At the restaurants in question, a day is divided into five work horizons (opening and breakfast, lunch, afternoon, dinner, evening and closing), for each of which a manager is assigned to run the restaurant operation. The manager normally starts to prepare for the work one hour before the work horizon begins. During this 'shift preparation time' the manager is required to prepare the production equipment, facility and inventory for services and review the sales data and employee schedules from the preceding work horizon.

The manager computes, records and monitors the gap between required and available capacity in real time. Available capacity is updated when employees do not report for their shifts. Capacity requirements are computed from actual sales data and the sales-to-staff conversion table. Actual sales data (dollar volume and transaction level) are kept track of by the POS (point-of-sales) system. Managers use a simple decision rule, similar to a typical control chart, in order to determine whether the observed gap is random. If the gap does not exceed pre-established threshold values, monitoring is continued and no other actions are initiated. However, if a significant imbalance is discovered, managers actively seek out the underlying causes by interacting with employees and customers. The implicit threshold values are 1–1.5 labour hours (amounting to $100–$150 in sales) for two consecutive time periods at the restaurants under discussions here. The capacity imbalance stemming from unexpected turnover or absenteeism normally triggers a schedule adjustment, since the absence of a worker exceeds the threshold values (the minimum shift length is 3 hours). If the imbalance arises from changing demand conditions, managers strive to identify the special events or causes and to revise the forecast for the remaining work horizon. During this process, they actively interact with employees and customers, and often utilise the 'special event' log book that includes the history of recurring events and their impact on sales. By comparing the sales patterns between the days of the similar events, they can estimate the sales for the remainder of the day. However, if managers are not able to identify the causes of demand changes or are not familiar with the event which is occuring, they are inclined to use a simple extrapolation technique, using the observed forecast errors during the early period of the day. For instance, if sales increase or decrease by 20% during the morning, the sales forecast for the remainder of the day is adjusted upwards or downwards by 20%.

In this phase, based on updated available and required capacity, service managers decide the amount of capacity adjustment and develop a revised work schedule in detail, using a diversity of adjustment actions. If available capacity falls short of the required capacity, the managers may ask the staff to return from a break, stay longer and start earlier. In addition, the managers may call in extra staff, sometimes even from other sister restaurant sites. In contrast, if the available capacity exceeds the required capacity, staff members maybe asked to finish early, start late, and be sent on a break or to help with other tasks. In particular, training is often conducted during this period. Moreover, task assignments should be revised accordingly by taking into account the positioning guide and individual skill strength. In the adjustment process, managers try to achieve multiple goals associated with customer service, cost control, worker utilisation and schedule stability:

- fast delivery: maintain the crew size as close to the target level as possible.

- cost: minimise direct labour costs.

- utilisation: maximise overall productivity.

- stability: minimise crew schedule changes and station changeovers.

Managers seek to minimise the imbalance between available and required capacity, which aims to achieve the target customer service level and to reduce potential employee burnout resulting from high work intensity (fast delivery). This goal is viewed as most important because the daily accumulated capacity gap is being used as a measure for their operating performance. Managers also strive to minimise direct labour costs, recognising that direct labour costs significantly affect profitability. They also attempt to maximise productivity by assigning workers to workstations at which they perform best ('all aces are in their places'), especially during the peak demand periods (utilisation). Managers also consider managerial burden and/or worker dissatisfaction that may rise from excessive work schedule modification and frequent changes in task/station assignment (stability).

The adjustment decision is an important management action within the store, responding to needed changes. Subjective estimates by the owner and managers indicate that between 25% and 35% of all days require staff adjustments in a typical store, with over half due to changes in demand level.

Source: Hur *et al*. 2004.

Notes

[1] See Parasuraman and Varadarajan 1988; Desiraju and Shugan 1999.

[2] See Klassen and Rohleder 2002.

[3] Sometimes, authors differentiate between demand management and capacity management (e.g. Klassen and Rohleder 2001). However, services marketing in general focuses on managing demand, while capacity management aims specifically at utilising as many capacities as possible. Therefore, in this book, capacity management encompasses both measures to change the quantities of service capacities and influencing the demand in order to utilise the capacities.

[4] See Davis and Heineke 1994.

[5] See Betts *et al*. 2000.

[6] See for example Heskett *et al*. 1990.

[7] See Klassen and Rohleder 2001.

[8] See Mabert 1986; Shemwell and Cronin 1994.

[9] The first two types are partly comparable with the general capacity management strategies offered by Crandall and Markland 1996: 'match' demand, 'provide' a maximum capacity, 'control' demand at an average level and 'influence' demand in order to reduce dynamics.

[10] See for an overview Adenso-Díaz *et al*. 2002.

[11] See Hur *et al*. 2004.

[12] See Ng *et al*. 1999.

[13] See Pullman and Moore 1999.

[14] See Morrow 1984.

[15] See Fitzsimmons and Fitzsimmons 1994; Lovelock and Wirtz 2003.

[16] See e.g. Desiraju and Shugan 1999.

[17] See Daudel and Vialle 1992.

PART 5

The external and internal environment of value-oriented services marketing

The predominant focus of services marketing are a service firm's activities in order to manage customer interactions and relationships, the two primary value processes of services marketing. However, these interactions and relationships are not isolated from a broader environment in which service providers (and customers) are participating. Although a service firm's major purpose is to service its customers, there are further **stakeholders** whose interests and expectations are to be considered by a service provider and services marketing as well as those who set conditions for services marketing activities. There are internal and external stakeholders.

It terms of the *external stakeholders*, the *consumer market* as the aggregation of the individual customer relationship is an important precondition and management figure of services marketing. On a more strategic level, services marketing decides which market segments are to be marketed to. These decisions influence the general definition of the service concept. Along with the consumer markets, *other provider markets* determine services marketing. This expression encompasses competitors, suppliers and customer firms, and other providers in the supply chain of a service provider. The behaviour of these firms as well as optional own behaviours regarding these firms, affect the design and success of value-oriented services marketing. A further, non-market-related group of external stakeholders consists of *politics and society*, which influence services marketing for example by setting the legal conditions.

Within service firms, there are *internal* stakeholders who influence services marketing. The *service organisation* as a construct affects services marketing. In this context, the top management, the departments within a firm, the department heads and employees are stakeholders whose behaviour affects the realisation of a services marketing concept. The **shareholders** as the owners of the service firm naturally directly influence services marketing to some extent. The main requirement by the shareholders is the value creation by services marketing. The 'representation' of the shareholders within the firm – not necessarily in terms of organisation but in terms of task, i.e. examining and managing the value creation by services marketing – is the controlling function.

This final part of *Services Marketing* deals with these considerations. Chapter 11 focuses on the external stakeholder, i.e. 'the markets' and explains what decisions service providers take regarding market strategies, international services marketing, service networks and service outsourcing. Chapter 12 concentrates on the internal stakeholders. First, implementation issues of value-oriented services marketing are examined, and secondly, a controlling concept based on the Service Value Chain is presented.

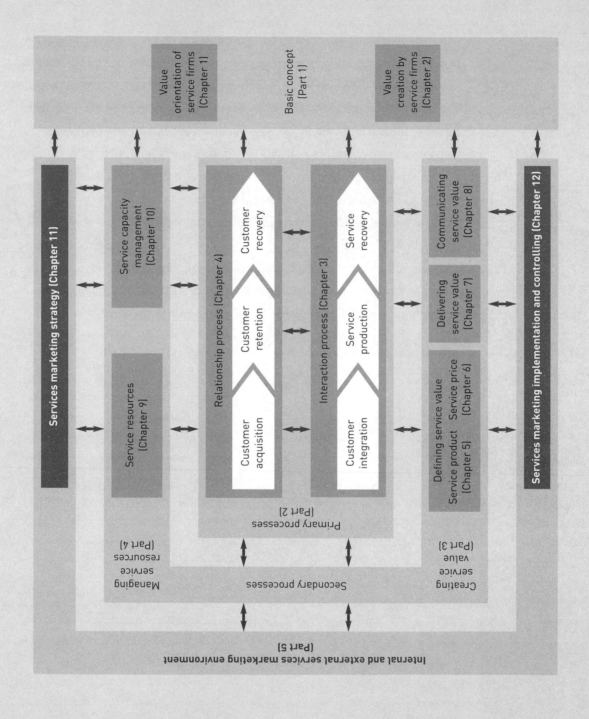

Value orientation of service firms (Chapter 1)

Basic concept (Part 1)

Value creation by service firms (Chapter 2)

Services marketing strategy (Chapter 11)

Service capacity management (Chapter 10)

Service resources (Chapter 9)

Relationship process (Chapter 4)

Customer recovery

Customer retention

Customer acquisition

Interaction process (Chapter 3)

Service recovery

Service production

Customer integration

Communicating service value (Chapter 8)

Delivering service value (Chapter 7)

Defining service value

Service price (Chapter 6)

Service product (Chapter 5)

Services marketing implementation and controlling (Chapter 12)

Primary processes (Part 2)

Managing service resources (Part 4)

Secondary processes

Creating service value (Part 3)

Internal and external services marketing environment (Part 5)

378

11 Services marketing and the markets: Market strategies, international services marketing, service networks and service outsourcing

Until now the primary focus of this book has been on how service providers behave towards their individual customers, customer segments or their target group in general. We assumed that the target group is given, that the firm has already decided on who are the potential customers of the firm. However, the value which is created by a service provider is not only influenced by the behaviour of the specific customer(s) but also by decisions on a more strategic market level.

The general concept of this book has a strategic focus by basing services marketing on the value of a service provider and interpreting services marketing activities from a value perspective. However, it is not only the management of service interactions and customer relationships, by employing different types of service resources, which affect the value that is created by a service provider – strategic decisions regarding the different markets also influence a provider's ability to create value.

This chapter focuses on *two parts of the markets* by examining the options of a service provider regarding its behaviour towards the markets. The first part concerns the market decision of a service provider and the *consumer markets* (see Figure 11.1). While the first ten chapters of the book discuss how the target group can be managed we now explore the general decision regarding the target group and outline different types of *market strategies*. Within these market strategies, as well as in the current discussions in business practice and service research, is the internationalisation strategy. Accordingly, *international services marketing* will also be covered in this chapter.

Another important part of the market which is strategically relevant to a service firm, is made up of the *other providers in the market* (see Figure 11.1). A service firm can have distinctive relationships with other providers. Some are competitors (another competitor airline), suppliers of the firm (caterers who provide the airline with meals for the passengers) or providers in other markets or market segments (a car rental firm). From a broad relationship marketing perspective,[1] managing these relationships is as important as managing customer relationships. To get an idea of what decisions regarding other providers are about, we explore two instruments of managing these relationships in more detail, *service networks* and *service outsourcing*.

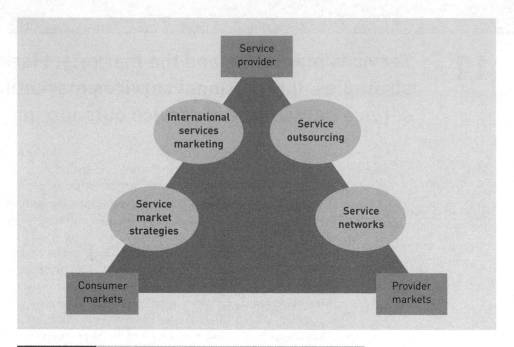

FIGURE 11.1   Decisions regarding consumer and provider markets

Summing up these introductory considerations, this chapter focuses on the following learning objectives (see Figure 11.2):

1. Understanding the decisions service providers take regarding consumer and provider markets.

2. Knowing how service providers proceed when deciding on the defined target market.

3. Defining and understanding how an international services marketing strategy can be implemented.

4 Learning how service outsourcing as a form of co-operation with other service providers works.

5. Realising how service providers behave towards other providers through the management of service networks.

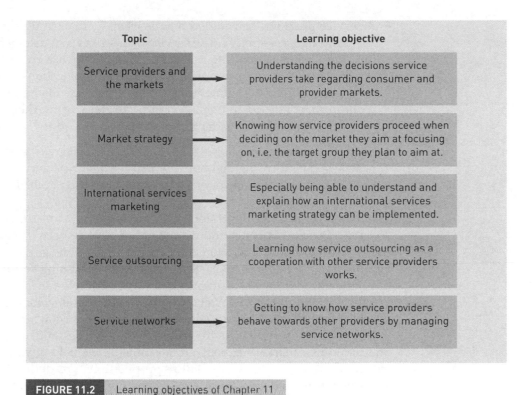

Topic	Learning objective
Service providers and the markets	Understanding the decisions service providers take regarding consumer and provider markets.
Market strategy	Knowing how service providers proceed when deciding on the market they aim at focusing on, i.e. the target group they plan to aim at.
International services marketing	Especially being able to understand and explain how an international services marketing strategy can be implemented.
Service outsourcing	Learning how service outsourcing as a cooperation with other service providers works.
Service networks	Getting to know how service providers behave towards other providers by managing service networks.

FIGURE 11.2   Learning objectives of Chapter 11

Market segment strategies

A service provider's decision about which target group it plans to focus on is taken within the decision on market segment strategies.[2] According to the services marketed and the markets distinguished, four *types of market segment strategies* can defined (see Figure 11.3):

- When a service firm concentrates on existing services and markets, then it follows a *market penetration strategy*. The firm aims at exploiting the current customer segments with its existing services. Possible tactics in this area are gaining customers from competitors, cross-selling services to existing customers who do not use all the services currently offered by the provider, or customer recovery, regaining lost customers, by compensation offers.

- A *service development strategy* concerns focusing on existing market segments with new services. The newly developed services can be sold to existing customers via cross-selling campaigns, or can play a role as a switching barrier – when a provider succeeds in positioning itself as an innovation leader in the market – and can also be used for customer recovery when customers have cancelled their relationship with the provider due to unsatisfactory services.

- A service provider focusing on new markets with existing services follows a *market development strategy*. The service firm strives for customer acquisition by offering its new services to market segments which were not previous customers of the firm. An example is a mobile communications provider who has only offered private customer services and now extends its service offering to include corporate customers. A typical strategy of market development is regional expansion or broader international expansion.

- Finally, a further option for service providers is a *diversification strategy*, which is achieved by focusing on both new markets and new services, for example a bank operating in Europe offering insurance products in the USA.

The four types of strategies differ according to their *relevance to services marketing decisions*. The market penetration strategy has already been discussed in the section which covered the relationship process which aims at recruiting, retaining and regaining customers in existing markets with existing services. The service development strategy plays an important role within the management of service products within the Service Value Chain. The market development strategy was discussed within the considerations of service channels when several multiple strategies were outlined. As diversification means establishing a new service offering to new market segments, it falls outside the field of value-oriented services marketing, as far as new value propositions are defined. An important strategy which has not yet been touched on in this book is the internationalisation strategy as part of the market development strategy. International penetration is a predominant strategy in many service industries today, although the service characteristics dramatically complicate an internationalisation programme, as we will see. Therefore, the following section will focus on this topic in more detail.

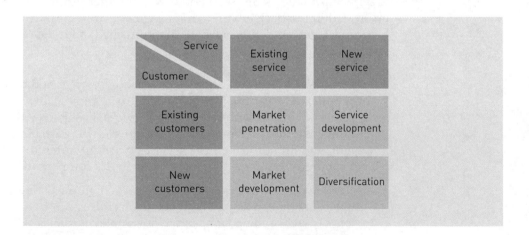

FIGURE 11.3 Market segment strategies of a service provider

Source: Ansoff 1966.

Market development through international services marketing

Value creation through international services marketing

In the field of services marketing, there are several conditions influencing a ser-vice provider's decision on marketing its services internationally. The predominant influence factor is the market situation. In *saturated markets* with high competition, service providers have difficulties in the continuous creation of value. Market saturation complicates customer acquisition and high competition makes customer retention a challenge. By extending the provider's focus market to other countries, a significant amount of *new revenue potentials* are realised. Furthermore, in many cases the internationalisation of the company necessitates the internationalising of the services offered to the customers. This *'following clients'* strategy is often found in business-to-business markets,[3] e.g. a management consultancy which follows its expanding customer companies to where the service firm may not yet be established. Furthermore, on the *cost side*, an internationalisation strategy might be used to realise economies of scale as well as synergies. Services marketing in action 11.1 illustrates several value effects of an internationalisation of service providers.

SERVICES MARKETING IN ACTION 11.1:

Cost and revenue synergies of international affairs at Air France-KLM

Air France-KLM, Europe's largest airline, said yesterday it was achieving cost benefits from the co-ordination of its international sales and station organisations abroad, faster than forecast. Patrick Alexandre, executive vice-president of international commercial affairs and operations at Air France, said the savings in international markets for the combined group in its sales and foreign stations were forecast to total 92 million euros within four years. This would account for more than 15 per cent of the total 580 million euro synergy benefits forecast for the whole group from the merger.

The takeover of KLM, the Dutch flag carrier, by Air France last year was a pioneering step in the consolidation of the fragmented European airline sector, and has been followed by Lufthansa's acquisition of Swiss International Air Lines. The combined Air France-KLM has 225 international destinations, 107 long-haul and 198 short-haul, with the international operations accounting for 58 per cent of total passenger revenues.

While merging at shareholder level and consolidating financial reporting, Air France-KLM has continued to pursue a strategy of 'one group, two airlines' by

▶

maintaining separate brands and fleet operations. A large part of the synergy benefits is planned to come from increased revenues generated by the combination of the two groups' global networks, centred on its twin hubs at Paris Charles de Gaulle and Amsterdam Schiphol airports. Around the world it is seeking to save costs by co-ordinating sales strategies on international routes and by rationalising its presence at international destinations.

Mr Alexandre said the biggest savings had come from the joint procurement of services, such as passenger and baggage handling and catering. Wherever possible the two airlines are seeking to rent offices and ticket offices jointly and to renegotiate station handling services.

Synergy benefits in the first year to 31 March 2005 in international commercial affairs had totalled 8.3 million euros, up from the 7 million euros originally forecast, while the forecast for cumulative annual savings after four years had been raised from 78 million euros to 92 million euros, said Mr Alexandre.

Source: Done 2005. Reproduced with permission from Financial Times Limited.

Challenges of international services marketing

While the most important motive is market-related, the *service characteristics* represent potential challenges for international services marketing. The central characteristic of services is customer integration, the customer's participation in service production and delivery. The consequences of this customer integration are further enforced within an international services marketing strategy:

- The necessity that similar internal factors or external factors are available to the new service delivery location complicates internationalisation. The *geographical distance* between provider and customer affects the possibility of service delivery and the cost of transporting the factors to the location of service delivery.

- Due to the direct contact between customer and service resources, many service elements are perceived directly and unfiltered by the customer. Although most service elements can be prepared in some manner (advertising material, employee training, etc.), service interactions are so dynamic that not every service element can be planned beforehand. This difficulty is aggravated by *cultural distance*. In some cultures, several behaviours are perceived differently (colours have different meanings in Europe compared to in Japan). This cultural difference affects cognitive and communication gaps within service interactions between customer and provider.[4] Services marketing in action 11.2 shows the importance of the consideration of the target country's specifics.

SERVICES MARKETING IN ACTION 11.2:

The rise and fall of coffeeshops in Switzerland

In 2000, a coffeeshop hype was forecast in Switzerland. Both foreign providers, such as Starbucks and McDonald's, and national providers, such as Mövenpick, planned to establish a total of 150 new coffeeshops. Today, most of the providers have ceased in their efforts and either closed their shops or at least stopped the original expansion plans. For example, the Swiss Globus retailing group planned to open 25 coffeeshops within the franchising chain 'Caffé-Nannini'. The expansion stopped at six shops in 2002. The original idea to open further shops was revised due to unsatisfactory test results and location analyses. Further, the opened shops were sold to the franchiser firm Nannini.

To explain this development, two major reasons are identified. First, coffeeshops are only profitable in highly frequented areas and in Switzerland, there are not too many of these areas, and then they are expensive. Secondly, in contrast to the US, a high coffee culture already exists, even before the coffeeshop chains emerged. The coffeeshop concept did not improve the coffee culture and theorefore had a less significant USP in Switzerland. Consequently, two important regional factors were not taken into consideration by the expanding coffeeshop chains, which led to a substantial failure in realising the set targets.

Source: Handelszeitung 2003.

The need for customer integration varies according to the service type. Consequently, the service type also affects the possibilities of international services marketing. Two *types of service* can be differentiated according to the integration characteristics of a service:[5] *hard services*: architectural design, education, life insurance and music, and *soft services*: foodservice, healthcare, laundry and lodging. For producing and delivering hard services, service production and consumption can be partially separated. The type of contact between provider and customer does not necessitate the provider having a local presence. In contrast, *soft services* are produced and consumed simultaneously and these services cannot be offered in a meaningful manner without the local presence of the provider. It is obvious that internationalisation is complicated for soft services which are confronted with specific challenges caused by service characteristics, while with hard services internationalisation does not differ significantly from the marketing of international consumer goods.[6] Table 11.1 lists typical international services. For the insurance industry, Services marketing in action 11.3 discusses some issues regarding market entry.

TABLE 11.1	International service industries

Accounting	Funeral services
Advertising	Healthcare
Banking	Insurance
Broadcasting	Investment banking (brokerage)
Computer services	Leasing
Computer software	Legal services
Construction	Lodging
Consulting	Maintenance and repair
Contract research	Media
Data entry	• Cinema
Data processing	• Internet
Design and engineering	• Newspapers/magazines
Distribution (including service distributors)	• Radio
• Agents, brokers and representatives	• Television
• Franchising	Reservation systems
• Freight forwarders and customs brokers	Restaurants
• Retailing	Royalities and licensing
• Shopping malls	Security systems
• Warehousing	Tourism
• Wholesaling	Telecommunications
Education	• Online services
• Executive and management development	• Mobile
• Institutions of higher learning	• Paging
• Vocational and technical	• Telephone
Entertainment	Transportation (courier)
• Music and other audio	• Express delivery
• Theme parks	• Package delivery
• TV productions, motion pictures	Transportation (merchandise)
• Spectator sports	Transportation (passenger)
• Theatre, live performances	Utilities

Source: Samiee 1999, p. 326.

SERVICES MARKETING IN ACTION 11.3:

International insurers going to China

Foreign insurers are preparing a significant expansion of their Chinese operations with the removal of tight restrictions on what products they can sell and where they can operate on the mainland. Foreign insurers such as Allianz, Prudential and Tokio Marine & Fire have already laid the groundwork for expanding their China operations in readiness for the substantial new liberalisation of the market, from December 11 2004. China agreed to remove geographical and product restrictions on the 30 existing foreign companies and their joint venture partners, under its accession to the World Trade Organisation.

China is now the third largest insurance market in Asia, between South Korea, which is second, and Australia, which is fourth and with about a tenth of the total premium income of $479bn of the leader, Japan. Xu Peihua, professor at the department of insurance, Fudan University in Shanghai, said the further opening of the Chinese market would force local companies to improve.

'Competition from foreign companies will make local insurers improve their credibility with customers [who are cautious because of previous widespread fraud]', said Mr Xu. The impact will not be immediate, as foreigners will still need licences to operate in newly opened cities and for each new product they wish to sell. 'I don't think it is going to happen overnight, by December 12, but over the next 6 to 12 months, you are going to see a lot of activity', said Stuart Leckie, a Hong Kong-based consultant. 'This is a relatively new industry in China and a lot of people are new to selling these products in China, and you are going to get lots and lots of problems along the way', said a Hong Kong-based analyst.

Foreigners now have a 14 per cent share of the market in the three major cities already open for business – Beijing, Guangzhou and Shanghai. But most of that is held by the local subsidiary of the American International Group. In the long term, the foreigners will concentrate on profitable niches, rather than market share. 'The issue won't be whether they get 30 per cent of the market, because they most certainly won't', said the Hong Kong-based analyst. 'The issue will be how good they are at marketing profitable products.'

Source: McGregor 2004. Reproduced with permission from Financial Times Limited.

Types of international penetration strategy

A major decision regarding the internationalisation of a service firm is the *international penetration strategy* of the firm, how the company enters the foreign markets. Although the decision on the market entry mode is not fixed and may be revised, it still determines the future steps of the internationalisation process and is therefore an important strategic decision. Overall, there are various types of international entry modes, as depicted in Figure 11.4, ranging between the two extremes 'service export' and 'affiliate'.[7]

A service export in the classic form of a *direct export* is only feasible in the case of hard services (see above). Then, the service (outcome) is transferred to a customer in a foreign country without the necessity of service resources in the home country. An example is the service of an institute conducting blood tests in one country for customers who are situated in other countries. Blood samples are collected and sent to a central blood bank and testing service and the results are sent back via email to the customers situated in the various countries. In this case, the service is delayed and the service can only be produced when the consignment of blood arrives for testing. In other circumstances, services can be provided electronically, such as providing databases for literature research, and thus the service export is a realistic strategy.

However, for many services, there is a need for a local presence of service resources. This local presence can be realised by *direct or indirect market entries*.[8]

A *direct entry* is realised by establishing the service organisation's own service facilities in the foreign country.[9] This entry mode concerns the other extreme on the list of entry modes and is conducted by establishing subsidiaries or affiliates in the foreign country. In this case, the provider fully owns the service provider outfits offering its services to the foreign customers. Establishing a new service organisation in foreign markets, is often associated with diverse problems, such as recruiting employees with experience in the foreign market or prejudices of the local customers. These trends are avoided by realising direct entry via company acquisitions.

When a service 'exporter' aims at facilitating management issues as well as decreasing the business risk associated with the internationalisation process, co-operation with experienced firms in the respective markets is initiated. There are various forms of co-operation which all represent the character of an *indirect entry* into the market. The corresponding entry modes are licence agreements, franchising systems, strategic alliances and joint venture; take for example the internationalisation achieved by car rental firms such as Avis, Hertz. While for the first two entry modes, the service provider can restrict its internationalisation

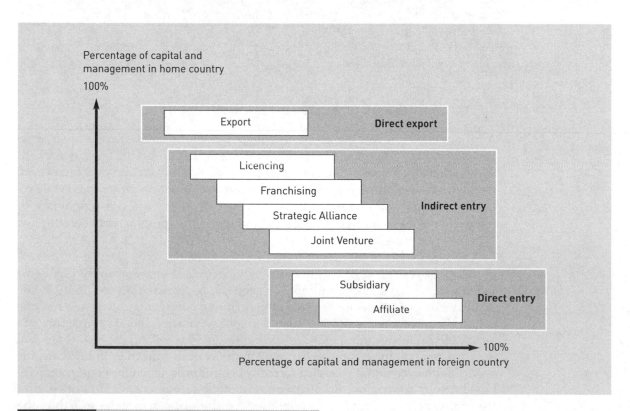

FIGURE 11.4 Types of international penetration strategy

to the export of its service idea, the latter two are associated with substantial financial and even physical investments in the foreign country.

Besides the service type – hard services versus soft services – there are various other *factors affecting a service provider's decision* regarding the international entry mode. In service industries where new technologies and e-commerce can be utilised for service delivery, service exports are easier to realise.[10] The firm size influences the firm's ability to finance a direct market entry.[11] For smaller firms with less financial power, indirect entry modes, such as licence agreements, are more feasible. Services marketing in action 11.4 shows the internationalisation strategy implemented by Tesco and its financial success.

SERVICES MARKETING IN ACTION 11.4:

Tesco's international success

Retailing is local. That maxim may well resonate with the several UK retailers that have retreated from unsuccessful ventures overseas. It is also one of the principles set out by Tesco, which yesterday reported underlying profit from its international operations up by one-fifth to £370m.

With a 29.5 per cent share of the UK grocery market, Tesco has had to look beyond the UK to drive growth. Stores in the UK still greatly outnumber those overseas, totalling about 80 per cent of the total 2,318 stores it operates. It has 261 stores in the rest of Europe and 179 in Asia. Hungary, Tesco's first foray abroad in 1994 – is set to be the biggest beneficiary of its new European expansion plans – with 16 new stores planned in 2005–06, taking the total number of stores in the country to 85.

Sir Terry Leahy, Tesco chief executive, is not known for being overly communicative about the secrets of Tesco's success. But he used the full-year results presentation to explain its approach to international expansion. Apart from being local, the key points were: being flexible about the requirements of each market; focusing and being prepared to make a long-term effort; having a multi-format approach that runs from convenience stores to hypermarkets; sharing skills and capabilities within the group; and taking time to build the brand.

This makes it seem deceptively easy. Looking at where expansion went wrong throws a different light on matters. Sir Terry mentioned three general errors: simply transplanting what worked very well in the domestic market; going overseas on the basis of opening a few stores in a capital city instead of being prepared for a long-term, large-scale commitment; and being distracted by weakness or instability in the home business.

The international growth has given Tesco plenty of opportunities to show its principles in action. In some European markets, such as the Czech Republic and Slovakia, it faced local price competition from German discounters last year, and had to respond by cutting prices to safeguard sales growth. The result was underlying international sales up 5.5 per cent in the first quarter.

Sources: Smith 2005; Killgren 2005. Reproduced with permission from Financial Times Limited.

Operational issues of an internationalisation strategy

The success of an international services marketing strategy not only depends on the international market entry mode, but also on the consideration of *operational issues* of international services marketing. In international services marketing, the geographical and cultural distances (see above) represent preconditions of the design and implementation of marketing instruments. All secondary processes of the *Service Value Chain* – directly influencing the primary processes – are affected by an international services marketing strategy:

- Regarding the *service product*, service customers in different countries evaluate service quality differently. Often, the relevance of service quality dimensions varies between countries. A further, special aspect of service quality evaluation is the so-called 'country of origin' effect[12] which affects service quality evaluations via consumer prejudices towards the foreign services and their providers. Another difference between countries with relevance to the service product concerns the normality of value-added services being offered to the customer. Regularly offered value-added services in a certain country represent essential quality characteristics for a new entrant.

- *Service pricing* is also affected by the international strategy of a service provider. Since in every country there are different levels of purchasing power affecting the demand for a service, the service provider's pricing strategy in a specific country must focus upon this purchasing power. McDonald's is assumed to be so professional in this field that the so-called 'Big Mac Index' considering the differences between prices for a Big Mac in different countries is interpreted as an indicator of a country's purchasing power (Services marketing in action 11.5).

- *Service communications* use several modal elements, words, names, colours, music, whose interpretation is affected by the culture in the foreign country. For example, in Western countries, 'white' is interpreted as being fresh or open, while in Japan it is perceived as a sign of mourning.

- Regarding *service delivery channels*, the practices of doing things in the foreign country must be taken into consideration. For example, in a country where internet usage by private households is not widespread, this avenue has less relevance than in countries with higher usage rates.

- In terms of international *human resources management*, a physcial presence in the respective country is essential when recruiting and training employees.[13]

- International *service tangibles* underlie comparable specifics, as do service communications. The design of service tangibles can influence the perceptions and emotions of customers differently.

- Regarding *service technology*, the acceptance of technology usage is an important determinant of a certain service technology in a country.

SERVICES MARKETING IN ACTION 11.5:

The Big Mac Index

The Economist's Big Mac Index is based on the theory of purchasing-power parity (PPP), the idea that exchange rates should move to equalise the prices of a basket of goods and services across different countries. The Economist's basket here is the Big Mac. For example, the cheapest burger on the chart is in China, at $1.26, compared with an average American price of $3. This implies that the yuan is 58% undervalued relative to its Big Mac dollar-PPP. On the same basis, the euro is 25% overvalued, the yen 17% undervalued (see Figure 11.5).

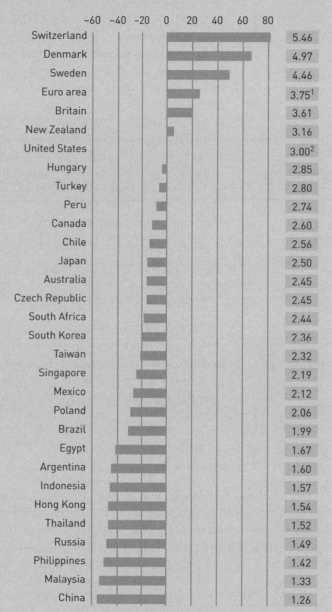

Switzerland	5.46
Denmark	4.97
Sweden	4.46
Euro area	3.75[1]
Britain	3.61
New Zealand	3.16
United States	3.00[2]
Hungary	2.85
Turkey	2.80
Peru	2.74
Canada	2.60
Chile	2.56
Japan	2.50
Australia	2.45
Czech Republic	2.45
South Africa	2.44
South Korea	2.36
Taiwan	2.32
Singapore	2.19
Mexico	2.12
Poland	2.06
Brazil	1.99
Egypt	1.67
Argentina	1.60
Indonesia	1.57
Hong Kong	1.54
Thailand	1.52
Russia	1.49
Philippines	1.42
Malaysia	1.33
China	1.26

Legend: Local currency under (–)/over (+), Valuation against the dollar, %, at market exchange rate (13 December 2004), [1]weighted average of member countries, [2]average of four cities

Figure 11.5 Big Mac Index

Source: The Economist 2004.

Strategies regarding other providers

Service providers concentrate not only on the consumer parts of the markets but also on the provider side of the markets: A firm's behaviour is determined by the behaviour of other providers. The most important field regarding other providers is the competition, providers of the same or comparable services as the provider. In some service industries there are smooth transitions between markets (e.g. between banks and insurance within the financial service industry), and it is often difficult to state categorically whether another service provider is a competitor, a supplier or a customer firm. Thus, a service provider's behaviour regarding other service firms is differentiated regarding whether the provider applies innovative (active) or imitative (passive) behaviour.[14] Further, the firm's behaviour can be evasive or confrontational.[15] A combination of these two dimensions results in four types of provider-related strategies:

- co-operation: passive/confronting (joint ventures);
- conflict: active/confronting (classic aggressive behaviour regarding competitors);
- evasion: active/evasive (innovation);
- adaptation: passive/evasive (price reductions when a competitor reduces prices).

While the value-oriented marketing presented in this book deals with several aspects of conflict, evasion and adaptation strategies, in this chapter we concentrate on the co-operation strategy. In several service industries, providers aim to create value through co-operation with other service providers. Two approaches to co-operating are emphasised in this chapter: service outsourcing and service networks.

Service outsourcing strategy

An important strategy regarding other service providers in a market relevant to the service firm is the outsourcing strategy. Outsourcing means eliminating a process from its own value chain, by not conducting the respective process itself any more, but letting this process be conducted by another service provider (e.g. outsourcing of a call centre by a bank). From a strategic perspective, outsourcing is an important mechanism to ensure a service provider concentrates on its core competencies (see also Services marketing in action 11.6).[16] By outsourcing non-core processes to be delivered by other providers, the provider's managerial, technological and financial competencies can focus on the firm's most important processes for delivering value to the customer. More specifically, service outsourcing affects value creation in several ways:[17]

SERVICES MARKETING IN ACTION 11.6:

Citibank's technology outsourcing

At the end of the 1990s, a quiet but radical revolution occurred within Citibank regarding the technology system of the bank. For 30 years, Citibank was a technology hothouse, a place where many of today's leading financial technologists got their technology training – foremost among them Citibank chairman and CEO John S. Reed. The bank is credited with inventing or rolling out on an unprecedented scale such now-ubiquitous banking technologies as branch-wide networks of automated teller machines, credit card authorisation systems, electronic payment networks and transaction processing systems.

At the end of the 1990s, however, Citibank began to unwind its centralised technology bedrock, estimated to cost over $1.8 billion annually – the highest in the industry – in favour of a more decentralised technology organisation. Of all financial services organisations that have structured major technology outsourcing strategies in recent years, perhaps most fascinating to observe is the 'standards'-based technology outsourcing strategy now unfolding at Citibank. If all technology providers both within and outside the bank 'are working to the same set of standards – on the network, the desktop, the LAN – the entire infrastructure, then you have control, you can communicate uniformly with suppliers, with members of your team, with customers', said Stan Welland, Citibank's global technology infrastructure chief.

One example of this outsourcing strategy was a $750 million deal with AT&T solutions in 1998 to consolidate 11 disparate global data networks the bank had used into a single new network managed by AT&T. It was the single largest global networking outsourcing agreement in the banking industry at the time.

Source: Levinsohn 1998.

- The outsourcing firm – the firm offering the outsourced service – is supposed to be able to deliver the respective process *more efficiently* due to superior management skills and technology than the original provider.[18] While the outsourced process is not the core competency of the original firm, it is indeed the core competency of the outsourcing firm. In the case of a call centre operator: the outsourcing firm concentrates on the process of 'handling calls' and trains its employees to ensure professionalism; the bank, the original provider, can now focus on what it does best, managing money.

- A further objective for a service provider in outsourcing certain processes is to *reduce capacity problems*. For example, the call centre of a bank illustrates the capacity problems described in Chapter 10. When the bank does not manage the call centre by itself, the problem is transferred to the outsourcing company, which then charges the bank a fee for these services. These call centres often offer services to several providers, thus achieving economies of scale, high levels of efficiency and correct capacity utilisation.

- Outsourcing specific services helps service providers to *reduce investments in new technology* as well as reducing the risk involved with these investments. In the case of the call centre, regular investments in new call centre technologies are no longer a decision problem for the bank.

- On the revenue side, as the outsourcing firm has specialist knowledge of the process which was outsourced by the actual service provider, it can ensure a *higher service quality for the respective process* than the actual provider. In consequence, customer satisfaction and retention might be increased resulting in higher revenues.

- Thus the service provider is able to concentrate on the *core competencies*, and its employees are better able to serve the customers at a *high-quality level*, a bank employee now concentrates on advising the customer instead of handling simple account queries, with greater efficiencies being achieved. Interestingly, by outsourcing, both the outsourced processes as well as the remaining processes can be improved.

Outsourcing is perceived as a strategic decision. Consequently, it is important for service providers to apply a *systematic approach* to the outsourcing decision. The following steps are a guide to the outsourcing decision (see Table 11.2):[19]

- evaluating whether it is a valuable strategy for the service firm to outsource processes against the strategic goals of the firm;

- analysing and assessing information of services outsourced and service deliverables, defining the outcomes which are expected from a certain process;

- selecting an appropriate outsourcing firm;

- agreeing on a contract which allows flexibility for the service provider to handle unplanned events;

- developing a transition plan for transferring the outsourced processes to the outsourcing firm;

- developing guidelines for the reappointment of the outsourcing firm;

- developing a service contract that clearly stipulates expected service standards and desired outcomes.

From a services marketing perspective, outsourcing processes by service providers or manufacturers allows *opportunities for new service development* and the foundation of new service firms. By an increase in the importance of processes and the increasing relevance of technologies in services (and manufacturing), the outsourcing firms' process specialism could observe a growing demand. One example is the call centre industry which has risen exponentially in the past decade.

TABLE 11.2 Steps of systematic service outsourcing

Steps	Actions
1. Evaluate whether outsourcing is a viable strategy for the organisation given its current strategic goals and objectives.	1. Develop a clear understanding of the strategy for the function being outsourced. Consider the impact on achievement or organisational mission and strategy, including cost, quality, flexibility and timeliness. Consider changes in the environment that require a change in strategy.
2. Analyse and access information on services outsourced and service deliverables.	2. Identify services to be outsoured and the expected level of performance. Ensure a clear definition of services to be outsourced and their value. Protect and retain core services and capabilities. Be clear about the scale of costs and potential saving by including all costs.
3. Select the appropriate vendor.	3. Identify the number of viable vendors, and document vendor's technical and managerial capabilities, culture and fit. Explicitly state and agree on expected service levels.
4. Secure a contract that protects the organisation yet is flexible enough to accommodate unplanned events.	4. Negotiate an agreement that is fair and equitable. Specify expected performance from each partner and how it will be measured and compensated and how disputes will be settled. Specify contingency clause and how subcontractors will be managed.
5. Develop a transition plan for transferring outsourced activities to vendor.	5. Establish a temporary transition team to organise and supervise the transition. Involve employees that may be affected, and make sure that key executives and managers from the outsourced function or department are involved.
6. Develop guidelines for reappointment of vendor.	6. Review service provisions in the contract, and measure actual outcomes against expected outcomes to decide if vendor's performance warrants reappointment.

Source: Roberts 2001, p. 245. Used with permission from Health Administration Press.

Although service outsourcing is associated with a list of value effects, as discussed above, there are also some *risks* involved with the decision to outsource certain service processes:

- Defining exactly what the core competencies of a firm are is not always obvious. Service providers (and also manufacturers) tend to see their core competencies in the products and internal processes. However, most service providers' core competency is – due to the characteristics of services – customer contact (as with the interaction and relationship processes in the Service Value Chain). When outsourcing customer contact, e.g. via call centres, there is the risk of losing information about the customer and also reducing influence on the customer.

- When service employees perceive it as their job to serve a customer comprehensively, outsourcing services might lower the morale of these employees.

- There is some risk involved in letting the outsourcing firm handle the customer relationships, as the firm has access to sensitive customer and company information.

- There is a risk of dependency of the provider upon the outsourcing firm.

Service network strategy

Nature and value creation of service networks

One strategy for service providers to utilise the relationships with other providers such as competitors, suppliers or customer firms is a service networking strategy. *Service networking* involves co-operation with other service providers regarding specific internal or external processes. Internal processes concern the provision of service resources by more than one firm (more or less without the customer's recognising the different providers). External processes concern activities where the customer is involved: the customer booking a flight to Houston, Texas, with British Airways – by flying first to New York with British Airways itself and then on to Houston with America West Airlines. Within a network, several providers take several tasks of service delivery – a constellation which can be labelled as '*out-partnering*'[20] instead of 'out-sourcing', since certain providers let certain partners conduct certain activities in order to realise an overall service delivery. For an example of a service network, see Services marketing in action 11.7.

A networking strategy has several positive value effects for a service provider which concern both revenues and cost. On an aggregate level, 'network companies continue to outperform because they own fewer assets, leverage the resources of partner companies, require less capital and return higher revenue per employee than conventionally run companies'.[21] But how are these financial

SERVICES MARKETING IN ACTION 11.7:

Advertising agency network of the year

The advertising industry typifies an industry where providers are organised in networks. As an example, one of these networks is TBWA – named the '2004 Global Agency Network of the Year' by *Advertising Age* magazine.

'This recognition is always nice and to be honored is an important milestone in the life of the . . . network. It's also a terrific affirmation of the success we have achieved over the last several years, and proves that we're founded on 237 centres of excellence – not just a handful', said Jean-Marie Dru, president and CEO, TBWA Worldwide, addressing the TBWA network with 237 network members.

The network members are partly TBWA affiliates and partly independent agencies. Moreover, they are distributed all over the world, e.g. 'Media Direction OMD' in South Africa, in China, TBWA China and 'Tequila China', and in the UK 16 agencies, e.g. TBWA Edinburgh, TBWA UK Group, London, Maher Bird Associates, London, and MKP, Manchester.

The network won the award as a result of outperforming its competitors in four categories:

- net growth (business wins and substantial organic account expansion/contraction);

- agency management (hirings, restructures, substantial new initiatives, operational or strategic change);

- creative quality (both excellence in traditional creative and creative innovation, such as new ways in which agencies have engaged consumers);

- marketing effectiveness (achieving substantive measurable results for clients).

Sources: Miller 2005; TBWA 2005.

results realised by installing a network with other service providers? A positive *effect on revenues* can be realised using the following levers (see Figure 11.6):

- By installing a network with other providers, a service firm can *ensure demand* due to the increased service offering/range. By being a member of the network, a service firm extends its ability to fulfil its customers' needs and expectations. In the airline example, a customer wanting to fly from London to Houston would necessarily have to contact a second airline if British Airways did not co-operate with other airlines. This would result in a higher search cost for the customer, resulting in lower convenience and lower satisfaction. Moreover, the customer would extend its evoked set of possible airlines to choose by involuntary 'testing' of a new airline. Conversely, by being able to offer the entire flight from London to Houston, British Airways ensures the customer's loyalty by improving the customer's service experience and pre-venting a conscious perception of competitor providers by the customer.

- Regarding customer acquisition, a service provider possibly extends its *acquisition potential* by co-operating with providers that have closer contact with the consumers or by implementing a wide distribution system. A life insurance company which does not have a personal distribution system multiplies its acquisition potential by co-operating with a retail bank which already has an extensive distribution system with huge customer bases and direct contact with these customers.

A networking strategy for service firms not only affects value via revenues but also on the *cost* side (see Figure 11.6):

- Service providers co-operating with others realise *cost synergies* across diverse processes. Co-operating with other providers over purchasing supplies helps to ensure bigger amounts of the supply good or service and results in lower prices due to increased amounts and market power. One example of this is the bakeries that co-operate in purchasing associations in order to purchase flour and other materials.

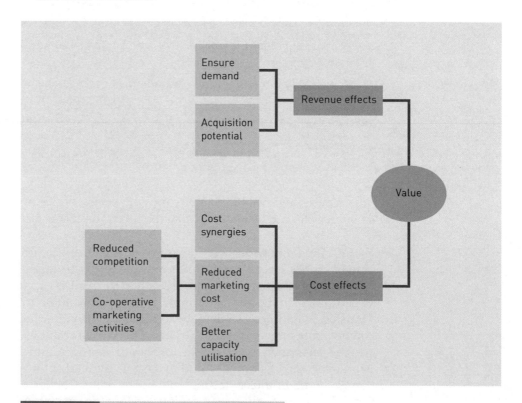

FIGURE 11.6   Value creation by service networks

- Service firms aligning in networks partly reduce competition between themselves. *Reducing competition* results in reduced cost for the providers. Elements of the marketing activities which are applied in a confrontational, competitive situation (aggressive advertising), are reduced in a co-operative market situation.

- Furthermore, some marketing activities are conducted by the co-operating providers together in the form of *co-operative marketing campaigns*, which also result in reduced marketing costs for the individual service provider. The airlines in an alliance often reduce their own marketing budget whilst on the alliance level advertising is conducted jointly, for the entire group.

- A better *capacity utilisation* can be realised by using networks. By sharing service resources with other providers, deviations of individual providers can be averaged by the network. Service providers that install a call centre together with other providers compensate their own usage deviations by those of the other providers.

These potential value effects of service networks have resulted in intensive efforts for building networks in several service industries. Services marketing in action 11.8 illustrates the value effects to which airlines aspire through their alliances. The various value effects are relevant for different types of networks.

SERVICES MARKETING IN ACTION 11.8

The alliances battle

Since May 1997, when Star Alliance was founded, airlines have been confederating in international co-operations. Increasing numbers of co-operations arose because airlines realised that by this strategy competition could be reduced and markets more or less strictly defined. The airlines within such a network align their flight timetables, shift passengers where a partner airline has a better offer, and co-operate in customer retention programmes as well as in purchasing materials and aeroplanes. The passenger profits from this networking using internationally aligned timetables, short transfer times and value-delivering retention programmes. However, one aspect the airlines liked in particular was the reduction of competition in markets which had recently been opened up to competition.

The competition of airlines changed into a competition between airline alliances (see Figure 11.7 and Figure 11.8 for the alliances' market shares in 2003). At the peak there were five alliances. The alliance demise started with Swiss International Airlines closing its co-operation 'Qualifier' in order to switch transitionally (today Swiss is an affiliate of Lufthansa and thus part of 'Star Alliance') as a junior partner to the network 'Oneworld' of British Airways and American Airlines. Air France and KLM subsequently merged, resulting in the closing down of the network 'Wings' with Continental, KLM and Northwest, and KLM's integration into Air France's network 'Skyteam'.

This merger relegated 'Oneworld' to third place in the alliances ranking. This alliance is not as successful as 'Star Alliance' because its main members, British Airways and American Airlines, do not have an Open-Sky agreement, resulting in missing synergy effects on North Atlantic traffic.

▶

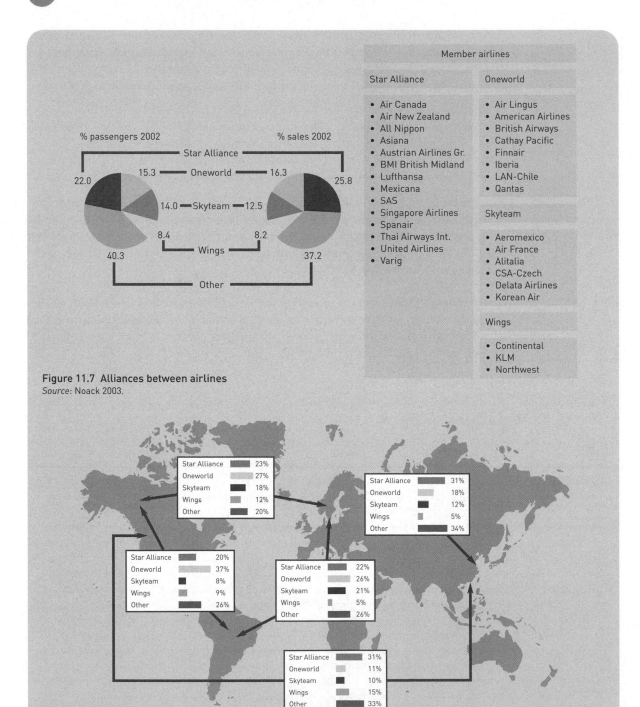

Figure 11.7 Alliances between airlines
Source: Noack 2003.

Figure 11.8 Capacity shares in the intercontinental airline market
Source : Noack 2003.

For the international airline market, it is expected that there will be further mergers, and there will remain four or five international EU airlines, completed by niche airlines in the low-cost segment as well as regional airlines.

Source: Noack 2003.

Types of networks

Networks between service providers concern co-operation relating to specific service processes. These two concepts, 'co-operation' and 'processes' are the basis for differentiating different network types with different value consequences and consequences for value-oriented services marketing.

Regarding the co-operation between network partners a differentiation of centrifugal and polycentric networks is made.[22]

Centrifugal networks are controlled strategically by a so-called 'focal firm' which represents the centre of the network. This firm dominates the network due to its size, market access and/or resource superiority. The focal firm determines the strategy and the kind and content of the inter-organisational relationships. Often, these networks are planned on a continuous basis and aim at open and assuring competitively relevant potentials.[23] They exhibit stable inter-organisational relationships which are often defined within framework agreements in order to ensure that the network-specific investments of the individual firms are profitable.[24]

Polycentral networks are a loose association of mostly smaller or medium-sized firms. In most cases, there is no strategic leadership by one partner, and balanced mutual dependencies exist. The inter-organisational relationships are merely informal.[25] Often, the co-operation has a project-like character.[26]

In terms of the *processes* which concern the service network, different network types can be differentiated according to the *stage in the supply chain* which is concerned with the co-operation. A simplified view of the supply chain differentiates between relationships to suppliers, competitors and customers. Allowing the simultaneous installation of co-operation on more than one level leads to three *types of service networks*:

- *Co-operating with suppliers* is often conducted in order to increase the efficiency of supply processes which represent a preparation for the actual service delivery, for example co-operation between an airline and a caterer. This co-operation can help to improve the service, by speeding up the service provision, or to reduce costs by lowering storage costs as a result of improved efficiency in consumer response systems between retailer and manufacturers.

- *Co-operating with competitors* mainly aims at reducing competition and widening the service range offered as well as realising cost synergies. The airline market is a typical example of a market where networks between competitors can be observed.

- Following the basic definition of networking as *co-operation between firms, co-operating with customers* concerns a service provider's collaboration with other service providers which utilise the delivered service for their own service delivery. This type concerns the converse perspective from the first type – an airline co-operating with a travel agency. Moreover, a network which integrates *end consumers* is applied by some service providers in order to get a closer contact with end consumers and their needs and expectations.

Figure 11.9 illustrates the three types of service networks according to the supply chain for an airline and more specifically for British Airways.[27]

Service providers engage in the type of network which is most relevant for their own *value creation*, in terms of the competitive situation in the respective market. When there is competition amongst the suppliers in a market, a provider will co-operate with suppliers. In competitive situations where service providers compete heavily with their own resources, co-operation with competitors is sought after, and when individual customers influence the competition, co-operation with them is essential in order to create value.

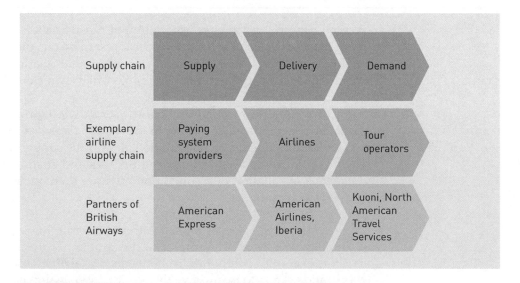

FIGURE 11.9 Partners of British Airways in the supply chain

Evaluation of networks

When a service provider aims to install a service network with other service providers, it is important to be aware of the criteria for evaluating potential partners and to decide on a specific partner. The specific criteria differ according to various attributes such as the industry concerned or the processes which are the object of the co-operation. On an aggregate level, three central *dimensions of the quality of co-operation between firms* were identified (see Figure 11.10):[28]

- The quality of a co-operation agreement is determined by the prevention of, or the *harmonisation of conflict*. In every instance of co-operation, conflicts can arise since the co-operating partners may have conflicting objectives, e.g. regarding the question of how costs generated by one partner's activities for the network are compensated. When a network succeeds in handling these conflicts by finding acceptable compromises instead of formal agreements, the result will be improved partnership quality.

- The more interdependent the relationship between firms is, the more stable it is. The *interdependence between partners* is determined by the degree to which a firm's realising its objective depends on the partner's behaviour. For example a car rental company co-operating with an airline depends on the airline's willingness to promote the co-operation in its own communications.

- The quality of a partnership further depends on the *information exchange* between the partners. The frequent exchange of relevant information is an indicator of the partner's willingness to co-operate and thus an indicator of the partnership quality. A travel agency which informs an airline about complaints from customers regarding the airline delivers important information for the airline to improve its services – assuming the airline is willing to receive and utilise such information.

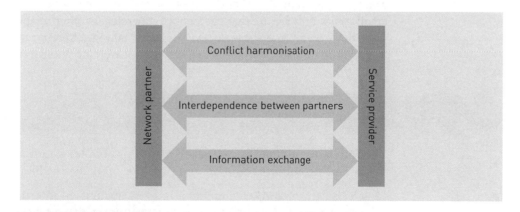

| FIGURE 11.10 | Dimensions of the quality of cooperation between firms |

Source: after Wiertz *et al.* 2004.

Risks of service networks

Although networks established by service providers help realise various value effects, the pursuit of a network strategy is to a certain extent also associated with risk:[29]

- Being part of a network reduces the freedom of choice and strategy flexibility of a service provider. When engaging in a network following a quality-oriented strategy, the member firm does not have the choice of following a price leadership strategy.

- An important quality dimension of a network is the openness between the network members regarding strategic relevant information. However, these open communications increase the chances that competitors who are not members of the network or – more complex – competitors who are part of the network regarding certain processes, but not regarding others, gain information relevant to the competition between the network members.

- Often, the processes which relate to the co-operation have to be redesigned in order to even out the process diversity before installing the network. This process redesign may possibly affect other processes of the service provider which are dependent on, or influence, the network process and therefore possibly induce negative value effects through these influences.

- Comparable with the higher inflexibility of huge corporations in contrast with small firms, networks are also less flexible in terms of their strategic behaviour in contrast to the individual service provider, due to the interdependence of the network partners and complicated decision rules regarding the processes which are the object of the co-operation.

The thoughts in this chapter demonstrate that service providers influence their value creation not only by the management of concrete customer relationships and interactions but – on a more strategic level – also by taking different market decisions, such as the internationalisation decision, service outsourcing and service networks.

 ## Summary

The following lessons can be taken from this chapter about a service provider's behaviour regarding consumer and provider markets (see Figure 11.11):

1. Decisions on market segment strategies such as an internationalisation strategy, service outsourcing and service networks can all have significant effects on value, as well as affecting the service provider's behaviour towards its customers, the market and other suppliers in other markets.

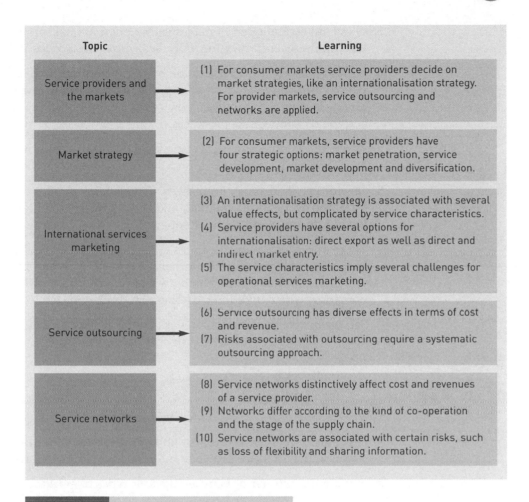

Topic	Learning
Service providers and the markets	(1) For consumer markets service providers decide on market strategies, like an internationalisation strategy. For provider markets, service outsourcing and networks are applied.
Market strategy	(2) For consumer markets, service providers have four strategic options: market penetration, service development, market development and diversification.
International services marketing	(3) An internationalisation strategy is associated with several value effects, but complicated by service characteristics. (4) Service providers have several options for internationalisation: direct export as well as direct and indirect market entry. (5) The service characteristics imply several challenges for operational services marketing.
Service outsourcing	(6) Service outsourcing has diverse effects in terms of cost and revenue. (7) Risks associated with outsourcing require a systematic outsourcing approach.
Service networks	(8) Service networks distinctively affect cost and revenues of a service provider. (9) Networks differ according to the kind of co-operation and the stage of the supply chain. (10) Service networks are associated with certain risks, such as loss of flexibility and sharing information.

FIGURE 11.11 Learning summary for Chapter 11

2. Regarding its market segment strategy, a service provider has four options: market penetration, service development, market development and diversification. Market penetration strategies as well as service development have been treated in detail earlier in this book. Diversification is not the focus of this book. Market development, especially internationalisation, is a strategically relevant decision, still to be discussed.

3. International services marketing is influenced by value considerations on the one hand and complicated by service characteristics on the other.

4. There are several types of international market penetration strategies ranging on a continuum from export via indirect entry to direct entry with distinct advantages and disadvantages.

5. There are several operational issues for international services marketing concerning the secondary value processes within the Service Value Chain.

6. Service outsourcing affects value by implementing more efficient processes, which result in reduced capacity problems, reduced investments in new technologies as well as a higher service quality of both the outsourced process and the remaining core processes.

7. Nevertheless outsourcing is also associated with some risks, resulting in the need to apply a systematic approach to decisions on outsourcing.

8. Service networks affect both revenues (ensuring greater demand proportion, increased acquisition potential) and costs (lower prices, fewer capacity problems, reducing competition, co-operative marketing campaigns).

9. There are several network types according to the kind of co-operation (centrifugal versus polycentric networks) and to the stage in the supply chain which is concerned with the networking (co-operation with suppliers, co-operation with competitors, co-operation with customers).

10. Service networks are involved with different risks for network members, like a loss in flexibility and the risk of sharing information.

Knowledge questions

1. Explain the relevance of internationalisation, outsourcing and networking strategies for a service provider and how these tools are linked to each other.

2. Explain the differences between the four types of market segment strategies.

3. Describe the value considerations which lead to the enforcement of service internationalisation.

4. Outline how international services marketing is impacted upon by the characteristics of services.

5. Describe and differentiate the various market entry modes for penetrating foreign markets.

6. Explain how an internationalisation strategy of a service provider interacts with the secondary value processes of the service provider.

7. How does outsourcing create value?

8. What steps can a service provider follow when taking an outsourcing decision?

9. What are the risks involved in an outsourcing decision?

10. Explain the value effects of service networking.

11. Describe the different types of networks. What are their advantages and disadvantages?

12. Which dimensions are used to evaluate the quality of a partnership between service providers?

13. Explain the risks involved with service networking.

Application and discussion questions

1. For each of the four market segment strategy types, find one real-life example of a firm that realised the strategy in focus.

2. Collect examples of hard and soft services and discuss whether an internationalisation strategy for the respective service is feasible or not.

3. Suppose you were the owner of a café bar and you plan market entry into a foreign country. Discuss the feasibility of the various market entry modes.

4. Spin out the café bar example. What would be the operational issues you would have to deal with?

5. Discuss decisions to employ an external call centre for customer requests in a retail bank and an internet research database. Define your answers based upon the associated value and risk considerations.

6. How does an airline's membership of an airline network affect its value creation?

7. What networking options does your university have? Discuss them considering the different network types.

8. Imagine you are the owner of a small niche music store. Discuss your options of service networking considering different network types. Apply the partnership quality dimensions and outline how you would potentially evaluate your optional network partners. What risks would be involved with the network for you and your store?

CASE STUDY: IKEA'S GLOBALISATION STRATEGY

For the past five years, IKEA has grown steadily. The company owns 180 stores worldwide and realised 31 billion euros in sales in 2004. An important facet of this growth is the internationalisation strategy. In 2004, the top five countries in terms of sales were Germany (20 per cent), UK (12 per cent), USA (11 per cent), France (9 per cent) and Sweden (8 per cent).

However, IKEA itself is unsatisfied with its progress in the USA. Ikea has 20 US stores, opening its first in 1985, but initially it struggled with a reputation for poor service and difficulty in sourcing goods locally. 'We were still very small then. We started late compared with Europe, and then we had a few years of consolidation when we didn't open any stores at all; it's only in the last few years that we have started to open stores again', Mr Dahlvig, IKEA's CEO, says.

In Europe, expansion is targeted at Germany, France, Spain and Italy, but in the UK, disputes with planning authorities meant that the group has not opened a new store in England since 1999. Last month, the government rejected IKEA's latest attempt outside Stockport in north-west England. The government fears large-scale out-of-town retail developments will kill city centres and increase car traffic.

Mr Dahlvig, says he is 'disappointed and frustrated' by the government's attitude and that the group should have a further 10 stores in the country. Next year will see an opening in Edmonton, north London, made possible by the special development status of the site, but no others are in the pipeline.

Further afield, IKEA is opening in Japan, while sales at its two Chinese stores rose 50 per cent last year. The group is hoping for 10 more in the next six to eight years, and Mr Dahlvig says South Korea is the next logical step in the region.

However, while many Western companies are moving into China, few are as bold as IKEA when it comes to Russia. Apart from stores in Moscow and St Petersburg, in April the group opened in Kazan, capital of Tatarstan. 'It's really testing out the provinces to see how it works. It's still early days. There are a lot of things to settle in there, teething problems, and so I can't give you forecasts. But it's a very interesting endeavour', says Mr Dahlvig. 'We will probably open two or three stores in the provinces now instead of one, to see how it works. We are looking at 10 cities and we will pick the ones that produce the best offer and site.'

IKEA is also moving into the Ukraine – a decision has been made to open a store in Kiev and a site is being located, Mr Dahlvig says. 'We are not a public company and we can afford to take more long-term decisions, not just look at very quick revenues. You can take all these as an example of where we believe very strongly that going early into these markets has some advantages. One is that you can acquire good locations at reasonable prices, and then international competition is not too heavy so you can establish brand recognition', he says. 'With 180 stores worldwide, one store in Kiev is not going to make or break the business if it fails.'

Source: George 2004. Reproduced with permission from Financial Times Limited.

CASE STUDY: NETWORKING AT NEXCOM

Nexcom Online Services was founded in 1996 and developed from an internet agency emphasising the design of websites of industrial customers to an IT system provider with service offerings ranging from 'mediaservices' (internet solutions, multimedia) through 'application services' (e-business, communities, database web applications) to 'systems services' (e.g. network, hosting and security services).

Nexcom's first orders were initiated by private contacts of the firm's founder, Markus Schewe. Only when co-operation with the press agency 'Pressehaus Stanossek' was established did the demand for the firm's services stabilise. The agency's director facilitated access to business networks in the information and communication technology industry, e.g. to industry associations or the 'Multimedia' division of Deutsche Telekom. The market leader in the German telecommunications market was Nexcom's first important partner. Since 1998, the partners have provided their customers with integrated multimedia solutions, ranging from website design to intranet and datawarehouse design. The roles are clearly defined. Deutsche Telecom delivers the technical know-how and the hardware, while Nexcom develops individual design concepts as well as the programming. Comparable partnerships and networks with other organisations could establish a wide network of business relationships.

For Markus Schewe, a critical success factor for SMEs in service industries is the ability to provide the customer with comprehensive all-in-one solutions as well as organisational flexibility, especially by realising synergies out of the established networks.

As a result of the established networks, Nexcom can maintain its internal success factors, which for Markus Schewe are the small company size (14 employees) and its creative team character. Every employee knows the other's projects and can contribute to them. By this, Nexcom realises optimal utilisation of its service resources.

The relationships with the external partners have been strengthened based on personal network relationships as well as positive project experiences. The latter were used to initiate new projects and business relationships. The embedding of the programmers and web designers in their professional networks offers access to various 'Communities of Practice'. The efficient organisation of Nexcom allows it to absorb newly required knowledge and distribute this information throughout the firm, effectively.

Source: Welge and Borghoff 2003.

Notes

[1] See Gummesson 2002.
[2] See Ansoff 1966.
[3] See Nigh *et al*. 1986; Terpstra and Yu 1988.
[4] See Clark *et al*. 1996.
[5] See Erramilli 1990.
[6] See Ekeledo and Sivakumar 1998.
[7] Based on Meissner and Gerber 1980.
[8] See Grönroos 1999.

9   See Grönroos 1999.
10 See Ekeledo and Sivakumar 1998.
11 See Winsted and Patterson 1998.
12 See Javalgi *et al*. 2003.
13 See Erramilli and Rao 1993.
14 See Miller and Friesen 1982.
15 See Easton 1987.
16 See Roberts 2001.
17 See for various aspects Quinn 1999.
18 See Roberts 2001.
19 See Roberts 2001.
20 See Peters 1994.
21 See Hacki and Lighton 2001.
22 See Stauss and Bruhn 2003.
23 See Jarillo 1993; Sydow 1992.
24 See Letmathe 2001, p. 552.
25 See Sydow 1995, p. 630.
26 See Letmathe 2001, p. 553.
27 For information about British Airways' partners, see British Airways 2005.
28 See Wiertz *et al*. 2004.
29 See Bruhn 2002b.

12 Services marketing and the service firm: Implementing and controlling services marketing

Services marketing, by definition, focuses on the external stakeholders, and principally on the customers. By managing the interactions and relationships with the customers, value is created. However, successful value-oriented services marketing is determined by strong interdependencies between all stakeholders within the service firm.

In order to be able to produce value, it is not enough that a marketing manager takes some decisions. As has already been discussed on various occasions and especially in Chapter 9 about service resources, the employees and above all the customer contact employees play an important role in service delivery. However, a service employee is not an isolated individual, focused only on individual interactions and relationships with the customer. In most service industries, service employees' behaviour is even more influenced by internal factors, e.g. the colleagues' and supervisors' behaviours, as well as the systems and the culture of the firm. All these are factors of *services marketing implementation* which *support the realisation of the services marketing concept* in the firm.

The firm not only supports services marketing implementation, conversely, services marketing supports the firm's efforts to create value. As has been explored in detail earlier in this book, services marketing contributes to a firm's value creation in many diverse ways. However, services marketing only represents a subgroup of the value drivers of a firm, and not every services marketing activity contributes to a firm's value to the same extent. Since financial resources are frequently scarce in companies, service providers conduct an *examination of services marketing activities according to their value contribution*, as an all-firm activity. This is the task of controlling a firm. Thus, next to services marketing implementation, we explore the possibilities of *services marketing control* as a second element in the connection between services marketing and the rest of the firm.

Based on these considerations, Chapter 12 highlights three learning objectives (see Figure 12.1):

1. Getting to know the value contribution of services marketing implementation and control.

2. Understanding the company-internal factors which support the implementation of value-oriented services marketing,

3. Learning how service providers control their value-oriented services marketing activities.

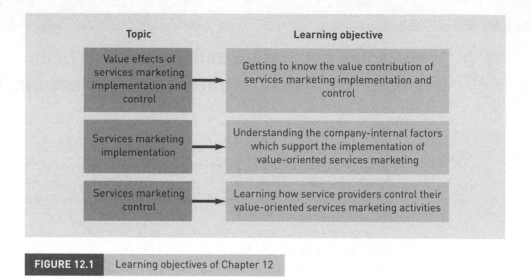

FIGURE 12.1   Learning objectives of Chapter 12

Value contribution of services marketing implementation and control

In contrast to the value effects of the primary and secondary value processes, the value effects of the internal preconditions of services marketing are more indirect. In fact, implementation and control support the systematic realisation of the activities in the value processes of the provider. More specifically:

- Considering and managing *implementation factors of services marketing* not only facilitates the realisation of value-oriented marketing, it also makes it possible. To illustrate this, take one important implementation factor as an example: company culture. When a service firm is characterised by a company culture which is not customer-oriented and where the top management ignores the opinions of the subordinates, it is unlikely that the employees will behave in a value-oriented sense. At least, they will not aim to contribute to a realisation of the firm's objectives. Furthermore, they will not behave in a customer-oriented manner as they are not motivated to be customer focused. The consequences are dissatisfied customers, slower service processes with the respective negative consequences for firm value.

- *Services marketing control* is the core of a recursive process: controlling both examines the value creation by services marketing activities and, through this, delivers the basis for the planning of future value-oriented measures. Services marketing control provides value-oriented performance figures which allow the management to assess whether the activities of the service firm contribute to firm value and the reasons for the value effects. Since knowledge is an important determinant for management decisions, controlling delivers the fundamentals for value creation through services marketing.

Implementing services marketing: Adapting a service firm's structure, systems and culture

Value-oriented services marketing underlies the principle that all activities aim to create value for the firm. According to the interdependence between the Service Value Chain and the service profit chain, value creation through marketing is realised when the firm is successful in delivering value to the customers whose behaviour in turn helps create financial value to the firm (see Chapter 2 for the link between the Service Value Chain and service profit chain). Based on this premise, the services marketing decisions consider the value implications of marketing activities. Interactions and relationships with customers are supposed to create value, as are the secondary value activities which concern the definition, delivery and communication of service value as well as the value-oriented employment of service resources. These decisions and activities are not isolated from other decisions in the firm. For example, the budget for services marketing represents the frame within which services marketing managers can take decisions. Consequently, when the top management pursues other strategically important topics, services marketing might have to manage on a reduced budget.

This argument concerns the support of the service firm for the *implementation of value-oriented services marketing*. The design of the service firm in general determines the possibilities for value-oriented services marketing. There are three main features of this 'design':

- structure of the service firm;

- systems of the service firm;

- culture of the service firm.

The design of these features can take on a variety of forms; from a value perspective, their design can be more or less value-oriented. Being value-oriented means in this context, whether a firm's structure, systems and culture are designed in such a way as to enable or support value creation by services marketing, i.e. whether the implementation drivers support services marketing's ability to deliver value to the customers and in turn create financial value for the company. Consequently, service firms which follow a value-oriented strategy regularly audit their structures, systems and culture regarding their value-orientation and undertake adaptations if necessary and possible.

Value-oriented company organisation

The company organisation describes first who is responsible for what tasks in a firm, e.g. who is responsible for measuring service quality, and how the different tasks are prioritised, e.g. does the person who is responsible for service quality measurement report to the person who is responsible for managing service quality or vice versa or are they both independent from each other? These questions concern the company structure as a first part of a company's organisation. The organisation structure arranges the different tasks in a firm. Since tasks often overlap, a second important part of a firm's organisation concerns the links between the different tasks. These links are defined by the process organisation of the firm.

Structural organisation of a service firm

The **structural organisation** of the firm describes how the activities and responsibilities in a firm are arranged. Typical aspects of structural organisation are the definition of organisational entities, e.g. departments, the allocation of responsibilities to these entities and the authorities between and within these departments. Over the course of time, three *basic types of organisational structures* have emerged:[1]

- functional organisation;
- object organisation;
- matrix organisation.

When a functional organisation is applied in a service firm, the second level of the organisational chart under the top management is determined by homogeneous groups of activities. Typical functional activities in a service firm are human resources, controlling, operations, service, IT or marketing.

A functional organisation's *advantages and disadvantages* are diverse. From the perspective of value-oriented services marketing, the following aspects appear to be most relevant:

- Functional organisations result in clear company structures. It is well defined who is responsible for which tasks, such as who is responsible for managing customer interactions and relationships. This clear definition of responsibilities generally facilitates the fulfilment of services marketing tasks.

- By the centralisation of decisions, synergies can be realised and coordination costs reduced. For example, when only one department is responsible for service communications, the communicative activities of the company can be integrated more easily.

- In functional organisations, every organisational entity specialises in its particular area. This specialisation leads to increased efficiency.

- However, the centralised decision-taking also results in standardised decisions. There are behavioural rules defined for many conceivable situations. However, not every situation can be planned. Especially in service industries, due to the direct contact between provider and customer, unplanned situations are frequent, e.g. when failures happen in the service delivery and the customer is annoyed. The standardisation of decisions can be diminished by increasing the decision-making authorities of service employees e.g. by empowerment (see Chapter 9).

- In functional organisations, there is often only one entity which is explicitly responsible for marketing activities and that is the marketing department. However, in typical functional organisations, an *isolation of the marketing function* can be observed.[2] The marketing function encompasses only some elements of value-oriented services marketing, like communications or product management. Consequently, many other services marketing elements are neglected or dependent on the value orientation of the other departments. Only when the human resources department is aware of the marketing role of all employees, can a company-wide service orientation be realised. Moreover, the links between the different elements of value-oriented services marketing are more difficult to translate into practice. For example, service value as it is perceived by customers consists of the service received as well as the price paid. When the services and the service range are defined by one entity and the service price by another entity, decisions are probably not taken under consideration of their value implications.

- When marketing decisions are taken by a certain functional unity, the objectives of this function dominate the decisions. These objectives often do not support value creation at its best (see Services marketing in action 12.1 'Marketing decisions in the airline industry').

Another type of structural organisation is an *object organisation*. Typical 'objects' which are used for structuring a firm are service products, customer groups or geographical regions. Typical examples are a bank's division into private and corporate clients or a consultancy's division into regional areas and consulting topics, such as strategic consulting, marketing consulting or process consulting. A further example is described in Services marketing in action 12.2 on 'Service profit responsibility at Reuters'. This type of organisation results in quasi-independent subdivisions of a service firm, which are often profit centres or even independent companies. These entities then have direct profit responsibility. At some level within the structure, there will also appear a functional organisation. But then, for example, the marketing for private clients is managed by the private client division and the marketing for corporate clients by the corporate client division. An *evaluation of the object organisation* with respect to value-oriented services marketing concerns the following aspects:

SERVICES MARKETING IN ACTION 12.1:

Marketing decisions in the airline industry

In airlines, capacity management often plays a strong role within the marketing organisation. Capacity management is responsible for the route planning and the filling of the capacities for these routes. In these organisations, strategic marketing targets are defined by the given routes. When certain routes are defined, based on past routes and/or general market conditions, marketing then starts filling these routes.

Applying this approach, the value of marketing activities is sub-optimal compared to alternative procedures. A customer value-oriented approach could be conducted when the airline would look first at the value potentials which are given in their customer relationships. The route needs of the most valuable segments of the airline would be analysed and then, the routes would be planned accordingly. This approach would result in better value creation by marketing activities through better exploitation of customer potential.

- Within an object organisation, the decision takers are closer to the '*object*', i.e. the service, the customer or the (geographical) market. This implies a higher value orientation since value creation by the services and the service programme, and the respective customer-directed decisions, directly influence the organisations' profit. For example, a customer-segment-based organisation aims to optimise the value for certain customer groups by orienting towards their service needs and consequently helping to ensure the value created by these segment behaviours. Alternatively, an organisation with geographical divisions contributes to the ability to consider cultural differences in international services marketing.

- The profit responsibility of the division leads to *increased motivation* on the part of the division heads and employees to realise the division's objectives and in consequence the firm's.

- Object-based divisions further allow *faster reactions to specific marketing situations*. Due to the division's responsibility for the business regarding a certain object, decisions can be taken without involving the top management.

- However, from the perspective of the service firm as a whole, marketing activities are *less integrated*. When communications are designed for every 'object' it is more difficult to integrate the effects for the whole firm, e.g. the company's brand image which again also influences the success of the individual divisions. For example, private clients of a bank possibly also perceive advertisements for corporate clients. The messages of the bank in these advertisements might be irritating for the private clients when they do not conform with the private client advertisements.

- Furthermore, the dynamics of the independent divisions might result in *synergy losses*. For example, service communications are planned and conducted for every service category resulting in higher communications costs than if communications were planned centrally.

As a third type of organisational structure, the *matrix organisation* combines at least two other organisational forms, optimally both functional and object organisational forms. By this, the matrix organisation aims to integrate the advantages of the two other organisational types. The basic principle of a matrix organisation is that, should coordination conflicts occur, there is no dominant organisational level, neither the functional nor the object organisation. The two sides are supposed to resolve conflicts. The following *advantages and disadvantages* are attributed to the matrix organisation:

- By the crossing of functional and object-oriented organisations, an *integration of internal and external needs* is achieved. For example, a customer-segment organisation (object orientation) is supposed to consider the needs of the different customer segments, while the functional orientation considers the internal needs in its decisions.

SERVICES MARKETING IN ACTION 12.2:

Service profit responsibility at Reuters

Reuters, the electronic information and media group, has launched a new phase in its £440m restructuring by making hundreds of managers directly responsible for the profit or loss of their products. The company, which is cutting its product portfolio from 1,300 trading systems and services to just 50, is rolling out a management tool dubbed Profitability Insight to monitor operating efficiency across the organisation. The initiative came as Reuters tried to overcome intense competition from Bloomberg and Thomson Financial in the $6bn to $7bn (£3.29bn to £3.84bn) market for data information and trading systems.

Under the scheme, to be introduced initially in areas such as sales and marketing, Reuters managers will be set profit targets that will be built into their bonus schemes – augmenting existing incentives built round sales performance. David Grigson, finance director, said: 'In Reuters, it is a new discipline. In the past, the overall level of complexity in the organisation thwarted this but now we can take this forward as part of the re-organisation and simplification of the company.

'It is just beginning now to give greater profit responsibility to individuals who previously had revenue or cost responsibility', said Mr Grigson. 'Anyone with product responsibility at a global level or in certain geographies will be responsible for profits in their areas.'

The initiative will help Reuters to break down the profit of different divisions for the first time.

Source: Burt 2004. Reproduced with permission from Financial Times Limited.

- Furthermore, internal communication channels are shorter, resulting in *more efficient communications*.

- Also, decisions are more likely to be based on a *holistic view* of the firm and its environment.

- However, processes are often characterised by a *higher complexity*. This can result in a lack of a sense of responsibility.

- *Decelerated decision-taking* often results from the need to reach a consensus between the two organisational forms.

- The success of a matrix organisation strongly depends on *personal abilities and relationships* between the organisation's members. Consequently, activities in firms with a matrix organisation are less predictable and less easy to plan.

Summing up, all three basic types of structural organisation are associated with advantages and disadvantages regarding value-oriented services marketing. And all three types are concerned with certain coordination problems. This is valid for a company's organisation in general, but especially crucial for service organisations. Due to the direct contact between service resources, e.g. the service employee, and the customer, a broader organisational interface is necessary.[3] This is provided by a firm's process organisation.

Process organisation of a service firm

The major organisational criteria of a **process organisation** are not the functions or objects or both, but processes, the entities of workflows in a service firm which are connected with each other.[4] This connectivity concerns the chronological order of workflows, i.e. the sequences of activities. A process orientation does not replace other organisational forms. A firm still might be functionally organised with a marketing and a controlling department. However, the *coordination between these* functions is realised by the process organisation (see Figure 12.2).

A process-oriented organisation uses the core processes of a firm as an organisational criterion. Processes are managed according to their value creation. For processes where several organisational entities are involved, often process owners are defined (see Figure 12.2). These are individuals who are responsible for the effectiveness and efficiency of a specific process. The process owners often assemble process teams in order to coordinate the participation of different entities at the process. Overall, the processes are coordinated by a managing team. The team members define the core processes and the process owners.

From the perspective of value-oriented services marketing, a process organisation is an important tool to realise the aim of value creation by services marketing. The Service Value Chain defines the primary processes 'interaction process' and 'relationship process' which are supported by secondary processes. By organising the service firm around these processes, value creation by them can be optimised.

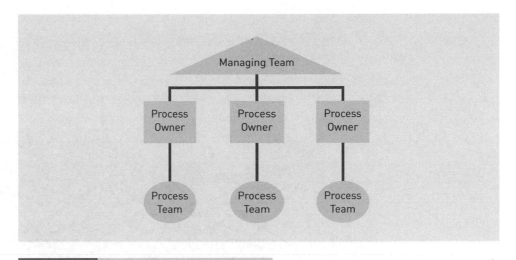

FIGURE 12.2   Model of a process organisation

Source: Kamiske and Füermann 1995, p. 146

For example, a customer interaction or a series of customer interactions often involves several departments, e.g. for a flight passenger. These series of interactions are often depicted in blueprints (see Chapter 3) in order to indicate the respective responsibilities. As the customer perceives the service process as a whole, the service provider can only deliver value to the customer when it also perceives the process as a whole. When it is not possible or efficient that the customer is served by one and the same employee during the whole process, a process organisation helps to design the process as a whole from the firm's perspective.

Regarding a process organisation based on the relationship process, Figure 12.3 illustrates how such an organisation can appear. Then, a firm's process organisation is built around the single processes of the relationship process, i.e. customer acquisition, customer retention, relationship enhancement[5] and customer recovery. Out of every functional unit, representatives are affiliated into organisational teams for each process step in order to jointly manage the respective phase of the relationship process. An institutionalisation of the relationship process within the firm's organisation is often found in direct marketing oriented service firms such as mail-order businesses. These often have clearly defined 'customer acquisition', 'customer retention' and 'customer recovery' departments.

Value-oriented company systems

A further driver of services marketing's implementation are a company's systems.[6] Systems describe how certain processes (e.g. complaint management process or reservation process) are organised, i.e. which individual steps the

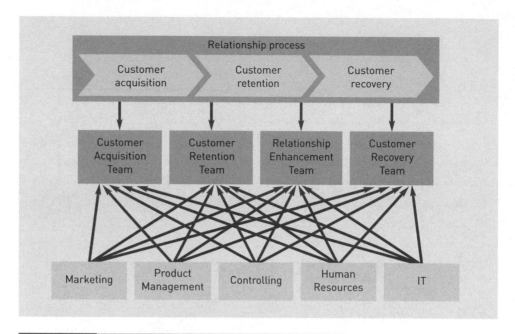

FIGURE 12.3   Example of a relationship process organisation

respective process contains. Sometimes, the expression 'systems' is perceived as being synonymous with 'technology'. However, even though there are also systems which use technologies which are important for services marketing, a system (e.g. complaint management system) is not necessarily synonymous with technology. There are three types of company systems which are closely connected with value-oriented services marketing. These are:

- information systems;
- communications systems;
- management systems.

Information systems are utilised in order to generate, process and transfer information regarding aspects which are relevant for services marketing. These can be internal – information regarding service range and prices – and external information. Consequently, there are internal and external information systems which are utilised for value-oriented services marketing. In services marketing, *internal information systems* support the service resources, e.g. employees, with internal information needed in the customer contact. Examples of these systems are:

- reservation systems which provide employees of airlines or hotels with information regarding the current reservation status for a certain service delivery time;

- service range systems which provide the employee or the electronic channel with service product specifications (e.g. interest rate, duration, etc. of a certain credit product by a bank);

- service pricing systems provide the employee or the electronic channel with information regarding the price for a specific service; these systems are especially necessary in the case of real-time pricing.

External information systems provide the service resources with external information, most importantly with information about the customer.[7] Customer databases collect many different types of information on the customer which can be used for analyses about the customer, such as customer segmentations or selecting customers for specific communicative activities. Figure 12.4 depicts how a customer database is structured. The core of the database are four groups of customer-related data: customer data (e.g. age, customer duration), potential data (e.g. customer interests), action data (e.g. last communication activity that was directed to a specific customer) and reaction data (e.g. the customer's reaction concerning a certain communicative activity). This data is used for customer analyses, planning of services marketing activities and marketing control. A frequent problem for

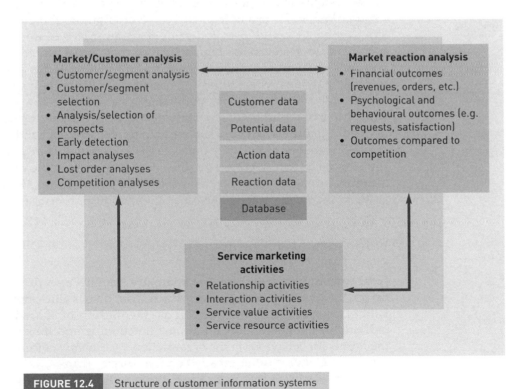

| **FIGURE 12.4** | Structure of customer information systems |

Source: Link and Hildebrand 1993, p. 45

service providers is that a lot of information exists in the company which is not utilised for services marketing. A central task of external information systems is to gather that information and to make it usable for marketing activities.

Communication systems design the communication processes with relevance for services marketing. There are internal and external communication processes which influence the success of services marketing. The *internal communication processes* ensure the top–down (supervisor to employee), bottom–up (employee to supervisor) and horizontal information flows (e.g. employee of one department to employee of another department). *External communication processes* concern the communication between the service provider and the customer. In order to ensure the information flows relevant for the firm's success, service providers employ internal and external communication systems which organise the utilisation of the different communication instruments within services marketing.

Management systems support a service provider's management to take decisions and are utilised to structure and initiate as well as control services marketing activities. There are *internal management systems* which are directed to the members of the service organisation. As employees are an important service resource, employee-directed management systems play an important role in services marketing. Examples are remuneration systems, qualification systems, career systems or workforce scheduling systems. Crucial for value-oriented services marketing, for example, is the value orientation of the respective systems. One option for value-oriented remuneration systems are customer-oriented remuneration systems. See Figure 12.5 for customer-oriented remuneration systems in service organisations. Quality management systems aim to structure the internal activities which build the basis for ensuring high service quality and service value for the customer. Budgeting systems define how budgets within the firm (e.g. marketing budget, technology budget, human resources budget) are defined. *External management systems* help to plan, conduct and control customer-directed activities. Often, they translate the information stored and transferred by the external information systems into concrete marketing measures. Examples are a complaint management system, Customer Relationship Management (CRM) systems, marketing automation, sales automation and service automation.

Value-oriented company culture

Next to company structure and company systems as a third implementation driver, the company culture affects the realisation of value-oriented services marketing. *Company culture* is defined as 'the pattern of shared beliefs that help individuals understand organisational functioning and thus provide them with the norms for behaviour in the organisation'.[8] Company culture is a multi-faceted construct. Cultures differ greatly between service firms. From the perspective of value-oriented services marketing, the question arises how a culture can be described that is best suited to support the implementation of value-oriented services marketing.

Company	Customer-oriented pay
Fedex	Managers must realise defined targets regarding customer satisfaction and employee satisfaction in order to participate in the bonus pool of the firm.
Hallmark	Depending on an employee's position, variable pay is between 5 and 10 per cent. One of the indicators for variable pay is customer satisfaction.
K-Mart	The firm has introduced a variable pay system in connection with the programme 'Super Service Initiative'. Within this initiative, associates receive a quarterly bonus which is calculated based on the 'Super Service Index (SSI)'.
Pizza Hut	50 per cent of branch managers' quarterly bonus pay is based on the results of customer satisfaction surveys as well as a 'Customer Loyalty' index.
Sears	The proportion of variable incentives are widely used at Sears and based on customer satisfaction.

FIGURE 12.5   Examples of customer-oriented remuneration systems

Sources: Tuzovic 2004; for Fedex: Brown 1992; Hallmark: Verespej 1996, p. 20; K-Mart: Estell 2001; Pizza Hut: McNerney 1996, p. 5; Sears: Driscoll 1994; Hallowell and Schlesinger 2000.

A central feature of value-oriented services marketing is the *customer-oriented culture*[9] of a service firm. It allows customer needs to be fulfilled and delivers a service of high value to the customers, as well as initiating and maintaining high value relationships for the customer. In consequence, customers exhibit types of behaviour, such as loyalty, which help to create value for the service firm. That it is not simple to realise such a customer orientation within a firm is illustrated below in Services marketing in action 12.3.

SERVICES MARKETING IN ACTION 12.3:

Problems with implementing customer value orientations

For value-oriented services marketing, both a customer and a customer value orientation are important. Customer orientation means that the provider and their

▶

employee focus on customer needs when planning and conducting marketing activities. Customer value orientation means that the provider and their employees not only have the customer's needs in mind, but also the firm's interests. In consequence, a concentration of the needs of the most valuable customers follows.

However, this approach is connected with various implementation problems, especially regarding the employees' behaviour. When the customer contact personnel are not convinced of value-oriented approaches, then a customer value orientation can result in a disaster in the customer contact.

This happened to a mobile communications provider who applied a multi-level pricing system, with different levels depending on the value of the respective customers, i.e. more valuable customers had to pay lower rates than less valuable customers. One day, a customer went into a shop of the mobile provider and asked for a certain tariff plan. On being given the information by the sales person, the customer claimed that he knew that a friend of his would be on a lower rate, to which the sales person replied: 'Yes, that is because you are a C customer within our A-B-C ranking.'

Such miscommunications can only be prevented when employees, first, are prepared correctly for customer contact, and secondly are convinced of the firm's value-oriented philosophy.

There is some research regarding the identification of *company culture types* and their effects on the customer orientation of the firm. One ostensive approach uses two dimensions in order to describe company cultures:[10] The first dimension differentiates whether a culture is internally or externally oriented and the second dimension differentiates organic processes, with focus on flexibility and spontaneity in contrast to mechanistic processes, which focus on control, order and stability. Combining these two dimensions results in the distinction of four *types of company culture*[11] (see Figure 12.6):

- clan culture: internal, organic;

- adhocracy culture: external, organic;

- hierarchy culture: internal, mechanistic;

- market culture: external, mechanistic.

In an empirical study it was found that the market and the adhocracy cultures outperformed the two other culture types.[12] Consequently the external orientation of the company culture is an important driver of a service firm's customer orientation and thus value orientation.

For establishing and maintaining a customer culture, service firms use three *types of instruments* which influence the culture within a company (see Figure 12.7). A first group of instruments describes measures which define and commu-

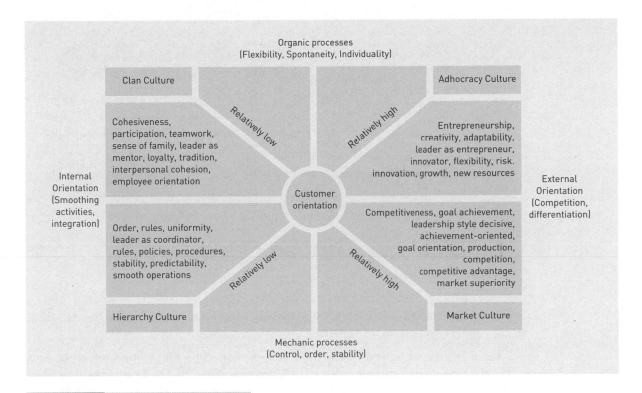

Organic processes
(Flexibility, Spontaneity, Individuality)

Clan Culture

Cohesiveness,
participation, teamwork,
sense of family, leader as
mentor, loyalty, tradition,
interpersonal cohesion,
employee orientation

Relatively low

Adhocracy Culture

Entrepreneurship,
creativity, adaptability,
leader as entrepreneur,
innovator, flexibility, risk.
innovation, growth, new resources

Relatively high

Internal
Orientation
(Smoothing
activities,
integration)

Customer
orientation

External
Orientation
(Competition,
differentiation)

Order, rules, uniformity,
leader as coordinator,
rules, policies, procedures,
stability, predictability,
smooth operations

Competitiveness, goal achievement,
leadership style decisive,
achievement-oriented,
goal orientation, production,
competition,
competitive advantage,
market superiority

Relatively low

Relatively high

Hierarchy Culture

Market Culture

Mechanic processes
(Control, order, stability)

FIGURE 12.6   Types of company culture

Source: adapted from Deshpandé *et al.* 1993, p. 25.

nicate the self-image of the service firm. Corresponding instruments are the company vision and behavioural rules. A second group concerns the communication and motivation of employees. Here internal communication instruments and the leadership style can be mentioned as measures.[13] The third group encompasses training and active collaboration, such as workshops or one-to-one conversations with employees.

An important role for the realisation of a company culture is the behaviour of the top management both externally as well as internally. When the CEO of the service firm communicates externally in a way contradictory to the culture of the firm, this behaviour is perceived by employees and affects their behaviour, too. More directly, the internal behaviour of the top management influences the company culture. The leadership style of the top management is transferred by the employees into their own behaviour.[14] Three *types of the leadership style* of a service firm's top management can be distinguished:[15]

- A participative leadership style is shown when the management involves subordinates when taking decisions.

Self-image	Communication/ Motivation	Trainings/ Active collaboration
• Company guidelines • Company vision • Behavioural rules • Systematic design of artefacts (e.g. ritual, myths, language, architecture)	• Posters • Brochures • Company magazine • Leadership style • Leadership instruments • Events	• Seminars • Workshops • Individual interviews

FIGURE 12.7　Instruments for managing company culture

Source: Bruhn 2002, p. 237.

- A supportive leadership style means that the management cares for its subordinates and offers them help.

- An instrumental leadership style is represented by behaviours which neglect the opinions of the subordinates and just issue directions for their work.

It was found empirically – as common sense would suggest – that the first two leadership styles help to ensure a customer orientation, while the instrumental leadership style contradicts the efforts to realise a customer and value orientation.

The inter-relations between different implementation drivers, i.e. structures, systems and culture, are illustrated in Services marketing in action 12.4.

SERVICES MARKETING IN ACTION 12.4:　

Bonus culture in investment banks

Chief executives of investment banks love to talk about culture. But it is difficult for them to do so in a manner that differentiates them from rivals, because the phrases they use – 'client-focused' and 'teamwork oriented' – have become platitudes through overuse in marketing ephemera. It is money that talks when it comes to culture on Wall Street. What really sets the winners apart from the losers is who gets compensation right. That will become clear this week when the bosses of Wall Street begin telling their charges the size of their bonuses. For employees, bonuses often represent the bulk of their compensation, especially for senior staff. A top-performing managing director – the highest rank at many investment banks – should earn about $900,000 in awards this year, according to Alan Johnson, a compensation consultant. Select staff will receive seven- and even eight-figure payouts. Chief executives use bonuses to attract and retain talent as well as to create what is referred to in business as an 'ownership culture'.

This term has rung hollow at Credit Suisse First Boston. CSFB used to be known for pay guarantees doled out to cowboy traders and bankers who considered their pay more important than the success of the investment bank. When John Mack joined CSFB from Morgan Stanley, one of his first steps as chief executive was to remove pay agreements in an effort to return the bank to profitability. But after some junior staff threatened to quit over 2003 bonuses, some received guarantees, exposing the long road CSFB's staff still had to travel before the investment bank could be united in its cause of catching up on rivals. Rival investment banks that could report record profits this year have done better.

Dick Fuld, chairman and chief executive of Lehman Brothers, considers stock awards an important step in retaining and attracting talent, as well as in convincing employees to worry about the strength of all businesses run by the investment bank, not just their own department. When Lehman was sold to the public a decade ago, Mr Fuld made sure to compensate his staff with stock. So much has been handed out that employees now own more than a third of shares, which have outperformed most rivals. This does more to explain Lehman's 'One Firm' slogan than any pamphlet.

Goldman Sachs, which ended a 130-year-old partnership when it sold itself to the public five years ago, set up a rank above managing director, which it calls the partnership pool, to keep the partnership culture alive. These people get a $600,000 salary and share a special bonus pool that is linked to the investment bank's overall profits. No matter what department they work in, they are meant to think as a team. Partners are named biennially. There were 99 additions this year. The plan explains Goldman's business principle list better than any of the 14 items on it, including 'we stress teamwork in everything we do'.

Source: Wells 2004. Reproduced with permission from Financial Times Limited.

Controlling services marketing: Assessing services marketing's value drivers

Controlling services marketing by value drivers

The leading purpose of services marketing – as understood in this book – is to create value for the service firm. In order to manage services marketing activities from a value perspective, a systematic controlling of these activities is necessary. Only when the service company is aware of how successful its marketing activities, i.e. its Service Value Chain, was and is, can it direct future activities towards maintenance or even expansion of its value creation.

A value-oriented, services marketing control aims at identifying whether the services marketing objectives are realised and what activities help to influence these value objectives. In order to examine these questions, services marketing control is geared towards value-oriented performance figures, so-called value drivers. A (services marketing) value driver represents a factor which directly or indirectly influences the value created by a firm's (services marketing) activities.

Categories of value drivers

There are various possible value drivers which can be relevant for a service organisation's success. They are derived from the basic concept of value-oriented services marketing, the Service Value Chain which affects value via the service profit chain. Consequently, each of the primary and secondary *processes of the Service Value Chain* contains certain value drivers (see Figure 12.8):

- *Relationship value drivers* encompass customer acquisition drivers, customer retention drivers, relationship enhancement drivers and customer recovery drivers.

- *Interaction value drivers* are divided into customer integration drivers, service encounter drivers and service recovery drivers.

- *Service value drivers* can be service product drivers, service price drivers, service delivery drivers and service communications drivers.

- *Service resources value drivers* are human resources drivers, tangible resources drivers, technology drivers and capacity drivers.

There are diverse value drivers within these categories. The individual value drivers differ regarding their *'closeness' to a firm's value*. There are drivers which influence a value directly (e.g. revenues with new customers) and there are drivers whose impact on value is more indirect (e.g. perceived friendliness of employees). Conceptually, the distinction of the different drivers can be structured by the integration of the Service Value Chain and the service profit chain. Based on this, four categories of value drivers are distinguished (see Figure 12.9):

- value parameters;

- perceptual value drivers;

- behavioural value drivers;

- financial value drivers.

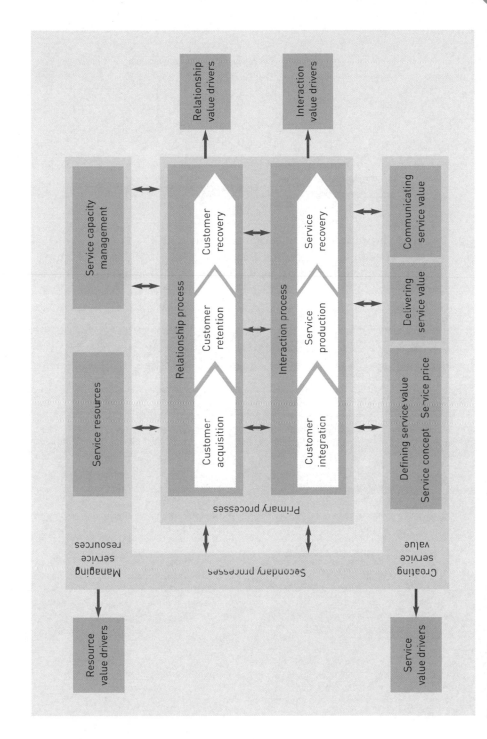

 FIGURE 12.8 Categories of value drivers

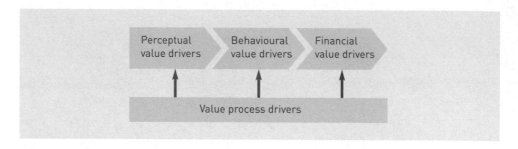

Mapping the Service Value Chain with the Service Profit Chain results in very specific *drivers of value-oriented services marketing* (see Figure 12.10). Before exploring the different driver categories according to the Service Profit Chain in depth,

Value process drivers	Perceptual value drivers	Behavioural value drivers	Financial value drivers
Relationship value drivers	• Trust in adviser • Mutual knowledge of processes • Perceived value of staying in relationship	• Customer acquisition rate • Customer retention rate • Customer regain rate	• Revenues with new customers • Revenues with retained customers • Revenues with regained customers
Interaction value drivers	• Perceived service quality • Availability of provider • Perceived individualisation	• Involvement of customer in service process • Customer's indicating of service failures	• Service profitability • Cost of rework due to service failures
Service value drivers	• Ease of contact service provider • Awareness of service provider • Perceived service–price combinations	• Cross-buying due to broad programme • Initial purchase due to price promotion	• Profitability of services marketing activities • Coverage of marketing activities
Resource value drivers	• Perceived competence of employees • Perceived usability of service technologies	• Service resource loyalty • Open communications in contact with provider	• Service resource productivity • Service resource cost

FIGURE 12.10   Drivers of value-oriented services marketing

we should consider Services marketing in action 12.5, 'Value drivers of department stores', which provides a basic idea of the concept of value drivers.

SERVICES MARKETING IN ACTION 12.5:

Value drivers of department stores

Karstadt was a leading department store in Germany in the 1980s. However, the firm has encountered some problems recently and in 2005 was still in the throes of a financial and strategic crisis.

When asked the reasons for this crisis and his ideas for the future, Helmut Merkel (Karstadt's former CEO) answered that the biggest mistake Karstadt could make was to neglect service to the customer. Over time, due to the financial problems, cost reductions were conducted repeatedly, with most of the cost reductions affecting the service levels. Therefore, in 2005 Merkel emphasised a strategy to re-invest in customer service as this would be the main value driver in the industry.

This vision of course raised the question of how investments in service could be increased with the financial problems still pending. Merkel explained that they found their service employees had to perform many activities which were not customer-directed, such as getting merchandise on to the shelves. Therefore, he planned to unburden service employees from non-service activities in order to give them more time to serve customers. The non-service activities would then to be conducted by lower-paid, non-service employees.

In this case, the process 'getting merchandise on to the shelves' proved too costly because it was conducted by highly paid service employees. Furthermore, these employees could not fulfil their original task properly and thus also did not deliver sufficient service and customer satisfaction to create firm value.

Source: Seidel 2004.

Value parameters are concrete specifications which describe the respective value processes. There are quantitative and qualitative value parameters. *Quantitative parameters* indicate objective attributes of the value processes (e.g. number of customer contact employees, percentage of trained employees as parameters of the secondary process 'human resources management'). Qualitative parameters concern descriptive attributes of the processes (e.g. qualification level of customer contact employees, breadth in content of trainings).

Perceptual value drivers substantiate degrees of customer perceptions with relevance for the service firm's value (e.g. perceived service quality, image of the service firm). Again, there are quantitative value drivers (e.g. customer satisfaction rate as the percentage of customers who are satisfied with the service firm);

and qualitative value drivers (e.g. level of satisfaction with a certain service characteristic).

Behavioural value drivers describe the characteristics of customer behaviours with relevance for the firm's value creation. Customer behaviour can be measured either as actual or real behaviour or as behavioural intentions. Accordingly, real behaviour (e.g. number of customers retained) and intentional behaviour drivers (e.g. number of customer committed to the firm) are distinguished.

Financial value drivers represent financial figures which can be directly attributed to services marketing activities and are components of overall financial figures and finally the firm's value. According to the definition of value, three categories of financial value drivers can be distinguished:

- Input-related drivers rate the negative financial consequences of services marketing activities, i.e. *cost*.

- Output-related drivers concern positive value consequences of services marketing, i.e. especially *revenues*.

- Input–output drivers contrast both positive and negative value consequences, e.g. *service productivity* and *return on services marketing*.

Cost, revenues, productivity and return on services marketing

As the consequence of negative value, *costs of services marketing* represent the direct financial consequences of the services marketing processes. When one more service employee is employed, cost for human resources increase. As some part of marketing costs are easily comprehensible – especially compared to services marketing's revenue effects – they are often the main financial figure for an evaluation of marketing activities (e.g. advertising budget or cost). These costs are direct costs which can be directly attributed to a certain marketing activity (e.g. cost for broadcasting a TV spot). However, significant parts of services marketing costs are indirect costs which cannot fully be attributed to a particular marketing activity. For example, many service employees participate in many service processes. Therefore, their cost cannot be attributed to only one activity. Furthermore, the costs attributed to unused capacities are difficult to determine because of the long-term character of many service facilities.

A method which aims at quantifying the indirect cost of services marketing processes is the so-called *activity-based costing*.[16] This method defines a service firm's processes, based on the Service Value Chain. Then, by thorough analyses of existing data complemented by activity analyses and interviews with employees, the inputs for every process are determined (e.g. for making a hotel reservation, a hotel receptionists needs 2 minutes of customer interaction and 5 minutes of further internal activities, like documentation, etc.). Then, by calculating cost ratios (e.g. cost of £15 per employee hour), the cost for a certain process can be determined (e.g. £1.75 as the employee's portion of costs of the total cost for the reservation process).

The performance figures which represent the positive value consequences of services marketing are *revenues*. The revenues from retained customers are a value driver of the customer retention process, the revenues caused by successful service recoveries are a driver within the service recovery process and revenues caused by the customer's appreciation of the service firm's price level are a value driver within the service pricing process. As becomes obvious, a major difficulty with revenues is not their general determination – most service firms track their sales and revenues on a regular basis – but rather that it is difficult to attribute revenues to specific value processes. In most cases it is not obvious to what extent the revenues of a firm are caused by a certain marketing activity.

One approach for estimating process-caused revenues is *interaction and relationship blueprinting*. Adapting the service blueprinting method, customers are asked to reconstruct the process of a certain interaction or their relationship to the provider by redrawing important situations in the course of the interaction or relationship. For the relationship blueprint, important stages – according to the relationship lifecyle – are – from the customer's perspective – relationship initiation, relationship beginning, relationship enhancement, relationship problems and possibly relationship termination. Then for each of the stages the customer is asked about the factors which influenced behaviour most, e.g. what where the reasons for his initial decision to use the services of the focal provider (see Figure 12.11). Services marketing in action 12.6 illustrates how value drivers can be identified using this method. By quantifying the reasons over a representative sample of customers, the service provider gets a first impression of the revenue drivers. For some uses of value drivers, e.g. the forecasting of a process revenue, quantitative measures of the value drivers and its impacts are needed. When the value drivers are known (e.g. derived from a blueprint analysis) and can be measured using customer usage data (e.g. for behavioural drivers) or customer survey data (e.g. for perceptual drivers), the statistical relationships between the drivers can be measured. It is possible to quantify which influence the customers' perception regarding a certain quality criterion (e.g. accessibility) has on customer behaviours (e.g. customer retention) and the latter on the financial drivers (e.g. revenues).[17]

Service providers are not only interested in isolated information about the cost and revenues such as the input and output figures of services marketing, but also in an evaluation of *input–output relations*. Two central figures based on input–output relations are service productivity and return on services marketing.

Service productivity is a ratio between output and input of service marketing activities. When the input is decreased with a constant output or the output is increased with a constant input, then there are increases in service productivity.[18] Service

Relationship initiation	Relationship enhancement	Relationship termination
• How had you become aware of provider X? • Did you compare provider X with other providers? • What information did you get about provider X? • What were the most important characteristics that you perceived of provider X? • What were the final reasons that you choose provider X?	• How did your relationship to provider X proceed? • After your first interaction, how were further interactions initiated? By you or by provider X? • What reasons did you have to contact provider X again? • Did you think about using more services of provider X? Why? • Did you think about using the services of provider X more often? Why?	• Did you ever perceive problems with provider X? Which? And how severe? • Did you communicate these problems to provider X? What was the reaction? • Which possible actions by provider X would have kept you from switching to another provider?

FIGURE 12.11   Exemplary relationship blueprint and questions for identifying value drivers

SERVICES MARKETING IN ACTION 12.6:

Application of the relationship blueprint

Blueprint: Mrs. K had bought a relatively large amount of stock and therefore had relatively frequent contact with her bank.
Value driver: Channel usage of customers, contact frequency of customers.

Blueprint: She is contacted by the branch manager and advised that her account is too labour-intensive for the bank and she should use direct banking.
Value driver: Contacting customers, communication behaviour of manager.

Blueprint: The customer officially complains to the branch manager and explains that she does not perceive such behaviour as good service.
Value driver: Complaint behaviour of customer.

Blueprint: The branch manager responds: We have too much work, too few people, etc., etc.

Value driver: Communication behaviour of manager.

Blueprint: The customer calls the branch in order to make a stock transaction. The information is not transferred to the trader.
Value driver: Internal communication processes.

Blueprint: The customer's complaint is responded to with, 'That's bad luck, you must have talked to a trainee.'
Value driver: Complaint reactions.

Blueprint: The branch is closed, the stock price is falling, and the customer cannot sell.
Value driver: Accessibility of service provider, availability of service.

Blueprint: The customer calls headquarters five times. Nobody admits responsibility.
Value driver: Accessibility of service provider, availability of service, determination of responsibility.

Source: Michalski 2002.

productivity can be specified according to the service resources applied. Labour productivity for example is defined as a firm's total sales divided by the number of employees.[19] Compared to productivity ratios of manufacturers, the calculation of the total productivity of a service provider is more complex due to the characteristics of services, especially due to the customer integration into service processes. One important refinement of service productivity compared to the traditional productivity definition is that the customer influences service productivity.[20] Service productivity varies with the customer's inputs into the service process. For example, service productivity decreases when the customer has difficulties in explaining their service requirements or when they arrive too late for the service delivery appointment. Moreover, service productivity is influenced by the ratio of capacity usage because unused capacity resulting in unused service units decreases service productivity because they cannot be stored and used on a later occasion.

Another input–output-related performance figure is the *return on services marketing*. This figure is based on the traditional return on investment (ROI) as one of the most important performance figures in controlling. Return on services marketing is the ratio between the profit from marketing activities, i.e. revenues minus cost – divided by the cost. The calculation of this figure integrates the problems of cost and revenue attribution to services marketing activities. However, application of the approaches presented to resolve these problems, i.e. activity-based costing and the interaction and relationship blueprint approach, helps to quantify the return on services marketing.

For every process of the Service Value Chain, value parameters, perceptual, behavioural and financial value drivers can be identified. Since there is a multitude of possible value drivers, it is important to *prioritise these value drivers*. Based on the relationships between the different drivers, service providers can calculate the relative importance of a driver. For example, when the firm's value is most influenced by revenues with retained customers which are most influenced by the customer retention rate which is influenced by the evaluation of the firm's retention programme which again is determined by the rebates which are offered to the customer, then these rebates are a priority value driver.

Utilising value drivers of services marketing

Identifying the value drivers of services marketing is the basis for controlling services marketing activities. When a service provider has determined its marketing's value drivers, this information can be used for various *controlling activities*:

- *Determining value objectives*: Future-oriented control not only evaluates past services marketing activities ex-post, but also aims to support the management of these activities by ensuring value-oriented services marketing. The hierarchy of value drivers is the basis for defining objectives. The inter-relationships between the value drivers indicate which drivers help most to influence drivers on a higher level. Moreover, the current results for the respective value drivers are one starting point for the formulation of objectives.

- *Value-based budgeting*: When the anticipated impacts of the various drivers on the overall value are known, then budgets can be allocated to the different drivers in accordance with the underlying value processes.

- *Target-actual comparison*: In retrospect, the objectives set can be compared with the actual results for the different value drivers. By this, service providers find out which value processes overperform and which underperform. This information offers an insight into the necessities for changes regarding future objectives.

- *Making processes operational*: Focusing on value drivers helps services marketing managers to define their value processes more concretely. Then, not only tasks within the respective processes are described but there are also specific figures provided by which the processes can be quantified.

A value-oriented services marketing control based on value drivers is the basis for a systematic realisation of value-oriented services marketing. A value orientation is only reached when there is information regarding the value-relevant factors and the available inter-relationships. Further, operational figures help managers to orient their decisions at some checkpoint. And finally, a value-oriented control helps marketing to get attention through the overall control of the firm and the top management.

Summary

Regarding services marketing implementation and control, this chapter provides the following lessons (see Figure 12.12):

1. Services marketing implementation and control represent the internal conditions which determine the realisation and success of value-oriented services marketing.

2. Services marketing implementation affects value creation by enhancing and supporting value-oriented marketing activities.

3. Services marketing control is at the core of a recursive process by examining past services marketing activities and providing the basis for future activities' objectives.

4. The realisation of value-oriented services marketing is supported by three implementation factors: company structure, systems and culture.

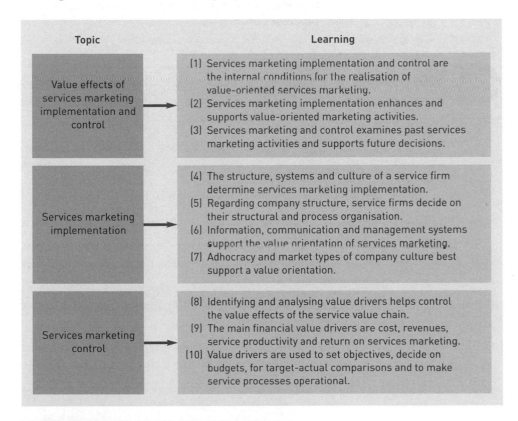

Topic	Learning
Value effects of services marketing implementation and control	(1) Services marketing implementation and control are the internal conditions for the realisation of value-oriented services marketing. (2) Services marketing implementation enhances and supports value-oriented marketing activities. (3) Services marketing and control examines past services marketing activities and supports future decisions.
Services marketing implementation	(4) The structure, systems and culture of a service firm determine services marketing implementation. (5) Regarding company structure, service firms decide on their structural and process organisation. (6) Information, communication and management systems support the value orientation of services marketing. (7) Adhocracy and market types of company culture best support a value orientation.
Services marketing control	(8) Identifying and analysing value drivers helps control the value effects of the service value chain. (9) The main financial value drivers are cost, revenues, service productivity and return on services marketing. (10) Value drivers are used to set objectives, decide on budgets, for target-actual comparisons and to make service processes operational.

FIGURE 12.12   Learning summary for Chapter 12

5. Regarding company structure, the structural organisation (e.g. functional, object or matrix organisation) and the process organisation influence the value-orientation of services marketing.

6. The information, communication and management systems of the service provider also affect value creation by services marketing.

7. There are several types of company culture from which an adhocracy and a market culture most affect the value orientation of services marketing.

8. Services marketing control is conducted by identifying and analysing the value drivers of marketing which can be differentiated based on the Service Value Chain and the 'closeness' of the driver to total firm value according to the service profit chain.

9. The basic financial value drivers of services marketing are cost, revenues, service productivity and return on services marketing. They all include specifics caused by the service characteristics.

10. Value drivers of services marketing are utilised for setting objectives, deciding on marketing budgets, conducting target-actual comparisons and making service processes operational.

Knowledge questions

1. Explain the value relevance of services marketing implementation. In this context, dwell on the indirect impact on value via the Service Value Chain.

2. How is value affected by services marketing control?

3. Explain the differences between the different organisational structures.

4. How does the organisational structure affect the value orientation of services marketing?

5. Explain how a process organisation helps to make the Service Value Chain operational.

6. Describe the influence of the different company systems on value creation by services marketing.

7. Explain the differences between different types of company culture. Explore further why there are differences in the value orientation of the different types.

8. What is a value driver? Which categories of value drivers can be differentiated?

9. Define the basic financial figures of services marketing.

10. How is the determination of the basic financial figures of services marketing affected by the service characteristics?

11. Explain how the use of the value drivers of services marketing help to ensure value-oriented services marketing.

Application and discussion questions

1. An airline lost 25 per cent of its customers last year. Develop a case for explaining this fall in customer numbers utilising your knowledge of services marketing implementation and control.

2. Research on the internet the organisational chart of some organisation. Interpret it based on your knowledge of the value-orientation of organisational structures. Which value effects would you assume? Compare these with observable value effects (how does the firm perform?).

3. A bank has purchased standard CRM software in order to store customer information and to derive decisions regarding segment-specific marketing activities. The software even provides the firm with customer segmentation, and the firm incorporated new customer data especially for the analytical tools offered by the software. However, in the next year, both revenue and profits drop. Discuss possible reasons for this development.

4. Choose a specific company – regardless of how small – that you know a little bit about from the inside (e.g. from an internship, your parents' stories about their firms, etc.). Try to determine the culture of this firm. Is the value effect suggested by theory observable in this case?

5. Imagine that you represent the mobile communications market. Based on your own behaviour, try to develop a value driver hierarchy in this market.

6. What are the factors influencing service productivity in a restaurant?

7. Discuss the influence factors of the cost of a customer interaction at the post office.

CASE STUDY: VALUE DRIVERS IN THE AIRLINE INDUSTRY

In an American study, the impact of services marketing activities on customer and firm value was analysed for several industries, e.g. the airline industry, and several providers within these industries, e.g. American Airlines within the airline industry.

First, the CLV for the customers participating in the study was calculated using the probabilities for customer switching as well as average purchase amounts in the airline industry. To extend the CLV figures to the firm's US customer equity, US Census data was used to determine the number of adults in the United States (187,747,000), and then this was combined with the percentage of US adults who were active users of airline travel (23.3%), yielding a total number of US adult airline customers of 43,745,051. To approximate the total customer equity, this number was multiplied by the average CLV across all study respondents.

As CLV is a major financial value driver, some insights can be obtained from examining American Airlines' CLV distribution. For example, the $0–$99 category includes more than 60% of American's customers, and the $500-plus category includes only 11.6% of customers, indicating that the bulk of American's customers have low CLV. Also, the analysis reveals that American's customers are fickle. Almost half of American's customers have a 20% or less, share-of-wallet (by CLV) allocated to American. Only 10.5% give more than 80% of their CLV to American. This percentage shows dramatically that the vast majority of American's customers cannot be considered monogamously loyal.

For analysing value drivers on the perceptual level, the study identified three groups of perceptual drivers:

- Service value, i.e. quality, price and convenience.

- Brand equity, i.e. advertising awareness, information, corporate citizenship, community events, ethical standards, image-personality-fit.

- Relationship management, i.e. investment in a loyalty programme, preferential treatment, knowledge of airline's procedures, knowledge of customer by airline, customer's recognition as being special by airline, community, trust.

The respondents' evaluations of these drivers can be used to analyse the financial impact of improvement efforts for any of the usual marketing expenditures. For example, American Airlines recently spent a reported $70 million to upgrade the quality of its passenger compartments in coach class by adding more leg room. Is such an investment justified? To perform an analysis such as this, the amount of ratings shift and the costs incurred in effecting the ratings shift are calculated. In this way, the recent American Airlines seating improvement was analysed. The $70 million cost figure reported by the company was used. Assuming that the average for the item that measures quality of the passenger compartment (a sub-driver of quality) increases by .2 rating points on the five-point scale, the analysis indicates that customer value will improve by 1.39%, resulting in an improvement in customer equity of $101.3 million nationally, or an ROI of 44.7%, which indicates that the programme has the potential to be a considerable success.

Source: Rust *et al*. 2004.

Notes

1 See Bruhn 2002a.
2 See Grönroos 1994.
3 See Laing and McKee 2000.
4 See Kennedy *et al*. 2003.
5 In this example, two example processes 'customer retention' and 'relationship enhancement' are distinguished because of the diversity of tasks associated with these two processes.
6 See Strong and Harris 2004.
7 See Dobni 2002.
8 See Deshpandé and Webster 1989, p. 4.
9 See Parasuraman 1987.
10 See Deshpandé *et al*. 1993.
11 See Deshpandé *et al*. 1993.
12 See Deshpandé *et al*. 1993.
13 See Dobni 2002.
14 See Krefting and Frost 1985; Bass 1985.
15 See Harris and Ogbonna 2001.
16 See Mabberley 1998.
17 See Chapter 2.
18 See Gummesson 1998.
19 See Anderson *et al*. 1997.
20 See Martin *et al*. 2001.

Glossary

Brand equity: Brand equity is defined as the future income streams which can be attributed to a brand.

Brand image: The brand image is a cluster of attributes and associations that consumers connect to a brand name. The totality of these attributes determine the value that is delivered to the consumer by a brand.

Capacity gap: A capacity gap is the result of a service demand exceeding the service capacity available.

Core service: The core service describes the parts of a service process which determine the main value creation by a service (e.g. flying from A to B is an airline's core service) (see also **supplementary services**).

Critical incidents: Due to their process character, services are seldom perceived as an entity by the customer. Rather, the customer perceives distinctively the different passages within a service interaction. When this perception is especially positive or negative, the customer perceives a critical incident which possibly affects their total evaluation of a service significantly.

Cross-buying: When a customer who already uses certain services of a provider (e.g. renting a hotel room) and then additionally uses further services (e.g. eating in the hotel's restaurant), they cross-buy.

Customer acquisition: A customer relationship starts with customer acquisition, i.e. the provider attracting potential customers and their conducting first purchases.

Customer enhancement: Customer enhancement describes the process of focusing on the expansion of an existing customer relationship.

Customer expectations: Expectations represent an individual's psychological state that relates to future behavioural consequences for that person. Customer expectations are this state regarding future service usages. Customers have normative expectations, which indicate the customer's requirements regarding a service provider, and predictive expectations which indicate the service level which is probable from the customer's perspective.

Customer integration: The customer (or one or more of their objects) is integrated into the service process as the '**external factor**' in order to produce a service. Within the Service Value Chain, 'customer integration' is the process of integrating the external factor into the service process – a process that takes place more or less significantly prior to the actual service production.

Customer Lifetime Value: Customer Lifetime Value is the present value of future income streams of a specific customer for the rest of the duration of his relationship to the provider.

Customer recovery: Customer recovery is the re-activation of relationships to former customers who have terminated a former relationship with the provider.

Customer relationship: A customer relationship is a series of linked interactions between service provider and customer. The existence of consecutive interactions is not a sufficient precondition of a relationship. It is important that the interactions are linked with each other, e.g. that information from prior interactions is used in current interactions.

Customer relationship lifecycle: This concept describes the typical course of a customer relationship. The variations in relationship intensity are depicted in dependence from relationship duration. A typical relationship consists of three phases: customer acquisition, customer retention and customer recovery.

Customer retention: Customer retention describes the repeated using of a provider's services by a specific customer.

Customer satisfaction: Customer satisfaction is a customer's emotional reaction to the evaluation of a service provider and its services. It is the result of the customer comparing the services received and their expectations regarding the services.

Customer switching: The customer's terminating a relationship to a specific provider and starting a relationship with another provider is called customer switching (e.g. switching from one mobile communications provider to another).

Customer value: The value of a customer generally means the financial contribution of a customer or a customer relationship to a firm's value. More concretely, there are a variety of customer value definitions depending on the purpose of the customer valuation (e.g. for decisions on which customers are to be retained possibly other value considerations are important compared to decisions about which customers to select for cross-selling activities). Typical components which are used to define customer value are profitability and potential as current/future income streams from a customer as well as loyalty and lifetime as the current/future indicator of the time component of customer value.

Demand gap: When there are more capacities than are requested by consumers, the service capacity exceeds the demand and a demand gap results.

Empowerment: Empowerment is a specific approach of service-oriented human resources management. It aims at augmenting the responsibilities of customer contact personnel. By this, service employees are supposed to react faster to customer requests or problems and to increase customer satisfaction.

External factor: The external factor is the customer or a customer's object which is integrated into a service process in order to produce the service. Without this integration, the service cannot be produced. Typical examples for external factors are the customer themselves (e.g. at the hairdresser), the customer's money (e.g. for banking services) or the customer's car (e.g. in the car wash).

Firm value: See **value**.

Franchising: A typical form of a **multiplication of service delivery** is via franchising (e.g. in the fast-food industry). The so-called franchisor offers a marketing concept which is utilised by the franchisees. The latter pay a franchise fee for the franchisor who in turn cares for the overall marketing strategy of the franchising chain.

Interactions: see **service interaction**.

Multi-channelling: Multi-channelling means the systematic offering of various **service channels** to the customers.

Multiplication of service delivery: The basic service delivery is between one service provider consisting of one service resource (e.g. shoe polish) and one customer. By multiplying the service delivery simultaneous conduct of several service deliveries, possibly at several places, is made possible.

Nonverbal communications: Nonverbal communications are the part of human communications which do not use the conventional rules of language, but kinesics, paralanguage, proxemics and the physical appearance of communicators.

Organisation: see **structural organisation** and **process organisation**.

Perceived service value: Customers attribute a value to a service used according to the benefits (e.g. perceived service quality) and the cost (e.g. price paid) they perceive in the context of using the service.

Price bundling: The procedure of offering a package of services for one single price (e.g. package holiday) is called price bundling.

Price discrimination: When service providers apply a pricing system which offers different prices according to specific criteria, they apply price discrimination. Typical characteristics for discriminating prices are customer characteristics (e.g. age), offering characteristics (e.g. number of service units purchased) and usage characteristics (e.g. channel used).

Primary value processes: Primary value processes create value directly. The main influence factor of a service provider's value creation is its ability to attract and retain customers. The relationship process encompassing customer acquisition, retention and recovery is one primary value process. A second one is the interaction process which encompasses customer integration, service production and service recovery.

Process organisation: The major organisational criteria of a process organisation are not functions or objects or both, but processes, i.e. entities of workflows in a service firm which are connected with each other.

Relationships: See **customer relationship**.

Secondary value processes: These processes support the primary value processes but do not create value directly. There are two groups of secondary processes: creating service value, as in the firm's activities in order to provide value to the customer (i.e. service product, price, delivery and communications decisions) as well as the firm's activities to manage service resources (employees, tangibles, technology) as well as the capacities of these resources.

Service blueprinting: Service blueprinting is a method for designing and analysing service processes. A service blueprint depicts the different stages in a service blueprint. For each stage, quality characteristics and cost effects are determined and analysed.

Service capacity: The service capacity describes the amount of service resources (e.g. number of hotel rooms, number of receptionists) which are available for service production and delivery. Due to the direct contact between these service resources and the customer or their objects which are integrated in the service process, a service provider can only deliver as many service units as service capacities are available.

Service channel: Service channels are the means via which service resources and customers interact. There are personal (e.g. branch system, franchising) and electronic service channels (service machines, telephone, internet, mobile channel).

Service characteristics: From an economic perspective, services account for the biggest part of the Third Sector of the Three-Sector Theory (with agriculture and forestry as the First Secor and industry as the Second Sector). In marketing, services are distinguished from consumer goods which are the object of traditional marketing approaches. Compared to consumer goods, services exhibit various specifics which can be summed up under the notion that 'services are processes'. This notion emphasises that services are produced and delivered in a process where the customer or some objects of the customer take part as an '**external factor**'. The external factor meets the internal factor, the **service resources**, in order to produce the service. Based on this specific further service characteristics follow, such as the intangibility, perishability and non-transportability of services.

Service delivery: The process of making a product or process service available for consumption or use.

Service elimination: When a service is taken out of the service programme of a provider, this is called service elimination.

Service employees: The employees of a service provider play an important role in service delivery by interacting with the customer. From a marketing perspective, customer contact employees are an important source of the customer's evaluation of a provider.

Service encounter: Service encounter is the situation in which service provider and customer meet in order to conduct service interactions and to produce the service.

Service innovation: Service innovation is the first stage of the service product lifecycle. A service innovation is a service which is new to a specific subject (e.g. own firm versus market).

Service interaction: Service interactions are exchanges of physical goods, information, performances, money or other elements which are necessary to produce a service.

Service location: A service location is the place where a service provider's resources (e.g. employees) are located (e.g. offices of a management consultancy, place of a restaurant). Service locations are evaluated by market-, position- and profitability-oriented criteria. The relevance of these criteria varies between service types.

Service modification: A service modification exists when certain elements of a service are changed (e.g. changing the element 'being served' in the transition from a classic restaurant to a cafeteria-type restaurant).

Service place: Service place is the location where the service is produced, i.e. either the provider's place (e.g. bank branch), the customer's place (e.g. internet banking at home) or a third party's place (e.g. stock exchange).

Service Profit Chain: The Service Profit Chain structures the effects of services marketing value processes. Services marketing activities influence customer perceptions (e.g. perceived service quality, perceived service value, customer satisfaction), customer behaviour (e.g. customer loyalty) and customer value (i.e. the financial contribution of a concrete customer for the firm).

Service quality: The customer evaluates a service by comparing the service received according to the service's characteristics with their expectations regarding these characteristics. The specific service characteristics (e.g. friendliness, empathy, convenience) are grouped into so-called service quality dimensions in order to make them operational. There are various approaches for service quality dimensions. The most important one is based on the SERVQUAL approach differentiating five dimensions: tangibles, reliability, responsiveness, assurance, empathy.

Service recovery: As services are produced when the customer is present, service failures cannot be totally prevented and are often perceived by the customer. Service recovery measures aim at reacting to service failures in order to prevent customer dissatisfaction.

Service resources: The elements or members of a service provider that interact with the customer in service delivery are called service resources. There are three basic types of service resources: service employees, tangibles and technology.

Service Value Chain: The Service Value Chain structures the activities of a service provider in order to create value. These are activities which directly affect the firm's value (e.g. cost generated by a marketing activity) or indirectly by creating value to the customer. According to the Service Profit Chain, this results in positive evaluations and behaviours of the customer which lead to increased revenues. The Service Value Chain differentiates **primary value processes** and **secondary value processes**.

Services marketing: Services marketing encompasses all activities of analysis, planning, realisation and control which aim at providing a service to the customer. From a value-oriented perspective, services marketing encompasses all customer-directed activities which help to create value. Primarily, services marketing is the marketing of service firms. However, the approach can also be applied to the services of industrial firms.

Servicescape: The servicescape is the physical location where the service is delivered.

Shareholder: A shareholder is an individual or company (including a corporation), that legally owns one or more shares in a joint stock company.

Stakeholder: A stakeholder was originally a person who held money or other property while its owner was being determined. The situation often arises when two persons bet on the outcome of a future event and have a third person act as the stakeholder, holding the money (or 'stake[s]') they have both wagered (or 'staked') until the event occurs. Regarding companies, a stakeholder is a person or organisation who has a legitimate interest in the company. Typical stakeholders are customers, employees, shareholders, vendors, and even members of the community or society in general.

Structural organisation: The structural organisation of the firm describes how the activities and responsibilities in a firm are arranged. Typical aspects of the structural organisation are the definition of organisational entities (e.g. departments), the allocation of responsibilities to these entities and the authorities between and within these departments.

Supplementary services: A core service in most cases is complemented by supplementary services. These can be mandatory (e.g. check-in by an airline) or value-added services (e.g. providing the customer with newspapers on an aircraft).

Tangibles: Services are intangible in nature. However, each service consists of a certain number of elements which can be perceived physically – the tangibles (e.g. facilities, furniture, appearance of employees).

Value: A firm's value is defined as the sum of the discounted future income streams of a company. From a marketing perspective, a central component of firm value is the so-called contribution, i.e. the difference between revenues and variable costs. Moreover, a central objective of services marketing is to create **customer value**.

Value driver: A value driver represents a factor which directly or indirectly influences the value created by a firm's (services marketing) activities.

Word-of-mouth communications: Customers tend to talk with their friends about their experiences with service providers. These word-of-mouth communications can be directed positively (e.g. recommendations) and negatively (e.g. dissuading others from using a certain provider's services).

Yield management: In some industries where capacity problems are very significant and relevant for value creation (e.g. the airline industry, travel industry, hotel industry), capacity-oriented and demand-oriented approaches of capacity management are combined by the concept of 'yield management'. 'Yield' expresses that this management approach aims at balancing capacity and demand according to profitability criteria.

Bibliography

4hoteliers (2004) 'Hotel profitability levels fall across Europe for 2nd consecutive year', cited from: *HotelBenchmark*, 11 July 2003, http://www.4hoteliers.com/4hots_ fshw.php?mwi=150, access: 14 May 2004.

Adams, M. (2003) 'E-mail works its way onto business-minded flights', article from *USA Today*, 24 June 2003, http://www.infobeat.com/index.cfm?action= article&id=894, access: 16 November 2004.

Adenso-Díaz, B., González-Torre, P. and Garcia, V. (2002) 'A capacity management model in service industries' *International Journal of Service Industry Management* **13** (3/4)   pp. 286–302.

Agnihothri, S., Sivasubramaniam, N. and Simmons, D. (2002) 'Leveraging technology to improve field service' *International Journal of Service Industry Management* **13** (1) pp. 47–68.

Alam, I. and Perry, C. (2002) 'A customer-oriented new service development process' *Journal of Services Marketing* **16** (6) pp. 515–33.

Anderson, E.W., Fornell, C. and Rust, R.T. (1997) 'Customer satisfaction, productivity, and profitability: differences between goods and services' *Marketing Science* **16** (2) pp. 129–46.

Angoujard, R. (2005) 'Exceeding customer expectations at Novotel' *Strategic HR Review* **4** (2) pp. 8–9.

Ansoff, H.I. (1966) *Management Strategies*, Munich: Verl. Moderne Industrie.

Arnold, D.R., Hoffman, K.D. and McCormick, J. (1989) 'Service pricing: A differentiation premium approach' *Journal of Services Marketing* **3** (3) pp. 25–33.

Avlonitis, G. and Indounas, K.A. (2004) 'Pricing strategy and practice: The impact of market structure on pricing objectives of service firms' *Journal of Product & Brand Management* **13** (5) pp. 343–58.

Avlonitis, G.J. and Indounas, K.A. (2005) 'Pricing objectives and pricing methods in the services sector' *Journal of Services Marketing* **19** (1) pp. 47–57.

Avlonitis, G., Papastathopoulou, P.G. and Gounaris, S.P. (2001) 'An empirically-based typology of product innovativeness for new financial services: success and failure scenarios' *Journal of Product Innovation Management* **18** (5) pp. 324–42.

Balci, R. (2005) *MediaMarkt: Abmahnung wegen Rabattaktion*, http://www.computerbase.de/news/wirtschaft/2005/januar/media_markt_abm ahnung_rabattaktion/, access: 30 March 2005.

Barber, H. (2004) 'Analyse offline bankers to help them shift online' *New Media Age* 14 October 2004 p. 11.

Bass, B.M. (1985) *Leadership and Performance Beyond Expectation*, New York: Free Press.

Bateson, J.E.G., Eiglier, P., Langeard, E. and Lovelock, C.H. (1978) *Testing a Conceptual Framework for Consumer Service Marketing*, Marketing Science Institute, Cambridge, MA: Marketing Science Institute.

BBC (2004) http://news.bbc.co.uk/, several articles, access: 16 November 2004.

Beard, L.H. and Hoyle, V.A. (1976) 'Cost accounting proposal for an advertising agency' *Management Accounting* **58** (4) pp. 38–40.

Bebko, C.P. (2001) 'Service encounter problems: Which service providers are more likely to be blamed?' *Journal of Services Marketing* **15** (6/7) pp. 480–5.

Bendl, H. (2004) 'König Kollege' *McK. Das Magazin von McKinsey* **3** pp. 122–7.

Berger, P.D. and Nasr, N.I. (1998) 'Customer lifetime value: Marketing models and applications' *Journal of Interactive Marketing* **12** (1) pp. 17–30.

Berry, L.L. (1983) 'Relationship marketing' *Emerging Perspectives on Services Marketing*, Chicago, IL: American Marketing Association.

Berry, L.L. (1986) 'Big ideas in services marketing' *Creativity in Sevices Marketing. What's New, What Works, What's Developing*, Venkatesan, M., Schmalensee, D.M., and Marshall, C. (eds), Chicago, IL: American Marketing Association, pp. 6–8.

Berry, L.L. (2000) 'Cultivating service brand equity' *Journal of the Academy of Marketing Science* **28** (1) pp. 128–37.

Berry, L.L. (2001) 'The substance of success', http://www.crstamu.org/images-managed/RetailingLetter/RecentIssues/AMRetIssues7-01%207-20-01.pdf, access: 30 March 2005.

Berry, L.L. and Parasuraman, A. (1991) *Marketing Services: Competing Through Quality*, New York: Free Press.

Betts, A., Meadows, M. and Walley, P. (2000) 'Call centre capacity management' *International Journal of Service Industry Management* **11** (2) pp. 185–96.

Biel, A.L. (1992) 'How brand image drives brand equity' *Journal of Advertising* **32** (6) pp. 6–12.

BIS (ed.) (1999) 'Mr. Wellink speaks about trends in the European banking industry and in banking supervision'. Speech given by Dr A.H.E.M. Wellink, President of De Nederlandsche Bank, at the launch of the Netherlands Society of Investment Professionals on 6 October 1999, in: *BIS Review* 107/1999.

Bitner, M.J. (1992) 'Servicescapes: The impact of physical surroundings on customers and employees' *Journal of Marketing* **56** (2) pp. 57–71.

Bitner, M.J., Booms, B.H. and Tetreault, M.S. (1990) 'The service encounter: Diagnosing favorable and unfavorable incidents' *Journal of Marketing* **54** (1) pp. 71–84.

Bitner, M.J., Ostrom, A.L. and Meuter, M.L. (2002) 'Implementing successful self-service technologies' *Academy of Management Executive* **16** (4) pp. 96–109.

Blattberg, R.C. and Deighton, J. (1996) 'Manage marketing by the customer equity test' *Harvard Business Review* **74** (4) pp. 136–44.

Blois, K.J. (1974) 'The marketing of services: An approach' *European Journal of Marketing* **8** (2) pp. 137–45.

Body Shop (2005) 'Customer Club', http://www.uk.thebodyshop.com/web/tbsuk/customer_club.jsp, access: 21 January 2005.

Bolton, R.N. (1998) 'A dynamic model of the duration of the customer's relationship with a continous service provider: The role of satisfaction' *Marketing Science* **17** (1) pp. 45–65.

Booms, B.H. and Bitner, M.J. (1981) 'Marketing strategies and organizational structures for service firms' *Marketing of Services, American Marketing Association*, Donnelly, J.H. and George, W.R. (eds), Chicago, IL: American Marketing Association.

Boulding, W., Kalra, A., Staelin, R. and Zeithaml, V.A. (1993) 'A dynamic process model of service quality: From expectations to behavioral intentions' *Journal of Marketing Research* **30** (1), pp. 7–27.

Bowen, D.E. and Lawler, E.E. III (1992) 'The empowerment of service workers: What, why, how and when' *Sloan Management Review* **33** (3) pp. 31–9.

Brady, D. (2004) 'Cult brands' *Business Week*, August 9–16 2004 pp. 64–8.

Brady, M.K. and Cronin, J.J. (2001) 'Some new thoughts on conceptualizing perceived service quality: A hierarchical approach' *Journal of Marketing* **65** (3) pp. 24–49.

Britannia Travel (2004) *Tour Conditions*, http://www.britannia.com/PriorityTravel/conditions.html, access: 7 October 2004.

British Airways (2005) www.ba.com, access: 20 April 2005.

Brown, M.G. (1992) 'Paying for quality' *Journal for Quality and Participation* **15** (5) pp. 38–43.

Brown, S.W., Fisk, R.P. and Bitner, M.J. (1994) 'The development and emergence of services marketing thought' *International Journal of Service Industry Management* **5** (1) pp. 21–48.

Bruhn, M. (2002a) *Integrierte Kundenorientierung*, Wiesbaden: Gabler.

Bruhn, M. (2002b) *Relationship Marketing: Managing Customer Relationships*, Harlow: Pearson Education.

Bruhn, M. (2003) 'Markteinführung von Dienstleistungen. Vom Prototyp zum marktfähigen Produkt' *Service Engineering: Entwicklung und Gestaltung innovativer Dienstleistungen*, Bullinger, H.-J. and Scheer, A.-W. (eds), Berlin: Springer.

Bruhn, M. (2004) *Qualitätsmanagement für Dienstleistungen*, Berlin: Springer.

Bruhn, M. and Frommeyer, A. (2005) 'Conceptualising and measuring communication quality', unpublished working paper, University of Basel.

Bruhn, M. and Grund, M. (2000) 'Theory, development and implementation of national customer satisfaction indices: The Swiss Index of Customer Satisfaction (SWICS)' *Total Quality Management* **11** (7) pp. 1017–18.

Budden, R. (2004a) 'Customer growth for Virgin Mobile' *Financial Times*, 30 July 2004.

Budden, R. (2004b) 'Naked brand power', FT.com site; 12 July 2004, http:// search.ft.com/search/article.html?id=040712006790&query=naked+brand+power &vsc_appId=powerSearch&offset=0&resultsToShow=10&vsc_subjectConcept=&v sc_companyConcept=&state=More&vsc_publicationGroups=TOPWFT&searchCat =-1, access: 10 April 2005.

Budden, R. and Pesola, M. (2004) 'Virgin Mobile's maiden numbers' *Financial Times*, 19 November 2004.

Burgers, A., de Ruyter, K., Keen, C. and Streukens, S. (2000) 'Customer expectation dimensions of voice-to-voice service encounters: A scale-development study' *International Journal of Service Industry Management* **11** (2) pp. 142–61.

Burt, T. (2004) 'Reuters to give managers profit responsibility' *Financial Times*, **21** August 2004.

Cadotte, E.R., Woodruff, R.B. and Jenkins, R.L. (1987) 'Expectations and norms in models of consumer satisfaction' *Journal of Marketing Research* **24** (3), pp. 305–14.

Callender, C. (2004) 2002/03 'Student income and expenditure survey: Students' income, expenditure and debt in 2002/03 and changes since 1998/99', http://www.dfes.gov.uk/research/data/uploadfiles/RR487.pdf, access: 30 September 2004.

Carlzon, J. (1987) *Moments of Truth*, New York: Harper & Row.

Carman, J. (1990) 'Consumer perceptions of service quality: An assessment of the SERVQUAL dimensions' *Journal of Retailing* **66** (1) pp. 33–55.

Cespedes, F.V. and Corey, R. (1990) 'Managing multiple channels' *Business Horizons* **33** (4) pp. 67–77.

Churchill, G.A. (1979) 'A paradigm for developing better measures of marketing constructs' *Journal of Marketing Research* **16** (2) pp. 64–73.

Ciao (2000) 'Absorbed parking ticket', http://www.ciao.co.uk/ Avis_Rent_A_Car__Review_5007074, review posted on 14 December 2000, access: 16 November 2004.

Clark, T., Rajaratnam, D. and Smith, T. (1996) 'Toward a theory of international services: Marketing intangibles in a world of nations' *Journal of International Marketing* **4** (2) pp. 9–28.

Coelho, F. and Easingwood, C. (2003) 'Multiple channel structures in financial services: A framework' *Journal of Financial Services Marketing* **8** (1) pp. 22–34.

Coelho, F.J. and Easingwood, C. (2004) 'Multiple channel systems in services: Pros, cons and issues' *The Service Industries Journal* **24** (5) pp. 1–29.

Collins, V.R. (2004) 'All change for travel sector', http://www.eurograduate.com/ career_planning/travel.html, access: 13 May 2004.

Corsten, H. (2001) *Dienstleistungsmanagement*, Stuttgart: Oldenbourg.

Crandall, R.E. and Markland, R.E. (1996) 'Demand management: Today's challenge for service industries' *Production and Operations Management* **5** (2) pp. 106–20.

Croft, J. (2004) 'Barclays embarks on radical shake-up' *FT.com*, 6 June 2004, http://search.ft.com/search/article.html?id=040606001319&query=Barclays+embarks+on+radical+shake-up&vsc_appId=powerSearch&offset=0&resultstoShow=10&vsc_subjectConcept=&vsc_companyConcept=&state=More&vsc_publicationGroups=TOPWFT&searchCat=-1, access: 15 April 2005.

Cronin, J.J. and Taylor, S.A. (1992) 'Measuring service quality: A reexamination and extension' *Journal of Marketing* **56** (3) pp. 55–68.

Curran, J. and Stanworth, J. (1983) 'Franchising in the modern economy: Towards a theoretical understanding' *International Small Business Journal* **2** (1) pp. 8–26.

Czepiel, J.A., Solomon, M.R. and Surprenant, C.F. (1985) *The Service Encounter: Managing Employee/Customer Interaction in Service Businesses*, Lexington, MA: Lexington Books.

Daniel, K. and Johnson, L.W. (2004) 'Pricing a sporting club membership package' *Sport Marketing Quarterly* **13** (2) pp. 113–16.

Daudel, S. and Vialle, G. (1992) *Yield Management*, Frankfurt/New York: Campus.

Davis, M.M. and Heineke, J. (1994) 'Understanding the roles of the customer and the operation for better queue management' *International Journal of Operations & Production Management* **14** (5) pp. 21–34.

Deloitte (2004) 'Hotel benchmark study', http://www.hotelbenchmark.com/frames.htm?http%3A//www.hotelbenchmark.com/know_today.htm, access: 13 May 2004.

Deshpandé, R. and Webster, F.E. Jr. (1989) 'Organizational culture and marketing: Defining the research agenda' *Journal of Marketing* **53** (1) pp. 3–15.

Deshpandé, R., Farley, J.U. and Webster, F.E. Jr. (1993) 'Corporate culture, customer orientation, and innovativeness in Japanese firms: A quadrad analysis' *Journal of Marketing* **57** (1) pp. 23–37.

Desiraju, R. and Shugan, S.M. (1999) 'Strategic service pricing and yield management' *Journal of Marketing* **63** (1) pp. 44–56.

DHL UK (2005) 'Tariff and transit time guide', http://www.dhl.co.uk, access: 21 January 2005.

Dobni, B. (2002) 'A model for implementing service excellence in the financial services industry' *Journal of Financial Services Marketing* **7** (1) pp. 42–53.

Dobni, D., Zerbe, W. and Ritchie, J.R.B. (1997) 'Enhancing service personnel effectiveness through the use of behavioral repertoires' *Journal of Services Marketing* **11** (6) pp. 427–45.

Docters, R., Reopel, M., Sun, J.-M. and Tanny, S. (2004) 'Capturing the unique value of services: why pricing of services is different' *Journal of Business Strategy*, **25** (2) pp. 23–8.

Domegan, C.T. (1996) 'The adoption of information technology in customer service' *European Journal of Marketing* **30** (6) pp. 52–69.

Donabedian, A. (1980) *The Definition of Quality and Approaches to its Assessment: Explorations. Explorations in Quality Assessment and Monitoring*, Vol. I, Ann Arbor, MI: Health Administration Press.

Done, K. (2005) 'Air France-KLM ahead on savings', 12 April 2005, http://news.ft.com/cms/s/05affbdc-aaf1-11d9-98d7-00000e2511c8.html, access: 14 April 2005.

Doney, P.M. and Canon, J.P. (1997) 'An examination of the nature of trust in buyer–seller relationships' *Journal of Marketing* **62** (2) pp. 1–13.

Donnelly, J.H. Jr. (1976) 'Marketing intermediaries in channels of distribution for services' *Journal of Marketing* **40** (1) pp. 55–7.

Doubledaves (2005) 'Location evaluation', http://www.doubledaves.com/, access: 15 January 2005.

dpa (2005) 'Mediamarkt', http://de.news.yahoo.com/050105/3/4d2em.html, access: 5 January 2005.

Drake, L. and Llewellyn, D.T. (1995) 'The pricing of bank payments services' *International Journal of Bank Marketing* **13** (5) pp. 3–11.

Driscoll, P.A. (1994) 'Sears to link incentives for auto service sales to customer satisfaction' *Marketing News* **28** (8) p. 8.

Dwyer, F.R. (1997) 'Customer lifetime valuation to support marketing decision making' *Journal of Direct Marketing* **11** (4) pp. 6–13.

Easton, G. (1987) 'Competition and marketing strategy' *European Journal of Marketing* **21** (2) pp. 31–49.

EasyJet (2004) 'Onboard service – easyJet kiosk', http://www.easyjet.com/EN/Flying/easykiosk.html, access: 16 November 2004.

Edmondson, A.C. (2003) 'Framing for learning: Lessons in successful technology implementation' *California Management Review* **45** (2) pp. 34–54.

Ekeledo, I. and Sivakumar, K. (1998) 'Foreign market entry mode choice of service firms: A contingency perspective' *Journal of the Academy of Marketing Science* **26** (4) pp. 274–92.

Ennew, C., Wright, M. and Watkins, T. (1989) 'Personal financial services: Marketing strategy determination' *International Journal of Bank Marketing* **7** (6) pp. 3–8.

Epstein, M.J. and Westbrook, R.A. (2001) 'Linking actions to profits in strategic decision making' *MIT Sloan Management Review* **42** (3) pp. 39–49.

Erramilli, M.K. (1990) 'Entry mode choice in service industries' *International Marketing Review* **7** (5) pp. 50–62.

Erramilli, M.K. and Rao, C.P. (1993) 'Service firms' international entry-mode choice: A modified transaction-cost analysis approach' *Journal of Marketing* **57** (3) pp. 19–38.

Estell, L. (2001) 'A green light for incentives' *Incentive* **175** (10) pp. 114–15.

Euromonitor (2004) 'Consumer foodservice in Germany – executive summary', June 2004, http://www.euromonitor.com/Consumer_Foodservice_in_Germany, access: 12 April 2005.

Fähnrich, K.P., Meiren, T., Barth, T., Hertweck, A., Baumeister, M., Demuß, L., Gaiser, B. and Zerr, K. (1999) *Service Engineering. Ergebnisse einer empirischen Studie zum Stand der Dienstleistungsentwicklung in Deutschland*, Stuttgart: IRB.

Fair Isaac (2004) 'Case study: Retention plan builds card issuer's bottom line with integrated analytics and consulting', http://www.fairisaac.com/NR/rdonlyres /C23520E3-60E7-442B-9C82-6CBF3872B058/0/StrategyScienceRetentionCS.pdf, access: 1 November 2004.

Farrell, A.M., Souchon, A.L. and Durden, G.R. (2001) 'Service encounter conceptualisation: Employees' service behaviours and customers' service quality perceptions' *Journal of Marketing Management* **17** (5/6) pp. 577–93.

Feuchtwanger, A. (1997) 'Business day: Supermarkets are queuing up to be the superbanks' *Evening Standard*, 28 November 1997.

FIFA (2002) 'Interview with Beckenbauer: "Football will take pride of place"', 30 November 2002, http://fifaworldcup.yahoo.com/06/en/021130/4/52.html, access: 12 April 2005.

FIFA (2005) 'Ticket overview', http://fifaworldcup.yahoo.com/06/ en/tickets/overview.html, access: 12 April 2005.

Fitzsimmons, J.A. and Fitzsimmons, M.J. (1994) *Service Management for Competitive Advantage*, New York: McGraw-Hill Education.

Fließ, S. and Kleinaltenkamp, M. (2004) 'Blueprinting the service company: Managing service processes efficiently' *Journal of Business Research* **57** (4) pp. 392–404.

Fornell, C., Johnson, M.D., Anderson, E.W., Jaesung C. and Bryant, B.E. (1996) 'The American customer satisfaction index: Nature, purpose, and findings' *Journal of Marketing* **60** (4) pp. 7–18.

George, N. (2004) 'IKEA continues to build on global success' *Financial Times*, 28 September 2004, p. 21.

Georgi, D. (2000) *Entwicklung von Kundenbeziehungen*, Wiesbaden: Gabler.

Gist, M.E. and Mitchell, T.R. (1992) 'Self-efficacy: A theoretical analysis of its determinants and malleability' *Academy of Management Review* **17** (2) pp. 183–211.

Goodwin, C. and Ross, I. (1990) 'Consumer evaluations of responses to complaints: What's fair and why' *Journal of Consumer Marketing* **7** (2) pp. 39–47.

Greene, W.E. (1994) 'Internal marketing' *Journal of Services Marketing* **8** (4) pp. 5–13.

Greenyer, A. (2004) 'The impact of different media channels on consumers and the wastage of potential advertising opportunities through existing customer communications' *Journal of Financial Services Marketing* **8** (3) pp. 279–90.

Griffith, T.L., Zammuto, R.F. and Aiman-Smith, L. (1999) 'Why new technologies fail' *Industrial Management* **41** (3) pp. 29–34.

Griffiths, K. (2005) 'McDonald's turns new leaf with salad sales boost' *The Independent*, 9 February 2005.

Grönroos, C. (1994) 'From marketing mix to relationship marketing: Towards a paradigm shift in marketing' *Management Decision* **32** (2) pp. 4–20.

Grönroos, C. (1999) 'Internationalization strategies for services' *Journal of Services Marketing* **13** (4/5) pp. 290–97.

Grönroos, C. (2000a) 'Creating a relationship dialogue: Communication, interaction and value' *The Marketing Review* **1** (1) pp. 5–14.

Grönroos, C. (2000b) *Service Management and Marketing: A Customer Relationship Management Approach*, 2nd edn, Chichester: John Wiley & Sons.

Grove, S.J., Carlson, L. and Dorsch, M.J. (2002) 'Addressing services' intangibility through integrated marketing communication: An exploratory study' *Journal of Services Marketing* **16** (5) pp. 393–411.

Guiltinan, J.P. (1987) 'The price bundling of service: A normative framework' *Journal of Marketing* **51** (2) pp. 74–85.

Gummesson, E. (1995) 'Services marketing and the interaction between quality, productivity and profitability' *European Journal of Marketing* **29** (5) pp. 77–9.

Gummesson, E. (1998) 'Productivity, quality and relationship marketing in service operations' *International Journal of Contemporary Hospitality Management* **10** (1) pp. 4–15.

Gummesson, E. (2002) *Total Relationship Marketing: Rethinking Marketing Management*, Oxford: Butterworth-Heinemann.

Gutman, J. (1982) 'A means–end chain model based on consumer categorization processes' *Journal of Marketing* **46** (2) pp. 60–72.

Gutman, J. and Miaoulis, G. (2003) 'Communicating a quality position in service delivery: An application in higher education' *Managing Service Quality* **13** (2) pp. 105–11.

Hacki, R. and Lighton, J. (2001) 'The future of the networked company' *The McKinsey Quarterly* 2001 No. 3, pp. 26–40.

Håkansson, H. and Snehota, I. (1993) *The Content and Functions of Business Relationships*, Paper at 9th IMP Conference, Bath: IMP.

Hallowell, R. and Schlesinger, L.A. (2000) 'The service profit chain: Intellectual roots, current realities and future prospects' *Handbook of Services Marketing & Management*, Swartz, T.A. and Iacobucci, D. (eds), Thousands Oaks, CA: Sage Publications.

Handelszeitung (2003) 'Lauwarmes Geschäft mit Kaffee' *Handelszeitung* (43) p. 29.

Harness, D.R. (2003) 'The end stage of a financial service product' *Journal of Financial Services Marketing* **7** (3) pp. 220–29.

Harris, L.C. and Ogbonna, E. (2001) 'Leadership style and market orientation: An empirical study' *European Journal of Marketing* **35** (5/6) pp. 744–64.

Hart, C.W.L., Heskett, J.L. and Sasser, W.E. (1990) 'The profitable art of service recovery' *Harvard Business Review* **68** (4) pp. 148–65.

Hartline, M.D. and Ferrell, O.C. (1996) 'The management of customer-contact service employees: An empirical investigation' *Journal of Marketing* **60** (4) pp. 52–70.

Hartman, D.E. and Lindgren, J.H. Jr. (1993) 'Consumer evaluation of goods and services' *Journal of Services Marketing* **7** (2) pp. 4–15.

Harvard Business School (2004) 'Singapore Airlines: Customer Service Innovation – Abstract', http://harvardbusinessonline.hbsp.harvard.edu/b01/en/common/item_detail.jhtml?id=504025, access: 16 November 2004.

Heskett, J.A., Sasser, W.E. and Hart, C,W. (1990) *Service Breakthroughs*, New York: Free Press.

Heskett, J.L., Sasser, W.E. and Schlesinger, L.A. (1997) *The Service Profit Chain*, New York: Free Press.

Heskett, J.L., Jones, T.O., Loveman, G.W., Sasser, W.E. and Schlesinger, L.A. (1994) 'Putting the service-profit chain to work' *Harvard Business Review*, **72** (2) pp. 164–70.

Hightower, R., Brady, M.K. and Baker, T.L. (2002) 'Investigating the role of the physical environment in hedonic service consumption: An exploratory study of sporting events' *Journal of Business Research* **55** (9) pp. 697–706.

Hite, C.F. and Hite, R.E. (1991) 'Quality uncertainty, brand reliance, and dissipative advertising' *Journal of the Academy of Marketing Science* **19** (2) pp. 115–21.

Hoffman, K.D. and Turley, L.W. (2002) 'Atmospherics, service encounters and consumer decision making: An integrative perspective' *Journal of Marketing Theory and Practice* **10** (3) pp. 33–47.

Hotels (2002) 'Leading Hotels extends its line' *Hotels* **36** (9) pp. 22–4.

Howe, U. (2003) 'Der tollste Laden der Welt' *Textilwirtschaft* (35) pp. 72–4.

Humby, C., Hunt, T. and Phillips, T. (2003) *Scoring Points: How Tesco is Winning Customer Loyalty*, London: Kogan Page.

Hur, D., Mabert, V.A. and Bretthauer, K. (2004) 'Real-time schedule adjustment decisions: A case study' *Omega – The International Journal of Management Science* **32** (5) pp. 333–44.

Iacobucci, D. and Ostrom, A. (1993) 'Gender differences in the impact of core and relational aspects of services on the evaluation of service encounters' *Journal of Consumer Psychology* **2** (3) pp. 257–86.

IBM (1998) 'British Airways teams up with IBM to roll-out self-service kiosk technology', http://www-1.ibm.com/industries/travel/doc/content/bin/BAkiosk.pdf, access: 11 April 2005.

Jackson, B.B. (1985) 'Build customer relationships that last' *Harvard Business Review* **63** (6) pp. 120–8.

Jarillo, J.C. (1993) *Strategic Networks: Creating the Borderless Organization*, Oxford: Butterworth-Heinemann.

Javalgi, R.G., Griffith, D.A. and White, D.S. (2003) 'An empirical examination of factors influencing the internationalization of service firms' *Journal of Services Marketing* **17** (2) pp. 185–201.

JD Power (2004) 'Hotel guest satisfaction continues to improve in some segments, despite economic challenges', August 2003, http://www.jdpower.com/awards/industry/pressrelease.asp?StudyID=767, access: 14 May 2004.

Judd, R.C. (1964) 'The case for redefining services' *Journal of Marketing* **28** (1) pp. 58–9.

Kamiske, G.F. and Füermann, T. (1995) 'Reengineering versus Prozessmanagement. Der richtige Weg zur prozessorientierten Organisationsgestaltung' *Zeitschrift Führung und Organisation* **64** (3) pp. 142–8.

Keaveney, S.M. (1995) 'Customer switching behavior in service industries: An exploratory study' *Journal of Marketing* **59** (2) pp. 71–82.

Keller, K.L. (2003) *Strategic Brand Management: Building, Measuring, and Managing Brand Equity*, New York: Prentice-Hall.

Kelley, S.W., Hoffman, K.D. and Davis, M.A. (1993) 'A typology of retail failures and recoveries' *Journal of Retailing* **69** (4) pp. 429–53.

Kennedy, K.N., Goolsby, J.R. and Arnould, E.J. (2003) 'Implementing a customer orientation: Extension of theory and application' *Journal of Marketing* **67** (4) pp. 67–81.

Killgren, L. (2005) 'Tesco's international empire', 12 April 2005, http://news.ft.com/cms/s/99f698c2-aa66-11d9-98d7-00000e2511c8.html, access: 14 April 2005.

Klassen, K.J. and Rohleder, T.R. (2001) 'Combining operations and marketing to manage capacity and demand in services' *Service Industries Journal* **21** (2) pp. 1–30.

Klassen, K.J. and Rohleder, T.R. (2002) 'Demand and capacity management decisions in services: How they impact on one another' *International Journal of Operations and Production Management* **22** (5) pp. 527–48.

Kleijnen, M.M., Wetzels, M. and de Ruyter, K. (2004) 'Consumer acceptance of wireless finance' *Journal of Financial Services Marketing* **8** (3) pp. 206–17.

Köhler, R. (2005) 'Kundenorientiertes Rechnungswesen als Voraussetzung des Kundenbindungsmanagements' in *Handbuch Kundenbindungsmanagement*, Bruhn, M. and Homburg, C. (eds), 5th edn, Wiesbaden: Gabler Verlag, pp. 400–33.

Korea Times (2005) 'Mobile learning gains foothold', *Korea Times*, 27 January.

Kotler, P. (1973) 'Atmospherics as a marketing tool' *Journal of Retailing* **49** (4) pp. 48–64.

Krefting, L.A. and Frost, P.J. (1985) 'Untangling webs, surfing waves, and wildcatting: A multiple-metaphor perspective on managing culture' in *Organization Culture*, P.J. Frost *et al.* (eds), Beverly Hills, CA: Sage.

Krugman, D.M., Reid, L.M., Dunn, S.W. and Barban, A.M. (1994) *Advertising: Its role in Modern Marketing*, 8th edn, Fort Worth, TX: Dryden Press.

Laing, A.W. and McKee, L. (2000) 'Structuring the marketing function in complex professional service organizations' *European Journal of Marketing* **34** (5/6) pp. 576–97.

Latoski, S.P., Pal, R. and Sinha, K.C. (1999) 'Cost-effectiveness evaluation of Hoosier Helper Freeway Service Patrol' *Journal of Transportation Engineering* **125** (5) pp. 429–38.

Lawchannel (2005) '"Lass dich nicht verarschen" – MediaMarkt abgemahnt', http://www.lawchannel.de/lawchannel/cont/channel/chann_full.php?vall=16&feed=12128, access: 30 March 2005.

Lawn, J. (2004) 'At your service!', http://www.food-management.com, August, pp. 33–40.

Lentell, R. (2000) 'Untangling the tangibles: "Physical evidence" and customer satisfaction in local authority leisure centres' *Managing Leisure* **5** (1) pp. 1–16.

Letmathe, P. (2001) 'Operative Netzwerke aus der Sicht der Theorie der Unternehmung' *Zeitschrift für Betriebswirtschaft* **71** (5) pp. 551–70.

Levinsohn, A. (1998) 'Citibank recharts its technology course' *ABA Banking Journal* **90** (5) pp. 40–8.

Lewis, M.A. (2002) 'Selecting and implementing service technology: Control, uncertainty and competitive advantage' *Service Industries Journal* **22** (2) pp. 17–42.

Liljander, V. (1994) 'Modeling perceived quality using different comparison standards' *Journal of Consumer Satisfaction, Dissatisfaction and Complaining Behavior* **7** pp. 126–42.

Liljander, V. and Strandvik, T. (1993) 'Different comparison standards as determinants of service quality' *Journal of Consumer Satisfaction, Dissatisfaction and Complaining Behavior* **6** pp. 118–32.

Liljander, V. and Strandvik, T. (1995) 'The nature of customer relationships in services' *Advances in Services Marketing and Management Research and Practice*, Swartz, T.A., Bowen, D.E. and Brown, S. W. (eds), Vol. 4, Greenwich/London: JAI Press, pp. 141–67.

Lindqvist, L.J. (1987) 'Quality and service value in the service consumption' *Add Value to Your Service*, Suprenant, C. (ed.), Proceedings Series, Chicago, IL: American Marketing Association.

Lindsell Marketing (2004) 'The danger of defection: A comparative study into winning back lost customers', www.lindsellmarketing.com, access: 1 November 2004.

Link, J. and Hildebrand, V. (1993) *Database Marketing und Computer Aided Selling*, Munich: Vahlen.

Lockyer, T. (2003) 'Hotel cleanliness: How do guests view it? Let us get specific. A New Zealand study' *International Journal of Hospitality Management* **22** (3) pp. 297–305.

Lovelock, C. and Wirtz, J. (2003) *Services Marketing*, 5th edn, New York: Prentice-Hall.

Lovelock, C. and Wirtz, J. (2004) *Services Marketing: People, Technology, Strategy*, Upper Saddle River, NJ: Pearson/Prentice-Hall.

Mabberley, J. (1998) *Activity Based Costing in Financial Institutions: How to Support Value-based Management and Manage Your Resources Effectively*, London: Pitman Publishing.

Mabert, V. (1986) 'Staffing and equipment decisions for services: An experimental analysis' *Journal of Operations Management* **6** (3/4) pp. 273–81.

Mangold, W.G. and Babakus, E. (1991) 'Service quality: The front-stage vs. the back-stage perspective' *Journal of Services Marketing* **5** (4) pp. 59–70.

Mankila, M. (2001) 'Application of price bundling strategies in retail banking in Europe', Handelshögskolan vid Göteborgs Universitet, FE-rapport 2001–379, Göteborg.

Mankila, M. (2004) 'Retaining students in retail banking through price bundling: Evidence from the Swedish Market' *European Journal of Operational Research* **155** (2) pp. 299–316.

Market Wire Incorporated (2005) 'Groundbreaking new service delivers museum-quality high resolution art and photography into the home on flat panel TVs and PCs', 11 January.

Marn, M.V. and Rosiello, R.L. (1992) 'Managing price, gaining profit' *Harvard Business Review* **70** (5) pp. 84–94.

Martin, C.R. and Horne, D.A. (1993) 'Services innovation: Successful versus unsuccessful firms' *International Journal of Service Innovation Management* **4** (1) pp. 49–65.

Martin, C.R. Jr., Horne, D.A. and Chan, W.S. (2001) 'A perspective on client productivity in business-to-business consulting services' *International Journal of Service Industry Management* **12** (2) pp. 137–48.

Matanovich, T. (2003) 'Pricing services vs. pricing products: Don't buy into the duality myth. Focus on value to the customer' *Marketing Management* **12** (4) pp. 12–13.

McDougall, G.H.G. and Levesque, T. (2000) 'Customer satisfaction with services: Putting perceived value into the equation' *Journal of Services Marketing* **14** (4/5) pp. 392–409.

McGregor, R. (2004) 'Foreign insurers gear up for push into China' *Financial Times*, 1 December.

McKosker, P. (2001) 'A brief history of cinema exhibition in the UK', http://www.mediasalles.it/crl_cosker.htm, access: 13 May 2004.

McNerney, D.J. (1996) 'Compensation: The link to customer satisfaction' *HR Focus* **73** (9) pp. 3–6.

Meenaghan, T. and Shipley, D. (1999) 'Media effect in commercial sponsorship' *European Journal of Marketing* **33** (3/4) pp. 328–47.

Meffert, H. and Bruhn, M. (2003) *Dienstleistungsmarketing*, 4th edn, Wiesbaden: Gabler.

Meffert, H. and Bruhn, M. (2005) *Dienstleistungsmarketing*, Wiesbaden: Gabler.

Meissner, H.G. and Gerber, S. (1980) 'Die Auslandsinvestitionen als Entscheidungsproblem' *BFuP* **32** (3) pp. 223–45.

Meuter, M.L., Ostrom, A.L., Roundtree, R.I. and Bitner, M.J. (2000) 'Self-service technologies: Understanding customer satisfaction with technology-based service encounters' *Journal of Marketing* **64** (3) pp. 50–64.

Michalski, S. (2002) *Kundenabwanderungs- und Rückgewinnungsprozesse*, Wiesbaden: Gabler.

Miller, D. and Friesen, D.H. (1982) 'Innovation in conservative and entrepreneurial firms: Two models of strategic momentum' *Strategic Management Journal* **3** (1) pp. 1–25.

Miller, J.A. (1977) 'Exploring satisfaction, modifying models, eliciting expectations, posing problems, and making meaningful measurement' in Hunt, H.K. (ed.) *Conceptualization and Measurement of Consumer Satisfaction and Dissatisfaction*, Cambridge, MA: Marketing Science Institute, pp. 72–91.

Miller, J. (2005) 'TBWA Worldwide named 2004 global agency network of the year by Advertising Age', press release from 10 January, http://www.tbwa.com/view_release.php?id=43, access: 14 April 2005.

Mittal, B. and Baker, J. (2002) 'Advertising strategies for hospitality services' *Cornell Hotel and Restaurant Administration Quarterly* **43** (2) pp. 51–63.

Monroe, K.B. (1991) *Pricing: Making Profitable Decisions*, 2nd edn, New York: McGraw-Hill.

Morgan, R.M. and Hunt, S.D. (1994) 'The commitment-trust theory of relationship marketing' *Journal of Marketing* **58** (3) pp. 20–38.

Morrow, L. (1984) 'Waiting as a way of life' *Time* **124** (4) p. 65.

Moustfield, N. (2003) 'Financial services survey', http://www.credo-group.com/ftp/finserv_jan2003.pdf, access: 29 September 2004.

Mövenpick (2004) *Kennzahlen, Mövenpick Wein*, http://www.moevenpick-group.com/NR/rdonlyres/CA259AFD-3369-4328-BB7B-9B1D4C11DAD7/0/MPW_050322d_wein.pdf, access: 30 March 2005.

Mybasel.com (2003) 'Evaluation of the cinema "Küchlin 1"', http://www.mybasel.com/, access: 5 May 2005.

Naylor, J.C., Pritchard, R.D. and Ilgen, D.R. (1980) *A Theory of Behavior in Organizations*, New York: Academic Press.

Netonomy (2004) 'Fujitsu/Netonomy self-service for mobile users report', http://www.netonomy.com/resourceslib/rl_fnssr.html, access: 7 October 2004.

Newton, R. (1998) 'The silver screen turns to gold: the days of the flea pit cinema have gone' *Sunday Telegraph*, 25 January 1998.

Ng, I.C.L., Wirtz, J. and Lee, K.S. (1999) 'The strategic role of unused service capacity' *International Journal of Service Industry Management* **10** (2) pp. 211–44.

Ngobo, P.V. (1997) 'The standards issue: An accessibility-diagnosticity perspective' *Journal of Consumer Satisfaction, Dissatisfaction and Complaining Behavior* **10** pp. 61–79.

Nickell, J.A. (2001) 'To voice mail hell and back', *Business 2.0* **6** (14) pp. 49–53.

Nigh, D., Kang, K.C. and Krishnan, S. (1986) 'The role of location-related factors in US banking involvement abroad: An empirical examination' *Journal of International Business Studies* **17** (3) pp. 59–72.

Noack, H.-C. (2003) 'Der Auslese der Fluggesellschaften folgt das Allianzsterben' *Frankfurter Allgemeine Zeitung*, 29 September, No. 226, p. 13.

Oliver, R.L. (1980) 'A cognitive model of the antecedents and consequences of satisfaction decisions' *Journal of Marketing Research* **17** (4) pp. 460–69.

Oliver, R.L. (1996) *Satisfaction: A Behavioral Perspective on the Consumer*, New York: McGraw-Hill.

O'Loughlin, D., Szmigin, I. and Turnbull, P. (2004) 'Branding and relationships: Customer and supplier perspectives' *Journal of Financial Services Marketing* **8** (3) pp. 218–30.

Olson, J.C. and Dover, P.A. (1979) 'Disconfirmation of consumer expectations through product trial' *Journal of Applied Psychology* **64** (2) pp. 41–50.

Olson, J.C. and Reynolds, T.J. (1983) 'Understanding consumers' cognitive structures: Implications for advertising strategy' *Advertising and Consumer Psychology*, Percy, L. and Woodside, A. (eds), Vol. 1, Lexington, MA: Lexington Books.

Organ, D.W. (1988) *Organizational Citizenship Behaviour: The Good Soldier Syndrome*, Lexington, MA: Lexington Books.

Parasuraman, A. (1987) 'Customer-oriented corporate cultures are crucial to services marketing success' *Journal of Services Marketing* **1** (1) pp. 39–46.

Parasuraman, A. and Varadarajan, P.R. (1988) 'Future strategic emphases in service versus goods businesses' *Journal of Services Marketing* **2** (4) pp. 57–66.

Parasuraman, A., Zeithaml, V.A. and Berry, L.L. (1985) 'A conceptual model of service quality and its implications for future research' *Journal of Marketing* **49** (1) pp. 41–50.

Parasuraman, A., Zeithaml, V.A. and Berry, L.L. (1988) 'SERVQUAL: A multiple-item scale for measuring consumer perceptions of service quality' *Journal of Retailing* **64** (1) pp. 12–40.

Parasuraman, A., Zeithaml, V.A. and Berry, L.L. (1994) 'Alternative scales for measuring service quality: A comparative assessment based on psychometric and diagnostic criteria' *Journal of Retailing* **70** (3) pp. 201–30.

Patil, P. and Chung, B. (1998) 'Changes in multiunit restaurant compensation packages' *Cornell Hotel and Restaurant Administration Quarterly* **39** (3) pp. 45–53.

Patrício, L., Fisk, R.P. and Falcão e Cunha, J. (2003) 'Improving satisfaction with bank service offerings: Measuring the contribution of each delivery channel' *Managing Service Quality* **13** (6) pp. 471–82.

Payne, A., Holt, S. and Frow, P. (2001) 'Relationship value management: Exploring the integration of employee, customer and shareholder value and enterprise performance models', *Journal of Marketing Management* **17** (7/8) pp. 785–817.

Peck, H., Payne, A., Christopher, M. and Clark, M. (1999) *Relationship Marketing: Strategy and Implementation*, Oxford: Butterworth-Heinemann.

Performix Technologies (2005) 'Conduit plc: Employee motivation builds productivity for directory services provider', http://www.performix technologies.com/contentmgr/showdetails.php/id/1259, access: 10 April 2005.

Perkins, C. (2005) 'Hours-of-service rules can raise costs, lower productivity' *Nation's Restaurant News*, **39** (8) p. 32.

Peters, T. (1994) *Crazy Times Call For Crazy Organizations*, New York: Vintage Books.

Porter, M.E. (1998) *Competitive Advantage: Creating and Sustaining Superior Performance*, New York: Free Press.

PR Newswire (2004) 'Shopping habits likely to be affected by Euro 2004, 10 June 2004, http://www.prnewswire.co.uk/cgi/news/release?id=124651, access: 12 April 2005.

Pullman, M.E. and Moore, W.L. (1999) 'Optimal service design: Integrating marketing and operations perspectives' *International Journal of Service Industry Management* **10** (2) pp. 239–61.

Quinn, J.B. (1999) 'Strategic outsourcing: Leveraging knowledge capabilities' *Sloan Management Review* **40** (4) pp. 9–21.

Rafiq, M and Pervaiz, A. (1993) 'The scope of internal marketing: Defining the boundary between marketing and human resource management' *Journal of Marketing Management* **9** (3) pp. 219–32.

Rathmell, J.M. (1966) 'What is meant by services?' *Journal of Marketing* **30** (4) pp. 32–6.

Ratza, C.L. (1993) 'A client-driven model for service pricing' *Journal of Professional Services Marketing* **8** (2) pp. 55–64.

Redding Electric Utility (2005) 'Frequently asked questions (FAQs): customer service', http://reuweb.reddingelectricutility.com/custsvc/csfaqs.html#contact, access: 12 April 2005.

Reed, D. (1997) 'Direct response TV: In the line of fire' *Marketing Week* **20** (33) pp. 55–9.

Regan, W.J. (1963) 'The service revolution' *Journal of Marketing* **27** (3) pp. 57–62.

Reichheld, F.F. and Sasser, W.E. (1990) 'Zero defections: Quality comes to services' *Harvard Business Review* **68** (5) pp, 105–11.

Reid Smith, E. (2004) 'Building B-t-B e-loyalty' *CRM Today*, http://www.crm2day.com/editorial/EpAyFykAypKoNeXRGa.php, access: 1 November 2004.

Reuters (2004) 'Reuters business insight: The European wealth management and private banking market outlook: Optimizing customer value in a demanding marketplace', http://www.reutersbusinessinsight.com/rbi/content/rbfs0058m.pdf, access: 18 October 2004.

Riley, G. (2003) 'Economics case study: The European airline market', http://www.tutor2u.net/Case_Study_European_Airlines.pdf, access: 13 May 2004.

Ritz-Carlton (2004a) *Awards*, http://www.ritzcarlton.com/corporate/about_us/awards.asp, access: 13 May 2004.

Ritz-Carlton (2004b) *MBNQA Application Summary*, http://www.ritzcarlton.com/resources/rcappsum.pdf, access: 13 May 2004.

Roberts, V. (2001) 'Managing strategic outsourcing in the healthcare industry' *Journal of Healthcare Management* **46** (4) pp. 239–49.

Rogers, J.D., Clow, K.E. and Kash, T.J. (1994) 'Increasing job satisfaction of service personnel' *Journal of Services Marketing* **8** (1) pp. 14–26.

Roos, I. and Strandvik, T. (1997) 'Diagnosing the termination of customer relationship', paper presented at *New and Evolving Paradigms: The Emerging Future of Marketing*, 12–15 June, Dublin: American Marketing Association.

Ross, S.D., Norman, W.C. and Dorsch, M.J. (2003) 'The use of conjoint analysis in the development of a new recreation facility' *Managing Leisure* **8** (4) pp. 227–44.

Royal Bank of Scotland (2004) 'E-billing services', http://www.rbs.co.uk/CBFM/Brochures_&_Publications/downloads/Brochures/Payments_and_Cash_Management/e-Billing_Services.pdf, access: 16 November 2004.

Rust, R., Zeithaml, V.A. and Lemon, K. (2000) *Driving Customer Equity: How Customer Lifetime Value is Reshaping Corporate Strategy*, New York: Free Press.

Rust, R.T., Lemon, K.N. and Zeithaml, V.A. (2004) 'Return on marketing: Using customer equity to focus marketing strategy' *Journal of Marketing* **68** (1) pp. 109–27.

Rust, R.T., Zahorik, A.J. and Keiningham, T.L. (1994) *Return on Quality: Measuring the Financial Impact of Your Company's Quest for Quality*, Chicago, IL.: Irwin Professional Publishing.

Samiee, S. (1999) 'The internationalization of services: Trends, obstacles and issues' *Journal of Services Marketing* **13** (4/5) pp. 319–28.

Sampathkumaran, S. (1994) 'Migration analysis helps stop customer attrition' *Marketing News* **28** (18) pp. 18–19.

Scheidegger, N. and Taaks, G. (2004) 'Umsatzsteigerungen mit Multichannel-Marketing bei der Mövenpick Wein AG' FHBB Case Study, Basel, http://experience-de.fhbb.ch/cases/experience.nsf/2c074be346c8febac1256d1e003f02c3/d51ceeb99039f639c1256f35004c4497?OpenDocument&Highlight=0,m%C3%B6venpick, access: 30 March 2005.

Scheuing, E.Z. and Johnson, E.M. (1989) 'A proposed model for new service development' *Journal of Services Marketing* **3** (2) pp. 25–34.

Schulz, A. (2001) 'Die deutsche Franchisewirtschaft im internationalen Vergleich' in *Handbuch Franchising and Cooperation: Das Management kooperativer Unternehmensnetzwerke*, Ahlert, D. (ed.), Neuwied: Luchterhand.

Seidel, H. (2004) 'Wir haben an der falschen Stelle gespart' *Die Welt*, 25 October, p. 12.

Shannon, R. (2002) 'Grasping the direct marketing advantage' *Journal of Financial Services Marketing* **7** (1) pp. 75–9.

Sharma, N. and Patterson, P.G. (1999) 'The impact of communication effectiveness and service quality on relationship commitment' *Journal of Services Marketing* **13** (2/3) pp. 151–70.

Shemwell, D.J. Jr. and Cronin, J. Jr (1994) 'Service marketing strategies for coping with demand/supply imbalances' *Journal of Services Marketing* **8** (4) pp. 14–24.

Shostack, G.L. (1977) 'Breaking free from product marketing' *Journal of Marketing* **41** (2) pp. 73–80.

Shostack, G.L. (1982) 'How to design a service' *European Journal of Marketing* **16** (1) pp. 49–63.

Shostack, G.L. (1984) 'Designing services that deliver' *Harvard Business Review* **62** (1) pp. 133–9.

Silverman, G. (2004a) 'Amex expands net marketing' *Financial Times*, 9 November 2004.

Silverman, G. (2004b) 'Advertisers go back to the future', FT.com site, 24 October 2004, http://search.ft.com/search/article.html?id=041024002941&query=Advertisers+go+back+to+the+future&vsc_appId=powerSearch&offset=0&resultsToShow=10&vsc_subjectConcept=&vsc_companyConcept=&state=More&vsc_publicationGroups=TOPWFT&searchCat=-1, access: 10 April 2005.

Silvestro, R. and Cross, S. (2000) 'Applying the service profit chain in a retail environment' *International Journal of Service Industry Management* **11** (3) pp. 244–68.

Simon, H. and Damian, A. (1999) 'Preispolitik für industrielle Dienstleistungen' *Wettbewerbsfaktor Dienstleistung: Produktion von Dienstleistungen – Produktion als Dienstleistung*, Corsten, H. and Schneider, H. (eds), Munich: Vahlen.

Six Continents Hotels (2004) 'Prelimary results – twelve months to 31 December 2003', http://www.ihgplc.com/investors/prelims03/presentation/slides.pdf, access: 13 May 2004.

Sixt (2004) *http://www.e-sixt.co.uk/*, access: 10 November 2004.

Smith, A. (2005) 'Sir Terry's formula for foreign fortune: Tesco's international profits rise sharply', 13 April, http://news.ft.com/cms/s/6ee6632a-abb9-11d9-893c-00000e2511c8.html, access: 14 April 2005.

Solomons, R. (2002) 'Six Continents Hotels, presentation at Crédit Lyonnais Conference 2002', http://www.ihgplc.com/investors/presentations/credit_lyonnais_conf/credit_lyonnais_conf.pdf, access: 13 May 2004.

Space.com (1999) 'Pizza Hut puts pie in the sky with rocket logo', posted at 30 September 1999, http://www.space.com/businesstechnology/business/pizza_hut_990930_wg.html, access: 16 November 2004.

Stafford, M.R. (1996) 'Tangibility in services advertising: An investigation of verbal versus visual cues' *Journal of Advertising* **25** (3) pp. 13–28.

Stamper, C.L. and van Dyne, L. (2003) 'Organizational citizenship: A comparison between part-time and full-time service employees' *Cornell Hotel and Restaurant Administration Quarterly* **44** (1) pp. 33–42.

Stauss, B. and Bruhn, M. (2003) 'Dienstleistungsnetzwerke – Eine Einführung in den Sammelband' in *Jahrbuch Dienstleistungsmanagement – Dienstleistungs-netzwerke*, Bruhn, M. and Stauss, B. (eds), Wiesbaden: Gabler.

Steinke, S. (2005) 'Germanwings: profitable growth' *Flug Revue* (3) p. 24, http://www.flug-revue.rotor.com/FRheft/FRHeft05/FRH0503/FR0503d.htm.

Stern, L.W., El-Ansary, A.I. and Coughlan, A.T. (1996) *Marketing Channels*, 5th edn, Hemel Hempstead: Prentice Hall.

Stevens, T. (2005) 'Arola launches home service in Barcelona' *Caterer and Hotelkeeper* **193** (4352) p. 14.

Stone, M., Bearman, D., Butscher, S.A., Gilbert, D., Crick, P. and Moffett, T. (2004) 'The effect of retail customer loyalty schemes: Detailed measurement or transforming marketing?' *Journal of Targeting, Measurement and Analysis for Marketing* **12** (3) pp. 305–18.

Storbacka, K. (1997) 'Segmentation based on customer profitability: Retrospective analysis of retail bank customer bases' *Journal of Marketing Management* **13** (5) pp. 479–92.

Strong, C.A. and Harris, L.C. (2004) 'The drivers of customer orientation: An exploration of relational, human resource and procedural tactics' *Journal of Strategic Marketing* **12** (3) pp. 183–204.

Sundaram, D.S. and Webster, C. (2000) 'The role of nonverbal communication in service encounters' *Journal of Services Marketing* **14** (4/5) pp. 378–89.

Sweeney, J.C. and Soutar, G.N. (2001) 'Consumer perceived value: The development of a multiple item scale' *Journal of Retailing* **77** (2) pp. 203–20.

Sydow, J. (1992) *Strategische Netzwerke. Evolution und Organisation*, Wiesbaden: Gabler.

Sydow, J. (1995) 'Netzwerkorganisation. Interne und externe Restrukturierung von Unternehmungen' *Wirtschaftswissenschaftliches Studium* **24** (12) pp. 629–34.

TBWA (2005) 'Offices and contacts', http://www.tbwa.com/pdf/tbwa_contacts. pdf, access: 14 April 2005.

Terpstra, V. and Yu, C.-M. (1988) 'Determinants of foreign investments of US advertising agencies' *Journal of International Business Studies* **19** (1) pp. 33–46.

Tetra Pak (2004) 'The Company History', http://www.tetrapak.com, access: 16 November 2004.

The Economist (2004) 'Big Mac Index' *The Economist*, 16 December, http://www. economist.com/markets/bigmac/displayStory.cfm?story_id=3503641, access: 14 April 2005.

The Times 100 (2004) 'FTSE case study', http://www.thetimes100.co.uk/case_ study.php?cID=4&csID=19&pID=1, access: 16 November 2004.

The Times 100 (2005) 'McDonald's: Recruiting, selecting and training for success', http://www.thetimes100.co.uk/case_study.php?cID=28&csID=194&pID=1, access: 12 April 2005.

Tse, D.K. and Wilton, P.C. (1988) 'Models of consumer satisfaction formation: An extension' *Journal of Marketing Research* **25** (2) pp. 204–12.

Tung, W., Capella, M. and Tat, P.K. (1997) 'Service pricing: A multi-step synthetic approach' *Journal of Services Marketing* **11** (1) pp. 53–65.

Tuzovic, S. (2004) *Kundenorientierte Vergütungssysteme im Relationship Marketing*, Wiesbaden: Gabler.

United Nations (ed.) (2003) *Statistical Yearbook of the Economic Commission for Europe*, New York and Geneva: United Nations.

Van Looy, B., Gemmel, P., Desmet, S., Van Dierdonck, R. and Serneels, S. (1998) 'Dealing with productivity and quality indicators in a service environment: Some field experiences' *International Journal of Service Industry Management* **9** (4) pp. 359–76.

van Raaij, W.F. (1991) 'The formation and use of expectations in consumer decision making' *Handbook of Consumer Behavior*, Robertson, T.S. and Kassarjian, H.H. (eds), Englewood Cliffs, NJ: Prentice-Hall.

Varian, H.R. (2002) *Intermediate Economics: A Modern Approach*, 6th edn, New York, London: W. W. Norton.

Verespej, M.A. (1996) 'More value for compensation' *Industry Week* **245** (12) pp. 19–20.

Voneche, F. (2005) 'Yield management in the airline industry', http://www.luc.edu/faculty/eventa/archive/su483we/yield.htm, access: 12 April 2005.

Waters, H.R. and Hussey, P. (2004) 'Pricing health services for purchasers: A review of methods and experiences' *Health Policy*, **70** (2) pp. 175–84.

Weatherly, K.A. and Tansik, D.A. (1993) 'Managing multiple demands: A role-theory examination of the behaviors of customer contact service workers' *Advances in Services Marketing and Management*, Swartz, T.A., Bowen, D.E. and Brown, S.W. (eds), Vol. 2, Greenwich, NY: JAI Press.

Welge, M.K. and Borghoff, T. (2003) 'Die Globalisierung der Netzwerkbildung von professionellen Dienstleistungsunternehmen: Fallbeispiele von drei Start-up-Unternehmen' *Jahrbuch Dienstleistungsmanagement – Dienstleistungs- netzwerke*, Bruhn, M. and Stauss, B. (eds), Wiesbaden: Gabler.

Wells, D. (2004) 'Money talks in culture of compensation' *Financial Times*, 11 December.

Werder Bremen (2005) 'Tageskarten-Preise der Saison 2004/2005', www.werder-online.de, access: 21 January 2005.

Wiertz, C., de Ruyter, K., Keen, C. and Streukens, S. (2004) 'Cooperating for service excellence in multichannel service systems: An empirical assessment' *Journal of Business Research* **57** (4) pp. 424–36.

Winsted, K.F. and Patterson, P.G. (1998) 'Internationalization of services: The service exporting decision' *Journal of Services Marketing* **12** (6) pp. 294–311.

Yelkur, R. and Herbig, P. (1997) 'Differential pricing for services' *Marketing Intelligence and Planning* **15** (4) pp. 190–94.

Youth Hostels Association (YHA) (2005) 'Membership discounts', http://www.yha.org.uk/Join_YHA/Offers/Membership_Discounts.html, access: 21 January 2005.

Zeithaml, V.A. (1981) 'How consumer evaluation processes differ between goods and services' *Marketing of Services*, Donnelly, J.H. and George, W.R. (eds), Chicago, IL: American Marketing Association, pp. 186–90.

Zeithaml, V.A. (1988) 'Consumer perceptions of price, quality and value: A means–end model and synthesis of evidence' *Journal of Marketing* **52** (2) pp. 2–22.

Zeithaml, V.A., Berry, L.L. and Parasuraman, A. (1993) 'The nature and determinants of customer expectations of service' *Journal of the Academy of Marketing Science* **21** (1) pp. 1–12.

Index

Entries in **bold** are defined in the Glossary.

abandoner role 85
ABC analysis 40, 41
accessibility of location 238
acquisition communication 273
activity-based costing 432–3
adaptability 350
advertising agencies 397
after-sales service 159, 160
Air France-KLM 383–4
airline industry
  alliances and mergers 8, 399–400, 401
  capacity management 416
  and competition 8, 399–400
  cost and revenue synergies 383–4
  critical incident analysis 80
  e-mail facilities 171–2
  frequent flier programmes 111, 122
  pricing 325, 362
  self-service kiosks 340–1
  service blueprint 92
  service elimination 181–2
  time flexibility 242
  value creation 18, 20–1
  value drivers 440–1
  yield management 367–8
alignment 120, 121
always-a-share markets 117
American Airlines 367–8, 440–1
American Express 289
Arola, Sergi 229
assurance 52, 55
atmospherics 321
ATMs 252
attribution 95–6
automation 77, 180–1, 367–8
autonomous processes 68
AVIS 160

banking
  bonus culture 426–7

competition in 7–8, 9
customer communications 274
customer satisfaction 307
customers' channel preferences 226, 257, 258
outsourcing 393
pricing practices 197–8, 214–15
risk distribution 165
segmentation 41–2
Service Profit Chain 64–5
switching bank accounts 114, 129
value creation 17–18
Barclays 307
barriers to switching 120–1
behaviour of customers *see* customer behaviour
behaviour of employees 307–10, 339
  evaluation of 312
  repertoires 311
behaviour-based communication 288
behavioural value drivers 432
benefits 48, 90, 279–80
Big Mac index 391
billing systems 158–9, 220
blueprinting *see* service blueprinting
Body Shop, The 211
bonding 120–1
bonus culture 426–7
booking databases 366
  see also reservation systems
branch systems 249–50
brand communication 275–81
  firm-level brands 275
  laddering approach 290–1
  means-end chain approach 279–82
  quality indicators 276
brand equity 276–8, **442**
brand experience 276
brand image 267, 268, 275–6, 279, 280, 291, 293, **442**
British Airways 340–1, 402
budgeting 436
bundling
  price bundling 213–15, **444**
  service bundling 178–9, 359–60

call centres 107, 178, 253–4, 326, 357, 393
Canadian Imperial Bank of Commerce 64–5
cancellation fees 85
capacity gap 343–4, 347, 347–9, **442**
capacity management *see* service capacity
car rental industry 164
centralisation 414–15
centrifugal networks 400–1
channels *see* service channels
children's playgrounds 156
China 386–7
cinemas 8, 50
Cisco Systems 329
Citibank 393
cleanliness 322–3
Club Med Cancun 97
Clubcard 123, 142–3
co-operative marketing campaigns 399
co-producer role 85–6
co-user role 86–8
coffeeshops 385
commitment 337–9
communication 267–97
   behaviour-based 288
   brand communication 275–81
   as a core service 271–2
   for customer acquisition 273
   for customer retention 273
   customised 287–90
   degree of standardisation 283
   direct 287
   face-to-face 283
   in-process 272
   integrated 293–5
   interactional 271–2
   internal 28–9, 316–17
   and internationalisation 390
   Internet 287–90
   mass communication 291–3
   non-verbal 286
   perceived quality 285
   personal 284–6
   post-process 272
   pre-process 272
   relational 273–4
   and service capacity 346, 362
   and service recovery 99, 273–4
   as a supplementary service 272
   value contribution 268–70
   word-of-mouth 119, 126, **448**

communication systems 422
communication-related services 156–8
company culture 412, 422–7
company organisation 414–19
   matrix 417–18
   object 415–17
   structural 414–18
compensation packages 316, 422, 426–7
competences 313
competition 7–10, 237, 399–400, 403
   co-operation with competitors 402
   and customer switching 128
   and internationalisation 392
   and pricing 205
competitive advantage 315
complaints 94, 98
   see also service failure
complex services 160, 167
conceptual focus 11
Conduit 326
conjoint measurement method 200–1, 204, 208
consultation services 157
contact technologies 328–9, 331
content integration 294
contract-related services 158–60
contribution analysis 39–40
control 411–12
   costs of 432–3
   interaction and relationship blueprinting 433–5
   productivity 12, 308, 326, 433–5
   return on services marketing 435
   revenues 433
   value contribution 412–13
   value drivers 427–32, 436
core competencies 394, 396
core service 149, 151–2, **442**
   capacity gap 347
   and communication 271–2
   and customer switching 149–50
   and differentiation 151
   and gender 161
   and innovation 177
   and the interaction process 152
   relative importance 160–1
   and the Service Value Chain 152
   tangibles 322
costs
   allocating 38–9
   cost oriented pricing 195–6
   cost–benefit relationship 48

of marketing control 432–3
synergies 166, 383–4, 398
and technology 258, 326–8
credit card industry 133–4, 135–6
critical incidents 78–82, 130–1, **442**
critical path analysis 130–2
cross-buying 45, 126, 163–4, 166, **442**
cruise operators 81
culture
company culture 412, 422–7
national culture 384
customer acquisition 18, 116–17, 118–20, **442**
and differentiation 118–19
inducements 119–20
reducing customer uncertainty 118
and service networking 398
customer behaviour 31, 35–6, 44–6
behaviour-based offers 288
loyal customers 123, 126
misbehaviour 84, 85, 86–7
and pricing 192–3, 365–6
problem customers 86
and service location 235
third-party behaviour 82
tracking 45
see also segmentation
customer contact technologies 328–9, 331
customer enhancement 442
customer equity 12
customer expectations 50, 54–7, **442**
customer integration 17, 74–6, **442**
and service location 235
customer interaction process *see* service interaction
Customer Lifetime Value (CLV) 37, 42–4, 440–1, **443**
customer loyalty 33, 37, 62–5, 94
behaviour of loyal customers 123, 126
and purchase frequency 126
see also loyalty programmes
customer mitigation analysis 46
customer orientation 308, 309, 423–4
customer perceptions 35–6, 48–57
of communication quality 285
of service quality 49–54
of tangibles 319–20, 324
of value 12, 48–9, 144–5, 191
customer preparation activities 84
customer recovery 19, 117, 127–34, **443**
inducements 133
persuasion 132
customer relationship 35–6, 57, 109–40, **443**

always-a-share markets 117
core phases 116
critical path analysis 130–2
criticisms of 111–12
familiarity 138
initiating a relationship 118
intensity of relationship 114–15
linkages between interactions 113–14
lost-for-good markets 117–18
membership relationships 120
quality of relationship 136–8
reciprocal dependence 138
relational communication 273–4
relationship pricing 194, 195–6, 210–12
relationship profit chain 136
relationship value drivers 428
and technology 324–5
termination 45, 128–32
trust 137, 138
value contribution 110–12, 134
customer relationship lifecycle 114–18, **443**
customer retention 18, 117, 120–7, **443**
alignment 120, 121
bonding 120–1
lock-in effects 121
see also loyalty programmes
customer roles
abandoner role 85
co-producer role 85–6
co-user role 86–8
and customer characteristics 87
specifyer role 83–4
transferer role 84–5
customer satisfaction 33, 54, 128, **443**
in banking 307
service recovery paradox 96
customer surveys 200, 204
customer switching 127–32, 149–50, **443**
barriers to switching 120–1
competition-related reasons 128
customer-related reasons 127–8
industry defection rates 135–6
provider-related reasons 128
customer value 12, 33, 36–9, **443**, 447
ABC analysis 40, 41
contribution analysis 39–40
definition 36–7, 38
potential analysis 37, 39–40
profitability analysis 37, 39–40
revenue analysis 39

customer value (*continued*)
   time and value orientations 38–9
   20:80 rule 40
   types of 37
customer-related price differentiation 361
customised communication 287–90

databases *see* information systems
definitional focus 11
delivery *see* service delivery
demand
   adjustments 351, 358–62, 371–4
   analysis 352, 354
   demand-related capacity management 349–50
   dynamics 350, 352
   growth in demand 7
   matching to capacity 343–4, 355–6
   patterns 343–4, 350
   and pricing 192, 193, 199–204
demand gap 343–4, 347–9, **443**
department stores 431
development strategy 381
DHL 216
differentiation 118–19, 151, 401–2
   differentiation pricing 199, 361–2
   segment-specific differentiation 360
dimensions of employee behaviour 307–10, 339
direct communication 287
direct distribution and delivery 246, 247
direct exports 387
direct market entry 388
direct marketing 9, 287
disconfirmation paradigm 54
discounts 217
distribution *see* **service delivery**
diversification strategy 382
divided service delivery 247
dynamic pricing 361

e-mail
   campaigns 265
   facilities on planes 171–2
e-services 161–2, 325, 327
easyJet 181
electronic service delivery 251–6, 258
   cost advantages 258
   interactive kiosks 106–8, 252–3, 340–1
   Internet 254–5
   mobile channels 255–6
   telephone 253–4, 287

empathy 52, 55
employees *see* service employees
empowerment 28, 102, 311–12, **443**
enviousness effects 218
error rectification 102
evaluation of employees 312
expert opinion 199–200
external factor 14–15, 74, 76, 77–8, **443–4**, 445
externalisation 179, 180, 181
externally-oriented behaviour 307, 309

face-to-face communication 283
facilitating processes 90
facilitating products 90
facilitating services 154
fail points 90
favouritism 311
feedback 312
financial resources 353–5
financial services industry 182–4
   see also banking; insurance industry
financial value drivers 432
firm orientation 309
firm value 9, 16, 31, 428, **444**
firm-level brands 275
fitness clubs 8
flat rate pricing 218
flexibility 242–3, 404, 405
flexible working hours 357
foodservice industry 354
football club pricing strategy 219, 224–5
FootFall 350
formal integration 294
formality factor 177
franchising 250–1, **444**
freeway patrol service 244
frequent flier programmes 111, 122
FTSE4Good index 169, 170
Fujitsu Consulting 106–8
functional organisation 414–15
furniture retailing 245

GalleryPlayer 231, 233–4
GAP model 11, 49–51, 175
general service usage 44
geographical distance 384
geographical extension 248–9
German tour operators 8
Germanwings 362
globalisation *see* internationalisation strategy
grocery market 19, 61–4

hard services 385
harmonisation of conflict 403
heterogeneity of services 14, 49
hierarchical integration 294
historical data and pricing 200
Hoosier Helper program 244
hospital foodservices 172–3
hospitality services 157–8
hotels
    cleanliness 322–3
    employee commitment 337–9
    pricing 206–7
    Ritz-Carlton 27–9, 134
human resources management 306–7
human resources marketing 315

IKEA 85, 156, 408–9
image adulteration 167
immobile tangibles 322
implementation 411–27
    company culture 412, 422–7
    company organisation 414–19
    systems 419–22
    value contribution 412–13
in-process communication 272
in-process services 154–5
in-process technologies 330
incentive schemes 217, 318–19
indirect distribution and delivery 247
indirect market entry 388–9
inducements 119–20, 133
information exchange 403
information services 156
information systems 420–2
information technology see service technology
innovation see service innovation
inside-out pricing 193–4, 195–7
insurance industry 83–4, 182–4, 259, 386–7
intangibility of services 14, 49
integrated communication 293–5
integration-related services 155–6
interactions see service interaction
interactive kiosks 106–8, 252–3, 340–1
Interbrand 276–8
interdependence between partners 403
Interdiscount department store 134
internal communications 28–9, 316–17
internal Service Profit Chain 306
internal technologies 331
internalisation 179

internally-oriented behaviour 307–8
internationalisation strategy 382, 383–91, 408–9
    and communications 390
    and competition 392
    cultural distance 384
    and delivery channels 390
    direct entry 388
    direct exports 387
    and employees 390
    geographical distance 384
    hard services 385
    indirect entry 388–9
    operational issues 390
    penetration strategies 387–9
    and pricing 390
    and products 390
    and retailing 389
    and service characteristics 384
    soft services 385
    and tangibles 390
    and technology 390
    value creation 383
Internet 254–5, 287–90
interpersonal communication quality 285
inventions 170
investment banks 426–7
Iridium 185

Karstadt 431
kinesics 286

laddering approach 290–1
leadership 315, 425–6
Leading Hotels of the World 164, 165
length of delivery 241–2
life cycles of products 167
life insurance industry 83–4, 182–4, 259, 386–7
line extension 169
line innovation 169
location see service location; service place
lock-in effects 121
lost-for-good markets 117–18
loyalty programmes 122–7, 166
    and competitive offers 125
    and data collection 122–3
    frequent flier programmes 111, 122
    hard rewards 124
    and marketing resources 124
    member-only events 125
    soft rewards 124

loyalty programmes (*continued*)
  Tesco Clubcard 123, 142–3
  see also customer loyalty

m-commerce 255–6
McDonald's 269–70, 314–15, 317, 371–4
management systems 422
market-pull innovation 169
marketing mix 11
markets
  development strategies 382
  penetration strategies 381, 387–9
  saturated markets 383
  segmentation 40, 41–2, 47, 193, 360, 365, 381–2
mass communication 291–3
materialisation strategy 291–2
materials 321–2
matrix organisation 417–18
means–end chain approach 279–82
measurement focus 11–12
Mediamarkt 235, 236
membership relationships 120
methodological competence 313
mobile distribution channels 255–6
mobile learning 231, 232–3
mobile tangibles 322
moments of truth 12
motivation 28, 317–19
Mövenpick Wein Corporation 263–5
multi-channelling 256–9, 263–5, 361, **444**
multi-level pricing 217–18
multi-step synthetic service pricing 204–8
multi-usage of capacity 357
multiplex cinemas 8, 50
multiplication of service delivery 246–7, 248–9, **444**

national culture 384
negative value effects 93
Neiman-Marcus 124–6
nesting 366
networking *see* service networking
new service processes 169
new service products 169
new-to-the-company innovation 169
new-to-the-market innovation 169
Nexcom Online Services 409–10
non-verbal communications 286, **444**
normative expectations 54–5
Novotel 337–9

object organisation 415–17
objectives 436
one-to-one distribution 246
opening times 243–4
operational focus 12
optimal prices 193
optimal service level 348–9, 366
order and delivery time-lags 244–5
organisation *see* process organisation; structural organisation
organisational citizenship behaviour 308–9
out-partnering 396
outside-in pricing 194, 198–204
outsourcing 392–6, 393
overbooking 366

para-language 286
parking lots 156
payment process 159
penetration strategies 381, 387–9
perceived communication quality 285
perceived service quality 49–54
perceived service value 12, 48–9, 144–5, 191, **444**
perceptual value drivers 431–2
perishability of services 14, 49
permanence of service availability 243–4
permission marketing 287–8, 289
personal communication 284–6
personal service delivery 248–51
personification strategy 291–2
physical appearance 286
Pizza Hut 153
pizza restaurants 239
polycentral networks 401
post-process communication 272
post-process services 155
post-process technologies 330–1
potential analysis 37, 39–40
potential customers 320
pre-process communication 272
pre-process services 154
pre-process technologies 330–1
predictive expectations 54
price bundling 213–15, **444**
price discrimination 208–20, **444**
  and billing systems 220
  distribution channel pricing 215
  dynamic developments 219
  enviousness effects 218
  exploiting free capacity 209

flat rate pricing 218
incentive plans 217
internal problems 220
multi-level pricing 217–18
and personal characteristics 210
price bundling 213–15
regional price differences 215
and the relationship lifecycle phase 210
relationship pricing 210–12
service level pricing 212
and service place 215
skimming the willingness to pay 208–9
and time of service use 215–16
volume-based price discrimination 217–18
see also service pricing
price sensitivity 365–6
prick-eared market research 175
primary value processes 16–19, 68, 345–6, **444**, 447
prioritising 426
problem customers 86
process organisation 418–19, **444**
processes 13–15
facilitating processes 90
process focus 12
product *see* service product
production factors 14–15
productivity 12, 308, 326, 433–5
professional communication quality 285
professional competence 313
profit chain *see* Service Profit Chain
profitability
analysis 37, 39–40
profit premiums 197
responsibility for 417
and service location 238
prototypes 175–7
proxemics 286
psychological competence 313
psychometric testing 317
purchase volume
discounts 217
increasing 45
volume-based price discrimination 217–18
volume-related price differentiation 361
purchasing decisions 235
purchasing frequency 120, 126, 194
purchasing power parity 391
purchasing trigger 193, 194

qualifying employees 313
quality *see* service quality

range systems 421
real-time pricing 361
recovery communication 273–4
recreational centre pricing 201–4
recruitment 28, 313–17
reference items 57
REI 188–90
relationships *see* customer relationship
reliability 52, 55
remuneration packages 316, 422, 426–7
repeat purchases 120
reservation systems 155–6, 357–8, 366–7, 420
resources *see* service resources
responsiveness 52, 55
restaurants 229, 235, 239, 316
retention communication 273
return on services marketing 435
Reuters 417
revenues
analysing 39
effects of networking 397–8
and marketing control 433
risk distribution 165
risks of service networking 404–5
Ritz-Carlton 27–9, 134
Robert Wood Johnson University Hospital 172–3
role clarity 311
role conflict 311
role management 310–12
see also customer roles
room capacity 238
room costs 238
room quality 238
Royal Bank of Scotland 214–15, 258

safekeeping services 156
sales price relationship 192, 193
saturated markets 383
scheduling systems 356–7, 372
secondary value processes 20–1, 58, 346, 358, **445**, 447
segmentation 40, 41–2, 47, 193, 360, 365, 381–2
self-service 106–8, 340–1
service blueprinting 12, 88–91, 433–5, **445**
airline industry 92
benefit identification 90
fail points 90
and innovation 175
of interactions and relationships 433–5
service process identification 90
standards and tolerances identification 90–1

service bundling 178–9, 359–60
service capacity 343–68, **445**
  adaptability 350
  airline industry 416
  capacity gap 343–4, 347–9
  capacity-related capacity management 350
  demand adjustments 351, 358–62, 371–4
  demand dynamics 350, 352
  demand gap 343–4, 347–9
  demand level analysis 352, 354
  demand–capacity matching 343–4, 355–6
  demand–related capacity management 349–50
  determination of capacity levels 351, 352–6
  and financial resources 353–5
  flexible working hours 357
  multi-usage of capacity 357
  nesting 366
  optimal service level 348–9, 366
  overbooking 366
  and pricing 361–2
  and primary value processes 345–6
  reservation systems 155–6, 357–8, 366–7, 420
  and secondary value processes 346, 358
  segment-specific differentiation 360
  and service bundling 359–60
  and service communications 346, 362
  and service networking 399
  and service resources 347
  short-term adjustments 351, 356–8
  and tangibles 356
  threshold curves 366, 373
  value contribution of capacity management 343–7
  waiting time management 351, 362–4
  workforce scheduling 356–7
  yield management 364–8
service channels 228, 246–59, **445**
  branch systems 249–50
  and capacity management 361
  channel conflict 259
  direct distribution and delivery 246, 247
  distribution channel pricing 215
  divided service delivery 247
  electronic service delivery 251–6, 258
  franchising 250–1
  indirect distribution and delivery 247
  mobile channels 255–6
  multi-channelling 256–9, 263–5, 361
  one-to-one distribution 246
  personal service delivery 248–51
service characteristics 13–14, 384, **445**

service concept 21
service definition 11
service delivery 144–5, 226–59, **445**
  and capacity management 361
  electronic 251–6
  and flexibility 242–3
  and geographical extension 248–9
  and internationalisation 390
  length of delivery 241–2
  multiplication of deliveries 246–7, 248–9
  order and delivery time-lags 244–5
  permanence of availability 243–4
  personal delivery 248–51
  and service location 227, 235–40
  and service place 228–34
  and service standardisation 245
  and service timing 228, 241–3
  value contribution 227–8
service elimination 181–4, **445**
service employees 17, 21, 306–19, **445**
  behaviour-based evaluation 312
  behavioural repertoires 311
  commitment 337–9
  communication methods 316–17
  compensation packages 316, 422, 426–7
  competences 313
  and competitive advantage 315
  and customer orientation 308, 309
  dimensions of behaviour 307–10, 339
  empowerment 28, 102, 311–12, **443**
  evaluation 312
  externally-oriented behaviour 307, 309
  favouritism 311
  feedback 312
  firm orientation 309
  human resources management 306–7
  incentive schemes 318–19
  internally-oriented behaviour 307–8
  and internationalisation 390
  motivation 28, 317–19
  organisational citizenship behaviour 308–9
  productivity 12, 308, 326, 433–5
  qualifying employees 313
  recruitment 28, 313–17
  role management 310–12
  and service failures 98, 102
  and tangibles 320
  teamworking 308
  training 28, 313–17, 338–9
  value effects 306–7

service encounter 71–2, 76–8, 82, **446**
service environment 321
service failures 72, 91–4, 98, 102
    attribution of 95–6
    complaints 94, 98
    consequences of 73
    controllability 96
    and customer loyalty 94
    external failures 94
    identification 98
    internal failures 93–4
service improvements 328
service innovation 167–77, **446**
    core service relationship 177
    formality factor 177
    innovation process 173–5
    inventions 170
    line extension 169
    line innovation 169
    market-pull innovation 169
    new service processes 169
    new service products 169
    new-to-the-company innovation 169
    new-to-the-market innovation 169
    prick-eared market research 175
    prototypes 175–7
    and service blueprinting 175
    service modifications 170
    and service place 231
    success drivers 177
    technology-push innovation 169
service interaction 17, 27, 36, 57–8, 68–9, 71–104, 152, **446**
    blueprinting 433–5
    and communication 271–2
    costs of 74
    customers' roles 83–8
    interaction time 90–1
    and pricing 193–4
    service encounter 71–2, 76–8, 82, **446**
    technologies 325, 330
    value creation 73–4, 106–8
    value drivers 428
    see also customer integration
service inventions 170
service level pricing 212
service location 74–6, 227, 235–40, **446**
    accessibility 238
    and competition 237
    customer behaviour effects 235

customer integration 235
    deciding on a location 236–40
    market-related factors 236–7
    position-related factors 237–8
    profitability-related factors 238
    and purchasing decisions 235
    room capacity 238
    room costs 238
    room quality 238
    and service quality 235
    service type influences 239
service machines 106–8, 252–3, 340–1
service modification 170, 177–81, **446**
    automation 77, 180–1, 367–8
    externalisation 179, 180, 181
    internalisation 179
    service bundling 178–9, 359–60
    value-added service offers 178
service networking 396–405, 409–10
    and capacity utilisation 399
    centrifugal networks 400–1
    co-operative marketing campaigns 399
    and competition 399, 403
    competitor co-operation 402
    cost synergies 398
    customer acquisition 398
    customer co-operation 402
    flexibility 404, 405
    harmonisation of conflict 403
    information exchange 403
    interdependence between partners 403
    out-partnering 396
    quality of networks 403, 404
    revenue effects 397–8
    risks 404–5
    supplier co-operation 402
    supply chain differentiation 401–2
    value creation 396–9
service place 228–34, **446**
    customer's place 228–31
    design of 235
    multi-option strategy 234
    and pricing 215
    provider's place 228–31
    and service innovations 231
    splitting 230–1
    strategies 231–4
    third-party place 228–31
service pricing 48, 191–220
    airline industry 325, 362

service pricing (*continued*)
  in banking 197–8, 214–15
  competition-driven base price 205
  conjoint measurement method 200–1, 204, 208
  cost oriented approach 195–6
  and customer behaviour 192–3
  and customer surveys 200, 204
  demand function pricing 192, 193, 199–204
  differentiation pricing 199, 361–2
  dynamic pricing 361
  and expert opinion 199–200
  and historical data 200
  inside-out approach 193–4, 195–7
  and the interaction process 193–4
  and internationalisation 390
  and market segmentation 193
  multi-step synthetic service pricing approach 204–8
  optimal prices 193
  outside-in approach 194, 198–204
  and perceived value 191
  pricing systems 421
  profit premiums 197
  and purchasing frequency 194
  as a purchasing trigger 193, 194
  as a quality indicator 193
  and the relationship process 194, 195–6
  sales-price relationship 192, 193
  and service capacity 361–2
  and service recovery 99
  and service resources 194
  and service units 196–7
  value contribution 192–4
  see also price discrimination
service product 147–62
  e-services 161–2, 325, 327
  facilitating products 90
  and internationalisation 390
  life cycles 167
  and service elimination 181–4
  and service innovation 167–77
  and service modification 177–81
  and the service programme 150–1, 163–7
  value contribution 148–50
  see also core service; supplementary services
service production 12, 71, 73
Service Profit Chain 31, **446**
  banking case study 64–5
  grocery store case study 61–4
  integrating the Service Value Chain 33–6
  internal profit chain 306

service programme 150–1, 163–7
  and complexity 167
  cost synergies 166
  cross-buying 163–4, 166
  design 164, 165
  image adulteration 167
  loyalty effects 166
  negative side effects 167
  risk distribution 165
  switching barriers 166
service prototypes 175–7
service quality 11–12, 91–3, 422, **446**
  dimensions 51–4
  network quality 403, 404
  perceived quality 49–54
  quality indicators 193, 276, 320, 324
  relationship quality 136–8
  and service location 235
service recovery 17, 72, 91–102, **446**
  and attribution 95–6
  communication measures 99
  effects of 94
  management of 97–102
  paradox 96
  place-related measures 99
  pricing measures 99
  product-related measures 99
  in retailing 100–1
  speed of error rectification 102
  unacceptable strategies 100–1
service resources 21, 75, 82, 304–5, 445, **446**
  and pricing 194
  and service capacity 347
  types of 77
  value drivers 428
service standardisation 158, 245
service technology 21, 324–34
  cost effects 326–8
  customer contact technologies 328–9, 331
  and employees' work 325
  implementation 331–4
  in-process 330
  and the interaction process 325
  interaction technologies 330
  internal technologies 331
  and internationalisation 390
  locus of utilisation 328–9
  multi-usage 358
  outsourcing 393
  post-process 330–1

pre-process 330–1
and the relationship process 324–5
and service improvements 328
and the Service Value Chain 324–5
support technologies 329–30
and tangibles 325
value effects 326–8
value-oriented typology 328
see also e-services
service timing 76, 228, 241–3
time flexibility 242
time integration 294
time of service use 215–16
time and value orientations 38–9
time-related price differentiation 361
service units 196–7
Service Value Chain 5–22, 57–8, **447**
and competition 7–10
developmental stages 10–12
primary processes 16–19, 68, 345–6, **444**, 447
secondary processes 20–1, 58, 346, 358, **445**, 447
services as processes 13–15
structure of value processes 16–22
and technology 324–5
value creation 4, 7–10
see also core service; customer value
service value drivers 428
servicescape 320–1, **447**
services marketing 2, 6, **447**
developmental stages 10–12
see also control; implementation
SERVQUAL 11–12, 52–4, 235
see also service quality
shareholders 377, **447**
shopping habits 350
short-term capacity adjustments 351, 356–8
SIXT 164
skimming the willingness to pay 208–9
social competence 313
soft services 385
space tourism 153
special offers 264
specifyer role 83–4
stakeholders 376–7, **447**
standardisation 158, 245
structural organisation 414–18, **447**
sunk costs 196
supplementary services 149–50, 152–60, **447**
and communication 272
communication-related services 156–8

contract-related services 158–60
facilitating services 154
and gender 161
in-process 154–5
integration-related 155–6
post-process 155
pre-process 154
relative importance 160–1
service programme design 165
value-added services 154
see also tangibles
supplier co-operation 402
supply chain differentiation 401–2
support technologies 329–30
switching barriers 166
Switzerland 385
Sydney Swans 224
systematic role management 311
systems 419–22
communication systems 422
information systems 420–2
management systems 422

tangibles 21, 52, 55, 235, 319–24, **447**
and core services 322
and customer perceptions 319–20, 324
and employees 320
immobile 322
and internationalisation 390
mobile 322
multi-usage 358
and potential customers 320
and quality signals 320, 322
and service capacity 356
service environment 321
service materials 321–2
servicescape 320–1
and supplementary services 322
and technology 325
value effects 319–20
teamworking 308
technology *see* service technology
technology-push innovation 169
telephone 253–4, 287
termination of relationships 45, 128–32
Tesco 389
Tesco Clubcard 123, 142–3
Tetra Pak 150–1
third-party behaviour 82
Three-Sector Theory 5–6, 445

threshold curves 366, 373
throughput of customers 16, 18, 68, 73
ticketing procedures 360–1
Times Square car race 290
timing *see* service timing
tourism industry 8, 20
    cancellation fees 85
    cruise operators 81
    service programme design 164, 165
    service recovery 97
    space tourism 153
    see also hotels
training 28, 313–17, 338–9, 425
transactional marketing 118
transferer role 84–5
transportability of services 14, 49
trust 137, 138
20:80 rule 40

universities 280, 281–2
USP (unique selling proposition) 151

value 4, 7–10, **447**
    and capacity management 343–7
    and communication 268–70
    and customer relationships 110–12, 134
    and implementation and control 412–13
    and internationalisation 383
    and marketing control 412–13
    negative value effects 93
    and networking 396–9
    objectives 436
    parameters 431

perceived value 12, 48–9, 144–5, 191, **444**
    and pricing 192–4
    and service delivery 227–8
    and service employees 306–7
    and service interaction 73–4, 106–8
    and service product 148–50
    structure of value processes 16–22
    and tangibles 319–20
    and technology 326–8
    see also customer value; Service Value Chain
value drivers 17, **448**
    airline industry 440–1
    categories 428–32
    in marketing control 427–32, 436
    prioritising 426
value-added service offers 178
value-added services supplementary services 154
value-based budgeting 436
Virgin Mobile 299–300
vision 425
volume *see* purchase volume

waiting time management 351, 362–4
Wells Fargo 329
Werder Bremen 219
willingness to pay 365
wine retailing 263–5
word-of-mouth communications 119, 126, **448**
workforce scheduling 356–7, 372

yield management 364–8, **448**
Youth Hostels Association 211–12